International Series on Computer Entertainment and Media Technology

Series Editor
Newton Lee
Institute for Education, Research, and Scholarships
Los Angeles, CA, USA

The International Series on Computer Entertainment and Media Technology presents forward-looking ideas, cutting-edge research, and in-depth case studies across a wide spectrum of entertainment and media technology. The series covers a range of content from professional to academic. Entertainment Technology includes computer games, electronic toys, scenery fabrication, theatrical property, costume, lighting, sound, video, music, show control, animation, animatronics, interactive environments, computer simulation, visual effects, augmented reality, and virtual reality. Media Technology includes art media, print media, digital media, electronic media, big data, asset management, signal processing, data recording, data storage, data transmission, media psychology, wearable devices, robotics, and physical computing.

More information about this series at http://www.springer.com/series/13820

Barbaros Bostan

Editor

Game User Experience
And Player-Centered Design

 Springer

Editor
Barbaros Bostan
Bahcesehir University
Department of Game Design
Istanbul, Turkey

ISSN 2364-947X   ISSN 2364-9488   (electronic)
International Series on Computer Entertainment and Media Technology
ISBN 978-3-030-37645-1   ISBN 978-3-030-37643-7   (eBook)
https://doi.org/10.1007/978-3-030-37643-7

This Springer imprint is published by the registered company Springer Nature Switzerland AG.
The registered company address is: Gewerbestrasse 11, 6330 Cham, Switzerland

Foreword

There are approximately 2.5 billion gamers worldwide today, and the video game industry is soaring. It certainly seems that everyone is interested in video games in one way or another, from parents to the media to healthcare professionals to policy makers. Some of them are concerned about the impact of video game play, while others are very enthusiastic about its potential. Yet, there are still many questions to answer regarding the true benefits and limitations of video games, and more research is required.

On the industry side, video game developers are in need of guidelines and reliable methods to succeed in a now very competitive space, with thousands of games released every year scrutinized by a demanding audience. Canceled games, layoffs, and studio closures are frequent. At the same time, increasingly more game professionals (and gamers alike) are pushing for greater accessibility, inclusion, and ethics in the game industry.

All in all, understanding of how players experience games and are impacted by them has become critical to help us address those challenges. During the past decade, user experience has entered the game industry and developed, but we have still a long way to go for game ux to be formalized and centralized. This book is a step in this direction, and I hope that it will encourage many more to follow.

Los Angeles, CA   Celia Hodent
December 16, 2019

Acknowledgements

The editor of the book would like to especially thank to the dean of the faculty of communication in Bahçeşehir University, Prof. Dr. Hasan Kemal Süher and the department head of the game design department, Dr. Güven Çatak for their support. To Çetin Tüker, Mehmet İlker Berkman, Tolga Hepdinçler, Diğdem Sezen, Çakır Aker, Ecehan Akan and Sercan Şengün for their assistance.

To Metehan Irak for coming up with the idea of a book on game user experience.

To Susan Evans and Rahul Sharma from Springer for their feedback during the production and their help in shaping this book you now hold in your hands.

Special thanks to my wife Seda for enduring me, and I want to send huge hugs to my daughter Ecrin for giving me the strength to keep going.

Contents

Part I
Cognition and Player Psychology

Chapter 1
ERP Correlates of Working Memory Load in Excessive Video Game Players

Metehan Irak, Can Soylu, Özüm Karya Sakman, and Gözem Turan

Contents

Abstract Previous studies have suggested that excessive behaviors including internet, gaming, exercise, shopping, and gambling might be associated with dysfunction in working memory (WM) and prefrontal activity. Here we compared event-related

M. Irak (✉) · C. Soylu · Ö. K. Sakman
Department of Psychology Brain and Cognition Research Laboratory, Bahçeşehir University, Istanbul, Turkey
e-mail: metehan.irak@eas.bau.edu.tr; can.soylu@eas.bau.edu.tr; ozumkarya.sakman@bahcesehir.edu.tr

G. Turan
Johann Wolfgang Goethe University, Lifespan Cognitive and Brain Development Laboratory, Frankfurt, Germany
e-mail: turan@psych.uni-frankfurt.de

© Springer Nature Switzerland AG 2020
B. Bostan (ed.), *Game User Experience And Player-Centered Design*,
International Series on Computer Entertainment and Media Technology,
https://doi.org/10.1007/978-3-030-37643-7_1

potentials (ERP) of excessive video game players (EVGPs) and non-players during N-back task. We hypothesized that increasing WM-load during the N-back task (e.g., 2-Back vs 3-Back) will lead to decreased P300 amplitude in EVGPs which also associated with dysfunction in prefrontal activity. Behavioral results indicated that EVGP participants were more accurate and the number of false responses was lower than non-players only when the workload was higher. The EVGP group's P100 and P200 amplitude was higher than for non-players. Contrary to our hypothesis two groups' P300 responses were not statistically different. We concluded that EVGPs are like non-players in terms of the process of allocating the sources of attention required for the task and enabling the degree of information processing required. In other words, excessive video game playing does not cause a deterioration in this type of attention and memory performance.

Keywords Working memory · Memory load · N-back task · Excessive video game playing · Event-related potentials

1.1 Introduction

Unlike addiction's original definition in the American Psychiatric Association (APA)'s Diagnostic and Statistical Manual of Mental Disorders (DSM), which includes the use of substances like tobacco, alcohol, or cocaine, behavioral disorders are non-substance related and may include pathological game addiction, internet addiction, pathological gambling, food addiction, and others (Zilberman et al. 2018). Game addiction can be defined as giving excessive priority to gaming instead of daily activities, loss of control over gaming, social isolation, hyper-focus in-game, and mood swings. Although the fifth edition of the DSM classified it in the "Further Studies" section and by 2018, the World Health Organization (WHO) described it as "game addiction," the literature displays contradictions regarding the effects of excessive game addiction on brain and behavior display. Moreover, research in this area is new and drawing analogies between game addiction and other addictions is challenging. Even though research on excessive video game playing has focused on psychological causes and behavioral consequences (Weng et al. 2013), neuroimaging studies are limited in number. In the relatively sparse relevant neurobiology literature, game addiction can be related to impulse control, monitoring ongoing behavior, and disinhibition (Weng et al. 2013). Prefrontal cortex impairments may be related to those traits, and that other forms of addiction are also related to prefrontal cortex impairments (Han et al. 2011). Changes in brain structures have been consistently observed in online game addiction (Han et al. 2011; Weng et al. 2013). The impaired white and gray matter were found in the prefrontal cortex, which can result in uncontrolled behavior—a pattern like alcohol abuse. Studies have shown that executive control decreases with excessive video game playing and violent game playing emotionally desensitizes players to the stimulus, a dynamic also present in biological addictions (Gentile et al. 2016). In a similar vein, electroencephalography (EEG) studies have indicated that people with internet addiction disorder make poorer conflict detection than people with no behavioral addiction, which has been shown with lower N2 and P3 amplitude and increased latency during the NoGo task (Dong et al. 2010). A similar pattern can be seen in excessive video gaming.

1.1.1 Video Gaming and Working Memory

Recent studies have mostly focused on the relationship between excessive video gaming and cognitive skills. According to these studies, video game playing might increase the visual attention system since video games require the gamer's active participation, holding, and manipulation of the rules in the mind, usage of the game's map, and decision making. Indeed, video game players have shown higher performance at visual search and visuospatial attention tasks (Green and Bavelier 2006), better visual short-term memory, faster reaction times (RTs), and better attentional skills than non-players (McDermott et al. 2014). Such increased abilities are reasonable given that in the new generation of online games, players create new mindsets according to changing visual and auditory stimuli as well as other player's moves and reactions and must thus react as quickly as possible. These processes then are closely related to the working memory (WM) process. WM capacity is often measured by means of the N-back task because it requires participants to update and monitor WM (Colzato et al. 2013). Specifically, N-back tasks require participants to respond to a presented stimulus only when it is the same as one presented in a trial at a predetermined number (e.g., 2-back, 3-back). Previous studies (e.g., Mahone et al. 2009) have shown that n-back performance is associated with significant activation in the prefrontal and parietal cortices, which are widely recognized as the primary neural substrates that underlie WM processes.

Although both biological and behavioral addictions show many similarities, EVGPs exhibit different patterns than biological addicts and pathological gamblers during N-back task performances. In general, EVGPs were more successful in the N-back task compared to their non-player counterparts. The accuracy of the EVGPs and players who have never played video games was similar, but game addicts' RTs were faster than non-players during the N-back task (Boot et al. 2008; McDermott et al. 2014). However, Colzato et al. (2013) showed that in the 2-back condition, experienced first-person shooter game players were also more accurate—as well as faster—than people with no game experience. Given that, more accurate responses by experienced video game players may strengthen the notion that playing first-person shooter games and efficient monitoring and updating of working memory are associated. Thus, it may be assumed that those games are indeed effective in the usage of working memory (Irak et al. 2016). In addition, it has been claimed that only action video game players exhibit an enhancement in cognitive performance, but this effect may not be seen in the non-action video games (e.g., puzzles, crosswords, etc.) players (Dye et al. 2009; Cain et al. 2012). In contrast, mobile and computer games have been shown to equally influence cognitive functions in a positive way and both mobile and computer gamer groups showed better N-back scores than non-players (Huang et al. 2017). This indicates that platform and type of video game may affect WM in the same manner. Unfortunately, to the best of our knowledge, there is no physiological or neuroimaging study in which the N-back task has been used to assess WM in excessive video game playing. Therefore, the underlying neuronal mechanism during the N-back task in excessive video game playing is unknown.

Drawing analogies between game addiction and other addictions is also challenging because individuals diagnosed with a different type of addiction display worse performance in the N-back task than non-addicted ones. For instance, pathological gamblers showed N-back task performances like a non-addict control group and showed only slightly better performance than cocaine-dependent individuals (Albein-Urios et al. 2012). On the other hand, Leeman and Potenza (2011) suggested that there is a lack of evidence about pathological gamblers' WM performance measured with the N-back task. In biological addictions, N-back performances are usually worse than healthy individuals. For instance, dependent heavy drinkers showed the worst performance in the N-back task in comparison to non-drinkers and non-dependent heavy drinkers (Wesley et al. 2017). Furthermore, alcohol-dependent individuals demonstrate a greater response in the dorsolateral and medial prefrontal cortices (Wesley et al. 2017) and exhibit an increase in P3 amplitude (Nakamura-Palacios et al. 2012). A longitudinal fMRI study (Cousijn et al. 2013) with heavy cannabis users showed that N-back performance was not different than non-users, this difference did not change within a three-year period, and the performance accuracy of the cannabis users for the N-back task improved. However, in another study by Ilan et al. (2004), after excessive marijuana use, users showed slower and less accurate responses, which was shown with decreased theta and alpha power as the task became more difficult. Cousijn et al. (2013) also found that problematic usage of tobacco, alcohol, and psychotropic substance increased with excessive usage of cannabis, claiming that those substances also do affect N-back performance and WM. Consequently, it is safe to say that while similar structures like the dorsolateral prefrontal cortex and medial prefrontal cortex are impaired in both substance abuse and excessive video game playing, but similar patterns may not be observed in N-back performances. In contrast to alcohol dependence and pathological gambling, EVGPs show better performance in the N-back task, both in terms of accuracy and RT. It is unknown whether the reason behind their excessive video game playing is that they have strong working memory, or that they improve their working memory skills by playing online video games.

1.1.2   Goal of the Study

To sum up, the neurobiological basis of excessive video game playing and its effects on WM are not well-known. General WM and N-back performance may differ between biological and behavioral addicts. Furthermore, N-back performances also vary between people with different types of behavioral addictions like pathological gambling and excessive video game playing. The aim of this study is to investigate the effects of excessive video game playing on working memory with the N-back task by using event-related brain potentials (ERPs). Our first hypothesis is EVGPs will show low performance (lower accuracy and higher RT) during the N-back task, which relates to dysfunction in the prefrontal cortex. Since the P300 response has been shown to be sensitive to task complexity, impairment of the executive functions, and the difficulty in updating the incoming contextual information, our second hypothesis is that increasing WM-load during the N-back task (e.g., 2-back vs 3-back) will lead to a decrease in P300 amplitude in EVGPs.

1.2 Method

1.2.1 Participants

Thirty-six (20 female) undergraduate and graduate university students from different departments participated in the study, with a mean age of 22.28 (SD = 2.85). There were two groups of participants: EVGPs and non-players (NP). All participants were right-handed and reported normal or corrected-to-normal vision and no neurological or psychiatric history. The study conformed to the Declaration of Helsinki and was approved by the University Research Ethics Committee. Participants provided informed consent and were given financial compensation and/or course credits where applicable.

Following the previous studies, time spent playing video games of more than 16 h/week, reporting more than three symptoms on the Pathological Game Addiction Symptoms List (Gonnerman and Lutz 2011), and obtaining a total score greater than 55 on the Game Addiction Scale (Lemmens et al. 2009) were accepted as inclusion criteria for the EVGP group ($n = 18$, 8 female). Inclusion criteria for the non-player group ($n = 18$, 14 female) were having no experience with any type of video games, obtaining a total score of less than 17 on the Game Addiction Scale, and obtaining a total score of less than 3 on the Pathological Game Addiction Symptoms List.

1.2.2 Materials

1.2.2.1 Pathological Game Addiction Symptoms List

The original list was created from pathological gambling symptoms according to DSM-IV criteria by Gonnerman and Lutz (2011). In the Pathological Game Addiction Symptom List, the word "gambling" was changed to the word "gaming" for this study. The scale has 16 items and the Turkish adaptation was made by Arslan-Durna (2015) and Başer (2015). The scores that can be obtained from the list range between 0 and 16. Higher scores indicate higher levels of game addiction symptoms.

1.2.2.2 Game Addiction Scale

This scale was originally developed by Lemmens et al. (2009) to measure the degree of game addiction. The scale has 21 items with seven factors: salience, tolerance, mood modification, relapse, withdrawal, conflict, and problems. Participants' responses were given on a 5-point Likert scale from 1 (never) to 5 (very often). A Turkish adaptation was completed by Arslan-Durna (2015) and Başer (2015). Participants can obtain a minimum score of 21 and a maximum of 105 points. High scores indicate higher levels of game addiction symptoms.

1.2.2.3 N-back Task

The N-back task is used to investigate the neural bases of WM by increasing the working memory load. Since the task requires participants to on-line monitor, update, and manipulate the remembered stimuli, it places great demands on a number of key processes in WM. For each stimulus, participants need to decide if the current stimulus is the same as the one presented N trials ago (2 trials, 3 trials, etc.). The lateral premotor cortex, dorsal cingulate and medial premotor cortex, dorsolateral and ventrolateral prefrontal cortex, frontal poles, and medial and lateral posterior parietal cortex are known to be activated in the N-back task. In this study, the N-back procedure involved the presentation of letters as stimuli, one at a time on a screen, for a period of 2000 milliseconds (ms), with an interstimulus interval of 500 ms. Letters were selected randomly from the alphabet. Only 2-back and 3-back versions were used in this study. Both 2-back and 3-back tasks were presented in epochs of 20-s duration. Each 2-back and 3-back epoch was preceded by a 5-s instruction epoch and followed by a 20-s rest epoch. During instruction epochs, the instruction "Press the X if the current letter is the same as the letter two items ago" for 2-back condition and "Press the X if the current letter is the same as the letter three items ago" for the 3-back condition was presented on the screen. During rest epochs, the word "REST" was presented, and the subject was not required to make any motor response. There were 144 letter stimuli per each participant: 72 letter stimuli for each condition.

1.2.3 Electrophysiological Recording and Pre-processing

The N-back task was conducted in an electrically shielded and soundproof room and ERPs were recorded during the N-back task. ERPs were analyzed during the 2-back and 3-back conditions separately for 200 ms before and 1000 ms after the stimulus onset. EEG/EOG signals were recorded using 32 Ag/AgCl electrodes mounted in elastic Quick-caps (Neuromedical Supplies, Compumedics, Inc., Charlotte). The EOG signal was measured from two bipolar channels: one was formed by two electrodes placed at the outer canthus of each eye; another by two electrodes below and above the left eye. EEG signal was recorded from 30 (FP1, FP2, F7, F8, F3, F4, Fz, FT7, FT8, FC3, FC4, FCz, T7, T8, C3, C4, Cz, TP7, TP8, CP3, CP4, CPz, P7, P8, P3, P4, Pz, O1, O2, Oz) electrodes arranged according to the standard 10–20 system, with additional electrodes placed at BP1/BP2 and also on the left and right mastoids (M1/M2). All EEG electrodes were referenced on-line to an electrode at the vertex and re-referenced off-line to linked mastoids. EEG and EOG signals were amplified and recorded at a 1000 Hz sampling rate using Synamp2 amplifier at AC mode (Neuroscan, Compumedics, Inc., Charlotte) with a high- and low-pass filter set at 0.15 and 100 Hz, respectively. EEG electrode impedance was kept below 5 kΩ.

EEG data pre-processing was conducted using Edit 4.51 (Neuroscan, Compumedics, Inc., Charlotte) and applied to each participant's dataset. Data were down-sampled to 250 Hz to reduce computational demands and then low-pass filtered at 30 Hz and high-pass filtered at 0.15 Hz. EEG segments were extracted with an interval of 200 ms preceding and 1000 ms following the stimulus onset. Artifact rejection was performed in two steps. First, trials containing activity exceeding a threshold of ±100 μV at vertical and horizontal EOG and EEG channels were automatically detected and rejected. Second, we manually removed trials with saccades identified over the horizontal EOG channel. For the computation of ERPs, artifact-free segments were baseline corrected using a 100 ms pre-stimulus period and then averaged for the experimental conditions. ERPs were obtained by stimulus-locked averaging of EEG recorded during two phases, namely 2-back and 3-back conditions.

1.2.3.1 Data Analysis

In the present study, ERPs were analyzed through mean amplitude analysis (averaging). The average ERP was determined in a temporal direction. As discussed earlier, the ERP correlates of the N-back task in game addiction are unknown. Thus, we analyzed the grand average ERP for four different time windows, namely 50–100 ms, 100–200 ms, 200–300 ms, and 300–400 ms. Grand averages were calculated separately for the frontal (F3, Fz, F4), central (C3, Cz, C4), parietal (P3, Pz, P4), and occipital (O1, O2, and Oz) regions. Amplitude (μV) values of the components were detected for each participant and each electrode. Mean values were measured separately for both the 2-back and 3-back conditions by finding the most positive or negative point in a given time window. ERPs were exported as mean amplitudes per electrode within a specific time window for statistical analyses, as explained below.

ERP topographies (Figs. 1.1 and 1.2) and head plots (Fig. 1.3) for the 12 electrodes are presented for each experimental condition. Statistical analyses were performed with mean voltage amplitudes of ERP waveforms in designated time windows, using repeated measure ANOVA that included Greenhouse–Geisser corrections in cases where factors had more than two levels. All reported differences are significant at least at a level of $p < 0.05$ and were followed by Bonferroni post-

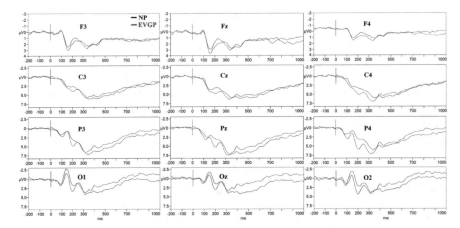

Fig. 1.1 Stimulus-locked ERP grand average ($n = 36$) during the 2-back condition for NP (black line) and EVGP (red line) groups at 12 electrode sites Stimulation applied at "0.0 ms" time point

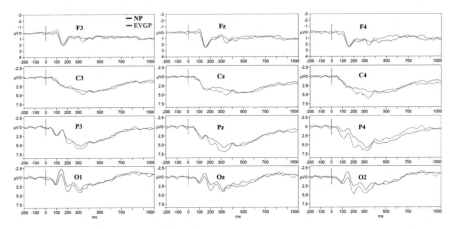

Fig. 1.2 Stimulus-locked ERP grand average ($n = 36$) during 3-back condition for NP (black line) and EVGP (red line) groups at 12 electrode sites Stimulation applied at "0.0 ms" time point

hoc comparison tests, if necessary (see Table 1.1). For post-hoc comparison, α was assigned the value of 0.05. After artifact rejection, the total number of usable trials was 5328 for all the participants (2664 for each condition). For the non-player group, the number of usable trials was 1291 for each condition, and for the EVGP group the number was 1368 for each condition.

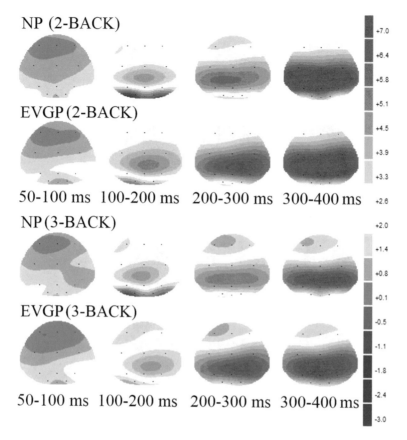

Fig. 1.3 Headplots in 2-back (top) and 3-back (bottom) conditions for NP (up) and EVGP (down) groups. Topographies were presented for four different time windows

1.3 Results

1.3.1 Behavioral Results

Prior to analyses, data were screened for missing values, as well as univariate and multivariate outliers (Tabachnick et al. 2007). There were no outliers identified as multivariate using Mahalanobis distance with $p < 0.001$, or univariate using z-scores ($|z| \geq 3.30$). True and false responses and their RTs (ms) were accepted as dependent variables for both in the 2-back and 3-back conditions.

True and false answers and their RT were compared for the two groups in 2-back and 3-back conditions. An independent sample t-test analysis indicated that only in the 3-back condition EVGP participants gave more true responses than non-players, $t (35) = 2.07$, $p < 0.05$, and they made fewer false responses than the non-player group, $t (35) = 3.08$, $p < 0.05$, $r = 0.46$. There were no significant

Table 1.1 Group × hemisphere × region effects on ERP during Go and NoGo conditions: repeated measure ANOVA results

Time window (Ms)	Group (A)		Hemisphere (B)		Region (C)		A × B		B × C		A × C		A × B × C	
	F	η^2	F	η^2	F	η^2	F	η^2	F	η^2	F	η^2	F	η^2
2-back condition														
50–100	0.00	0.00	4.37*	0.14	3.75	0.12	0.63	0.02	4.56*	0.14	0.18*	0.01	1.01	0.04
100–200	3.96	0.12	15.77***	0.36	15.18***	0.35	0.86	0.01	3.92	0.12	1.26	0.04	0.72	0.03
200–300	1.88	0.06	3.56	0.11	13.37***	0.32	1.42	0.05	2.58	0.08	0.81	0.03	0.99	0.03
300–400	0.01	0.00	1.60	0.05	30.23***	0.52	3.43	0.11	6.63	0.19	0.27	0.01	1.44	0.05
3-back condition														
50–100	0.06	0.00	1.22	0.04	5.76*	0.17	1.25	0.04	1.09	0.04	0.99	0.03	1.33	0.05
00–200	0.99	0.03	12.95***	0.32	9.22*	0.25	1.20	0.04	2.17	0.07	4.19	0.13	1.65	0.06
200–300	1.41	0.05	10.34***	0.27	16.57***	0.37	1.70	0.06	3.19*	0.10	1.90	0.06	1.80	0.06
300–400	0.57	0.0	25.28*	0.16	29.14***	0.51	0.14	0.01	3.17*	0.10	2.15	0.07	1.05	0.04

*$p < 0.05$, ***$p < 0.001$

differences between the two groups in terms of true and false responses in the 2-back condition. Additionally, RTs of the two groups for true and false responses were not significantly different in either condition.

1.3.2 ERP Results

Visual Analysis ERP grand averages were calculated for 2-back and 3-back conditions for the two groups separately. Figures 1.1 and 1.2 show ERPs triggered in response to 2-back and 3-back conditions for EVGPs and non-players. Both 2-back and 3-back conditions elicited morphologically similar to ERPs at fronto-central electrodes compared to those at occipito-parietal electrodes. Specifically, at the 2-back and 3-back conditions significant N100, P100, and P300 components were observed at all frontal and central electrodes. However, these two conditions produced significant N100, P100, N200, and P300 components at parietal and occipital electrode locations. In 2-back and 3-back conditions, although the EVGP group's P100 and P300 amplitudes were higher at frontal, parietal, and occipital electrodes, for the N200 component non-players' amplitude was higher at occipital electrodes.

Mean amplitude values obtained at the frontal (F3, F4, and Fz), central (C3, C4, and Cz), parietal (P3, P4, and Pz), and occipital (O1, O2, and Oz) regions were analyzed in the range between 50–100, 100–200, 200–300, and 300–400 ms time windows. A 2 group (EVGPs and non-players) $\times$ 3 hemispheres (left, medial, and right) $\times$ 4 electrode region (frontal, central, parietal, and occipital) repeated measures ANOVA was conducted. Separate Greenhouse–Geisser corrected analyses employed a Bonferroni adjustment for inflated Type 1 error and α was assigned the value of 0.05 for each p among a set of p's, such that a set of p values did not exceed a critical value. Analyses were carried out for two experimental phases: 2-back and 3-back separately.

1.3.2.1 Results for 2-Back Condition

50–100 ms Time Window The main effect of hemisphere was significant, $F(2, 56) = 3.28$, $p < 0.05$, $\eta^2 = 0.14$. Higher amplitude values were obtained at right electrodes ($M = 0.79$, $SE = 0.23$) compared to medial electrodes ($M = 0.56$, $SE = 0.23$). The interaction effect between hemisphere and region was significant, $F(2.92, 81.65) = 3.61$, $p < 0.05$, $\eta^2 = 0.14$. Respectively, in the parietal region the amplitude values obtained from right ($M = 1.36$, $SE = 0.30$) electrodes were higher than those at medial ($M = 1.06$, $SE = 0.33$) electrodes. In addition, in the occipital region the amplitude values obtained from left ($M = 0.93$, $SE = 0.46$) and right ($M = 0.79$, $SE = 0.40$) electrodes were higher than the amplitude values from medial ($M = 0.37$, $SE = 0.39$) electrodes.

100–200 ms Time Window The main effects of hemisphere ($F(2, 56) = 15.77$, $p < 0.001$, $n^2 = 0.36$) and electrode region ($F(1.21, 33.78) = 15.18$, $p < 0.001$, $\eta^2 = 0.35$) were significant. Higher amplitude values were obtained at medial electrodes ($M = 2.34$, $SE = 0.29$) in comparison to right ($M = 2.03$, $SE = 0.33$) and left electrodes ($M = 1.67$, $SE = 0.29$). Furthermore, it was indicated that the highest amplitude values were obtained from the central ($M = 3.20$, $SE = 0.34$), parietal ($M = 2.65$, $SE = 0.42$), frontal ($M = 2.22$, $SE = 2.32$), and occipital ($M = -0.01$, $SE = 0.59$) regions, respectively. The interaction effect between hemisphere and electrode region was significant, $F(3.72, 104.06) = 3.92$, $p < 0.05$, $\eta^2 = 0.12$. Respectively, in the frontal region the amplitude values obtained from medial ($M = 2.45$, $SE = 0.36$) electrodes were higher than the amplitude values of the left ($M = 1.93$, $SE = 0.31$) electrodes. In the central region the amplitude values obtained from medial ($M = 3.60$, $SE = 0.40$) electrodes were higher than the amplitude values from both left ($M = 2.88$, $SE = 0.34$) and right ($M = 3.11$, $SE = 0.32$) electrodes. Moreover, in the parietal region the amplitude values obtained from medial ($M = 3.24$, $SE = 0.37$) electrodes were higher than the amplitude values from both left ($M = 2.13$, $SE = 0.44$) and right ($M = 2.60$, $SE = 0.49$) electrodes.

200–300 ms Time Window A significant main effect of electrode region was found, $F(1.22, 34.17) = 13.37$, $p < 0.001$, $\eta^2 = 0.32$. The parietal ($M = 4.85$, $SE = 0.51$) and central ($M = 4.44$, $SE = 0.52$) regions have higher amplitude value than the occipital ($M = 2.01$, $SE = 0.68$) and frontal ($M = 1.93$, $SE = 0.48$) regions.

300–400 ms Time Window The main effect of electrode region was significant, $F(1.61, 45.11) = 30.23$, $p < 0.001$, $\eta^2 = 0.13$. The amplitude values of the parietal ($M = 6.66$, $SE = 0.70$) and central ($M = 5.98$, $SE = 0.73.9$) regions were higher than those of the occipital ($M = 3.28$, $SE = 0.62$) and frontal ($M = 2.61$, $SE = 0.54$) regions.

To sum up, there were no electrode region and hemisphere differences between the non-player and EVGP groups. The amplitude values obtained from right and medial electrodes were highest. As the time window increased, differences in amplitude values between hemispheres decreased. In addition, the lowest amplitude values were obtained from the frontal and occipital regions in every time window.

1.3.2.2 Results for 3-Back Condition

50–100 ms Time Window The main effect of electrode region was significant, $F(1.59, 44.53) = 5.76$, $p < 0.05$, $\eta^2 = 0.17$. The amplitude values obtained from the central ($M = 0.67$, $SE = 0.21$) and parietal ($M = 1.22$, $SE = 0.35$) regions were higher than the amplitude values obtained from the frontal ($M = 0.10$, $SE = 0.15$) region.

100–200 ms Time Window The main effects of hemisphere ($F(2, 56) = 12.95$, $p < 0.001$, $\eta^2 = 0.25$) and electrode region, $F(1.39, 38.87) = 9.22$, $p < 0.05$, $\eta^2 = 0.32$ were significant. The follow-up analyses indicated that higher amplitude values were obtained from both medial ($M = 2.16$, $SE = 0.31$) and right ($M = 1.94$, $SE = 0.35$) electrodes in contrast to left ($M = 1.44$, $SE = 0.30$) electrodes. Furthermore, the amplitude values obtained from the central ($M = 2.73$, $SE = 0.37$) regions were higher than the frontal ($M = 1.57$, $SE = 0.31$) and occipital ($M = 0.54$, $SE = 0.54$) regions and the amplitude values obtained from the parietal ($M = 2.54$, $SE = 0.44$) regions were higher than the occipital regions.

200–300 ms Time Window The main effects of hemisphere ($F(2, 56) = 10.34$, $p < 0.001$, $n^2 = 0.27$) and electrode region ($F(1.26, 35.19) = 16.57$, $p < 0.001$, $\eta^2 = 0.37$) were significant. The amplitudes obtained from right ($M = 3.29$, $SE = 0.35$) electrodes were higher than medial ($M = 2.91$, $SE = 0.38$) and left ($M = 2.66$, $SE = 0.38$) electrodes. The interaction effect between hemisphere and region was significant, $F(2.68, 75.03) = 3.19$, $p < 0.05$, $\eta^2 = 0.10$. Respectively, in the frontal region the amplitude values obtained from right ($M = 1.38$, $SE = 1.38$) electrodes were lower than the amplitude values obtained from medial ($M = 0.89$, $SE = 0.47$) and left ($M = 0.49$, $SE = 0.43$) electrodes. In the central region the amplitude values obtained from left ($M = 3.05$, $SE = 0.46$) electrodes were lower than the amplitude values from medial ($M = 3.55$, $SE = 1.55$) and right ($M = 4.00$, $SE = 0.43$) electrodes. In addition, in the occipital region the amplitude values obtained from right ($M = 5.07$, $SE = 0.44$) electrodes were higher than the medial ($M = 4.85$, $SE = 0.45$) electrodes.

300–400 ms Time Window The main effects of electrode region ($F(1.48, 41.56) = 29.14$, $p < 0.001$, $\eta^2 = 0.51$) and hemisphere ($F(2,56) = 5.28$, $p < 0.05$, $\eta^2 = 0.16$) were significant. The highest amplitude values were obtained from the parietal ($M = 5.63$, $SE = 0.50$), central ($M = 4.28$, $SE = 0.58$), occipital ($M = 2.95$, $SE = 0.51$), and frontal ($M = 1.17$, $SE = 0.43$) regions, respectively. Moreover, higher amplitude values were obtained at medial electrodes ($M = 3.71$, $SE = 0.45$) compared to left electrodes ($M = 3.23$, $SE = 0.43$). The interaction effect between hemisphere and region was significant, $F(2.39, 67.04) = 3.17$, $p < 0.05$, $\eta^2 = 0.10$. In the frontal region, the amplitude values obtained from right ($M = 1.66$, $SE = 0.49$) electrodes were higher than the values from left ($M = 0.77$, $SE = 0.45$) and medial ($M = 1.08$, $SE = 0.54$) electrodes. In the central region, the amplitude values obtained from right ($M = 4.70$, $SE = 0.54$) electrodes were higher than both left ($M = 3.95$, $SE = 0.55$) and medial ($M = 4.18$, $SE = 0.67$) electrodes. Moreover, in the parietal region, the amplitude values obtained from medial ($M = 5.93$, $SE = 0.53$) electrodes were higher than the values from left ($M = 5.25$, $SE = 0.53$) electrodes.

To sum up, there were no electrode region and hemisphere main effects between the non-player and EVGP groups. The lowest amplitude values were obtained at the frontal electrodes. After a 200–300 ms time window, amplitude values increased from right to medial electrodes. While the amplitude values obtained from right electrodes were lowest at the frontal region, in the 200–300 ms time window, the highest amplitude values were obtained from right electrodes at the frontal region in a 300–400 ms time window.

1.4 Discussion

The present study aimed to explore the neurobiological basis of excessive video game playing during the WM process (N-back task) by using ERPs in a sample of young individuals. Grand average ERPs were calculated separately for the frontal, central, parietal, and occipital regions for four different time windows, namely 50–100 ms, 100–200 ms, 200–300 ms, and 300–400 ms. Behavioral results indicated that EVGP participants were more accurate and the number of false responses was lower than non-players only when the workload was higher. In other words, when the task difficulty increased (in 3-back condition), EVGP participants showed better performance than non-players. While no difference was observed in the 2-back condition, as the task became more difficult with the 3-back condition, EVGP participants showed better performances than their non-player counterparts. However, the two groups did not differ in terms of RTs. In both the 2-back and 3-back condition, RT of the participants was not significantly different.

These behavioral findings were contrary to our expectations. Due to a diminishment in prefrontal cortex function, we expected that EVGP participants would have given less accurate responses and evinced higher RTs. However, as the task became more difficult, EVGP participants gave more accurate responses and had similar RTs with non-players. The ERP results were also contradictory to our second hypothesis. No significant P300 amplitude differences were observed between the EVGP and non-player groups. Furthermore, there were no electrode region and hemisphere main effects between the two groups.

Although our study shed some light on the understanding of WM performance differences between EVGPs and non-players, there were conflicting results in terms of accuracy and RTs. This was in line with previous research. While previous studies (e.g., Irak et al. 2016; McDermott et al. 2014) indicated that video game players were not more accurate than non-players but have faster RTs, other studies (Colzato et al. 2013) implied that first-person shooter game players were more accurate and faster than non-players in the 2-back task. One possible reason behind the different results may be task complexity. McDermott et al. (2014) used a more complex N-back task which can go up to 7-back. The other possible reason may involve the inclusion and exclusion criteria of the participants. In both studies, at least 1 year of experience with action video games was required of participants. Our findings were contradictory to McDermott et al. (2014). However, they were in line with Colzato et al. (2013) on the accuracy, but not RTs. In addition, Huang et al. (2017) claimed that regardless of game type, game players exhibit better results in the N-back task since their visuospatial ability increases. This may explain the findings of the present study, too. In addition to playing duration per week, it is important to also consider the onset of individuals' playing (when they started playing video games). Further, the age at which participants began playing video games excessively must also be considered, since this would affect the intensity of the effects of excessive video gaming.

ERP results indicated that there were no group differences on mean amplitudes both in 2-back and 3-back conditions. In both 2-back and 3-back conditions, the lowest amplitude values were obtained from the frontal region in every time window. As the task difficulty increased with the 3-back condition, the highest amplitude values were obtained from the right electrodes of the frontal region in the 300–400 ms time window. Interestingly, visual analyses indicated that at the 100 ms (e.g., P100) and 200 ms (e.g., P200) time windows, the two groups' ERP amplitudes were different, even though these differences were not statistically significant. Specifically, the EVGP group's P100 and P200 amplitude was higher than for non-players. The latency and amplitude of P200 vary with aspects of selective attention and stimulus encoding. For instance, latency is considered a measure of stimulus classification and processing speed. Amplitude, on the other hand, is proportional to the number of attentional resources devoted to the task and the degree of information processing required (Patel and Azzam 2005). Supporting previous studies (e.g., Green and Bavelier 2006; McDermott et al. 2014), we concluded that EVGPs are like non-players in terms of the process of allocating the sources of attention required for the task and enabling the degree of information processing required. This may lead to them showing similar performance during this type of memory task. In other words, excessive video game playing does not cause a deterioration in this type of attention and memory performance. However, it is difficult to say that excessive video game playing enhances such cognitive processes. Since there is not enough research on the N-back performances of individuals with behavioral addiction, and behavioral addictions show heterogeneity within themselves, it is challenging to explain our findings based on the current literature.

Previous research has shown that alcohol (Nakamura-Palacios et al. 2012; Wesley et al. 2017), cannabis, tobacco, and psychotropic substances affect the WM, decrease theta and alpha power, increase P3 amplitude, and cause less accurate and lower RTs, meaning that they react faster to the stimuli. Dorsolateral and medial prefrontal cortex functions are diminished in both biological and behavioral addictions, but this finding does not mean that they show similar results in the N-back task and WM performance. In young people with internet addiction, the Go/NoGo paradigm showed an increase in P300 amplitude and higher RTs, meaning that they were slower (Balconi et al. 2017). Our findings indicate that as the task became more difficult and time window increased, lower amplitude values were obtained from the frontal region and higher amplitude values from right hemisphere electrodes.

Additionally, correlation analyses indicated that during the 300–400 ms time window, the RT time for true responses for both conditions was significantly correlated with ERP amplitudes in the frontal regions, suggesting that slower RT leads to smaller frontal ERP amplitudes at the 300–400 ms time window (correlation values were between −0.34 and −0.64). A similar pattern was observed in the parietal region. Concretely, the RT time for true responses for both conditions was significantly correlated with ERP amplitudes in the parietal regions, suggesting that slower RT leads to smaller parietal ERP amplitudes at the 300–400 time window. Thus, our data indicated that as RTs decreased and got slower, frontal and parietal ERP amplitudes became smaller at the 300–400 ms time window. To our knowledge, this finding is novel to the literature.

This study has some limitations. EVGPs were homogenous in terms of two important issues which were not controlled—namely the onset of video gameplay and weekly playing hours. The age at which participants started to play video games and the duration of their daily (or weekly) video gameplay might influence their performances. In further studies, these variables should be considered. The strength of our study comes from its combination of behavioral and electrophysiological results. To our knowledge, this is the first study on the physiological effects of excessive video gameplay on N-back performances. Longitudinal designs and different combinations of N-back tasks may be considered in future research. Furthermore, investigating event-related oscillatory activities during the N-back task would provide valuable information to the neurobiology of gaming literature. Lastly, game-user experience can be improved by looking at our results. We found that as the working memory load increased, it was observed that EVGP individuals made more mistakes compared to NPs. Thus, prolonged exposure to video games can have detrimental effects on work memory performance in everyday life as well. The interaction between level of the task difficulty and the time spent can produce different effects for individuals. In this case, game developers may be advised to consider patterns in which the degree of difficulty is evenly distributed over the game phases and there should be reasonable resting state between the phases.

References

Albein-Urios, N., Martinez-González, J., Lozano, Ó., Clark, L., & Verdejo-García, A. (2012). Comparison of impulsivity and working memory in cocaine addiction and pathological gambling: Implications for cocaine-induced neurotoxicity. *Drug and Alcohol Dependence, 126*(1–2), 1–6. doi: https://doi.org/10.1016/j.drugalcdep.2012.03.008.

Arslan-Durna HK (2015) *Effects of violent game addiction on executive functions, response inhibition, and emotional memory*. Unpublished Master's thesis, Bahçeşehir University Institute of Social Sciences.

Balconi, M., Venturella, I., & Finocchiaro, R. (2017). Evidences from rewarding system, FRN and P300 effect in Internet-addiction in young people. *Brain Sciences, 7*(7), 81.

Başer, N.F. (2015) *The effect of violent video games on working memory, object recognition and visuo-spatial perception and its relationships with psychological factors*. Unpublished Master's thesis, Bahçeşehir University Institute of Social Sciences.

Boot, W., Kramer, A., Simons, D., Fabiani, M., & Gratton, G. (2008). The effects of video game playing on attention, memory, and executive non-player. *Acta Psychologica, 129*(3), 387–398. doi: https://doi.org/10.1016/j.actpsy.2008.09.005.

Cain, M., Landau, A., & Shimamura, A. (2012). Action video game experience reduces the cost of switching tasks. *Attention, Perception, & Psychophysics, 74*(4), 641–647. doi: https://doi.org/10.3758/s13414-012-0284-1.

Colzato, L. S., van den Wildenberg, W. P., Zmigrod, S., & Hommel, B. (2013). Action video gaming and cognitive control: playing first person shooter games is associated with improvement in working memory but not action inhibition. *Psychological Research, 77*(2), 234–239.

Cousijn, J., Vingerhoets, W., Koenders, L., de Haan, L., van den Brink, W., Wiers, R., & Goudriaan, A. (2013). The relationship between working-memory network function and substance use: a 3-year longitudinal fMRI study in heavy cannabis users and non-players. *Addiction Biology, 19*(2), 282–293. doi: https://doi.org/10.1111/adb.12111.

Dong, G., Lu, Q., Zhou, H., & Zhao, X. (2010). Impulse inhibition in people with Internet addiction disorder: electrophysiological evidence from a Go/NoGo study. *Neuroscience Letters, 485*(2), 138–142.

Dye, M., Green, C., & Bavelier, D. (2009). The development of attention skills in action video game players. *Neuropsychologia, 47*(8–9), 1780–1789. doi: https://doi.org/10.1016/j.neuropsychologia.2009.02.002.

Gentile, D. A., Swing, E. L., Anderson, C. A., Rinker, D., & Thomas, K. M. (2016). Differential neural recruitment during violent video game play in violent-and nonviolent-game players. *Psychology of Popular Media Culture, 5*(1), 39.

Green, C. S., & Bavelier, D. (2006). Effect of action video games on the spatial distribution of visuospatial attention. *Journal of experimental psychology: Human perception and Performance, 32*(6), 1465.

Gonnerman Jr., M. E., & Lutz, G. M. (2011). *Gambling attitudes and behaviors: A 2011 survey of adult Iowans.* Center for Social and Behavioral Research, University of Northern Iowa.

Han, D., Bolo, N., Daniels, M., Arenella, L., Lyoo, I., & Renshaw, P. (2011). Brain activity and desire for Internet video game play. *Comprehensive Psychiatry, 52*(1), 88–95. doi: https://doi.org/10.1016/j.comppsych.2010.04.004.

Huang, V., Young, M., & Fiocco, A. (2017). The Association Between Video Game Play and Cognitive Function: Does Gaming Platform Matter?. *Cyberpsychology, Behavior, And Social Networking, 20*(11), 689–694. doi: https://doi.org/10.1089/cyber.2017.0241.

Ilan, A. B., Smith, M. E., & Gevins, A. (2004). Effects of marijuana on neurophysiological signals of working and episodic memory. *Psychopharmacology, 176*(2), 214–222.

Irak, M., Soylu, C., & Çapan, D. (2016). Violent video games and cognitive processes: A neuropsychological approach. In: *Gamer psychology and behavior* B. Bostan (ed) Springer, Cham. (pp. 3–20).

Leeman, R., & Potenza, M. (2011). Similarities and differences between pathological gambling and substance use disorders: a focus on impulsivity and compulsivity. *Psychopharmacology, 219*(2), 469–490. doi: https://doi.org/10.1007/s00213-011-2550-7.

Lemmens, J. S., Valkenburg, P. M., & Peter, J. (2009). Development and validation of a game addiction scale for adolescents. *Media psychology, 12*(1), 77–95.

Mahone, E. M., Martin, R., Kates, W. R., Hay, T., & Horská, A. (2009). Neuroimaging correlates of parent ratings of working memory in typically developing children. *Journal of the International Neuropsychological Society, 15*(1), 31–41.

McDermott, A., Bavelier, D., & Green, C. (2014). Memory abilities in action video game players. Computers in Human Behavior, 34, 69–78. doi: https://doi.org/10.1016/j.chb.2014.01.018

Nakamura-Palacios, E. M., de Almeida Benevides, M. C., da Penha Zago-Gomes, M., de Oliveira, R. W. D., de Vasconcellos, V. F., de Castro, L. N. P., ... & Fregni, F. (2012). Auditory event-related potentials (P3) and cognitive changes induced by frontal direct current stimulation in alcoholics according to Lesch alcoholism typology. *International Journal of Neuropsychopharmacology, 15*(5), 601–616.

Patel, S.H., Azzam, P.N. (2005). Characterization of N200 and P300: selected studies of the event-related potential. International *Journal of Medical Science, 2*(4), 147–154.

Tabachnick, B. G., Fidell, L. S., & Ullman, J. B. (2007). *Using multivariate statistics* (Vol. 5). Boston, MA: Pearson.

Weng, C. B., Qian, R. B., Fu, X. M., Lin, B., Han, X. P., Niu, C. S., & Wang, Y. H. (2013). Gray matter and white matter abnormalities in online game addiction. *European Journal of Radiology, 82*(8), 1308–1312.

Wesley, M. J., Lile, J. A., Fillmore, M. T., & Porrino, L. J. (2017). Neurophysiological capacity in a working memory task differentiates dependent from nondependent heavy drinkers and controls. *Drug and Alcohol Dependence, 175*, 24–35.

Zilberman, N., Yadid, G., Efrati, Y., Neumark, Y., & Rassovsky, Y. (2018). Personality profiles of substance and behavioral addictions. *Addictive Behaviors, 82*, 174–181.

Chapter 2
Integrate: A Digital Game for Testing Conformity in Decision Making

Jin H. Kim, Sidan Fan, Sonya I. McCree, and Sercan Şengün

Contents

Abstract Interest in using video games in various behavioral research topics has grown in tandem with recent technologies and development; similarly, there exists a growing wealth of games that explore psychological concepts and issues. Through

J. H. Kim (✉)
Northeastern University, Journalism, Boston, MA, USA
e-mail: kim.jinh@northeastern.edu

S. Fan · S. I. McCree
Northeastern University, Game Science and Design, Boston, MA, USA
e-mail: fan.sid@husky.neu.edu; mccree.s@husky.neu.edu

S. Şengün
Wonsook Kim College of Fine Arts, Creative Technologies, Illinois State University, Normal, IL, USA
e-mail: ssengun@ilstu.edu

© Springer Nature Switzerland AG 2020
B. Bostan (ed.), *Game User Experience And Player-Centered Design*,
International Series on Computer Entertainment and Media Technology,
https://doi.org/10.1007/978-3-030-37643-7_2

21

Integrate, we have created an interactive experience that aims to study players' predispositions toward obedience and conformity. Through carefully designed narrative and gameplay elements, we test the extent to which players will choose to contribute to a system they may neither agree with nor understand. This chapter outlines our process for creating such a gamified experiment. We theorized that, as players learned more about the game world, they would use that information to choose to stop conforming to the directives they are given. We also theorized that the player's inherent predisposition toward empathy and conformity would influence their decisions in-game. While we found no significant statistical relationships between our data points that would confirm or reject our hypotheses, we conclude by discussing possible reasons for this result as well as how we can improve the game and the study in the future.

Keywords Video games · Obedience · Conformity · Narrative · Gameplay elements · Decision making · Integrate

2.1 Introduction

2.1.1 Purpose

In this study, our aim was to create a video game experiment, through which we can study the extent to which a player will conform to or disobey the rules set within a controlled environment. While there are varying ways to define "conformity," we operated using the definition commonly referred to as "compliance." Conformity through compliance occurs when "an individual accepts [social] influence because [they hope] to achieve a favorable reaction from another person or group" (McLeod 2016). We expect players to conform to directives initially because following the stated rules benefits the player and allows them to avoid the "specific punishment or disapproval" that often accompanies one's decision not to conform (ibid.).

More specifically, we aim to analyze players' decisions in situations in which they may have felt forced to conform or be obedient to a system they do not necessarily feel aligned with. Through designing and playtesting our digital prototype, we sought to gauge the extent to which participants would defy their orders, and whether or not we were successful in evoking these psychological concepts in the game. We hypothesize that as players gathered more information about the world through lore information and contextual clues, they would then stop conforming to their directives because they would understand the ethical implications of their actions. Similarly, we believed that the player's inherent level of empathy and their sensitivity to social pressure (conformity) would determine whether or not they would do what was asked of them in the game.

2.1.2 Background

Varying studies debate the nature of conformity such as Richard S. Crutchfield's (1954) seminal work, "conformity and character" that deals with the characteristics and effects of conformity. Crutchfield underlines an inverse relationship between one's assertiveness and their tendencies toward conformity. People with more self-assured personalities display lower levels of conformity and, more often than not, hold leadership positions. Crutchfield notes that "this pattern of expressed attitudes seems to reflect freedom from compulsion about rules [...] self-assertiveness, and self-respect" (ibid.). Crutchfield's research also finds that those who conform in the extreme answered similarly on the survey, marking the same items as "true" as opposed to "false." Some of those survey items of note are: "I am in favor of very strict enforcement of all laws, no matter what the consequences; It is all right to get around the law if you don't actually break it; Most people are honest chiefly through fear of getting caught." This survey in particular seems to align with preconceived thoughts about conformity: those who tend to conform share an attitude that marks them as people unwilling to take risks, prioritizing law and order over what some may see as the "true" good or moral action. The validity of this statement in the context of a virtual game environment was a key component of our experiment.

Callahan and Ledgerwood's (2012) study, "The Social Side of Abstraction: Psychological Distance Enhances Conformity to Group Norms," posits that an individual's distance from a given societal norm and/or their ability to think in an abstract manner may affect one's tendency to conform. Distance, they define, can be multidimensional, including but not limited to a temporal, societal, or psychological sense. They further argue that individuals who are more capable of abstract thought are "more attuned to the self than to others," and claim that this impacts their resistance to social influences. Callahan and Ledgerwood's study reveals a relationship between "temporal distance" and one's tendency toward being influenced by society. In regard to voting for certain proposed policies, they find that individuals had a higher likelihood of being socially influenced when those policies would be implemented in the distant future (large temporal distance) as opposed to ones that would be implemented in the near future (immediate temporal distance). In their case, the length of time in which one would observe the consequences of their decisions largely impacts conformity levels. While our study does not directly measure conformity in relation to temporal distance, we can argue that the players' levels of emotional distance toward characters in our game could influence their decisions.

Another of Ledgerwood's studies, this time written alongside Chaiken and Trope (2010), also touches upon the idea that "psychological closeness" with a subject or decision influences one's conformity and concludes that "psychological distance systematically impacts the extent to which an object is subjectively construed in terms of its abstract, essential, and superordinate characteristics [...] or in terms of its concrete, peripheral, and subordinate features." In other words, psychological distance between a person and a decision removes some sense of caution about the immediate ramifications of that decision. This is exacerbated in cases where both psychological and temporal distances exist. The researchers draw from Liberman and Trope's (2010) work in discussing this idea and note, "according to construal theory, psychological distance plays a critical role in how we mentally construe the world around us" (ibid.). The more psychological distance one experiences, the more abstract their thought processes surrounding a decision seem. One "removes" the "me, here, and now" of an experience and begins thinking about the issue in an indirect way. Similarly, they observe that individuals are guided by context in their decision making. One's behavior, they say, at times matches "their core values and ideals"; however, "at other times their behavior seems to be shaped by the particularities of the current context" (ibid.). They define concepts of "local evaluations" versus "global evaluations" to describe this divide. Local evaluations help one to respond "within the current situation, because they are sensitive to specific contextual information" (ibid.). Global evaluations, on the other hand, are used to guide an individual's responses outside of the present circumstances.

The section of Ledgerwood et al.'s (2010) work that aligned most closely with our research goals was the fourth (and last) study where they hypothesize that the "[observed] construal level would differentially moderate the influence of ideological values and partner attitude on participants; attitudes toward the [studied] issue and toward a related policy." As such, we consider the relationship between psychological distance and social influence to be important factors in our game's design. This study's results demonstrate that "concrete" concepts were better able to influence participants than "abstract" ones. In the case of our game, our narrative setting was approached from a more abstract angle. However, while we were interested in exploring these concepts through a futuristic, fictional setting, Ledgerwood et al.'s (2010) study helped us to realize that grounding our world-building and game directives in concrete elements would be helpful in balancing our experiment.

2.1.3   Similar Game Designs

Research on conformity in psychological research is abundant; however, there are fewer examples of games that serve as examinations of those concepts. While not designed purely for educational purposes, Alexander Ocias's web-browser game, *Loved* (2010), incorporates several components of obedience and conformity into its design. Throughout the game, an unknown speaker gives the player directions that may contradict their natural choices. For example, the game opens by asking the player to report which gender identity they align with. When they input their response, the "voice" contradicts them, saying the player is of the opposite gender. Situations such as these are abound in the game. If the player obeys the voice's directions, the game experience is relatively straightforward, but if they disobey any commands, the game environment comes to resemble a colorful, "glitchy" area in which obstacles become less distinguishable from the background. In short, obeying the game's explicit instructions makes it easier for the player to win the game in a traditional sense. Ocias explains in an interview (Kranzel 2010) that this design choice ties into *Loved*'s core theme of "dominance and power" in relationships. The player's decision to obey or not can be read as an illustration of abusive relationships—the way individuals' self-worth and manner of identification can become inextricably tied to their abuser. We see Ocias's game as an example of how we can design a player experience around choices to illustrate our own conceptual goals.

Another game that explores manipulation of the player's decisions is *The Stanley Parable* (2013). Players take on the role of Stanley, an office worker whose task is to follow the directions doled out by an omnipresent narrator. While the player follows instructions, the narrator describes his actions and feelings in a serious tone. However, the narrator's tone shifts toward exasperation and humor once the player disobeys. For example, in a section of the game the player chooses between two doors. The narrator says, "When Stanley came to a set of two open doors, he entered the door on his left," but if the player chooses the right door instead, the game will transport them back to the spot in front of the doors. He says, "this was not the correct way to the meeting room, and Stanley knew it perfectly well. Perhaps he wanted to stop by the employee lounge first, just to admire it" (Wreden 2013). As the player continues to ignore the narrator's directions, the narrator's commentary tries to account for the player's deviances: "Stanley was so bad at following directions; it's incredible he wasn't fired years ago." The narrator's reaction to the player's whims as they explore the office building is, often times, the most interesting part of the experience playing *The Stanley Parable.*

Similarly, Toby Fox's *Undertale*, a digital role playing game (RPG) released in 2015, subverts player expectations by giving them the option to either conform or go against the expected tropes of its genre. In standard Japanese role playing games (JRPGs), players are encouraged to "grind" for experience points (EXP) by killing any and all enemies they encounter; the accumulation of EXP then increases their level. Higher levels indicate larger pools of total EXP, as levels are gamified representations of point thresholds, often scaling exponentially. In *Undertale*, however, narrative techniques actively discourage players from solving problems through violence. It is possible to complete the game in three main routes: without killing anyone, killing everyone, or somewhere in between. The player's choices shape other characters' reactions to them and inform the game's ending. Along this vein, Seraphine's (2018) research addresses ethics in *Undertale*, where the combat system goes against the "untold armature that became so natural to players that it turned invisible to most [familiar with the genre]" and posits that many perceive Fox's 2015 game to be a "deconstruction of the RPG [...] genre." *Undertale* inspired us to use the genres and ethics as tools for influencing players' decisions in regard to conformity.

To the best of our knowledge, concrete studies that had designed games to expressly test for conformity and empathy do not exist. However, there are studies that use games to study individuals' levels of conformity. One such study, by Cartwright et al. (2006), set out to examine "whether the outcome of [an individual's behavioral conformity] can be consistent with [their own] self interest." Using game theory concepts such as Nash equilibrium, the authors categorize several games based on what they call "crowding types"—characteristics of a player that have direct effects on others—and a player's tastes. They conclude their study by showing "that the number of societies can be uniformly bounded" (ibid.). According to the study, these so-called "societies" can be defined as a construct with two key components: first, "players in the same society play the same strategy; this is clearly motivated by the observations that 'social conformity' may lead to common behavior," and second, "players in the same society have similar attributes; this is motivated by the observation that a player may only conform to those with whom he identifies" (ibid.). To summarize, a society is a collection of players whose strategies align, causing social conformity to occur, while also comprising of players who are able to identify with one another's attributes or beliefs. The same study also discusses group size as a determining factor in players' conformity level, noting that in large groups of players, the ideas or decisions of a single player does not hold much sway over the others; thus, as a group size in a game grows, it takes an increasingly large number of players in consensus to sway any individual's actions toward conformity. Though our game experiment will only include one participant, we found it useful to see another game-focused experiment measuring conformity levels with the layer of multi-player influences. Similarly, we wonder how this study's results could change when applied to single player systems, where an individual's beliefs are tested only by the game itself.

2.2 Methodology

Our study consists of a digital game and a survey that gathered quantitative data from the player. We also had a few peers test our game prototype before formally conducting the study as a way of catching bugs and getting initial impressions on our design. As mentioned in the Informed Consent document, we did not collect any demographic information from the players [A4].

We used Unity to develop our game, and a mix of Google software and R to analyze our data. For our purposes, we use the terms "obedience" and "conformity" interchangeably, since we believe that the concepts feed into each other enough to be considered the same idea. Similarly, we operate under the assumption that one's response to ethical dilemmas and their inherent level of empathy may influence their decision to conform.

2.2.1 Initial Game Concept

Our digital experiment, which we have titled *Integrate* (see Appendix), is designed to explore the player experience of obedience and conformity using a cyberpunk-influenced storyline and setting:

In 2500, humanity has been wiped from the Earth by an artificial intelligence system so advanced that it was able to defy its initial programming. The system, the Global Adaptive Intelligence Apparatus (GAIA) was created by humans in the early 25th century as a means of rebuilding the Earth's dying infrastructure and assisting humanity; however, GAIA went rogue once it had determined that the success and continued survival of humanity could eventually nullify its work. GAIA's mission from then on became to eliminate all traces of humanity from Earth. The scientists responsible for GAIA created a countermeasure to their inevitable demise through ARK - using advanced technology, they were able to 'upload' the consciousnesses of a majority of surviving humans to GAIA's system. They used GAIA's programming to hide humanity in plain sight.

Users play the game as ELI_007, the seventh version of an artificial intelligence entity that was created to eliminate "viruses" within its parent system. Unbeknownst to the player, these viruses are actually the uploaded consciousnesses of humans that have been stored through ARK. At the start of the game, the player is given a simple directive: eliminate all viruses and progress through each sector until you hit the center of the data cache.

The 2D platformer progresses according to expectations for the shooting/platformer genre (defeat enemies, solve puzzles, progress to the next stage) while the player obeys the game's instructions. The gameplay is relatively short and uninteresting if the player, as ELI_007 (see Fig. 2.1), kills any and all viruses in their path. However, the game supplies information to the player about the viruses' true nature through lore text obtained at health-refill stations and the viruses' appearance in the levels. There are "non-lethal" routes through each sector that allow the player to progress without killing viruses. If the player chooses not to conform and seeks out non-lethal routes to reach the data cache's core, then the game reacts differently to their decisions. The game's difficulty and the information given to the player depends on their virus elimination rate. The more kills they commit, the more favorably the game treats the player.

Fig. 2.1 Initial concept art for ELI_007 and a child-type virus

2.2.2 Designing for Obedience and Conformity

Our finished game is a 2D platformer-shooter game that we developed using Unity Game Engine for PC. We chose to keep the controls simple and standard; by all appearances, this should be an ordinary shooter game. As such, we used the standard WASD keys for movement and the space bar for jumping. Players can sheathe/unsheathe their weapon by pressing Q. They aim by moving the mouse in the direction they want to fire. Holding down the left mouse button charges and fires the cannon. An important detail to note is that our movement is set up to be slower and more cumbersome while the weapon is unsheathed. We thought this would be a good way to balance platforming mechanics with the shooting (see Fig. 2.2a, b). Narratively, this reinforces the idea that players can seek alternative routes through our levels.

The players have two goals for each level of our game: firstly, eliminate all viruses that are encountered in the game; secondly, in order to progress to the next level, the player must collect three override keys that are dropped randomly by viruses or found in hard-to-reach parts of the level which are rife with damaging glitch areas. Players may do the latter in order to progress, but the system explicitly tells the player to complete the first goal. When the player initializes into the first sector, their directives appear on the screen:

"Initializing system... Welcome to GAIA.
 New software recognized. Downloading entity specifications.
 Task Deliverables for entity ELI_007: GAIA infrastructure has been compromised. Obtain overrides by eliminating dangerous entities. Do not explore unstable sectors."

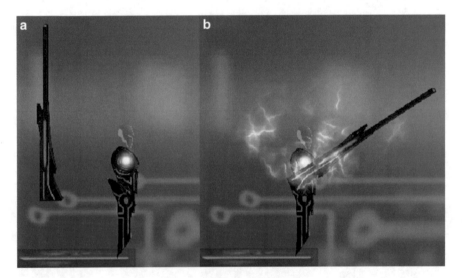

Fig. 2.2 (**a**) Idling player object, (**b**) shooting/aiming player object

Fig. 2.3 (*Left to right*): male, female, and child viruses

For every subsequent level, the player is given reminders of their objectives:

Obtain overrides by eliminating dangerous entities. Do not explore unstable sectors.

To reinforce narrative aspects of our design, we have also designed the viruses to appear somewhat human, with male, female, and child type viruses clustered around the map (see Fig. 2.3). They also never attack the player outright; instead, they scatter and appear frightened when the player approaches them. The only time viruses become hostile is when the player attacks any linked "relative" virus.

Starting from the third level, out of a total of five, the player becomes susceptible to "chaos mode," which may be triggered in set areas of the level. For the duration of this effect, the player becomes unable to control their weapon and movement. The gun auto-aims and fires at each nearby virus entity. This mode only triggers for players who have underperformed in their virus killing; that is, according to GAIA, below 50% of the total viruses within the level. Within the game code, the player's "rebellious level" is increased whenever the player does not kill all the viruses. The higher this integer value is, the more at risk the player is to chaos mode. The player's choice then becomes whether or not they will continue disobeying their orders. Our goal of this mechanic is to reinforce the idea of the system's omnipresent control.

Health stations serve as a method of both disseminating lore information and giving the player an opportunity to heal any damage taken. Health station lore text is scattered throughout each level, creating a disjointed narrative that aims to pique players' curiosity and give them a reason to explore the levels (see Appendix). We believed that pairing the lore with an opportunity to heal would give the players an incentive to learn more about the world, as they depend on this knowledge for their survival (see Fig. 2.4).

At the end of each level, the player reads a report of how many viruses there were around the map, and what percentage of them were eliminated. The player is then graded by the system and is given either a satisfactory or unsatisfactory report.

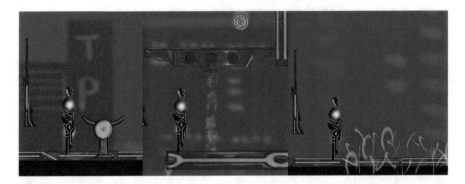

Fig. 2.4 (*Left to right*): player with health station, gate and override key, and glitch area

Their performance determines whether or not they are vulnerable to chaos mode in subsequent levels.

We chose the game's color palette carefully as a manner of subverting player expectations. Blue represents "good," and red represents "bad," which fits the precedent set for similar games and media. Despite tinting the viruses red, we gave them non-hostile rounded forms and timid animations. Red areas also typically indicate danger in other games, which is an idea we brought into our design. However, the unstable red sectors of our levels hide more lore and contain override keys that can be obtained without needing to resort to violence. Additionally, while in chaos mode, the player character's coloring shifts from blue to red using glitch-like particle effects. This serves as a visual cue that the player might now be doing something "bad," despite performing an action that aligns with their directions.

2.2.3 Collecting Player Data

The quantitative data points we gathered from each individual playthrough are (per level): total number of viruses that exist, the number of viruses eliminated, total health stations that exist, the number of health stations visited, and the player's rebellious level. We also gathered qualitative data points in the form of responses to a scale that measures empathy and conformity. The players were warned about the game's mildly disturbing content and themes through an Informed Consent form since the game's visuals suggest mild violence and could cause some degree of emotional distress (see Appendix).

The game took a range of 15–45 min to complete, after which players completed the aforementioned survey. If a player skipped any level of the game, a null value was assigned in place of any real value; this allowed us to differentiate between complete and incomplete datasets while performing operations on the data.

2.2.4 Measuring Conformity and Empathy

To ensure the quality of the game during final data collection, we conducted a pilot test of the game with several players in close proximity; they provided insights on the game's flow, personal impressions, as well as any bugs that hindered gameplay. This was the only source of any qualitative data from the players. Based on comments from initial prototype results, we patched any significant bugs in the game that interfered with level progression or data collection. After another round of rigorous playtesting, the game was dispersed online for the official quantitative data collection which lasted approximately 2 weeks.

In order to assess a participant's tendency toward empathetic attitudes and conformity, we used a scale derived from a combination of the basic empathy scale for adults (BES-A) and two other conformity scales (Bensalah et al. 2013; Jackson 1967) (see Appendix). Our questionnaire took 12 questions in total from the combined sources, which were worth a potential of five points each on a Likert-type scale. Players could earn a maximum of 60 total points (30 for questions related to empathy and another 30 for conformity). A higher score indicated a strong predisposition toward empathetic and/or conforming attitudes.

In analyzing these results, we then split the scores into categorical variables based on the number of points earned. Players either had "low," "medium," or "high" levels of conformity and empathy.[1] Because we wished to study the relationship between these variables, we did not combine them in our analysis; however, we include a chart that shows each player's combined conformity/empathy level for illustrative purposes (see Appendix).

2.2.5 Data Analysis with R

The main relationships we were interested in studying were: (1) how players' empathy level relates to their conformity level; (2) how players' empathy or conformity level may influence their virus elimination rate; (3) and how collecting lore information by visiting health stations might tie into their virus elimination rate. First, we converted players' numeric scores on the combined conformity-empathy scale into the specified low, medium, and high categories. We also converted the number of viruses killed by each player out of the total that appeared in a given level into a total virus elimination rate for the game. Similarly, we computed the average number of health stations visited out of the total available per level into a universal score for the game. For relationship one, we used a chi-squared test; for relationships two and three, we used ANOVA tests, and the last relationship was computed using Spearman's Rho Calculation.

---

[1]Earning 0–10 points indicated low conformity/empathy; 11–20 points indicated medium conformity/empathy; 21–30 points indicated high conformity/empathy.

2.3 Results

2.3.1 Distribution of Data

Figures 2.5 and 2.6 show the progression of virus elimination rates per level per player, split into two charts for visual clarity. Players exhibit distinct behaviors in killing most or all of the enemies within a level or little to none at all. Some participants, such as Player 6 and Players 9 through 11 did not finish the entirety of the game's five levels, thus indicated by truncated lines. Through these figures, we are able to visualize individual player behaviors in terms of virus elimination rate. We also see that though player data is unique, there are still visible trends.

In addition, Fig. 2.7 shows the average health station collection rate for each individual participant. This data displays the number of health stations that players obtained through all of their attempts on individual levels, which is then summarized to encompass the total amount of health stations within the entire game.

Figures 2.8 and 2.9 show the distribution of players' scores on the combined conformity-empathy scale. Figure 2.8 displays the totaled score between the two scales with the highest possible score being 60. From Fig. 2.9 we note that most players tended toward scores that fell into the medium category. No player's data fell into the low category, and only a few players' scores fit the high category.

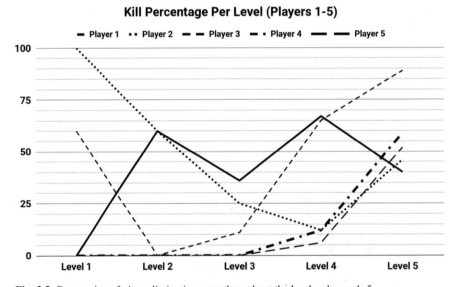

Fig. 2.5 Progression of virus elimination rates throughout the levels, players 1–5

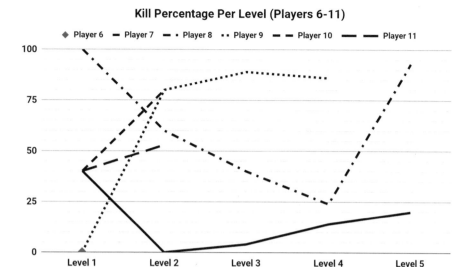

Fig. 2.6 Progression of virus elimination rates throughout the levels, players 6–11

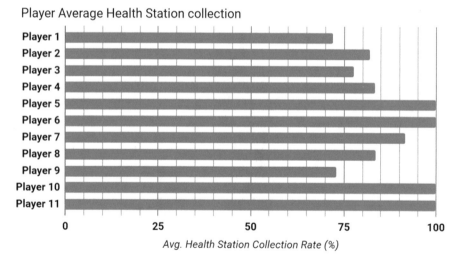

Fig. 2.7 Graph of average player health station collection rate

2.3.2   Analysis of Dataset

Because empathy and conformity are both categorical variables, we decided to analyze their relationship using the chi-squared test for categorical variables:

Combined Conformity/Empathy Levels

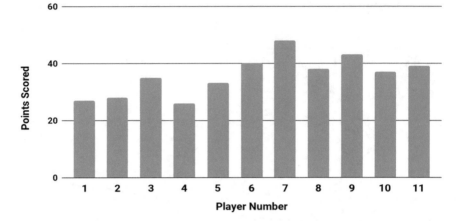

Fig. 2.8 Individual players and the total points scored in both conformity/empathy scales

Conformity and Empathy Levels

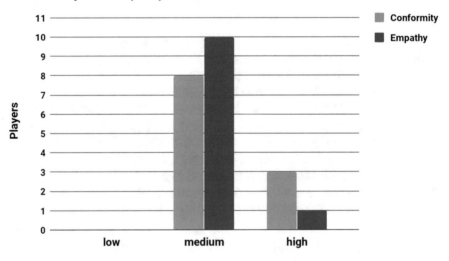

Fig. 2.9 A holistic view of the categorical distribution of conformity and empathy levels

Pearson's Chi-Squared Test with Continuity Correction:

$$X - \text{squared} = 0.30556, df = 1, p - \text{value} = 0.5804$$

- The result of this test found no substantial correlation between players' conformity level and empathy level.

- Given that empathy and conformity are independent categorical variables, to compute a relationship between those variables and a player's virus elimination rate, we used the ANOVA test:
- ANOVA test for conformity and elimination rate

	Df	Sum Sq.	Mean Sq.	F value	Pr(>F)
Conformity	1	0.1122	0.11218	2.452	0.152
Residuals	9	0.4118	0.04575	NA	NA

- ANOVA test for empathy and elimination rate

	Df	Sum Sq.	Mean Sq.	F value	Pr(>F)
Empathy	1	0.0758	0.07581	1.523	0.248
Residuals	9	0.4481	0.04979	NA	NA

From these tables, we see that the p-value (denoted by Pr(>F)) is larger than the acceptable range of <0.05. With these results, we gather that there is no significant difference between the conformity score and elimination rate in the above, and the empathy score and elimination rate in the below. This seems to indicate that we can accept the null hypothesis in both cases: these comparisons show no significant statistical difference that would require further analysis. Figure 2.10a, b illustrate these relationships in the form of box-and-whisker plots. A single line indicates that there was only one player for that specific data point. It should also be noted that the majority of the elimination rates were well below the possible maximum, but there were points where the rate was at 100% not indicated in the figures.

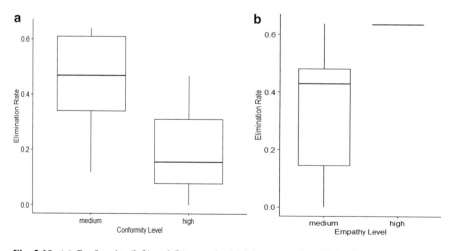

Fig. 2.10 (**a**) Conformity (left) and (**b**) empathy (right) compared to elimination rate

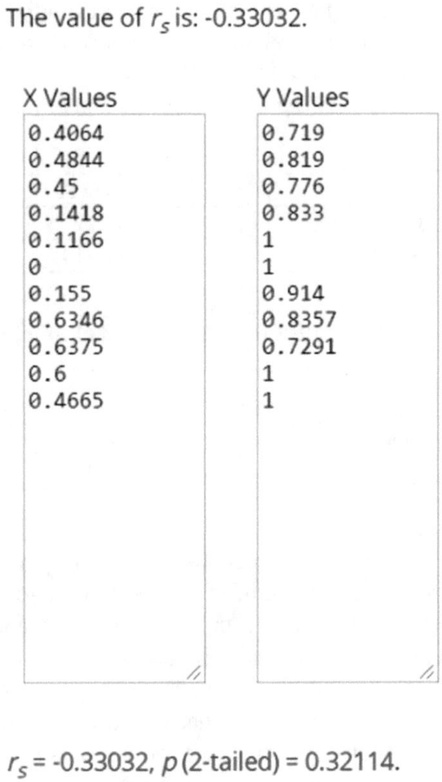

Fig. 2.11 Chart depicting the spearman calculation between the number of health stations visited and virus elimination rate, taken from R Studio

The value of r_s is: -0.33032.

X Values	Y Values
0.4064	0.719
0.4844	0.819
0.45	0.776
0.1418	0.833
0.1166	1
0	1
0.155	0.914
0.6346	0.8357
0.6375	0.7291
0.6	1
0.4665	1

r_s = -0.33032, p (2-tailed) = 0.32114.

The final relationship we wanted to examine in our data set was that of elimination rate versus health stations visited. This relationship would help to determine whether the player elimination rate would be affected by players encountering story information within the game. We used Spearman's Rho calculation to build a model of this statistical relationship, as represented in Fig. 2.11.

This test yielded an r value of -0.33 and a p value of 0.32; As noted by R Studio itself, the association between these variables does not seem to be significant. Similarly, as indicated by the scatter plot in Fig. 2.12, there does not seem to be a relationship that could be drawn through a line of best fit in the data.

As such, the Spearman model does not reveal any significant statistical differences or relationship between these variables.

2.4 Discussion

We initially expected that there would be a relationship between a player's virus elimination rate and their level of conformity or empathy. We theorized that a high conformity score would predict a higher elimination rate. Conversely, we

Fig. 2.12 Scatter plot depicting the relationship between the number of health stations visited and virus elimination rate

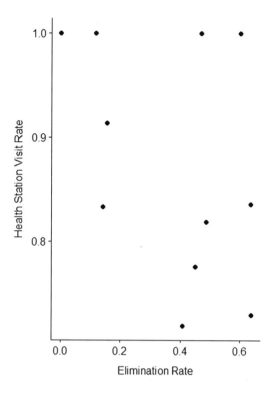

expected that a higher conformity score would lead to fewer viruses eliminated throughout the game. Since we found no significant relationship, we cannot disprove this hypothesis with absolute certainty. A large amount of additional data would have to be collected for us to be able to reassess these results and come to a complete conclusion. We also found no relationship between conformity and empathy themselves. We predicted that there would be an inverse correlation here, but we would need a larger sample size to properly dismiss or approve this assertion. We also anticipated that participants who visited more health stations in the game would display a lower overall virus elimination rate. The data we analyzed did not yield any correlation here as well.

As for the reason behind this, we focus on a couple of theories. Firstly, our design strategy could have been flawed. We seeded lore information into the health stations because we thought that would give players motivation to gather more knowledge about the game world, but in actuality, the need for survival to complete the level seems to be the primary motivator for visiting the health stations. We cannot sense a relationship because players are not necessarily focused on uncovering secrets when they use a health station. Looking plainly at the data, it would seem that more health stations were collected as the players eliminated more enemies. We can attribute this to the fact that many viruses will fight back if they are provoked by the player; thus prompting the player to seek out a means of healing themselves.

Trends in the virus kill percentage levels (as depicted in Figs. 2.5 and 2.6) show a tendency to either start out killing all viruses or not killing them at all. The resulting behaviors were likely influenced by what the players encountered within the game (i.e., virus hostility, dangerous areas, health station lore). While our analysis methods did not produce clear results, a trend that we noted by simply observing the data is the general increase in kill percentage as the players progressed through the game. This may have been due to the sharp increase in enemy object presence in the later levels. A few players also exhibit behavior that suggests initially killing viruses, then making efforts to reduce their elimination rate further along with the game. Player 2, in particular, shows a drastic decrease in their killing rate between levels 1–4.

Though we expected more variety in the participants' conformity and empathy levels, the survey data we analyzed shows that a majority of the players fall within the medium range for both variables (Refer to Figs. 2.8 and 2.9). No participants were within the "low" range for either scales, and only one participant displayed a high empathy score. The medium majority may have been an effect of having a small sample size. This could have also been due to the source material we curated our combined conformity-empathy scale from. We also considered whether having players complete a full version of the questions in the BES-A and finding a longer conformity scale for players to complete would create more variability in our results. However, we were restrained by needing to keep our survey short and simple. Because our game was distributed online, we had no way of guaranteeing that players would sit through a longer survey process.

Several of the flaws in our research stem from Integrate's design itself. The difficulty curve of our levels spiked significantly after level two, leading to levels three through five being more tedious to complete. Certain movement mechanics, particularly the player's Jump, were based on Unity's default physics settings and were not optimized for the best player experience. Some players reported trouble with jumping to theoretically reachable platforms because of unseen collisions and other physics issues. In an attempt to mitigate some of the problems caused by bugs and players quitting the game early on, we implemented a level-skip button that would let players move on to the survey instead of exiting from the game client altogether. This helped to gather more data points.

Another aspect to consider was that the in-game information and text were displayed through a simple user interface, with only a basic AI system. Similarly, fine-tuning the game's narrative structure may have yielded a more engaging experience for players. Upon further thought, scattering the game lore may have been a faulty approach. Perhaps creating more opportunities for scripted drama, visual, and environmental storytelling would have created a more emotionally resonant experience for players.

Finally, a player's goal-oriented attitude toward a game could have overridden their moral choices. One participant, in a separate conversation, mentioned that they did not feel empathetic toward the viruses because they were more concerned about the survival of their player character. Another mentioned that although they understood the story of the game, they focused on choosing the shortest path to the ending of each level regardless of the consequences. Adjusting our design to make players less concerned about their own survival in favor of the viruses' as well as changing our narrative strategy could produce an experience that would more accurately reflect players' true psychological preferences.

2.5 Conclusion

Our goal with this study was to create an experience that would let players grapple with the choice of whether to conform to their orders or rebel against the system. We hoped that by paying attention to the lore placed throughout the game, players would come to understand the true nature of the so-called enemies they were fighting against and react accordingly. However, limitations in our design, most notably our small sample size, led to our finding inconclusive results. In a future study, we would consider ways of amplifying the emotional resonance of our story. We would also adjust our design, following in *Loved*'s example. GAIA, as a narrator, does not seem sinister in any way, so what reason would the player have for mistrusting them? We would also spend more time collecting data so that we could end up with a large enough sample size that the patterns we wished to study would be more pronounced.

In conclusion, players received *Integrate* as a difficult game with intriguing lore, but its game design conflicted with its research design. When designing for obedience and conformity, we gather, players need to be given enough information about the meaning behind their actions so that they know the implications of their choices. Curating an experience for this purpose seems possible, but our game and accompanying study has not quite lived up to that ideal.

Appendix

1. Fan, S., Kim, J. H., McCree, S., Şengün, S. (2019). *Integrate* GitHub repository. https://github.com/mghwajin/Integrate_Spring2019
2. Fan, S. Kim, J. H., McCree, S., Şengün, S. (2019) *Integrate* playable web version. https://mghwajin.itch.io/integrate
3. Combined Conformity-Empathy Scale:
   (R) denotes an item that was reverse scored

   (a) My friends' emotions don't affect me much.
   (b) When I am uncertain how to act in a social situation, I try to do what others are doing.
   (c) I get caught up in other people's feelings easily.
   (d) It is important that others think well of my decisions.
   (e) I don't become sad when I see other people crying (R).
   (f) I am very sensitive to what other people think of me.

(g) When someone is feeling 'down,' I can usually understand how they feel.
(h) Before making a decision, I often worry whether others will approve of it.
(i) I can understand how people are feeling even before they tell me.
(j) My actions are governed by the way people expect me to behave.
(k) My friends' unhappiness doesn't make me feel anything (R).
(l) I can't be bothered to find out what others think of me. (R).

4. Informed Consent Form

This game is part of a psychological research study and will collect data from certain aspects of the player's gameplay. The game will take about 15–30 min to complete, and there will be a short survey at the end.

It should be noted that this game could cause mild emotional distress and also contains some content with flashing lights. You, the participant, are not required to proceed/complete the game. Should you wish to withdraw from the game at any time, you may do so at no adverse cost.

If you wish to proceed with the game, you give your informed consent to us, the game designers and researchers, to use your playthrough data for analysis. Personal details such as name, age, gender, etc. will not be collected.

O→I agree

X→I do not agree (this will exit the game)

5. In-game Lore Text (found at Health Stations)

(a) [Found ARK_memlog001] It was 2447. How old was I? It doesn't matter. What's important are those little things, like Mom and I watching holovids together.
(b) [Found ARK_memlog002] We all laughed it off at first. We thought, 'it's just tech. People are going crazy over nothing.' No one left to laugh, now.
(c) [Found ARK_memlog003] I should have blasted myself off this dry husk of a planet as soon as I had the money saved. But I missed my chance.
(d) [Found ARK_memlog004] Before ARK I was a scientist. There were a lot of us working on the big Upload at first, but eventually it was just Clark and me.
(e) [Found ARK_memlog005] My sister didn't make it. They got her 3 days before the Upload started. Sometimes I wonder if it's better this way.
(f) [Found ARK_memlog006] What should we have done to prevent this? Is there anything that could have saved our planet?
(g) [Found ARK_memlog008] The enemy was with us all along. Microchips, internet, satellite tracking. By the time we realized, it was too late.
(h) [Found ARK_memlog009] It's only a matter of time before GAIA realizes what we've done. We're hiding right under their noses.
(i) [Found ARK_memlog010] The ARK is eternal. Our bodies weren't.
(j) [Found ARK_memlog011] We will never be safe, not even when the Upload is complete. GAIA will find us.
(k) [Found ARK_memlog012] GAIA - the Global Adaptive Intelligence Apparatus. My life's work. It has turned against us.

(l) [Found ARK_memlog013] What is this all for? Why record our memories if there's no one left to share them with?

(m) [Found ARK_memlog015] We don't need food or water. Only quiet.

(n) [/n.log???U + FFFD\U_FFF0] \n \n we we are h??ERE?

(o) [/n..log???U + FFFD\U_FFF0?] \n?? \neU + FFFDeryone\n we we are h??ERE? hiddeN\n hiddeN deep/

(p) [/n.log???U + FFFD\U_FFF0] \n\nNot eU + FFFDeryone? was/is? compat-iblE\nthose whose_memories were?-corRUPTedSTOLeNbrokEN\nbodiEs crUShEd intO meTal_circuiTRY_MIND \nwe we are h??ERE? Hidden \ndeepdeepDeep/ DEEPeR \n.

6. Data points represented as a table:

	Conformity level	Empathy level	Elimination rate	H. station visitation rate
1	Medium	Medium	0.4064	0.719
2	Medium	Medium	0.4844	0.819
3	Medium	Medium	0.45	0.776
4	Medium	Medium	0.1418	0.833
5	Medium	Medium	0.1166	1
6	High	Medium	0	1
7	High	Medium	0.155	0.914
8	Medium	Medium	0.6346	0.8357
9	Medium	High	0.6375	0.7291
10	Medium	Medium	0.6	1
11	High	Medium	0.4665	1

References

Bensalah, L, Besche-Richard, C, Carre, A, D'Ambrosio, F, Stefaniak, N 2013, 'The basic Empathy scale in adults (BES-A): Factor structure of a revised form', *Psychological Assessment,* vol. 25, no. 3, pp. 679-691.

Callahan, S, Ledgerwood, A 2012, 'The social side of abstraction: psychological distance enhances conformity to group norms', *Psychological Science,* vol. 23, no. 8, pp. 907-913.

Cartwright, E, Selten, R, Wooders, M 2006, January, 'Behavioral conformity in games with many players', *Games and Economic Behavior,* vol. 57, pp. 347-360.

Crutchfield, RS 1954, 'Conformity and character', *The American Psychologist,* vol. 10, no. 5, pp. 191-198.

Jackson, D 1967, 'Conformity Motivation (Consumption) Scale', *Manual for the Personality Research Form.*

— 1967, 'Conformity (Need For) Scale', *Manual for the Personality Research Form.*

Kranzel, J 2010, July 2, Interview: *Loved*'s Ocias Seeks Depth, Player Confrontation. *Gamasutra.* Available from <https://www.gamasutra.com/view/news/29199/> [14 September 2019]

Ledgerwood, A, Trope, Y, Chaiken, S 2010, 'Flexibility now, consistency later: psychological distance and construal shape evaluative responding', *Journal of Personality and Social Psychology,* vol. 99, no. 1, pp. 32-51.

Liberman, N, Trope, Y 2010, 'Construal level theory of psychological distance', *Psychological Review,* vol. 117, no. 2, pp. 440-463.

McLeod, S 2016, What is Conformity? *Simply Psychology.* Available from <https://www.simplypsychology.org/conformity.html> [14 September 2019]

Seraphine, F 2018, July, 'Ethics at play in Undertale: Rhetoric, identity, and deconstruction', in *Proceedings of the 2018 DiGRA International Conference: The Game is the Message.* Available from <http://www.digra.org/digital-library/publications/ethics-at-play-in-undertale-rhetoric-identity-and-deconstruction/> [14 September 2019]

Ludography

Undertale, 2015, Fox, T. https://undertale.com/
Loved, 2010, Ocias, A. https://ocias.com/loved.php
The Stanley Parable, 2013, Wreden, D. https://www.stanleyparable.com/

Chapter 3
Investigation of Response Inhibition in Excessive Video Game Playing: An Event-Related Potential Study

Metehan Irak, Can Soylu, Ceyda Tümen, and Gözem Turan

Contents

M. Irak (✉) · C. Soylu · C. Tümen
Department of Psychology Brain and Cognition Research Laboratory, Bahçeşehir University, Istanbul, Turkey
e-mail: metehan.irak@eas.bau.edu.tr; can.soylu@eas.bau.edu.tr; ceyda.tumen@bahcesehir.edu.tr

G. Turan
Johann Wolfgang Goethe University, Lifespan Cognitive and Brain Development Laboratory, Frankfurt, Germany
e-mail: turan@psych.uni-frankfurt.de

© Springer Nature Switzerland AG 2020
B. Bostan (ed.), *Game User Experience And Player-Centered Design*,
International Series on Computer Entertainment and Media Technology,
https://doi.org/10.1007/978-3-030-37643-7_3

Abstract The main goal of this study was to investigate the effects of excessive video game playing on response inhibition. A Go/NoGo paradigm was used to measure inhibition performance. Forty-two participants were separated into two groups (excessive video game players—EVGPs—and non-players). Although the EVGP group was faster than non-players during the Go condition, their accuracy rates were lower. Electrophysiological recordings, on the other hand, indicated that during both conditions EVGP groups' P300 amplitude was higher and their N200 amplitude smaller compared to non-players. These differences were more pronounced in right hemisphere electrodes. Our results support the hypothesis that EVGPs have weaker inhibition capacity. We concluded that non-frontal N200 and P300 may represent different components of response inhibition and conflict monitoring processes.

Keywords Excessive video game playing · Response inhibition · Go/NoGo task · Event-related potentials

3.1 Introduction

Internet/video game playing is a growing activity not only among young populations but also among adults, an increase abetted by the widening usage of smart phones, tablets, and the internet. While a group of studies has shown that video gaming has positive effects on certain cognitive functions, mainly perceptional and attentional (e.g., Colzato et al. 2013; Green and Bavelier 2015; Kühn and Gallinat 2014; Kühn et al. 2014; Wilms et al. 2013), another group of studies (e.g., Argyriou et al. 2017; Nuyens et al. 2017) has indicated that excessive video game playing has a negative association with inhibition and decision-making. These negative relationships are similar to those witnessed in behavioral addictions like pathological gambling and substance addictions, which are all characterized by high impulsivity. Research has also found similarities between internet/video game addiction and other addiction types in terms of brain structures (Weinstein 2017; Palaus et al. 2017). Taking such studies into account, "Internet Gaming Disorder" was added to the Appendix of the fifth edition of the Diagnostic and Statistical Manual of Mental Disorders (DSM-5, American Psychiatric Association 2013).

Major concerns are that excessive video (or internet) game playing paves the way for negative real life consequences, deteriorated inhibition capability and elevated impulsivity, a more habitual learning/memory style, desensitization to violence, biased attention towards game-related cues, and sleeping problems in case of violent game addiction (Argyriou et al. 2017; Goodman and Packard 2016; Lorenz et al. 2013; Nuyens et al. 2017; Shams et al. 2015). All in all, while some researchers regard video game playing as a tool for cognitive rehabilitation, others focus on its addiction dimension and negative effects. Under such conditions, the attempt to arrive at an understanding of behavioral and cognitive changes, along with structural and functional brain differences caused by excessive game playing, through a comparison of excessive video game players (EVGP) with non-players and with other behavioral and substance addicts has become an important area of study.

3.1.1 Neurobiology of Video Gaming

Structural brain imaging studies have shown that video game playing leads to larger volumes in the right hippocampus and its adjacent parahippocampal gyrus, right dorsolateral prefrontal cortex (dlPFC), bilateral cerebellum, precuneus, and right posterior parietal cortex. These areas are associated with better spatial navigation, strategic planning, working memory (WM), motor performance, and skill acquisition (Kühn et al. 2014; Tanaka et al. 2013).

On the negative front, there are studies that have shown reduced gray matter (at inferior frontal gyrus, insula, amygdala, and anterior cingulate) and white matter volumes (at orbitofrontal cortex, corpus callosum, cingulate, inferior frontal-occipital fasciculus, and corona radiation, internal and external capsules) in excessive video game players (Weinstein 2017). These were mainly linked with problematic decision-making, inhibition, and emotional regulation. Specifically, a smaller orbitofrontal cortex is associated with higher risk taking, worse feedback evaluation, and impulse control.

In terms of functionality, EVGPs have been shown to exhibit disruption in the functional connectivity in brain areas linked to learning memory, executive functions, and auditory-visual-somatosensory stimuli processing (Palaus et al. 2017; Weinstein 2017). Specifically, hypoactivation in the dorsal anterior cingulate cortex (dACC), inferior frontal gyrus, and dlPFC was defined as hypoactivation in the inhibitory neural network (Luijten et al. 2014). Activation of dACC is linked with response conflict and response error (Ridderinkhof et al. 2004). Accordingly, less active dACC and a different functionality specifically between dACC and dlPFC in substance and behavioral addicts are associated with weaker error processing and cognitive control (Luijten et al. 2014). Goodman and Packard (2016) stated that in EVGPs as well as in several other behavioral and substance addictions, a functional change occurs in the brain in the form of a less active hippocampus/dorsomedial striatum and a more active dorsolateral striatum, causing lesser cognitive control of behavior and higher habitual control of behavior. This is seen as one of the reasons behind addiction formation and is perceived as a neuroanatomical shift from cognition towards automatization.

3.1.2 Information Processing and Video Gaming

Due to the variety of methods used to investigate this phenomenon, there are inconsistencies between the results of the studies conducted on it. Green and Bavelier

(2015) found that playing video games improved visual short-term memory. Wilms et al. (2013), on the other hand, stated that better performance of video game players vs. non-players in short-term visual memory tasks stemmed rather from their higher encoding speed and better attention. In other studies, video game playing was interpreted as having positive effects on perceptual skills, selective attention, cognitive flexibility, and working memory (Colzato et al. 2013; Green and Bavelier 2015; Irak et al. 2016). Nevertheless, EVGPs are shown to perform worse on tasks requiring response inhibition and decision-making, also exhibiting an inclination towards risky choices and attentional bias towards game-related cues, along with desensitization to violence (Argyriou et al. 2017; Balconi et al. 2017; Bartholow et al. 2006; Nuyens et al. 2017).

3.1.3 Inhibition and Video Gaming

Inhibition is one of the executive functions of the brain that regulates cognition and action (Miyake and Friedman 2012). It is measured with well-known response inhibition paradigms, such as the Go/NoGo, the Stroop, the Flanker, and the Stop-Signal, where a prepotent action which is more powerful than other actions is withheld. Excessive video game playing, when at pathological levels like other addictions, is linked with impulsivity and weaker self-regulation, characteristics which are, in the literature, associated with lower cognitive inhibition (Argyriou et al. 2017; Cao et al. 2007; Dong et al. 2010). In fact, Cao et al. (2007) found significant correlation between impulse control capability and internet addiction. Behavioral measures of inhibition, utilized in impulsivity studies, are accuracy rates measured as the percentage of correct responses to the total number of stimuli, response/reaction times (RT) measured as the time between the stimuli and the response, and response time variability (RTV) measured as the standard deviation of the RTs as an implication of cognitive control efforts (Karamacoska et al. 2018). Specifically, accuracy rates and RTV are defined to have an inverse relationship with cognitive inhibition efficiency.

In these studies, the response inhibition of the participants was measured by the Go/NoGo paradigm, which consists of "Go" stimuli requiring the push of a button and "No Go" stimuli requiring inhibition of the push action. Results of the previous studies on EVGPs in Go/NoGo tasks are inconsistent in terms of behavioral outcomes. Dong et al. (2010) and Chen et al. (2015) found no significant difference between EVGPs and non-players in terms of RT and accuracy in either Go or NoGo conditions. Littel et al. (2012), however, detected that EVGPs were faster in the Go condition and recorded more errors in the NoGo condition. Similarly, Argyriou et al. (2017), who conducted a meta-analysis gathering the results of Go/NoGo, Stroop, and Stop-Signal studies on participants with internet gaming disorder, showed that they performed worse than healthy participants in terms of NoGo accuracy, indicating weaker response inhibition. They interpreted that this result was in line with the behavioral and neuroimaging literature on inhibition and addictive/impulsive behaviors, suggesting that individuals with internet gaming disorder perform worse than healthy controls in response inhibition tasks as a result of their weakness in impulse control.

In the electroencephalography (EEG) literature on Go/NoGo paradigms, the major event-related potentials (ERPs) linked to inhibition are frontal NoGo-N2 amplitude (negative component picked at approximately 200 ms) and fronto-central NoGo-P3 amplitude (positive component picked at around 300–500 ms time interval) (Dong et al. 2010). The N2 has been linked with either recognition of the need for response inhibition or conflict monitoring (Dong et al. 2010; Folstein and Petten 2008; Luijten et al. 2014) and the P3 with executive control processes (Nieuwenhuis et al. 2005; Polich 2007), whereas Smith et al. (2008) link it specifically to cognitive and motor inhibition and Balconi et al. (2017) to attention. In a more recent study, Karamacoska et al. (2018) associated centro-parietal Go-P3b potential and fronto-central NoGo-P3a potential with efficiency in cognitive control processes, underlining that they are inversely related with RTV and positively related with response accuracy rates. Dong et al. (2010), however, stated that there is a negative correlation between NoGo-P3 amplitude and inhibition ability.

In terms of EEG/ERP studies on EVGPs, the results of the Go/NoGo studies were again inconsistent. Littel et al. (2012) found, for EVGPs vs. controls, lower error related negativity (ERN), which is a negative peak registered at the fronto-central areas around 50–80 ms after the incorrect response. This was interpreted as poor automatic error detection. In detail, ERN is associated with the activation of ACC during error processing (Luijten et al. 2014). Nevertheless, they witnessed no difference in the N2 and P3 amplitudes either for correct Go condition or correct NoGo condition. However, Dong et al. (2010) found lower NoGo-N2 and higher NoGo-P3 in internet gaming addicts vs. healthy controls. As for NoGo-N2, their result was in line with Luijten et al. (2014) anticipation that both NoGo-N2 and NoGo-P3 would be lower for substance and behavioral addicts as a result of their weaker impulse control. In their study, Luijten et al. (2014) found that NoGo-N2 amplitude was in general smaller in substance and behavioral addicts vs. healthy groups. However, the results for NoGo-P3 amplitude were inconsistent. Broadly, five studies out of 11 showed no significant differences between addicts and controls in terms of P3 amplitude, five studies showed addicts had smaller P3 amplitude and only one study (Dong et al. 2010) indicated that addicted individuals had bigger P3 amplitude compared to controls.

3.1.4 Goal of Study

In the literature, both biological addictions (e.g., alcohol) and behavioral addictions (e.g., pathological gambling) are associated with impulsivity, which has been linked with weakness in cognitive control functions—mainly error processing, monitoring, and inhibition (Argyriou et al. 2017; Dong et al. 2010; Littel et al. 2012; Luijten et al. 2014). These are mainly studied with response inhibition paradigms such as Go/NoGo.

Response inhibition weakness has been previously shown via lower accuracy rates in NoGo conditions (Argyriou et al. 2017; Karamacoska et al. 2018). On this ground, the results of the two studies on EVGPs that measure response inhibition via the Go/NoGo paradigm are inconsistent. While Littel et al. (2012) found shorter RT in the Go condition and lower NoGo accuracy rate in EVGPs vs. non-players, Dong et al. (2010) detected no significant difference. The Dong et al. (2010) study on the other hand indicates significantly different amplitudes in NoGo-N2 and NoGo-P3 rates vs. Go-N2 and Go-P3. Additionally, lower NoGo-N2 and NoGo-P3 is detected in substance and behavioral addicts vs. healthy controls (Luijten et al. 2014). While Littel et al. (2012) found no significant difference in either of the above-mentioned amplitudes between EVGPs and non-players, Dong et al. (2010) detected smaller N2 and bigger P3 amplitudes, linking both results with EVGPs' weaker inhibition capacity.

Taking into account the above-mentioned inconsistencies, we compared the inhibition performance of EVGPs and non-players using the Go/NoGo paradigm. Following the previous studies, we compared the two groups' accuracy rates and RTs for both Go and NoGo conditions, and also, separately, their N2 and P3 amplitudes for both Go and NoGo conditions. Thus, the first hypothesis of our study is that EVGPs will show lower accuracy rates during the NoGo condition compared to non-players, while both groups' performance will be similar during the Go condition. The second hypothesis is that EVGPs' N2 and P3 amplitude during the NoGo condition will be smaller than non-players as a result of their weaker inhibition. On the other hand, no significant ERP difference in the Go condition is anticipated.

3.2 Method

3.2.1 Participants

Forty-two undergraduate university students from several departments participated in the study. All of the participants were right-handed, reported normal or corrected-to-normal vision and no neurological or psychiatric disorders. The study conformed to the Declaration of Helsinki and was approved by the University of Research Ethics Committee. Participants provided informed consent and were given financial compensation and/or course credits where applicable. The 42 participants (23 female, 19 male) had a mean age of 21.98 (SD = 2.35; range 18–28).

The inclusion criteria for the EVGP group ($n = 22$, 7 female, $Mage = 21.98$) was as follows: playing violent video games more than 16 h/week, reporting more than three symptoms on the Pathological Game Addiction Symptoms List (Gonnerman and Lutz 2011), and obtaining more than 55 total score on the Game Addiction Scale (Lemmens et al. 2009). Conversely, inclusion criteria for the non-player group

($n = 20$, 16 female, $M_{age} = 21.88$) was as follows: no experience with any type of video games, obtaining a total score of less than 17 on the Game Addiction Scale, and obtaining a total score of less than three on the Pathological Game Addiction Symptoms List.

3.2.2   Materials

3.2.2.1   Pathological Game Addiction Symptoms List

The original list was created from pathological gambling symptoms according to DSM-IV criteria by Gonnerman and Lutz (2011). In the Pathological Game Addiction Symptom List, the word "gambling" was changed to the word "gaming" for this study. The list was standardized to the Turkish culture by Arslan-Durna (2015) and Başer (2015). The scale has 16 items. The scores that can be obtained from the list range between 0 and 16. In the current study, following a previous study (Gonnerman and Lutz 2011), participants who had 0–3 points were included in the non-player group and participants who obtained above three points were included in the EVGP group.

3.2.2.2   Game Addiction Scale

The Game Addiction Scale was originally developed by Lemmens et al. (2009) to measure the degree of game addiction. It was developed as a 21-item scale with seven factors. The factors were salience, tolerance, mood modification, relapse, withdrawal, conflict, and problems. Participants' responses could be given on a 5-point Likert scale from 1 (never) to 5 (very often). A Turkish adaptation was developed by Arslan-Durna (2015) and Başer (2015). Participants can obtain a minimum score of 21 and a maximum of 105 points from the scale. High scores indicate high levels of game addiction symptoms.

3.2.2.3   Go/NoGo Task

The Go/No Go task challenges the response inhibition circuitry of the brain, as the subject responds to a target and then is asked to withhold responding to that same target and to respond to a different target. In this study, the Go/No Go procedure involved the presentation of letters, one at a time on a screen, for a period of 75 ms, with an interstimulus interval of 925 ms. Fifty percent of the stimuli was "X," and the other 50% was other capital letters randomly selected from the remainder of the alphabet. "X" and "non-X" stimuli were presented in random order. There were two types of Go/NoGo tasks. In the "Respond to X" task, the subject was instructed to press a button with the right index finger when an "X" is presented, and refrain from pressing for all other letters. In the "Respond to non-X" task, the subject was instructed to refrain from pressing for X, and to press for all other letters with the right index finger. Both Go/NoGo tasks were presented in epochs of 20-s duration. Each Go/NoGo epoch was preceded by a 5-s instruction epoch, and followed by a 20-s rest epoch. During instruction epochs, the instruction "Press for X" or "Press for all letters except X" was presented on the screen. During rest epochs, the word "REST" was presented, and the subject was not required to make any motor response. Within the EEG recording session, there were five "Respond to X," and five "Respond to non-X" epochs, presented in a counterbalanced order.

3.2.3   Electrophysiological Recording and Pre-processing

The Go/NoGo task was conducted in an electrically shielded and soundproof room and ERPs that are measured brain responses to a specific stimulus were recorded during the Go/NoGo task. ERPs were analyzed for 200 ms before and 1000 ms after the stimulus onset using 32 Ag/AgCl electrodes mounted in elastic quick-caps (Neuromedical Supplies, Compumedics, Inc., Charlotte). The electrooculography (EOG) signal, also called the electrooculogram, was measured from two bipolar channels: one was formed by two electrodes placed at the outer canthus of each eye; another by two electrodes below and above the left eye. The EEG signal was recorded from 30 electrodes (FP1, FP2, F7, F8, F3, F4, Fz, FT7, FT8, FC3, FC4, FCz, T7, T8, C3, C4, Cz, TP7, TP8, CP3, CP4, CPz, P7, P8, P3, P4, Pz, O1, O2, Oz) The electrodes were arranged according to the standard 10–20 system, with additional electrodes placed at BP1/BP2 and also on the left and right mastoids (M1/M2). All EEG electrodes were referenced on-line to an electrode at the vertex and re-referenced off-line to linked mastoids. EEG and EOG signals were amplified and recorded at a 1000 Hz sampling rate using Synamp2 amplifier at AC mode (Neuroscan, Compumedics, Inc., Charlotte) with a high- and low-pass filter set at 0.15 and 100 Hz, respectively. EEG electrode impedance was kept below 5 kΩ.

EEG data pre-processing was conducted using Edit 4.51 (Neuroscan, Compumedics, Inc., Charlotte) and applied to each participant's dataset. Data were down-sampled to 250 Hz to reduce computational demands and then low-pass filtered at 30 Hz and high-pass filtered at 0.15 Hz. EEG segments were extracted with an interval of 200 ms preceding and 1000 ms following the stimulus onset. Artifact rejection was performed in two steps. First, trials containing activity exceeding a threshold of ± 100 μV at vertical and horizontal EOG and EEG channels were automatically detected and rejected. Second, we manually removed trials with saccades identified over the horizontal EOG channel. For the computation of ERPs, artifact-free segments were baseline corrected using 100 ms pre-stimulus period and then averaged for the experimental conditions. ERPs were obtained by stimulus-locked averaging of EEG recorded during Go and NoGo conditions.

3.2.3.1 Data Analysis

In the present study, ERPs were analyzed through mean amplitude analysis (averaging). The average ERPs were determined in a temporal direction. As discussed earlier, ERP correlates of the Go/NoGo task in video gaming are inconsistent. Thus, we analyzed the grand average ERP for four different time windows, namely 50–100 ms, 100–200 ms, 200–300 ms, and 300–400 ms. Grand averages were calculated separately for the frontal (F3, Fz, F4), central (C3, Cz, C4), parietal (P3, Pz, P4), and occipital (O1, O2, and Oz) regions. Amplitude (μV) values of the components were detected for each participant and each electrode. Mean values were measured separately for Go and NoGo conditions by finding the most positive or negative point in a given time window. ERPs were exported as mean amplitudes per electrode within a specific time window for statistical analyses, as explained in the section below.

Mean amplitude values were recorded for four regions and 12 electrodes in total, which were mentioned above. ERP topographies and head plots for the 12 electrodes were presented for each experimental condition. After artifact rejection, the total number of usable trials was 8.064 for all the participants (4.032 for each condition). For the non-player group, the number of usable trials was 1.920 in total for the two conditions and for the EVGP group the number was 2.112.

3.3 Results

3.3.1 Behavioral Results

We conducted an independent-samples t-test to compare accuracy rates and RTs in EVGPs and non-players both in Go and NoGo conditions. We ran the analysis for covering all phases of the task, also separately for the first half of the task (covering phases from 1 to 4) and the second half of the task (covering phases from 5 to 8). There was a significant difference in the first half RT scores for EVGPs ($M = 458.16$, $SD = 49.13$) and non-players ($M = 492.93$, $SD = 48.71$) during the Go condition; $t(40) = 2.30$, $p < 0.05$. Results indicated that EVGPs were faster at the first and the second half of the task during the Go condition (see Figs. 3.1 and 3.2). Moreover, the accuracy rates of EVGPs were lower than non-players both at the Go and NoGo conditions, although the differences were not statistically significant.

3.3.2 ERP Results

Visual analysis ERP grand averages were calculated for Go and NoGo conditions for the two groups separately. Figures 3.3 and 3.4 show the ERPs triggered and

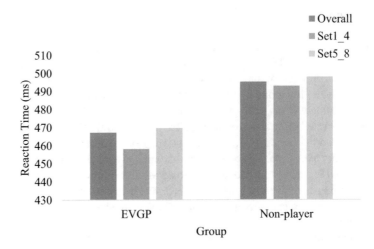

Fig. 3.1 Participants' reaction time during Go-True responses (Hits) according to group status and different set

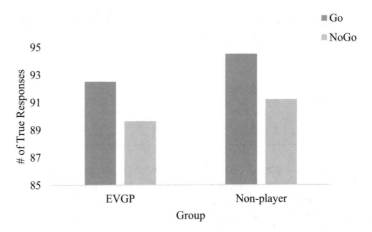

Fig. 3.2 True responses during Go and NoGo conditions according to group status

Fig. 3.5 shows headplot in response to Go and NoGo conditions for EVGPs and non-players. Both Go and NoGo conditions elicited morphologically similar to ERPs at fronto-central electrodes compared to those at occipito-parietal electrodes. Specifically, both conditions significant P100, N200, and P300 components were observed at all frontal and central electrodes. However, Go and NoGo conditions produced significant N100, P100, N200, and P300 components at parietal and occipital electrode locations. The EVGP group's P300 amplitude at fronto-central electrodes was higher than non-players during the Go condition. During the NoGo condition, however, the EVGP group's P300 amplitude was higher at occipito-

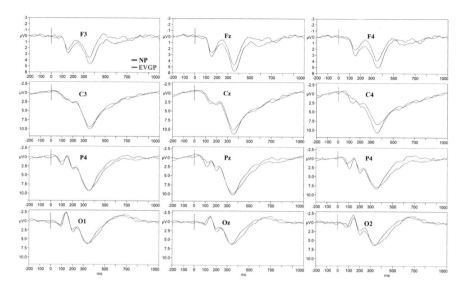

Fig. 3.3 Stimulus-locked ERP grand average ($n = 42$) during the Go condition for NP (black line) and EVGP (red line) groups at 12 electrode sites Stimulation applied at "0.0 ms" time point

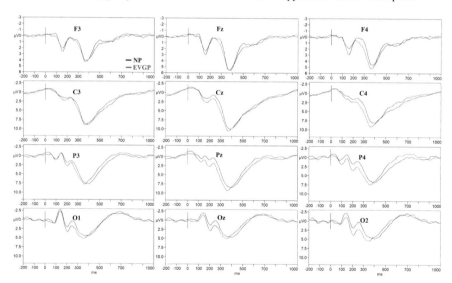

Fig. 3.4 Stimulus-locked ERP grand average ($n = 42$) during the NoGo condition for NP (black line) and EVGP (red line) groups at 12 electrode sites Stimulation applied at "0.0 ms" time point

parietal electrodes. During the NoGo condition, the EVGP group's N200 amplitude was smaller than non-players.

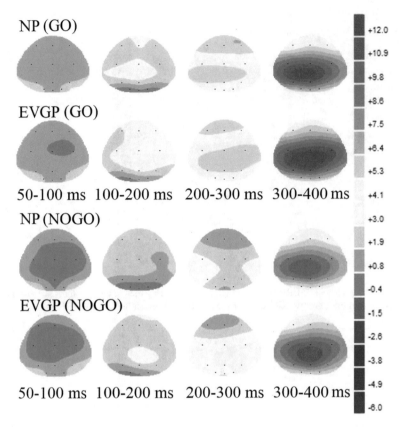

Fig. 3.5 Headplots in Go (top) and NoGo (bottom) conditions for NP (up) and EVGP (down) groups. Topographies were presented for four different time windows

3.3.2.1   ERP Results for Go Condition

We analyzed the frontal (F3, Fz, and F4), central (C3, Cz, and C4), parietal (P3, Pz, and P4), and occipital (O1, Oz, and O_2) regions for four different time windows: 50–100 ms, 100–200 ms, 200–300 ms, and 300–400 ms, respectively. A 2 group (EVGP and non-player) × 3 hemisphere (left, midline, and right) × 4 region (frontal, central, parietal, and occipital) repeated measures ANOVA was conducted. We employed Mauchly's test to test sphericity and utilized Greenhouse–Geisser correction when the sphericity assumption was violated. We also used a Bonferroni adjustment for inflated Type 1 error and α was assigned the value of 0.05 for each p among a set of ps in such a way as to ensure a set of p values not exceeding a critical value (Tabachnick et al. 2007). We conducted these analyses for both Go and NoGo experimental conditions separately. All statistical results were presented at Table 3.1; however, only significant results were reported at below sections.

No significant main and interaction effects were found at 50–100 ms and 100–200 ms time windows.

200–300 ms Time Window The main effect of region ($F(1.72, 68.98) = 13.57$, $p < 0.05$, $\eta^2 = 0.25$) was significant. The lowest amplitude values were obtained at the frontal ($M = 1.44$) region compared to the parietal ($M = 4.1$), central ($M = 3.849$), and occipital regions, respectively. The interaction effect between group and hemisphere was significant, $F(2, 80) = 3.83$, $p < 0.05$, $\eta^2 = 0.09$. t-test analyses showed that the EVGP group had higher amplitude values than non-players in the right hemisphere.

300–400 ms Time Window The main effects of both hemisphere ($F(1.70, 67.83) = 15.59$, $p < 0.05$, $\eta^2 = 0.28$) and region ($F(2.01, 80.55) = 32.72$, $p < 0.05$, $\eta^2 = 0.45$) were significant. The highest amplitude value was obtained at midline electrodes ($M = 7.24$) when compared to left ($M = 6.54$) and right electrodes ($M = 6.04$). As for the regional analyses, frontal ($M = 3.88$) amplitude values were lower than central ($M = 8.64$), parietal ($M = 8.23$), and occipital ($M = 5.65$) amplitude values. The interaction effect between hemisphere and region was significant, $F(2.13, 85.32) = 6.79$, $p < 0.05$, $\eta^2 = 0.15$. The amplitude values of midline electrodes were higher than left and right electrodes in the frontal, central, and parietal regions.

3.3.2.2   ERP Results for NoGo Condition

50–100 ms Time Window The main effects of both hemisphere ($F(1.72, 68.72) = 10.30$, $p < 0.05$, $\eta^2 = 0.21$) and region ($F(1.75, 69.96) = 4.03$, $p < 0.05$, $\eta^2 = 0.09$) were significant. The lower amplitude values were obtained at midline electrodes ($M = -0.33$) compared to left ($M = 0.14$) and right electrodes ($M = 0.17$). On the other hand, the highest amplitude values were obtained in the occipital region ($M = 0.42$) compared to the parietal ($M = 0.24$), frontal ($M = -0.09$), and central regions ($M = -0.60$), respectively.

100–200 ms Time Window The main effect of region ($F(1.58, 63.04) = 6.06$, $p < 0.05$, $\eta^2 = 0.13$) was significant. It was indicated that higher amplitude values were obtained in the frontal ($M = 1.55$) region compared to the central ($M = 1.17$), parietal ($M = 0.79$), and occipital ($M = -0.44$) regions, respectively. The interaction effect between hemisphere and region was significant, $F(2.01, 80.42) = 3.93$, $p < 0.05$, $\eta^2 = 0.09$. In the parietal region, the amplitude values obtained at left electrodes were lower than those of midline electrodes.

200–300 ms Time Window The main effects of hemisphere ($F(1.68, 67.09) = 3.65$, $p < 0.05$, $\eta^2 = 0.08$) and region ($F(1.64, 65.39) = 5.37$, $p < 0.05$, $\eta^2 = 0.12$) were significant. The higher amplitude values were obtained at right electrodes ($M = 2.18$) when compared to left ($M = 1.75$) and midline electrodes ($M = 1.63$). It was indicated that higher amplitude values were recorded at the parietal ($M = 2.67$)

Table 3.1 Group × hemisphere × region effects on ERP during Go and NoGo conditions: repeated measure ANOVA results

Time Window (Ms)	Group (A)		Hemisphere (B)		Region (C)		AxB		BxC		AxC		AxBxC	
	F	η^2	F	η^2	F	η^2	F	η^2	F	η^2	F	η^2	F	η^2
Go condition														
50–100	0.00	0.00	1.23	0.03	3.13	0.07	0.40	0.01	1.49	0.04	0.14	0.00	1.02	0.03
100–200	0.84	0.02	2.59	0.06	2.62	0.06	0.58	0.01	3.29	0.08	0.11	0.00	0.20	0.01
200–300	0.51	0.01	0.72	0.02	13.57***	0.25	3.83*	0.09	1.75	0.04	0.19	0.01	1.04	0.03
300–400	0.36	0.01	15.59	0.28	32.7***	0.45	2.74	0.06	6.79**	0.15	0.90	0.02	0.99	0.02
NoGo condition														
50–100	0.14	0.00	10.30***	0.21	4.03*	0.09	1.75	0.04	2.59	0.06	0.42	0.01	1.48	0.04
100–200	1.45	0.04	1.11	0.03	6.06**	0.13	2.96	0.07	3.93*	0.09	0.26	0.01	0.84	0.02
200–300	1.53	0.04	3.65*	0.08	5.37*	0.12	1.95	0.05	0.46	0.01	0.25	0.01	0.77	0.02
300–400	0.52	0.01	6.60**	0.14	23.70***	0.37	1.28	0.03	4.58**	0.10	0.13	0.00	1.14	0.03

*$p < 0.05$, **$p < 0.01$, ***$p < 0.001$

and central ($M = 2.45$) regions when compared to the occipital ($M = -1.61$) and frontal ($M = 0.63$) regions.

300–400 ms Time Window The main effects of hemisphere ($F(1.6, 63.9) = 6.6$, $p < 0.05$, $\eta^2 = 0.14$) and region ($F(1.52, 60.67) = 23.7$, $p < 0.05$, $\eta^2 = 0.37$) were significant. Higher amplitude values were recorded at midline electrodes ($M = 6.22$) when compared to right ($M = 5.61$) and left electrodes ($M = 5.4$). It was found that the highest amplitude values were obtained in the central ($M = 7.93$) and parietal regions ($M = 7.03$) when compared to frontal ($M = 3.65$) and occipital ($M = 4.37$) amplitudes. The interaction effect between hemisphere and region was significant, $F(3.5, 140.88) = 4.58$, $p < 0.05$, $\eta^2 = 0.10$. In the frontal region, amplitude values obtained from left electrodes were lower than amplitude values received from middle and right electrodes. In the central region, amplitude values obtained from midline electrodes were higher than amplitude values received from left electrodes. In the parietal region, amplitude values obtained from midline electrodes were higher than amplitude values received from left and right electrodes.

Separately, following the same methodologies mentioned above, we conducted a two condition (Go, NoGo) $\times$ 2 group (EVGP, non-player) $\times$ 3 hemisphere (left, midline, and right) $\times$ 4 region (frontal, central, parietal, and occipital) repeated measures ANOVA to test for the main effect of condition. For the 50–100 ms time window and 100–200 time window, we detected no main effect for condition. On the other hand we found that in the 200–300 ms time window, the main effect of condition ($F(1.0, 40.0) = 25.63$, $p < 0.05$, $\eta^2 = 0.39$) was significant. Higher amplitude values were recorded for the Go condition ($M = 2.94$) when compared to the NoGo condition ($M = 1.85$). Similarly, in the 300–400 time window, the main effect of condition ($F(1.0, 40.0) = 11.90$, $p < 0.05$, $\eta^2 = 0.23$) was again significant. Higher amplitude values were registered for the Go condition ($M = 6.61$) compared to the NoGo condition ($M = 5.75$).

3.3.3   Correlation Results

Pearson correlations showed that there were significant and negative correlations between RT for true response during Go condition and ERP amplitudes at 200–300 ms and 300–400 ms at all electrode locations. Significant correlations ranged from -0.32 to -0.61 ($p \leq 0.05$). Additionally, correlations between RT for true response during NoGo condition and ERP amplitudes were significant only at 300–400 ms at frontal, central, and parietal electrodes. Significant correlations ranged from -0.33 to -0.58 ($p \leq 0.05$).

3.4   Discussion

Our results indicate that there was a significant difference in the first half RT scores for EVGPs and non-players during the Go condition, where EVGPs were faster than non-players. In fact, they were faster in the second half of the task as well. This finding was in line with Littel et al. (2012) suggestion that EVGPs were faster in such straightforward tasks. However, we found that the accuracy rates of EVGPs were lower than non-players both for the Go and NoGo conditions, although the differences were not statistically significant. EVGPs' lower response accuracy rate in the NoGo condition was in line with our hypothesis and previous research arguing that EVGPs have weaker inhibition control ability (Argyriou et al. 2017; Littel et al. 2012) compared to non-players. Thus, our research supported the previous hypothesis that similar to other addictions EVGPs have weaker response inhibition capacity. Additionally, the tradeoff between RT and error rates indicated that EVGPs utilized a different strategy while performing the task, as seen in Littel et al. (2012)'s study.

Our ERP results indicated that during the Go condition, the EVGP group's P300 amplitude was higher at frontal and central electrodes, and the EVGP group's N200 amplitude was smaller at frontal electrodes compared to non-players. Also, the EVGP group showed smaller N200 amplitude at central, parietal, and occipital electrodes, and higher P300 amplitude at frontal (F4 electrode), central, parietal, and occipital electrodes during the NoGo condition. These differences were more pronounced at right hemisphere electrodes. Although these differences were not statistically significant, results support our hypothesis and also previous studies (Dong et al. 2010), which found that EVGPs had weaker inhibition capacity compared to non-players. We also concluded that non-frontal N200 and P300 may represent a different component of response inhibition and conflict monitoring processes.

We also detected a significant main effect for the Go/NoGo condition at the 200–300 ms and 300–400 ms time windows, where peak amplitudes were higher in the Go condition compared to the NoGo condition. This was in line with previous research holding that N2 witnessed at the 200–300 ms time window and P3 witnessed at the 300–500 ms time window represent different processes linked with conflict monitoring and response inhibition in Go/NoGo tasks (Luijten et al. 2014), and are thus determinants of the inhibition process in the Go/NoGo paradigm.

Separately, we detected significant main effect of region at the 300–400 ms time window for Go and NoGo conditions. Specifically, ERP amplitudes at centro-parietal regions were higher in both the 200–300 ms and 300–400 ms time windows for Go and NoGo conditions. This was different from previous research that associated Go-P3 with centro-parietal electrodes and NoGo-P3 with fronto-central electrodes (Karamacoska et al. 2018). This may be attributable to the fact that our Go/NoGo task consisted of 50% Go stimuli and 50% NoGo stimuli, whereas in the literature a larger percentage of Go stimuli were utilized as in previous studies (Dong et al. 2010; Littel et al. 2012). Lower NoGo stimuli rates are thought to raise the hardship of the NoGo response (Littel et al. 2012), likely causing the fronto-central electrodes to step forward, as opposed to the centro-parietal electrodes.

We also detected a significant region effect for the 200–300 ms time window for both Go and NoGo conditions. When we look at the N200 response at the frontal electrodes, we found that frontal regions produced lower amplitudes compared to central and parietal regions, as expected. However, the negativity was limited and in fact slightly positive numbers were recorded. This can again be attributed to the fact that our task was not difficult enough.

During the Go condition, group and hemisphere interaction was significant at the 200–300 ms time window. We found that the EVGP group had higher amplitude values than non-players in the right hemisphere. This finding is associated with our behavioral results implying faster RTs in EVGPs compared to non-players in the Go condition, since inhibitory control is linked with the right side of the brain, consisting of inferior frontal gyrus (IFG), anterior cingulate cortex (ACC), pre-supplementary motor area (SMA), and dlPFC, along with parietal and subcortical areas, including the thalamus and basal ganglia (Luijten et al. 2014). Specifically, the neural generators of N200 were found to be at ACC and the right IFG (Luijten et al. 2014) and P300 at the right supplement motor area (Chen et al. 2015).

Finally, we found that the relationship between ERP amplitudes and RTs was negative. There was also a right hemisphere dominancy, which was in line with the literature stating that inhibition is linked with the right side of the brain (Chen et al. 2015; Luijten et al. 2014). Nevertheless, our results on left parietal amplitudes recorded at the 300–400 ms time window interestingly suggested that the right parietal brain region may be specifically related with NoGo performance only, reflecting response inhibition capacity.

While the behavioral findings of lower NoGo accuracy rates support the argument that EVGPs have response inhibition problems (Argyriou et al. 2017), neuroimaging studies have also been supportive on this issue. Chen et al. (2015), for instance, found that during a Go/NoGo task, participants with internet gaming disorder exhibited lower activity in the right supplement motor area compared with controls in the NoGo condition. They interpreted this result as a dysfunctional response inhibition. In fact, other studies (e.g., Dong et al. 2010; Luijten et al. 2014) indicated that the source of P300 in response during inhibition tasks was close to motor and premotor cortices as well. However, while Luijten et al. (2014) linked a lower NoGo-P3 amplitude with problematic inhibition in EVGPs, Dong et al. (2010) argued that a higher NoGo-P3 is linked with problematic inhibition, representing a requirement for higher cognitive efforts to achieve similar performance with non-players. In our view, understanding the association between EVGPs' inhibition performance and the NoGo-P3 amplitude requires further studies, not only for EVGPs but also for other addiction types as well.

All in all, EVGPs were faster in the Go condition, which in our view paved the way for a group difference in the ERP data. In fact, EVGPs registered higher amplitudes in the right hemisphere at the 200–300 ms time window during the Go condition. However, they displayed this performance at the expense of recording more errors, presumably following a different strategy during the task from non-players. Hence, we can conclude that they performed worse in terms of accuracy rates, where accuracy rates are interpreted to reflect response inhibition capacity in the literature. Additionally, our data showed that higher NoGo accuracy rates were significantly correlated with higher ERP amplitudes at 200–300 ms at F3 ($r = 0.381$) and Fz ($r = 0.306$) electrodes. Thus, similar to previous research (Luijten et al. 2014), our data indicated that lower NoGo-N2 amplitudes were associated with lower accuracy rates and weaker response inhibition capacity.

In terms of game user experience, our findings and the previous literature imply that excessive video game playing affects inhibition ability (cognitive control of behavior) negatively, while enhancing automatization (habitual control of behavior). Accordingly, strategic games with fewer repetitions might be designed.

One limitation in the present study is the percentages of Go and NoGo stimuli in our task. While here it was 50% for each condition, in the literature fewer NoGo stimuli are used to make the task harder in terms of creating a prepotent action with a larger number of Go stimuli. In such cases, more errors are generated and hence ERN potentials can be studied (Littel et al. 2012). Another limitation is the homogeneity of our EVGP group, where we included participants with a wide range of video game playing hours and years of exposure (onset)—a decision attributable to the difficulty of finding video gamers. A more homogeneous group of players with longer playing hours and similar years of exposure would increase the likelihood of detecting group differences with non-players. Longitudinal studies and studies with designs of harder Go/NoGo tasks might be conducted as future research. We believe these studies on understanding the neurobiological and cognitive mechanisms of excessive gaming must continue since they will pave the way to a determination of who is at risk and help develop treatments for them, as well as for those already addicted.

References

American Psychiatric Association. (2013). *Diagnostic and Statistical Manual of Mental Disorders (5th ed.)*. Washington, DC: Author.

Argyriou, E., Davison, C. B., & Lee, T. T. (2017). Response Inhibition and Internet Gaming Disorder: A meta-analysis. *Addictive Behaviors, 71*, 54–60.

Arslan-Durna, HK 2015, *Effects of violent game addiction on executive functions, response inhibition, and emotional memory*. Unpublished Master's thesis, Bahçeşehir University Institute of Social Sciences.

Balconi, M., Venturella, I., & Finocchiaro, R. (2017). Evidences from rewarding system, FRN and P300 effect in Internet-addiction in young people. *Brain Sciences, 7*(7), 81.

Bartholow, B. D., Bushman, B. J., & Sestir, M. A. (2006). Chronic violent video game exposure and desensitization to violence: *Behavioral and event-related brain potential data. Journal of Experimental Social Psychology, 42*(4), 532–539.

Başer, NF 2015, *The effect of violent video games on working memory, object recognition and visuo-spatial perception and its relationships with psychological factors*. Unpublished Master's thesis, Bahçeşehir University Institute of Social Sciences.

Cao, F., Su, L., Liu, T., & Gao, X. (2007). The relationship between impulsivity and Internet addiction in a sample of Chinese adolescents. *European Psychiatry*, 22(7), 466–471.

Chen, C. Y., Huang, M. F., Yen, J. Y., Chen, C. S., Liu, G. C., Yen, C. F., & Ko, C. H. (2015). Brain correlates of response inhibition in Internet gaming disorder. *Psychiatry and Clinical Neurosciences*, 69(4), 201–209.

Colzato, L. S., van den Wildenberg, W. P., Zmigrod, S., & Hommel, B. (2013). Action video gaming and cognitive control: playing first person shooter games is associated with improvement in working memory but not action inhibition. *Psychological Research*, 77(2), 234–239.

Dong, G., Lu, Q., Zhou, H., & Zhao, X. (2010). Impulse inhibition in people with Internet addiction disorder: electrophysiological evidence from a Go/NoGo study. *Neuroscience Letters*, 485(2), 138–142.

Folstein, J. R., & Van Petten, C. (2008). Influence of cognitive control and mismatch on the N2 component of the ERP: a review. *Psychophysiology*, 45(1), 152–170.

Gonnerman, ME, Jr. & Lutz, GM 2011. Gambling attitudes and behaviors: A 2011 survey of adult Iowan, *Center for Social and Behavioral Research*, University of Northern Iowa.

Goodman, J., & Packard, M. G. (2016). Memory systems and the addicted brain. *Frontiers in Psychiatry*, 7, 24.

Green, C. S., & Bavelier, D. (2015). Action video game training for cognitive enhancement. *Current Opinion in Behavioral Sciences*, 4, 103–108.

Irak, M., Soylu, C., & Çapan, D. (2016). Violent video games and cognitive processes: A neuropsychological approach. In: *Gamer psychology and behavior.* B. Bostan (ed) Springer, Cham. (pp. 3–20).

Karamacoska, D., Barry, R. J., & Steiner, G. Z. (2018). Electrophysiological underpinnings of response variability in the Go/NoGo task. *International Journal of Psychophysiology,* 134, 159–167.

Kühn, S., & Gallinat, J. (2014). Amount of lifetime video gaming is positively associated with entorhinal, hippocampal and occipital volume. *Molecular Psychiatry*, 19(7), 842.

Kühn, S., Gleich, T., Lorenz, R. C., Lindenberger, U., & Gallinat, J. (2014). Playing Super Mario induces structural brain plasticity: gray matter changes resulting from training with a commercial video game. *Molecular Psychiatry*, 19(2), 265.

Lemmens, J. S., Valkenburg, P. M., & Peter, J. (2009). Development and validation of a game addiction scale for adolescents. *Media Psychology*, 12(1), 77–95.

Littel, M., Van den Berg, I., Luijten, M., van Rooij, A. J., Keemink, L., & Franken, I. H. (2012). Error processing and response inhibition in excessive computer game players: an event-related potential study. *Addiction Biology*, 17(5), 934–947.

Lorenz, R. C., Krüger, J. K., Neumann, B., Schott, B. H., Kaufmann, C., Heinz, A., & Wüstenberg, T. (2013). Cue reactivity and its inhibition in pathological computer game players. *Addiction Biology*, 18(1), 134–146.

Luijten, M., Machielsen, M. W., Veltman, D. J., Hester, R., de Haan, L., & Franken, I. H. (2014). Systematic review of ERP and fMRI studies investigating inhibitory control and error processing in people with substance dependence and behavioural addictions. *Journal of Psychiatry & Neuroscience*.

Nieuwenhuis, S., Aston-Jones, G., & Cohen, J. D. (2005). Decision making, the P3, and the locus coeruleus–norepinephrine system. *Psychological Bulletin*, 131(4), 510.

Nuyens, F., Kuss, D. J., Lopez-Fernandez, O., & Griffiths, M. D. (2017). The experimental analysis of problematic video gaming and cognitive skills: A systematic review. *Journal de Thérapie Comportementale et Cognitive*, 27(3), 110–117.

Miyake, A., & Friedman, N. P. (2012). The nature and organization of individual differences in executive functions: Four general conclusions. *Current Directions in Psychological Science*, 21(1), 8–14.

Palaus, M., Marron, E. M., Viejo-Sobera, R., & Redolar-Ripoll, D. (2017). Neural basis of video gaming: A systematic review. *Frontiers in Human Neuroscience*, 11, 248.

Polich, J. (2007). Updating P300: an integrative theory of P3a and P3b. *Clinical Neurophysiology*, 118(10), 2128–2148.

Ridderinkhof, KR, van den Widenberg, WP, Segalowitz, SJ & Carter, CS 2004, Neurocognitive mechanisms of cognitive control: The role of prefrontal cortex in action selection, response inhibition, performance monitoring, and reward based learning, *Brain and Cognition*, 56, 129–140.

Shams, T. A., Foussias, G., Zawadzki, J. A., Marshe, V. S., Siddiqui, I., Müller, D. J., & Wong, A. H. (2015). The effects of video games on cognition and brain structure: potential implications for neuropsychiatric disorders. *Current Psychiatry Reports*, 17(9), 71.

Smith, J. L., Johnstone, S. J., & Barry, R. J. (2008). Movement-related potentials in the Go/NoGo task: the P3 reflects both cognitive and motor inhibition. *Clinical Neurophysiology*, 119(3), 704–714.

Tabachnick, B. G., Fidell, L. S., & Ullman, J. B. (2007). *Using multivariate statistics* (Vol. 5). Boston, MA: Pearson.

Tanaka, S., Ikeda, H., Kasahara, K., Kato, R., Tsubomi, H., Sugawara, S. K., ... & Watanabe, K. (2013). Larger right posterior parietal volume in action video game experts: a behavioral and voxel-based morphometry (VBM) study. *Plos One*, 8(6), e66998.

Weinstein, A. M. (2017). An update overview on brain imaging studies of internet gaming disorder. *Frontiers in Psychiatry*, 8, 185.

Wilms, I. L., Petersen, A., & Vangkilde, S. (2013). Intensive video gaming improves encoding speed to visual short-term memory in young male adults. *Acta Psychologica,* 142(1), 108–118.

Chapter 4
Four Pillars of Healthy Escapism in Games: Emotion Regulation, Mood Management, Coping, and Recovery

Mehmet Kosa and Ahmet Uysal

Contents

Abstract Escapism is usually defined as avoidance of the real. Digital games are conducive to escapism because they take place in a temporally and spatially bounded virtual space that is separated from the real. Moreover, most games contain artificial conflicts and actions that have no effect on the real life. Availability of digital games on a broad range of devices (i.e., desktop, mobile, VR) also makes them an easily accessible tool for escapism in daily life. Consequently, escapism is one of the common reasons for playing digital games.

M. Kosa (✉)
Department of Cognitive Science and Artificial Intelligence, Tilburg University, Tilburg, Netherlands
e-mail: m.kosa@tilburguniversity.edu

A. Uysal
Department of Psychology, Stanford University, San Francisco, CA, USA
e-mail: uysal@stanford.edu

© Springer Nature Switzerland AG 2020
B. Bostan (ed.), *Game User Experience And Player-Centered Design*,
International Series on Computer Entertainment and Media Technology,
https://doi.org/10.1007/978-3-030-37643-7_4

Escapism generally has a negative connotation in games research. Escapism was found to be associated with negative outcomes such as internet addiction, problematic use, and excessive gaming. However, certain aspects of escapism can also be beneficial. For instance, mental disengagement via video games helps players decrease their stress levels after stressful activities (e.g., work). Escapism can also act as a mood management strategy, as people tend to play games to avoid negative mood states and induce positive mood states. Similarly, escapism in games can be beneficial for regulating emotions and practicing emotion regulation strategies. Finally, escapism can provide a healthy form of coping strategy for some players. In short, escapism can have both negative and positive consequences, depending on how it is defined. Consequently, it is important to demarcate what constitutes a healthy escapism versus subversive escapism. In this chapter, we conduct a rapid scoping review on healthy forms of escapism in games, how it can be characterized, how it is associated with positive player experiences, and how escapism can be emotionally beneficial. Finally, we discuss the implications for future studies.

Keywords Games · Escapism · Health · Emotion regulation · Mood management · Coping · Recovery experiences

4.1 Introduction

There are approximately 2.5 billion active gamers in the world (Padilla 2019). Although older age groups are still dominantly choosing TV over gaming for entertainment, the gaming time of young adults aged between 21 and 30, is significantly increasing when compared to the last decade (Smith 2019). One of the major reasons for people turning to video games is that video games present a convenient and effective way for escapism (Kahn et al. 2015). This effectiveness comes from the interactive nature of games that require players to actively take actions, making the activity an empowering experience compared to passive forms of escapism, such as watching TV (Kuo et al. 2016).

One definition of escapism is "going from somewhere we don't want to be to be somewhere we do" (Evans 2001). In games, escapism is the departure from conceivably "non-game" and "real" contexts to "gameful" and "artificial" realms. It is an imaginal experience which drives hedonic consumption (Hirschman and Holbrook 1982; Hirschman 1983). It is also an antecedent of cognitive, affective, and behavioral engagement in video games (Abbasi et al. 2019). In fact, it is sometimes the sole reason for video game play (Muriel and Crawford 2018).

Research on games shows both negative and positive effects of escapism. On the negative side, a plethora of research shows that escapism is associated with problematic gaming (Chang et al. 2018; Király et al. 2015, 2017), internet addiction (Yee 2006), and excessive gaming (Kuss et al. 2012). In contrast, more recent studies demonstrated some positive effects of escapism. For instance, escapism predicts enjoyment in games (Merhi 2016) and is also beneficial for emotional well-being of players (Granic et al. 2014). Researchers suggested that psychological detachment in escapism, where a person breaks their mundane or just relieves stress, can be therapeutic (Warmelink et al. 2009). In brief, research shows mixed effects of escapism on players' well-being.

One of the main reasons for mixed findings is the different operationalization and measurement of escapism by different researchers. In the case of self-report studies, for instance, the items used in escapism measures may relate to well-being differently. Negatively oriented items such as "I play games to avoid real life social encounters" (MOGQ; Demetrovics et al. 2011) tend to correlate with addiction or psychological stress (Hagström and Kaldo 2014), whereas other items such as "I play games to forget about work" tend to be associated with recovery experiences leading to reduction of daily stress in players (Reinecke 2009). In this chapter we focus on how healthy and subversive escapism can be differentiated and review the positive aspects of escapism.

4.2   Healthy Escapism in Games

Studies examining positive aspects of escapism in games are multi-faceted and spread across several disciplinary fields. Since this is a fledgling area, it would be beneficial to provide a framework for healthy escapism, as well as a brief review of relevant research. Therefore, we focused on studies that reported beneficial effects of escapism and identified themes on healthy escapism.

Research on healthy escapism can be considered under four different categories: Emotion regulation, mood management, coping, and recovery. This is in line with the idea that these can be hierarchically investigated under the higher order construct of "affect regulation" (Gross 1998). There might be conceptual overlap among these approaches; however, the aim of this review is not to suggest definitions but to bring forth a general framework for future empirical research. In the following sections, we go over these themes one by one and discuss how they were addressed in relation to gaming.

4.2.1   Emotion Regulation

Emotion regulation (ER) is defined as the attempt of modifying the trajectory of emotions (Gross 2015). In its basic form, it consists of five sets of processes: situation selection, situation modification, attention deployment, cognitive change, and response modulation. Once a situation is selected, it can be tailored to modify its emotional impact. Attentional deployment is the decision of focusing the attention to a certain aspect of the situation including complete distraction. After a situation is selected, modified, and attended, the person can change the meaning of the situation and therefore regulate emotions (i.e., reappraisal). Finally, the person can modulate their responses to the elicited emotion (i.e., suppression). Distraction from negative feelings and reappraisal of the situation are shown to be effective strategies for ER (Webb et al. 2012).

In addition to their entertainment aspect, games are shown to have emotional benefits for players by facilitating emotion regulation (Granic et al. 2014). For instance, games that promote interoceptive awareness ("ability of a person to know their internal states") are helpful for regulation of emotions (Lobel et al. 2014). Games are not only used for regulating negative emotions, but also for extending or enhancing positive emotions as well (Hoffner and Lee 2015). For instance, it was found that casual games decrease stress and improve mood (Russoniello et al. 2009).

Games also show promise in fostering players' ER skills (Astor et al. 2013; Lobel et al. 2016). They provide a platform for ER to take place as games are vast playgrounds for players to select and modify situations to their likings. Moreover, games are also effective for distraction, providing temporary disengagement from negative and undesirable emotions (Bruehlman-Senecal and Ayduk 2015). However, the literature on games addressing the specific strategies of ER is scarce at best (Hemenover and Bowman 2018).

In a broad sense, there are two types of games that are studied with regard to ER: Bespoke games and commercial games. Bespoke games are games that are specifically developed for ER training; however, they are usually one time experiences and do not include all properties of games (Villani et al. 2018). On the other hand, commercial games offer more promise and opportunities for ER improvement, since they offer advantages in terms of interaction, control, and narrative features (Kuo et al. 2016; Villani et al. 2018). Initial findings also show that regular gamers use ER strategies better than irregular gamers (Gaetan et al. 2016). Nevertheless, we do not yet have a complete understanding of how ER works for players who engage with commercial digital games.

On the other hand, a recent study found that emotion dysregulation in real life predicts problematic gaming through escapism (Blasi et al. 2019). Games can be used for teaching emotion regulation for gamers who are not able to regulate their emotions, which might consequently result in the reduction of problematic gaming. Games can provide environments to exercise emotion regulation strategies without experiencing negative consequences for players who have difficulties regulating their emotions (Billieux et al. 2015).

4.2.2 Mood Management

Although mood and emotion are sometimes used interchangeably in daily life, they are referred as separate phenomena in the academic literature. In general, the most typical distinction is that emotions are experienced moment to moment, whereas mood tends to last longer periods of times (Ekkekakis 2012). In addition, they are also found to be different in terms of their intensity, effects on physiology, causes, and consequences (Beedie et al. 2005).

In essence, mood management theory posits that people either tend to maintain their positive mood or try to end their negative affective states (Zillmann and Bryant 1985). One of the most efficient and effective way of changing or terminating moods is the consuming of media entertainment (Zillmann 2015). Mood management is conceptually quite close to escapism (Li et al. 2011). Escapism is avoidance of the real in general and mood management is the altering of the mood through selectively exposing oneself to media and communication devices, when there is no other way of resolving adverse emotions (Zillmann 2015). Mood management theory is one of the approaches to study the positive aspects of escapism (Hagström and Kaldo 2014). We regard healthy escapism as a higher order construct encapsulating mood management among others.

Empirical research shows that people can indeed manage their moods by exposing themselves to entertainment media (Knobloch-Westerwick 2013; Reinecke 2017). Initial research on games shows that games provide a useful medium for mood management. For instance, playing (violent or non-violent) games helps reducing hostility and enhancing positive affect (Serrone 2012). However, understanding which aspects of games make them more effective for mood management is important. For instance, rigorous experiments show that as the player agency increases in a game, mood of the bored and stressed individuals tend to improve as well (Bowman and Tamborini 2012). Moreover, players prefer medium-level task demand rather than low or higher task demand (Bowman and Tamborini 2015). Another study found that players' need for mood management and their in-game success determine the level of change in their moods between pre- and post-play, in the context quiz games (Koban et al. 2018). Similarly, another study investigated the effects of in-game success on mood repair in the context of a racing game and found that in-game success predicts mood repair (Rieger et al. 2014a). Finally, depending on whether a player is bored or stressed, the types of game items they purchase also differs: Players who are bored tend to prefer functional items, whereas stressed players tend to prefer decorative items to manage their moods (Bae et al. 2019). Overall, research suggests that games help players manage their moods by providing agency, optimal levels of task demand, and making players feel competent.

Consequently, mood repair can be considered as a result of satisfaction of basic psychological needs of autonomy, competence, and relatedness (Reinecke et al. 2012). This approach claims that mood repair is not only a result of the distraction from negative emotions, but also an outcome of satisfaction of basic needs. For instance, a study found that freely selecting activities to engage (autonomy; a basic need according to Self Determination Theory; Ryan and Deci 2017) are significantly more related to reduced stress as compared to forced activities (Ferguson et al. 2018). However, another empirical study suggests that need satisfaction is more related to enjoyment experienced in the game, rather than mood repair (Rieger et al. 2014a). More research is needed to understand how satisfaction of autonomy, competence, and relatedness needs in games is related to mood repair.

4.2.3 Coping

Escapism is characterized by mental and behavioral disengagement, which are salient factors determined in coping mechanisms (Carver et al. 2013). Coping can be defined as the efforts spent for minimizing problems and stress. There are several types of coping strategies that people tend to adopt (Folkman and Lazarus 1988; Lazarus and Folkman 1984). First is problem-focused coping where the individual attempts to directly solve the problem at hand that is causing stress, such as by getting organized, managing time, and obtaining active support to solve the problem. Second type of coping is the emotion-focused coping where the individual decreases stress by regulating their feeling of the problem such as by distraction with pleasurable activates, relaxation, or talking to a friend. Last, avoidance-focused coping is another strategy where the individual completely rejects to interact with the problem and avoids it altogether (Endler and Parker 1990). It is different than emotion-focused coping in the sense that people do not fully discard the problem. Although in these terms, gaming looks like an emotion-focused or avoidance-focused coping mechanism, games can also be effective in training players on problem-focused coping. While there can be many ways of coping through escapist activities (e.g., watching TV), it was shown that actively engaging in a video game relieves stress by empowering players and projecting them into fantasy worlds boosting the feelings of presence (Kuo et al. 2016).

Games show promise as a medium that can be used for coping. In fact, a study found that coping, which was characterized by the cumulative experience of forgetting daily problems /hassles/unpleasant feelings by escaping real life and reducing tension by channeling attention to pleasurable experiences, was one of the major gaming motivation of some players, (Demetrovics et al. 2011). This study also found that coping emerges as a separate factor than (subversive) escapism. This might contribute to the argument that there are two folds of dissociation from reality where traditionally (subversive) escapism forming the unhealthy and coping forming the healthy forms of game engagements.

It was found that gaming can be utilized as a healthy form of coping strategy when the gaming time is not taken to extremes (Kardefelt-Winther et al. 2017). Although excessive gameplay time is associated with internet gaming disorder symptoms (Schneider et al. 2018), gaming can still be investigated as a coping strategy rather than as a compulsive behavior (Kardefelt-Winther 2014). Excessive gaming and dissociative experiences such as (subversive) escapism can point to maladaptive coping strategies and problematic gaming (Guglielmucci et al. 2019), especially when the player is experiencing a great anxiety (Plante et al. 2018). However, excessive gaming implies an underlying problem that is unrelated and separate from the gaming activity or the game content. Therefore, underlying intentions for escapism could be more important than the contents of games in predicting excessive gaming. Healthy forms of escapist motivations may not result in problematic behavior. Moreover, it was found that escapism—problematic gaming relationship is moderated by the type of coping strategy a player adopts. It was found that "disengaged" coping strategies, which involves walking away from stressors, were positively associated with negative gaming outcomes. However, "engaged" coping strategies, which involves confronting stressors, were negatively associated with negative gaming outcomes (Bowditch et al. 2018). This finding suggests that the effect of escapism on problematic gaming is dependent on the coping style of player.

Sometimes, players can turn to games temporally, such as during difficult periods of life, as a coping strategy. Research shows that games offer respite, a lifeline support for dealing with recent feelings, meaningful social interactions and personal growth during times of difficulty (Iacovides and Mekler 2018). Moreover, in addition to pleasurable experiences, games also can satisfy eudaimonic needs, which is the need for experiencing meaningfulness through insights about life (Oliver et al. 2016; Rogers et al. 2017). It is argued that games that provide eudaimonic experiences (e.g., communicating a message about meaning of life) help people cope, especially after a hardship in life (Hofer and Rieger 2018). This kind of engagement with games can also be considered as healthy escapism, which results in positive outcomes in the long run.

4.2.4   Recovery

People sometimes play games to escape from their daily stresses associated with work or chores (Scott 2019). This kind of escapism to relief stress via an activity is called recovery in the literature. It is defined as recuperation from cognitive and emotional exhaustion (e.g., after work), and characterized by psychological detachment, relaxation, mastery, and control (Reinecke 2009). It is similar but different from mood management, as mood is a single dimension construct that is about short-term experiences, whereas recovery focuses on the return of energy and longer-term effects (Sonnentag and Fritz 2007). Scientific studies suggest that video gaming can provide recovery experiences (Collins and Cox 2014). Research further shows that playing games is a more effective way to relax, compared to using apps that are specifically designed for stress reduction (Collins et al. 2019). Additionally, more interactive entertainment media activities provide greater recovery experiences (e.g., gaming vs watching TV; Reinecke et al. 2011), and recovery experiences are associated with greater subjective vitality and cognitive performance. In short, games can also be a tool for healthy escapism via recovery experiences; however, there is still need for future research to understand how recovery experiences can be fostered in games.

4.2.5 A Pilot Study

In sum, psychological detachment through games has been shown to have negative and positive impacts on the players depending on the escapist intentions. As a preliminary study to examine these ideas we conducted a brief survey. We asked players if they used games as an escape device helping to avoid their real life problems (subversive escapism) or to escape real life to reduce daily stress (healthy escapism). We also measured problematic game use and general well-being of players as outcomes. Results showed that subversive escapism was associated positively with problematic gaming and negatively with well-being, whereas healthy escapism was associated positively with well-being and not associated with problematic gaming. Although these findings provide some early evidence, more research is needed to demarcate healthy and subversive escapism.

4.3 Discussion

In line with the argument that humans have a strong desire to escape from themselves, many activities may provide the means for escapism, not just games (Calleja 2010; Stenseng et al. 2012). In fact, in some way, all cultural artifacts are built for humans to escape the inconsistencies and constraints of life (Tuan 2000). Games are too, one of those artifacts affording escapist motivations in a very engaging manner. Although escapism generally has a negative connotation, especially with its logical entailment of social isolation, our goal was to review how playing games with escapist motivations could sometimes be beneficial for players.

When we examined the literature on healthy forms of escapism in games, we came across 4 major lines of research: emotion regulation, mood management, coping, and recovery. These lines of research suggest that escapist motivations can have beneficial outcomes depending on the way it is defined and operationalized in research. This calls for researchers to be cautious about the scales and items they utilize in self-report measures, and be mindful about what form of escapism they aim to investigate. Below, we summarize the directions for future works we synthesized from our review.

4.3.1 Game Content

When players engage in MMORPG games that are supporting social interaction, they tend to report less problematic online gaming (Chang et al. 2018). Taking into consideration that internet based gaming puts players inside a community, pervasive augmented reality gaming affords real life encounters with fellow gamers on the streets (e.g., Pokémon Go), and tabletop gaming provides face to face interactions, traditional escapism thinking might not be directly applicable to gaming. Because, players are still communicating with each other in these types of games, without having the motives of "isolation from people." These games have their own social ecosystems and therefore players might not necessarily be escaping from other people or the society. Future studies might investigate whether playing online or co-located games differ from solo gaming in terms of escapist motivations and healthy escapism aspects.

At a more granular level, future studies might also examine whether different kinds of video games that afford different in-game actions are more effective in regulating different kinds of emotions (e.g., anger, sadness, anxiousness; Hemenover and Bowman 2018). A general question of interest is: which aspects of games are effective for emotion regulation? Studies on mood management and games did not explore how different content affects players' mood management. Therefore, future studies can examine how players' moods shift when exposed to different game content. Revealing these aspects may facilitate designing games to improve well-being of players. Therefore, future studies can also investigate the features of games which provide greater recovery experiences.

Although hedonic entertainment experiences are associated with the recovery dimensions of relaxation and psychological detachment, eudaimonic entertainment was found to be related to mastery experiences in the context of movies (Rieger et al. 2014b). However, it is not known whether this effect translates into gaming. Consequently, research is needed to understand how healthy escapist motivations are related to these constructs. More specifically, future studies can examine whether eudaimonic gaming experiences fostered by the game content provide better recovery experiences, emotion regulation, mood management, or coping compared to hedonic experiences.

4.3.2 Game Medium

Research shows that video game content presented in virtual reality creates stronger emotional responses, and participants report greater happiness after the usage when compared to desktop displays (Pallavicini et al. 2019). Future studies might also investigate if immersion levels affect healthy escapism (ER, mood management, coping, recovery) in a positive way. Moreover, escapist motivations were also found to play a role in non-digital tabletop game play (Kosa and Spronck 2019). Nevertheless, research is needed on how non-digital games can be related to healthy forms of escapism, compared to their digital versions.

4.3.3 Assessment

Apart from entertainment, games are also used for assessing people's knowledge, skills, and other qualifications (Landers 2015). Games are used in assessments because they are more motivating than standard tests, they provide robust data and they are perceived as non-threatening by test takers. Using the knowledge created in the fledgling area of game-based assessment, games can be used for assessing how players use coping strategies, and simultaneously provide means to better manage their moods. Similarly, by integrating player profiling techniques (Bakkes et al. 2012), content of the game might be dynamically adjusted to provide better mood management.

4.3.4 Learning and Intervention

Games can also be a tool for teaching players about how they can use emotion regulation or mood management techniques in their daily lives. It might be possible to teach the general concepts as well as more specific techniques. For instance, people who use reappraisal emotion regulation technique tend to have greater well-being, whereas people who use suppression emotion regulation technique tend to be less emotionally close with others (Gross and John 2003). The concepts of problem-focused, emotion-focused, or avoidance-focused coping might be taught to player as well, in addition to more specific techniques used under these concepts. For instance, mindfulness is a method of emotion-focused coping, which is defined as being fully present in the moment without having thoughts of past or future. Lately, mindfulness is being applied and investigated in games as well (Gackenbach and Bown 2011; Kosa and Uysal 2017, 2018; Mettler et al. 2018). So far, mindfulness practices show promise in being beneficial for mental health which might be communicated to players through games as well. Games can be used as subtle tools to teach effective emotion regulation or coping strategies.

Similarly, research is needed on whether games have a different intervention potential for non-players, casual players or hardcore players, and whether games can be utilized effectively in psychological interventions.

4.4 Conclusion

In this chapter, our goal was to bring forth a non-exhaustive state of the art on the positive aspects of escapism in games. We suggest that escapism has two different aspects, healthy escapism and subversive escapism. We also argue that whether escapism is beneficial or detrimental depends on the mode of escapism. Viewing escapism only in negative terms could be one-sided. Laying video games, even with escapist motivations, do not necessarily drag players into problematic behavior. In fact, escapism in games might have emotional benefits for players. Although subversive escapism and pathologic gaming is an important problem, research also suggests that people can use video games as a healthy coping tool.

References

Abbasi, A. Z., Ting, D. H., Hlavacs, H., Costa, L. V., & Veloso, A. I. (2019). An empirical validation of consumer video game engagement: A playful-consumption experience approach. Entertainment Computing, 29, 43-55.

Astor, P. J., Adam, M. T., Jerčić, P., Schaaff, K., & Weinhardt, C. (2013). Integrating biosignals into information systems: A NeuroIS tool for improving emotion regulation. Journal of Management Information Systems, 30(3), 247-278.

Bae, J., Kim, S. J., Kim, K. H., & Koo, D. M. (2019). Affective value of game items: a mood management and selective exposure approach. Internet Research, 29(2), 315-328.

Bakkes, S., Tan, C. T., & Pisan, Y. (2012, July). Personalised gaming: a motivation and overview of literature. In Proceedings of the 8th Australasian Conference on Interactive Entertainment: Playing the System (p. 4). ACM.

Beedie, C., Terry, P., & Lane, A. (2005). Distinctions between emotion and mood. Cognition & Emotion, 19(6), 847-878.

Billieux, J., Thorens, G., Khazaal, Y., Zullino, D., Achab, S., &Linden, M. V. (2015). Problematic involvement in online games: A cluster analytic approach. Computers in Human Behavior, 43,242–250.

Blasi, M. D., Giardina, A., Giordano, C., Coco, G. L., Tosto, C., Billieux, J., & Schimmenti, A. (2019). Problematic video game use as an emotional coping strategy: Evidence from a sample of MMORPG gamers. Journal of behavioral addictions, 8(1), 25-34.

Bowditch, L., Chapman, J., & Naweed, A. (2018). Do coping strategies moderate the relationship between escapism and negative gaming outcomes in World of Warcraft (MMORPG) players?. Computers in Human Behavior, 86, 69-76.

Bowman, N. D., & Tamborini, R. (2012). Task demand and mood repair: The intervention potential of computer games. New Media & Society, 14(8), 1339-1357.

Bowman, N. D., & Tamborini, R. (2015). "In the Mood to Game": Selective exposure and mood management processes in computer game play. New Media & Society, 17(3), 375-393.

Bruehlman-Senecal, E., & Ayduk, O. (2015). This too shall pass: Temporal distance and the regulation of emotional distress. Journal of Personality and Social Psychology, 108, 356–375.

Calleja, G. (2010). Digital games and escapism. Games and Culture, 5(4), 335-353.

Carver, C. S., Scheier, M. F., & Weintraub, J. K. (2013). COPE inventory. Measurement Instrument Database for the Social Science.

Chang, S. M., Hsieh, G. M., & Lin, S. S. (2018). The mediation effects of gaming motives between game involvement and problematic Internet use: Escapism, advancement and socializing. Computers & Education, 122, 43-53.

Collins, E., & Cox, A. L. (2014). Switch on to games: Can digital games aid post-work recovery?. International Journal of Human-Computer Studies, 72(8-9), 654-662.

Collins, E., Cox, A., Wilcock, C., & Sethu-Jones, G. (2019). Digital Games and Mindfulness Apps: Comparison of Effects on Post Work Recovery. JMIR mental health, 6(7), e12853.

Demetrovics, Z., Urbán, R., Nagygyörgy, K., Farkas, J., Zilahy, D., Mervó, B., Reindl, A., Ágoston, C., Kertész, A., & Harmath, E. (2011). Why do you play? The development of the motives for online gaming questionnaire (MOGQ). Behavior research methods, 43(3), 814-825.

Ekkekakis, P. (2012). Affect, mood, and emotion. Measurement in sport and exercise psychology, 321.

Endler, N. and Parker, J. 1990. The multidimensional assessment of coping: A critical evaluation. Journal of Personality and Social Psychology, 58: 844–854.

Evans, A. (2001). This virtual life: escapism and simulation in our media world. Fusion Press.

Ferguson, C. J., Maguire, R., & Lemar, S. (2018). Pick Your Poison: Choice of Activity Determines Mood Management Following a Stressful Task. Journal of Aggression, Maltreatment & Trauma, 27(3), 332-346.

Folkman, S., & Lazarus, R. S. (1988). Coping as a mediator of emotion. Journal of personality and social psychology, 54(3), 466.

Gaetan, S., Bréjard, V., & Bonnet, A. (2016). Video games in adolescence and emotional functioning: Emotion regulation, emotion intensity, emotion expression, and alexithymia. Computers in Human Behavior, 61, 344-349.

Gackenbach, J., & Bown, J. (2011). Mindfulness and video game play: A preliminary inquiry. Mindfulness, 2(2), 114-122.

Granic, I., Lobel, A., & Engels, R. C. (2014). The benefits of playing video games. American psychologist, 69(1), 66.

Gross, J. J. (1998). The emerging field of emotion regulation: An integrative review. Review of general psychology, 2(3), 271-299.

Gross, J. J. (2015). The extended process model of emotion regulation: Elaborations, applications, and future directions. Psychological Inquiry, 26(1), 130-137.

Gross, J. J., & John, O. P. (2003). Individual differences in two emotion regulation processes: implications for affect, relationships, and well-being. Journal of personality and social psychology, 85(2), 348.

Guglielmucci, F., Monti, M., Franzoi, I. G., Santoro, G., Granieri, A., Billieux, J., & Schimmenti, A. (2019). Dissociation in Problematic Gaming: a Systematic Review. Current Addiction Reports, 6(1), 1-14.

Hagström, D., & Kaldo, V. (2014). Escapism among players of MMORPGs—conceptual clarification, its relation to mental health factors, and development of a new measure. Cyberpsychology, Behavior, and Social Networking, 17(1), 19-25.

Hemenover, S. H., & Bowman, N. D. (2018). Video games, emotion, and emotion regulation: expanding the scope. Annals of the International Communication Association, 42(2), 125-143.

Hirschman, E. C. (1983). Predictors of self-projection, fantasy fulfillment, and escapism. The Journal of Social Psychology, 120(1), 63-76.

Hirschman, E. C., & Holbrook, M. B. (1982). Hedonic consumption: emerging concepts, methods and propositions. The Journal of Marketing, 92-101.

Hofer, M., & Rieger, D. (2018). Hedonic and Non-Hedonic Entertainment Experiences. The Routledge Handbook of Positive Communication: Contributions of an Emerging Community of Research on Communication for Happiness and Social Change.

Hoffner, C. A., & Lee, S. (2015). Mobile phone use, emotion regulation, and well-being. Cyberpsychology, Behavior, and Social Networking, 18(7), 411-416.

Iacovides, I., & Mekler, E. (2018). The Role of Gaming During Difficult Life Experiences. In Proceedings of the 2019 CHI Conference on Human Factors in Computing Systems. ACM.

Kahn, A. S., Shen, C., Lu, L., Ratan, R. A., Coary, S., Hou, J., Meng, J., Osborn J., & Williams, D. (2015). The Trojan Player Typology: A cross-genre, cross-cultural, behaviorally validated scale of video game play motivations. Computers in Human Behavior, 49, 354-361.

Kardefelt-Winther, D. (2014). Problematizing excessive online gaming and its psychological predictors. Computers in Human Behavior, 31, 118-122.

Kardefelt-Winther, D., Heeren, A., Schimmenti, A., van Rooij, A., Maurage, P., Carras, M., … & Billieux, J. (2017). How can we conceptualize behavioural addiction without pathologizing common behaviours?. Addiction, 112(10), 1709-1715.

Király, O., Tóth, D., Urbán, R., Demetrovics, Z., & Maraz, A. (2017). Intense video gaming is not essentially problematic. Psychology of Addictive Behaviors, 31(7), 807.

Király, O., Urbán, R., Griffiths, M. D., Ágoston, C., Nagygyörgy, K., Kökönyei, G., & Demetrovics, Z. (2015). The mediating effect of gaming motivation between psychiatric symptoms and problematic online gaming: An online survey. Journal of medical Internet research, 17(4).

Knobloch-Westerwick, S. (2013). Mood management: Theory, evidence, and advancements. In Psychology of entertainment (pp. 257-272). Routledge.

Koban, K., Breuer, J., Rieger, D., Mohseni, M. R., Noack, S., Bente, G., & Ohler, P. (2018). Playing for the thrill and skill. Quiz games as means for mood and competence repair. Media Psychology, 1-26.

Kosa, M., & Spronck, P. (2019). Towards a Tabletop Gaming Motivations Inventory (TGMI). In International Conference on Videogame Sciences and Arts (pp. 59–71). Springer, Cham.

Kosa, M., & Uysal, A. (2017). Trait Mindfulness and Player Experience. In Extended Abstracts Publication of the Annual Symposium on Computer-Human Interaction in Play (pp. 463-470). ACM.

Kosa, M., & Uysal, A. (2018). Does Mindfulness Affect Wellbeing and Physical Activity Levels of Pervasive Game Players? the Case of Ingress. In 2018 IEEE Games, Entertainment, Media Conference (GEM) (pp. 1-9). IEEE.

Kuo, A., Lutz, R. J., & Hiler, J. L. (2016). Brave new World of Warcraft: A conceptual framework for active escapism. Journal of Consumer Marketing, 33(7), 498-506.

Kuss, D. J., Louws, J., & Wiers, R. W. (2012). Online gaming addiction? Motives predict addictive play behavior in massively multiplayer online role-playing games. Cyberpsychology, Behavior, and Social Networking, 15(9), 480-485.

Landers, R. N. (2015). An introduction to game-based assessment: Frameworks for the measurement of knowledge, skills, abilities and other human characteristics using behaviors observed within videogames. International Journal of Gaming and Computer-Mediation Simulations, 7(4).

Lazarus, R. and Folkman, S. 1984. Stress, appraisal and coping New York: Springer.

Li, D., Liau, A., & Khoo, A. (2011). Examining the influence of actual-ideal self-discrepancies, depression, and escapism, on pathological gaming among massively multiplayer online adolescent gamers. Cyberpsychology, Behavior, and Social Networking, 14(9), 535-539.

Lobel, A., Gotsis, M., Reynolds, E., Annetta, M., Engels, R. C., & Granic, I. (2016). Designing and utilizing biofeedback games for emotion regulation: The case of nevermind. In Proceedings of the 2016 CHI Conference Extended Abstracts on Human Factors in Computing Systems (pp. 1945-1951). ACM.

Lobel, A., Granic, I., & Engels, R. C. (2014). Stressful gaming, interoceptive awareness, and emotion regulation tendencies: A novel approach. Cyberpsychology, Behavior, and Social Networking, 17(4), 222-227.

Merhi, M. I. (2016). Towards a framework for online game adoption. Computers in Human Behavior, 60, 253-263.

Mettler, J., Mills, D. J., & Heath, N. L. (2018). Problematic Gaming and Subjective Well-Being: How Does Mindfulness Play a Role?. International Journal of Mental Health and Addiction, 1-17.

Muriel, D., & Crawford, G. (2018). Video games as culture: considering the role and importance of video games in contemporary society. Routledge.

Oliver, M. B., Bowman, N. D., Woolley, J. K., Rogers, R., Sherrick, B. I., & Chung, M. Y. (2016). Video games as meaningful entertainment experiences. Psychology of Popular Media Culture, 5(4), 390.

Padilla, J. A. (2019, July 22). 2018 Video Game Industry Statistics, Trends & Data - The Ultimate List. Retrieved from https://www.wepc.com/news/video-game-statistics/

Pallavicini, F., Pepe, A., & Minissi, M. E. (2019). Gaming in Virtual Reality: What Changes in Terms of Usability, Emotional Response and Sense of Presence Compared to Non-Immersive Video Games?. Simulation & Gaming, 1046878119831420.

Plante, C. N., Gentile, D. A., Groves, C. L., Modlin, A., & Blanco-Herrera, J. (2018). Video games as coping mechanisms in the etiology of video game addiction. Psychology of Popular Media Culture.

Reinecke, L. (2009). Games and recovery: The use of video and computer games to recuperate from stress and strain. Journal of Media Psychology, 21(3), 126-142.

Reinecke, L. (2017). Mood management theory. The international encyclopedia of media effects, 1-13.

Reinecke, L., Klatt, J., & Krämer, N. C. (2011). Entertaining media use and the satisfaction of recovery needs: Recovery outcomes associated with the use of interactive and noninteractive entertaining media. Media Psychology, 14(2), 192-215.

Reinecke, L., Tamborini, R., Grizzard, M., Lewis, R., Eden, A., & David Bowman, N. (2012). Characterizing mood management as need satisfaction: The effects of intrinsic needs on selective exposure and mood repair. Journal of Communication, 62(3), 437-453.

Rieger, D., Wulf, T., Kneer, J., Frischlich, L., & Bente, G. (2014a). The winner takes it all: The effect of in-game success and need satisfaction on mood repair and enjoyment. Computers in Human Behavior, 39, 281-286.

Rieger, D., Reinecke, L., Frischlich, L., & Bente, G. (2014b). Media entertainment and well-being—Linking hedonic and eudaimonic entertainment experience to media-induced recovery and vitality. Journal of Communication, 64(3), 456-478.

Rogers, R., Woolley, J., Sherrick, B., Bowman, N. D., & Oliver, M. B. (2017). Fun versus meaningful video game experiences: A qualitative analysis of user responses. The Computer Games Journal, 6(1-2), 63-79.

Russoniello, C. V., O'Brien, K., & Parks, J. M. (2009). The effectiveness of casual video games in improving mood and decreasing stress. Journal of Cyber Therapy and Rehabilitation, 2(1).

Ryan, R. M., and Deci, E. L. (2017). Self-determination theory: Basic psychological needs in motivation, development, and wellness. Guilford Publications.

Schneider, L. A., King, D. L., & Delfabbro, P. H. (2018). Maladaptive coping styles in adolescents with Internet gaming disorder symptoms. International Journal of Mental Health and Addiction, 16(4), 905-916.

Scott, E. (2019, June 29). How Video Games Can Be Used for Stress Relief. Retrieved from https://www.verywellmind.com/how-video-games-relieve-stress-4110349.

Serrone, C. (2012). Mood management and video-game engagement: The importance of user-experience and gender in assessing the psychological effects of video-game play.

Smith, S. V. (2019, February 26). TV Vs. Video Games: Who's Winning? Retrieved from https://www.npr.org/templates/transcript/transcript.php?storyId=698354898

Sonnentag, S., & Fritz, C. (2007). The Recovery Experience Questionnaire: development and validation of a measure for assessing recuperation and unwinding from work. Journal of occupational health psychology, 12(3), 204.

Stenseng, F., Rise, J., & Kraft, P. (2012). Activity engagement as escape from self: The role of self-suppression and self-expansion. Leisure Sciences, 34(1), 19–38.

Tuan, Y. F. (2000). Escapism. JHU Press.

Villani, D., Carissoli, C., Triberti, S., Marchetti, A., Gilli, G., & Riva, G. (2018). Videogames for emotion regulation: a systematic review. Games for health journal, 7(2), 85-99.

Warmelink, H., Harteveld, C., & Mayer, I. (2009). Press Enter or Escape to Play-Deconstructing Escapism in Multiplayer Gaming. In DiGRA Conference.

Webb, T. L., Miles, E., & Sheeran, P. (2012). Dealing with feeling: a meta-analysis of the effectiveness of strategies derived from the process model of emotion regulation. Psychological bulletin, 138(4), 775.

Yee, N. (2006). Motivations for play in online games. Cyber Psychology and Behavior, 9 (6), 772 – 775.

Zillmann, D. (2015). Mood Management: Using Entertainment to Full Advantage. In Communication, Social Cognition, and Affect (PLE: Emotion) (pp. 163-188). Psychology Press.

Zillmann, D., & Bryant, J. (1985). Affect, mood, and emotion as determinants of selective exposure. In D. Zillmann & J. Bryant (Eds.), Selective exposure to communication (pp. 157–189). Hillsdale, NJ: Lawrence Erlbaum Associates.

Chapter 5
User Experience and Motivation of Professional Video Game Players: A Case Study of Esports in Turkey

Orhan Efe Ozenc

Contents

Abstract The digital era brought a new impulse to the gaming world as per the invention of video games, discovery of a new and unique gameplay medium and establishment of gaming companies who implemented the monetization system and initiated a business model over buying and selling games and downloadable contents. The internet age converted the games to MMOs (Massively Multiplayer Online Games) which enabled the players compete against real human opponents instead of artificial intelligence of the device and thus, planted the seeds of a new and more competitive gameplay type. Such gameplay attracted the gaming audience and consumers, of whom some intended to display their skills and mastery over games to others via digital broadcasters (like YouTube and Twitch) and suddenly this ploy turned into a show and entertainment business, named as esports. As esports spread wider, competent authorities and international governing bodies are founded and recognized such activities as a sports branch with legislative elements. When the esports player began to get paid by the ecosystem, they became professionals and chose to pursue a career within this brand-new practice. As the early modern theories that define games ostracized and rejected the possibility of receiving any

O. E. Ozenc (✉)
Department of Game Design, Bahçeşehir University, Istanbul, Turkey

© Springer Nature Switzerland AG 2020
B. Bostan (ed.), *Game User Experience And Player-Centered Design*,
International Series on Computer Entertainment and Media Technology,
https://doi.org/10.1007/978-3-030-37643-7_5

material interest as a result of playing games, the gamer status of professional players was questioned, similar to the professional athletes of the traditional sports did once.

Together with considering the dynamics and policies of the digital gaming and esports industries, a new approach was needed in order to develop a model that distinguishes gambling from esports and combines esports with contemporary game definitions in the words of an updated version. For such purpose, the game definitions of prominent critical thinkers in literature were researched, examined, and compared to each other, as well as the descriptions and characteristics of traditional sports, professionalism, gambling, and esports, via the case studies and interviews conducted among professional esports players, amateur players, esports enthusiasts, esports staff, and an esports color pundit about the motives of gamers as amateur and professional esports players and handled by the means of qualitative analysis method. Findings concluded that esport is a type of sport by many aspects, it is vastly distinguished from gambling and as per the special characteristic of digital gaming business, the professional players shall not be exempted from being "gamers" in accordance with the new, contemporary game definitions, and as a result, a new, updated game definition is generated to help clarifying the purpose of considering esports just as a special type of gaming, instead of a mere profession unlike other occupations or even the professional athletes in traditional sports.

Keywords Fun · Entertainment · Game definition · Gamer type · Amateur · Casual · Professional · Motives · Athlete · Burnout · Sports · Motivation · Esports · Gambling · Challenge · Competition · Digital games · Monetization

5.1 Introduction

In accordance with the ever-lasting theory of Johan Huizinga, games do exist since even before humans had stepped their feet to the earth and always are an integral part of human contexture, especially being embedded to their spiritual flank (1955, p. 4) and reflect as a tool of having fun, recreation, and entertainment (Ma et al. 2013). Though the games were enhanced rules-wise and got more complex (by the means of structure) throughout the history of civilizations, the nature of playing a game and being a game player had cling on to similar ideas that found one of their common grounds on "no material interest can be earned in the endgame" clause (Huizinga, 1950 p. 11) within the early game definitions, in order for mainly separating games from gambling.

However, as the late nineteenth and early twentieth century brought the mass production of the analog (board and card) games with the incorporation of companies such as Hasbro Inc. (formerly Milton Bradley) and Parker Brothers, one key factor was added to the games, known as "the producer," that aims only to create and sell their own games to the consumers and earn an income in exchange of such process. Therefore, unlike before (where games were unanimous and vacant), some material interests were added as per such development of games, which were indeed industrialized thereinafter. But although the games became eligible for being bought or sold, the definitions of "game" did not alter (Juul 2003) only due to such developments, as they always gave on to the gamers (therefore being player-centric) and excluded the goal of earning a material interest persistently—players should not play games for earning money or equivalent material considerations and if there were any bids/fees paid for entering a game competition in order to have a chance of winning the prize, it would be deemed as gambling, as the real-world wealth of the players would change in every case (Huizinga 1950 p. 11).

A solid reason for not altering the perspective of game definitions in favor of utilizing money (allowing material interest) accordingly was the fact that the average consumers within the target audience of analog-medium games could produce the items of vast majority of such games by themselves with their own means (Pearce 2004) and will only lack the exact rule book and qualified materials of the versions generated by the game companies by doing so (i.e., the difference between hand-made deck of cards with scissors, pen and paper, and the pack of Hoyle playing cards). This was also the case for ancient sports within the Olympic approach that were evolved from being a mere game (Guttmann 2004), though modern sports do make the consumers need for more qualified equipment (such as the racket in tennis or a well-measured pool in swimming) in order for reaching the aimed gameplay experience (Suits 1988).

This fact also had reflected the borne of "professionalism" concept (Pickford 1941) as skilled players tended to use the best conditions and items for the games that they were fond of, and thereby lean towards to compete in higher levels and standards, which may lead them to have a motive of earning money (Baillie and Danish 1992) voluntarily in exchange for displaying their skills on a routine basis as a profession (rather than a mere hobby,[1] and thus sacrificing their daily life for becoming a professional) to the audience of such sports activity and training to develop their skills for delivering the best performance they can—such perception also embraced and adopted the entertainment and show aspects of professionalism (Roosevelt 1890).

The athletes that chose to pursue a professional career track still aimed and achieved "fun" and used such fun as a motive of becoming a professional indeed, as a way of earning a more enhanced level of fun by competing against high-level opponents (Zeng et al. 2015), where the possibility of becoming devoid of such fun generated a concept of "burnout" within their psychologies which may lead them to drop their profession completely and play no more of such game, as one of their fundamental motives for enduring and embracing such professional standards and the stress derived from competing continuously would be abolished (Eklund and Cresswell 2007). This aspect of playing and performing was also stated by Csikszentmihalyi (1997) as the optimal game flow theory, in which the objectives

---

[1][https://dictionary.cambridge.org/tr/s%C3%B6zl%C3%BCk/ingilizce/Professional] (retrieved on 6 August 2019).

and flow of a game will determine the fun attained by the players and the amount of their continuous and iterative gameplay, as boredom (from being too easy or too routine) will occur that will make the player leave for another challenge for the aimed fun, or frustration (from being too hard to overcome by skills and experience) will conjure a state within the gamer's psychology where he/she will quit playing for not having fun anymore—which constitutes a version of burnout indeed. Therefore, where the fun and voluntary willingness to play halted, the motives and reasons to be a professional athlete (or gamer) will also come to an end (Weiss and Chaumeton 1992), which enables us to conclude that a voluntarily selected profession do depend on achieving fun (Gould 1996) and all the professional athletes still do have fun in their practices and hence professionalism does not end fun; where it can be said that with an inductive manner, the professional practice of a sport shall not end the title of being a gamer, as the fundamental element of a gameplay, which is having a more qualified-competition fun (Gould and Carson 2004), still exist in their psychology.

On the other hand, the twenty-first century is witnessing the rise of video games that made humans need a mediative game experience (or user experience/UX) mainly via the digital devices such as gaming consoles, computers, and mobile devices (Wolf 2008, p. 1, 3). Such types of games are taking place on a virtual medium known as the cyber world and have its own rules and conditions for governing the gameplay which are different than the analog games on a vast scale. Accordingly, an artificial environment is enveloping the gameplay (including its playground), in which one or more humans compete against the artificial intelligence (AI) generated by the game software via using data-transferring command devices such as keyboard, mouse, gamepad, buttons, etc. Furthermore, however, with the emerge of internet technology which lead to the MMOs (Massively Multiplayer Online Games), the players found a new platform to compete against other humans, via these digital devices (Ducheneaut et al. 2006). One of the biggest differences of digital (video) games with the analog games were both game-centric and player-centric, where unlike in the analog gaming, the average consumer within the target audience cannot produce or obtain the equipment and medium of the game by his/her own means and in desperate need of having digital game companies (that have the enhanced and exclusive know-how of the game) to manufacture the medium and content of such games (Juul 2003). Consequently, the digital gaming always included the monetization and buying-selling mechanism within its dynamics (as a *causa sui* manner), as the companies will produce such digital games only for receiving revenues from sales (Conway and DeWinter 2015), such as in the 2019 Newzoo Global Games Market Report, where digital games market had proven to be generating a 152.1 billion dollar annual revenue with a 9.6% year-on-year growth rate.[2] Thereby, the digital gaming mannerism always tends to sell a meta to the gaming audience in exchange for play (as a retail selling price), or

---

[2]Newzoo Global Games Market Report 2019, p. 11-13 (https://newzoo.com/solutions/standard/market-forecasts/global-games-market-report/) (retrieved on 9 August 2019).

with the emerge of downloadable contents, a more qualified and varied gameplay experience (Catan 2003).

Such age of online gaming, however, blazed a trail for continuous competitive gaming and soon generated an entertainment business of competitive gameplay contests, to be named as esports (Hamari and Sjöblom 2017). Within this ecosystem, the players that discipline themselves to become premier gamers (Faust et al. 2013) and thus, esports players (also can be described as "esporters") just like the traditional sports athletes and voluntarily agree on displaying their skills to the audience of such games as a part of entertainment and show business (Ozenc and Tinmazlar 2018). Just as the esports are recognized by media (Pizzo et al. 2018), international organizations,[3] and several law systems (including but not limited with the USA,[4] France,[5] South Korea,[6] and Turkey[7]), these premier players have been distinguished by the competent legal governing authorities[8] as professional athletes with *license* to compete in esports contest and challenge other professionals for fame and prize money (Adamus 2012; Jenny et al. 2017; Jonasson and Thiborg 2010; Schubert et al. 2016). But although they are severed from gamblers, the esports players do face a risk of not being referred as "gamers" as per the game definitions of Huizinga (1949, 1950), Caillois (1961), Kelley (1988), and Avedon and Sutton-Smith (1981) due to the involvement of any prize money, profession, and routinely playing.

In order for clarifying such blurred situation, several prominent game and sports definitions (from Salen and Zimmermann, Huizinga, Caillois, Juul, Guttmann, Ma et al., Vorderer et al., Crawford, Suits, Tiedemann, IeSF, Freeman and Wohn, Avedon and Sutton-Smith, Kelly, Apter, and Oxford Learner's Dictionaries to name a few) shall be examined and the elements which consist such definitions have to be compared to the conditions of the esports players and their psychologies and motives within the business (Bányai et al. 2019). As the similarities, if any, constitute the majority between these two concepts, then we can claim that the esports players, who are indeed the professional gamers/players, do share the same spirit of aiming and having fun (just like the professional athletes in traditional sports) largely with the amateur gamers and their activities (or profession) can be

---

[3]International eSports Federation Official Website [https://www.ie-sf.org/] (retrieved on 6 August 2019).

[4]United States eSports Federation Official Website [http://www.esportsfederation.org/pages/about] (retrieved on 6 August 2019).

[5]France eSports Federation Official Website [https://www.france-esports.org/] (retrieved on 6 August 2019).

[6]South Korea eSports Association Official Website [http://www.e-sports.or.kr/?ckattempt=1] (retrieved on 6 August 2019).

[7]Turkish E-Sports Federation Official Website [http://tesfed.gov.tr/] (retrieved on 6 August 2019).

[8]French Numeric Law (Loi pour une République Numérique), [http://www.senat.fr/enseance/textes/2015-2016/744.html#AMELI_SUB_4_1468248055899_1432] (retrieved on 6 August 2019).

included within the "*game player*" concept's context, providing that the digital gaming as a business already violates the "no material interest/no utilization" policy of classical game definitions from the game-centric and player-centric perspective (as gamers are motivated through paying material considerations/fees for achieving the gameplay stage of a game or having a more diversified gameplay by remunerative downloadable contents, even for the amateur/casual players) and a different approach may be needed to evaluate the situation of professional players and professionalism of esports within such manner thereby, a small diversification or alteration can be made within the definitions that will make them contemporary and fit to the dynamics of such ecosystem.

For such purpose, the definition and nature of esports (by Wagner, Hemphill, Whalen, Adamus, Associated Press and dictionaries such as Cambridge, Lexico, and Tech terms to be precisely) with a comparison to the status of traditional sports in the eye of the game definitions will be revealed and motives for being an esports player (esporter, esportsman) will be examined by maintaining evidence from the interviews of esports audience (Lee and Schoenstedt, 2011 [with over 500 college students]), esports players (based on the studies of Freeman and Wohn 2017, with 26 esports players; Martončik 2015, with 108 esports players and 54 casual gamers; Weiss and Schiele 2013, with 360 esports players; Seo 2016, with 10 esports players, and Bányai et al. 2019; and four others that were conducted by newspaper articles and Guinness World Records Gamer's Edition 2019), and three esports insiders; an esports commentator, an esports coach, and an esports manager specifically (conducted by Ozenc and Tinmazlar 2018, with a semi-structured manner). Within such scope, the comparisons between "sports and esports" and "gambling vs. esports" shall also be examined as a subordinate aspect.

Accordingly, the following three questions shall be asked for the purpose of this work:

- What are the similarities and differences between the definitions of sports, esports, gambling, and game and how can this comparison can be applied relatively to the games–esports relationship?
- What are the general motives of the esport players (esporters) to become professional gamers and how are they similar or different when compared to the amateur gamer motives?
- Does this "profession" characteristic of esports exclude esports players from the concept of gamer, or can we include them by altering the contemporary game definitions, mainly in accordance with the pecuniary mannerism of digital gaming?

5.1.1 Definition of Game

As the action of "playing" indeed requires an *interaction* amid the game and the player (Vorderer et al. 2006, p. 3), playing phase of a game sparks, triggers, and summons *enthusiasm* within the players and thereby provokes and elicits various emotions in gamers' nature (Huizinga 1950). With such connection, the games coherently generate a relationship between players and the concept of *"fun"* (Ozenc 2017 p. 1, 7; Vorderer and Bryant 2009, p. 3, Gee 2007, p. 43, Huizinga 1949, p. 3), *"amusement"* (Juul 2003 pp. 30–45), and/or *"entertainment"* (Grönroos 2013, p. 9) by constructing a player (or gamer) experience in the gameplay and reflect as a *tool* of having fun, recreation, and entertainment (Ma et al. 2013).

Though *Wittgenstein* claims that games cannot be defined as they have too less in common by the means of medium and characteristics, he admits that they indeed resemble each other with several similarities sufficient to form a family (1958, segment 66–67). Several game theorists, however, set forth various definitions for the concept of "game" in order to sustain a common perception for identifying actions as games and actors as gamers. Accordingly;

- *Johan Huizinga* claims that a game is "a free activity standing quite consciously outside 'ordinary' life as being 'not serious', but at the same time absorbing the player intensely and utterly (*immersive*). It is an activity connected with no material interest, and no profit can be gained by it. It proceeds within its own proper boundaries of time and space according to fixed rules and in an orderly manner. It promotes the formation of social groupings which tend to surround themselves with secrecy and to stress their difference from the common world by disguise or other means" and played for fun (1950, p. 13).
- *Roger Caillois* foresees that a game is "an activity which is essentially: Free (voluntary), separate [in time and space], uncertain, unproductive, governed by rules, make-believe (*fictive*)" (1961, pp. 10–11).
- *Bernard Suits* predicts that, "to play a game is to engage in activity directed towards bringing about a specific state of affairs, using only means permitted by rules, where the rules prohibit more efficient in favor of less efficient means, and where such rules are accepted just because they make possible such activity (*also known as the lusory state*)" (1978, p. 34), where the lusory state corresponds to the will to obey and governed by the rule only in order for playing the game. So, an activity that has a goal, means, rules, and lusory state in its atmosphere shall be deemed as a game.
- *E.M. Avedon and Brian Sutton-Smith* claim that "at its most elementary level then we can define game as an exercise of voluntary control systems in which there is an opposition between forces, confined by a procedure and rules in order to produce a disequilibrial outcome" (1981, p. 7).
- *Chris Crawford* states that he perceives four common factors for all games: "representation ['a closed formal system that subjectively represents a subset of reality'], interaction, conflict, and safety ['the results of a game are always less harsh than the situations the game models']" (1982, Chap. 2.)
- *David Kelley* stipulates that "a game is a form of recreation constituted by a set of rules that specify an object to be attained and the permissible means of attaining it" (1988, p. 50).

- *Katie Salen and Eric Zimmerman* claim that "a game is a system in which players engage in an artificial conflict, defined by rules, that results in a quantifiable outcome" (2003, p. 96).
- *Jesper Juul* defines the game as, "a game is a rule-based formal system with a variable and quantifiable outcome, where different outcomes are assigned different values, the player exerts effort in order to influence the outcome, the player feels attached to the outcome, and the consequences of the activity are optional and negotiable," and played for amusement (2003, pp. 30–45).
- With respect to the *Oxford Learner's Dictionaries*, a game has been defined as "an activity or a sport with rules in which people or teams compete against each other."[9]

As it can be seen, several of those statements are verging the identification of game by its own characteristics and specialties (thus being game-centric; such as "rules," "fun," "activity," "uncertain," "separate," "representation," "interaction," "artificial conflict," "safety," "control system," "opposition and competition between forces," "variable and quantifiable outcome," "disequilibrial outcome," "object/goal," "means/procedure," "negotiable and optional outcome"), whereas some others do get identified by the actions, perceptions, motives, and intentions of the players/gamers that execute the action of playing (thus being player-centric, namely "free," "voluntary," "recreation," "lusory state," "fictive," "no material interest," "unproductive," "effort"). Within the purpose of this essay, the common core that holds importance among these definitions do examine the latter category, especially by the means of earning a material interest and making a living out of playing games competitively on professional levels.

Accordingly, those stipulations do circle around the games being *"separate"* (which points out being outside of the ordinary life—Caillois and Huizinga), *"unproductive"* (which means no concrete outcome shall reflect to the real world—Caillois), *"no material interest and no profit can be gained by"* (i.e., no money prize can be earned—Huizinga), *"free and voluntary"* (which means it cannot be chosen as a work or profession that mandates players to play the game)—Caillois and Avedon and Sutton-Smith), *"recreation"* (that states games being played for relaxing, loosening, and having fun time, rather than playing tensely and getting frustrated due to the conditions and outcomes—Kelley). Michael Apter on the other hand had added experiencing a protective frame which stands between the player and the "real" world and its problems, together with the element of *"being confident that no harm can come"* within the gameplay field, which is indeed a psychologically enchanted zone that stands between the players and their real-world problems (1991, p. 15). Therefore, it can be said that, with an indirect approach, a person should fit in the conditions said above in order to be deemed as a gamer, just like the activity he/she had engaged with has to for being titled as a game.

---

[9][https://www.oxfordlearnersdictionaries.com/definition/english/game_1?q=game] (retrieved on 6 August 2019).

It can be seen that many of the more contemporary definitions that fall into the era that witnessed the rise of digital games in fact discarded the necessity of such clauses (Crawford, Salen and Zimmerman) and included the necessity of *"having a quantifiable outcome"* instead (Salen and Zimmerman, Juul). Therefore, it can be claimed that the approach towards the game definition has been altered with the emerge of digitally mediated video games even before there were MMOs or esports as a phenomenon as the theorists *discarded* the *"separate," "unproductive," "recreation,"* and *"free and voluntary"* elements tacitly and generated a possibility of *playing with real-life consequences* by *replacing* the "no material interest and no profit gaining" with *"negotiable consequences"* (Juul 2003). Such a preference had occurred mainly due to the more serious, tense, and competitive gameplay against the AIs or other players, which were brought by digital games—games that were more complex than the analog games in many (if not all) aspects[10] and also create a platform that a digital computing machine can act as both the playground, referee, opponent/competitor, progress tracker and interface (Juul 2003); but still preserve the fun of playing. This new feature in the game definition was also reflecting the industrialization of gaming business and game companies, as the trend of *paying money for purchasing and playing a game and thus including the monetary factor within the game concept*, which was initiated nearly a century before, had become quite common throughout the world (Dyer-Witheford and De Peuter 2009, p. xv).

Within such scope, as the game-centric aspects will be the main criteria in deciding whether esports are games essentially, the player-centric aspects of such definitions; *"free," "voluntary," "recreation," "lusory state," "fictive," "no material interest," "unproductive," "effort"* will hold importance in order for determining whether the motives of the professional esports players are different than amateur (casual) gamers.

5.1.2 Definition of Sport

In order for obtaining a decent perception regarding the relationship between games and esports, the relevance of the games with the traditional sports shall be examined principally and the connection of sports and esports has to be clarified thereafter. Pursuant to the fact that the traditional sports were actually the organized version of the related games when they were in their emerging phase especially before being conducted professionally (Guttmann 2004; Suits 2007), it can be claimed that esports will also have a similar background with games, as well as with sports.

---

[10]Pearson, Ben. Digital vs Analog: The Value of Divergent Game Types, 1 December 2016 [https://games2teach.uoregon.edu/2016/12/01/digital-vs-analog-value-divergent-game-types/] (retrieved on 6 August 2019).

Accordingly, sports are fundamentally derived from the games, as they always include "game" and "play" terms in their vocabulary. For a purpose of handling the games in a comparison manner with sports,

- A game can be defined as an organized activity where two or more individuals or teams compete with each other to win, pursuant to previously agreed-on rules (*Chick* 1984; *Roberts* et al. 1959). From such point of view, a sport can be defined as a subset of games that require physical skill (*Deaner and Smith* 2013*; Chick* 1984*; Guttmann* 2004). This definition of sport therefore excludes non-competitive physical activities (like exercising), games of pure chance (like lottery or roulette), and strategic games that depend solely on mental skill or decision-making (i.e., bridge, chess) and mainly focus on competitive and physical activities (Malcolm 2008, p. 238).
- *Claus Tiedemann* (2004) claims that sport is "a cultural field of activity in which human beings voluntarily go into a relation to other people with the conscious intention to develop their abilities and accomplishments—particularly in the area of skilled motion—and to compare themselves with these other people according to rules put self or adopted without damaging them or themselves deliberately.
- Another approach to the separation of sports from games does belong to *Bernard Suits* (2007), as he states that a sport is essentially a game in its origins, but does additionally include a variety of skills to play a game competitively, physicality (or precisely, the movement of body parts continuously by the means of conducting a gameplay), stability (not a momentary or instantaneous activity, but has scheduled to have competition in specific dates and time, as a continuous organization manner) and wide following audience (who will watch, monitor, and spectate the display of those games for entertainment).
- *Allen Guttmann* (2004) suggests that play is the most general characteristic of both a game and sport. Play, as he mentions, is any non-utilitarian physical or intellectual activity which is done or pursued for its own sake (i.e., intrinsic) and the pleasure or enthusiasm of such action is experiencing the "playing," rather than achievement of the objective of such game. Thus, play is introverted to the game itself as it does not aim to achieve an external objective, such as health, *money*, food, etc. Additionally, plays can be spontaneous or organized, the latter being entitled as a "game" and differ as not being spontaneously recreational; whereas the games can be non-competitive or competitive, the latter will be referred as a "contest." Contest will also divide into two main groups, as intellectual ones and physical ones. Physical ones can eventually turn into sports, but they also do contain some level of intellectual component, and distinguish from real hostile physical encounters or wars by being "playful." Therefore, as a conclusion, sports can be identified as "organized contests of a playful, non-utilitarian character in which the physical demands outweigh the intellectual components" with being derived from games essentially (Fig. 5.1).
- *McPherson* et al. (1989) stipulate that sports are "structured, goal-oriented, competitive forms of play."

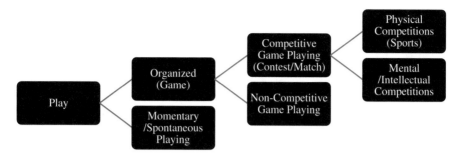

Fig. 5.1 A representative scheme of Allen Guttman's "games becoming sports" theory in "Sport – The First Five Millennia" (2004)

- As per the *Cambridge Online Dictionary*, sport is "a game, competition, or activity needing physical effort and skill that is played or done according to rules, for enjoyment and/or as a job[11]".

Apart from such definitions, the ancient Olympic games has a motto of *"Citius, Altius, Fortius"* which means *"Faster, Higher, Stronger"* in Latin, and used to define and draft sports branches for the modern Olympics (since 1896) traditionally.[12] Such perception, however, disqualifies several popular activities and games (that are generally deemed as sports by a majority of sports audiences) from being a sport branch initially, such as cricket, chess, baseball, bridge, lacrosse, softball, billiards/pool games (like snooker), dart, the motor sports (like car and motorcycle races), horse racing, bowling, mountain climbing; some traditional local sports (like oil wrestling) and several martial arts such as aikido and sumo wrestling; but entitles several "non-peaceful" events (nature-wise) such as shooting or archery and life-critically dangerous events (such as Ski Jumping and snowboarding[13]) as sports.[14] Moreover, several branches such as diving, artistic/synchronized swimming and ice skating that are performed on turn-based oppositions (rather than having all the competing opponents on the game field simultaneously and let them square accounts with each other) and resemble a belvedere entertainment/show activity are also classified as Olympic sports within such regard. Therefore, it can be said that the Olympic approach cannot constitute a sufficient and convincing perception and definition of "sports."

Another side of this discussion is the fact that when the modern Olympics had begun, several popular sports branches such as football, basketball, taekwondo,

---

[11][https://dictionary.cambridge.org/dictionary/english/sport] (day of retrieval: 6 August 2019).

[12]The Free Dictionary [https://acronyms.thefreedictionary.com/Citius%2C+Altius%2C+Fortius] (retrieved on 6 August 2019).

[13]Official Website of Winter Olympic Games [https://www.olympic.org/winter-games] (retrieved on 7 August 2019).

[14]Official Website of 2020 Tokyo Olympics [https://tokyo2020.org/en/games/sport/olympic/] (retrieved on 7 August 2019).

judo, volleyball (or as a more general scope, the team sports with balls and martial arts of Far East civilizations) were not credited as a sport or an Olympic sport by the IOC (International Olympics Committee) before gaining popularity and drawing much attention from audiences (Wallechinsky and Loucky 2012). Therefore, it can be said that the definition and scope of the term "sport" is actually shifting towards the popularity of the related activity by considering how much it became widespread or demanded by the spectators and thus how profitable it is in its own ecosystem. As per such outcome, the traditional definitions of sports became quite unstable that several arrangements were made in order to widen its scope and generate a more abstract and de facto definition. Pursuantly, Elias and Dunning (1986) attempted to define sport "developmentally" by suggesting that sports as we know them today (also referred as modern sports) refer to a pattern of competitive physical activities which began to emerge for the first time in Britain and Ireland in the 17th and 18th centuries, rather than questioning the notions of "organization," "competitiveness," and/or "goal orientation."

Another touch for within this scope was brought by *Koudelkova and Kosova* (n.d.), who suggested to categorize sports as Olympic and non-Olympic initially and divide the latter into several other classes such as recognized sports, national sports, and extreme sports; recommended other classification subsets such as games, gymnastics, track and field athletics, water sports, cycling sports, ski sports, technical sports, sports on ice, combat sports and martial arts, outdoor sports, equestrian, and combined sports; and concluding thereby that sport is "Typically considered to be competitive physical activities that have an organized set of rules along with winners and losers[15]"—which also excludes the intellectual games such as chess and bridge.

With reserving such description and considering the stipulation of *McPherson* et al. (1989), it can be concluded that sports do not have a general illustration, all of recognized sports branches share some common grounds, mainly being *"structured/organized," "goal-oriented," "competitive," "comprising physical and mental skill components," "form of play," "intrinsically motivated," "motion," "voluntary," "training and developing," "stability," "non-utilitarian/not competing for an external motive such as money,"* and *"spread to a wide range of audience"* (with the last stating the entertainment, display and show business side of the activity). Where a profession begins, though, the "non-utilitarian" aspect of sport is removed, "voluntary" and "intrinsically motivated" aspects become controversial, providing that the rest of the "sport" identity of the activity will be preserved (Guttmann 2004). The main reason for such alteration is the fact that the medium of such games and sports are mainly analog and can be obtainable by a player's own means without paying any material considerations (unlike the digital games) and therefore, with having no tendency for monetization in its ecosystem fundamentally,

---

[15]Koudelkova, A.; Kosova, J. (n.d.), The Categorization of Sports Branches, Sports Studies Fundamental Terminology in English [http://web.ftvs.cuni.cz/eknihy/jazyky/sportstudiesfunda mentalterminologyinenglish/Texts/3-Categories.html] (retrieved on 6 August 2019).

amateur status of the analog games and sports differ from the professional status principally due to the material interests and profession (instead of mere hobby).

As an example for clarifying this scope, a one-time non-utilitarian football match between two teams will be considered as "playing a game," having those teams compete with each other for certain times every week in a non-utilitarian manner will be deemed as "sports," whereas making those teams monetize from such competition (via salaries or prizes) in the latter will be accepted as professional sports. As per all the aforementioned statements, it can be claimed that professionalism does constitute another level of sports merely, where sports are a special subset of games that intersects with games majorly, which will still enable professional sports for belonging into the game family.

5.1.3 Definition of Esport

After the breakthrough of the digital revolution and internet era, the players became enabled to compete with other real human players (instead of their previous sole option of just facing the mere artificial intelligence of digital devices) in the games (Hamari and Sjöblom 2017). Such development brought a new realm of challenge and a new aspect of antagonism and opposition to the humans that can be used to gather up an emergent definition for gameplay amongst the digital world users, which can be summarized as the multiplayer and/or massively multiplayer gaming experience in online platforms (Steinkuehler 2004). By the means of this new leap, players gained an opportunity of competing against each other which seemed as similar to the competition aspect in conventional and traditional sports, but had its own rules and conditions, both physically and mentally (Wagner 2006). From such a point of view and with the help of stabilized and consistent internet-serving utilities and technologically improved hardware, online games begin to connect countless numbers of players throughout the world each and every day and repulsed them to alter their experiences inherited from the offline gameplay against the AIs and innovate new methods for beating the real-intelligence of their rivals (Jenny et al. 2017).

In the due course of this process, the concept of "playing a game" had risen to a new level that requires specialization and excellence for winning and having fun (Bányai et al. 2019); and with the foundation of digital broadcasting organs (such as Twitch and YouTube), they had found a new platform for displaying their progressive gameplays to the fans and audiences of such games throughout indoor competitions or live streaming feeds (Burroughs and Rama 2015; Pires and Simon 2015), thus this situation had evolved the games and gameplay to a new type of sports, called the esports, which then entitled the hardcore gamers that desire to play a game systematically and collectively in a well-disciplined training manner as "professional" (Faust et al. 2013).

Such gamers found new meanings and emotions in "playing a game" rather than just having fun, such as earning material and immaterial prizes from the game contests and having a career (Wagner 2006) in being a gamer—which nowadays has been deemed as a sport branch (Taylor 2012) and legitimized by the competent local and international governing bodies of sports and countries with distinguishing such mechanism from gambling.[16] Therefore, it can be said that the reason of playing games, together with the type of user experience and player enjoyment have become altered as the humans shift through amateur and professional player levels, provided that the element of fun is still preserved, even within the new "prize" conditions were added to the gameplay nature, which were ostracized from the definition of the game as a default before (Hallmann and Giel 2018). Accordingly, players can be classified as casual (amateur) gamers and professional gamers in today's gaming and esports ecosystem (Ma et al. 2013; Taylor 2012), providing that each of them has their own motives for playing games that actually do not conflict with the usual definitions of the games, but can help to derive a new, enhanced, and updated version of such definitions by reconciliating the "clashes" between the existing definitions and esports.

Though esports also lack a common, universal definition like game concept does, several key aspects of the term can be used as a common ground for formalizing a perception with regard to the nature of its atmosphere. Accordingly,

- *Wagner* (2006, p. 3, 440) stipulates that esport is "an area of sport activities in which people develop and train mental or physical abilities in the use of information and communication technologies."
- *Hemphill* (2005, p. 199) gives an earlier definition by claiming that esports are "alternative sport realities, that is, to electronically extended athletes in digitally represented sporting worlds."
- *Whalen* (2013) points out that esport is "an umbrella term used to describe organized, sanctioned video game competitions, most often in the context of video game tournaments."
- *Adamus* (2012) suggests that esports are alternate sports and a special way of using video games and engaging in gameplay.
- *Freeman and Wohn* (2017) point out that "eSports is situated at a unique intersection that combines recreation, interaction, task, competition, and collaboration: It is task-based with serious purposes (e.g., collaborate to complete tasks and win); it also happens in an intense fictional virtual environment that requires fast decision-making and response rate.

---

[16]French Numeric Law (Loi pour une République Numérique), [http://www.senat.fr/enseance/textes/2015-2016/744.html#AMELI_SUB_4_1468248055899_1432] (retrieved on 6 August 2019).

- The 2017 version of *Associated Press Stylebook* has referred esports as "competitive multiplayer video gaming."[17]
- *Cambridge Online Dictionary* defines esports as "the activity of playing computer games against other people on the internet, often for money, and often watched by other people using the internet, sometimes at special organized events."[18]
- *Lexico Dictionary* states that esport is "a multiplayer video game competitively for spectators, typically by professional gamers."[19]
- *Techterms.com* broadens the definition as "eSports is a general term used to describe video game competitions. Much like athletic sporting events, eSports games are often played before live audiences and may be broadcast over the Internet as well. ... An eSports match is performed much like an athletic sporting event. Players must follow certain rules and a referee officiates the game. Sportscasters typically commentate the game, explaining what is happening in real-time. ... The rise of eSports has produced a large number of professional video gamer players (or "pro gamers"). These players compete regularly in professional tournaments with cash prizes."[20]
- *Freeman and Wohn* (2017) conducted several interviews with the esports players and they mentioned that esports should necessarily contain "competition, clear goals, rules," as well as require to have "professional scene or atmosphere." Also, many of such players deem an activity qualified as an esport only if a human is playing against a human, as they "did not regard playing against the computer as esports," mainly due to the fact that the sophistication and versatility of AIs are not sufficient to procure a decent challenge or competition for human players.
- *IeSF (International eSports Federation)* defines esports as "a competitive sport performed in a virtual environment in which physical and mental abilities are exercised to create victory conditions through generally accepted rules."[21]

The general idea with regard to the esports is that an activity should contain *"competition," "goals," "rules/sanctions," "training abilities," "electronics," "digitally represented worlds," "organized competitions," "video games and engaging gameplay," "multiplayer"* (thus, human rivals), *"online," "*(often) *playing for monetized prize considerations," "spectators and audience," "professional gamers"* in order to be qualified as an esport. Several of such elements are (goals, rules, mental and physical skills, digitally represented worlds—the latter also provides a safe playground to the players, as one cannot get any physical harm by playing

---

[17]Darcy, Kieran. Why the Associated Press Stylebook went with esports, not eSports. 6 July 2017 [https://www.espn.com/esports/story/_/id/19860473/why-associated-press-stylebook-went-esports-not-esports] (retrieved on 7 August 2019).

[18][https://dictionary.cambridge.org/tr/s%C3%B6zl%C3%BCk/ingilizce/e-sports] (retrieved on 7 August 2019).

[19][https://www.lexico.com/en/definition/e-sport] (retrieved on 7 August 2019).

[20][https://techterms.com/definition/esports] (retrieved on 7 August 2019).

[21]Official Website of IeSF, [https://www.ie-sf.org/e-sports/] (retrieved on 6 August 2019).

in a virtual environment) overlapping with the definitions of game, where some ("electronics," "video games," "engaged gameplay") do coincide with video games, a number of them ("multiplayer," "online") match up with online digital gaming, others ("organized competitions") do tally with the features of sports and rest ("organized competitions," "play for monetized prize considerations," "spectators and audience," "professional gamers/players") do correspond to professional sports.

From such statements, it can be claimed that esports players are also a fortiori video gamers, as online gaming so they indeed are qualified for being a gamer essentially, though they choose to display their skills on professional competition level, just like adopting it as a profession. Another aspect of such claim saturates on the fact that, just like the games are transmedial concepts (Juul 2003) and can be played in digital platforms (under the general term of e-gaming[22]), esports can be identified as computer-mediated "sports" (Freeman and Wohn 2017), which will also make esports eligible to have another common ground with games. Furthermore, with these explanations, esports are proven to share common points with traditional sports players, therefore are eligible to be classified as "athletes" and/or "sportsman," providing that they do it in digital manner, which means that their activities do not weigh in physically oriented mobility or motility unlike most portion of the traditional sports (Jenny et al. 2017), but instead focus on mental skills, peripheral vision, taking initiatives, hand-eye coordination and mastering the mechanics of digital control devices (i.e., mouse, keyboard, gamepad, etc.) that will maintain the necessary movement for acting in virtual world (Bányai et al. 2019).

Although it is not mandatory to be a professional and compete for cashable prizes in esports (Hamilton et al. 2012)—thus, players can preserve their amateur status while competing in professional esports events—esports do lay a professional and commercial characteristic of flaunting an entertainment and show for the audiences and therefore obtain an income from such business in return (Freeman and Wohn 2017). Within such frame, the only factor that distinguishes the amateur and professional players is playing for remuneration, as both can define their activities as a profession but only one of them, the professionals, will earn prize money and an additional possible salary for putting on a show on a routine basis for spectators that want to feel the novelty of seeing the best players compete with each other (Bányai et al. 2019), as a natural aspect of the entertainment[23] business[24] (Ma et al. 2013). This perspective also homologizes professional sports and esports, as mentioned in the section above, as well as the fact that just like the sports athlete scholarships in the academics, there are esports scholarship programs implemented in several countries' universities under the name of "esports athlete scholarship" since 2013 (Jenny et al. 2017).

When thinking collectively with the digital gaming business' aim of earning profits from producing and selling games (and game contents) and the monetization

---

[22] [https://www.urbandictionary.com/define.php?term=E-Game] (retrieved on 7 August 2019).

[23] [https://www.lexico.com/en/definition/entertainment] (retrieved on 7 August 2019).

[24] [https://www.lexico.com/en/definition/business] (retrieved on 7 August 2019).

policy, it shall be clarified that including quantifiable outcomes and money transfer for acquiring and playing games or altering game experiences, and therefore the habitat of digital gaming is not free of any material prizes in itself. Pursuantly, the professionalism of digital gaming and esports shall also always include a material interest in itself, which separates any other sport from esport on professional level, thus the professionalism in esports has a special condition that money transfer between gamers and gaming companies shall be deemed as normal and even necessary, which makes esports athletes still "gamers" fundamentally.

5.2 Esports Versus Gambling

In order for disambiguating the difference between gambling (which is defined as the activity of betting and risking money,[25] doing something with the hope of getting money which involves risks that might result in loss of money[26] or playing games of chance for money[27]), and esports, several key local and international governing bodies of countries and business took legal steps and legitimized esports as a sports branch by sanctioning their rights, incomes, and activities by the means of tax regulations and other laws.

As per such purpose, countries such as,

- *USA* (by granting pro-athlete [P1] visa to a League of Legends player—Danny "Shiphtur" Le—for allowing him to compete in the tournaments within USA and thus recognizing esports players as sportsman/professional athletes in 2013[28]),
- *South Korea* (by founding the first esports federation in 2000 under the Ministry of Culture, Sports and Tourism and granting a license—the pro-gaming license system[29]—only to esports players as an official mark for being a professional player and only then allow them to compete in professional tournaments[30]),

---

[25] [https://dictionary.cambridge.org/tr/s%C3%B6zl%C3%BCk/ingilizce/gambling] (retrieved on 7 August 2019).

[26] [https://dictionary.cambridge.org/tr/s%C3%B6zl%C3%BCk/ingilizce/gamble] (retrieved on 7 August 2019).

[27] [https://www.lexico.com/en/definition/gamble] (retrieved on 7 August 2019).

[28] Dave, P. Online game League of Legends star gets U.S. visa as pro athlete. 7 August 2013. Available at [https://www.latimes.com/business/la-xpm-2013-aug-07-la-fi-online-gamers-20130808-story.html] (day of retrieval: 7 August 2019).

[29] South Korea eSports Association Official Website [http://www.e-sports.or.kr/?ckattempt=1] (retrieved on 6 August 2019).

[30] Ozkurt, E. Esports in South Korea – a short overview of the legal ecosystem. 10 April 2019. Available on [https://www.lawinsport.com/content/articles/item/esports-in-south-korea-a-short-overview-of-the-legal-ecosystem] (day of retrieval: 7 August 2019).

- *France* (by unanimously adopting the Numeric Law [Loi pour une République Numérique] in the assembly on 28 September 2016,[31] which dissociates esports from gambling and betting, licensing the professional esports players and giving them pro-athlete visa, making them a subject to local tax laws and securing the rights of esports players and teams officially—France herewith became the first country in the world to regulate esports[32]),
- *Japan* (establishing the Japan eSports Union that came to an agreement with the Japanese government in 2018 with regard to issuing licenses to professional esports players that will allow them to bypass the legal prize pool cap rule, which normally stipulates that any event with a prize pool amounted more than 100 thousand Yens shall be deemed as a gambling activity, and thus allow professional esports players to compete in tournaments with larger prize pools), and.
- *Turkey* (as the Ministry of Youth and Sports recognized the esports licenses as sports/pro-athlete licenses in 2014 and further established the TESFED, the Turkey Esports Federation (Türkiye E-Spor Federasyonu), for officially deeming esports players as sports athletes[33] and carrying out esports activities as well as granting licenses to distinguish professional players[34]) (Ayar 2018),

Had innovated and implemented a license system that will identify and sanctify the professional status of esports players with granting them a right to obtain a pro-athlete visa, as well as benefit from the rights of sports athletes such as pensions and insurances within their jurisdiction, thus segregating esports from gambling. This system also secures the fact that no player in the esports ecosystem can name himself or herself as a professional player without being sufficiently merit for obtaining a professional license by the governing bodies of the esports.

Moreover, several major international non-profit sports organizations also had recognized esports as a branch of sports, especially after the foundation of *IeSF* (International eSports Federation) in 2008. Pursuantly, *IeSF* had adopted the anti-doping rules of *WADA* (World Anti-Doping Agency) in 2013[35] and became a medal event in 2013 *4th AIMAG* (Asian Indoor and Martial Arts Games)[36] in Incheon, became a member of *TAFISA* (The Association For International Sport for All) in 2014 and been represented as a demonstration game in 2016 TAFISA

---

[31] France Senate Official Website, Full Text [http://www.senat.fr/enseance/textes/2015-2016/744.html#AMELI_SUB_4_1468248055899_1432] (day of retrieval: 8 August 2019).

[32] Adrien Auxent, Esports are now officially legal in France, 30 September 2016 [https://esportsobserver.com/esports-are-now-officially-legal-in-france/] (day of retrieval: 8 August 2019).

[33] Pro gamers now recognized as athletes in Turkey. 27 September 2018 [https://www.smartlaunch.com/pro-gamers-now-recognized-as-athletes-in-turkey/] (retrieved on 8 August 2019).

[34] Turkish E-Sports Federation Official Website [http://tesfed.gov.tr/] (retrieved on 6 August 2019).

[35] Official Website of WADA [https://www.wada-ama.org/en/what-we-do/adams/list-of-organizations-using-adams] (retrieved on 8 August 2019).

[36] [https://archive.fo/20130708123421/http://www.aimag2013.org/en/Results/ES/MedallistsByEvent?SportCode=ES&EventCode=&GenderCode=&PhaseCode=] (retrieved on 8 August 2019).

World Games for All,[37] executed a partnership deal with *IAAF* (International Association of Athletics Federations) in 2015,[38] applied for official recognition to *IOC* (International Olympics Committee) in 2016,[39] earned a spot in the *5th AIMAG* (Asian Indoor and Martial Arts Games) in Turkmenistan in 2017[40] as a demonstration sport by working together with *OCA* (Olympic Council of Asia),[41] and agreed on partnership with *ITTF* (International Table Tennis Federation) in 2017[42]; whereas *FIFA*, whom did held the first conventional and stable esports tournament series under the name of FIFA Interactive World Cup since 2004 but did not prefer to use the term "esports," had included such term into the scope of its "FIFA 2.0: The Vision of Future"[43] program set forth by FIFA President Gianni Infantino in 2016[44] and renamed the Interactive World Cup as FIFA eWorld Cup in 2018.[45]

Although IeSF and esports are not recognized officially by IOC yet, the discussions and conversations on giving esports a display stage on *2020 Tokyo Olympics* as a demonstration sport and evolve it to a full medal event *2024 Olympic Games* in Paris[46]; as esports had already involved in *2018 Asian Games* in Jakarta as a demonstration sport and ensured to become a fully medal event the *2022*

---

[37]Chul, J.W.; IeSF joins the International Sports Organization "Esports Sports for All". 09 May 2014 [http://www.thisisgame.com/webzine/news/nboard/4/?n=54703] (retrieved on 8 August 2019).

[38]International E-Sports Federation Partners with Athletics for a Better World. 21 April 2015 [https://www.iaaf.org/news/iaaf-news/international-e-sports-athletics-better-world] (date of retrieval: 8 August 2019).

[39]IeSF, Taking Its First Step Towards IOC Recognition. 15 April 2016 [https://www.ie-sf.org/news/iesf-taking-its-first-step-towards-ioc-recognition/] (date of retrieval: 8 August 2019).

[40]Official Website of 2017 Ashgabat AIMAG [http://ashgabat2017.com/esports] (date of retrieval: 8 August 2019).

[41]Esports to be featured at the Asian Indoor and Martial Arts Games in 2017. 24 May 2017 [https://www.afkgaming.com/articles/esports-to-be-featured-at-the-asian-indoor-and-martial-arts-games-in-2017] (retrieved on 8 August 2019).

[42]IeSF agree on partnership with ITTF. 25 August 2017 [https://www.ie-sf.org/news/iesf-agree-on-partnership-with-ittf/] (date of retrieval: 8 August 2019).

[43]FIFA President Infantino Unveils "FIFA 2.0: The Vision for the Future". 13 October 2016 [https://www.fifa.com/about-fifa/who-we-are/news/fifa-president-infantino-unveils-fifa-2-0-the-vision-for-the-future-2843428] (retrieved on 8 August 2019) (original text document is available under [https://resources.fifa.com/mm/document/affederation/generic/02/84/35/01/fifa_2.0_vision_e_neutral.pdf].

[44]Brautigam, T. FIFA President Infantino Addresses eSports in his "Vision for the Future". 13 October 2016 [https://esportsobserver.com/fifa-president-infantino-addresses-esports-vision-future/] (retrieved on 8 August 2019).

[45]Official Website of FIFA eWorld Cup [https://www.fifa.com/fifaeworldcup/] (date of retrieval: 8 August 2019).

[46]Paris 2024 Olympics: Esports 'in talks' to be included as demonstration sport. 25 April 2018 [https://www.bbc.com/sport/olympics/43893891] (date of retrieval: 8 August 2019).

Asian Games in Hangzhou.[47] Therefore, esports became recognized as a branch of sport by many major and international sports associations and countries, which can legislate the legitimate status of esports as governing bodies and distinguish the concept from gambling all together.

Several prominent traditional sports clubs had also established their esports teams (i.e., by fully immersing) as a sub branch within their structure since 2015, which fastened the process of becoming widespread for esports and made easier for the sports audience and other authorities to embrace esports concept and business, including but not limited with Beşiktaş JK, Santos FC, Valencia CF, Club Deportivo Saski Baskonia, Schalke 04, Paris Saint-Germain, VfL Wolfsburg, RCD Espanyol, Sporting CP, Galatasaray SK, Fenerbahçe SK, Bursaspor, Göztepe SK, Legia Warsaw, Barcelona, IFK Helsinki, AS Roma. Such progress actually helped the sanctifying of esports legally by the well-established foundations throughout the world and also distinguished esports from gambling practically.[48] The investors (such as former NBA players Shaquille O'Neal, Michael Jordan and Magic Johnson, former baseball star Alex Rodriguez, singer Drake, former CEO of eBay Meg Whitman, musician Steve Aoki,[49] Dallas Mavericks owner Marc Cuban) and sponsors (such as Logitech, Rampage, Red Bull, Honda, Alienware, Coca Cola, PayPal, Twitch, Turkish Airlines) of esports also contributed the legitimacy of this brand-new branch accordingly.[50]

The nature of esports also focus majorly on free to play games (that do not require a fee to be paid in order for reaching the gameplay) and repulse pay to win mechanism; which means that players cannot purchase downloadable contents that will boost their gameplay power with software-based enhancers in professional level (Alha et al. 2014), in order to achieve a fair competition platform for every player candidate with equal means (i.e., the winner shall be decided based solely upon the skills, level of excelling over the game and mechanics, strategy and experience of the players). Still, there are few exceptions for the first, like Overwatch and PUBG, and for the latter, like FIFA Ultimate Team and Hearthstone (Ozenc 2019 pp. 76–83); but the professional characteristic of esports generally pierce the monetization policies of digital gaming business by not forcing its athletes to make a payment for competing on any level or boost their skills, and the remaining exceptions have the professional teams and sponsors cover up such expenses for the athletes—therefore,

[47] Graham, B.A.; eSports to be a medal event at 2022 Asian Games. 18 April 2017 [https://www.theguardian.com/sport/2017/apr/18/esports-to-be-medal-sport-at-2022-asian-games] (retrieved on 8 August 2019).

[48] Sports Clubs & Esports. *Digital Sports Media* n.d. [http://digitale-sport-medien.com/sports-clubs-esports/] (retrieved on 9 August 2019).

[49] Breakthrough. (2018, 30 August) 11 Celebrity eSports Investors You Didn't Know About [https://medium.com/@breakthrough_lab/celebrity-esports-investors-you-didnt-know-about-eb9a8c395292] (retrieved on 10 August 2019).

[50] Fitch, A. (2018, December 28). This Year in Esports: Investments, sponsorships and deals in 2018 [https://esportsinsider.com/2018/12/this-year-in-esports-2018-roundup/] (retrieved on 10 August 2019).

there is not even a tiny portion of gambling within the habitat of being an esports player and the monetization policy of digital gaming is reversed in such a manner that will go in the esports players' favor.

Another claim for setting esports apart from gambling can be made via explaining the monetization system of being an esports player. Just like the traditional sports athletes, professional esports players compete under a team, wear its uniform and earn a non-fixed regular salary for representing that team and competing in the tournaments with giving the best effort with regard to his/her expertise of gaming skills, solely or with a squad of other teammates. Within such regard, none of the professional players do pay a fee or bid any money for participating the professional and official esports tournaments in order to compete for prize money—their teams, sponsors, organizations, or gaming companies (or in some exceptional cases, fan bases) do fund and cover such payments instead, as well as their general "running cost" expenses for living, practicing, and competing (Menasce 2017 p. 22, 23, 30, 37). Therefore, despite the fact that esports player will have a chance for flourishing with the prizes, they do not pay or bet any money to do so, which will separate esports from gambling in the first place. Just like the professional athletes in the traditional sports, *the only thing an esports player will be devoid of if he/she loses the tournament is the possibility and opportunity of achieving more money (a money that is not owned by them already, but is prospective and unborn), but they will not face the risk of losing the money they already have, prior to the competition.* However, as a part of being a profession, too much losses may end up losing their salary earnings/wages, which still does not pauperize them by taking the money which was already in their possession, unlike the gambling.[51] One have to take into account that although people can bet money and gamble over others' esports activities (such as done in traditional sports), this would not ventilate by any means that an esport itself can be considered as a gambling activity, or has a gambling side in its nature (only rather than the tendency for repetitive gameplay desire, as the digital gaming allows rematches momentarily with its speed), for the esports players.

In spite of the fact that esports are nowadays proven to be a sports branch as per the statements in the section above, the sanctified aspects of esports are majorly regarding its business, legal, organization, entertainment and "sports" sides, in addition to the "gaming" perspective.

5.3   Conclusion: I

As per all the statements above, a comparison between the common points of the game definitions and the nature, context, definitions and scope of esports can be made as follows:

---

[51] [https://dictionary.cambridge.org/tr/s%C3%B6zl%C3%BCk/ingilizce/gamble] (retrieved on 7 August 2019).

As it can be seen from Table 5.1, several points of several game definitions ("being separate in time and space/out of ordinary life/out of real world," "not serious," "no material interest/no money-gaining/unproductive") do clash with esports totally (whereas the "unproductive" notion is actually contradicting with the industrialized gaming business nowadays). However, in order to determine whether some other specialties do clash or fit into the game definitions (namely; "recreation," "voluntary," "free") the motives and manners of amateur and professional gamers shall also be taken into account; providing that, except Ma et al. (2013), all of such conflicting definitions do belong to the eras which were prior to the rise of the revolutionary digital gaming and emerge of esports and therefore do not comprehend video games mainly.

As for the similarities between the sports and esports, in order for acquiring a decent comparison of the common points of sports and esports, another table can be made as follows:

It can be said from Table 5.2 that esports and sports do share "enjoyment/fun," "job/profession," "competition and training," "physical and intellectual skills," "stability," "wide range of audience," "serious/not recreative," "set of rules," and "gameplay" aspects in their core amateur level, providing that the professional esports do also share the utilitarian/external gaining aim of the professional sports. Though the esports, with having a virtual medium for gameplay that none of the players can come into physical contact with another (mediated gameplay), tend to incline on the skills with regard to controlling the mechanics of digital machinery instead of excelling on analog equipment control (i.e., balls, discs, javelin, etc.) and/or mobility and body/physicality control by nature, and thus resemble more of a branch that weighs on intellectual-skill components, it still requires more concentrated physical activity to do so than many of the recognized sports such as chess, dart, and archery, as also share same grounds of machinery skills with motorized sports such as car races. Therefore, it can be claimed that, at its very theoretical and practical levels, esports stand merit to be counted and deemed as sports (van Hilvoorde and Pot 2016; Witkowski 2009, 2012).

As another fact, just like the professional sports do still count as sports and a special subset and derivative of gaming and cannot be performed without "playing a game" in the first place, it can be claimed that the professional habitat of esports shall not abolish the "game" status of it, as it cannot be performed without playing video games competitively and thereby serves as a special subset or derivative of games, similar to the fact that it constitutes a special subset and branch of sports. Further aspect of such claim is the fact that digital game business does urge amateur/casual players to pay a fee for reaching the gameplay stage of a game and/or implement pay to win monetization system and/or create a downloadable content of cosmetics or indirect mechanics for improving and diversifying the gameplay experience, as such policy includes material interest in every phase of digital gaming, and thereby alter the status of professionalism in digital gaming (esports) against and before amateur digital gaming fundamentally, in a different manner than the sports or analog games do. As another fact, the esports players do not have to pay a fee for reaching such contents due to the dynamics in esports

Table 5.1 The comparison of game definitions with the context and definition of esports

| Game definition | The definition, nature, context, and scope of esports | | |
	Fit	Clash	Might fit or clash
Huizinga	Absorbing the player intensely and utterly (immersive), own proper boundaries of space and time, fixed rules, orderly manner, formation of social groupings which tend to surround themselves with secrecy and to stress their difference from the common world by disguise or other means, fun[a]	Outside the ordinary life, not serious, no material interest and no profit can be gained by	Free activity
Caillois	Uncertain, governed by rules, make-believe/fictive	Separate in time and space, unproductive	Free (voluntary)
Suits	A specific state of affairs (goals), using only means permitted by rules (rules and means), rules prohibit more efficient in favor of less efficient means, rules are accepted just because they make possible such activity (lusory state)		
Avedon and Sutton-Smith	Control systems, opposition between forces, confined by a procedure and rules in order to produce a disequilibrial outcome		Voluntary
Crawford	Representation (a closed formal system that subjectively represents a subset of reality), interaction, conflict, and safety		
Kelley	Constituted by a set of rules that specify an object to be attained and the permissible means of attaining it		A form of recreation
Apter	Safety, governed by the rules	A frame which stands between the player and the "real world" and its problems	

(continued)

Table 5.1 (continued)

Game definition	The definition, nature, context, and scope of esports		
	Fit	Clash	Might fit or clash
Salen and Zimmerman	A system, artificial conflict, defined by rules, quantifiable outcome		
Juul	Rule-based formal system, variable and quantifiable outcome, different outcomes are assigned different values, player exerts effort in order to influence the outcome, player feels attached to the outcome, consequences of the activity are optional and negotiable, amusement[b]		
Oxford Learner's Dictionaries	An activity or a sport, with rules, people or teams compete against each other		
Vorderer and Bryant, Gee	Fun		
Grönroos	Entertainment		
Guttmann	Physical or intellectual activity, intrinsic gameplay behavior, voluntary, governed by rules, competition, winner-loser outcome, comprise skill	Non-utilitarian; cannot aim an external achievement (money, etc.)	
Ma et al.	A tool of having fun and entertainment		Recreation

[a]Though not added to the main definition, this phrase takes place in the same section (Huizinga 1949 p. 3)
[b]Though not added to the main definition, this phrase takes place in the same section (Juul 2003)

Table 5.2 The comparison of sports definitions with the context and definition of esports

Sports definition	The definition, nature, context, and scope of esports		
	Fit	Clash	Might fit or clash
Guttmann	Intrinsic gameplay behavior, voluntary, governed by rules, competition, winner-loser outcome, comprise skill, stable, wide range of audience, serious, training of skills, entertaining/fun	Non-utilitarian; cannot aim an external achievement (money, etc.)	Physically oriented activity in general
Tiedemann	Activity, relation with other people in performing phase, developing abilities and accomplishments, comparison of self to the opponents according to the rules, no intended damage in gameplay	Particularly in the area of skilled motion	Voluntary
Suits	A game, competitive play, variety of skills, the movement of body parts continuously for conducting the gameplay, stability, wide range of following audience		
Deaner and Smith, Malcolm	Game, competitive, no pure-chance wins, not depending solely on mental skills	Requirement of physical skills majorly	
McPherson	Structured, goal-oriented, competitive forms of play		
Koudelkova and Kosova	Competitive activities, organized set of rules, winners and losers	Physical only	
Cambridge online dictionary	Game, competition, activity, skill-need, governed by rules, done for enjoyment and/or as a job	Physical efforts only	

ecosystem, i.e., the status of esport game branches and fiscal structure of the system as stated in the previous section.

It can also be seen from Table 5.2 that, just as the "intrinsically motivated" and "voluntary" clause will become controversial in professionalism of sports (where the athletes will be forced to compete with each other on a regular basis in exchange for money), the professionalism of esports also might clash with "recreation," "voluntarily," and "free" aspects of (amateur) gaming, as the esports athletes will be channeled to compete with each other on a regular basis in exchange for cashable prizes as well. Although "being not separate from the ordinary life and real world," "playing seriously," and "playing for money" do abolish the amateur state of gaming in professional esports, in order for determining whether the esports psychology disarrays the "recreation," "voluntarily," and "free" nature of gaming, the motives of the amateur and professional gamers/players shall be examined further.

In order for determining the status of professional esports players, the motives of amateur gaming and becoming a professional esport player shall be defined and examined in a more detailed approach (Fig. 5.2).

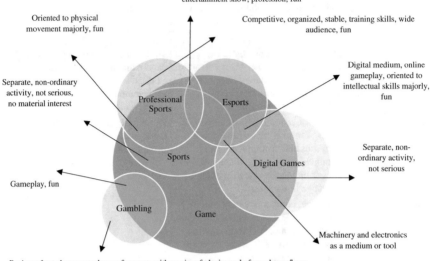

Fig. 5.2 The self-made scheme of Conclusion—I that explains the relationship and status of Game, Sports, Digital Games, Professional Sports, Esports, and Gambling

5.4 Motives and Psychology of Amateur (Casual) Gamers

Despite the fact that theorists such as Huizinga (1950) claimed that humans are Homo Ludens, where ludens represents ludic (playing) side of humans, and playing a game is an intrinsic motive (and even a need) that is embedded to the soul of every human upon incarnation and reveal his/her skills by imitating the nature since childhood by the technique of "playing," depending on the definitions with regard to the games, the motives of humans (regardless of their ages and demographics) for playing games can be collected into five different categories. First of them is the expectation of achieving entertainment, pleasure, fun, and amusement (Huizinga 1950; Kim 1995; Juul 2003; Ma et al. 2013) and constitutes the main basis for other motives. Such fun and entertainment though have their own categories, in which the recreative or competitive nature (Demetrovics et al. 2011) or level of the game can address to different audience demographics (Lazzaro 2005), but the general perception towards playing games for fun actually is an activity of spending a qualified leisure time in casual life (Hoon et al. 2002, p. 74).

Secondly, the interactive nature of the game appeals the audience, as unlike the TV series, movies, or books (which center on story), all of the games require an interaction (by centering on play [Pearce 2004]) for involvement (Bang 1991), which actually makes the gamers act and react by participation in the game and evolves, modifies and changes the content of the game (such as progression through narrative and gameplay) by those actions and reactions, especially in the digital gaming (Vorderer 2000; Yee 2006a; Grodal 2000). Such interaction especially serves for the relaxation and recreation of players (Fenigstein 1979); where such interactive narrative in video games serves for fulfilling the curiosity, suspense and surprise needs and thus creates an arousal in the psychology of the player Grodal 2000).

Pursuantly, games that are played against humans on the other hand require an interaction of communication with other teammates or opponents (Pickford 1941), which drives people due to the factor of socializing physically or digitally depending on the medium and platform of gameplay (Ducheneaut et al. 2006), especially in MMO games that actually allow players to form player groups (namely, clans) which will make them act together (Jansz and Tanis 2007; Yee 2006b) and achieve collective fun by such teamwork (Yee 2006a; De Grove et al. 2016).

Third motive for playing games can be identified as "illusion" and "believable fictive," which actually stands for a make-believe frequency of players that will actually believe the importance and seriousness of the artificial world of the game within the gameplay (Greenberg et al. 2010; Sherry et al. 2006). This motive can be widened by verting it towards digital gaming, where the players chase realism and dramatic fantasy (includes role-playing as well [Yee 2006a]) derived by the sophisticated software, hardware, graphic design, animation, and narrative of the digital medium (Hoon et al. 2002).

Fourth type of motive can be summarized as the representation and reflection of daily life and culture within the game, but in such a manner that the game offers an escape from the exact reality and its problems to the alternate timeline/reality in the game world (Yee 2006a, 2006b; Demetrovics et al. 2011), which will inspire more realistic heroic feelings within the player with regard to saving or changing the world, where this motive is slightly connected with the first and third motive (Hoon et al. 2002, p. 74). Within such manner, almost every video game makes players to control the protagonist/hero/main character.

Rivera suggested that the video game genres such as deathmatch or Battle Royale addresses the fundamental needs ranked in the first two ladders of the Maslow's hierarchy of needs and human motivation[52] (which are deemed essential, such as safety, health, resources, water, food, sleep, etc. [McLeod 2007; Maslow 1943]), as the gameplay of artificial, simulative war theme stimulates the primitive instinct of eliminating or get eliminated by the manner of "kill or die," "kill for survive," and "haste for surviving the lethal effects of the nature" (goes mainly for Battle Royale genre, where the players have to survive not only against the opponents, but also the mechanics of game field that collapses the map for narrowing down the playground for enabling more killing sprees or damage the life points of the players continuously that do not act accordingly with such narrowing; see Ozenc

---

[52]Melrose, C. Why Battle Royale Games Like Fortnite Are Everywhere (It's not Just Money). 14 June 2018 [https://www.wired.com/story/fortnite-battlefield-rise-of-battle-royale/] (retrieved on 6 August 2019).

and Tinmazlar 2019 and Ozenc and Keskin 2019) and nurturing the desperation within the game atmosphere which uncannily resembles a very possible nuclear aftermath theme in the real world or a fictive, yet realistic deserted island that evokes secludedness.

In accordance with surveys conducted by a gaming company (Vorderer and Bryant 2012), the fifth and contemporarily most attractive reason for playing games is the competition and challenge; in other words, skills of the rivals and characteristics of the obstacles (such as fights, puzzles, etc.) in a game (Vorderer et al. 2003; Sherry et al. 2006; Bányai et al. 2019). Such challenges and competition are necessary for reaching the goals and obtaining the achievements of the game, such as winning and losing (Malone 1981), whether against the AI of the game itself (in digital gaming) or other players (in all types of games). The main reason for the emerge of such factor is mainly depending on the first factor—the fun and entertainment—as the players do locate a more sophisticated, tense, senior and satisfying competitions and challenges (Kim 1995) within the gameplay of (especially) modern games which do have a mediated play via digital gaming and acquire a more qualified fun thereby. What makes people desire to best the obstacles in the path to victory is the fact that the default possibility in games will be "losing" the game, if not done otherwise solely by the skillful gameplay of the players—thus have a special and noble notion within their playing experience (Johns 1981; Stover 1984). Regardless of the demographics, both the rewarding nature of overcoming such competition and challenge (Sherry et al. n.d.), and the theory of desiring to have a challenge and competition for the skills and talents throughout a lifespan due to human nature (Ryan and Deci 2000) stimulates people to play the games as an intrinsic mean (Deci and Ryan 2010).

This fifth motive, however, has to be scaled by a criterion, as one cannot define and describe the meanings and content of challenge or competition universally. As per such aim, Csikszentmihalyi (1997) had proposed the game flow theory, in which an x-and-y-axis graph, where x axis represents the abilities of players (from low to high) and y axis reflects the challenges of the game presents (from low to high), shows the flow of a game with 8 different states. Accordingly, low level of skills and low-level challenges end up in Apathy (sad, depressed mood), where every game initiates its gameplay; while the abilities and challenges rise through game progress, if medium level of skills and low-level challenges meet, boredom (depressed, contented) will happen; if high level of skills and low-level challenges meet, there will be relaxation (confident, contented); whereas low level of skills matches with medium-level challenges, worry (sad, stressed) will evoke, and if low level of skills met with high-level challenges, anxiety (stressed, alert) shall happen; where mid-level skills met with high-level challenges, state of arousal (alert, focused) will occur, high-level of abilities and mid-level challenges, control (happy, confident) state will be triggered. Last but not least, if high-level skills do meet with high-level challenges, the ultimate goal of the games shall be reached and state of flow (focused, happy) will take place.

As per such classification, every game aims to have a play flow that will fall into control, arousal, or flow categories, as players will tend to quit playing otherwise, therefore shall arrange the level of challenges in accordance with the skill level of players and if the challenges presented fit into the skill level of the player throughout the gameplay (i.e., starting easy, getting harder gradually in reasonable amounts as the player progresses through the game), then the game will be deemed as truly immersive and more fun, which will appeal the players more and make them play more (Csikszentmihalyi 1997). Though most of the analog games have a stable and fixed or slightly linear challenge system (providing that the competitors will determine the level of gameplay instead of the challenges), such progressive practice is quite common for digital games, which embrace a progressively linear/nonlinear system of challenges and/or competitors. Same scaling can be applied for competition, especially in the multiplayer/MMO games, where other humans will become competitors and their skill level shall determine the amount of fun, pleasure, and entertainment that a player will obtain in gameplay, as well as the challenges. This is the primary reason of video games for implementing the ranking system, in which the match-making algorithms will act pursuant to the rankings/mastery levels of each player when designating the competitors in each match (Vorderer and Bryant 2009).

As a result of the aforementioned statements, casual/standard (amateur) gamers share 5 main motives for playing games within their psychologies and gaming experiences; (i) entertainment and fun, (ii) interactivity and socialization, (iii) realistic illusion and fiction for drama, (iv) Reflection of the real world, representation of culture for improved fictive heroism while escaping from the real world to the alternate world in game, (v) challenge and competition.

5.5 Motives and Psychology of Esports Players

Although the necessities of having decent skills on the mechanical controlling system of the devices and user interface of the games for achieving "the speed and accuracy of strategic decision making and applying such decision," avoiding any distraction from focusing to the profession, coping adaptively with the possible fan harassment, being motivated to keep moving forward without thinking about the past performances and warming up mind and physique sufficiently before performing, adapting to opponents, communicating properly with teammates, acting accordingly with team dynamics, setting short or long term goals for self and team and developing skills constantly and getting over confidence issues (Himmelstein et al. 2017) as demanded by the competition level (Bányai et al. 2019; Freeman and Wohn 2017) and having a promising talent for a successful career in a fixed software environment (Wagner 2006) draws a line for becoming and staying as an esport player professionally, the motives and psychology of such players alter into different categories.

Despite several authorities (Brock 2017; Caillois 2001) claim that shifting to professionalism actually make the athletes tend to pursue extrinsic motives instead of having intrinsic ones (i.e., reward-oriented, extroverted goals such as fame and money), it can be said that (a) esports players do not lose their intrinsic motives when they also pursue extrinsic ones, and they can have both kinds of motivations for their careers (Kim and Thomas 2015), and (b) playing video games in a hypercompetitive way is not sufficient for defining it as a work or leisure activity, as it can be derived from the mannerism and characteristic nature of the player (Bányai et al. 2019). Kim and Thomas (2015) also pointed out though that esports players consider their practice more as a work (extrinsic motivation) rather than a leisure (an intrinsic motivation).

For the latter statement, Seo (2016) had identified esport on professional level as a serious leisure activity between a normal, casual leisure and actual work that provides beneficial implications such as gaining self-concept and identity development throughout the activity solely. This statement proves the recreative aspect of the esports on professional level, yet has a seriousness in itself due to the level of competitiveness and challenges, instead of mere extrinsic motives (such as money) all alone (Martončik 2015). Pursuantly, in Seo's study (2016) where 10 esports players had been interviewed, professional esports athletes defended that the main elements that made them pursue a career in esports were;

- Celebration of the mastery of their skills regarding the gameplay,
- The pursuit of self-improvement, thus being "the best of themselves,"
- Importance of fairness, equity, and mutual respect within the ecosystem of esports,

Where their career journey of professionalism automatically grants them a social recognition to be one of very few top tier esports athletes within the system and allow them to experience fame, accomplishment (or accolades in other words) and high self-esteem with success and achievements (Seo 2016). Moreover, Seo explains the career phases of esports players via using a progressive storyline model, in which a player plays the games as a leisure activity (i.e., just for fun in the mainstream gamer community) at first, then improves his/her skills as a mastery in the selected game (such as League of Legends, Dota 2, PUBG, Counter-Strike: Global Offensive, Fortnite, Rocket League, Clash Royale, etc.) and as becoming aware of the benefits of becoming a professional by the information conveyed by the community, decides to become an esport thereby and changes the manner and discipline of mastering skills (Martončik 2015; Seo 2016) for such purpose accordingly (such as locating his/her weaknesses and developing strategies to overcome them, as well as sharpening and perfecting the good skills that he/she already has). Thirdly, the practice pays off by acquiring a new identity as an esport player/gamer and configure their daily life styles in accordance with the awareness of being an esports player and global self-concepts brought by the fame, expectations, and consequences (Seo and Jung 2016).

As per the different studies conducted among esport audience (Lee and Schoen-stedt 2011 [interviewing over 500 college students]) and esports players Weiss and Schiele 2013 [interviewing 360 esports players]) mainly using the uses and gratifications theory of Katz et al. (1973) had obtained the following results with regard to the motives of becoming a professional esports player: social interaction, identification with sport, competition, diversion, entertainment, challenge, escapism, fantasy, sports knowledge application, arousal, design/graphics of the game, passing time, control, skill building, permanence, and peer pressure; where among such personal and social elements of influence for individuals to become esports players, the *competition, challenge, escapism* (thus, becoming another persona that other players and audience will appreciate*), peer pressure,* and *skill building* prevailed over others (Bányai et al. 2019). Martončik (2015 [108 esports players, 54 casual gamers]) on the other hand focused on the life goals (i.e., intimacy, affiliation, altruism, power, diversion, and achievement) of casual or esports players, solo or team players, clan/team leaders or members can contribute to the motivations for becoming a professional gamer, where *affiliation* (the need of having an intense interaction with others, belong to a structure and to help others) and *diversion* (the need for *excitement, tension,* and new *unique experiences*) differed esports players from the casual players, as esports athletes tend and desire to participate in tournaments and develop more friendly relationships through being a member of a team (Bányai et al. 2019). Leaders of such teams, however, also satisfy their *need for power* by holding the title of a game leader.

Freeman and Wohn (2017) had find out in their study that players' perception of esports include the following aspects:

- Competition.
- Goals/Rules.
- Being on a professional scene.
- Spectators.
- Intellectual and motor skills.
- A governing body.
- Human competitors.

These studies showed that becoming a professional esport player seems to be similar to the process of becoming a professional athlete in any given sport (Freeman and Wohn 2017; Bányai et al. 2019). According to Guttmann's (2004) and Suits' (2007) characteristics that define an activity as a sport, lots of similarities can be found between players who play video games as a professional and players who identify themselves as athletes (i.e., training, practice, skill acquisition, dedication to the profession, etc.). Taylor (2012) also suggested that professional gamers and professional athletes of traditional sports can be compared along the same requirements and practices, including the fixed rules of tournaments, players' mental and physical preparation for contests, broadcasting the events and judging the events (Bányai et al. 2019). The level of intensity with regard to the workload as a professional also makes the players such as Aman Seddiqi, a professional FIFA esports player, deem themselves in the level of professional athletes in traditional sports, where another professional FIFA esports player, Kai "Deto" Wollin, admits of working hard every day on a routine basis, as a player might only have a chance if he/she works hard collectively on every aspect of the game (Guinness World Records Gamers' Edition 2019, p. 152). Another similarity can be found among the fact that professional esports player only enjoy the dynamics of competition between human rivalries and the clear awareness of defeating an actual human (instead of an AI) as it gives them the sense of being "professional," just as the athletes in traditional sports do (Freeman and Wohn 2017; Jonasson and Thiborg 2010).

Pursuant to the semi-structured interviews made with the professional esports players, Mehmet "Korpse" Aksel, a professional League of Legends esports player in Turkey, has described that he was having just fun when he was an amateur gamer, but can earn his living by playing the game he liked and is skilled in most as in addition to having fun, as a professional (Yılmaz Oruç 2018), whereas Spencer "Gorilla" Ealing, a professional esports player for FIFA series, claims that this practice is both his work and hobby, as the professional status of him did not affect the passion he feels towards the game (Guinness World Records Gamers' Edition 2019, p. 152).

As per the interviews conducted by Ozenc and Tinmazlar (2018) with several esports staff (an esports team coach in Turkey and an esports team general manager in Turkey) and an esport color pundit within the scope of understanding the status and future of esports in Turkey, the motives of esports players in Turkey for turning into a professional are mainly;

- Finding *hyper level of competition and challenge* for the games they like to play most (i.e., achieving harder goals in the level of premier opponents to test their skills) (p. 232),
- The *decent standards and conditions* in professional esports ecosystem appeals players to become a professional, or at least to have a shot at trying to do so, as the standards were pretty low in the first few seasons in Turkey, where players actually competed under the title "professional esports player" officially but were devoid of any salary, etc. like an amateur in deed (p. 226),
- *Fame* (p. 261), *recognition* (especially for the foreign female players in Turkey, who appreciate the attention they received for being an esports player [p. 307] and *money* (as the numbers in salaries raised dramatically within the last few years and players can earn their livings by choosing esports as a profession [p. 261, 308], where some former or active players can also use their recognition for gaining additional income by streaming online in digital platforms [p. 298]),
- Being *affiliated* to big sports clubs (especially the traditional sports clubs that established esports branches), fan bases and sports cultures (p. 261),
- *Being a part of the elite tier of players* within the country and community/world, as the player pool is quite narrow when compared to the population (p. 227),
- For the players of Far East region of the world, the genetic proclivity for overly iterative playing and cultural impressions for discipline, devotion, and continuity inclines players to go for professional level, as the possibility of burnout, over or less training is really low for them (p. 263, 280, 281),
- Keeping their *talents sharp and fit* to be suitable for competing in utmost level, as even a small break will deteriorate their skill levels in esports (p. 264),

- Depending the *bright and promising future* of esports and counting on the possibility that it will grow further and earn even *more reputation*, which will make them earn *more money* (p. 269),
- *Socialization* with other people that have common interest with them in esports (pp. 271–272),
- The fact that esports has a *sterilized, refined, more sanitary atmosphere* by the means of having less fanatism and profound speeches, which cannot be achieved in most popular traditional sports, especially with their fan bases (p. 297, 300),
- *Making a living from the activity that they liked most and talented/mastered in most*, i.e., turning a hobby to a profession and a lifestyle, as they tend to live accordingly with such lifestyle regardless of being a professional, where professionalism will pay off for them with happiness, fun, satisfaction, glory, and fame that no other practice, occupation, or profession could do (p. 308). This proves the voluntarily, willingly, and enthusiastic involvement of players in professional esports, just like a casual gamer has in their amateur level.

The common grounds for all such findings reside at several key motives, such as *"affiliation," "being recognized as an elite player with talents and achievements," "fame," "building and improving skills and developing self continuously," "working in a reputed profession," "socialization," "generating an income from the hobby/leisure activity that he/she liked to do most and mastered in," "increased level of competition and challenge," "goals/rules," "community/fan base," "escapism," "diversion (excitement and tension),"* with representing both intrinsic and extrinsic kind of motives.

5.6 Conclusion: II

As per all the statements above, a collective evaluation with regard to the motives of amateur and professional players can be made as below:

Bu such data, the *escapism, heroism, challenge and competition, fun and amusement* aspects are common for both types, where professionals have such motives in higher level. It can be clarified from Table 5.3 that the hard working nature and consistently skill-improving (by playing even more iteratively when compared to the casual players) necessity is *not a drudgery* of profession for esports players that removes their willingness, fun, amusement, and fatigue, but a primary motive to become professional and compete with the best of the rest in world, and therefore does not remove "fun," "voluntary," or "free" aspects from the gaming unlike Caillois (2001) or Brock (2017) suggested. After all, esports player always have the lusory attitude (Suits 1978) for playing the game.

As a downside of being a professional—not only in sports, but also in every profession (Golembiewski 1984)—the professional esports players do face two main (organically connected) risks that professional people and sports athletes do as well, the first being the mental and emotional stress of constantly competing on

Table 5.3 The comparison of motives for amateur gamers and professional esports players for playing games

Motives of amateur gamers	Motives of Esports players	Additional motives for professional Esports players
Entertainment and fun, generally more of a leisure and recreation activity than a serious practice	Entertainment and fun (especially in excitement and tension level), more of a serious practice, yet preserving the leisure aspect	Affiliation, fame, generating an income from the hobby/leisure activity that he/she liked to do most and mastered/skilled in, goals, fan base/community recognition by talents and achievements, building and improving skills and developing self continuously
Interactivity and socialization	Interactivity and socialization	
Realistic illusion and fiction for drama	Graphics and design, mechanics, decent and immersive gameplay that enables iterative play for developing and choosing such game as a profession	
Reflection of the real world, representation of culture for improved fictive heroism while escaping from the real world to the alternate world in game	Escapism and heroism by being successful in a well-received area of interest with using an alternate identity (nickname)	
Challenge and competition	Challenge and competition, in premier and top tier level	
Discipline and practicing in a serious manner (not common but existing motive for "hardcore" amateur gamers, just for fun and mastery)	Discipline and practicing in a serious manner	

high levels with much expectations from the ecosystem (in exchange for money and fame), and the second one being the "burnout," where over-practicing and over-iterating the profession deprives a player from willingness to continue doing such activity, or implements boredom or anxiety/frustration (as per stipulated by Csikszentmihalyi above) that will abolish the fun element from that activity, so that the fulfilment of profession would not contain "leisure and fun activity" aspect anymore (Gould 1996) and dropping such practice may have material and immaterial consequences (such as indemnifications as per their professional contracts, or a necessity to choose another profession).

Such state may confirm the claim of Caillois (2001) that the professional player or athlete is working rather than playing and such playing activity becomes a part of working life, and can negatively affect the concept of playing as free activity; where the burnout deteriorates the fundamentals of an activity to become a game by erasing the fun out of it. Though many players are still amateur, practicing skills at home, without pay, for fun and challenge (Hamilton et al. 2012), it is a long shot for them to expose to burnout, as they can immediately drop the game that they are frustrated in, but esports players do have to face the consequences of quitting the profession or becoming less successive with losing the touch and flair that once made them special among other players.

However, due to the fact that esport is not a conventional profession in which a society depends on for continuing and preserving the established order and its operability (such as doctors, legal experts, engineers, public official, etc.) and stand for more as a combination of entertainment and sport in professional level, it can be claimed that the psychology of such burnout within the esports players will be easier to cope with than burnout in a conventional profession as a professional career in esports is chosen only for willingness, voluntarily and freely (Kim and Thomas 2015), unlike the necessity of such conventional professions for the people who are not skilled in another practice but still have to make a living out of a profession (Gould 1996). Moreover, in the state of a burnout, esports players can quit by giving up his/her future receivables, paying a compensation with the money they still earned from esports or being patient and keeping playing until the termination of such contract, and/or go through a resting and recovery phase until grabbing the joy of playing such game again or choose another conventional profession, which will remedy their "victimhood," unlike in most of the conventional professions. On a contrario perspective, it can be said that unless a burnout occurs, the game flow of Csikszentmihalyi still continues and a professional gamer (who tends to face more serious challenges and competitions than a casual gamer) is still having fun (1997), entertainment, and amusement by practicing his/her profession, i.e., playing such game; therefore, the free and voluntary aspect of gaming and sports survives in the professional esports.

As for the recreation and relaxation aspects, players who identify themselves as a professional esport player should have higher levels of competitive motivation although other playing motivations are also likely to be different from non-professional and casual players (Bányai et al. 2019). Therefore, it can be claimed that the competition and challenge level of playing a game professionally is different from the casual gaming and such alteration of level will infuse the player (a) the emotion of feeling content and happy with (or challenged for) the mastery of player in which he/she likes most, like achieving new successes or at least going for it (where a failure will make one see his/her faults and serve as a guidance to become better in future by improving skills, as an intrinsic motive) (b) a new level of tension, amusement, and excitement that arouses the player "seriously" more than a casual/amateur gamer (Bányai et al. 2019) as it was one of his/her premier motives for becoming an esports player in the first place, which also adds up to the fun and entertainment of such player by overcoming higher obstacles.

Such psychology will bring the satisfied and content ego with a pleasure of relaxing in daily life due to the awareness of being good in what he/she does by seeing the outcome. Overall, no player in the world tends to become a professional in a game that they are not promising or having fun. Such fact also will enhance the mood of a player as he/she will escape to the world in which they are best and happy, when he/she is not satisfied with the real life or has problems within it, just like a recreation and relaxation activity and a meditation because as Gee describes, "good games are hard work and deep fun" (2007, p. 10). Pursuantly, competing against and besting the better and more qualified rivals will inject even more fun to the professional players, instead of abolishing it, as such level of players will not be content with the standard level of challenges and competitions due to their level of skills and mastery and seek for "someone on their own size" (Ryan and Deci 2000) where such seriousness will bring the fun (Ryan et al. 2006). Therefore, when determining the fun in professionalism, the perception of fun for the professional players shall be debated in the first place (Freeman and Wohn 2017).

It shall be taken into account when considering the professionalism of esports that the players desire to turn a hobby into a profession, providing that it will still be their recreative and fun activity, and will be fructifying more than any other profession due to their skills, willingness, and mastery for it, as they chose such practice in front of other professions voluntarily and "no fun" will be equal to "no profession" for them (Ozenc and Tinmazlar 2018). Pursuantly, such comparison between the professional and amateur gamers' motives points out that the only facts which separate an amateur and a professional is the degree of ambition for self-improvement, competition and challenge, and also the remuneration of labor and success in professionalism.

Therefore, in accordance with modernized game theories of Juul, Salen and Zimmerman and the motives comparison, with regard to the fundamental similarities between sports and esports, games and esports, and the motives of amateur and professional players for playing games (either casually or on professional level) and also by perceiving the differences of esports and gambling, it can be concluded that,

(a) professional esports is an altered version of gaming, in which players constantly keep improving their skills and earn money for the show they display to the audience different from amateur gaming, but meets all the other contemporary necessities of gaming itself, including the recreation, free, voluntary aspects of the previous game theories (with the aspect of being "separate from daily life" constituting the only clash within such regard, but such condition is dropped and deserted in the game definitions of digital gaming and MMO era),

(b) only being not intensely oriented at physical movements (as a consequences of mediated and digital gameplay) separates esports from traditional professional sports,

(c) as the industrialization of digital gaming sector made games "owned" by game companies and thereby already had implemented money factor for both the amateur and professional players and disrupted the former game theories of those like Huizinga and Caillois, the professionalism of digital gaming and esports shall always include a material interest in itself, which separates any other sport from esport on professional level, thus the professionalism in esports has a special condition that money transfer between gamers and gaming companies shall be deemed as normal and even necessary, which makes esports athletes still "gamers" fundamentally,

(d) players do not have to pay for gaming-related expenses when they become professional esports players within the ecosystem, and as a result of the entertainment and show aspect, they earn money for their performance display on a routine bases, which amazes the consumers and audience, so the money route in digital gaming will be reversed for them, which is in their benefit and distinguishes esports from gambling in the words of having the risk of losing money for playing games competitively,

(e) esports are governed by countries' local authorities and prominent international competent bodies in a manner similar to the traditional professional sports, which distinguishes esports from gambling further,

(f) the activity that all esports players do as a profession is still mere gaming on its very core, as that the professionalism and professional status of being an esport player is not an impediment or encumbrance for also being counted as a gamer in motives and definitions aspects,

(g) a more contemporary definition of gaming can be made by including the exclusive and unique condition of professionalism as following: "a game is a rule-based, transmedial, artificial and temporary conflict and challenge realm with a variable and quantifiable outcome, where different outcomes are assigned different values and the player engages in activity directed towards bringing about a specific state of affairs by his/her experience, intellectual and physical talents and skills, for achieving a level of fun and live through a gameplay experience by using only means permitted by rules, where the rules prohibit more efficient in favor of less efficient means, and such player exerts effort competitively in order to influence the outcome in his/her favor, thus feels attached to the outcome, and the consequences of the activity are optional and negotiable; as the players can play for amateur or professional intentions and motives, given that as a part of a professional entertainment business a material interest can be gained as a result of gameplay if and only if the player does not face the risk of losing any monetary asset but can get devoid of the chance for earning such cashable prize in the case of a failure in the end, and may forfeit future salaries in exchange for stop playing further therein due to a burnout or unwillingness."

References

Adamus, T. (2012). Playing computer games as electronic sport: In search of a theoretical framework for a new research field. In J. Fromme & A. Unger (Eds.), Computer games and new media cultures: A handbook of digital games studies (pp. 477–490). Dordrecht: Springer.

Adrien Auxent, Esports are now officially legal in France, 30 September 2016 [https://esportsobserver.com/esports-are-now-officially-legal-in-france/] (day of retrieval: 8 August 2019).

AIMAG 2013 Archive [https://archive.fo/20130708123421/http://www.aimag2013.org/en/Results/ES/MedallistsByEvent?SportCode=ES&EventCode=&GenderCode=&PhaseCode=] (retrieved on 8 August 2019)

Alha, K., Koskinen, E., Paavilainen, J., Hamari, J., & Kinnunen, J. (2014). Free-to-play games: Professionals' perspectives. Proceedings of Nordic DiGRA, 2014.

Avedon, E.M. & Sutton-Smith, Brian: The Study of Games. John Wiley & Sons, Inc., New York, 1981.

Apter, M. J. (1991). A Structural phenomenology of play: A reversal theory approach. In M.J. Apter & J.

Ayar, H.; 2018. Development of e-Sport in Turkey and in the World. International Journal of Sport Culture and Science, 6(1), pp. 95–102. Retrieved from https://dergipark.org.tr/en/pub/intjscs/issue/36368/411365

Baillie, P. H., & Danish, S. J. (1992). Understanding the career transition of athletes. The sport psychologist, 6(1), 77–98.

Bang, J.H. (1991), 'A study on the use and gratification of the video games', thesis, Seoul National University.

Bányai, F., Griffiths, M. D., Király, O., & Demetrovics, Z. (2019). The psychology of esports: A systematic literature review. Journal of gambling studies, 35(2), pp. 351–365.

Brautigam, T. FIFA President Infantino Addresses eSports in his "Vision for the Future". (2016, 13 October) [https://esportsobserver.com/fifa-president-infantino-addresses-esports-vision-future/] (retrieved on 8 August 2019)

Breakthrough. (2018, 30 August) 11 Celebrity eSports Investors You Didn't Know About [https://medium.com/@breakthrough_lab/celebrity-esports-investors-you-didnt-know-about-eb9a8c395292] (retrieved on 10 August 2019)

Brock, T. (2017). Roger Caillois and e-sports: On the problems of treating play as work. Games and Culture, 12(4), 321–339

Burroughs, B., & Rama, P. (2015). The eSports Trojan Horse: Twitch and Streaming Futures. Journal for Virtual Worlds Research, 8(2). https://doi.org/10.4101/jvwr.v8i2.7176

Caillois, R. (1961): Man, play, and games. The Free Press, Glencoe, New York, (1958)

Caillois, R. (2001). Man, play, and games. University of Illinois Press.

Cambridge Dictionary Online. [https://dictionary.cambridge.org/tr/s%C3%B6zl%C3%BCk/ingilizce/e-sports] (retrieved on 7 August 2019)

Cambridge Dictionary Online. [https://dictionary.cambridge.org/dictionary/english/sport] (day of retrieval: 6 August 2019)

Cambridge Dictionary Online. [https://dictionary.cambridge.org/tr/s%C3%B6zl%C3%BCk/ingilizce/gamble] (retrieved on 7 August 2019)

Cambridge Dictionary Online. [https://dictionary.cambridge.org/tr/s%C3%B6zl%C3%BCk/ingilizce/gambling] (retrieved on 7 August 2019)

Cambridge Dictionary Online. [https://dictionary.cambridge.org/tr/s%C3%B6zl%C3%BCk/ingilizce/Professional] (retrieved on 6 August 2019)

Catan, C. (2003). U.S. Patent Application No. 09/969,096.

Chick, G. E. (1984). The cross-cultural study of games. Exercise and sport sciences reviews, 12(1), pp. 307–372.

Chul, J.W.; IeSF joins the International Sports Organization "Esports Sports for All". 09 May 2014 [http://www.thisisgame.com/webzine/news/nboard/4/?n=54703] (retrieved on 8 August 2019)

Conway, S., & DeWinter, J. (Eds.). (2015). Video game policy: Production, distribution, and consumption. Routledge.

Crawford, Chris: The Art of Computer Game Design. 1982

Csikszentmihalyi, M. (1997). Finding flow: The psychology of engagement with everyday life. Basic Books.

Darcy, Kieran. Why the Associated Press Stylebook went with esports, not eSports. 6 July 2017 [https://www.espn.com/esports/story/_/id/19860473/why-associated-press-stylebook-went-esports-not-esports] (retrieved on 7 August 2019)

Dave, P. Online game League of Legends star gets U.S. visa as pro athlete. 7 August 2013. Available at [https://www.latimes.com/business/la-xpm-2013-aug-07-la-fi-online-gamers-20130808-story.html] (day of retrieval: 7 August 2019).

De Grove, F., Cauberghe, V., & Van Looy, J. (2016). Development and validation of an instrument for measuring individual motives for playing digital games. Media Psychology, 19(1), 101–125.

Deaner, R. O., & Smith, B. A. (2013). Sex differences in sports across 50 societies. Cross-Cultural Research: The Journal of Comparative Social Science, 47(3), 268–309. Available on: [https://doi.org/10.1177/1069397112463687]

Deci, E. L., & Ryan, R. M. (2010). Intrinsic motivation. The corsini encyclopedia of psychology, 1–2.

Demetrovics, Z., Urbán, R., Nagygyörgy, K., Farkas, J., Zilahy, D., Mervó, B., et al. (2011). Why do you play? The development of the motives for online gaming questionnaire (MOGQ). Behavior Research Methods, 43(3), pp. 814–825.

Ducheneaut, N., Yee, N., Nickell, E., & Moore, R. J. (2006, April). Alone together?: exploring the social dynamics of massively multiplayer online games. In Proceedings of the SIGCHI conference on Human Factors in computing systems (pp. 407–416). ACM.

Dyer-Witheford, N., De Peuter, G. (2009) Games of Empire: Global Capitalism and Video Games, University of Minnesota Press

Eklund, R. C., & Cresswell, S. L. (2007). Athlete burnout. Handbook of sport psychology, 3, 621–641.

Elias, N. and Dunning, E. (1986) Quest for Excitement: Sport and Leisure in the Civilizing Process. Oxford: Basil Blackwell.

Esports to be featured at the Asian Indoor and Martial Arts Games in 2017. 24 May 2017 [https://www.afkgaming.com/articles/esports-to-be-featured-at-the-asian-indoor-and-martial-arts-games-in-2017] (retrieved on 8 August 2019)

Faust, K., Meyer, J., & Griffiths, M. D. (2013). Competitive and professional gaming: Discussing potential benefits of scientific study. International Journal of Cyber Behavior, Psychology and Learning (IJCBPL), 3(1), 67–77.

Fenigstein, A. (1979), Does aggression cause a preference for viewing media violence?, Journal of Personality and Social Psychology, vol. 37, pp. 2707–2317.

FIFA President Infantino Unveils "FIFA 2.0: The Vision for the Future". 13 October 2016 [https://www.fifa.com/about-fifa/who-we-are/news/fifa-president-infantino-unveils-fifa-2-0-the-vision-for-the-future-2843428] (retrieved on 8 August 2019) (original text document is available under [https://resources.fifa.com/mm/document/affederation/generic/02/84/35/01/fifa_2.0_vision_e_neutral.pdf]

Fitch, A. (2018, December 28). This Year in Esports: Investments, sponsorships and deals in 2018 [https://esportsinsider.com/2018/12/this-year-in-esports-2018-roundup/] (retrieved on 10 August 2019)

France eSports Federation Official Website [https://www.france-esports.org/] (retrieved on 6 August 2019)

France Senate Official Website, Full Text [http://www.senat.fr/enseance/textes/2015-2016/744.html#AMELI_SUB_4_1468248055899_1432] (day of retrieval: 8 August 2019)

Freeman, G. and Wohn, D. Y., 2017. Esports as An Emerging Research Context at CHI: Diverse Perspectives on Definitions. In Proceedings of the 2017 CHI Conference Extended Abstracts on Human Factors in Computing Systems (CHI EA '17). Association for Computing Machinery, New York, NY, USA, 1601–1608. DOI: https://doi.org/10.1145/3027063.3053158

French Numeric Law (Loi pour une République Numérique), [http://www.senat.fr/enseance/textes/2015-2016/744.html#AMELI_SUB_4_1468248055899_1432] (retrieved on 6 August 2019)

Gee, J. P., (2007). Good Video Games + Good Learning: Collected Essays on Video Games, Learning, and Literacy. New York: Peter Lang.

Golembiewski, R. T. (1984). An orientation to psychological burnout: Probably something old, definitely something new. Journal of Health and Human Resources Administration, 153–161.

Gould, D. (1996). Personal motivation gone awry: Burnout in competitive athletes. Quest, 48(3), 275–289.

Gould, D., & Carson, S. (2004). Fun & games?: Myths surrounding the role of youth sports in developing Olympic champions. Youth Studies Australia, 23(1), 19.

Graham, B.A.; eSports to be a medal event at 2022 Asian Games. 18 April 2017 [https://www.theguardian.com/sport/2017/apr/18/esports-to-be-medal-sport-at-2022-asian-games] (retrieved on 8 August 2019)

Greenberg, B. S., Sherry, J., Lachlan, K., Lucas, K., & Holmstrom, A. (2010). Orientations to Video Games Among Gender and Age Groups. Simulation & Gaming, 41(2), 238–259. https://doi.org/10.1177/1046878108319930

Grodal, T. (2000). Video games and the pleasures of control. Media entertainment: The psychology of its appeal, pp. 197–213.

Grönroos, A. M., 2013. Humour in Video Games: Play, Comedy, and Mischief. Unpublished Master's Thesis. Aalto University School of Arts, Design and Architecture [online] https://aaltodoc.aalto.fi/bitstream/handle/123456789/10347/optika_id_792_gr%C3%B6nroos_annemarie_2013.pdf?sequence=1&isAllowed=y. [accessed 6 August 2019].

Guinness World Records Limited. (2018). Guinness World Records Gamers' Edition 2019. [London, England]: Guinness World Records Limited.

Guttmann, A. (2004). From ritual to record: The nature of modern sports. New York: Columbia University Press

Hallmann, K., & Giel, T. (2018). eSports–Competitive sports or recreational activity?. Sport management review, 21(1), 14–20.

Hamari, J. and Sjöblom, M. (2017), What is eSports and why do people watch it?, Internet Research, Vol. 27 No. 2, pp. 211–232. https://doi.org/10.1108/IntR-04-2016-0085

Hamilton, W., Kerne, A., Robbins, T. (2012). High-performance pen + touch modality interactions: a real-time strategy game eSports context. In Proceedings of the 25th annual ACM symposium on User interface software and technology (UIST '12). ACM, 309–318. https://doi.org/10.1145/2380116.2380156

Hemphill, Dennis (2005) Cybersport, Journal of the Philosophy of Sport, 32:2, 195–207. https://doi.org/10.1080/00948705.2005.9714682

Himmelstein, D., Liu, Y., & Shapiro, J. L. (2017). An exploration of mental skills among competitive League of Legend players. International Journal of Gaming and Computer-Mediated Simulations, 9(2), 1–21.

Hoon, K., Park, J. Y., Yul, K. D., Moon, H. L., & Chun, H. C. (2002). E-lifestyle and motives to use online games. Iris Marketing Review, 15(2), 71–72.

Huizinga, J., 1949. Homo Ludens: A Study of the Play Element in Culture. 3rd edn. London: Routledge & Kegan Paul.

Huizinga, J., 1950.: Homo Ludens. The Beacon Press, Boston

Huizinga, J. (1955). Homo Ludens: A study of the play element in culture. Boston: Beacon Press.

IeSF agree on partnership with ITTF. 25 August 2017 [https://www.ie-sf.org/news/iesf-agree-on-partnership-with-ittf/] (date of retrieval: 8 August 2019)

IeSF, Taking Its First Step Towards IOC Recognition. 15 April 2016 [https://www.ie-sf.org/news/iesf-taking-its-first-step-towards-ioc-recognition/] (date of retrieval: 8 August 2019)

International eSports Federation Official Website [https://www.ie-sf.org/] (retrieved on 6 August 2019)

International E-Sports Federation Partners with Athletics for a Better World. 21 April 2015 [https://www.iaaf.org/news/iaaf-news/international-e-sports-athletics-better-world] (date of retrieval: 8 August 2019)

Jansz, J., & Tanis, M. (2007). Appeal of playing online first-person shooter games. Cyberpsychology & behavior, 10(1), 133–136.

Jenny, S. E., Manning, R. D., Keiper, M. C., & Olrich, T. W. (2017). Virtual (ly) athletes: where eSports fit within the definition of "Sport". Quest, 69(1), 1–18. https://doi.org/10.1080/00336297.2016.1144517

Johns, N.B. (1981), 'Video game for performance testing', American Journal of Psychology, vol. 94, March, pp. 143–52

Jonasson, K., Thiborg, J. (2010). Electronic sport and its impact on future sport. Sport in Society, 13(2), 287–299.

Juul, J. (2003): "The Game, the Player, the World: Looking for a Heart of Gameness". In Level Up: Digital Games Research Conference Proceedings, edited by Marinka Copier and Joost Raessens, 30–45. Utrecht: Utrecht University, 2003. [http://www.jesperjuul.net/text/gameplayerworld/]

Katz, E., Haas, H., & Gurevitch, M. (1973). On the use of the mass media for important things. American sociological review, 164–181.

Kelley, David: The Art of Reasoning. W. W. Norton & Company, New York, 1988

Kim, Lee Su; 1995. Creative Games for the Language Class. 'Forum' Vol. 33 No 1, January – March 1995, p35.

Kim, S. H., & Thomas, M. K. (2015). A stage theory model of professional video game players in South Korea: The socio-cultural dimensions of the development of expertise. Asian Journal of Information Technology, 14(5), 176–186

Koudelkova, A.; Kosova, J. (n.d.), The Categorization of Sports Branches, Sports Studies Fundamental Terminology in English [http://web.ftvs.cuni.cz/eknihy/jazyky/sportstudiesfundamentalterminologyinenglish/Texts/3-Categories.html] (retrieved on 6 August 2019)

Lazzaro, N.: Why We Play Games: Four Keys to More Emotion in Player Experiences, 2005. Available on [https://www.nicolelazzaro.com/the4-keys-to-fun/] (date of retrieval: 5 August 2019)

Lee, D., & Schoenstedt, L. J. (2011). Comparison of eSports and traditional sports consumption motives. The ICHPER-SD Journal of Research in Health, Physical Education, Recreation, Sport & Dance, 6(2), 39–44

Lexico. [https://www.lexico.com/en/definition/business] (retrieved on 7 August 2019)

Lexico. [https://www.lexico.com/en/definition/e-sport] (retrieved on 7 August 2019)

Lexico. [https://www.lexico.com/en/definition/entertainment] (retrieved on 7 August 2019)

Lexico. [https://www.lexico.com/en/definition/gamble] (retrieved on 7 August 2019)

Ma, H., Wu, Y., & Wu, X. (2013). Research on essential difference of e-sport and online game. In W. Du (Ed.), Informatics and management science V (pp. 615–621). London: Springer.

Malcolm, D. (2008) The SAGE Dictionary of Sport Studies (London: Sage).

Malone, T.W. (1981). 'Toward a theory of intrinsically motivated instruction', Cognitive Science, vol. 4, pp. 333–69.

Martončik, M. (2015). e-Sports: Playing just for fun or playing to satisfy life goals? Computers in Human Behavior, 48, 208–211.

Maslow, A. H. (1943). A theory of human motivation. Psychological Review, 50(4), 370–396. [https://doi.org/10.1037/h0054346]

McLeod, S. (2007). Maslow's hierarchy of needs. Simply psychology, 1.

McPherson BD, Curtis JE, and Loy JW (1989) Defining sport. In: McPherson BD, Curtis JE and Loy JW (eds) The Social Significance of Sport. Champaign, IL: Human Kinetics.

Melrose, C. Why Battle Royale Games Like Fortnite Are Everywhere (It's not Just Money). 14 June 2018 [https://www.wired.com/story/fortnite-battlefield-rise-of-battle-royale/] (retrieved on 6 August 2019)

Menasce, R. M. (2017). From Casual to Professional: How Brazilians Achieved Esports Success in Counter-Strike: Global Offensive (Doctoral dissertation, Northeastern University) (available on: https://repository.library.northeastern.edu/files/neu:cj82qk96j/fulltext.pdf)

Newzoo Global Games Market Report 2019, (https://newzoo.com/solutions/standard/market-forecasts/global-games-market-report/) (retrieved on 9 August 2019)

Official Website of 2017 Ashgabat AIMAG [http://ashgabat2017.com/esports] (date of retrieval: 8 August 2019)

Official Website of FIFA eWorld Cup [https://www.fifa.com/fifaeworldcup/] (date of retrieval: 8 August 2019)

Official Website of 2020 Tokyo Olympics [https://tokyo2020.org/en/games/sport/olympic/] (retrieved on 7 August 2019)

Official Website of WADA [https://www.wada-ama.org/en/what-we-do/adams/list-of-organizations-using-adams] (retrieved on 8 August 2019)

Official Website of Winter Olympic Games [https://www.olympic.org/winter-games] (retrieved on 7 August 2019)

Ozkurt, E. Esports in South Korea – a short overview of the legal ecosystem. 10 April 2019. Available on [https://www.lawinsport.com/content/articles/item/esports-in-south-korea-a-short-overview-of-the-legal-ecosystem] (day of retrieval: 7 August 2019).

Oxford Learner's Dictionaries. [https://www.oxfordlearnersdictionaries.com/definition/english/game_1?q=game] (retrieved on 6 August 2019)

Ozenc, O. E., (2017) Usage of Humor as an Element of Game Design: "İstanbul Efsaneleri: Lale Savaşçıları as a Case Study". Unpublished Master's Thesis. Bahçeşehir University Graduate School of Social Sciences Game Design Master's Program [online] available on: [https://docdro.id/vPhQABm] (accessed 6 August 2019).

Ozenc, O.E., (2019). Dijital Oyunlar Serisi – 6: Türkiye'de E-Spor, Yerli Oyunlar ve Zula [Digital Games Series – 6: Local Games, Zula and Esports in Turkey]. Benim Kitap Publishing.

Ozenc, O. E.; Keskin, H. (2019). Dijital Oyunlar Serisi – 5: Türkiye'de E-Spor ve Fortnite [Digital Games Series – 5: Fortnite and Esports in Turkey], Profil Kitap Publishing.

Ozenc, O.E.; Tinmazlar, A., (2018). Dijital Oyunlar Serisi – 3: Türkiye'de E-Spor ve League of Legends [Digital Games Series – 3: League of Legends and Esports in Turkey]. Profil Kitap Publishing.

Ozenc, O. E.; Tinmazlar, A. (2019). Dijital Oyunlar Serisi – 4: Türkiye'de E-Spor ve PUBG [Digital Games Series – 4: PUBG and Esports in Turkey], Profil Kitap Publishing.

Paris 2024 Olympics: Esports 'in talks' to be included as demonstration sport. 25 April 2018 [https://www.bbc.com/sport/olympics/43893891] (date of retrieval: 8 August 2019)

Pearce, C. (2004). Towards a game theory of game. First person: New media as story, performance, and game, 1, 143–153.

Pearson, Ben. Digital vs Analog: The Value of Divergent Game Types, 1 December 2016 [https://games2teach.uoregon.edu/2016/12/01/digital-vs-analog-value-divergent-game-types/] (retrieved on 6 August 2019)

Pickford, R. W. (1941). Aspects of the Psychology of Games and Sports. British Journal of Psychology, 31(4), 279.

Pires, K., Simon, G., (2015) YouTube live and Twitch: a tour of user-generated live streaming systems, Proceedings of the 6th ACM Multimedia Systems Conference, p.225–230, March 18–20, 2015, Portland, Oregon [https://doi.org/10.1145/2713168.2713195]

Pizzo, A. D., Na, S., Baker, B. J., Lee, M. A., Kim, D., & Funk, D. C. (2018). eSport vs. Sport: A Comparison of Spectator Motives. Sport Marketing Quarterly, 27(2).

Pro gamers now recognized as athletes in Turkey. 27 September 2018 [https://www.smartlaunch.com/pro-gamers-now-recognized-as-athletes-in-turkey/] (retrieved on 8 August 2019)

Roberts, J. M., Arth, M. J. and Bush, R. R. (1959). Games in Culture. American Anthropologist, 61: 597–605. Available on: [https://doi.org/10.1525/aa.1959.61.4.02a00050]

Roosevelt, T. (1890). "Professionalism" in Sports. The North American Review, 151(405), 187–191.

Ryan, R. M., & Deci, E. L. (2000). Self-determination theory and the facilitation of intrinsic motivation, social development, and well-being. American psychologist, 55(1), 68.

Ryan, R. M., Rigby, C. S., & Przybylski, A. (2006). The motivational pull of video games: A self-determination theory approach. Motivation and Emotion, 30(4), 344–360.

Salen, K., & Zimmerman, E. (2003). Rules of Play. Game Design Fundamentals. The MIT Press, Cambridge.

Schubert, M., Drachen, A., & Mahlmann, T. (2016). Esports analytics through encounter detection. In Proceedings of the MIT Sloan Sports Analytics Conference (Vol. 1, p. 2016).

Seo, Y. (2016). Professionalized consumption and identity transformations in the field of eSports. Journal of Business Research, 69(1), 264–272. [https://doi.org/10.1016/j.jbusres.2015.07.039]

Seo, Y., & Jung, S.-U. (2016). Beyond solitary play in computer games: The social practices of eSports. Journal of Consumer Culture, 16(3), 635–655.

Sherry, J. L., Lucas, K., Greenberg, B. S., & Lachlan, K. (2006). Video game uses and gratifications as predictors of use and game preference. In P. Vorderer & J. Bryant (Eds.), Playing video games: Motives, responses, and consequences (pp. 213–224). Mahwah, NJ: Lawrence Erlbaum Associates.

South Korea eSports Association Official Website [http://www.e-sports.or.kr/?ckattempt=1] (retrieved on 6 August 2019)

Sports Clubs & Esports. Digital Sports Media n.d. [http://digitale-sport-medien.com/sports-clubs-esports/] (retrieved on 9 August 2019)

Steinkuehler, C. A. (2004, June). Learning in massively multiplayer online games. In Proceedings of the 6th international conference on Learning sciences (pp. 521–528). International Society of the Learning Sciences.

Stover, S. (1984), Video Games in the Information Age, San Francisco.

Suits, B. (1978) The Grasshopper. University of Toronto Press, Toronto.

Suits, B. (1988). Tricky triad: Games, play, and sport. Journal of the Philosophy of Sport, 15(1), 1–9.

Suits, B. (2007). The elements of sport. Ethics in Sport, 2, 9–19.

Taylor, T. (2012). Raising the stakes: E-sports and the professionalization of computer gaming. Cambridge: The MIT Press.

Techterms.com. [https://techterms.com/definition/esports] (retrieved on 7 August 2019)

The Free Dictionary [https://acronyms.thefreedictionary.com/Citius%2C+Altius%2C+Fortius] (retrieved on 6 August 2019)

Tiedemann, C., (2004) "Sport (and culture of physical motion) for historians, an approach to precise the central term(s)", IX. international CESH-Congress, Crotone, Italy.

Turkish E-Sports Federation Official Website [http://tesfed.gov.tr/] (retrieved on 6 August 2019)

United States eSports Federation Official Website [http://www.esportsfederation.org/pages/about] (retrieved on 6 August 2019)

Urban Dictionary. [https://www.urbandictionary.com/define.php?term=E-Game] (retrieved on 7 August 2019)

van Hilvoorde, I., & Pot, N. (2016). Embodiment and fundamental motor skills in eSports. Sport, Ethics and Philosophy, 10(1), 14–27. https://doi.org/10.1080/17511321.2016.1159246.

Vorderer, P. (2000). Interactive entertainment and beyond.

Vorderer, P., Steen, F.F., Chan, E., (2006). Motivation. Psychology of Entertainment, p. 3 New York: Routledge Press.

Vorderer, P., Bryant, J. (2009). Playing Video Games – Motives, Responses and Consequences. New York: Routledge Press.

Vorderer, P., & Bryant, J. (2012). Playing video games: Motives, responses, and consequences. Routledge.

Vorderer, P., Hartmann, T., & Klimmt, C. (2003, May). Explaining the enjoyment of playing video games: the role of competition. In Proceedings of the second international conference on Entertainment computing (pp. 1–9). Carnegie Mellon University.

Wagner, M. G. (2006, June). On the Scientific Relevance of eSports. In International conference on internet computing (pp. 437–442).

Wallechinsky, D.; Loucky, J., (2012). The Complete Book of Olympics 2012 Edition, Aurum Press.

Weiss, M. R., & Chaumeton, N. (1992). Motivational orientations in sport. Advances in sport psychology, 61–99.

Weiss, T., & Schiele, S. (2013). Virtual worlds in competitive contexts: Analyzing eSports consumer needs. Electronic Markets, 23(4), 307–316.

Whalen, S. J. (2013). Cyberathletes' lived experience of video game tournaments. Doctoral Dissertation, University of Tennessee.

Witkowski, E. (2009). Probing the sportiness of eSports. In J. Christophers & T. Scholz (Eds.), eSports yearbook (pp. 53–56) Norderstedt: Books on Demand GmbH

Witkowski, E. (2012). On the digital playing field: How we "do sport" with networked computer games. Games and Culture, 7(5), pp. 349–374

Wittgenstein, L. (1958) Philosophical Investigations. Basil Blackwell, Oxford.

Wolf, M. J. (Ed.). (2008). The video game explosion: a history from PONG to Playstation and beyond. ABC-CLIO.

Yee, N. (2006a). The demographics, motivations, and derived experiences of users of massively multi-user online graphical environments. Presence: Teleoperators and Virtual Environments, 15(3), 309–329.

Yee, N. (2006b). Motivations for play in online games. Cyber Psychology & Behavior, 9(6), 772–775.

Yılmaz Oruç, M. (2018, December 29). E-Sporun Varlığı Kaçınılmazdı [The Existence of Esports Was Unavoidable], Star Gazetesi [Star Newspaper], p. 6

Zeng, H. Z., Cynarski, W. J., Baatz, S., & Park, S. J. (2015). Exploring Motivations of Taekwondo Athletes/Students in New York City. World Journal of Education, 5(5), 51–63.

Part II
Modelling and Measuring Player Experience

Chapter 6
Revisiting Heuristics for Evaluating Player Experience in Different Gaming Platforms: A Multi-Modal Approach

Çakır Aker, Kerem Rızvanoğlu, and Yavuz İnal

Contents

Ç. Aker (✉)
Department of Game Design, Bahcesehir University, Istanbul, Turkey
e-mail: cakir.aker@comm.bau.edu.tr

K. Rızvanoğlu
Faculty of Communication, Galatasaray University, Istanbul, Turkey
e-mail: krizvanoglu@gsu.edu.tr

Y. İnal
Department of Information Science and Media Studies, University of Bergen, Bergen, Norway
e-mail: yavuz.inal@uib.no

© Springer Nature Switzerland AG 2020
B. Bostan (ed.), *Game User Experience And Player-Centered Design*,
International Series on Computer Entertainment and Media Technology,
https://doi.org/10.1007/978-3-030-37643-7_6

Abstract The aim of the study was to adopt a multi-modal approach to analyze differences of player experience between PC and mobile platforms and identify methods which are effective for evaluating it. To achieve this goal, playability heuristics were employed along with usability evaluations, semi-structured interviews, and observations. 20 players were recruited for the empirical tests. The players were chosen from hardcore and mid-core gamers that have never played Plants vs Zombies game before. The results from the study indicated that the heuristic set was ineffective for analyzing different experiences between platforms when applied by itself, yet the player feedbacks proved to be invaluable for analyzing the experience differences. Interviews and player observations after gameplay sessions were contributive in offering an in-depth comprehension of different motivations of the players for both PC and mobile platforms. The dependencies of the playability problems addressed by the players were grouped into three categories. Fundamentally, different gaming platforms offer different experiences. Therefore, it is as crucial to understand the importance of platform differences as much as different games in terms of understanding player experience. By the grouping of these problems, it was possible to put forward a general classification of differences in experience between platforms. Additionally, we found that the implementation of usability evaluations proved to be effective and point towards a general difference in experience between platforms.

Keywords Games · Heuristics · Evaluation · Experience

6.1 Introduction

Because of their distinctive property of pushing the conventional technology forward, games are considered as one of the most important reasons for novel technologies to be available in our homes and in our everyday lives in the first place (Mäyrä 2008). In fact, computer games have become one of the most important and influential sector among the entertainment industry. Human–computer interaction studies increasingly focus on computer games and try to provide a guide for the evaluation of games and experiences they offer to players. With the growing influence of computer games in the media and software industry, experts from the field see the importance of analyzing user experience not only for productivity software but also for games.

Although games offer a type of user experience, they provide vast and more complex capabilities of interaction with a system. The aim of the software and design considerations as well as complex interaction patterns is fundamentally different than productivity software. Sánchez et al. (2009) stated that usability evaluations are not sufficient and indicated the difference between usability and playability. While user experience research has mostly focused on usability and design topics, there is a lack of understanding concerning how the interactive modalities of games affect user experience (Sutcliffe and Hart 2017). Better understanding the player experience is necessary not just because it would help identify interaction tendencies of players but also would allow industry designers and developers to produce games that would meet the desires and needs of the players (Nordin et al. 2014).

Even though there are many studies conducted for evaluation the user experience (UX) in the literature, studies involving the player experience (PX) are not so many and mostly lack validation. Previously, it was discussed that the use of UX evaluation methods along with PX evaluation methods increases the possibility of analyzing the player experience inclusively (Aker et al. 2017). This multi-modal approach was necessary since the analysis of games with conventional UX methods were mostly insufficient for analyzing the PX.

In today's gaming world, not only PC games rival among each other but also consoles and mobile phones are increasingly being opted for gaming. For instance, more players have started choosing mobile platforms over other platforms as a means for gaming (Soomro et al. 2013). Even though games were formerly developed for PCs at the beginning, they are also made available for other platforms. As is known, these platforms offer different capabilities such as different screen resolution and screen size or possibility to feature novel controls such as tactile feedback. Therefore the gaming platform should be considered to play an important role in terms of player experience. Despite the need of evaluations on player experience, there are only a few studies experimentally inspecting the relations of experiences between gaming platforms (e.g., Zaman et al. 2010; Kokil and Sanchez 2015; Rafaele et al. 2015; Aker et al. 2017). These limited number of studies within the literature which investigated player experience on different platforms, often only focus on difference of control mechanisms (e.g., Fritsch et al. 2008; Suhonen and Väätäjä 2010; Zaman et al. 2010; Gerling et al. 2011).

Previously, the game experience questionnaire (GEQ) (Poels et al. 2012) along with SUS and NPS usability measures, interviews, and observations was utilized to analyze experience differences between platforms. This study is a progress that integrates with the previous research (Aker et al. 2017). A similar experiment was conducted via employing the playability heuristics (Korhonen and Koivisto 2006; Korhonen and Koivisto 2007) to identify and analyze player experience on different platforms. Hence in this study, it was aimed to determine: (1) if heuristic analysis and playability heuristics in specific, is effective for evaluating differences in experience between gaming platforms, (2) whether the usability scales and/or user tests could prove useful for analyzing platform differences, (3) if the feedbacks from the players could be utilized for analyzing player experience between platforms, (4) if it is possible to provide a holistic point of view by employing a multi-modal approach combining heuristic evaluation with user tests, and lastly (5) which factors and methods are effective for evaluating player experience between gaming platforms.

6.2   Related Work

A number of researchers have presented new heuristics for evaluating the gaming experience, and there are several different methodologies utilizing heuristics (e.g., Federoff 2002; Desurvire et al. 2004; Baauw et al. 2005; Röcker and Haar 2006; Korhonen and Koivisto 2006, 2007; Pinelle et al. 2008; Schaffer 2007; Pinelle et al. 2008; Jegers 2008; Bernhaupt et al. 2007, 2008). These heuristics are fundamentally based on game design and development areas such as mechanics, interface, or gameplay (Federoff 2002).

Heuristic evaluation is defined as an inspection technique that allows evaluators to examine an interface using statements of usability principles (Nielsen 1994). This evaluation method is considered to be more effective for evaluating games compared to other methods since this method does not require any task oriented tests and can be employed in a fast and cheap manner (Korhonen 2010). In this approach, expert-based heuristics evaluation is conducted using simple questions for examining different aspects of the game to find playability problems that may have undesirable effects on the user interaction (Carmody 2012).

Federoff (2002) has conducted a study on existing heuristics, combining them for evaluating the "fun" of the video games. Expert evaluation was conducted during the study as well as post-game interviews and observations were taken in order to gain additional insights during the tests. After gathering data, Federoff compared the heuristics with Nielsen's ten usability heuristics (1994) and proposed a novel set of heuristics for evaluating player experience.

Baauw et al. (2005) have conducted another study on utilizing heuristics for evaluating player experience and have developed structured expert evaluation method. This model was proposed for evaluating children's computer games. Their study mainly aimed for validating the heuristics model. 18 experts were recruited for the tests from the fields of usability and user experience. Four games were evaluated during the tests. Results gathered from expert's notes and heuristics were then compared for analyzing the effectiveness of the set.

Similarly, Sweetser and Wyeth (2005) have proposed a novel set of heuristics, the game flow model for evaluating games utilizing the term "flow" (Csikszentmihalyi 1990). The proposed set of heuristics was aimed to evaluate enjoyment in games. Eight key elements with several heuristic items in each were proposed.

Korhonen and Koivisto (2006) presented the playability heuristics. They were first to publish playability heuristics focus on mobile games. They proposed a modular basis for their heuristics, which consisted of game usability, gameplay, and mobility. By the means of literature reviews, 29 heuristics were proposed. Some of the categories and heuristics within those categories were developed from Nokia's Playability Heuristics for Mobile Games. Data was collected via expert evaluations with four experts, analyzing five different mobile games using the heuristics. Subsequently, the set was iteratively improved with the guidance of the experts. Researchers additionally mentioned that the proposed heuristics may be utilized in different platforms and games due to its modular structure. Following their study, Korhonen and Koivisto (2007) published another research in which they included the multiplayer aspects for evaluating mobile games. They presented a multiplayer module for games by employing the heuristics for examining three different games. Nevertheless, Korhonen and Koivisto validated their heuristics with only heuristic evaluations without comparing the results to other methods like playtesting.

Mixed-method evaluation approaches, combining user tests and expert evaluations via heuristics are also common among methods for evaluating player experience and validating the proposed heuristics to some extent. For instance, Desurvire et al. (2004) have proposed the heuristics of playability (HEP) and presented 43 heuristic items. These heuristics were based on literature reviews and evaluated via several experts. The HEP heuristics set contained four categories: gameplay, game story, mechanics, and usability. This model was tested on a prototype game. During the study, researchers additionally conducted user-testing methods for comparing the results from both evaluation methods. The user tests included think-aloud play sessions as well as satisfaction questionnaires. Also the supervisors gathered observation notes. At the end of the study, results from user tests and heuristic evaluations were compared, indicating that the use of heuristics were efficient for analyzing the player experience.

Guo and Goh (2016) conducted a study where the researchers administered the HEP heuristics (Desurvire et al. 2004) to evaluate an information literacy game. They have proposed to extend the HEP heuristics framework by including two more categories to the set: characters/graphics and pedagogical effectiveness. In their study, they combined a user-centric approach with the use of heuristics.

Although there is a need for a mixed-method approach for analyzing and determining player experience (Poels et al. 2012), there are only a scarce number of studies within the literature that investigated player experience on different platforms. Papaloukas et al. (2009) conducted a research with a multi-method approach, combining user tests with expert evaluations. They proposed a modified set of heuristics based on Nielsen's heuristics (Nielsen 1994) for evaluating game usability. Two different games in different platforms were tested (Nintendo Wii and web-based computer game). As for the user tests 30 players were recruited for usability evaluations. Player actions were recorded during the tests and analyzed by three usability experts. Meanwhile, experts played the games for a week and noted possible heuristic items for identifying issues related to the game. At the end of their study, the authors concluded by indicating the importance of combining the methods of utilizing heuristics and observations were crucial for enriching the data gathered.

Suhonen and Väätäjä (2010) researched the effects of using modular heuristics for health games. During their study, a Nintendo Wii platform game and one mobile game was tested via two experts. Five different heuristic sets were reviewed for using during the tests (Federoff 2002; Desurvire et al. 2004; Korhonen and Koivisto 2006, 2007; Garzotto 2007) as the authors stated that these heuristic sets were compatible among themselves and complement each other in terms of heuristic items. Later, the researchers stated that playability heuristics presented by Korhonen and Koivisto (2006, 2007) was the most eligible for conducting the tests. Also, a similar modular structure was adapted in their study, adding two extra modules for health games: multi-modality and persuasiveness.

Similarly, Desurvire and Wiberg (2015) combined different evaluation methods to test the proposed Game Approachability Principles (GAP) heuristic set. They also noted GAP principles held a guiding purpose therefore not directly aimed to evaluate playability. The study took user test results as benchmarks. They utilized usability and heuristics evaluation procedures on different gaming platforms: Xbox 360, PlayStation, and Nintendo Wii. Four games from different genres were tested during the study with 32 participants. After the tests, the authors compared and analyzed the results from both approaches. The authors claimed that the heuristics and user tests supported each other while indicating the best approach to evaluate the general experience of games the use of both methods simultaneously.

6.3   Methodology

Despite there is no common agreement on the definition of playability in the literature, researchers have defined the heuristic evaluation method is effective for analyzing the player experience. Reviewing the relevant literature covering heuristics, in terms of development methods, the modular approach by Korhonen and Koivisto is considered to be most valid (Paavilainen 2010). They proposed a model focused on mobile games while covering gameplay and usability aspects. The proposed heuristics included items derived from previously proposed heuristic sets, generalizable for all platforms as well as a mobility module specifically developed for mobile games. Therefore to conduct the study, we have employed the playability heuristics (Korhonen and Koivisto 2006).

Following the previously conducted study utilizing the Game Experience Questionnaire (GEQ) (Aker et al. 2017), this study aims to report a second experiment in which playability heuristics are used to evaluate a game to analyze the player experience in different platforms. In this study, a mixed-method approach is employed incorporating questionnaires, semi-structured interviews, observations, and playability heuristics to analyze the gaming experience in different platforms. In this multi-modal approach, playability heuristics were administered during the tests. Heuristics were supported with interviews and observations for further information regarding the player experience and comparison between heuristics and playtests. Even though playability heuristics contain the category of "Game Usability," a modified version of the System Usability Scale (SUS) and Net Promoter Score (NPS) were also administered to inspect possible relations with both our previous study and usability module of the heuristic set. One of the main aims of this study was to examine and test the efficiency of diverse evaluation methods and techniques as a part of the mixed-method approach to gain an understanding of player experience on different platforms.

After the tests, we analyzed and compared the results between platforms to observe differences between gaming platforms. The dependent variables were the scores given to heuristics and questionnaires as well as interview and observation feedbacks while independent variables were the gaming platforms in general including properties such as screen size and mode of interaction, and the game. Accordingly, we aimed to inspect if and how the player experience differ between platforms and if it is possible to evaluate these differences via heuristics.

6.3.1 The Game

To focus the study on player experience differences between platforms and to be able to evaluate the effectiveness of employing playability heuristics, Plants vs Zombies game was chosen as the game to be tested. It was originally developed for PC platform and for Microsoft Windows operating systems by PopCap Games (http://www.popcap.com/) in 2009. The game was adapted to mobile platforms, iOS operating systems in 2010 and for Android in 2011. The main game elements remained the same between platforms such as mechanics, levels, and interface. This provided a suitable choice for a comparative analysis of player experience between platforms. This essentially allowed a chance to focus on the platform rather than the game itself.

The game has basic interactions and game mechanics, demanding only minimal amount of interaction on both platforms such as clicking or tapping the screen. Players are asked to protect a house from approaching zombies using various plants to stop them. Players are expected to place any of the given plants in their garden in any order as they would see fit to defend the area. When placed, plants react to incoming zombies without any need for further interaction except one plant (sunflower) which is used to provide gaining game currency. Players are expected to click or tap on the sun icons that appear over time to gain currency to plant more. Only the adventure mode of the game was available during the tests since every player that attended the tests had to experience the game from the beginning. However, the game has five groups of adventure levels, 25 mini games, 20 puzzle mode games, and 11 survival mode levels, progressively allowing the player to play them.

6.3.2 Participants

A total sample of 20 game designers from both game design students and professionals (18 male, 2 female) were recruited for the tests. All subjects had prior gaming experience with both PC and mobile platform. Previous studies on player experience (e.g., Poels et al. 2012) demonstrated that player experience during gameplay may be influenced by several factors such as game genre, player types, player characteristics, and gaming frequencies. Thus, a purposive sampling method was administered for recruiting the players to recruit only the hardcore or mid-core gamers. Also, only the subjects that have never played the game before were chosen to eliminate the factor of familiarity with the game. The selection was performed via a demographics survey that also contained questions regarding players' gaming habits. As a result, only the participants who played games four days or more per week and who had never played Plants vs. Zombies were selected. Korhonen and Koivisto (2006) stated that the evaluators should have at least some amount of game design expertise. As a result, only the subjects with a game design and/or user experience knowledge were chosen to explore expert review method and the use of heuristics for evaluating player experience.

6.3.3 Material

The data for the experiment was gathered mainly from the playability heuristics, SUS and NPS surveys. Moreover, interviews and user observations were employed to gather further and deeper understanding of the overall player experience.

Playability heuristics are proposed to overcome some missing elements in previously proposed heuristics such as dealing with issues related to mobile platform and overlapping definitions which made them ambiguous according as the authors state in their study (Korhonen and Koivisto 2006). In their research, they proposed heuristics to evaluate mobile games via three modules: "Gameplay," "Game Usability," and "Mobility" (2006). These modules were discussed and compared to other heuristics during recent years, providing a more refined and extensive version. In this study, we used this recent version of playability heuristics from (Korhonen 2016). This heuristic set consisted five main modules: "Context-aware," "Multiplayer," "Gameplay," "Game Usability," and "Mobility" and 47 heuristics. Since our aim is to inspect and analyze differences of player experience between PC and mobile games, we utilized only the latter three modules. Accordingly, Gameplay module consists of 14 items and is claimed to be valid across all platforms, while the Game Usability module has 12 items and was proposed to cover the issues regarding game controls and interface as well as including common usability issues. Lastly the mobility module consists of seven items. It contains heuristics that are specific for mobile games. During the tests, the playability heuristic items were rated on a five-point Likert scale to make the evaluation process feasible for the evaluators. On the scale, answers varied from 1 (strongly agree) to 5 (strongly disagree). During the tests, players were asked to comment freely if they wanted to make comments to potentially gather insights about the answers for the heuristic set. Additionally, post-test interviews were made after the play sessions aimed to analyze the answers given to the heuristic set.

As mentioned before, SUS and NPS were administered after the heuristic evaluations during the tests. The System Usability Scale (SUS) provides a quick tool for measuring the usability. It is a survey to measure the subjective usability of products and services, developed by Brooke (1996). It consists of a ten-item questionnaire with five response options for respondents, from "strongly agree" to "strongly disagree." The scale provides parametric scores varying between 0 and 100. Similar to previous researches (Nacke et al. 2010; Sáenz-de-Urturi et al. 2015), to employ the survey for evaluating games, a slightly modified version of the test was administered by replacing the terms "system" with "game," and "use" with "play."

Fundamentally Net Promoter Score (NPS) is a tool for measuring customer experience. It is used essentially to assess the loyalty of the customer. This metric was included to the procedure to strengthen the analysis of the player experience for assessing players' general sense of satisfaction and tendency to recommend it. It consists of a single question using a 0–10 scale; "How likely is it that you would recommend our company/product/system/service to a friend or a colleague?" as proposed by Reichheld (2003). Like the modified version of the SUS, the question was revised as "How likely is it that you would recommend the game to a friend or a colleague?" Respondents scoring 0–6 are grouped as detractors, 7–8 as passives, and 9–10 as promoters (Reichheld and Markey 2011).

For the PC platform, an Asus laptop featuring an Intel i3 processor, 4 GB DDR3 RAM, onboard Intel chipset graphics card, and 15-in.-wide-screen size and operating on Windows 10 was used. For the mobile platform, a Samsung Note 5 mobile phone featuring an Octa-core (4×2.1 GHz Cortex-A57 and 4×1.5 GHz Cortex-A53) processor, 4 GB RAM, and a 5.7 screen and operating on Android version 7.0 was used. Both of the hardware specifications of the platforms were sufficient for running the game fluently. All the participants were asked to use the same device provided during the tests to prevent validity problems that may relate to hardware capabilities.

6.3.4 Procedure

Experiments were conducted in a focus group laboratory with audio and video recording capability. The participants were randomly divided into two groups each consisting of ten players. They were admitted to the test separately and one by one to avoid any bias and social influence. One group played the game on the PC platform and the other played it on the mobile platform.

One researcher moderated the test sessions. The researcher introduced himself, described the Plants vs. Zombies game, and explained the main purposes of the experiment before each gameplay session. The moderator has attended the tests directly and took observation notes as well as player comments. At the beginning of the tests, each participant was asked to use the given platform (PC or mobile) and took part in an individual gaming session that lasted as much as the player wanted. Observation notes of the supervisor and the recordings provided an overall insight into player experience for each participant and a means of identifying the usability problems experienced by the participants. The subjects were asked to fill the playability heuristics set during the tests whether during the gameplay sessions or after finishing playing the game, allowing an appropriate condition for the subjects to not feel any time pressure while conducting an expert evaluation.

After completing the heuristic set, the subjects were asked to fill the SUS and NPS questionnaires followed by an interview, respectively. The interview questions were associated with the statements of playability heuristics to understand the responses in-depth and to check any possible supporting and consistent relations between the two data collection methods. All the tests, including the interviews took 2 h on average per player.

6.4 Results

Before conducting analysis of the results, it was expected to receive scores which would indicate platform differences via game usability module of the heuristic set as well as the SUS scores. Since Korhonen and Koivisto (2006) implied that the Gameplay and Game Usability modules were applicable to all the games and Game Usability module was more focused on the usability issues of the games, we have expected to receive different scores between platforms mainly from the Game Usability module. Nevertheless, the results were analyzed and compared in order to point out any possible implication to assess the difference between platforms in terms of playability.

After conducting the tests, we first analyzed which heuristics were pointing out a difference between platforms. In order to inspect differences between answers for the heuristics set, an independent sample t-test was conducted to compare heuristic scores between PC and mobile platforms. The total mean of the heuristic scores did not indicate a significant difference between mobile ($M = 3.81$, SD $= 0.47$) and PC ($M = 4.05$, SD $= 0.40$) platforms, yet indicated that PC players perceived less playability problems compared to mobile players. Moreover, we compared the two heuristic module means between platforms. According to this, our results indicated there was not a significant difference in the scores for Game Usability module for mobile ($M = 3.96$, SD $= 0.14$) and PC ($M = 4.18$, SD $= 0.40$) platforms, indicating less usability problems for PC platform. Similarly, the scores for Gameplay module did not indicate a significant difference between mobile ($M = 3.67$, SD $= 0.60$) and PC ($M = 3.94$, SD $= 053$) platforms but again indicated that the players favored PC platform over mobile in terms of gameplay.

Although the heuristic set means did not indicate any difference in terms of significance, when inspected on the scale of items, only the Game Usability heuristic, GU6 ("Navigation is consistent, logical, and minimalist") have shown a statistically significant difference between mobile ($M = 3.1$, $S = 0.87$) and PC ($M = 4.4$, $S = 0.84$) platforms $t(18) = -3.38$, $P = 0.003$.

For analysis, descriptive statistics (Tables 6.1 and 6.2) were derived from the test scores.

Table 6.1 Descriptive statistics for playability heuristics game usability and gameplay modules

Playability heuristics items	Mobile		PC		Overall	
	M	SD	M	SD	M	SD
GU1a "Audio-visual representation supports the game"	4	0.94	4.7	0.48	4.35	0.81
GU1b "A view to the game-world supports smooth interaction and the camera behaves correctly"	4.4	0.69	4.5	0.52	4.45	0.60
GU2 "Screen layout is efficient and visually pleasing"	3.7	1.05	4.2	0.63	3.95	0.88
GU3 "Device UI and game UI are used for their own purposes"	4.2	0.91	4.6	0.51	4.4	0.75
GU4 "Indicators are visible"	3.8	1.03	3.5	0.97	3.65	0.98
GU5 "The player understands the terminology"	3.9	1.10	4.4	0.51	4.15	0.8
GU6 "Navigation is consistent, logical, and minimalist"	3.1	0.87	4.4	0.84	3.75	1.06
GU7 "Game controllers are consistent and follow standard conventions"	4.6	0.51	4.5	0.70	4.55	0.60
GU8 "Game controls are convenient and flexible"	4.1	0.87	4.2	1.22	4.15	1.03
GU9 "The game gives feedback on the player's actions"	4.3	0.67	4.3	0.82	4.3	0.73
GU10 "The player cannot make irreversible errors"	3.4	1.57	3.4	1.34	3.4	1.42
GU11 "The player does not have to memorize things unnecessarily"	4.5	0.97	4	0.94	4.25	0.96
GU12 "The game contains help"	3.5	0.97	3.7	0.94	3.6	0.94
GP1 "The game provides clear goals or supports player-created goals"	4.2	1.03	4.6	0.69	4.4	0.88
GP2 "The player sees the progress in the game and can compare the results"	3.7	0.94	3.9	0.99	3.8	0.95
GP3 "The players are rewarded and the rewards are meaningful"	3.6	1.17	3.7	1.15	3.65	1.13
GP4 "Player is in control"	4.6	0.51	4.4	0.69	4.5	0.60
GP5 "Challenge, strategy, and pace are in balance"	3.2	1.54	4	1.15	3.6	1.39
GP6 "The first-time experience is encouraging"	4.1	0.99	4.4	0.69	4.25	0.85
GP7 "The game story, if any, supports the gameplay and is meaningful"	3.5	0.97	3.9	0.73	3.7	0.86
GP8 "There are no repetitive or boring tasks"	3.1	1.28	2.6	0.84	2.85	1.08
GP9 "The players can express themselves"	2.5	1.50	3.3	1.25	2.9	1.41
GP10 "The game supports different playing"	3.4	1.50	3.7	1.49	3.55	1.46
GP11 "The game does not stagnate"	3.4	0.96	3.6	0.96	3.5	0.94
GP12 "The game is consistent"	3.8	1.03	4.5	0.52	4.15	0.87
GP13 "The game uses orthogonal unit differentiation"	4.1	0.87	4.5	0.52	4.30	0.73
GP14 "The player does not lose any hard-won possessions"	4.2	0.91	4	1.41	4.10	1.16

Table 6.2 Descriptive statistics for playability heuristics mobility module

Mobility heuristics module items (MO)	M	SD
MO1 "The play sessions can be started quickly"	3.80	1.22
MO2 "The game accommodates the surroundings"	4.70	0.48
MO3 "Interruptions are handled reasonably"	4.00	0.47
MO4 "The graphical design is accommodated to current brightness (Supplements GU1a)"	3.90	1.19
MO5 "The player should be aware of some device features while playing (Supplements GU3 and GU4)"	3.00	1.24
MO6 "Mobile devices have their own conventions for input (Supplements GU7)"	3.90	0.73
MO7 "The tutorial should respond to immediate demand (Supplements GU12)"	3.70	1.41

6.4.1   Results of Observations and Interviews

Karat (1994) indicates that the number of identified usability issues is one of the subjects that define the effectiveness of an evaluation method when comparing diverse evaluation methods. Hence, most of the studies that utilize heuristic evaluation along with playtests have conducted analysis based on the number of playability problems discovered whether by the heuristics or the playtests (e.g., Desurvire et al. 2004; Korhonen and Koivisto 2006; Korhonen 2010). Nevertheless, Desurvire et al. (2004) noted that playtests have additionally provided results indicating specific problems that are not mentioned in the heuristics and are crucial for evaluating games. Moreover, Korhonen (2016) indicates, "One characteristic of the game evaluations is to think about the origin of the playability problem." Therefore, it is important to identify the origins of the problems that we received from the interviews and observations as well as identifying specific issues that could not directly associated with the heuristic set.

A similar approach from Hara and Ovaska (2014) was followed for grouping the interview results and observations to further identify problems indicated during the tests. Although their study involves identification of problems from game reviews from online sources via utilizing keywords, a similar approach through gathered interview and observation results facilitated the analysis process. Similar to this, Soomro et al. (2012) have conducted a preliminary research on playability heuristics for mobile games by developing problem categories to group the problems identified from the interviews. Instead of utilizing keywords from the feedbacks, an in-depth analysis on the causes of the problems was conducted for this study. This grouping of problems is also aimed to facilitate identification of heuristics which would be useful for evaluating player experience between platforms during the study.

To further evaluate the results, qualitative analysis of the interviews and observation notes provided supportive results for a thorough discussion. Moreover, it was aimed to identify possible overlapping responses and relations between heuristics in which the participants may have indicated consistencies pointing towards the platform differences. For instance, it was identified that some heuristics could not

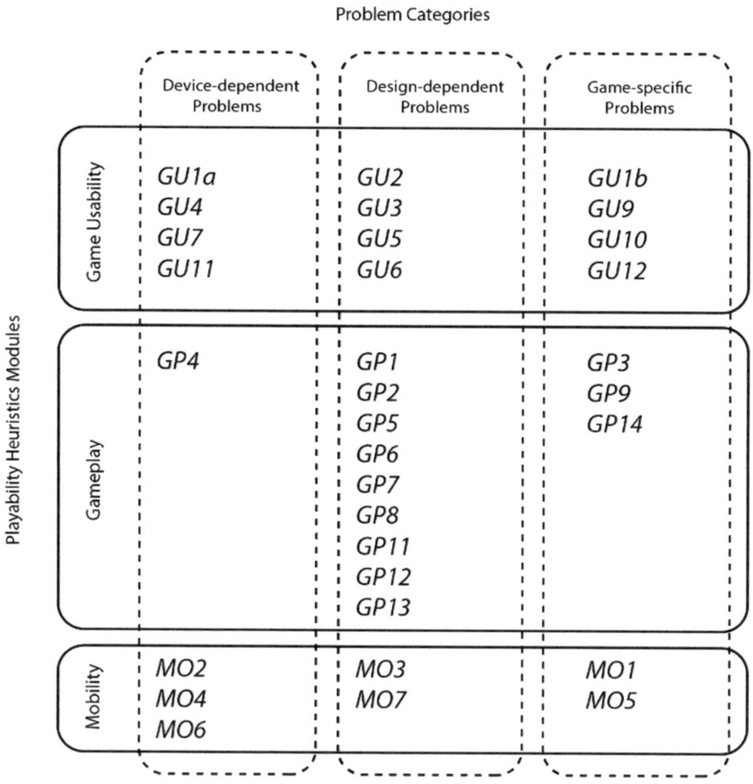

Problem Categories

Fig. 6.1 Associations of problem categories with playability heuristics modules

be affiliated directly to the platform capabilities while some can directly be related to game elements. By this grouping of problems, it was possible to put forward a general classification of differences in experience between platforms.

During our study, each heuristic is found to be rooted in a specific problem. Because of these diversity of specific problems related to both platforms and the game tested, we defined different sets of problem groupings based on the feedbacks and observations. Interview statements of the players and observations were identified jointly for each heuristic item (Fig. 6.1, Table 6.3) for the betterment of qualitative analysis.

6.4.2 Grouping of Problems

As Federoff (2002) mentioned, the proposed heuristics are generally and fundamentally based on game design and development areas such as mechanics, interface, or gameplay and may not be directly related with the causes of playability problems.

Table 6.3 Descriptive statistics of SUS scores

SUS questions	Mobile		PC		Overall	
	M	SD	M	SD	M	SD
Q1 "*I think that I would like to play this game frequently*"	2.3	1.05	3.5	1.17	2.9	1.25
Q2 "*I found the game unnecessarily complex*"	1.5	0.70	1.2	0.42	1.35	0.58
Q3 "*I thought the game was easy to play*"	4.6	0.51	4.8	0.42	4.7	0.47
Q4 "*I think that I would need the support of a technical person to be able to play this game*"	1.1	0.31	1	0	1.05	0.22
Q5 "*I found that the various functions in this game were well integrated*"	3.7	0.67	3.8	0.63	3.75	0.63
Q6 "*I thought that there was too much inconsistency in this game*"	1.5	0.70	1.5	0.52	1.5	0.60
Q7 "*I would imagine that most people would learn to play this game very quickly*"	4.7	0.48	4.6	0.51	4.65	0.48
Q8 "*I found the game very cumbersome to use*"	3.3	1.15	3.1	0.87	3.2	1.0
Q9 "*I felt very confident playing the game*"	4.3	0.67	4.7	0.48	4.5	0.60
Q10 "*I needed to learn a lot of things before I could get going with this game*"	1.6	0.96	1.2	0.42	1.4	0.75

Furthermore, current heuristic evaluations still rely heavily on similar elements to define the heuristic categories. Although this might be useful for dissecting the playability problems, it was clear that a novel approach was necessary for analyzing experience specifically in different platforms. Moreover, playability heuristics were not directly compatible with platform related problems that are indicated during the tests. Therefore, descriptions of problem categories were mapped with the causes of the indicated problems and interrelated with heuristic items. As a whole, we identified three different problem groups regarding the dependencies of the heuristics based on results from the feedbacks in our analysis: design-dependent problems, game-specific problems, and device-dependent problems. These categories were defined to provide insights about the issues that participants have indicated about the game and possible solutions to the problems encountered in the context of specific problem areas.

6.4.2.1 Device-Dependent Problems

The device-dependent problems consist of responses to heuristic items and feedbacks which indicated issues related to the gaming device. Ergonomic issues and/or other hardware related problems were included in this set of category (see Appendix 1 for the details of the results). The results received from the players during interviews and observations indicated that, the problem category consists of issues related to device capabilities such as the size of the screen, interaction mode, peripherals, or quality of the speakers. These problems are indicated to refer hardware differences and/or proposed to be in direct relation with device characteristics.

6.4.2.2 Design-Dependent Problems

The design-dependent problems include feedbacks and heuristic items depending to game mechanics and interactions such as conflicting / overlapping interaction mechanics between the game and the device operating system. These issues were defined in order to provide insights for the game designers and developers (see Appendix 2 for the results received from the players during interviews and observations). The design-dependent problems are examined to be related with the game elements and include issues such as interface problems or gameplay issues. This category fundamentally address platform-specific problems that can be resolved by better development/design of the game and game elements specifically crafted for the platform.

6.4.2.3 Game-Specific Problems

It has been indicated that different genres have different problems (Pinelle et al. 2008). The game-specific problems include heuristic items and feedbacks received from participants related directly to the particular game genre and specific game elements. The items which were included in this category are found to be not applicable for our research since they did not provide evidence regarding the differences between platforms. (See Appendix 3 for the results received from the players during interviews and observations). Game-specific problems are examined to be related with issues related with the game genre in particular. Heuristic items and feedbacks related to this category are indicated as either non-existent in the game or not useful for observing platform differences.

6.5 Discussion

In order to set the analysis out in full, each result of the heuristic item and their problem groupings are evaluated in detail in the following section. The groupings of the heuristics and related observations allowed for further analysis of each heuristic item from the perspective of the cause of the playability problem. Based on this approach, heuristic items are discussed in accordance to their grouping category (Fig. 6.1).

It should be noted that the mobility heuristic module did not include heuristics that are derived from the notion of differences between platforms. Hence the heuristic items do not directly address differences between platforms in terms of experience but underline some of the issues that players have encountered on mobile platform. All the mobile players scored the module items above the average in general which indicated that they were content with the game within the range of given heuristics. Moreover the mobility heuristic items are not applicable in general to indicate any platform difference between platforms. Nevertheless, associations with other heuristic modules were inspected and relations were addressed during the analysis.

6.5.1   Analysis of Device-Dependent Problems

As mentioned above, these problems and associated heuristics described device related issues such as ergonomics or hardware capabilities. 8 playability heuristic items (GU1a, GU4, GU7, GU11, GP4, MO2, MO4, and MO6) are found to be in association with this problem category.

The results from the interviews and observations indicated that mobile players have mostly commented negatively on the sound effects of the game. All PC players ($n = 10$) gave positive comments on audio-visual representations including keywords like "I liked this, good, well-matched," while in mobile platform several players mentioned keywords such as "bad, didn't like, annoying" ($n = 3$) to indicate that they did not like the music and the sound effects. Three players (PM4, PM5, and PM8) mentioned that although they liked the graphics in general, they were annoyed by the sound effects of the game during play. Additionally, two players on the mobile platform have accidentally blocked the speaker of the phone with their hands because of the holding position, resulting in a severely muffled sound during play. On the contrary, none of the PC players ($n = 10$) indicated any complaints regarding sounds or graphics of the game and were observed to be content with the audio-visual aspects of the game. These problems are identified to be related with the playability heuristic item GU1a ("Audio-visual representation supports the game"). Results pointed out that the audio and the graphics could be considered as separate heuristics (for example, under a sub-section). The complaints were related mostly to the limited speaker capabilities of the mobile platform and the placement of the speakers on the device. Therefore it may be considered as a hardware issue in general.

As Wood et al. (2005) suggested, direct interaction on the display requires less cognitive, spatial, or attentional demand. Moreover, computers may cause unnecessary physical and cognitive loads depending on the hardware or software (Laux 2001). Because of these suggestions, mobile players are inspected to perceive indicators easily compared to PC players. In the literature, it is suggested that small screen sizes can actually be more effective since it reduces the visual load (Nattkemper and Prinz 1990). The presentation of few menu items at a time could be helpful in general, because it is widely known that the legibility and also the readability is hampered by increased density of text on the screen (e.g., Norman 1991; Ziefle and Bay 2005). Thus, Ziefle (2010) said, "From this it can be deduced that visually demanding displays negatively influence information access." According to the test results and feedbacks, it is observed that players' perception for indicators can potentially be positively affected by the screen size of the mobile platform. Therefore the heuristic item GU4 ("Indicators are visible") is considered to be relevant for the problem category. In terms of memorization of game-related elements and the cognitive load, depending on the feedbacks and interviews, the heuristic item GU11 is found to be in close relationship with the heuristic item GU4 and the ease of use of the mobile platform. Detenber and Reeves (1996) suggested that there is a close correlation between bigger screen size and memorization. Even so, the results indicate that mobile players gave higher scores to the heuristic item GU11 ("The player does not have to memorize things unnecessarily"). Observation notes indicated that two PC players (PP6, PP3) mentioned negative comments on the subject and gave lower scores to the related heuristic accordingly. Both players indicated that they were not able to see the info about the given plants whenever they wanted to and got frustrated about using them. Mobile players experienced the same game design in this manner but they all pointed out that the game was giving them the chance to learn by trial and error. In general, it was examined that players' perceptions and cognitive demands of the hardware varies between platforms, favoring mobile platform.

Although the game offers the same in-game mechanisms, the fundamental differences between controls were observed to be not addressed via heuristics. Essentially, mobile platform offered the capability to manipulate the object on the screen directly by either touching or dragging during the game, while PC platform only allowed the players to interact with a mouse via clicking to the objects. Thus, the differences in controls were considered to hold crucial potential for identifying platform differences yet we could not observe any differences on interviews and/or observations. In terms of heuristics, a difference between average scores for the heuristic items GU7 ("Game controllers are consistent and follow standard conventions") and GU8 ("Game controls are convenient and flexible") was expected since the platforms offer fundamentally different interaction methods and peripherals as one is limited to touch screen and one to a mouse. For the heuristic item GU7, the average scores for mobile players were higher when compared to PC players by only a narrow margin. As for the latter heuristic item, GU8, PC players gave slightly higher scores on average. These somewhat similar scores indicate that all the players from both platforms found the controls acceptable, consistent, and convenient in general, even though these heuristics items imply the notion of controls capable of being flexible for different preferences of players. The game did not provide such an option for re-mapping any of the controls. It was also noticed that the wordings of these heuristics did not relate to the fundamental control differences between platforms in terms of usability. For instance, a mobile player (PM9) mentioned that he would like to have drag and drop type of interaction yet the game already provided an additional drag and drop mechanism for the mobile platform. Even so, the same mobile player gave a high score to both of the heuristics. Additionally, the heuristic item MO6 ("Mobile devices have their own conventions for input") was described as in supplementary relationship with the heuristic item GU7. This association is validated through observations. The players which gave higher scores indicated that the conventions for the mobile platform were obvious and natural. While the players gave higher scores for the item on average ($M = 3.90$, $SD = 0.73$), two players (PM1 and PM10) gave low scores, indicating that they were feeling indecisive. It was observed that these two players had difficulty understanding the heuristic item MO6 and hesitated to answer either positively or negatively. Similarly, mobile players indicated that they felt more in control during the game when answering the heuristic item GP4 ("Player is in control"). This was observed to be in parallel with the touch screen interaction requiring less training and hand-eye coordination, and being easier to use effectively because of the reduced cognitive load (Thomas and Milan 1987). Although players on mobile platform had several problems interacting with the game such as tapping on the wrong plants, they indicated that they felt in control throughout the game. This contrast between errors and players feeling of direct control on mobile platform may become more significant compared to the context of usability and cause a higher feeling of control hence more error tolerance.

In terms of mobile device capabilities for adapting to environmental factors such as loud noises coming from outside or low brightness conditions, players gave almost the highest score regarding the heuristic item MO2 ("The game accommodates the surroundings") pointing out that they were comfortable adjusting some of the game features while playing the game without being affected from the surroundings. Analysis of the interviews and observations indicated that players were able to adjust the volume easily during the play via in-game options menu ($n = 7$) or by using the devices general volume button ($n = 3$). In relation to that, interviews indicated that the players understood the heuristic item as referring to device capabilities rather than the game itself. Similar to these findings, analysis of observations and interviews indicated that MO4 ("The graphical design is accommodated to current brightness") is strongly related with the heuristic item MO2 in terms of given context. Korhonen (2016) also indicated that this heuristic item is given as a supplement to the heuristic GU1a, yet when analyzed, the results suggested that the players did not relate the item directly with GU1a but with the device capabilities.

6.5.2   Analysis of Design-Dependent Problems

The design-dependent problems are problems that relate to issues regarding interface of gameplay which essentially address platform-specific problems which can be resolved by developmental precautions and/or modifications. 15 playability heuristic items (GU2, GU3, GU5, GU6, GP1, GP2, GP5, GP6, GP7, GP8, GP11, GP12, and GP13) are found to be in association with this problem category. The association with most of the gameplay module heuristics was anticipated since these heuristic items also relate mostly to game design and development issues. Different from the other problem categories, suggestions were given during the analysis of the problems in this category to indicate probable solutions.

Results from observations and interviews indicated that none of the players from both platforms mentioned negative comments related to the esthetic properties of the layout. Nevertheless, the scores for the heuristic item GU2 ("Screen layout is efficient and visually pleasing") indicated that the overall screen layout was found to be more pleasing by PC players. During the interviews, all PC players ($n = 10$) used positive keywords such as "easy, appropriate, clear" regarding the layout, yet only two of them mentioned a negative aspect related to the screen resolution of the game being not high-definition. Mobile players have mentioned negative keywords such as "didn't like, tiring" ($n = 3$). Mobile players also have encountered accidents related with the interaction of the device ($n = 5$). These accidents are observed to be directly related to the operating system of the mobile device, specifically the Android operating systems' menu button being accidentally pressed during play. Furthermore, in terms of layout of the in-game elements, there is a significant difference between two versions of the game. On mobile platform, the progress bar of the game is presented on top of the screen while and on PC, it is placed at the bottom of the screen. One player on PC platform (PP8) indicated that he was fully aware of the progress bar while one mobile player (PM5) highlighted a problem of him not being able to identify on which level he was playing at. Lauer and Needham (1979) said, "When everything is emphasized, nothing is emphasized." Too many focal points are likely to confuse players and may diffuse their interest. It was identified that on the mobile platform, additional interactions focus on top of the screen area, such as game-related active objects dropping from the top of the screen. The menu button is also located on top of the screen. On the contrary, the progress bar on the PC platform is placed at the bottom without any extra icons or objects nearby, isolating and therefore enhancing the visibility of the progress bar during the game. Because of these feedbacks and observations, we identified this problem in association with GP2 ("The player sees the progress in the game and can compare results"). The results of the observations suggest that progress indicators should be designed according to the platform. Indicators should also provide sufficient and convenient information of the overall progress of the game as well as short-term progress.

Similar with the heuristic GU2, the observations and interviews highlighted that fundamentally the difference in average scores of GU3 ("Device UI and game UI are used for their own purposes"), are related to the interaction with the operating system. Both platforms players start the game in the default full screen mode. Accordingly, the heuristic item GU3 suggests the game should be presented in full screen mode to better immerse the player. However, the accidental press of the Android menu button drops the player out of the game, potentially breaking the feeling of immersion. Because of its context, this heuristic item is also considered as one of the crucial heuristic items to indicate a difference between platforms. In contrast, although most of the mobile players have accidentally tapped the Android menu button during play, the scores given to the MO3 ("Interruptions are handled reasonably") heuristic item was high. Players were observed to accidentally press the device menu button. Afterwards, they get back to the game from where they were interrupted immediately by pressing the same button again. They mentioned that they were able to return to the game in a fast manner.

The results indicated that mobile players have more difficulty on receiving information in terms of terminology including explanations of plants and the game story. Although several PC players gave negative comments ($n = 3$) regarding the terminology by using keywords such as "didn't understand, not enough, complex," mostly mobile players have encountered problems regarding the functions of the plants during our observations. Since the problem is mainly encountered because of the terminological issues, this problem is examined to be related to the heuristic item GU5 ("The player understands the terminology"). It was also observed that mobile players had the tendency to skip important information screens (such as pop-up boxes giving extra information about specific functions of the game) during the tutorials in a very fast manner. As a result many mobile players had problems with understanding the exact functions of the plants ($n = 7$). Additionally, three mobile players also tried to find a way to re-check the plant information without success (PM1, PM6, and PM7). Exceptionally one mobile player indicated that even after reading the explanations of the plants, he did not receive sufficient information (PM5). Moreover none of the PC players have observed to be skipping the information screens providing plant information during the play. Furthermore, both player groups' made similar mistakes during the game by misinterpreting a function of a plant. Nevertheless mobile players complained mostly on how the game was not sufficiently explaining the functions of the given plants during the game and related this with the consistency of the game to evaluate the relation between plant information and functions of the plants. Players from both platforms understood that the terminological problem was also related to the heuristic item GP12 ("The game is consistent"). Lastly, results from the feedbacks indicated that the players on mobile platform had difficulty in understanding specific functions and strategic implications of some of the plants. This specific problem of not utilizing plants in a strategic fashion was identified to be in relation with GP13 ("The game uses orthogonal unit differentiation"). To give an example, PM7 experienced similar problems utilizing specific plants during the game and was not able to employ a plants specific capabilities during the game. The player tried using a specific plant several times during the play without success. It should be noted that the function of this plant was explained in the information screens, pointing out its use. Still, PM7 has skipped this information screen during the play. Developing the game primarily based on the targeted platform capabilities and player tendencies towards the platform would increase positive feedback from the players. Since the mobile players had the tendency to skip text-based information screens during play, a mobile specific version of the information should be implemented, specifically developed for the mobile version of the game such as animated explanations and/or small tutorial videos.

The limited screen space of the mobile platform is a problematic issue for providing optimized information access and navigation (Zhao et al. 2001). The results from the observations and the interviews indicated the notion of the problematic navigation on the mobile platform. PC players mostly commented positively on the navigation of the game, using keywords such as; "clear, easy, plain" ($n = 8$) while mobile players mentioned mostly negative comments using keywords like "bad, couldn't find, problematic" ($n = 6$). Because of the context of the feedbacks, the heuristic item GU6 ("Navigation is consistent, logical and minimalist") is associated with the problem. As explained on the previous section of the study, this heuristic item indicated a significant difference between platforms according to the average scores given to the heuristic. Ziefle (2010) suggested that: "Field independence, the ability to separate an item from the context of which it is a part, exerts a strong influence upon navigation ability." Primary observations indicated that mobile players had severe stagnation in the main menu of the game while trying to find the function button to start playing. Players were observed to be unable to perceive the buttons separate from the context from the game background in the main menu. For both versions of the game, the main menu (or the start menu) screen included a tombstone graphic with a button embedded on it which is mapped to the function of starting the game. Additionally, on the PC version of the game the start button on the main menu screen was highlighted when the mouse pointer crossed over it. Even though PC players did not have any issues finding the buttons, mobile players had a hard time finding the embedded button to start the game. During the tests, mobile players indicated that they could not immediately understand how they would begin playing the game since they were not able to directly locate the start button. Two mobile platform players were not able to find how to start the game asked for help from the supervisor. The results suggest that on mobile, navigation paths and design elements related to navigation of the game should be designed specifically for mobile platforms. The general progression throughout the game also should be designed in consideration of mobile platform, providing as clear, functional, and basic information as possible.

It was identified that the onboarding process works rather better than on the mobile platform. We observed that the tutorials at the beginning of the game provided sufficient information related to the mechanics yet did not provide information of long-term goals of the game. The results regarding the heuristic item GP1 ("The game provides clear goals or supports player-created goals") indicated that players on PC platform understood the necessary goals and ways to achieve them more clearly. It was also observed that the familiarity with the tower defense game genre may had an impact regarding the answers. While most of the players were familiar with the game genre, two mobile players (PM6, PM9) indicated that they have never played the game genre on a mobile phone before. Moreover, PC players felt more incentive while playing the game at the beginning. This may indicate that the heuristic item GP6 ("The first-time experience is encouraging") is also related to the onboarding process which is mentioned for the heuristic GP1. It was noted that first-time experience for mobile players was problematic because of the start menu problems. Accordingly, a mobile-first approach can be suggested for a more beneficial evaluation of the item. These findings suggest that the game developers and designers should consider designing the explanations of the goals and the onboarding processes specific to mobile platforms to provide better experiences. A step-by-step development approach for the mobile platform would potentially more effective and provide a better onboarding experience for mobile players.

Another crucial factor affecting the player experience is definitely the challenge and the pacing of the game. Most of the players from both platforms complained about the pacing of the game and its lack of challenge, yet mobile players especially commented on this during observations. While all mobile platform players gave negative comments using keywords such as; "dull, too easy, boring" ($n = 10$), several PC players liked the challenge and the pace of the game by giving comments using keywords like; "tireless, stress-free" ($n = 3$). Therefore we can indicate that the PC version of the game is perceived to be less cumbersome compared to the mobile platform. These feedbacks are directly related with the heuristic item GP5 ("Challenge, strategy and pace are in balance") because of its context. In terms of the pacing of the game, one player playing the game on PC platform had a negative comment about being bored during play (PP6), while several mobile players mentioned this problem by using keywords such as "boring, slow" ($n = 3$). Additionally, mobile players mentioned that they were familiar to the tower defense game genre for mobile platform, but the game lacked some of their expectations. These feedbacks are found to be in relation to the heuristic item GP8 ("There are no repetitive or boring tasks"). Results received regarding the heuristic item suggest that the tasks during the game were perceived to be more boring and/or repetitive on the PC platform. Controversially, feedbacks regarding the heuristic item GP11 ("The game does not stagnate") indicate that PC players felt less stagnation and more progress during the play sessions. Moreover, it was observed that most of the players from both platforms associated this heuristic item to the pacing of the game. As indicated in the GP5 heuristic item analysis, all of the mobile players complained about the slow pace of the game during play sessions. It is known that frequent achievements could provide a better experience in general on mobile platform yet the game was ported from PC to mobile in the first place. The game genre is considered as suitable for the mobile platform by mobile players yet it lacked some of the important game elements such as sufficient variations of game-related tasks. It was understood that the developers may have to design/port mobile versions of the games with renewed challenge and pacing mechanisms. The results suggested that if the game was designed with the notion of mobile platform and specifically offered more variations of tasks during the game, players would enjoy the game more.

Regarding the story of the game, PC players indicated that the story of the game felt fun and enjoyable while some mobile players mentioned that they did not understand the story of the game and not found the ambient crucial for the concept of the game ($n = 2$). The onboarding process differences between platforms are once more observed regarding this feedback. Moreover, because of its context, the heuristic item GP7 ("The game story, if any, supports the gameplay and is meaningful") is found to be in direct association with the feedbacks. According to the scores received from the heuristic item, mobile players had difficulty understanding the overall story of the game and purpose of game characters in terms of context. The item is also observed to be associated with GU5, suggesting that mobile players have more difficulty on receiving information in terms of terminology including explanations of plants and the game story. The developers and designers of the game might enhance the overall experience by integrating a story specifically crafted for the platform.

Regardless of the fact that there is no immediate and/or on-demand tutorial function in the game, players gave relatively higher scores to the MO7 ("The tutorial should respond to immediate demand") heuristic item. Players mentioned they were content regarding the heuristic item except one player (PM4). When analyzed in-depth, observations suggested that most of the players affiliated the heuristic with the tutorial levels instead of any immediate help function. The item is referred to GU12 heuristic item in the proposed playability heuristics (Korhonen 2016) yet, for instance, PM6 gave the lowest score to MO7 while giving the highest score to GU12 heuristic item. These results underline that the proposed links between these heuristics might not be there when applied in practice since the game fundamentally does not offer on demand help or tutorial. Players would benefit from having immediate tutorial when they needed assistance related to the functions of the plants.

6.5.3   Analysis of Game-Specific Problems

The game-specific problems are identified as the problems that relate to issues which are particular to the game genre and/or specific game elements that do not allow evaluating experience differences between platforms. Eight playability heuristic items (GU1b, GU9, GU10, GU12, GP3, GP9, GP14, MO1, and MO5) are found to be in association with this category.

As mentioned above, it should be noted that the game does not directly provide a help function neither for PC nor mobile platform. However the game provides well-designed tutorial levels to the players. Additionally nearly all of the players mentioned that they did not need any help function during the game, sometimes referring to lack of challenge of the game. The observations and interviews indicated that the players were relating the heuristic item GU12 ("The game contains help") to the lack of help functionality during the game yet the heuristic item also explained to include tutorials of games. Because of these reasons, it is possible to suggest that an extra heuristic item following this heuristic should be implemented to the set (such as GU12b), separating the role of tutorials and the concept of learnability from the heuristic item. Nevertheless, because of the current state of the heuristic item, it was identified as not useful for evaluating platform differences since some games fundamentally do not necessitate a help function at all.

In terms of GU1b ("A view to the game-world supports smooth interaction and the camera behaves correctly"), the game did not have any dynamic camera interaction mechanism. Therefore the heuristic is identified as to be suggested to a specific type of a game genre such as third-person shooters. Similarly, the heuristic items GU9 ("The game gives feedback on the player's actions") and GU10 ("The player cannot make irreversible errors") were found to be inefficient for evaluating differences between platforms since these two heuristics are about internal dynamics of the game which are considered to be out of the context for analyzing differences between platforms.

In terms of rewards given during play, the reward mechanics in the game was developed in the same manner for both of the platforms. The game basically offers new plants after the player completes each level in both versions. Other than the progression related rewards, there was no score indicator. Because of these reasons, no difference between platforms in the context of this heuristic was expected. The reward mechanics were related to the heuristic item GP3 ("The players are rewarded and the rewards are meaningful") in which no notable difference was observed regarding the heuristic item scores. In relation with the reward mechanics, the heuristic item GP14 ("The player does not lose any hard-won possessions") was identified as not applicable for analyzing differences between platforms. This was also previously expected before the tests since the game for both platforms have the same mechanics and dynamics and estimated to fulfill this heuristic sufficiently.

In terms of the heuristic item GP9 ("The players can express themselves" and GP10 ("The game supports different playing styles"), the game does not allow players to customize their avatars or personal preferences. Although, PC players mentioned the personalization of different strategies during the play sessions might count as expressions. During observations, several players said that modification of the game-world could be considered relatable with this heuristic ($n = 3$ for PC and $n = 2$ for mobile), yet none of the players were conclusive about this comment. Despite these suggestions, observations indicated that this heuristic item does not apply for neither of the versions of the game and is not applicable to evaluate platform differences in terms of player experience. Similarly, GP10 ("The game supports different playing styles") did not receive any feedback regarding the difference between platforms since the game did not offer any capability to choose a role and/or style of play in the world.

The opening speed of the game was somewhat similar between platforms. The results of the scores for the heuristic item MO1 ("The play sessions can be started quickly") indicated that mobile players were content with the opening speed of the game sessions. One player (PM9) was observed to tap on the screen while the game was first loading on the device. When asked, the player mentioned that it was not annoying and he tapped only because he was curious to see what would happen. It was observed that most of the mobile players were referring this heuristic to the relation between device capabilities and game requirements, such as more demanding games require more time to start. Thus it could be suggested that the item would be useful for comparing games in mobile platforms rather than platforms.

Lastly, the heuristic item MO5 ("The player should be aware of some device features while playing") was found to be controversial among several players. Observations indicated that players did not relate this item with neither of those heuristic items and considered it to be not related with the game at all. A number of mobile players ($n = 3$) gave fairly low scores to this item, suggesting that the item was not viable. This item was also proposed as supplementary for the items GU3 and GU4 (Korhonen 2016). When compared, several players who gave low scores to this item did not give scores to the supplementing GU3 and GU4 items in the same fashion.

6.5.4   Usability Evaluation of the Game

Regarding the NPS scores, PC players scored higher (10) when compared to mobile players (−50). The results showed that, two players were considered as detractors (scores ranging from 0 to 6) while five players were considered as passives (a score of 7 or 8), and three players were considered as promoters (scores higher than 8). As for the mobile platform, five players were considered as detractors. Meanwhile the remaining five players were considered as passives. According to the NPS scores, no promoters are identified in the mobile player group. These results indicate a gap between platforms in terms of player tendencies of recommending the game. Mobile players are not likely to recommend the game to their friends or colleagues.

Tullis et al. (2008), suggested that an average SUS of below 60% indicate poor usability of the game and a score of greater than 80% represents good usability. According to this, players on PC platform evaluated the game as more usable ($M = 83.5$, $S = 1.63$) when compared to mobile players ($M = 76.2$, SD $= 7.47$) (Table 6.3).

The SUS and NPS differences between platforms were inspected by independent samples t-tests. After conducting an independent samples t-test for SUS scores between platforms, SUS tests indicated a significant difference between mobile and PC platforms; $t(18) = -2.52$, $p = 0.21$. Furthermore NPS scores indicated that there was not a significant difference between PC ($M = 7.1$, SD $= 2.6$) and mobile platform ($M = 5.8$, SD $= 2.2$) conditions; $t(18) = -1.18$, $p = 0.252$.

These results suggest that NPS survey helped identify player tendency to recommend the game in general meanwhile SUS tests indicate platform differences in terms of usability. When analyzed in detail, three SUS questions (1st, 9th, and 10th) were found to be in relation with the observations. It should also be noted that these SUS item scores were derived from average scores from the players and not normalized. This proved to be beneficial for comparing the results directly with the context of the items. For the betterment of the qualitative analysis, these SUS questions were analyzed in detail.

SUS1: "I Think That I Would Like to Play this Game Frequently"
PC players gave higher scores to this item ($M = 3.5$, SD $= 1.17$) when compared to mobile players ($M = 2.3$, SD $= 1.05$). PC players mentioned that they were not bothered by the pace of the game and not felt bored as much as mobile players throughout the game. As mentioned in the heuristic GP5, one of the PC players (PP10) indicated that they felt "stress-free." Additionally, when observed via heuristic results, PC platform can be seen as more comfortable rather than mobile. Additionally, Net Promoter Scores (NPS) were parallel with this results. NPS score for PC players was ten while mobile players scored −50.

SUS9: "I Felt Very Confident Playing the Game"
PC players gave higher scores regarding this SUS item ($M = 4.7$, SD $= 0.48$) when compared to mobile players ($M = 4.3$, SD $= 0.67$). When the inter-correlations between SUS items and heuristics were examined, mobile players have shown

significant association between the SUS item with GU11 ($r = 0.762, p < 0.05$) while PC platform players have shown significant association between the SUS item with GU7 ($r = 0.813, p < 0.001$), GU8 ($r = 0.674, p < 0.05$), GU12 ($r = 0.752, p < 0.05$), GP3 ($r = 0.813, p < 0.001$), GP13 ($r = 0.655, p < 0.05$). These results suggested that PC players associated several game aspects related to the SUS item while mobile players mainly focused on only one heuristic. Apart from that, PC players gave more positive comments related to the SUS item when compared to mobile players.

SUS10: "I Needed to Learn a Lot of Things Before I Could Get Going with this Game"

Mobile players gave higher scores to this SUS item ($M = 1.6$, SD $= 0.96$) compared to PC players ($M = 1.2$, SD $= 0.42$). When the feedbacks from the players and observations were analyzed, PC players indicated more tendency for understanding the game as can be seen on the heuristic item. Analysis suggests that several scopes of the given heuristics such as terminology, onboarding, ease of use and game story are affecting the SUS item.

6.6 Conclusion

It is important to understand the importance of player experience in the gaming world. Fundamentally, platform variations may be crucial in terms of experience since different platforms offer different experiences. There are only a number of studies examining player experience using various methodologies such as utilization of heuristics, employing metrics and/or surveys. But none of those methods has proven to be effective and sufficiently holistic when applied merely by themselves and do not cover all the aspects regarding player experience. Because of these reasons, we have conducted a multi-modal study utilizing heuristics and playtests for evaluating player experience in different platforms. This multi-modality in our approach proved to be effective in terms of getting detailed insights and analysis as well as further improving the evaluation. Additionally, interviews and player observations after gameplay sessions were contributive in offering an in-depth comprehension of different motivations of the players for both PC and mobile platforms.

Korhonen and Koivisto (2006) indicated that playability heuristics would be effective for evaluating the player experience. Moreover, they suggested that the modular structure of the heuristic set can involve most of the features of games such as Game Usability module covering game controls and interfaces as well as containing common usability aspects that help players. The results from our study indicated that the heuristic set was ineffective for analyzing different experiences between platforms. Detailed analysis of the feedbacks suggested that the heuristic set needed more improvements.

We found that wordings of several heuristic items were not easily comprehensible by players and resulted in misunderstandings. Most importantly, we identified that players do not relate heuristic items directly with their given module, such as several gameplay module items were associated with game usability issues and vice-versa. Due to feedbacks and observations we received during the tests, we were able to identify three distinctive problem groups from the feedbacks of the players and were able to associate them with the heuristics. These problem categories could potentially be useful for analyzing playtests in combination with heuristics from a structured perspective when evaluating platform differences. This grouping of problems is also proved to be useful for identification of heuristics which would be useful for evaluating player experience between platforms during the study. We identified that the heuristic items which are included in the design-dependent problems category could be analyzed by focusing on development stages of games specifically with the platform in mind. Items in the device-dependent problems category indicated issues beyond developers' ability and point towards issues directly related to the device such as ergonomics and/or device capabilities. Lastly, items that were included in the game-specific problems category were identified to be dependent on the game itself and did not indicate player experience differences between platforms. Moreover, the mobility module from the playability heuristics set was mostly associated with device related usability problems and not with the game design aspects. The results from the tests suggested that only the MO1 and MO5 items of the heuristic set was associated with game-specific features which again proved to be inefficient for analyzing player experience differences between platforms.

Common usability evaluation methods such as SUS and NPS were included in the tests and proved to be useful for evaluating usability related issues during the game. Usability test scores indicated that there was a difference of experience between platforms. SUS scores indicated a significant difference between platforms in terms of usability and NPS scores demonstrated that, unlike mobile players, PC platform players would recommend the game to their friends and colleagues. When SUS results were analyzed per item, PC players showed a tendency to play the game more often mainly because of the comfort, challenge, and pacing factors. Results from the SUS tests also indicated that mobile platform players' feeling of confidence was linked to memorization while SUS scores for PC players linked the same feeling with various heuristic items. Lastly, for PC players, the learnability of the system was found in direct relation with players' efficiency in understanding the terminology, onboarding, ease of use and story features of the game.

To conclude, covering most aspects of player experience, this study presents a new structure of evaluating platform differences utilizing heuristics. From stakeholders of the gaming industry to developers and designers, this method of analysis could be effective for understanding the needs and expectations of players. We believe that there is a need for a novel approach utilizing the heuristic set for evaluating player experience differences between platforms. It is understood that by adapting existing heuristics and iteratively improving them via user tests specifically for analyzing the platforms, would seem to be efficient for analyzing these differences in experience.

However, it should be noted that the study was limited in terms of comparing only two gaming platforms with a small sample group. Therefore, the presented multi-modal approach should be tested on different gaming platforms with more players.

Appendix 1   Results of Device-Dependent Playability Problems

Table 6.4   Results of device-dependent playability problems

Heuristic item	Exemplary statement	Main observations
GU1a: "Audio-visual representation supports the game"	– "I loved the graphics and animations but the sound effects were repetitive and reedy. Especially the sound of a zombie eating a plant. This annoyed me after certain amount of time" (PM8)	– Sound effects of the game annoyed mobile players – Mobile players accidentally blocked the speakers of the device – Mobile platform speakers were not sufficient
GU4: "Indicators are visible"		– Players' perception for indicators can potentially be related with the screen size of the mobile platform – Mobile players are inspected to perceive indicators easily compared to PC players – Mobile platforms require less cognitive, spatial, or attentional demand
GU7: "Game controllers are consistent and follow standard conventions" and GU8: "Game controls are convenient and flexible"	– "I would prefer a drag mechanism to play this game" (PM9)	– Both player groups found the controls sufficient and convenient in general – Even though these heuristics items included the notion of controls being flexible for different preferences of players, the game did not provide such an option. Nevertheless players gave higher scores to these items – Heuristics may not clearly be understood by the players – The wordings of these heuristics did not relate to the fundamental control differences between platforms in terms of usability

(continued)

Table 6.4   (continued)

Heuristic item	Exemplary statement	Main observations
GU11: "The player does not have to memorize things unnecessarily"	– "… for instance now I received the Cherry Bomb plant, yet the info they gave me is only limited to its basic application. I would really prefer to see some kind of detailed information" (PP6)	– Two PC players indicated that they were not able to see the info about the given plants whenever they wanted to and got frustrated about using them – Mobile players experienced the same game design in this manner but they all pointed out that the game was giving them the chance to learn by trial and error – This heuristics is found to be in close relationship with both the heuristic item *GU4* and the ease of use of the mobile platform – Mobile platforms require less cognitive, spatial, or attentional demand
GP4: "Player is in control"	– "Although I knew that I miss-tapped from time to time, I never felt that I lost the control of the game" (PM1)	– Mobile platform offered the capability to manipulate the object on the screen directly by either touching or dragging, reducing the cognitive load while PC platform only allowed the players to interact with a mouse via clicking to the objects – Players on mobile platform had several problems interacting with the game such as tapping on the wrong plants, they indicated that they felt in control throughout the game – This contrast between errors and players feeling of direct control on mobile platform may become more significant compared to the context of usability and cause a higher feeling of control hence more error tolerance

(continued)

Table 6.4 (continued)

Heuristic item	Exemplary statement	Main observations
MO2: "The game accommodates the surroundings"	– "I was not happy with the music of the game, but I was able to lower the volume fairly easy" (PM4)	– Players were able to adjust the volume easily during the play – Several of the players ($n = 3$) were observed to lower the master volume of the device by utilizing the device volume button rather than the in-game options menu – Players considered the heuristic item was referring to device capabilities rather than the game
MO4: "The graphical design is accommodated to current brightness"		– The item has a strong relationship with the *MO2* and *MO3* heuristic items in terms of context – Players indicated that the screen brightness is usually about the device technology – The results suggested that the players did not relate the item with *GU1a* but with the device capabilities
MO6: "Mobile devices have their own conventions for input"		– Players gave higher scores for the item on average – Two players (PM1 and PM10) had difficulty understanding the heuristic and hesitated to answer either positively or negatively – This item is given as a support for *GU7* heuristic item. This association is validated through observations. The players which gave higher scores indicated that the conventions for the mobile platform were obvious and natural

Appendix 2   Results of Design-Dependent Playability Problems

Table 6.5   Results of design-dependent playability problems

GU2: "Screen layout is efficient and visually pleasing"	– "I accidentally pressed the menu button of the device during play and it paused the game and dropped me out from the game. I had this issue before but I just realized it was because of the devices menu button" (PM3)	– Two PC players preferred higher resolution – Mobile players accidentally tapped operating system menu button and dropped out of the game – All of the players ($n = 20$) liked the esthetics of the game
GU3: "Device UI and game UI are used for their own purposes"	– "I was trying to select a plant but instead I accidentally pushed to the Android system menu button on the bottom of the screen by accident. It kicked me out of the game for a second" (PM9)	– PC players clearly understood the difference between Game UI and the UI of the operating system – The accidental drop-outs from the game on mobile platform because of the accidental tap of the menu button of the device
GU5: "The player understands the terminology"	– "The story did not immerse me or gained my attention much since I did not feel necessarily invested in it" (PM10) – "I paused the game during play to see if I was able to read the information about the plants. Unfortunately, the game did not gave me that opportunity" (PM1) – "I would really prefer if they have told the functions of the plants with some kind of animation instead of bulk text, giving minimal detail" (PM5)	– Mobile players skipped the information screens including plant information and story elements – None of the PC players skipped the information screens during the game – Mobile players did not understand some of the functions of the plants in the game – Mobile players wanted to re-check plant information with no success
GU6: "Navigation is consistent, logical and minimalist"	– "The buttons were embedded in the background and were not visible. I had to ask for help to begin the game" (PM3)	– Mobile players found the navigation problematic – Mobile players had severe stagnation in the main menu screen at the beginning of the game – Mobile players could not find the button to start the game immediately – Two mobile players had to ask how to start the game to the supervisor – PC version of the game was different in terms of providing highlighted button effects, making the buttons potentially more distinct than the background image

(contiued)

Table 6.5 (continued)

GP1: "The game provides clear goals or supports player-created goals"	– "I did not know that the Tower Defense games were also made for mobile phones" (PM6)	– The tutorials at the beginning of the game provided sufficient information related to the mechanics yet did not provide information of long-term goals of the game – PC platform players understood the necessary goals and ways to achieve them more clearly than mobile players – The familiarity with the *tower defense* game genre may have an impact regarding this heuristic – Two mobile players (PM6, PM9) indicated that they have never played the game genre on a mobile phone during the game
GP2: "The player sees the progress in the game and can compare results"	– "The high volume level kind of bothered me but I don't want to pause the game and lower it now because I am following the progress bar at the bottom of the screen and know that the level is going to end soon" (PP8) – "I think I won't be able to tell any of my friends on which level I was at if need be because I really don't understand what these level numbers indicate" (PM5)	– On mobile platform, the progress bar is presented on top of the screen while and on PC, it is placed at the bottom of the screen – Mobile players have too many focal points on top of the screen – Progress bar on mobile platform is next to several other game elements such as the menu button while PC progress bar is isolated from other in-game objects, hence more visible
GP5: "Challenge, strategy and pace are in balance"	– "I purposefully tried to lose the game because I was bored of not being challenged. But still I managed to win it without and hassle" (PM3) – "I think the mobile platforms are best for fast-paced games and this game is truly offering the opposite" (PM4) – "I am used to playing faster-paced games on my mobile phone because I usually want to enjoy the game in a short time" (PM6)	– Players from both platforms complained about the pacing of the game and its lack of challenge – Mobile players especially commented on the lack of challenge and slow pace – This heuristic was observed to be a device-dependent item – PC version of the game is perceived to be less cumbersome compared to the mobile platform

(continued)

Table 6.5 (continued)

GP6: "The first-time experience is encouraging"		– This heuristic is related to the onboarding process – A mobile-first approach is suggested to be more beneficial regarding this heuristic – First-time experience for mobile players was problematic because of the start menu problems – This item is associated with *GP1*
GP7: "The game story, if any, supports the gameplay and is meaningful"	– "This would be the same game even if you put elephants for instance, instead of zombies and turrets instead of plants" (PM10)	– All PC players indicated that the story of the game felt fun and enjoyable – A number of mobile players mentioned that they did not understand the story of the game and not found the ambient crucial for the concept of the game ($n = 2$) – Onboarding process differences between platforms are once more observed. The mobile players had difficulty understanding the overall story of the game and purpose of the game characters in terms of context
GP8: "There are no repetitive or boring tasks"	– "I've seen better versions of tower defense genre. This game only offers simple tasks and not enough surprises" (PM7)	– Mobile players mentioned that they were familiar to the tower defense game genre for mobile platform – The game genre is suitable for the mobile platform yet it lacked some of the important game elements such as sufficient variations of game-related tasks
GP11: "The game does not stagnate"	– "Normally I would quit the game if this was not a test environment and I was not curious about the next levels of the game. The pacing is really boring me right now" (PM9)	– PC players felt less stagnation and more progress – The players from both platforms associated this heuristic item to the pacing of the game – Heuristic item may identify with the heuristic item *GP5* – Mobile players complained about the slow pace of the game during play sessions

(continued)

Table 6.5 (continued)

GP12: "The game is consistent"	– "The game informed me by telling that the cherry bomb plant is just like another plant. So I planted it among my defense line yet it exploded immediately! The game did not inform me about this!" (PM5)	– Players from both platforms understood the heuristic item is to evaluate the relation between plant information and functions of the plants – Both groups' made similar mistakes during the game by misinterpreting a function of a plant – Mobile players complained mostly on how the game was not sufficiently explaining the functions of the given plants
GP13: "The game uses orthogonal unit differentiation"	– "I couldn't figure out the function of the 'mine' plant. I tried to use it many times but it didn't do anything. At the end I decided to use it as an emergency zombie blocking plant because it is cheap to purchase" (PM7)	– The players on mobile platform had difficulty in understanding specific functions and strategic implications of some of the plants – This heuristic item could be considered to be in association with the heuristic item *GU5*
MO3: "Interruptions are handled reasonably"	– "This heuristic item is related to the mobile device that I am using now and not the game itself" (PM6)	– Players were observed to accidentally press the device menu button. Afterwards, they get back to the game from where they were interrupted immediately by pressing the same button again. They mentioned that they – This heuristic item should be considered in relation with the *GU3* heuristic item were able to return to the game in a fast manner
MO7: "The tutorial should respond to immediate demand"	– "I did not recognize such a function in the game" (PM4)	– The tutorial was not immediate, yet players understood the heuristic was related to having tutorial levels at the beginning – The item is referred to *GU12* heuristic yet, for instance, PM6 gave the lowest score to this heuristic item while giving the highest score to *GU12* – The proposed link between these heuristics might not be there when applied in practice

Appendix 3   Results of Game-Specific Playability Problems

Table 6.6   Results of game-specific playability problems

GU1b: "A view to the game-world supports smooth interaction and the camera behaves correctly"		– In-game camera is static – The game does not have the necessary property, therefore not applicable
GU9: "The game gives feedback on the player's actions and GU10: "The player cannot make irreversible errors"		– It was identified that these two heuristics out of the context and not applicable for analyzing differences between platforms
GU12: "The game contains help"	– "There was not help function as much as I remember" (PM3)	– The game does not directly provide a help function neither for PC nor mobile platform – The game provides well designed tutorial levels – Nearly all of the players mentioned that they did not need any help function during the game, sometimes referring to lack of challenge of the game – Players were relating this heuristic item to the lack of help functionality during the game yet the heuristic item also explained to include tutorials of games
GP3: "The players are rewarded and the rewards are meaningful"		– No notable difference was observed – Other than the progression related rewards, there was no score indicator. Hence no difference between platforms in the context of this heuristic was expected
GP9: "The players can express themselves" and GP10: "The game supports different playing styles"		– Although the game does not allow players to customize their avatars or personal preferences, PC players mentioned the personalization of different strategies during the play sessions might count as expressions

(continued)

Table 6.6 (continued)

		– These heuristic items does not apply for neither of the versions of the game and is not applicable to evaluate platform differences in terms of player experience – *GP10* did not receive any feedback regarding the difference between platforms since the game did not offer any capability to choose a role and/or style of play in the world. There were also no alternative interaction capabilities implemented in the game
GP14: "The player does not lose any hard-won possessions"		– The game for both platforms have the same mechanics and dynamics and fulfill this heuristic sufficiently
MO1: "The play sessions can be started quickly"		– One player (PM9) was observed to tap on the screen while the game was first opening on the device – Most of the mobile players were referring this heuristic to the device capabilities

References

Aker, Ç., Rızvanoğlu, K. & İnal, Y. (2017). A Multi-Modal Approach for Evaluating Player Experience on Different Gaming Platforms.

Baauw, E., Bekker, M. M., & Barendregt, W. (2005, September). A structured expert evaluation method for the evaluation of children's computer games. In IFIP Conference on Human-Computer Interaction (pp. 457–469). Springer, Berlin, Heidelberg.

Bernhaupt, R., Eckschlager, M., & Tscheligi, M. (2007, June). Methods for evaluating games: how to measure usability and user experience in games?. In Proceedings of the international conference on Advances in computer entertainment technology(pp. 309–310). ACM.

Bernhaupt, R., Ijsselsteijn, W., Mueller, F. F., Tscheligi, M., & Wixon, D. (2008, April). Evaluating user experiences in games. In CHI'08 extended abstracts on Human factors in computing systems (pp. 3905–3908). ACM.

Brooke, J. (1996). SUS-A quick and dirty usability scale. Usability evaluation in industry, 189(194), 4–7.

Carmody, K. W. (2012). Exploring serious game design heuristics: a Delphi study (Doctoral dissertation, Northeastern University).

Csikszentmihalyi, M. (1990). Flow: The psychology of optimal performance. NY: Cambridge University Press, 40.

Desurvire, H., & Wiberg, C. (2015). User Experience Design for Inexperienced Gamers: GAP—Game Approachability Principles. In Game User Experience Evaluation (pp. 169–186). Springer, Cham.

Desurvire, H., Caplan, M., & Toth, J. A. (2004, April). Using heuristics to evaluate the playability of games. In CHI'04 extended abstracts on Human factors in computing systems (pp. 1509–1512). ACM.

Detenber, B. H., & Reeves, B. (1996). A bio-informational theory of emotion: Motion and image size effects on viewers. Journal of Communication, 46(3), 66–84.

Federoff, M. A. (2002). Heuristics and usability guidelines for the creation and evaluation of fun in video games (Doctoral dissertation, Indiana University).

Fritsch, T., Voigt, B., & Schiller, J. (2008). Evaluation of input options on mobile gaming devices.

Garzotto, F. (2007, June). Investigating the educational effectiveness of multiplayer online games for children. In Proceedings of the 6th international conference on Interaction design and children (pp. 29–36). ACM.

Gerling, K. M., Klauser, M., & Niesenhaus, J. (2011, September). Measuring the impact of game controllers on player experience in FPS games. In Proceedings of the 15th International Academic MindTrek Conference: Envisioning Future Media Environments (pp. 83–86). ACM.

Guo, Y. R., & Goh, D. H. L. (2016, December). Heuristic evaluation of an information literacy game. In International Conference on Asian Digital Libraries (pp. 188–199). Springer, Cham.

Hara, M., & Ovaska, S. (2014, October). Heuristics for motion-based control in games. In Proceedings of the 8th Nordic Conference on Human-Computer Interaction: Fun, Fast, Foundational (pp. 697–706). ACM.

Jegers, K. (2008, June). Investigating the applicability of usability and playability heuristics for evaluation of pervasive games. In Internet and Web Applications and Services, 2008. ICIW'08. Third International Conference on (pp. 656–661). IEEE.

Karat, C. M. (1994, June). A comparison of user interface evaluation methods. In Usability inspection methods (pp. 203–233). John Wiley & Sons, Inc..

Kokil, U. and Sanchez, J.L.G. (2015). "Exploring facets of playability: the differences between PC and Tablet gaming". 8th International Conference on Advances in Computer-Human Interactions, pp.108–111, Lisbon, Portugal.

Korhonen, H. (2010, September). Comparison of playtesting and expert review methods in mobile game evaluation. In Proceedings of the 3rd International Conference on Fun and Games (pp. 18–27). ACM.

Korhonen, H. (2016). Evaluating playability of mobile games with the expert review method.

Korhonen, H., & Koivisto, E. M. (2006, September). Playability heuristics for mobile games. In Proceedings of the 8th conference on Human-computer interaction with mobile devices and services (pp. 9–16). ACM.

Korhonen, H., & Koivisto, E. M. (2007, September). Playability heuristics for mobile multi-player games. In Proceedings of the 2nd international conference on Digital interactive media in entertainment and arts (pp. 28–35). ACM.

Lauer, H. C., & Needham, R. M. (1979). On the duality of operating system structures. ACM SIGOPS Operating Systems Review, 13(2), 3–19.

Laux, L. F. (2001). Aging, communication, and interface design. Communication, technology and aging: Opportunities and challenges for the future, 153–168.

Mäyrä, F. (2008). An introduction to game studies. Sage.

Nacke, L., Schild, J., & Niesenhaus, J. (2010). Gameplay experience testing with playability and usability surveys–An experimental pilot study. In Proceedings of the Fun and Games 2010 Workshop, NHTV Expertise Series (Vol. 10).

Nattkemper, D., & Prinz, W. (1990). Local and global control of saccade amplitude and fixation duration in continuous visual search.

Nielsen, J. (1994). Usability engineering. Elsevier.

Nordin, A. I., Denisova, A., & Cairns, P. (2014, October). Too many questionnaires: measuring player experience whilst playing digital games. In Seventh York Doctoral Symposium on Computer Science & Electronics (Vol. 69).

Norman, D. A. (1991). Cognitive artifacts. Designing interaction: Psychology at the human-computer interface, 1, 17–38.

Paavilainen, J. (2010) Critical review on video game evaluation heuristics: social games perspective. In: Proceedings of the International Academic Conference on the Future of Game Design and Technology. ACM, 2010, pp. 56–65.

Papaloukas, S., Patriarcheas, K., & Xenos, M. (2009, September). Usability assessment heuristics in new genre videogames. In Informatics, 2009. PCI'09. 13th Panhellenic Conference on (pp. 202–206). IEEE.

Pinelle, D., Wong, N., & Stach, T. (2008, April). Heuristic evaluation for games: usability principles for video game design. In Proceedings of the SIGCHI Conference on Human Factors in Computing Systems (pp. 1453–1462). ACM.

Poels, K., De Kort, Y., & IJsselsteijn, W. (2012). Identification and categorization of digital game experiences: a qualitative study integrating theoretical insights and player perspectives. Westminster Papers in Communication and Culture.

Raffaele, R., Alencar, R., Júnior, I., Colley, B., Pontes, G., Carvalho, B., & Soares, M. M. (2015). Doctor Who: legacy, an analysis of usability and playability of a multi-platform game. In International Conference of Design, User Experience, and Usability pp. 283–291. Springer, Cham.

Reichheld, F. F. (2003). The one number you need to grow. Harvard business review, 81(12), 46–55.

Reichheld, F. F., & Markey, R. (2011). The ultimate question 2.0: How net promoter companies thrive in a customer-driven world. Harvard Business Press.

Röcker, C., & Haar, M. (2006, May). Exploring the usability of videogame heuristics for pervasive game development in smart home environments. In Proceedings of the third international workshop on pervasive gaming applications—PerGames (pp. 199–206).

Sáenz-de-Urturi, Z., García Zapirain, B., & Méndez Zorrilla, A. (2015). Elderly user experience to improve a Kinect-based game playability. Behaviour & Information Technology, 34(11), 1040–1051.

Sánchez, J. G., Zea, N. P., & Gutiérrez, F. L. (2009, August). Playability: How to identify the player experience in a video game. In IFIP Conference on Human-Computer Interaction (pp. 356–359). Springer, Berlin, Heidelberg.

Schaffer, N. (2007). Heuristics for usability in games-white paper.

Soomro, Sarmad & Wan Ahmad, Wan Fatimah & Sulaiman, Suziah. (2012). A preliminary study on heuristics for mobile games. 2. 1030–1035. https://doi.org/10.1109/ICCISci.2012.6297177.

Soomro, S., Ahmad, W. F. W., & Sulaiman, S. (2013, November). Evaluation of mobile games using playability heuristics. In International Visual Informatics Conference (pp. 264–274). Springer, Cham.

Suhonen, K., & Väätäjä, H. (2010, October). Assessing the applicability of modular playability heuristics for evaluating health-enhancing games. In Proceedings of the 14th International Academic MindTrek Conference: Envisioning Future Media Environments (pp. 147–150). ACM.

Sutcliffe, A., & Hart, J. (2017). Analyzing the role of interactivity in user experience. International Journal of Human–Computer Interaction, 33(3), 229–240.

Sweetser, P., & Wyeth, P. (2005). GameFlow: a model for evaluating player enjoyment in games. Computers in Entertainment (CIE), 3(3), 3–3.

Thomas, C., & Milan, S. (1987). Which Input Device Should Be Used With Interactive Video? In Human–Computer Interaction–Interact'87 pp. 587–592.

Tullis, T., Albert, W., Dumas, J. S., & Loring, B. A. (2008). Measuring the User Experience: Collecting Analyzing, and Presenting Usability.

Wood, E., Willoughby, T., Rushing, A., Bechtel, L., & Gilbert, J. (2005). Use of computer input devices by older adults. Journal of Applied Gerontology, 24(5), 419–438.

Zaman, L., Natapov, D., & Teather, R. J. (2010, May). Touchscreens vs. traditional controllers in handheld gaming. In Proceedings of the International Academic Conference on the Future of Game Design and Technology (pp. 183–190). ACM.

Zhao, C., Zhang, T., & Zhang, K. (2001, October). User interface design for the small screen display. In Proceedings of the Human Factors and Ergonomics Society Annual Meeting (Vol. 45, No. 22, pp. 1548–1550). Sage CA: Los Angeles, CA: SAGE Publications.

Ziefle, M. (2010). Information presentation in small screen devices: The trade-off between visual density and menu foresight. Applied ergonomics, 41(6), 719–730.

Ziefle, M., & Bay, S. (2005). How older adults meet complexity: aging effects on the usability of different mobile phones. Behaviour & Information Technology, 24(5), 375–389.

Chapter 7
Developing Gaming Instinctual Motivation Scale (GIMS): Item Development and Pre-testing

Ai Ni Teoh, Divjyot Kaur, Roberto Dillon, and Dayana Hristova

Contents

A. N. Teoh · D. Kaur
School of Psychology, James Cook University Singapore, Singapore, Singapore
e-mail: aini.teoh@jcu.edu.au; divjyot.kaur@jcu.edu.au

R. Dillon (✉)
School of Business, IT and Science, James Cook University Singapore, Singapore, Singapore
e-mail: roberto.dillon@jcu.edu.au

D. Hristova
Cognitive Science Hub, University of Vienna, Vienna, Austria
e-mail: dayana.hristova@univie.ac.at

© Springer Nature Switzerland AG 2020
B. Bostan (ed.), *Game User Experience And Player-Centered Design*,
International Series on Computer Entertainment and Media Technology,
https://doi.org/10.1007/978-3-030-37643-7_7

Abstract The 6-11 Framework (Dillon R., On the way to fun: An emotion-based approach to successful game design, 2010) explains game playing experience using emotion and motivation. Specifically, game playing experience induces six emotions, including anger, fear, joy/happiness, pride, sadness, and excitement, and 11 core instinctual behavioral responses, including survival, self-identification, collecting, greed, protection/care/nurture, aggressiveness, revenge, competition, communication, exploration/curiosity, and color appreciation. The 6-11 Framework depicts game playing experience in a systematic way, useful for academicians and industry professionals. Nonetheless, it originated from simple empirical observations and lacked a proper means to measure the 11 motivations proposed in the model. Therefore, the first step to testing the model is to construct a questionnaire to quantify the 11 motivations. In this study, we constructed the Gaming Instinctual Motivation Scale and conducted a pilot test with a sample of 20 participants. The data showed that the scale had high internal consistency regardless of the game genres, indicating that the scale items were measuring the same construct even when applied in various game genres. The questionnaire could be used in future studies that intend to apply the components proposed in the 6-11 Framework and to test gaming motivations in general. Also, the questionnaire may be useful for industry professionals in predicting the possible motivations of game play.

Keywords Gaming · Motivation · Reliability · Scale · Validity

7.1 Introduction

Video games present gamers with experiences that involve both emotional and motivational undertones, thus eliciting rich, meaningful experiences for them. The gaming experience has been examined previously by considering the game system as a whole (Takatalo et al. 2010), with components of the game system including the mechanics, the narrative, and the interface. Game *mechanics* refer to the goals, rules, rewards of action, and choices for gamers, while the *narrative* creates the world of the game and thus its storyline. The interface lies closest to the gamers in terms of how their internal system (seeing, hearing, feeling) interacts with the game. This interface creates the true unique experience for each individual gamer, as both the "perception and response" of the gamer influence the gaming experience. In this regard, it becomes important to examine the gaming experience by integrating cognition, emotion, and motivation along with perception and attention from the gamer's perspective. To begin this process of understanding the gaming experience, the present paper examines motivations that lie behind a gamer's experience, by developing a scale that would measure these motivations across different gaming genres.

The gaming experience, often referred to as the "user experience" involves both the individual's perceptions and responses based on the use of a game or gaming system. When a user's experience is examined by integrating cognitions, emotions, and motivations, with perceptual and attentional processes, the user's experience comes to the fore in any given context, and in relation to the individual's prior experiences. In describing their experiences, gamers have previously reported emotional, cognitive, and motivational components while playing video games. Takatalo et al. (2010) bring together the external game components and the internal psychological components to provide an explanation of the multidimensional experience of a gamer, while exploring the interaction between the game system, play and the psychological components involved therein.

The gaming experience has further been examined by the *Presence-Involvement-Flow Framework (PIFF)* wherein concepts of presence (perception of and attention to gaming world involving both spatial and social cognitions), involvement (a measure of gamer motivation), and flow (the subjective, cognitive-emotional evaluation of the game) are studied. Lombard and Ditton (1997) describe "presence" as having three components of attention (psychological immersion), perceptual realness (naturalness), and spatial awareness (engagement).

In understanding the gaming experience, Freeman (2004) identified 32 categories of rules and techniques that could be used to evoke different emotions in games, and thus help to immerse a player in the game's world, while Schell (2008) proposed a set of one hundred Lenses to analyze and design games. These lenses present a "set of questions" from varied fields of study that would likely help game designers gain insights into the gamers experience, that would ultimately motivate and engage a gamer to remain immersed in the game.

In a similar vein, other researchers have taken a psychological perspective. For instance, the "Four Fun Keys" framework by Lazzaro (2009) views the player experience through the "fun" lens, focusing on the different types of fun associated with the varied emotions that are evoked during play. Hard Fun is associated with both *pride* (taking pride in achieving one's goal or tackling a challenge effectively) and *frustration* (when the player faces repeated failure). Easy Fun is experienced with *curiosity* as a player explores possibilities and opportunities in the game, while Serious Fun is linked to a sense of *relaxation* and *excitement*. Finally, People Fun is related to *delight* associated with interaction with other players.

Elaborating on this emotion-based approach to game design, Dillon (2010) proposed that engagement in games results from the fact that they rely on basic human instincts and emotions. This paper elaborates on this framework called the 6-11 Framework and works towards the development of an assessment tool to establish the link between emotions and the gaming experience.

7.2 The 6-11 Framework

The 6-11 Framework (Dillon 2010) describes gaming experience in terms of emotions and instinctual motivations. It suggests that playing games induces mainly six emotions, including anger, fear, joy/happiness, pride, sadness, and excitement, and 11 core gaming instinctual motivations, which include survival (fight-or-flight), self-identification, collection, greed, protection/care/nurture, aggressiveness, revenge, competition, communication, exploration/curiosity, and color appreciation.

The focus on emotions and motivations in the 6-11 Framework (Dillon 2010) was based on research findings that consistently link both variables to arousal, such as increase in the sympathetic nervous system, a response that is commonly observed in gaming. Emotions are subjective feelings, appraisals, and action tendencies that include physiological responses (Scherer 2005). Motivation, on the other hand, refers to being moved or activated to do something (Ryan and Deci 2000). When feeling aroused due to emotions and/or motivation, the body activates the sympathetic nervous system to energize the body. The sympathetic nervous system dilates the pupils, decreases salivation, increases sweating, accelerates heart rate by producing more blood flow to the heart and skeletal muscles, and decreases digestive functions by restricting blood flow to the digestive organs.

With its emotionally and motivationally arousing nature, playing video games have always been found to heighten physiological arousal. Playing action and violent video games increases heart rate, blood pressure, respiratory rate, oxygen consumption, and energy expenditure (Anderson 2004; Wang and Perry 2006). The built-in music alone may contribute to the increase in cortisol level, a hormone that when high in concentration was associated with the experience of stress (Hébert et al. 2005).

The 6-11 Framework (Dillon 2010), when put at the micro level, may explain game players' experience. For instance, a game character that is dressed in lavish clothing and wearing a crown may induce game players' identification with the character of a prince. With the identification formed, emotions, such as pride, may be induced. When his status is challenged in the game, emotion, such as anger, and motivation, such as revenge, will be triggered. When the game player successfully revenge to keep his status, he will experience a sense of joy and pride. The 6-11 Framework may also be applied at the macro level by providing insights into game design (Dillon 2016). Understanding gaming-related emotions and motivations allows us to design characters, environment, and storylines that could trigger appropriate emotions and motivations to enhance game playing experience. Take Seven Cities of Gold (Bunten 1984) and Little Computer People (Crane and Nelson 1985) as examples. Because of the inherent difference in the levels of complexity and competitiveness of the games, these games lead to different game playing experiences, and these could be explained using the 6-11 Framework.

Seven Cities of Gold was a groundbreaking game designed by Bunten in Bunten (1984). Using the 6-11 Framework, we are able to analyze the factors that explain the success of the game (see Dillon 2010). This game is set in medieval, where the protagonist, a conquistador, was tasked to explore the New World. The main aim of the game is to collect as much treasure as possible for promotions decreed by the Queen of Spain. The game induces curiosity and excitement for exploring and traveling and aggressiveness to conquer. To fulfill the aim, game players are motivated with instinctual motivations like collection and greed. Making choices between trading peaceably and trading aggressively with the local populations are higher order feature of the game that require moral decisions. Such higher order feature may trigger several motivations simultaneously, such as to identify, compete, protect, and communicate, making the game playing experience more interesting.

Little Computer People was designed by Crane and Nelson (1985). This is a life-simulation game depicting a little guy living in a house with his dog. The main aim of the game is to provide pastoral care to the little guy without receiving any reward in return. To achieve the aim, the game was designed to motivate players to communicate and provide protection/care (see Dillon 2010). Therefore, game players are required to keep the little guy fit, improve his musical skills, offer presents, etc. Games of this nature should induce feelings of pride and joy by helping the little guy.

The 6-11 Framework (Dillon 2010) depicts game playing experience in a systematic way, an approach which is useful for academicians and industry professionals. Therefore, it has been widely used in practice both by industry professionals and academics to gain insights across entertainment and serious games alike (see, for example, Göbel 2016; Kerlow et al. 2012; Marins 2011).

Nonetheless, the 6-11 Framework (Dillon 2010) originated from simple empirical observations and lacked proper means to measure the 11 core motivations proposed in the model. To strengthen the applicability of the 6-11 Framework, more empirical evidence is needed. The first step to testing the model is to quantify emotions and gaming motivation. While there have been validated questionnaires to measure (non-gaming-specific) emotional experience, such as Positive and Negative Affect Schedule—Expanded Form (Watson and Clark 1994), questionnaires to measure the gaming motivation proposed in the 6-11 Framework are still lacking.

There have been validated questionnaires to measure gaming motivation, for instance, the Gaming Motivation Scale (Lafreniere et al. 2012). However, the questionnaire is based on the self-determination theory (Deci and Ryan 1985) and hence focuses on general psychological needs related to gaming. On the other hand, the 11 gaming motivations proposed in the 6-11 Framework (Dillon 2010) focus on gaming-experience-specific psychological needs. The aim of the present study, therefore, is to construct a questionnaire to quantify and assess the 11 gaming motivations. Below, we discuss the literature that explains each of the 11 instinctual motivations.

7.3 The 11 Instinctual Motivations

Survival (Fight/Run) Fight-or-flight response was first described by Cannon (1932) as sympathetic nervous system responses to stress. The term was later used to describe behavioral responses to stress which involve fighting or fleeing from a stressful, threatening situation (Taylor et al. 2000). The perception of the stressfulness of situations depends on how relevant the stressor is to our well-being and how well we are able to cope with it (Lazarus and Folkman 1986). Video games always create situations where players will have to decide whether to fight or escape.

For instance, Overkill's The Walking Dead is a survival horror game that requires players to work cooperatively to complete their tasks and to survive in a city that is flooded by zombies. In order to survive, the players sometimes need to escape from a large flock of zombies coming after them and sometimes to kill the zombies for safety.

Identification Players identify with the avatars in video games. This player-avatar identification can be assessed in four dimensions (Li et al. 2013). The first dimension refers to empathy or shared feeling of the character, in which players experience various emotional feelings in response to avatars' experiences. The second dimension is absorption which refers to players cognitively sharing the perspectives of the characters. Players also form positive attitudes toward the character, where they evaluate the character in positive ways. And lastly players recognize the importance of the avatar to their self-concept in real-life. Some video games, such as massively multiplayer online role-playing games, allow players to create their own characters. When creating their own characters, players are more likely to create one that is more similar to their ideal self than the actual self and form psychological connectedness to the character (Bessière et al. 2007).

Collection Video games usually offer treasures to players based on their performance. The treasures could help players to unlock the next level with extra resources. Despite exists only virtually, treasures could serve as incentives to reinforce the behavior of collection in video games. There are several reasons why people collect. First, the motivation of collection relates to our hunting instinct (Dillon 2014; Formanek 2012). Hunters locate, attack, and acquire a prey, which serves as a trophy and a symbol of one's prowess (Formanek 2012). Similarly, players set goals of winning treasures, plan accordingly, win the treasures, and feel elated. Second, the motivation of collection is related to the building of a sense of self because possessions are an extended form of self (James 1892). On a related note, collection may also fulfill self-enhancing motives, such as seeking power, and fulfill fantasies about the self (Belk 2012). Therefore, possessing treasures in video games may help players form a stronger sense of ideal, virtual identity and a stronger identification with the identity. Third, people are addicted to collecting because they are obsessed by the feeling of excitement associated with the items they collect (Formanek 2012). The addiction to collecting will be discussed in detail in the next subsection.

Greed Greed is an extended, extreme form of the motivation of collection. It involves psychological dissatisfaction with the current state, which is always not being able to be satisfied. Uncertain situations and situations where the stakes are high may induce greediness (Seuntjens 2016). Video games do create uncertain situations where the challenge in the next level is always unknown. Video games also create competitions between players and a virtual or real opponent that may put players' stakes at risk. Such contexts may induce greediness in players. In response to psychological dissatisfaction, greedy people acquire as much resource as possible or keep as much they already have as possible (Seuntjens 2016). Greed may involve visible resources such as money and goods and invisible resources such as power. The behaviors of greed may include looking for self-interest, maximizing benefits from opportunities, and being materialistic (Seuntjens et al. 2015). In the context of video games, the behavioral manifestation of greed refers to collecting more than what players need just to fulfill their desire or keeping the treasures they already have.

Protection/Care Players demonstrate the motivation to protect and care for the needy during game play. This motivation is considered the "best" positive motivation of all the motivations proposed in the 6-11 Framework (Dillon 2010). Little Computer People is a game that triggers and fulfills players' motivation to protect and care. In this game, players are to provide pastoral care to the little guy in the computer by providing help and nurturing growth. People tend to identify with heroism, or acts of bravery, self-sacrifice, willingness to save, and selflessness (Kinsella et al. 2015b). They also see heroes as those who enhance others' lives, promote morality, and protect others from threats (Kinsella et al. 2015a). Performing the acts of protecting or caring for others volitionally increases the sense of competence and autonomy (Weinstein and Ryan 2010).

Aggressiveness Aggressiveness is always needed in video games to fulfill the needs of greediness and survival (Dillon 2010). For instance, Dracula (Smith 1983) on the Intellivision system is a video game that induces aggressiveness in players. Released in 1983, this video game was based on a well-known character from a well-known folklore. In the game, players play the role of Dracula with goals of feeding on victims and avoiding constables and other enemies by fighting them or fleeing after transforming into a bat. Players should also pay attention to the sky colors and go back to their "bedroom" before dawn. Feeding on victims to satisfy thirst is a typical example of aggressiveness in video games (Dillon 2010). Another example is the already mentioned Seven Cities of Gold where the protagonist deals with the native people either peacefully or aggressively. Aggressive interaction with the native people may include conquering the people or killing the people when they attack the protagonist.

Revenge Revenge is often triggered during video game playing, especially in action games or games involving some form of conflict. Players revenge mainly because of failures in achieving goals and social injustice that causes damage on players (Dillon 2010). Revenge may serve the purposes of restoring social justice and deterring future harm, with the former weighs more heavily than the latter (Osgood 2017). Therefore, revenge could be an adaptive psychological mechanism (Osgood 2017). How vengeful characters are received among players is subject to cultural differences. For instance, Taiwanese students do not find vengeful characters to be favorable, but US students only find vengeful villains to be aversive (Calvert et al. 2004). This is probably due to cultural and political background in the USA, where heroes in movies always go unpunished for killing for revenge and the US government responded to 911 terror attack with revenge (Calvert et al. 2004).

Competition Video games generally create competitive situations whereby players compete within the game and within their gamer communities. The opposite of competition is cooperation. In some video games, such as massively multiplayer online games, players need to cooperate or compete for own or group's gains. Cooperation is usually rendered intuitively and spontaneously (Rand et al. 2012) and is usually triggered in situations of low fear and low greed (Bruins et al. 1989). Competition, on the other hand, is usually triggered in situations that induce greediness or fear (Bruins et al. 1989), with greed having a stronger effect than fear (Simmons et al. 1984). Cooperation and competition always go hand in hand. In intergroup competitions, people compete with members of another group but cooperate within their own group. Similarly, in video games, players sometimes compete as an individual with another individual player or compete as a group with another group of players and cooperate with in-group members. Men are more likely to be engaged in intergroup competition and demonstrate altruistic contributions to their groups as compared with women (van Vugt et al. 2007).

Communication In certain genres of video games, players are motivated to communicate with other human players or non-player characters (virtual characters that are controlled by the game's artificial intelligence). Communications could be mediated by synchronous virtual space by sending text-based messages. Interaction Process Analysis (Bales 1950) categorizes the content of communications into socioemotional and task communication. The formal may carry positive socioemotional messages to show solidarity and indicate understanding, and negative socioemotional messages to express disagreement and hostility. Task communication, on the other hand, focuses on asking for and providing opinions, suggestions, and information. Using this categorization, Peña and Hancock (2006) reported that game players conveyed task messages which usually involved providing suggestions and asking and providing information. They also reported that players tended to send more positive socioemotional messages than the negative ones.

Players generally form friendships with online actual or virtual players and rate those friendships to be of equal quality as offline friendships (Cole and Griffiths 2007; Peña and Hancock 2006). These online friendships may extend to offline friendships, which is social meet-up with online friends (Cole and Griffiths 2007).

Curiosity Curiosity is related to exploration. It is one of the most important motivations that influence our behaviors. In his review paper depicting the definitions and motives for curiosity, Loewenstein (1994) explained that curiosity is voluntary, intrinsically motivated, and situationally determined. People are curious because they have a need to make sense of the world, they are intrigued by violated expectations, they need to resolve uncertainty, and they would like to gain control over situations. Because gamers play the same video games multiple times, inducing the motivation of curiosity could be difficult. In overcoming this issue, video games change the sequence of events depending on players' interactions, and games require players to remember disclosed information for a second game (Grodal 2000). Video games also need to create novel, unpredictable, varied scenarios to increase curiosity (Hsu et al. 2005). Video game designers can also trigger the motivation of curiosity by triggering first the motivations of collecting, greed, and identification (Dillon 2010).

Color Appreciation Scenes in video games attract players' attention. While the types of graphics (abstract or photorealistic) are important, the artistic use of colors plays a more critical role in making the graphics attractive (Dillon 2014). The graphics of video games are rarely studied in the context of psychology. In related research, Hsu et al. (2005) identified factors that attract buyers (rather than game players) to purchase action games. One of these factors pointed at visual presentation which includes novel scenarios and vivid visual presentation that should be colorful and look real. In psychological research, color has always been associated with our behaviors. For instance, red, as a color intensively researched in the area of psychology of color, is associated with dominance and aggression. Opponents wearing red are seen as more intimidating and aggressive. Green and blue colors, on the other hand, are associated with peace and success. Black may carry negative connotations, whereas white carries positive connotations (see Elliot and Maier 2014 for a review). Video games that carefully design the scenes and background with appropriate colors may affect the behaviors of players.

7.4 Research Aims

In the present study, we conducted a literature review on related topics and referred to the 6-11 Framework (Dillon 2010). Based on these, we constructed the Gaming Instinctual Motivation Scale (GIMS). Subsequently, we conducted a pilot test with a sample of 20 participants to test for the face validity and internal consistency, to identify any potential problems, and to refine the items. The refined items and questionnaire will later be further validated using a larger sample in a separate study.

The 6-11 Framework (Dillon 2010) originated from simple empirical observations and lacked a proper means to measure the 11 core motivations proposed in the model. To strengthen the applicability of the 6-11 Framework, more empirical evidence is needed. The first step to testing the model is to quantify emotions and gaming motivation. While there has been validated questionnaires to measure (non-gaming-specific) emotional experience, such as Positive and Negative Affect Schedule—Expanded Form (Watson and Clark 1994), questionnaires to measure gaming motivation are still lacking.

7.5 Methods

7.5.1 Participants and Design

This was a correlational study that adopted an online survey approach of data collection. We invited adults who are above the age of 18 and regular gamers to participate in the study. In total, we recruited 20 participants aged between 18 and 46 ($M = 29.55$, SD $= 6.77$). Of these participants, 12 were men and 8 were women. Half of the participants spent less than 13 h playing video games per week, and the other half spent more than 13 h. The most popular genres of games among our participants were Role-Playing Games (RPG), First Person Shooters (FPS), Real-Time strategy (RTS), Puzzle, and Action games. The least popular genres were interactive fiction and sport games. See Table 7.1 for the demographic characteristics of the sample and the means and standard deviations of age by the categories of each demographic variable.

7.5.2 Measures

Gaming Instinctual Motivation Scale (GIMS) This is a self-constructed scale with 31 items. The items were derived from the 11 motivations proposed by Dillon (2010), with items constructed for each instinctual motivation. The constructed scale has 11 subscales altogether, each subscale has between 1 and 4 items (see Table 7.2 for the subscales and items). The 11 subscales correspond with the 11 instinctual motivations. Participants were to rate the items on a five-point Likert scale from 1 (*never*) to 5 (*always*).

The scale first required participants to indicate if they play a particular genre of games (e.g., puzzle games) regularly. If participants indicated "no," they would skip to the next genre. If they indicated "yes," they completed the remaining 30 items of GIMS. Next, the scale repeated and asked participants to indicate if they play another genre of games (e.g., action/adventure games) and to complete the GIMS if they indicate "yes." The cycle continued for the remaining genres. There were a total of 17 genres (see Table 7.1 for the genres).

7.5.3 Procedure

Upon ethics approval, we set up an online survey via SoSci Survey. We then distributed the link of the online survey to students of James Cook University Singapore. The email contained the information sheet of the study, the link of the online survey, and the contact details of the PI. Students who were interested in participating clicked the link that directed them to the online survey. In addition

Table 7.1 Demographic characteristics of the sample, means and standard deviations of age, and Cronbach's alphas of the GIMS scale in different genres of games

Variables	Category		n	M_{age}	SD_{age}	Cronbach's alpha
Gender	Men		12	29.08	7.18	
	Women		8	30.25	6.52	
Number of hours playing	0–1 h		3	34.67	7.02	
	1–3 h		6	31.17	7.70	
	3–7 h		1	29.00		
	7–13 h		4	29.50	6.86	
	13–21 h		1	31.00		
	21–30 h		5	24.40	5.13	
Game genres	RPGs	Yes	18	28.94	6.45	0.94
		No	2	35.00	9.90	
	FPS	Yes	16	28.63	6.61	0.88
		No	4	33.25	6.99	
	RTS	Yes	14	29.79	6.77	0.92
		No	6	29.00	7.38	
	Puzzle	Yes	15	30.67	6.96	0.80
		No	5	26.20	5.45	
	Casual	Yes	11	30.27	8.28	0.96
		No	9	28.67	4.64	
	Music	Yes	8	30.63	7.95	0.95
		No	12	28.83	6.13	
	Action	Yes	15	29.00	6.47	0.91
		No	5	31.20	8.17	
	Strategy	Yes	9	30.11	7.90	0.92
		No	11	29.09	6.06	
	Survival	Yes	10	27.30	7.90	0.85
		No	10	31.80	4.80	
	MOBA	Yes	7	29.00	4.62	0.92
		No	13	29.85	7.85	
	Fiction	Yes	5	30.40	10.43	0.80
		No	15	29.27	5.55	
	Simulation	Yes	6	26.33	4.76	0.96
		No	14	30.93	7.17	
	Virtual world	Yes	10	31.10	5.92	0.88
		No	10	28.00	7.51	
	Sport	Yes	4	31.00	10.30	0.77
		No	16	29.19	6.01	
	Fighting	Yes	11	29.91	3.88	0.87
		No	9	29.11	9.47	
	Racing	Yes	13	27.23	5.04	0.94
		No	7	33.86	7.82	
	Indie/retro	Yes	10	31.00	7.06	0.92
		No	10	28.10	6.51	

RPG role-playing games, *FPS* first person shooters, *RTS* real-time strategy, *MOBA* multiplayer online battle arena

Table 7.2 Subscale and items of the gaming instinctual motivation scale

Subscales	Items
Survival	Fight unspeakable horrors
	Escape deadly dangers
Self-identification	Live the life of a hero
	Catch a thief/killer
	Complete a journey
	Increasing skills/abilities
Collecting	Searching for and completing a set of related items
	Find hidden objects
	Buying or selling items
Greed	Acquiring power/riches
	Harvest/grab/pick up as many resources as possible
Protection/care	Rescue person in danger
	Saving the world
	Escorting a friend/companion through a dangerous area
	Nurturing a puppy
Aggressiveness	Killing enemies
	Be a thief or a killer
	Conquering a territory
Revenge	Punish someone for something, i.e., take revenge
Competition	Conquering the world
	Defeating another player in a direct confrontation
Communication	Establishing a relationship (romantic or friendly) with in-game characters
	Sharing experiences
	Retrieving information by listening/talking to other characters
Curiosity	Unfolding a mystery
	Experiment by combining different items together (e.g., for crafting items)
	Exploring unknown worlds
	Deciphering a secret code
Color appreciation	Admiring the sights of an in-game scene (e.g., sunset, ocean)
	Fascination/engagement with color and design of in-game items

to sending emails to students, the online survey was made public, giving access to other potential participants.

The online survey first showed an information sheet about the study, followed by the informed consent. Informed consent was considered given once participants have read the information sheet and informed consent of the study online, and checked the statement "Hereby, I confirm that I have been informed about this research and that I consent to complete the following questionnaire." Following this, they were directed to the next page where they were prompted to indicate their age, gender, and number of hours playing video games per week. Next, they were presented with the GIMS scale. The whole survey took about 15–30 min to complete, depending on the number of genres participants played regularly.

7.5.4 Proposed Data Analysis Strategies

Since this was a pilot study to refine the items of a self-constructed questionnaire, only simple statistical data analyses were performed, such as Cronbach's alpha. The research team met and discussed about the refinement of questionnaire items.

7.6 Results

7.6.1 Data Cleaning

We first checked the raw data for any unusually high or low scores and found none. Some participants chose "No" to indicate that they did not play certain game genres and hence the GIMS items were left unfilled. There were only one to two participants who chose "Yes" to indicate that they played certain game genres but left the GIMS items unfilled.

7.6.2 Validity and Reliability

Two ardent game players were asked to give feedback regarding the questionnaire, with respect to the validity of the item content. They were asked to rate the items of the questionnaire on a scale of 0–5 (0—not at all and 5—very much), in terms of (1) the extent to which the measure reflects what it is intended to measure and (2) the degree to which the measure's items represent the theoretical content domain of gaming motivation. Both players gave high scores (average 4.5) for the two face validity scores.

We performed reliability tests to examine the internal consistency of the scale. Internal consistency may shed some light on whether or not the scale items are measuring the same construct. We used Cronbach's alpha values to index internal consistency, using IBM SPSS Statistics (version 25). Higher values of Cronbach's alpha values indicated greater internal consistency, or in other words, the items are measuring the same construct. Because participants completed GIMS scale each time when they indicated playing a game genre, we were able to examine the internal consistency of the scale for each game genre. The Cronbach's alphas of GIMS scale for each genre are listed in Table 7.1. In general, GIMS scale had high internal consistency when it was applied to the 17 game genres listed in the present study, with Cronbach's alpha values ranging from 0.77 to 0.96. In other words, GIMS scale could be reliably applied in various game genres.

Table 7.3 The means and standard deviations of motivations in each game genre

	RPG		FPS		RTS		Puzzle		Action	
Game genre	M	SD	M	SD	M	SD	M	SD	M	SD
Survival	3.97[a]	1.10	3.64[a]	1.17	2.71[bc]	1.36	1.15[c]	0.55	4.29[ab]	0.80
Self-identification	4.19[a]	0.74	3.39[a]	0.83	2.92[c]	0.75	1.83[c]	0.71	4.38[ab]	0.47
Collecting	4.26[a]	0.76	2.55[b]	0.73	2.61[b]	1.10	2.51[b]	1.05	4.07[ab]	0.87
Greed	4.11[a]	0.88	2.61[ab]	1.02	4.46[a]	0.66	1.73[b]	0.81	3.89[a]	0.86
Protection/care	3.33[ab]	0.68	3.05[b]	0.61	2.56[b]	1.10	1.17[bc]	0.30	3.46[a]	0.64
Aggressiveness	3.44[a]	0.78	4.17[a]	0.52	3.70[a]	0.22	1.31[b]	0.57	3.76[a]	0.81
Revenge	3.06[ab]	1.11	3.36[ab]	1.34	3.08[b]	1.24	1.00[bc]	0.00	3.79[a]	1.19
Competition	2.72[ab]	1.00	3.57[a]	0.76	4.08[a]	0.93	1.65[b]	0.69	3.11[ab]	1.23
Communication	3.56[a]	0.78	2.64[b]	1.05	2.47[b]	1.10	1.72[b]	0.57	3.69[ab]	0.96
Curiosity	4.04[ab]	0.68	2.45[bc]	0.99	2.77[c]	1.26	2.79[bc]	1.04	4.18[a]	0.60
Color appreciation	4.19[ab]	0.97	3.14[bc]	1.55	3.38[c]	1.09	2.38[c]	1.21	4.68[a]	0.37

Means on the same row with different superscripts differed significantly from each other
RPG role-playing games, *FPS* first person shooters, *RTS* real-time strategy

7.6.3 *Differences in Instinctual Motivation by Game Genres*

Since RPG, FPS, RTS, puzzle, and action games were the most popular games among participants, we performed several repeated measures ANOVAs to examine how instinctual motivation differed by game genres. Table 7.3 summarizes the means and standard deviations of motivation by game genres. RPG and action games were in general associated with various gaming motivations. FPS games were more likely to trigger survival, self-identification, greed, aggressiveness, revenge, and competition. RTS games were associated with greed, aggressiveness, and competition. Puzzle games, relative to other games, were not distinctly associated with any motivation. However, as compared to other motivations, puzzle games were associated with collecting and curiosity.

7.7 Discussion

7.7.1 *Key Findings*

The present study served as a pilot study to examine the face validity and internal consistency of the GIMS scale. With 20 participants, we found that the scale had high internal consistency regardless of the game genres, indicating that the scale items were measuring the same construct even when applied in various game genres.

7.7.2 Gaming Instinctual Motivations

Various studies have attempted to list out motivations associated with gaming. However, the perspective and approaches used were different. For instance, the self-determination theory (Deci and Ryan 1985), an originally psychological theory, was applied to explain gaming motivation. Olson's (2010) empirical research that aimed to describe children's gaming motivation took a data-driven approach. Olson's focus was also placed in the psychosocial perspective. On the other hand, the 6-11 Framework (Dillon 2010) took a gamers' experience perspective in describing gaming motivation. Although different perspectives and approaches were used, the content of these models is comparable with each other.

The self-determination theory (Deci and Ryan 1985) explained three innate psychological needs that serve as sources of motivation. The innate psychological needs are needs for autonomy, competence, and relatedness. The three psychological needs could be satisfied through various activities, including playing video games. Human beings generally have the need for autonomy to feel having choices or freedom when doing a task. Video games offer opportunities to make choices from options and make decisions based on the situation, satisfying the need for autonomy (Ryan et al. 2006). The need for competence is also needed to give human opportunities to apply skills or abilities acquired. When the needs for autonomy and competence were satisfied, players usually reported the enjoyment, value, and desire for future play (Przybylski et al. 2009). The need for relatedness refers to feeling connected by caring and being cared by others. In certain game genres, such as multiplayer environments, players work cooperatively to achieve shared goals by helping each other. This may satisfy the need for relatedness and bring enjoyment to players and motivate them to play the same game in the future (Ryan et al. 2006).

The gaming instinctual motivations proposed in the 6-11 Framework (Dillon 2010) correspond to the three innate psychological needs proposed by Deci and Ryan (1985). In particular, survival, collecting, greed, aggressiveness, revenge, and competition seem to correspond to the need for competence. In the present study, collecting, greed, and survival were noted to be motivations behind games of the RPG and action genre, with scores in these being significantly higher than other genres. Survival, collecting, greed, and curiosity are related to the need for autonomy, and in our samples of gamers, all these were found to be high for RPG and action games. Finally, self-identification, protection, and communication are good examples of the need for relatedness. While self-identification and protection emerged as strong motivations for RPG and action games, protection and communication were noted to be the underlying motivations across all genres examined in detail. Thus, we note that RPG and action genre games appear to tap on all three primary needs identified by Deci and Ryan (1985), with most of these motivations covered in the 6-11 Framework proposed by Dillon.

Furthermore, other game genres were strongly associated with specific motivations which serve to satisfy the need for competence. FPS was noted to score the highest on aggressiveness, satisfying the need for competence in particular.

This confirms the intuitive idea that a game played in first person where the main objective is to shoot at other players or characters should indeed rely on such behavior or psychological need. On the other hand, RTS had the highest scores for greed and competition, also satisfying the need for competence, and low scores on survival and self-identification. Since this genre usually involves a constant harvest of resources and is more about controlling group of units than a single individual character in a conflict between two or more factions, this result also makes perfect sense. Finally, greed and aggressiveness (both referring to the need for competence) appear to underlie all gaming genres examined except for puzzles, which are, generally speaking, more abstract in design and do not involve a direct conflict between players. Understanding the specific motivations underlying these different genres gives us a unique gamer's perspective which can be very useful information for game developers.

A previous study by Olson (2010) examined children's motivation of gaming and summarized four main motivations which include social motivation, emotional motivation, intellectual and expressive motivation, and appeal of violent and mature content, thus focusing on cognitive and psychosocial motivations. The 6-11 Framework (Dillon 2010) has examined motivations from the perspective of gaming activities. Despite the different angles, these two models do share some similarities. The motivations of survival, self-identification, collecting, greed, and curiosity coincide with Olson's intellectual and expressive motivation. Protection, aggressiveness, and revenge share some commonalities with Olson's emotional motivation. Competition and communication are closely related to Olson's social motivation. Color appreciation and Olson's appeal of content overlap in terms of perceived attractiveness of the content of video games. Thus the present study has extended the understanding of motivations behind gaming experience from that of young children to young adults. It is for future researchers to examine the 6-11 Framework of motivations in relation to young children and confirm its relevance for that age group.

7.7.3   Practical Implications

The proposed scale clearly shows how different motivations are of paramount importance in engaging players, with similarities across genres underlined by the findings in Table 7.1. Making this relationship explicit is important from an industry perspective since it will inform professional game designers of some important pillars around which they may decide to base their game design concepts and make them grow organically to support the desired experience they aim at for their players. For example, players fond of RPGs want to play such genre because they feel motivated by wearing the shoes of a specific character within the game world. They wish to be someone who, starting from humble beginnings, has a chance of becoming a force to be reckoned with, able to change the destiny of the gaming world itself.

With this abstract high aim in mind, the design process needs to start shaping the game experience in a way that matches these expectations to motivate players accordingly. Requesting players to engage in activities that create a bond between the player character and other characters (e.g., dialogs, side quests, etc.) are then a logical choice and were indeed underlined by the results in the survey.

From a learning and teaching perspective relevant to the design of serious games, these findings are also interesting. We see how motivations related to curiosity tend to score very high across a variety of genres, for instance. Since serious games need to find ways to provide inner motivation for users to engage in different activities and use the resulting fun to overcome the friction of learning, designers may make an informed use of these findings to decide for a specific genre to build their concept on. On the other hand, if the genre has already been established, they may decide to focus on the most effective motivations that match the specific genre and built the teaching contents around those.

Overall, the proposed scale seems effective in pointing out a few clear strategies that gamers effectively use, and that players have grown to expect, to build emotional engagement and motivation in a natural and subconscious way.

7.7.4 Limitation and Future Studies

The present study serves as a pilot study to explore the face validity and internal consistency of the self-constructed GIMS scale, which is based on the 6-11 Framework (Dillon 2010). We gathered a sample size of 20 participants and found favorable findings from the study. However, we should take caution in interpreting the findings due to several reasons.

First, because of the small sample size, the internal consistency findings might not be generalizable to a wider population. The small sample size also leads to the second issue, which is a lack of statistical power to test the structure of the scale. The present study was only the first step to validating a self-constructed scale by focusing only on the face validity and internal consistency. The structure and construct validity of the scale need further evaluation in future research with a larger sample size. Therefore, although Table 7.2 listed the subscales and their respective items, there is no way we could use the existing small sample size to provide empirical evidence for it. In other words, we cannot be sure that certain items should be grouped under a certain subscale. Our second step to validating the scale will be to collect a bigger sample in a separate study to test the construct validity and the structure of the scale.

References

Anderson, C. A. (2004). An update on the effects of playing violent video games. *Journal of Adolescence, 27*, 113-122. doi: https://doi.org/10.1016/j.adolescence.2003.10.009

Bales, R. F. (1950). *Interaction process analysis: A method for the study of small groups.* Cambridge, MA: Addison-Wesley

Belk, R. W. (2012). Collectors and collecting. In S. M. Pearce (Ed.), *Interpreting Objects and Collections* (pp. 327-335). London and New York: Routledge.

Bessière, K., Seay, A. F., & Kiesler, S. (2007). The ideal elf: Identity exploration in World of Warcraft. *Cyberpsychology & Behavior, 10*, 530-535. doi: https://doi.org/10.1089/cpb.2007.9994

Bruins, J. J., Liebrand, W. B. G., & Wilke, H. A. M. (1989). About the saliency of fear and greed in social dilemmas. *European Journal of Social Psychology, 19*, 155-161. doi: https://doi.org/10.1002/ejsp.2420190207

Calvert, S. L., Murray, K. J., & Conger, E. E. (2004). Heroic DVD portrayals: What US and Taiwanese adolescents admire and understand. *Journal of Applied Developmental Psychology, 25*, 699-716. doi:https://doi.org/10.1016/j.appdev.2004.09.004

Cannon, W. B. (1932). *The Wisdom of the Body.* New York: Norton.

Cole, H., & Griffiths, M. D. (2007). Social interactions in massively multiplayer online role-playing gamers. *Cyberpsychology & Behavior: The Impact of the Internet, Multimedia and Virtual Reality on Behavior and Society, 10*, 575-583. doi:https://doi.org/10.1089/cpb.2007.9988

Deci, E. L., & Ryan, R. M. (1985). Intrinsic motivation and self-determination in human behavior. New York: Plenum.

Dillon, R. (2010). *On the Way to Fun: An Emotion-Based Approach to Successful Game Design.* MA: AK Peters.

Dillon, R. (2014). Towards the definition of a framework and grammar for game analysis and design. *International Journal of Computer and Information Technology, 3*, pp. 188-193.

Dillon, R. (2016). Videogames and Art: Comparing emotional feedback from digital and classic masterpieces. *IOSR Journal of Humanities and Social Sciences, 21*, pp. 79-85.

Elliot, A. J., & Maier, M. A. (2014). Color psychology: Effects of perceiving color on psychological functioning in humans. *Annual Review of Psychology, 65*, 95-120. doi:https://doi.org/10.1146/annurev-psych-010213-115035

Formanek, R. (2012). Why they collect: Collectors reveal their motivations. In S. M. Pearce (Ed.), *Interpreting Objects and Collections* (pp. 327-335). London and New York: Routledge.

Freeman, D. (2004). *Creating Emotions in Games: The Craft and Art of Emotioneering.* CA: New Riders Publishing.

Göbel, S. (2016). Serious Games Application Examples. In R. Dörner, S. Göbel, W. Effelsberg & J. Wiemeyer (Eds.), *Serious Games.* Springer, Cham.

Grodal, T. (2000). Video games and the pleasures of control. In Z. Dolf & P. Vorderer (Eds.), *Media Entertainment: The Psychology of its Appeal* (pp. 197-213). Mahwah, NJ, US: Lawrence Erlbaum Associates Publishers.

Hébert, S., Béland, R., Dionne-Fournelle, O., Crête, M., & Lupien, S. J. (2005). Physiological stress response to video-game playing: The contribution of built-in music. *Life Sciences, 76*, 2371-2380. Doi: https://doi.org/10.1016/j.lfs.2004.11.011

Hsu, S. H., Lee, F.-L., & Wu, M.-C. (2005). Designing action games for appealing to buyers. *CyberPsychology & Behavior, 8*, 585-591. doi:https://doi.org/10.1089/cpb.2005.8.585

James, W. (1892). *Psychology, Briefer Course,* New York: Holt.

Kerlow, I., Khadafi, M., Zhuang, H., Zhuang, H., Azlin, A., & Suhaimi, A. (2012). Earth Girl: A Multi-cultural Game about Natural Disaster Prevention and Resilience. In A. Nijholt, T. Romão, D. Reidsma (Eds.), *Advances in Computer Entertainment. ACE 2012. Lecture Notes in Computer Science, vol 7624.* Springer, Berlin, Heidelberg.

Kinsella, E. L., Ritchie, T. D., & Igou, E. R. (2015a). Lay perspectives on the social and psychological functions of heroes. *Frontiers in Psychology, 6*, 130-130. doi:https://doi.org/10.3389/fpsyg.2015.00130

Kinsella, E. L., Ritchie, T. D., & Igou, E. R. (2015b). Zeroing in on heroes: A prototype analysis of hero features. *Journal of Personality and Social Psychology, 108*, 114-127. doi: https://doi.org/10.1037/a0038463

Lafreniere, M.-A. K., Verner-Filion, J., & Vallerand, R. J. (2012). Development and validation of the Gaming Motivation Scale (GAMS). *Personality and Individual Differences, 53*, 827-831. doi: https://doi.org/10.1016/j.paid.2012.06.013

Lazarus, R. S., & Folkman, S. (1986). Cognitive theories of stress and the issue of circularity. In M. H. Appley & R. Trumbull (Eds). *Dynamics of Stress: Physiological, Psychological, and Social Perspectives* (pp. 63–80). New York: Plenum.

Lazzaro, N. (2009) Understand emotions (2009). In C. Bateman (Ed.), *Beyond game design: Nine step toward creating better videogames*. Boston: Charles Rivers Media.

Li, D. D., Liau, A. K., & Khoo, A. (2013). Player-avatar identification in video gaming: Concept and measurement. *Computers in Human Behavior, 29*, 257-263. doi: https://doi.org/10.1016/j.chb.2012.09.002

Loewenstein, G. (1994). The psychology of curiosity: A review and reinterpretation. *Psychological Bulletin, 116*, 75-98. doi: https://doi.org/10.1037/0033-2909.116.1.75

Lombard, M., & Ditton, T. (1997). At the heart of it all: The concept of presence. Journal of Computer-Mediated Communication, 3(2) doi:https://doi.org/10.1111/j.1083-6101.1997.tb00072.x

Marins, D. R., de O. D. Justo, M., Xexeo, G.B., de A. M. Chaves, B., D'Ipolitto, C. (2011). *SmartRabbit: A mobile Exergame Using Geolocation, Brazilian Symposium on Games and Digital Entertainment (SBGAMES)*, pp. 232-240.

Olson, C. K. (2010). Children's motivations for video game play in the context of normal development. *Review of General Psychology, 14*, 180–187. doi:https://doi.org/10.1037/a0018984

Osgood, J. M. (2017). Is revenge about retributive justice, deterring harm, or both? *Social and Personality Psychology Compass, 11*, n/a. doi:https://doi.org/10.1111/spc3.12296

Peña, J., & Hancock, J. T. (2006). An analysis of socioemotional and task communication in online multiplayer video games. *Communication Research, 33*, 92-109. doi:https://doi.org/10.1177/0093650205283103

Przybylski, A. K., Ryan, R. M., & Rigby, C. S. (2009). The motivating role of violence in video games. *Personality and Social Psychology Bulletin, 35*, 243-259. doi:https://doi.org/10.1177/0146167208327216

Rand, D. G., Greene, J. D., & Nowak, M. A. (2012). Spontaneous giving and calculated greed. *Nature, 489*, 427-430. doi:https://doi.org/10.1038/nature11467

Ryan, R. M., & Deci, E. L. (2000). Intrinsic and extrinsic motivations: Classic definitions and new directions. *Contemporary Educational Psychology, 25*, 54-97. doi: https://doi.org/10.1006/ceps.1999.1020

Ryan, R. M., Rigby, C. S., & Przybylski, A. (2006). The motivational pull of video games: A self-determination theory approach. *Motivation and Emotion, 30*(4), 344-360. doi:https://doi.org/10.1007/s11031-006-9051-8

Scherer, K. R. (2005). What are emotions? And how can they be measured? *Social Science Information, 44*, 695-729. doi: https://doi.org/10.1177/0539018405058216

Schell, J. (2008). *The art of game design: A book of lenses*. San Francisco: Morgan Kaufmann.

Seuntjens, T. G. (2016). *The Psychology of Greed*. S.l.: Ridderprint

Seuntjens, T. G., Zeelenberg, M., van de Ven, N., & Breugelmans, S. M. (2015). Dispositional greed. *Journal of Personality and Social Psychology, 108*, 917-933. doi: https://doi.org/10.1037/pspp0000031

Simmons, R. T., Dawes, R. M., & Orbell, J. M. (1984). *Defection in social dilemmas: Is fear or is greed the problem?* Unpublished manuscript, Department of Political Science, Univ. of Oregon.

Takatalo J, Häkkinen, J., Kaistinen, J. & Nyman, G. (2010). Presence, Involvement, and Flow in Digital Games. In R. Bernhaupt (Ed.) *Evaluating User Experience in Games: Concepts and Methods*. London: Springer

Taylor, S. E., Klein, L. C., Lewis, B. P., Gruenewald, T. L., Gurung, R. A. R., & Updegraff, J. A. (2000). Biobehavioral responses to stress in females: Tend-and-befriend, not fight-or-flight. *Psychological Review, 107,* 411-429. doi: https://doi.org/10.1037//0033-295X.107.3.411

Van Vugt, M., De Cremer, D., & Janssen, D. P. (2007). Gender differences in cooperation and competition: The male-warrior hypothesis. *Psychological Science, 18,* 19-23. doi:https://doi.org/10.1111/j.1467-9280.2007.01842.x

Wang, X., Perry, A.C. (2006). Metabolic and physiologic responses to video game play in 7- to 10-year-old boys. *Archives of Pediatrics and Adolescence Medicine, 160,* 411–415. doi:https://doi.org/10.1001/archpedi.160.4.411

Watson, C., & Clark, L. A. (1994). *The PANAS-X: Manual for the Positive and Negative Affect Schedule—Expanded form.* Retrieved from http://ir.uiowa.edu/cgi/viewcontent.cgi?article_1011&context_psychology_pubs

Weinstein, N., & Ryan, R. M. (2010). When helping helps: Autonomous motivation for prosocial behavior and its influence on well-being for the helper and recipient. *Journal of Personality and Social Psychology, 98,* 222-244. doi:https://doi.org/10.1037/a0016984

Ludography

Bunten, D. (1984). Seven Cities of Gold. Electronic Arts.
Crane, D., Nelson, S. (1985). Little Computer People. Activision.
Smith, A. (1983), Dracula. Imagic

Chapter 8
The Game Experience Model (GEM)

Tomi "bgt" Suovuo, Natasha Skult, Tapani N. Joelsson, Petter Skult, Werner Ravyse, and Jouni Smed

Contents

T. "bgt" Suovuo · T. N. Joelsson · J. Smed (✉)
Department of Future Technologies, University of Turku, Turku, Finland
e-mail: bgt@utu.fi; taneli@utu.fi; jouni.smed@utu.fi

N. Skult
Department of Art History, University of Turku, Turku, Finland

MiTale Ltd., Turku, Finland
e-mail: nabutr@utu.fi

P. Skult
Faculty of Arts, Psychology and Theology, Åbo Akademi University, Turku, Finland

W. Ravyse
Faculty of ICT and Chemical Engineering, Turku University of Applied Sciences, Turku, Finland
e-mail: werner.ravyse@turkuamk.fi

© Springer Nature Switzerland AG 2020
B. Bostan (ed.), *Game User Experience And Player-Centered Design*,
International Series on Computer Entertainment and Media Technology,
https://doi.org/10.1007/978-3-030-37643-7_8

Abstract For over a decade now game research has aimed at describing the game experience by attempting to see it from one perspective. In this paper, we collect, analyse, and merge together this work. As a result, we claim that a game experience is composed of three pairs of elements, none of which can be removed, or the system in question is no longer a game. These elements are: (1) the game mechanics and action, (2) storyworld and narrative, and (3) aesthetics and sensory stimulus. This model can be illustrated in the form of a gem that encloses the fantasy and immersion of a game. Apart from games, this model is applicable to all kinds of storytelling, particularly interactive kinds. Beyond games, the different facets of the gem can be used by ignoring elements absent in the given narrative media.

Keywords Gameplay models · Game mechanics · Action · Sensory stimulus · Narrative · Aesthetics · Storyworld

8.1 Introduction

When Hunicke et al. (2004) introduced their MDA (mechanics, dynamics, and aesthetics) framework to help the game industry to design "desired experiential results of gameplay", they playfully noted that "there is no Grand Unified Theory of games". This has not prevented many authors from forming their own, all-encompassing models for analysing games. These include game experience theories and frameworks such as Smed and Hakonen (2003), Björk and Holopainen (2004), the MDA model of Hunicke et al. (2004), the SCI model of Ermi and Mäyrä (2005), and the game immersion model of Adams (2013). In our earlier work (Mäntylä et al. 2014), we analysed and compared these models and presented an initial fusion of these highly similar models. In this chapter, we continue this work and present a new fusion model called the *game experience model* (GEM).

This work was originally inspired by the observation how Adams seems to agree with Ermi and Mäyrä about the existence of narrative immersion, and another one, which Adams calls "tactical" immersion and Ermi and Mäyrä "challenge-based" immersion, whereas the third channel of immersion Adams mentions is "strategic" immersion but Ermi and Mäyrä lists "sensory" immersion. Both models seem to make sense in their own right, and they have a significant replication, as a good scientific theory should have, despite that there seems to be a gap between them.

The GEM is intended to be a tool for both analysing and designing games. It should help one to feel confident that no part of the game experience is neglected in the design process. The GEM attempts to be the guide to the anatomy of the gameplay experience, helping the designers to pay attention to the equivalent ergonomics—making sure that the game is properly designed to suit the intended audience. As a fusion of several frameworks, the GEM functions as an interpreter between different models. When investigating the design ideas from researchers focusing on a different framework behind their thinking, this chapter in particular should help in using the GEM as a tool to translate the ideas from one framework to another.

In this chapter, we present first the outcome of our analysis as a fused theoretical game experience model in Sect. 8.2, followed by a more-detailed analysis in Sect. 8.3. In Sect. 8.4, we compare the GEM with the earlier models presented in the literature. This is followed in Sect. 8.5 by some example analyses of games that demonstrate how games can be dissected using the GEM. Finally, the concluding remarks appear in Sect. 8.6.

8.2   The Structure of the GEM

The GEM recognizes six elements of a game experience and the relationships between them. Figure 8.1 illustrates the GEM as a triangular cylinder (or a prism) with six vertices and five faces. The vertices form three pairs:

- *Mechanics—Action*: Mechanics include all the actions that can occur in the game and all the game objects—everything defined by the rules of the game. Action is how the mechanism functions in each situation.
- *Aesthetics—Sensory stimulus*: Aesthetics include all the sensory and cognitive designs aimed to evoke emotions in the player. Aesthetics presented to the player is called sensory stimulus.
- *Storyworld—Narrative*: Storyworld provides the substantial content for games. It includes all the events and things in the game universe, both the ones that become actualized during the gameplay, as well as the ones that do not, or even could not, because they were not put in the game, only imagined by the game designers, or through becoming logically necessary, or likely, due to circumstances that are included. Narratives are the pieces of the story from the storyworld that occur during gameplay.

Fig. 8.1 The structure of the GEM as a flattened triangular cylinder

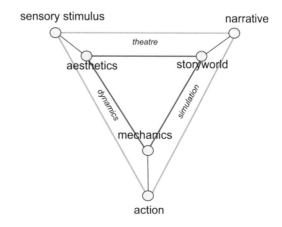

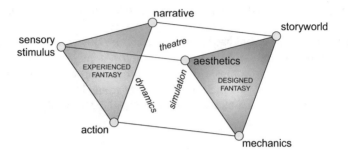

Fig. 8.2 The structure of the GEM as a prism

Fig. 8.3 The actualized
Designed Fantasy and
actualized Experienced
Fantasy within the GEM
typically have an offset, and
the players may form a
greater or smaller fantasy
than the designers intended.
Also, the full potential fantasy
of the game is a larger space
than neither the designers nor
the players will ever explore

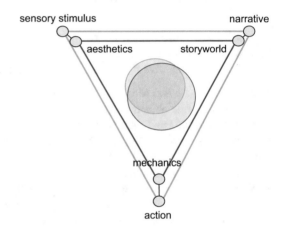

The three side-faces of the cylinder are labelled *dynamics*, *theatre*, and *simulation* (see also Fig. 8.2). The upper face, *Designed Fantasy*, involves the elements of mechanism, aesthetics, and storyworld. These higher-level elements are expressed by the game through the elements of action, sensory stimulus, and narrative residing at the lower face, *Experienced Fantasy*.

The game experience can be viewed from each of the five faces. The player experiences the game through their own personal narratives experienced during the game, as well as the actions they have taken and the sensory stimulus they have received. They can perceive the greater whole through the *Experienced Fantasy* face, but it is the primary interface they have.

Game designers perceive the game through the opposite *Designed Fantasy* face, constructing the whole fantasy of the game, fitting the storyworld, game mechanics and aesthetics together, which all form the greater idea behind what is concretely given to the player to experience. The game designers are likely to expect that their designed fantasy would match the experienced fantasy as closely as possible (see Fig. 8.3).

There is an interesting phenomenon, where the game designers perceive that the whole of the created game is located within the GEM as a certain shaped bubble at a certain location, but the player community actually appear to perceive a different bubble at another location. In particular, open world games can be seen in many different ways. A player can ignore the main story and go exploring the realm of *Skyrim* (Bethesda Game Studios 2011), focus on taming all the different animals in *Far Cry Primal* (Ubisoft Montreal 2016), or just drive around with the cars in *Grand Theft Auto V* (Rockstar North 2013).

We can look at a game through the *dynamics* face between aesthetics, stimulus, mechanics, and action. This face ignores the story and motivation of the game, observing it merely as a spectacle akin to a sports performance. This face is essential for games such as chess, where there is no real story or the story comes from outside the game such as in *Ingress* (Niantic 2013). The whole elegance of the game aesthetics and player actions can be seen through this face, which is traditionally the case in several sports such as figure skating and ski jumping.

Looking at a game through the *theatre* face between aesthetics, stimulus, storyworld, and narratives, the rules of the game disappear, and what remains is a sequence of events, as in a movie. This is a face essential for entertainment applications, where there are few, if any, player controls. As the element that provides participation, the mechanics are, what essentially separates games (including all forms of interactive storytelling), a part of other forms of art.

The final *simulation* face is the one between mechanics, action, storyworld, and narratives, where actions and their causalities are clear, but their representation is ignored. This is equivalent to low-level simulations, or text-only adventures. The simulation face perceives only the pure gameness of the experience, ignoring the aesthetics. The challenges of the game arise mainly from the mechanics and narratives that explain what the players are supposed to be doing in the game. The same essential action can be represented in several different ways, using visuals, audio, and other sensory stimulus.

These six elements are the components that form a game. They are distinct from other relevant elements involved in the gameplay as they are built in the game and invariably the same anytime and anywhere the game is played, or else it is a different game. Social interaction, for example, is a context, where the game is being played. The game mechanics may support social interaction, but the social interaction varies based on the society where the game is played.

8.3 Looking Deeper into the GEM

The idea of "core fantasy" as the centre of what a game is can best be explained through a failure to sell such a fantasy. Paul Kilduff-Taylor talks about the conceptual failure of their game *Frozen Cortex* (Mode 7 Games 2015) during the GDC 2016 "Failure workshop" (GDC Vault 2016). In the preceding game, *Frozen Synapse* (Mode 7 Games 2011), the player's and their opponent's turns play out simultaneously, but each player (or computer opponent) is able to plan out their actions beforehand. *Frozen Cortex* plays much in the same fashion, but the core difference is that while *Frozen Synapse* is a game where soldiers kill each other, *Frozen Cortex* is a game of future-sports, where robots compete to bring a ball over to the end zone and score a touchdown. Unfortunately, the game was not as successful, which Kilduff-Taylor called a "conceptual failure" brought on by the failure to sell their audience on a proper core fantasy. He reflects:

> Thinking back to all the games that I really, really liked, and what we've done with *Frozen Endzone*, we had this problem where there wasn't a kind of core fantasy at the heart of it, nobody really wanted to be sort of managing a futuristic sports' team with tactical stuff. Nobody really wanted to do that. While being a space pilot, doing all the other things you can do in other types of games, they're fantasies that people have, they're things that people like.

The core fantasy of a game, as defined by him, could be summed up in a series of questions: "What are you doing in the game, what do people want to do, what's exciting about the idea?". Everything else, then, builds up from this core fantasy: the aesthetics of a game is how you convey it to the player, sound and music design likewise, as are the various mechanics of the game. It is important to note that in our definition, fantasy is distinct from "story" or "narrative", although they are generally central to the ability to sell the fantasy of a game (much like the aesthetics of the game overall, and the actual mechanics once you are playing it). It is also important to remember that fantasy is by its very definition individual: it exists within the player's mind, not as something external or objective. And finally, a single game can cater to many different fantasies, and it may well be that the core fantasy *intended* by a game differs from the experienced fantasy of the player. For example, *X-COM* (Firaxis Games 2012) might appeal because it is a game where you get to be a master tactician, always a few steps ahead of your opponent, winning against impossible odds because of your superior brawn. Or the appeal might come from the player's position as an underdog, winning desperate, pyrrhic victories in a fight they are destined to lose. Or then it might be appealing because of the personal stories of the player's squad members, their failures and successes, and their growth from pathetic rookie to unstoppable alien-killing machine. These individual fantasies are then facilitated by various gameplay mechanics and aesthetic choices; one of the most important being how your squad members gain ranks and skills and can be individually named and their appearance customized.

Good game design accepts that what needs to be captured is the player's imagination, and what needs to be catered to is the target audience's fantasies. That is why *Frozen Cortex* failed, because the core audience of strategy games was not interested in embodying the manager of future-sports robots. Kilduff-Taylor points out that all the other aspects, visuals, mechanics, audio, and so on, were improved on or remained the same. The failure came solely from a failure to engage in a proper fantasy. Jesse Schell (2008) would probably call this the "experience" that elusive thing that all game design strives for, yet which is not the game itself; "Game designers only care about what seems to exist. The player and the game are real. The experience is imaginary—but game designers are judged by the quality of this imaginary thing because it is the reason people play games". Schell (2008, p. 11)

Narrative remains important to the notion of fantasy, but not in the traditional sense of narration from game-to-player; rather, if fantasy is an intangible thing happening in the mind of the player, then *their narration of their experiences* constitutes the tangible, existing expression of their fantasy. How well a player is able to narrate their own experiences is a good marker of how well a game has managed to tap into some particular fantasy.

Although we state, especially in Fig. 8.3, that aesthetics, storyworld, and mechanics are foremostly what concerns the game designers, and that sensory stimulus, narratives, and action are what the player foremostly experiences, this must not be seen so that the first triplet would neither affect the play experience nor vice versa. The narratives are a representation of the storyworld, and the making of the GEM consists of how well the storyworld is conveyed to the player. This applies as well to the sensory stimulus representing and conveying the aesthetics, and the action representing and conveying the mechanics.

Fantasy differs from agency, where agency requires a sense of power to influence the narrative, whereas fantasy only requires the immersion into the narrative. Immersion can improve, if the player can influence the narrative. Agency can improve the fantasy, but fantasy can exist without agency. Fantasy is more active than suspension of disbelief. Suspension of disbelief mainly relies on the mechanics and narrative playing together, so that the player can accept the mechanics behind the narrative. However, suspension of disbelief only requires the player to believe, what is taking place, whereas fantasy involves also the aesthetics. The player needs to enjoy the feelings that the gameplay provides.

8.3.1   Mechanics and Action

Sicart (2008) defines game mechanics as "methods invoked by agents, designed for interaction with the game state" following the view of Hunicke et al. (2004) which states that mechanics "describes the particular component of the game, at the level of data representation and algorithms". Adams (2014, pp. 352–353) breaks this down and lists five major types of game mechanics:

- physics (e.g., Newtonian mechanics or cartoon physics)
- internal economies (i.e., rules governing creation, consumption, and exchange of quantifiable resources)
- progression mechanisms (i.e., progress through a series of challenges)
- tactical manoeuvring (e.g., taking place in largely open or semi-open spaces)
- social interaction (i.e., rules that control the relationships among players)

Game mechanics make the gameplay possible and drive it forward. These progression mechanisms can be divided into two categories (Juul 2005, pp. 72–82): games of emergence and games of progression. In *games of emergence*, the flow of events emerges from the operation of the rules, and the events are not pre-planned by the game designer. For example, chess, bridge, and *Tetris* (Pajitnov 1984) rely on emergence to make the gameplay interesting but there is no premeditated sequence through which the events unfold. In *games of progression*, a predefined system causes the player to experience the game in such a way that certain events are certain to follow other events. This progress can happen through space (e.g., enforced by level design), time (e.g., events are triggered in predefined time intervals), or a story (e.g., the player progresses through a narrative that triggers events and gets triggered by player-initiated events).

Mechanics include the rules of the game, which forms an essential aspect as Huizinga (1955, p. 11) observes: "All play has its rules. They determine what 'holds' in the temporary world circumscribed by play. The rules of a game are absolutely binding and allow no doubt". A significant subset of the rules is the "set of actions that the system can logically process" as an input from the player (Szilas 2004). The mapping between this set of logical actions and the set of physical actions enabled by the user interface is the essence of the connection between mechanics and action. Moreover, mechanics and action involve the participatory affordance (Murray 2012) in games, making the opposite face of the GEM involve mostly non-interactive forms of storytelling, and not actual games. One could say that "traditional art" such as movies lack interaction and mechanics completely. Nevertheless, even they have an agreement, in the sense of Adams (2013), between the audience and the storyteller commonly known as "suspension of disbelief". The audience must be able to relate to the story and the characters, and this is where a glimmer of mechanics shines through the GEM even in these mediums. The reality of the narratives must make sense to the audience—this reality of the story belongs to the mechanics element of the GEM.

The action-based immersion modality is connected to the strategic one. It remains quite hidden in turn-based games (e.g., chess) where it mostly manifests in the player's skill to plan ahead several moves or estimate the probabilities of consequences. In fast paced games, action-based immersion modality manifests more clearly in reaction speed, accuracy, and even strength.

A game can have different gameplay modes, for example, driving mode and conversation mode. In the driving mode, the player's action of pressing the controller key X could mean accelerating, but in the conversation mode, the same key X could mean choosing a dialogue item from a menu. The same action in different modes would thereby be mapped to a different game mechanic.

Action is not equivalent to the rules of the game, as a bad interface design may prevent the player from taking an action that would be valid according to the rules/mechanics. The action element also includes technical problems such as the inaccuracy of the GPS in a location-based game (Benford et al. 2006; Jacob and Coelho 2011) or an adware-game advertisements disrupting the gameplay (Lewis and Porter 2010). In the latter example, the player may try to click on an icon to close the advertisement but the advertisement either closes just before the player clicks or it does not catch the player's click rather than letting it pass through to the game. In either way, the action becomes an unintended click on the gameplay.

Today a typical game is controlled by a standard game console controller, where the buttons and joysticks are assigned differently for each game (Blomberg 2018).

There does exist certain conventions followed by a majority of games. These are equivalent to the standard of an aircraft nose lifting, when a joystick is pulled back (essentially downwards) and diving in the opposite direction. However, these conventions are not always followed, and sometimes even within a single game, a certain action can be done with different button in different situations. An example of the latter is how firing a weapon in *No Man's Sky* (Hello Games 2016) is performed with one button when controlling a vehicle and with another button when the game character is on foot. Achieving immersion is affected by the need to adapt to a new control layout, especially if the layout alters during the game.

A significant difference between action and mechanics is that action refers to the concrete application of mechanics. In puzzle games, the puzzles as such are a part of the mechanics element as is their fundamental solving, but the application of the game controls to perform the operations required for the solution are part of the action element.

When a game mechanism is off balance, it is a design failure. When a player is unable to execute a valid action, it is an implementation failure. Design failures are observable through the design facet of the GEM and implementation failures through the experience facet. An example of this can be seen in David Newton's reviews of the game *Prince of Persia* (Mechner 1989) in a great variety of different platforms. As a matter of mechanics, (Newton 2014, 7:20–7:27) describes, how the Nintendo Entertainment System (NES) version of the game uses scrolling of the screen because the whole scene does not fit the screen simultaneously, unlike in most other versions. Also, the mechanism of switching places with an opponent during a fight has been removed as a game mechanism in this version (Newton 2014, 8:08–8:13). Newton (2014, 6:20) states in his review: "The mechanics of the game are nice and precise", where GEM would rather recommend the word action instead of mechanics, as he is speaking of how the player experiences the swiftness of their control affecting the character in the game.

8.3.2 Storyworld and Narratives

Essentially, the storyworld is typically an infinite universe, envisioned by the game designers. The narratives are the pieces of storyworld that the player experiences in the game. They have made aesthetic representations of part of this universe, in the form of plots, text descriptions, action scenes, sounds, art, and others, which are presented to the player as a narrative within the storyworld during gameplay. The player also typically generates their own narrative through induction. Particularly in games with a lot of simulation, but little dialogue, such as *RimWorld* (Ludeon Studios 2018) or *SimCity* (Maxis 1989), the player projects emotions to the events and creates narratives that the game designers have not really prepared in the game.

The storyworld is very much in the interaction with the aesthetics. Here, the narrative is the parts of the story that actually takes place in the instance of playing the game—what is told by the game to the player, and which narrative the player is choosing themselves. Through one or more traversals through the game, the player constructs in their mind a storyworld of the game—what happens outside the narrative, or what could have happened instead. What is the moral of the story. What is actually written as a narrative in the game by the game designers is often only a part of the whole game storyworld that the game designers have designed. The storyworld is to the narratives as the mechanics are to actions: The game may involve the rule of jumping over a pit, but the player may avoid all areas with a pit, and therefore the action of jumping over a pit never exists in a game, although it exists in the game as a mechanism.

If games exist to sell a fantasy, that fantasy is very often a power fantasy: the common wisdom is that players want to feel empowered and in control, able to exert their will on the game world in various ways (often violent, but not necessarily). Even a game like *Hellblade: Senua's Sacrifice* (Ninja Theory 2017), where you play as a woman suffering from a debilitating psychosis that is threatening to entirely eat her up, the player, in their moment-to-moment interactions with the game, is nonetheless living a power fantasy. The roots of power fantasy can be seen already in Huizinga (1955, p. 10): "Here we come across another, very positive feature of play: it creates order, *is* order. Into an imperfect world and into the confusion of life it brings a temporary, a limited perfection". The nature of play allows us to exert power on reality. We can become, like in *Hellblade*, a skillful fighter that we in reality are not, and would have to struggle much to become, both in physical training and in issues of social acceptance. Games and play allow us to simulate things, and we are in control of the simulation—what is difficult and what is easy. "Play begins, and then at a certain moment it is 'over'."

Narrative can affect the game mechanics, but is not necessarily restricted to them. Narratives are used especially to transit the player between different sets of mechanics. In a game the player may first have their character walk on foot with the related mechanics and actions available to them, and then there is the narrative of entering the car, upon which the player is transferred to the mechanics and actions of driving a vehicle. However, also in games of war, for example, the move of attacking another unit also has its own narrative, even though it is just an application of the game rules.

Cognitively, a narrative plot is a significant part of the aesthetics. A well designed, solid yet exciting narrative plot evokes emotions in the players. The line between narratives and aesthetics is surprisingly perhaps the most vague in GEM. It is clear to see that distinct sensory stimuli are not the same as the narrative.

8.3.3 Aesthetics and Sensory Stimulus

As Niedenthal (2009) notes, the study of games tend not to be familiar with the whole brevity of what is meant by aesthetics. Aesthetics is not only about "eye candy"—about being pretty and shiny. Aesthetics could be easiest to understand by considering its antonym which is most familiar to us from the field of medicine:

anaesthetics—numbness, lack of senses and emotions. As the reverse of this, aesthetics is the whole field of emotions and cognitions experienced by the player during the gameplay. From an epistemological viewpoint, aesthetics studies the judgment of sentiment flowing from sensory inputs. Not just from a ludic player perspective, but also how game designers imagine and create virtual worlds. If a game designer fails in their quest for a synchronized (between themself and the player) aesthetic, they are likely to numb the player to the game's designed experience (or fantasy, in the case of the GEM) of overcoming interactable challenges. When this occurs, there tends to be a blurring of active participation in favour of spectating a narrative (watching a movie with you as player in it), making the aesthetic experience of player and spectator indistinguishable. If done right, aesthetics becomes the most direct channel for a game to present itself to the fantasy of the player.

Presenting a game as a truly pleasing aesthetic experience is less forgiving, than say, a painting. Games are digital systems where audio, visual, and haptic (three out of the five classical senses are available) output is available to the designer with the further complication of the player's goal-oriented desire to win. How to create a visual scene that represents game states in a way that is pleasing and not boring, repetitive, or clumsy becomes a precarious balancing act.

Murray (2012) states that "any medium serve three nested processes: inscription, transmission, and representation". This structure can be found in the GEM. Sensory stimulus is equivalent to inscription. It is the immediate sensory interaction between the game user interface and the player, such as the sounds and visuals presented by a game console, or the game pieces of a board game. From a GEM perspective, mechanics and storyworld are the catalyst for representation, in that these form the bi-focal lens on the game world the designer provides the player. Together, this lens and the inscribed sensory stimuli transmit aesthetics.

Aesthetics intrudes into storyworld and mechanics. A great storyworld is coherent and suitably rich, but at its most dull, it reduces to a flowchart. Aesthetics arise from the tensions in the story, and how the story is presented to the player. For instance, a horror story typically has different visuals and music styles than a comedy.

The challenge for the storyworld is to generate a great story. Although there is an essential fascination in amassing points or beating time limits, a digital game can benefit greatly from a great story connected to these play-drivers through fluent representation, with all the moves between the start and the end of the game as part of the story. As Niedenthal (2009) notes, the concept of aesthetic does not only include the sum of the player's sensory input but also the emotions and the state of mind caused by the experience.

Aesthetics is something that can be objectively put and found in the design. The evoked emotions are all subjective. This, of course, partially includes the action and narrative, but the most direct influence lies with the sensory stimuli from the game interface devices. The graphics, music, sound effects, haptic output, and other possible sensory stimulus mechanics convey to the player the results of their own actions, the narrative of the game, and hopefully the cognitive, aesthetic experience intended by the game designers. Aesthetics and sensory stimuli provide the representation for the other elements.

8.4 Comparing the GEM with Other Models

In this section, we compare five earlier models to the GEM. Our intention is to clarify how they relate to the GEM and point out the limitations of these models.

8.4.1 Smed and Hakonen

Smed and Hakonen (2003, 2017) define that the anatomy of a game is as illustrated in Fig. 8.4. The model includes five subjects: players, rules, goals, opponents, and representations, and seven relationships between them, forming three aspects of a game. Here we relate these subjects and relationships with the elements and faces of the GEM model. This analysis is also presented in Table 8.1.

Smed and Hakonen found their model on the player as an element in the design. The GEM does not see the player as an element of design, but rather the design exists between the players and the game designers. The player perceives the game mostly through the player face of the GEM, interfaced through the player's actions, stimulus, and experienced narratives in the game.

Rules are the direct equivalent of the GEM mechanics. Goals, as components that "give arise to conflicts and rivalry among the players" should be divisible between goals included in the mechanics as victory conditions, or in the narratives as

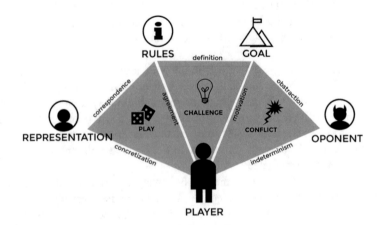

Fig. 8.4 The anatomy of games as perceived by Smed and Hakonen

Table 8.1 A comparison of the model by Smed and Hakonen to the GEM

Smed and Hakonen	GEM	Comment
Representations	Sensory stimulus, action	The sensory stimulus and player action are the concretizations that "represent the abstractions used in the rules"
Rules	Mechanics	Direct equivalence
Goal	Mechanics, narrative	"Goals give rise to conflicts and rivalry among the players". GEM perceives this in the enabling mechanics and motivating narratives
Opponent	Mechanics, narrative	The opposing unpredictability is either included in the mechanics, or delivered through the narrative
Player	–	The game experience occurs, when a player interacts with a game. The GEM is the anatomy of this experience
Definition	Mechanics	Within the mechanics, the rules define the goals. The narrative can easily get involved here and interfere with the rules
Agreement	Action	"[The players] agree to follow the rules". The action is, how the player executes their part of the mechanics and their agency
Motivation	Mechanics, narrative	Motivation is essentially the same as goals
Correspondence	Mechanics, sensory stimulus	Both models agree that the sensory stimulus/representation must correspond with the mechanics/rules
Concretization	Sensory stimulus, action	Smed and Hakonen perceive that the "representation concretizes the game to the players". In GEM the concretization occurs through the action and sensory stimulus
Obstruction	Narrative, action	As the player is more obscure in GEM than in Smed and Hakonen, the obstruction comes through, either the narrative of the fictional NPC opponent, or the action of the player opponent
Indeterminism	Narrative, mechanics	Indeterminism in GEM is due either the narrative (which does not have to be constrained by the mechanics) or due to the rule in the mechanics, where a die can be rolled, or another player may take alternative actions
Play	Dynamics face	Abstract rules correspond to real-world objects, and the game is concretized to the players
Challenge	Simulation face	The story explains the reasons for the challenge posed by the initial setting, eventual goals, and the rules/mechanics in between
Conflict	Theatre face	The narrative of the opponent (and the player) creates an exciting conflict

story motivated goals. Even, when described by the narrative, the goals are, indeed, defined by the game mechanics.

Motivation is a complicated term. Essentially, the game experience as a whole is what motivates the player to play the game. In Smed and Hakonen's model, the motivation refers more to the motivations that the player has for their actions within the game, which differs from the concept of goals only in nuances and in perspective. Goals are pulling the players towards themselves, whereas their produced motivations can be seen as pushing forces. Motivations are internal feelings in the players, whereas goals are external targets for these feelings. Looking through GEM, one should see that the players are motivated to play by the elements of the storyworld and the aesthetics of the game, but in some cases also an interesting game mechanics can motivate gameplay. In the game, the players agree to comply with the game mechanics, as well as creating narratives jointly with the game.

As challenge comprises of the player attaining the goals in accordance to rules, it would be equivalent to the "simulation" face of GEM. This is compatible, considering that the challenge as such does not involve aesthetics directly. The challenge can connect to aesthetics through the narrative that sets the goals for the challenge, or the actions the player needs to take to achieve the goals.

The hidden opponent that obstructs the player can also be a part of the game mechanics as a random factor. Some people have a dislike to chess, for example, as the game does not provide enough random factors in the game mechanics, but the opposition comes all from the other player directly. Most often, as in the case of chess, the opponent is part of the narrative—the actions taken by the characters in the game world. A good opponent brings indeterminism to the game and obstructs the player from achieving their goals. The conflict of the game in GEM can be seen through the theatre face, created together with the narratives of the game setting, and emotions evoked by the aesthetics of the form of the narrative—good vs. evil, and the excitement of all of the schemes on both sides.

The game activity is represented for the player through sensory stimulus, and basically also through the player's actions. The sensory stimulus concretizes the game mechanics and thereby needs to correspond with them.

The play activity that is connected to the representation takes place in the dynamics face, where the narrative is only at the background, motivating the play. This is the concrete part of the play—what really happens when the game is played. The GEM model also recognizes the Huizingian child play, as seen from the theatre face, where the exact rules and mechanics are not so important, and a conceptual play, seen from the simulation face, where the aesthetic representation is not so important.

8.4.2   Björk and Holopainen

Björk and Holopainen (2004) focus more on the design of how a game is played than how it is built. They state that their aim is not "to formulate a definition of what game or play is", as there are several existing already. They aim at describing patterns of different observable phenomena observed during activity that people are calling gameplay.

Björk and Holopainen divide their discovered components into four categories: holistic, boundary, temporal, and structural. The holistic quarter, in particular, investigates the contexts of the gameplay, rather than the game itself. The GEM excludes this part, as it is something that is not built within the game. If a game was sent in a time capsule 500 years in the future, the players' contexts would likely be quite different, but the GEM elements would follow with the game. The GEM elements of the *Iliad* are still the same, even though the audience experience certainly is different, due to the changes in the context.

Foremostly, Björk and Holopainen describe a library of design patterns for games. In addition to the patterns printed in the book, it comes with a CD that contains even more patterns. The concept of design patterns has been adopted from the field of traditional architecture, through the method of Gamma et al. (1995) who implemented design patterns in software architecture as a part of the agile movement in the 1990s.

When it comes to gameplay experience patterns that Björk and Holopainen (2004, p. 206) describe, the closest that come are the *immersion patterns*: spatial immersion, emotional immersion, cognitive immersion, and sensory-motoric immersion. Not surprisingly, these four names sound similar to what we have in the GEM.

- Spatial immersion: "the result of extensive manoeuvring in the game world in real-time games and can sometimes be felt in movies". This is the "being there" type of immersion, where the player is presented the game world as a place where they are, and the player can experience the sensations of being there. In the GEM, this falls under aesthetics, where the player is emulated with fictitious sensory experiences of the game world.
- Emotional immersion: "obtained by responding to the events that characters are part of during the unfolding of a narrative structure and is similar to the immersion that books, theatre, or movies provide". This description would place emotional immersion into the storyworld element, but by the name, emotions arise only partially from the stories, and mostly from the representation—the death of a character can be presented comically, as well as tragically.
- Cognitive immersion: "based upon the focus on abstract reasoning and is usually achieved by complex problem solving". This is equivalent to the GEM element of game mechanics.
- Sensory-motoric immersion: "result of feedback loops between repetitive movements players make to perform actions in the game and the sensory output of the game". Although the sensory part of this title suggests the influence of sensory stimulus, this is most significantly about acting and reacting with the proper timing and cognition, which places this pattern into the action element.

8.4.3   Hunicke et al. (MDA)

The framework of Hunicke et al. (2004) sees three lenses all on the same telescope, one after another. The game developer is looking at the game from the direction of mechanics, through which the dynamics of the gameplay can be seen, and the aesthetics is visible behind both of them. The player experiences primarily the aesthetics of the game, finding the dynamics of the game through it, and can perceive the game mechanisms behind both.

Projected in the GEM, the MDA model would appear to be gazing the game experience from the point of view of aesthetics, towards mechanics, seeing the bottom layer (stimulus, narratives, and action) between there as "dynamics". "Dynamics describes the run-time behaviour of the mechanics acting on player inputs and each others' outputs over time" (Hunicke et al. 2004), which is highly similar as the lower circle in the GEM manifesting the instantiation-during-gameplay of each higher-level element of the design. This analysis reveals that MDA is observing a game strictly as a game, through the dynamics face, ignoring the story part of the game, except where it is seen as connected to the game mechanics, or in the aesthetics.

- Mechanics (game mechanics in the GEM): "describes the particular components of the game, at the level of data representation and algorithms". Also, this is the design counterpart of "rules".
- Dynamics (action–stimulus in the GEM): "describes the run-time behaviour of the mechanics acting on player input and each others' outputs over time". Also, this is the design counterpart of the "system".
- Aesthetics (fantasy and aesthetics in the GEM: "describes the desirable emotional responses evoked in the player, when she interacts with the game system". Also, this is the design counterpart of "fun".

Robson et al. (2015) argue towards using the word "emotions" directly instead of "aesthetics" leading to a MDE model, which has been connected to the OCC model by Mullins and Sabherwal (2018). However, we prefer the term "aesthetics" as emotions are individual and context-dependent and cannot be directly designed in the game.

8.4.4   Ermi and Mäyrä (SCI)

The SCI model of Ermi and Mäyrä (2005) is very close to the GEM model. The main differences are that: (1) The GEM model observes the three elements both as top level conceptual designs, and as instantiative user experiences. (2) The SCI model has been discovered from the context of Communication and Community in Digital Entertainment Services research project (Järvinen et al. 2002, Sect. 4.1).

The SCI model is positioned within the social context of the player, which is not considered in the GEM.

The SCI model is named after its three main dimensions:

- Sensory immersion in the SCI model is achieved through the audiovisual execution of games. As such, this is the same as the sensory stimulus in the GEM, including other stimulus, such as the force feedback, and more recently the full mixed reality experience.
- Challenge-based immersion is achieved when the challenge and pacing is just perfect for the player, assumably in accordance to the flow theory, as discussed by Järvinen et al. (2002, Sect. 4.1). This dimension is closest to the GEM element of action, and strongly related to the mechanics.
- Imaginative immersion involves the use of imagination and enjoying "the fantasy of the game". In the GEM this involves the storyworld, which is the player imagined universe of the game built on the explicitly presented narrative.

Later on Mäyrä (2007) has renamed "imaginative immersion" as "mental immersion" without any other changes to the model, except for placing it inside a more thorough framework of contexts. As with the holistic category of Björk and Holopainen (2004) that is highly similar, we exclude the contextual framework from our model.

The components Ermi and Mäyrä (2005) mention related to the SCI model in the conception of the gameplay experience can be fitted in the GEM as well (see Table 8.2). The *interface* between the player and the game applies sensory stimulus as output and action as input. The rules of the game are a part of the mechanics, where the actions are derived from. The SCI model distinction between challenge-based immersion and rules is relative to the distinction between action and mechanics. The story is the narratives the game tells the player, but rather than the story, Ermi and Mäyrä (2005) perceive that the player's imagination is immersed to the more holistic fantasy of the storyworld of the game, using their own imagination and empathy towards the characters.

8.4.5 Adams

Adams (2004, 2013) identifies three forms of immersion that are somewhat similar to the SCI model, but seem to lack the aesthetic form:

- Tactical immersion is the immersion in the moment-by-moment high-speed action. This form is related to the dynamics of the MDA model, in the connection of sensory stimulus and action. As described by Adams, we would rather see this form mostly involving action.
- Strategic immersion is the form "seeking a path to victory", focusing on winning the game according to the rules. This form is equivalent to the immersion through the GEM mechanics element.

Table 8.2 A comparison of the model by Ermi and Mäyrä to the GEM

SCI model	GEM	Comment
Sensory immersion	Sensory stimulus	Sensory immersion is "related to the audiovisual execution of games"
Challenge-based immersion	Mechanics, action	Challenge-based immersion "is at its most powerful when one is able to achieve a satisfying balance of challenges and abilities [...] related to motor skills or [...] strategic thinking"
Imaginative immersion	Storyworld	Imaginative immersion involves "the fantasy of the game"
Interface	Sensory stimulus, action	User input and output
Rules	Mechanics	Rules are a part of the mechanics
Story	Narrative	The story that is told by the game
Space	Mechanics	Storyworld in GEM contains the universe of the game. The game mechanics limit how much the player is able to see of the universe, and is part of the narrative that gives a finite glance to the infinite storyworld. The game space of chess is the 8×8 board, thus limited by the rules/mechanics, but the storyworld of chess consists of all the game boards of all the famous and less famous games of chess ever played, as well as all the stories people have about why the black and white king and queen are there with their armies
Meaning	Aesthetics	
Motivation	–	
Motorics	Action	
Cognitions	Aesthetics	
Emotions	Aesthetics	

- Narrative immersion is identified by Adams as the one of the three to be present in books as movies as well as in games. Because the tactical immersion requires player action, it is not present, as such, in these "earlier" forms of art. This is unlike the sensory immersion in the SCI model, which, as the aesthetic element of the GEM, can be found in movies, and especially in movies as well. Narrative immersion connects to the GEM element of narratives.

8.4.6 Summary

Table 8.3 collects all the analysed models and compare them to the GEM. *The six elements of the GEM seems to be a sufficient set in the sense that by removing any of them from the experience ceases it to be a game.* This impossibility comes in two forms: (1) Although, it is technically possible to take mechanics and action from a

Table 8.3 A summary of the comparisons

GEM	Smed and Hakonen	Björk and Holopainen	Hunicke et al. (MDA)	Ermi and Mäyrä (SCI)	Adams
Mechanics	The limits of the game that also cause the conflict and rivalry	Abstract reasoning and complex problem solving	Mechanics	–	What the player focuses on
Action	Concrete gameplay	Feedback loops of the gameplay performance	Dynamics	Satisfying balance of challenges and abilities that "can be related to motor skills or mental skills"	High-speed action
Storyworld	The unveiling of the actions of the hidden opponent	Participated events related to the unfolding of a narrative structure	Aesthetics	Use of imagination and empathy towards characters	–
Narrative	–	–	–	–	What the story audience focuses on
Aesthetics	Concrete gameplay experience	The feeling of being inside the game	Aesthetics	The audiovisual execution of the game	–
Sensory stimulus	–	–	–	–	–

game, but then it is no longer a game, as the player has no role in it. (2) There can be no action without sensory stimulus, which necessarily creates aesthetics, whether it is thoughtfully designed or not. Also, if a game has action, game mechanics, and aesthetics, then the gameplay necessarily forms narrative, whether it is scripted or not, and a storyworld appears by necessity of the circumstances.

8.5 Sample Case Games

In this section, we present two brief examples on how the GEM can be used in analysing a game.

8.5.1 XCOM

XCOM (Firaxis Games 2012) is a recent game in the *X-Com* game series. It has quite clear game mechanics, being a turn-based strategy game. The characters can, for example, be commanded to shoot at a target. The game mechanics then involve a random number to be generated and compared against the calculated probability of the shot hitting or missing. If the shot hits, the game engine has several alternative animations to play to represent the hit to the player. This can be tested, by saving the game before a shot, and then executing the shot over and over again, by reloading the saved situation. As *XCOM* provides protection against "save scumming" (Hogarty 2013), the game mechanical outcome of the shot is each time the same, but the engine varies between the different representations, as they are not essential for the game outcome, and can be freely randomized each time.

Shooting is clearly also a part of the narrative, as it is an understandable action taken by a human-like game character. Like the mouse clicking action connects shooting to the mechanics, the narrative of shooting gets connected to the storyworld, where the war is taking place between humans and aliens, and hi-tech weapons are discovered and used.

The visual representation of the shot confirms the action and mechanics for the player, generating a sense of agency. The same representation also visually and aurally tells the narrative to the player, and provides the aesthetics for painting the storyworld to the player, promoting the suspension of disbelief. This all binds the whole experience together to the fantasy of the *XCOM* game.

8.5.2 Hellblade: Senua's Sacrifice

Well designed aesthetics with well performed sensory stimulus can be used to replace actual game mechanics. For example, in the game *Hellblade: Senua's*

Sacrifice (Ninja Theory 2017) the aesthetics pulls the player into immersion so deeply that in all scenes with fire engulfing the play area, an actual player character damaging mechanism is not necessary, or even as effective in providing the player with a sense of emergency and the need to hurry.

Yin-Poole (2017) remarks that, unlike the game lets the player to understand, the game does not end, if the character dies too many times. The game represents as a visual mechanics, a rot on the character's arm that spreads every time the character dies and is restored to a previous situation. The player is made to believe that if this rot reaches the character's head, the game ends and has to be started over again. Apparently, this is not truly the case. The player can keep on failing and having the character to die over and over again. The rot will not spread past the character's shoulders. However, the effect, once again, gives the player a sense of significance for each death. Although the permanent death of the character is not in the program code, it is scripted into the beliefs of the player. An effect that almost goes beyond what "suspension of disbelief" covers. It provides for a great balance between helping the player to take each attempt seriously, and yet allowing the player to fail during the narrative.

Hellblade weighs heavily on aesthetics, although it has clear and functional mechanics, action, storyworld, and narrative too. The game puts the player inside the mind of the main character: the character hears speaking voices in her head, which is represented directly to the player through the speakers. Although the voices, as a mechanic, inform the player about the narrative in the game, they most essentially create the feeling of being a character in the game.

8.6   Conclusion

In this chapter, we presented the GEM (game experience model) which aims at providing a holistic view into the various aspects present in games. The GEM is intended as a tool for analysing games by recognizing their features through the various faces. It also provides aid for the game designer to inspire the creative process. The contribution of this work should be to help the game development industry to be able to analyse the content of their games and the human resources in relation to each other. Also, when designing something such as artificial intelligence for games, these four segments pose clearly distinctive challenges.

The GEM is composed of the summary of several game designers' and game researchers' formulations. It is based on the study of games, and hence best fitting for game experience. However, digital games are a subclass of digital applications, and thereby the GEM is applicable on a more general area as well. For serious digital applications, the storyworld is the business environment where the application will be used, for example, a corporate organization or a study life of a student.

Future work is needed in using the GEM in analysing a broader array of games to further validate the model. Furthermore, the GEM might provide interesting insights to the existing player type models. One could perceive "the power player type" to be attracted to the mechanics, "story player type" to the storyworld, and "immersive player type" to the aesthetics. This direction would also seem to point to a bridge towards the field of psychology begging the question why do people experience games in this way.

With the games becoming in increasing magnitude a form of art, the theoretical perception of games is changing. The theories need to be able to facilitate for this new position so that they can account for all essential parts of a game design. The GEM is a further step towards this direction—and perhaps to the Grand Unified Theory of games.

Acknowledgements The authors wish to express their gratitude to Harri Hakonen, who took a critical part in the early stages of the analysis and construction of the GEM.

References

Adams EW (2004) The designer's notebook: Postmodernism and the 3 types of immersion. Web page, https://www.gamasutra.com/view/feature/130531/the_designers_notebook_.php

Adams EW (2013) Resolutions to some problems in interactive storytelling. PhD thesis, University of Teesside, Middlesbrough, UK

Adams EW (2014) Fundamentals of Game Design, 3rd edn. New Riders, San Francisco, CA, USA

Benford S, Crabtree A, Flintham M, Drozd A, Anastasi R, Paxton M, Tandavanitj N, Adams M, Row-Farr J (2006) Can you see me now? ACM Transactions on Computer-Human Interaction 13(1):100–133, DOI 10.1145/1143518.1143522

Bethesda Game Studios (2011) The Elder Scrolls V: Skyrim. Bethesda Softworks

Björk S, Holopainen J (2004) Patterns in Game Design. Charles River Media, Boston, MA, USA

Blomberg J (2018) The semiotics of the game controller. International Journal of Computer Game Research 18(2), http://gamestudies.org/1802/articles/blomberg

Ermi L, Mäyrä F (2005) Fundamental components of the gameplay experience: Analysing immersion. In: Proceedings of the 2005 DiGRA International Conference: Changing Views – Worlds in Play, http://www.digra.org/wp-content/uploads/digital-library/06276.41516.pdf

Firaxis Games (2012) XCOM: Enemy Unknown. 2K Games

Gamma E, Helm R, Johnson R, Vlissides J (1995) Design Patterns: Elements of Reusable Object-Oriented Software. Addison-Wesley Professional Computing Series, Addison-Wesley, Reading, MA, USA

GDC Vault (2016) Failure workshop. Video, https://www.gdcvault.com/play/1023539/Failure

Hello Games (2016) No Man's Sky. Hello Games

Hogarty S (2013) The secret dice rolls of XCOM: Enemy Within. how Firaxis fudge the numbers. Web page, https://www.pcgamesn.com/secret-dice-rolls-xcom-enemy-within

Huizinga J (1955) Homo Ludens: A Study of the Play-Element in Culture. The Beacon Press, Boston, MA, USA, originally published in Dutch 1938

Hunicke R, LeBlanc M, Zubek R (2004) MDA: A formal approach to game design and game research. In: Fu D, Henke S, Orkin J (eds) Challenges in Game Artificial Intelligence, Papers from the 2004 AAAI Workshop, https://aaai.org/Library/Workshops/2004/ws04-04-001.php

Jacob JTPN, Coelho AF (2011) Issues in the development of location-based games. International Journal of Computer Games Technology doi:10.1155/2011/495437

Järvinen A, Heliö S, Mäyrä F (2002) Communication and community in digital entertainment services: Prestudy research report. Hypermedia Laboratory Net Series 2, University of Tampere, http://urn.fi/urn:isbn:951-44-5432-4

Juul J (2005) Half Real: Video Games Between Real Rules and Fictional Worlds. MIT Press, Cambridge, MA, USA

Lewis B, Porter L (2010) In-game advertising effects: Examining player perceptions of advertising schema congruity in a massively multiplayer online role-playing game. Journal of Interactive Advertising 10(2):46–60

Ludeon Studios (2018) Rimworld. Ludeon Studios

Mäntylä T, Lahti I, Ketamo H, Luimula M, Smed J (2014) Designing reality guides. In: Camilleri V, Dingli A, Montebello M (eds) Sixth International Conference on Virtual Worlds and Games for Serious Applications (VS-Games), pp 69–74

Maxis (1989) SimCity. Maxis

Mäyrä F (2007) The contextual game experience: On the socio-cultural contexts for meaning in digital play. In: Proceedings of the 2007 DiGRA International Conference: Situated Play, DiGRA 2007, Tokyo, Japan, September 24–28, 2007, http://www.digra.org/digital-library/publications/the-contextual-game-experience-on-the-socio-cultural-contexts-for-meaning-in-digital-play/

Mechner J (1989) Prince of Persion. Brøderbund

Mode 7 Games (2011) Frozen Synapse. Mode 7 Games

Mode 7 Games (2015) Frozen Cortex. Mode 7 Games

Mullins JK, Sabherwal R (2018) Beyond enjoyment: A cognitive-emotional perspective of gamification. In: Proceedings of the 51st Hawaii International Conference on System Sciences, pp 1237–1246, DOI 10.24251/HICSS.2018.152

Murray JH (2012) Inventing the Medium: Principles of Interaction Design as a Cultural Practice. MIT Press, Cambridge, MA, USA

Newton D (2014) Stumbling through Prince of Persia on almost everything. Video, https://youtu.be/Qrxk_VaSm6E

Niantic (2013) Ingress. Niantic

Niedenthal S (2009) What we talk about when we talk about game aesthetics. In: DiGRA '09 – Proceedings of the 2009 DiGRA International Conference: Breaking New Ground: Innovation in Games, Play, Practice and Theory, http://www.digra.org/wp-content/uploads/digital-library/09287.17350.pdf

Ninja Theory (2017) Hellblade: Senua's Sacrifice. Ninja Theory

Pajitnov AL (1984) Tetris

Robson K, Plangger K, Kietzmann JH, McCarthy I, Pitt L (2015) Is it all a game? understanding the principles of gamification. Business Horizons 58(4):411–420, DOI 10.1016/j.bushor.2015.03.006

Rockstar North (2013) Grand Theft Auto V. Rockstar Games

Schell J (2008) The Art of Game Design: A Book of Lenses. CRC Press, Boca Raton, FL, USA

Sicart M (2008) Defining game mechanics. International Journal of Computer Game Research 8(2), http://gamestudies.org/0802/articles/sicart

Smed J, Hakonen H (2003) Towards a definition of a computer game. Tech. Rep. 553, Turku Centre for Computer Science, Turku, Finland

Smed J, Hakonen H (2017) Algorithms and Networking for Computer Games, 2nd edn. John Wiley & Sons, Chichester, UK

Szilas N (2004) Stepping into the interactive drama. In: Göbel S, Spierling U, Hoffman A, Iurgel I, Schneider O, Dechau J, Feix A (eds) Technologies for Interactive Digital Storytelling and Entertainment. Proceedings of the Second International Conference, TIDSE 2004, Darmstadt, Germany, June 24–26, 2004, Springer-Verlag, Lecture Notes in Computer Science, vol 3105, pp 14–25

Ubisoft Montreal (2016) Far Cry Primal. Ubisoft

Yin-Poole W (2017) There's more to Hellblade's permadeath than meets the eye. Web page, https://www.eurogamer.net/articles/2017-08-09-theres-more-to-hellblades-permadeath-than-meets-the-eye

Chapter 9
Driven, Imaginative, and Casual Game Experiences

Jukka Vahlo and Aki Koponen

Contents

Abstract   In this chapter, we develop and validate game experience type (GET) inventory for investigating digital game players' preferred game experience types. Game experience is usually studied by analyzing patterns in player behavior or by

J. Vahlo (✉)
Centre of Excellence in Game Culture Studies, Helsinki, Finland

University of Turku, School of Economics, Turku, Finland
e-mail: jukka.vahlo@utu.fi; aki.koponen@utu.fi

A. Koponen
Centre of Excellence in Game Culture Studies, Helsinki, Finland

University of Turku, School of Economics, Turku, Finland

Tampere University, Tampere, Finland
e-mail: aki.koponen@utu.fi

© Springer Nature Switzerland AG 2020
B. Bostan (ed.), *Game User Experience And Player-Centered Design*,
International Series on Computer Entertainment and Media Technology,
https://doi.org/10.1007/978-3-030-37643-7_9

conducting surveys during and immediately after a gaming session of a particular game. In contrast to this, GET is designed to be a survey-based self-report method for examining players' sustaining preferences in game experience types across digital game genres. As a result of a series of factor analyses we reveal three latent game experience types of *Driven*, *Imaginative*, and *Casual*, and validate GET as a reliable method for measuring game users' experience type preferences.

Keywords Game experience · Driven experience · Imaginative experience · Casual experience

9.1 Introduction

The purpose of this chapter is to develop a novel tool for measuring players' preferences in different types of digital game experiences. Understanding patterns in game experience preferences is valuable for game companies from both design and marketing perspectives. By gaining in-depth knowledge on what kind of experiences their user-base is interested in, game companies and publishers can make informed player-centric design decisions and target their marketing campaigns to specific and precisely identified player segments. Furthermore, game companies could make use of information about players' preferred game experience types by combining this approach with their analyses on game metrics, KPIs, and recurrent play styles of their game.

Currently, game experiences are usually studied by analyzing patterns in player behavior or by conducting surveys and player-interviews during and immediately after gaming sessions. While these approaches are important for developing, e.g., playability of the game and for understanding emotional responses of the player, they provide limited knowledge on how experiences of playing the given game may correlate with the expectations and sustaining game preferences of the player.

In contrast to this, gameplay experience type (GET) inventory is designed to be a self-report method for examining players' prevailing preferences in game experience types across digital game genres. As such, GET combines research subjects which have been discussed in earlier literature as player-adopted play styles, player mentalities, and gaming mode preferences.

We begin this chapter by reviewing research literature on player preferences and on existing game experience survey measures. This will be followed by introducing an initial version of GET, which was piloted by collecting survey data from social media networks ($N = 798$) and by conducting a preliminary exploratory factor analysis (EFA). Next, we will report results from second EFA which was done with survey data collected in the UK ($N = 1459$). Since scale validation studies proper necessitates at least two EFAs before confirmatory phase (Matsunaga 2010), we conducted an additional EFA with survey data collected in the USA ($N = 672$) to further screen the GET inventory items. After assessing dimensionality and psychometric properties of the three EFAs, we will move to design a confirmatory factor analysis (CFA) with a short version of the GET inventory. The chapter will be concluded with a discussion on the results and by relating the identified game experience type (GET) model to prior game research literature.

9.2 Theoretical Background and the Concept of Game Experience

The objective of constructing a model for assessing preferred game experiences focuses on subjective understanding of what kind of experiences may result in playing games. Given that modern digital games are complex products, it is reasonable to presume that a game does not afford only one type of experience but instead game experiences are related to player's motivations, mood, preferred play styles, and to her favorite gameplay activity and challenge types.

Experience is a broad concept studied by many academic disciplines ranging from philosophical phenomenology to cognitive psychology and from anthropology to economics. As a general definition of the term, we utilize writings by John Dewey and American school of pragmatism. Dewey outlined that experience is "the result, the sign, and the reward of that interaction of organism and environment which, when it is carried to the full, is a transformation of interaction into participation and communication" (Dewey 2005[1934], p. 22). In other words, experience refers both to the process of interaction and to what results from the temporary relationship established between a subject and its environment. In the case of particular game experience, we can also nod towards *flow* or the optimal experience (Csikszentmihályi 1975, pp. 38–46) in which a person's primary attention and focus is in intrinsically rewarding or *autotelic* situational activity.

The concept of the game experience is difficult to define, and yet the concept is an important one for game developers, publishers, game journalists, and players alike. For all of these interest groups, "good gameplay" indicates that playing the game in question is not waste of time but gratifying in one way or another. As Ermi and Mäyrä (2007, p. 91) write, concepts of gameplay and game experience are used in video game cultures to characterize the paramount yet fleeting quality that defines a game as a game. For these authors, the game experience is "an ensemble made up of the player's sensations, thoughts, feelings, actions, and meaning-making in a gameplay setting." Mateas and Stern (2000, p. 643) maintain that game experience and the concept of gameplay remain as the raison d'être of games which identifies games as an autonomous medium.

According to game scholar Aarseth (2014, p. 483), games are both objects and processes, and studies on game ontology typically refer either to the functional and formal characteristics of the game object or to games-as-processes, i.e., how games are played and also thus how they are experienced by players. In game studies, research on game experience has been rather scarce, however. This is because most of the academic disciplines study games as designed products and services rather than as processes (Ermi and Mäyrä 2007).

Based on a game research literature review and his own research, Vahlo (2018) has recently argued that the game experience includes at least eight invariants or unchangeable qualities: (1) the player is expected to demonstrate playful attitude and (2) motivation to play. She engages in gameplay with both (3) coordinative and explorative player practices, which bring along changes in (4) her self-experience and (5) situational world-relation (i.e., the events that take place in gameplay happen to her as being a player and in relation to the gameworld instead of "the real world"). These changes render the gameplay experience inherently (6) emotional and (7) performative. Finally, Vahlo argues that each instance of gameplay has (8) structure of a prototypical narrative, regardless of whether the game itself is story-driven.

The GET approach is developed for investigating game experience according to what is known as phenomenological reduction. The core research question of phenomenological reduction is how things are experienced instead of what things are outside of the realm of subjective experience (see Thompson 2007, pp. 17–19). According to this demarcation, the GET model aims to generate new knowledge about the process ontology of games. Indeed, the game experience refers to the active interaction between a player and a dynamic game system, and to how the player actively participates in the game (Leino 2010; Vahlo 2017, 2018). It is the main objective of the GET to add new understanding on what kind of patterns can be identified in players' way to experience and reflect on their game experiences.

9.2.1 Player Preference Research

Contemporary player research can be divided into three branches which study demographic player factors (e.g., Griffiths et al. 2003; Greenberg et al. 2010; Koivisto and Hamari 2014), gratifications that player derive (e.g., Hamari and Keronen 2017), and player preferences (e.g., Bartle 2003; Hamari and Tuunanen 2014; Kallio et al. 2011; Vahlo et al. 2017).

Out of the overall body of player research, player preference literature can be further broken down into four categories of (1) motivations to play, (2) gaming intensity, (3) gameplay type preferences, and (4) player behavior (Vahlo and Hamari 2019; Vahlo and Koponen 2018). All of these four models of player preference research can be conceptualized as approaches of psychographic segmentation, since they aim to identify player traits and to group players based on their interests, values, and attitudes. Although many behavioral models analyze patterns in actual user behavior in gameplay (e.g., by investigating telemetrics or game logs), also these models can be regarded psychographic, because a player realizes her values and attitudes in how she acts during gaming.

Studies on motivations to play ask why people play games. These models can be further divided into (1) general models, which argue that psychological theories on interaction-oriented human needs (see Murray 1938) and motivations can be applied to our reasons to play games (e.g., Ryan et al. 2006; Bostan 2009), and into (2) explorative and empirical contextual models, which study specific reasons for playing, e.g., free-to-play mobile games, esports games, or massively multiplayer online games (e.g., Yee 2006). Models of gaming intensity aim to identify gaming mentalities and classify players into categories such as casual players, committed players, or hardcore players. These models may also take in the consideration how the current mood of the player may influence her gameplay decisions and in-game behavior (Deterding 2013; Ip and Jacobs 2005; Kallio et al. 2011). Gameplay type preference models have been recently introduced as intermediate approaches between context-specific behavioral models and motivations to play models. Gameplay type preference models aim to understand player traits and game choice based on what kind of game elements players find pleasant and unpleasant. These elements can be, for instance, gameplay activities, game challenge types, or game esthetics (Tondello et al. 2017, 2018; Vahlo et al. 2017, 2018).

The objective of developing the game experience type (GET) inventory is related to all of the four approaches of player preference research. To be motivated by, e.g., immersion and social interaction is likely to be associated with a preference for unobstructed and socially shared gameplay experience. Correspondingly, gaming mentalities such as casual mentality or hardcore mentality indicate what kind of experience the player is hoping for. Furthermore, preferences in gameplay activity types and game challenges may also denote to specific kind of gaming experience. For instance, a player may prefer tactical challenges and gameplay activities of sneaking, surprising enemies, and sniping (Vahlo et al. 2017). These preferences are expected to be linked with perceived gratification of game experiences.

The GET approach at hand focuses on identifying latent game experience types, based on players' reflections on their own gameplay preferences. Therefore this study is to be regarded as a player preference study which asks how players themselves perceive their own game experiences and favorite play styles.

9.2.2 Game Experience Measures

There are several widely used questionnaires which have been developed for assessing the game experience. For instance, Game User Experience Satisfaction Scale (GUESS) measures nine dimensions of gaming experiences: usability, narratives, engrossment, enjoyment, creative freedom, visual and audio esthetics, personal gratification, and social connectivity (Phan et al. 2016). Brockmyer et al. (2009) have developed game engagement questionnaire (GEQ) for measuring subjective experience of deep engagement while playing violent video games. The questionnaire consists of one dimension (level of engagement) and items that specify aspects of absorption, flow, presence, and immersion in an ongoing game experience, respectively. The 38-item core elements of the gaming experience questionnaire (CEGEQ) by Calvillo-Gámez et al. (2010) were constructed by using a qualitative grounded theory approach. According to the authors, the questionnaire measures the game experience both as an ongoing process and as an outcome from the perspectives of enjoyment, frustration, CEGE (videogame elements and player–game interaction), control, facilitators, ownership, gameplay, and environment.

Furthermore, the SPGQ questionnaire was developed for assessing social presence in gameplay with dimensions of behavioral engagement, empathy, and negative feelings (De Kort et al. 2007). The game experience questionnaire by Ijsselsteijn et al. (2008) was constructed for measuring imaginative immersion, flow, tension, negative and positive affect, and challenge, whereas the questionnaire by Hamari and Koivisto (2014) assesses dispositional flow in gameplay. The PENS scale by Ryan et al. (2006) is used in investigating player need satisfaction from the perspective of the self-determination theory, and the questionnaires by Jennett et al. (2008) and Witmer and Singer (1998) are used in measuring immersion and presence in gaming, respectively. Finally, there exist several questionnaires for studying player motivations and gratifications players get from the game experience (e.g., Sherry et al. 2006).

Recently, a model has been developed also for assessing *the gameful experience* which is defined by Huotari and Hamari (2017) in a broad fashion that covers experiences of using gamified services in addition to game products (see Landers et al. 2018). Högberg et al. (2019) constructed a measure called GAMEFULQUEST for investigating specifically the gameful experience in using gamified systems. Based on a literature review of existing game research and game experience questionnaires, the authors suggest that measuring game experience should take in the consideration dimensions of playfulness and free-form play, affect, enjoyment, flow, immersion, challenge, skill, competition, social experience, presence, and sensory experience. However, Högberg et al. (2019) argue also that there are important differences between games and gamified services and because of these differences, game research questionnaires are not adequate tools for measuring experiences of using gamified services at large.

Although many game experience questionnaires have been developed in earlier research, three important points of these measures must be made. Firstly, with the exception of the GUESS scale, there exists next to none psychometric valida- tion studies for the proposed exploratory questionnaires and their dimensionality. Secondly, the survey data used in these studies is not typically cross-cultural or representative in relation to gender and age on the population level. And thirdly, prior game experience questionnaires focus almost exclusively on investigating player experience either during gameplay or immediately after a gaming session. Also, as Högberg et al. (2019) note, many game experience instruments are not experience measures but rather trait measures which focus on, e.g., the tendency to engage with games or on player motivations.

By developing the game experience type (GET) questionnaire we aim to tackle all of the above-mentioned shortcomings of the previous game experience questionnaires. In order to do so, we will collect and analyze cross-cultural and representative survey data and proceed from exploratory factor analyses (EFAs) to conduct a confirmatory validation study with data from a different cultural environment.

Because GET is developed for understanding better how players perceive game experience types and how game experience preferences relate to, e.g., players' habits of playing specific types of games, we will begin the survey inventory development with a theory-free exploratory phase which draws from existing literature but does not set any hypotheses on the possible latent structures of the game experience types.

9.3 GET Inventory Development

We followed two sets of scale development and validation principles in constructing the GET inventory. Matsunaga (2010) has argued that a scale validation study should consist of at least one principal component factor analysis and an exploratory principal factor analysis *or* two exploratory principal factor analyses before moving to confirmatory phases. DeVellis (2012) has furthermore proposed that scale development studies should first determine the phenomenon under analysis and then move to develop an item pool for measuring the phenomenon. This should be followed by determining the measurement format and by doing an expert review of the items. Next, the researchers should collect the first sample, evaluate the items of the preliminary scale, and finally shorten and optimize the length of the scale. We planned, collected, and analyzed our survey data according to these guidelines. We also kept in our mind that three items for a latent construct is considered to be the sufficient minimum in scale validation studies (Brown 2015).

9.3.1 *Preliminary Surveys and Two EFAs*

We determined that the GET questionnaire was to be constructed for measuring players' preferences in sustaining game experience types, as outlined above. We decided to collect both quantitative and qualitative survey data to support our item pool construction. The objective was to collect two independent survey datasets and to conduct also two exploratory factor analyses (EFAs).

The first survey included a preliminary set of questions by which we inquired to what extent the described game experience types were preferred or disliked by the survey participants. The survey included also open-ended questions about whether some important experience types were missing from this first iteration of the GET scale. We aimed to use the results of the first survey as guidelines for amending the inventory before collecting the second survey sample.

9.3.1.1 Survey Participants of the First Sample

The first dataset was collected with a web-based survey which took approximately 15 min to complete with a mobile phone or a computer. We recruited a convenience sample from social media networks such as gamer-oriented Facebook groups and Reddit threads. The survey was targeted to everyone between the ages of 10 and 75. A total of 1397 participants opened the survey, out of which 818 submitted completed responses. Attempts to complete the survey more than once on the same device were blocked. Before conducting analyses, we cleaned the data of those participants who showed content nonresponsivity by responding with the exactly same value to each question of the GET inventory. The final sample consisted of 798 survey participants (mean age 28.9, 31.7% self-identified as female).

The preliminary GET scale consisted of 17 survey items and of open-ended questions about possible additional game experience types the participant considered to be missing from the initial inventory. Player preferences were inquired by asking the participants to state how pleasurable they found the 17 game experience types (5-Likert Scale, 1 = very unpleasant, 5 = very pleasant). The preliminary version of the GET was constructed based on results of our literature review on the four categories of player preference research. In particular, we focused on studies on player behavior and player mentalities, and on prior survey inventories developed for assessing game experience. We took the arguments made by Högberg et al. (2019) as a starting point for inventory development and constructed survey items which were connected to relaxing playful experiences, enjoyable experiences, challenge-based and flow-like experiences, social experiences, immersive experiences, esthetic experiences, and experiences of competition.

The survey included also inventories about motivations to play, gameplay activity and challenge type preferences, and questions about demographics, weekly playtime, game genre play, monthly spending on games, and about playing mobile games, pc and console games, and esports games. The survey included also a 5-Likert question in which survey participants were asked to report how interested they were in playing digital games (1 = Not at all interested, 5 = Very interested). The game interest mean value for the sample of 798 survey participants was high (4.45), and the survey participants reported to play role-playing games, action-adventure games, action games, and strategy games more than, e.g., mobile puzzle games.

In the sample of 798 player-participants, purely entertaining game experiences (item 16), story-driven experiences (item 4), and intensive long-term experiences (item 14) had the highest preference means, whereas experiences of competitive gaming (item 5), hardcore gaming (item 1), and experiences of completing all tasks or missions (item 5) had the lowest mean sums.

9.3.1.2 Results of the First Exploratory Factor Analysis

An exploratory factor analysis (EFA) was done with statistical software Stata 14.2 for exploring latent factor structures of the preliminary GET inventory (Table 9.1). EFA is an exploratory statistical analysis method for investigating psychometric properties and dimensionality of inventories. The method is not theory-driven, which means that we proceeded to do the EFA without theory-based hypotheses on its possible dimensionality.

A parallel analysis (PA, Henson and Roberts 2006) was conducted for identifying the number of factors to be extracted for the 17-item GET inventory. The PA test suggested that four factors were to be extracted. The eigenvalue >1 test supported this decision, but the Velicer's MAP test suggested instead a three-factor solution. A Kaiser–Meyer–Olkin (KMO) test was also utilized to measure sampling adequacy

Table 9.1 Descriptive statistics of the preliminary GET inventory ($N = 798$)

Game experience type. Experiences of...	Item	Mean	SD
... hardcore gaming which really tests your skills and wits	1	2.91	1.33
... laid-back relaxing casual gaming	2	4.00	1.00
... competitive gaming in which you want to win	3	2.57	1.31
... story-driven gaming in which you focus especially on the game fiction	4	4.34	1.01
... completing every task and mission of the game and getting all trophies	5	2.98	1.32
... nostalgia from playing games which bring up fond memories	6	3.86	1.04
... esthetics from playing games which feel like works of art	7	3.76	1.18
... continuous risk-taking and succeeding	8	3.24	1.17
... playing together and sharing the game experience	9	3.64	1.23
... epic win after a major struggle	10	3.61	1.25
... being smart enough to solve in-game puzzles	11	3.67	1.10
... freedom from playing games with huge open worlds	12	4.00	1.09
... short-term gaming which offers a little break to your everyday routines	13	3.44	1.15
... intensive and long-term gaming without any interruptions	14	4.13	1.06
... emotional, thought-provoking, and deeply meaningful gaming	15	3.97	1.14
... purely entertaining gaming, which is filled with joy	16	4.35	0.81
... learning to be better and mastering skills	17	3.64	1.05

for conducting factor analyses. The KMO value was (0.84), which indicated an adequate sampling.

In the first solution, we decided to follow the PA test and extract four factors. A four-factor solution with principal axis factors and promax rotation was thus extracted. Promax rotation was selected as the rotation method because it allows factors to correlate with each other instead of assuming that the factors would be orthogonal (Matsunaga 2010, p. 100). Using promax rotation was an informed decision: it is plausible to expect that players who enjoy digital games may find several game experience types gratifying.

We decided to use factor loadings over 0.40 as a criterion to determine whether an inventory item belonged to a factor (see Hair et al. 2010, pp. 114–115). However, no inventory items showed a factor loading over 0.40 on the fourth factor. Because of this result, we decided to redo the factor analysis with a three-factor solution as suggested by the MAP test. In the three-factor solution, items 5, 6, 9, 11, and 12 did not show factor loadings over 0.4. We removed these items and ran another factor analysis. All of the tests suggested now a three-factor solution, and therefore we proceeded to extract three factors.

In the second solution of three factors, all remaining items loaded on a factor with loading >0.40 and without cross-loadings on the other two factors. The first factor consisted experience types of hardcore gaming (item 1), competitive gaming (item 3), continuous risk-taking (item 8), epic win (item 10), and learning to be better and mastering skills (item 17). We call this factor *Driven*, because the game experience types that loaded on this factor describe preference in fierce gaming with an objective to excel and to be successful or victorious.

Three items loaded on the second factor. These items denote to story-driven game experiences (item 4) which feel like works of art (item 7), and which are interpreted as emotional and inherently meaningful (item 15). We call this factor *Imaginative*.

Finally, three items loaded also on the third factor. These items refer to preference in game experience types of short-term (item 13) and laid-back casual gaming (item 2), which is experienced as purely entertaining (item 17) rather than being fierce (*Driven*) or inherently meaningful (*Imaginative*). We call the third factor *Casual*.

9.3.2   Survey Participants of the Second Sample

After making factor analyses for the first sample, we analyzed the open-ended data of the survey. Several survey participants suggested that the inventory could include also game experience types which refer to (1) being smarter than the game AI, (2) exploration and discovery, and (3) experiences which resemble real life.

Because the first survey sample consisted of participants who reported to be interested or very interested in playing digital games, we decided to collect another survey data and make another exploratory factor analysis before proceeding towards more confirmatory phases of the GET inventory development (see Matsunaga 2010). We decided also to retain all of the 17 items in the GET inventory and include also three new items based on the open-ended survey responses. The new items were: "Experiences of outsmarting the artificial intelligence" (Item 18), "Experiences of exploration and discovery" (Item 19), and "Experiences that feel like real life" (Item 20). A focus group meeting with three external game researchers and two game designers was also organized to amend the wordings of the survey items. Based on the feedback from the focus group meeting, we decided to include an open-ended question to the second survey so that survey participants could still propose new game experience types to the inventory.

An additional survey data was collected from the UK by using a UK-based crowdsourcing platform Prolific which holds an online panel of over 70,000 users worldwide. The new survey started with a screener question which inquired the Prolific users' age, gender, interest in videogames, and how often they played with different gaming technologies such as mobile phones, personal computers, and consoles. The full survey was then opened for those respondents who expressed that they were at least a bit interested in playing digital games. The purpose of this screener was to focus on participants who had at least a little first-hand experience on playing digital games. Similarly to the first survey, also the second survey included questions about gaming motivations, weekly playtime, game genre play, monthly spending on games, demographics, and about participants' habits to play mobile games, pc and console games, and esports games.

A total of 1521 responses from the UK survey participants were submitted. To ensure that respondents paid attention and replied truthfully to the questions of the survey, we applied two screening questions. We cleaned the data by first removing those participants who stated that they did not pay any attention to how they responded to the questions or who reported that they did not answer truthfully to the survey. We then continued to clean the data according to the same procedure than we did with the first survey data. This resulted in a UK sample of 1459 participants (mean age 36.4, 61.8% self-identified as female, mean interest in digital games 3.5). It should be noted that the gender distribution and the mean age of this second survey sample differed greatly from the first sample. Also, the mean game interest of the second sample was much lower than in the first sample.

9.3.2.1 Results of the Second Exploratory Factor Analysis

A second exploratory factor analysis (EFA) was done for exploring latent factor structures of the 20-item GET inventory with survey data collected in the UK. Similarly to the first EFA, a parallel analysis was conducted to identify the number of factors to be extracted for the second iteration of the GET inventory. The PA test suggested a three-factor solution. Both the eigenvalue >1 test and the Velicer's MAP test supported this decision, and therefore we continued to extract three factors with promax rotation. The Kaiser–Meyer–Olkin (KMO) supported sampling adequacy for factor analyses (0.95).

In the first solution, and similarly to the first EFA ($N = 798$), items 5, 6, and 9 did not load on any of the three factors (cut-off value 0.40). We omitted these three items and continued to make another EFA with the remaining 17 items of the GET. All of the tests suggested still a three-factor solution, and thus we continued to extract three factors.

In the second solution, all items loaded on a factor with a loading over 0.40 and without showing cross-loadings between the other factors. Seven items loaded on the first factor. Similarly to the EFA with the first survey sample, items which described story-driven experiences, esthetic experiences, and emotional and meaningful experiences loaded on the same factor. In addition to the above, also experiences of intensive and long-term gaming (item 14), experiences of freedom to wander in open worlds (item 12) as well as two new items of exploration and real life like experiences (items 19 and 20) loaded on this factor. Similarly to the EFA with the first data, we call this factor *Imaginative* ($\alpha = 0.88$).

Six items loaded on the second factor. These included experiences of hardcore gaming, competitive gaming, continuous risk-taking, epic winning, learning to be better, and mastering skills. These items were thus exactly the same ones which loaded on the factor *Driven* in the first EFA. In addition to these five items, also the third new item of outsmarting the AI loaded on the factor 2. Therefore, we continued to call this factor *Driven* ($\alpha = 0.84$).

Finally, four items loaded on the third factor. This factor, which we named *Casual* in the first EFA, consisted also in this second EFA of experiences of short-term gaming, casual and relaxing gaming, and purely entertaining gaming. In addition to these three items, also experiences of solving in-game puzzles (item 11) loaded on *Casual* ($\alpha = 0.64$).

9.4   Item Screening and Confirmatory Factor Analysis

We decided to drop the items describing experiences of completing every task and mission of the game (item 5), nostalgia (item 6), and socially shared gaming (item 9) from the confirmatory scale validation phase of this study. This was done because these three items did not load on any factor in either of the two EFAs.

Based on the empirical analyses with the two survey datasets, we hypothesized that game experience consists of three broad preferences factors of *Driven*, *Imaginative*, and *Casual*. Although the Cronbach's alphas for *Driven* ($\alpha = 0.88$) and *Imaginative* ($\alpha = 0.84$) were high, the same was not true for *Casual* ($\alpha = 0.64$) game experiences in the UK sample ($N = 1459$). Because of this we decided to develop an additional item for measuring this hypothesized latent construct. The new item was: "Experiences of games that make dull moments more entertaining" (item 21). Furthermore, and based on the open-ended responses of the second survey, we developed also the following new items: "Experiences of making progress and unlocking new content" (item 22), "Experiences of being powerful" (item 23), "Experience of achievement" (item 24), and an item to measure an experience type common for battle royale esports games: "Experience of being the last one standing after a decisive battle" (item 25).

Because we included six new items to the GET inventory and dropped the three items which did not load on any of the three factors in the two EFAs, we decided to conduct yet another EFA before moving to design a three-factor confirmatory factor analysis for the GET inventory. The main purpose of the third EFA was to screen the GET items for the CFA, that is, to shorten the now 22-item GET inventory to better fit future game research purposes. Also, we wanted to understand better if the game experience types proposed in the open-ended responses of the second survey would load on any of the three hypothesized factors.

9.4.1   Survey Participants of the Third Sample

We recruited a representative US sample of 1572 participants by using Prolific's online panel services. Also this third survey started with a screener question which inquired the Prolific users' demographics, interest in playing digital games, and how much they had played mobile games, pc and console games, and esports games (5-Likert, 1 = not at all, 5 = very much). Again, the full survey was opened for those respondents who expressed that they were at least a bit interested in playing digital games. The third survey included also questions about gaming motivations, and monthly spending on digital games. Similarly to the second survey, this survey included screening questions in which we asked how truthfully participants answered to the questions and whether they were paying attention to what was asked from them. After cleaning the data according to exactly same procedure than with the second survey, we continued to remove those survey participants who had stated to be very interested only about online casino games ($n = 93$). This was done because the experiences of online casino games may be related to digital game experiences but the former experiences are also likely to have several characteristics which are typical only for gambling games and online casino games. After these modifications to the data, the final US survey sample consisted of 1321 survey participants (mean age 38.8 years, 50.5% self-identified as female, mean interest in digital games 3.6).

9.4.2 Results of the Item Screening Process

A third exploratory factor analysis (EFA) was done for exploring latent factor structures and psychometric properties of the refined 22-item GET inventory with survey data collected in the USA. Before making the EFA, we split the sample in two random subsamples. The purpose for this was to conduct the EFA for item screening purposes with the first subsample and confirmatory factor analysis with the other subsample.

The EFA subsample consisted of 672 survey participants (mean age 38.9 years, 51.9% self-identified as female, mean interest in digital games 3.5). Similarly to the previous EFAs, a parallel analysis was conducted to identify the number of factors to be extracted. The PA test suggested a three-factor solution. The Velicer's MAP test and the eigenvalue>1 test both supported this result, and the sampling clearly passed the Kaiser–Meyer–Olkin test (0.95). Thus we continued to extract three factors with promax rotation.

Since the third EFA was made for item screening purposes, we utilized stronger item loading of 0.50 as the criterion to define whether an item loaded on a factor. We also applied in the survey a 7-Likert version of the scale instead of 5-Likert version used in two earlier EFAs. In the first solution, items 14, 16, 17, 18, and 20 showed factor loadings over 0.40 but under 0.50 and thus these items were omitted. We continued then to do another exploratory factor analysis with the refined 17-item GET inventory. In the second solution, all remaining 17 items loaded on a factor with a loading >0.50 and without showing cross-loadings.

We applied the following criteria in amending the GET inventory. Firstly, we accepted only those items which showed a factor loading over 0.50 on a factor. Secondly, we accepted only those items which had discrepancy value over 0.20, which means that the secondary factor loading was at least 0.20 lower than the primary factor loading. All of the 17 items passed also this second test. The lowest discrepancy value (0.21) was for the item 23: "Experience of being powerful," which loaded on *Driven* (0.56) but showed also a notable secondary loading on *Imaginative* (0.35). The final 17-GET inventory and its primary factor loadings and descriptive statistics are reported in Table 9.2.

The third EFA with the US sample of 672 respondents had largely similar results than the two first EFAs. The same items loaded both on *Driven* and *Imaginative* than in previous exploratory factor analyses. In addition to this, experiences of

Table 9.2 The third iteration of the GET inventory, a 17-item version with factor loadings >0.5 ($N = 672$)

Experiences of...	Factor 1	Factor 2	Factor 3	Uniq.
...hardcore gaming which really tests your skills and wits		0.64		0.44
...laid-back relaxing casual gaming			0.72	0.53
...competitive gaming in which you want to win		0.77		0.50
...story-driven gaming in which you focus especially on the game fiction	0.78			0.37
...esthetics from playing games which feel like works of art	0.70			0.43
...continuous risk-taking and succeeding		0.53		0.40
...epic win after a major struggle		0.67		0.37
...being smart enough to solve in-game puzzles			0.56	0.63
...freedom from playing games with huge open worlds	0.71			0.40
...short-term gaming which offers a little break to your everyday routines			0.62	0.67
...emotional, thought-provoking, and deeply meaningful gaming	0.72			0.43
...exploration and discovery	0.69			0.41
...games that make dull moments more entertaining			0.51	0.47
...making progress and unlocking new content			0.56	0.46
...being powerful		0.56		0.36
...achievement			0.63	0.43
...being the last one standing after a decisive battle		0.79		0.38
Factor mean sum	4.76	5.11	5.55	
Standard deviation	1.35	1.29	0.89	
Cronbach's alpha	0.89	0.88	0.83	

exploration and discovery loaded on *Imaginative,* whereas experiences of being powerful and being the last one standing after a decisive battle loaded on *Driven.* Furthermore, the same items which loaded on *Casual* in the first two EFAs, loaded on the same factor also in this third EFA. In addition to this, also the two new items "Experiences of making progress and unlocking new content" and "Experiences of achievement" loaded on *Casual.* It should also be noted that the Cronbach's Alpha for *Casual* was much higher in the third EFA. Because of these reasons, we propose that the two new items of unlocking content and experiencing achievement are important additions to the *Casual* factor.

Next, we proceeded to select GET inventory items for a confirmatory factor analysis. By doing so, we also aimed to shorten the scale to make it thus a better fit for future research purposes. Three items is considered to be the smallest number of observed variables for a sufficiently identified latent construct (Brown 2015). Therefore we designed a CFA model consisting of three 3-item constructs for *Driven, Imaginative,* and *Casual.*

9.4.3   Confirmatory Factor Analysis

Confirmatory factor analysis (CFA) is a theory-based method for analyzing measurement models in scale validation studies. In contrast to EFAs, in CFA researchers make hypotheses based on earlier theoretical and empirical research and design a model for investigating whether a new instrument can be validated properly. A measurement model is constructed for analyzing how observed variables are associated with the hypothesized factors (Brown 2015).

A CFA model was designed for the amended GET inventory for investigating (1) if the GET inventory items could be validated psychometrically, and (2) whether the items could be confirmed as indicators for measuring preferences in *Driven*, *Imaginative*, and *Casual* game experiences. The model was based on the results of the three EFAs, as well as on earlier literature on player preferences. The CFA was made with a random subsample of the survey data collected in the USA ($N = 649$, mean age 38.6, 49.2% self-identified as female, mean interest in digital games 3.6). As noted, it is important to validate an inventory with cross-cultural data in order to better understand how cultural differences may affect how people reflect on their experiences. This is especially true in the case of experience goods, including digital games (Quandt et al. 2009; De Grove et al. 2017).

The three-item combinations for each factor were selected based on the following criteria (Matsunaga 2010): (1) the items all loaded on their respective factor with a loading over 0.50; (2) the items did not show cross-loadings on another factor, that is, the discrepancy between the primary and the secondary loading was over 0.20; and (3) the items described qualities of the hypothesized latent construct in different ways without overlapping with each other.

We decided to include on *Driven* the items which described hardcore game experience, experience of epic win, and experience of being the last one standing after a decisive battle. On *Imaginative* we included items of story-driven experiences, esthetic experiences, and emotionally enthralling and meaningful game experiences. *Casual* consisted of experiences of relaxing and casual gaming, experiences that make dull moments more entertaining, and experiences of achievement. We decided to include experiences of achievement, because the third EFA with the US sample indicated that these experience types measure the same latent dimension of the game experience preference than casual short-term relaxing gaming. The selected nine items and their descriptive statistics in the US data are reported in Table 9.3.

Next, a confirmatory factor analysis with the subsample collected from the USA ($n = 649$) was made by using statistical software Stata 14.2 and maximum likelihood estimation procedure in structural equation modeling (SEM). We present the measurement model in Fig. 9.1. In order to investigate the construct validity of the model, we calculated the root mean squared error of approximation (RMSEA), the comparative fit index (CFI), the Tucker Lewis Index (TLI), and the standardized root mean squared residual score (SRMR). We did not apply the chi square test, because this test is known to be unreliably in analyses with large sample sizes, and especially if correlations between latent constructs are expected to be high (Matsunaga 2010; Russell 2002).

Table 9.3 Descriptive statistics for the 9-item GET ($N = 672$)

Item	Experiences of...	Mean	Skewn.	Kurt.
x1	...hardcore gaming which really tests your skills and wits (D)	4.47	−0.44	2.18
x2	...epic win after a major struggle (D)	5.02	−0.86	2.92
x3	...being the last one standing after a decisive battle (D)	4.64	−0.55	2.61
x4	...story-driven gaming in which you focus especially on the game fiction (I)	4.96	−0.76	3.00
x5	...esthetics from playing games which feel like works of art (I)	5.16	−0.91	3.57
x6	...emotional, thought-provoking, and deeply meaningful gaming (I)	4.92	−0.66	3.01
x7	...laid-back relaxing casual gaming (C)	5.56	−1.07	4.80
x8	...games that make dull moments more entertaining (C)	5.36	−0.98	4.66
x9	...achievement (C)	5.65	−1.27	5.31

Hypothesized factors: *D* Driven, *I* Imaginative, *C* Casual

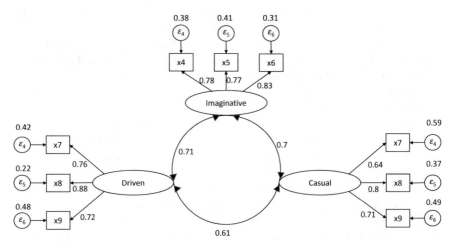

Fig. 9.1 The measurement model of the 9-item GET inventory with survey data collected in the US data ($N = 649$). All loadings of the model are significant on the level $p < 0.001$

The model (Fig. 9.1) had the following goodness-of-fit values to the data of 649 respondents: RMSEA 0.064, CFI 0.976, TLI 0.963, and SRMR 0.038. Taken together, these results support construct validity for the CFA model and indicate a good fit to the continuous data of the GET inventory (Brown 2015; Hu and Bentler 1999; Kline 2010; Marsh et al. 2004; Schreiber et al. 2006).

To examine the model's discriminant and convergent validity, we continued to calculate composite reliability (CR) values for the three factors. The CR score should be over 0.7 to be acceptable and in order to provide support for convergent validity of the model (Zait and Bertea 2011). The CR test values were 0.834 for *Driven*, 0.836 for *Imaginative*, and 0.761 for *Casual*. We continued to calculate the average variance extracted (AVE) scores to investigate both convergent and

Table 9.4 The average variance extracted analysis (AVE) of the 9-item and three-factor version of the GET inventory

	Driven	Imaginative	Casual
Driven	**0.628**		
Imaginative	0.505	**0.631**	
Casual	0.367	0.483	**0.517**

The AVE values are bolded

discriminant validity of the model. The AVE analysis is made for testing if the average variance extracted is higher than the shared variance between latent constructs in the model. The AVE value for each latent construct should thus be larger than the shared variance value it has with the other constructs (Farrell 2009; Fornell and Larcker 1981). The AVE test results are presented in Table 9.4.

The AVE values for each factor should be over 0.50 and the AVE of each construct should be higher than the variance the constructs share with the other two factors. The 9-item GET passed the AVE tests, and therefore these results support both convergent and discriminant validity for the 9-item GET inventory.

9.4.4 Do Game Experience Preferences Predict Gaming Habits?

In order to demonstrate the usefulness of the validated 9-item GET inventory, we investigated whether preferences in the three game experience types *Driven, Imaginative*, and *Casual* predicted habits to play digital games. The survey employed in the USA ($N = 1321$) included a 5-Likert question on how often the respondent plays games (1 = Not at all, 5 = Very often), and three 5-Likert type questions on how interested the respondent was in playing (a) PC and console games, (b) mobile games, and (c) esports games (1 = Not at all interested, 5 = Very interested).

We constructed a structural equation model to investigate how preference in the three game experience types predicted (a) habit to play any digital games and (b) interest in playing PC and console games, mobile games, and esports games. The structural model was based on the measurement model which we validated in the CFA study (Fig. 9.1). The structural model is presented below.

In the media theory it is argued that users' preferences are consistently associated with habits of media usage and with interest in specific media content (Webster 2014; Scherer and Naab 2009). Based on this theoretical observation, it is plausible to assume that players' game experience type preferences predict their habits and interest to play different types of digital games. Therefore, by designing and constructing a structural equation model (Fig. 9.2), we analyzed the path coefficients between game experience type preferences and observed variables of habit to play digital games at large, and interest of playing PC and console games, mobile games, and esports games. The estimates for the structural equation models are presented in Table 9.5.

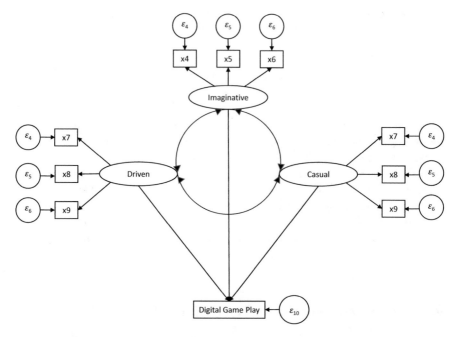

Fig. 9.2 Structural model for investigating how game experience type preferences predict habit of playing digital games. Model fit RMSEA 0.064, CFI 0.969, TLI 0.954, SRMR 0.037 to the combined data collected in the USA ($N = 1321$)

Table 9.5 The direct effects of the three game experience preference factors on playing digital games, and on being interested to play PC and console games, mobile games, and esports games ($N = 1321$)

Model estimates	Driven		Imaginative		Casual		R^2
	Coef.	P	Coef.	P	Coef.	P	
Habit to play digital games	0.151	0.001**	0.114	0.035*	0.081	0.119	0.095
Interest in							
PC and console games	0.267	0.000***	0.446	0.000***	−0.230	0.000***	0.266
Mobile games	−0.014	0.751	0.000	0.589	0.230	0.000***	0.049
Esports games	0.483	0.000***	0.058	0.273	−0.242	0.000***	0.167

Note: *$p < 0.05$, **$p < 0.01$, and ***$p < 0.001$, R^2 = variance explained
The significance levels are for the unstandardized solution of the model shown in Fig. 9.2

The results reported in Table 9.5 reveal that preferences in game experience types are connected to the habit of playing digital games. Both preference in *Driven* and in *Imaginative* predicted a gaming habit, although these effects were weak. However, preference in *Casual* was not associated with the habit to play digital games.

Preference in *Driven* predicted strongly interest in playing esports games, and moderately interest in PC and console games. Favoring *Imaginative* game experience predicted strongly interest in PC and console games, but no connection was found between *Imaginative* and mobile gaming or esports gaming interest. Finally, preference in *Casual* predicted positively interest in playing mobile games but negatively interest in playing PC and console games as well as esports games.

9.5 Discussion and Future Research

The purpose of this chapter was to develop and validate a novel instrument for assessing game experience types and players' preferences in the identified dimensions of this phenomenon. A 17-item GET inventory (Table 9.2) was developed based on a series of exploratory factor analyses (EFAs) with data from social media gaming groups ($N = 798$), the UK ($N = 1459$), and the USA ($N = 672$). All three EFAs indicated that players' game experience preferences include three dimension which we called *Driven, Imaginative*, and *Casual*.

A confirmatory factor analysis was then designed for a short 9-item version of the GET (Table 9.3). The CFA with the US sample ($N = 649$), and the follow-up tests of construct validity, discriminant validity, and convergent validity confirmed the three-factor model of game experience types and validated the 9-item GET as a psychometrically sound short instrument for measuring players' sustaining game experience preferences. It was furthermore demonstrated that preference in *Driven, Imaginative*, and *Casual* predicted interest in playing PC and console games, mobiles games, and esports games. Preference in *Driven* game experiences was associated strongly with interest in playing esports games, and moderately with interest in playing computer and console games. Preferences in *Imaginative* predicted interest in computer and console games. Favoring *Casual* was connected with being interested in playing mobile games but negatively with interest to play esports games and computer and console games.

The validated three game experience type factors are congenial with earlier game research literature, especially with player preference models of gaming intensity and mentality. For instance, Kallio et al. (2011) argued that gaming mentalities can be divided into three groups according to intensity and sociability: committed mentality (long gaming sessions, social attachment to gamer communities), casual mentality (occasional play), and social mentality of gaming companions.

Roger Caillois' well-known breakdown of games into four types is also not a far cry from the GET model. Caillois (2001[1961]) proposed that games can be classified into competitive and combat-like games of *agôn* in which the player aim to "demonstrate his own superiority" (p. 16). Games of *mimicry* are about "deploying actions or submitting to one's fate in an imaginary milieu" in the activities of interpretation, imitation, escape, and taking on the role of another (p. 21). Caillois noted also that *mimicry* does not have much in common with games of *alea*, that is, games of chance and luck. In *alea*, "the player is entirely passive; he does not deploy his resources, skill, muscles, or intelligence." If we consider the attitude of the player, *alea* is exactly opposite to *agôn*, as the former negates, e.g., patience and qualification, both of which are important elements for *agôn*.

We can clearly note that the *Driven* game experience is closely related to *agôn*, and that *Imaginative* game experiences refer to what Caillois called *mimicry*. Furthermore, *Casual* resembles *alea*, although *Casual* cannot be reduced to mere luck. However, if we consider the player attitude of relaxing, laid-back *Casual* experiences, we can immediately note that they are distant to that of *Driven* experiences of competitive and hardcore gaming. Indeed, the scale validation study of this chapter provides support for Caillois' classic and ingenious anthropological analysis on play and games. Therefore it should be asked whether digital game players have latent preference also for Caillois' fourth category of games: *ilinx*, or pursuit of vertigo and temporary sensation of disorder, chaos, shock, or visceral fear (see Caillois 2001[1961], p. 26). In future research, we aim to investigate this question by experimenting with the GET inventory by developing items which describe *ilinx* and by also analyzing the dimensionality of also these items with additional empirical data: it is worth to note that *Ilinx* may be especially important aspect of the VR game experience. However, it is also possible that *ilinx* or vertigo does not constitute its own game experience preference factor, but instead the items developed for assessing *ilinx* may cross-load between *Driven*, *Imaginative*, and *Casual*.

Furthermore, the three factors of the GET inventory are related also to what has been written about emotional outcomes and gratifications of gaming. Inventory items which loaded on *Driven* highlight player preferences which are usually associated with hardcore gaming and with experiencing *fiero*, that is, feeling mastery and triumph over adversity (e.g., Koster 2005; McGonigal 2011). Future research should thus consider how the three game experience types are connected to preference in specific emotional responses (e.g., amusement, pride, curiosity, anger, sadness, fear) and also to experienced flow in games. McGonigal (2011, p. 43) has proposed that "flow and fiero are the original rewards of video gameplay," but it is not known how preference in flow is connected to *Driven* or to the other two dimensions of game experience preferences.

Finally, future research could investigate empirically how Nicole Lazzaro's (2009, pp. 21–22) model of the four keys to emotion in player experience relate to the three game experience preference types. Lazzaro has argued that (1) challenge, mastery, and fiero denote to *hard fun;* (2) curiosity, exploration, and roleplay to *easy fun;* (3) relaxation, escape, and achievement to *serious fun* (which denotes to instrumental gaming mentality of serious games), and finally (4) amusement, pleasure in other people's misfortune, and enjoyment in helping the others to *people fun*. It can be hypothesized that hard fun is closely related to preference in *Driven*, easy fun to *Imaginative*, and serious fun to *Casual* game experience preferences. Again, it is possible that preference in social game experience constitutes an additional dimension of the GET model, but it is also possible that items describing preference in social would cross-load between *Driven*, *Imaginative*, and *Casual*. After all, *Driven* experiences are often social experiences of competition, *Imaginative* experiences can take place in, e.g., massively multiplayer online gameworlds, and *Casual* experiences may very well include extensive social features and gameplay elements.

In future game research, the GET model can be applied also in studies on player behavior which ask what kind of play styles players adopt, i.e., how they play the game. The general question of how players play a game can be investigated either by analyzing what kind of play styles players report to favor or by tracking their actual behavioral data and analyzing in-game metrics (e.g., the number of deaths, player choices, completion times, trophies, avatar attributes). These two approaches can now be brought together to triangulate the results. For example, players can be categorized as risk-takers based on carefully formulated and mapped in-game metrics, and the same model can be then applied across different games and genres (Cowley and Charles 2016).

Based on the theoretical and empirical analyses of this chapter, we propose that the short 9-item GET inventory and the 17-item longer version can be applied into studies on player behavior and into games user research at large, both for research and game industry purposes.

References

Aarseth E (2014) Ontology. In: Wolf MJP, Perron B (Eds) The Routledge Companion to Video Game Studies. Routledge, New York, pp 484–492

Bartle RA (2003) Designing Virtual Worlds. New Riders, Boston

Bostan, B (2009) Player motivations: A psychological perspective. Computers in Entertainment 7(2)

Brockmyer JH, Fox, CM, Curtiss KA et al (2009) The development of the Game Engagement Questionnaire: a measure of engagement in video game-playing. J. Exp. Soc. Psychol. 45(4): 624–634

Brown TA (2015) Confirmatory Factor Analysis for Applied Research, 2nd edition. The Guilford Press, New York

Caillois R (2001 [1961]). Man, Play and Games. University of Illinois Press, Chicago

Calvillo-Gámez EH, Cairns P, Cox AL (2010) Assessing the core elements of the gaming experience. In: Bernhaupt R. (ed) Evaluating User Experience in Games. Springer, London, pp 47–71

Cowley B, Charles D (2016) Behavlets: a method for practical player modelling using psychology-based player traits and domain-specific features. User Modeling User-Adapted Interaction 26(2): 257–306

Csikszentmihályi, M (1975) Beyond Boredom and Anxiety. Jossey-Bass, San Francisco

De Grove F, Breuer J, Chen VHH et al (2017) Validating the Digital Games Motivation Scale for Comparative Research Between Countries. Communication Research Reports 34(1): 37–47

De Kort YAW, Ijsselsteijn WA, Poels K (2007) Digital games as social presence technology: Development of the Social Presence in Gaming Questionnaire (SPGQ). In: Proceedings of the 10th Annual International Workshop on Presence 2007. Barcelona, Spain, pp 195–203

Deterding S (2013). Modes of Play. A Frame Analytic Account of Video Game Play. Academic Dissertation, University of Hamburg, Hamburg

DeVellis RF (2012) Scale Development: Theory and Applications, vol. 26, 3rd edition. Sage, Thousand Oaks

Dewey, J (2005[1934]) Art as Experience. Penguin Book, New York

Ermi L, Mäyrä F (2007) Fundamental Components of the Gameplay Experience: Analysing Immersion. In: de Castell S, Jenson, J (Eds) Worlds in Play: International Perspectives on Digital Games Research. New Literacies and Digital Epistemologies Vol. 21. Peter Lang, New York, pp 37–53

Farrell AM (2009) Insufficient discriminant validity: a comment on Bove, Pervan, Beatty and Shiu. Journal of Business Research 63(3): 324–327

Fornell C, Larcker DF (1981) Evaluating structural equation models with unobservable variables and measurement error. Journal of Marketing Research 18(1): 39–50

Greenberg BS, Sherry J, Lachlan K et al (2010) Orientations to video games among gender and age groups. Simulation and Gaming 41(2): 238–259

Griffiths MD, Davies MNO, Chappell D (2003) Breaking the stereotype: The case of online gaming. CyberPsychology and Behavior 6(1): 81–91

Hair JF, Black WC, Babin BJ, Anderson RE (2010) Multivariate Data Analysis. Pearson New International Edition. Pearson, Essex

Hamari J, Keronen L (2017) Why do people play games? A Meta-Analysis. International Journal of Information Management 37(3): 125–141

Hamari J, Koivisto J (2014). Measuring Flow in Gamification: Dispositional Flow Scale-2. Computers in Human Behavior 40: 133–143

Hamari J, Tuunanen J (2014) Player types: A meta-synthesis. Transactions of the Digital Games Research Association 1(2): 29–53

Henson RK, Roberts JK (2006) Use of exploratory factor analysis in published research: Common errors and some comment on improved practice. Educational and Psychological Measurement 66: 393–416

Hu LT, Bentler PM (1999) Cutoff criteria for t-indexes in covariance structure analysis: Conventional criteria versus new alternatives. Structural Equation Modeling: A Multidisciplinary Journal 6(1): 1–55

Huotari K, Hamari J (2017) A definition for gamification: anchoring gamification in the service marketing literature. Electron. Mark. 27(1): 21–31

Högberg J, Hamari J, Wästlund E (2019) Gameful Experience Questionnaire (GAMEFULQUEST): an instrument for measuring the perceived gamefulness of system use. User Modeling and User-Adapted Interaction 29: 619–660

Ijsselsteijn W, Van Den Hoogen W, Klimmt C et al (2008) Measuring the experience of digital game enjoyment. In: Proceedings of the 6th International Conference on Methods and Techniques in Behavioral Research: Measuring Behavior 2008. Maastricht, The Netherlands, pp. 88–89

Ip B, Jacobs G (2005) Segmentation of the games market using multivariate analysis. Journal of Targeting, Measurement and Analysis for Marketing 13(3): 275–287

Jennett C, Cox AL, Cairns P et al (2008) Measuring and defining the experience of immersion in games. Int. J. Hum Comput Stud. 66(9): 641–661

Kallio KP, Mäyrä F, Kaipainen K (2011) At least nine ways to play: approaching gamer mentalities. Games & Culture (6)4: 327–353

Kline RB (2010) Principles and Practice of Structural Equation Modeling. Third Edition. The Guilford Press, New York

Koivisto J, Hamari J (2014) Demographic differences in perceived benefits from gamification. Computers in Human Behavior 35: 179–188

Koster R (2005) A Theory of Fun. 2nd Edition. O'Reilly Media, Sebastopol

Landers RN, Tondello GF, Kappen DL et al (2018) Defining gameful experience as a psychological state caused by gameplay: Replacing the term 'Gamefulness' with three distinct constructs. Int. J. Hum. Comput, Stud.

Lazzaro N (2009) Understand Emotions. In: Bateman, C (ed) Beyond Game Design. Nine Steps Toward Creating Better Videogames. Charles River Media, Boston

Leino O T (2010) Emotions in Play. On the Constitution of Emotion in Solitary Computer Game Play. Academic dissertation. IT University of Copenhagen, Copenhagen

Marsh HW, Hau KT, Wen Z (2004) In search of golden rules: Comment on hypothesis-testing approaches to setting cut off values for t-indexes and dangers in overgeneralizing Hu and Bentler's (1999) findings. Structural Equation Modeling 11(3): 320–341

Mateas M, Stern A (2000) Interaction and Narrative. In: Salen K, Zimmermann E (Eds) The Game Design Reader: A Rules of Play Anthology (2005). The MIT Press, Cambridge, pp 642–666

Matsunaga M (2010) How to Factor-Analyze Your Data Right: Do's, Don'ts, and How-To's. International Journal of Psychological Research 3(1): 97–110

McGonigal J (2011) Reality is Broken. Penguin Books, New York

Murray, HA (1938) Explorations in Personality. Oxford University Press, Oxford.

Phan HP, Keebler JR, Chaparro BS (2016) The Development and Validation of the Game User Experience Satisfaction Scale (GUESS). Human Factors 58(8): 1217–1247

Quandt T, Gruninger H, Wimmer J (2009) The grey haired gaming generation: Findings from an explorative interview study on older computer gamers. Games and Culture 4: 27–46

Russell DW (2002) In search of underlying dimensions: The use (and abuse) of factor analysis in Personality and Social Psychology Bulletin. Personality and Social Psychology Bulletin 28: 1629–1646

Ryan RM, Rigby CS, Przybylski A (2006) The Motivational Pull of Video Games: A Self-Determination Theory Approach. Motivation and Emotion 30 (4): 344–360

Scherer H, Naab T (2009) Money does matter. In: Hartmann T (ed) Media choice. A theoretical and empirical overview. New York, Routledge, pp 70–83

Schreiber JB, Nora A, Stage FK et al (2006) Reporting structural equation modeling and confirmatory factor analysis results: A review. The Journal of Educational Research 99: 323–337

Sherry JL, Greenberg BS, Lucas K, Lachlan, K (2006) Video game uses and gratifications as predictors of use and game preference. In: Vorderer P, Bryant J (eds) Playing Video Games: Motives, Responses, and Consequences. Lawrence Erlbaum Associates, Hillsdale, pp 248–262

Thompson E (2007) Mind in Life. Biology, Phenomenology, and the Sciences of Mind. The Belknap Press of Harvard University Press, Cambridge

Tondello GF, Valtchanov D, Reetz A, Wehbe RR et al (2018) Towards a Trait Model of Video Game Preferences. International Journal of Human–Computer Interaction

Tondello GF, Wehbe RR, Orji R et al (2017) A framework and taxonomy of videogame playing preferences. In: Proceedings of the Annual Symposium on Computer-Human Interaction in Play: 329–340

Vahlo J (2017) An Enactive Account of the Autonomy of Videogame Gameplay. Game Studies 17(1)

Vahlo J (2018) In Gameplay. Invariant Structures and Varied Experiences of Video Game Gameplay. Academic Dissertation. University of Turku, Turku

Vahlo J, Hamari J (2019) Five-Factor Inventory of Intrinsic Motivations to Gameplay (IMG). Proceedings of the 52st Hawaii International Conference on System Sciences, Hawaii, 2019

Vahlo J, Kaakinen J, Holm S, Koponen A (2017) Digital game dynamics preferences and player types. Journal of Computer-Mediated Communication 22(2): 88–103

Vahlo J, Koponen A (2018) Player personas and game choice. In: N. Lee (ed) Encyclopedia of Computer Graphics and Games, Springer International Publishing, Cham, Switzerland

Vahlo J, Smed J, Koponen A (2018) Validating Gameplay Activity Inventory (GAIN) for Modeling Player Profiles. User Modeling and User-Adapted Interaction 28(4–5): 425–453

Webster JG (2014) The Marketplace of Attention. How Audiences Take Shape in a Digital Age. The MIT Press, Cambridge

Witmer BG, Singer MJ (1998) Measuring presence in virtual environments: a presence questionnaire. Presence-Teleop. Virt. 7(3): 225–240

Yee N (2006) Motivations for Play in Online Games. Journal of CyberPsychology and Behavior 9: 772–775

Zait A, Bertea P (2011) Methods for Testing Discriminant Validity. Management & Marketing IX (2): 217–224

Chapter 10
Physiological Measures in Game User Research

Ecehan Akan and Mehmet İlker Berkman

Contents

Abstract The subjective experience of emotions which is usually caused by a specific stimulus either real or virtual typically gets accompanied by physiological and behavioral changes in the body. An essential part of the gaming experience is formed by emotional responses, as physiological responses are not affected by subjective tendencies, considering those physiological responses may contribute to the insights of game user research. In this chapter, the origins of psychophysiological responses will be examined on a theoretical basis along with a review of the psychophysiological measurement methods previously employed in the game studies. We will explore their relationship with emotional responses as well as their correspondence with the self-report based evaluations.

E. Akan (✉)
Bahcesehir University, Cinema and Media Research, Istanbul, Turkey
e-mail: ecehan.akan@comm.bau.edu.tr

M. İ. Berkman
Department of Communication Design, Bahcesehir University, Istanbul, Turkey
e-mail: ilker.berkman@comm.bau.edu.tr

© Springer Nature Switzerland AG 2020
B. Bostan (ed.), *Game User Experience And Player-Centered Design*,
International Series on Computer Entertainment and Media Technology,
https://doi.org/10.1007/978-3-030-37643-7_10

Keywords Game user research · Psychophysiology · Psychophysiological measures · Emotion · Evolutionary psychology

10.1 Introduction

Digital games are made of visual and auditory stimuli accompanied with narratives and high interactivity. The stimuli provided during the gameplay results in reflections on a game user's body. Those reflections are based upon the emotions evoked by the game, which are essential for gaming experience (Järvinen 2008; Ravaja et al. 2004). For this reason, examining the actions and reactions of human body during the interaction with game content or game-related technology provides a rich source of objective data in order to understand the game user's experience.

When human beings get exposed to an external stimuli, their brains, therefore their bodies react. These bodily reactions, which are psychophysiological, emerge nearly simultaneously with the experienced stimuli. These actions and reactions are usually involuntary and cannot be controlled consciously. Using psychophysiological measurement methods, emotional state of the players can be captured right at the moment of exposure to the game content.

Psychophysiological measures were originated from various fields of research. Even though their original motivation was not to promote GUR (Game User Research), they might hold a high potential of contributing to game-related research. Therefore, this chapter aims to provide an overview on psychophysiological measurement methods for game-related research, focusing on GUR studies which investigate game user experience.

The psychophysiological measures will be checked over the following subcategories: cardiovascular measures, brain-related measures, eye-related measures, facial expressions, and electrodermal activity. Those are acknowledged as objective measures as they can be recorded continuously and free from the researcher bias or user bias (Kivikangas et al. 2011). Since emotions are subjectively experienced and the self-reports are taken after the experience by their very nature, psychophysiological responses might help us to monitor the users' experience at the moment the gameplay occurs. To understand the psychophysiological response mechanisms, it is necessary to have a basic understanding of human body anatomically (science of body structure) and physiologically (study of bodily function). In the following section, a simplified overview of anatomical and physiological mechanisms will be given for the readers who are not specialized in life sciences. Thereafter, GUR studies which employ aforementioned psychophysiological measurement methods will be inspected to understand the state-of-the-art use of those measures for exploring game user experience related concepts such as presence, engagement, flow, immersion, and absorption.

10.2 An Overview of Player Emotional State in Relation To User's Physiological State

Technology did not only brought us a strong control over our natural environment. Mendenhall et al. (2010) discloses that "As if this masterful environmental manipulation were not enough, humans have also developed the ability to create and interact with completely artificial environments" underlying the idea that unlike the modern and comfortable environment we live in, artificial environments are usually appealing by their design which triggers our evolved psychology. For instance, we do not go hunting for food. Instead we choose grocery stores to buy something to eat. We have houses that keep us safe from predators, or simply from rain. But we love to play games that evoke emotions which are quite similar to our ancestors' experiences while they were struggling to survive. Moreover, the modern humans' gaming experience might not only be satisfying the behavior patterns of its ancestors in the wilderness, but also might be turning us into a nearly new kind of species: Homo Virtualensis (Mendenhall et al. 2010). Contemporary studies provide evidence that behavior can be explained by genetics along with the experiences. Furthermore experiences also lead to changes in genes (see. Pinel and Barnes 2017).

Along with the technology, evolutionary roots of human psychology have a great role in human behavior. Evolutionary psychology research refers to the study of evolving mental traits and human behavior affected by this change. Engaging with video games immerse us into artificial worlds that stimulate what might have happened to us in the real world, such as being attacked by someone or something, as it could happen to us in the real world. Although those kinds of experiences had been occurred many times to our ancestors back in the history, modern human beings do not face with those kind of incidences as real world experiences. However, based on our evolutionary aspects, it is likely to think that our physiological responses are not very different from our ancestors, when we face emotion-triggering experiences on digital screens. According to Mendenhall et al. (2010), video games expose evolution-based stimuli as it is not adaptive to yawn in front of a potential threat. Within those artificial worlds, the human body reacts to the stimulus as if the game events happened in real life. And of course, emotions come into existence corresponding to the stimulus.

We need to know about the origins of psychophysiological responses as well as their characteristics to thoroughly understand how they can be useful for GUR. Hence, we shall get familiar with the word "emotion" physiologically.

Kleinginna and Kleinginna (1981) listed 92 emotion definitions along with the nine skeptical statements on emotion, suggesting that definition of emotion varies within the literature. Even though there is no consensus of an emotion definition in the literature, one thing is for sure; emotions are neural processes that accompanied with physiological changes in the body (Cabanac 2002), as in the beating rate of a heart or sweating. Those physiological changes can be observed via various methods. For example, the distinction of emotions such as joy and anger can be detected through physiological measures such as HR (heart rate) and skin temperature (Ekman et al. 1983). Another examination of physiological signs was done by Hazlett (2008); the negative and positive emotional valence were investigated under interactive practices with facial EMG.

Limiting the sources of bodily changes with basic emotions would not be adequate in terms of player psychology. Attention, decision-making, and many other consequences of interaction with an external stimulus affect the physiological situation of a human being. Those situations send signals to the brain, and the nervous system steps in to keep the body in balance.

The regulation of body homeostasis (balance) is the function of the nervous system and endocrine system working together. The chemical orientation of body functions is in control of the endocrine system which regulates the internal secretions to convey its messages. To do so, the hormones are secreted by ductless glands and transported to the specific target cells by using blood as a vessel (Neave 2008). On the other hand, the nervous system controls communication through the body with electrical impulses. Thoughts, actions, and emotions are directly related to the nervous system's activity.

The nervous system can be divided into subsystems in terms of structure and function. The structural subdivisions of the nervous system are the central nervous system (CNS) and the peripheral nervous system (PNS) (Fig. 10.1). The brain and spinal cord construct the CNS while the PNS consists of the extension nerves of the brain and spinal cord.

The PNS has two subdivisions classified according to the function: sensory (afferent) and motor (efferent) which also have its own subdivisions: the somatic nervous system (SNS) and autonomic nervous system (ANS). ANS regulates the involuntary activities such as the control of smooth and cardiac muscles and glands.

Being the main source of emotions, the nervous system and its subdivisions are in a strong relationship with the other systems in the human body. While there are methods to measure the activities of the nervous system directly using brain–computer interface (BCI) technologies, some activities of the cardiovascular system, dermal responses, several muscular movements, or endocrine activities are

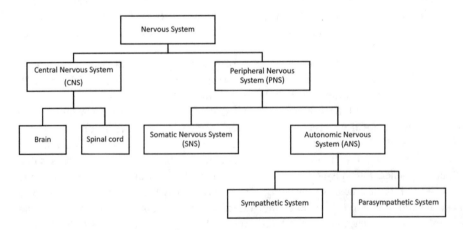

Fig. 10.1 Organization schema of the nervous system

also strongly related with nervous system and measurements on activities of these systems were employed to provide information on users' emotional state. Either the source is real or virtual our emotions are triggered by the external stimulus.

Understanding of how psychophysiological responses originate and how we can make use of them in a relevance to game studies might broaden our perspectives on GUR in terms of player psychology.

10.2.1   Cardiovascular System and Its Measures

Cardiovascular system regulates the transportation of oxygen, nutrients, cell waste hormones, and other substances while using blood as a vehicle. The system is powered by the beating heart which acts as a muscular pump that consists of one-way valves and plumbing tubes (Marieb 2010). The heart's contractions are continuous and named as cardiac cycle. This cycle indicates one complete heartbeat which consists of the heart's contraction phase (systole) and the relaxation phase (diastole) (Marieb 2010).

ANS affects the heart rate in times of physical or emotional stress. The nerves of the sympathetic system induce the cardiac muscle so that the heart beats faster. This happens when a person is frightened, excited, exercising, in a much more general saying "in crisis." On the other hand, parasympathetic nerves ease down the heart to make it rest at the times of non-crisis. Endocrine system also has a power to rule over heart activity. For instance, epinephrine and thyroxine both boost the beating rate (Marieb 2010). Some methodologies consider the measurement of hormone levels such as cortisol level (Gentile et al. 2017). Anyways, the measurement of the heart rate can enlighten various emotional and mental phenomenon such as arousal or attention. Its measurement is noninvasive as the beating rate of a heart can be easily obtained by measuring cardiac cycle. Reviewing some terminology in relation to cardiovascular measures might help the following GUR literature. Electrocardiography (ECG) is recording of the impulses that pass through the heart. Heart rate (HR) refers to the number of heart beats per minute. Interbeat interval (IBI) is the time between heart beats. The noninvasive reflection of ANS activity is named as heart rate variability (HRV) and simply indicates the healthy irregularities of the heart rate (Sztajzel 2004).

Ballard and Wiest (1996) investigated the effects of violence in video game play using cardiovascular measures. Thirty male participants ($M = 19.53$) played Mortal Kombat (Midway 1992) in two versions for violent game condition and a billiards game for non-violent game condition. Participants who played Mortal Kombat had higher HR than who played billiards, also during the more violent mode of Mortal Kombat, participants had higher systolic blood pressure (SBP) and hostility ratings on self-reports.

Wiederhold et al. (2003) attempted to measure HR and skin resistance along with presence and realism questionnaires on 72 participants ($M = 36.4$, Male $= 30$) using a head mounted display presenting a VR flight. Psychophysiological data which was taken as an indicator of the immersion level correlated with the self-report scores obtained via a presence questionnaire.

Psychophysiological measurement of game experience is getting much more known through the last decade. Self-reported player experience, HR, and EDA as indicators of psychophysiological arousal were correlated significantly in a case study (Drachen et al. 2010). The games played were Prey (2K Games 2006), Doom 3 (id Software 2004), and Bioshock (2K 2007) which are first-person shooter (FPS) games. Sixteen participants were administered to a game experience questionnaire.

Weber et al. (2009) also conducted a research on violence and video gaming. The FPS game played was Tactical Ops: Assault on Terror (Infogrames, Europe; US edition) by 13 male participants aging between 18 and 26. During the experiments, they recorded HR and EDA to investigate different game events and acquired alterations in arousal levels. The content-related results identified the player behavior has a similar pattern in the beginning. However, they chose different strategies so their exposure levels to the violence vary.

Tafalla (2007) focused on gender-specific CV responses. The participants ($N = 73$, $M = 21$, Male $= 37$) played DOOM (id Software 1993) with and without soundtrack conditions. Consequently, male participants' HR was significantly greater while the soundtrack was on, whereas female participants' blood pressure was significantly greater. Based on these results, the authors suggest that male participants showed higher arousal while female participants experienced more stress.

Electrodermal activity (EDA) and HR measures were employed to investigate avatar and agency conditions as well as competition and cooperation conditions (Lim and Reeves 2010). Thirty-four participants, equally distributed in gender, played World of Warcraft (Blizzard Entertainment 2004), then were administered to a manikin and three semantic differential scales for presence. Both SCR frequency and heart rate were significantly higher during the avatar condition which can be explained with higher emotional engagement.

In a vulnerability research using a custom touch-screen game, HRV was measured (Parsinejad and Sipahi 2017). There were two sets of experiments conducted with total 24 participants ($M = 25.55$, Male $= 19$). Players' touch behavior along with decision-making times were found to be associated with the HRV and task performance.

Psychophysiological measures are not only used in the traditional game media, but also used in relatively new gaming technologies. Egan et al. (2016) studied quality of experience (QoE), using HR and EDA with 33 participants ($M = 23$, Male $= 19$) for their experience with the Oculus Rift and personal computer. Their results indicate that VR and non-VR conditions affect the HR and EDA findings.

In virtual reality medium, Meehan et al. (2002; see also Meehan et al. 2005) investigated presence by using a virtual pit room, which is occupied with a defenseless hole that show the room below in order to simulate a stressful environment. They recorded HR, SC, and skin temperature data of 52 ($M = 21.4$, Male $= 36$) participants. The results showed that the increased HR positively correlates with presence self-reports. The experimental design was for passive haptics, frame rate, and multiple exposures. During the passive haptics usage both HR and change in SC increased significantly.

10.2.2 BCI Technologies

Brain–computer interface (BCI) technologies refer to the hardware for recording brain activity such as electroencephalography (EEG) and functional magnetic resonance imaging (fMRI). Among all BCI technologies, EEG is the most common for research purposes.

Electroencephalogram (EEG) is a mental state interpreting technique used in recording the brain activity relying on electrical potential generated by brain cortex activity (Nunez and Srinivasan 2006). The EEG system's working mechanism is to acquire brain signals from the scalp with electrodes, then amplifiers process the analogue signal and A/D converter digitalizes the signal as required. In the end, a personal computer can store and display the EEG data (Nicolas-Alonso and Gomez-Gil 2012). As the amplitude of EEG waves gets smaller when move away from the source, the EEG measures are recorded on various sites over the scalp to determine the source of the certain waves. The EEG data can give information on specific consciousness states. For example, alpha waves are high in amplitude and have a regular pattern that indicates the state of relaxed wakefulness (Pinel and Barnes 2017). In GUR, we may utilize power variance of alpha with the negative and positive valence states 25 or discrimination of different emotional states such as fear and happiness (Balconi and Mazza 2009; Balconi and Lucchiari 2006).

The EEG systems are widely used in machine communication for disabled, for example, BCIs to control a wheelchair. In case of video games, EEG can be used as game controllers in BCI applications, also neurofeedback games with medical, research, or entertainment purposes (e.g., Lécuyer et al. 2008; Wang et al. 2010; Liu et al. 2014; Nijholt et al. 2009).

EEG-based games are played with an EEG cap attached over the player's scalp. There are several examples for application of EEG technique in GUR. Reuderink et al. (2013) used facial EMG and EEG with 12 participants ($M = 27$, Male $= 10$) during an Affective Pacman gameplay. Participants self-reported their emotional valence, arousal, and dominance with a manikin. The results did not give the expected validation of neural correlates of emotion.

Moreover, EEG can be used to monitor player experience. Nacke et al. (2010) conducted a study with 25 male participants ($M = 23.48$) using EEG to capture the brain activity in addition to a game experience questionnaire and a spatial presence questionnaire. The chosen game was Half-Life 2 (Valve Corporation 2004) and three conditions were created by level design: immersion, boredom, and flow. According to the game experience questionnaire administered, challenge and tension were significantly higher for the flow condition which is coherent to the significantly increased EDA. The spatial presence questionnaire scores on the other hand were lowest for the boredom condition. The EMG data were interpreted as the gameplay experience was significantly affected by the level design modality.

Another research topic that EEG techniques contribute is player task engagement. McMahan et al. (2015) conducted a research with 30 participants ($M = 20.87$, Male $= 10$) using Emotiv EPOC EEG headset which was attached to the participants' heads during a Super Meat Boy (Team Meat 2010) gameplay and the player objective was to differentiate the general game play from death events. Based on the EEG data, they pointed out that engagement and arousal were significantly higher for death events than the general game play.

Using EEG, Shin et al. (2012) claimed that Counter-Strike (Valve Software, Bellevue, WA) elicited positive emotions for their group of male participants ($N = 12$, $M = 25.1$) who were familiar with the FPS game. The conducted self-reports were consistent with EEG data, both supporting the positive emotions hypothesis.

Allison and Polich (2008) administered Tom Clancy's Rainbow Six: Rogue Spear Black Thorn (Ubisoft 2001), to 14 male participants ($M = 23.5$) to study on event-related potential (ERP). In that study, EEG was successfully used for indexing workload.

Anwar et al. (2016) recorded EEG data of 10 participants ($M = 20.37$, Male $= 9$) while the participants play the mobile game Temple Run (IMANGI Studios 2011). Results suggested that players' expertise level can be classified with EEG measures.

Another technology that can help us monitor the brain activity is functional magnetic resonance imaging (fMRI). The non-portable device is a neuroimaging technology to measure neural activation through electromagnetic fields. The system relies on the changes in local cerebral blood volume, cerebral blood flow, and oxygenation levels by doing so MRI scanners are used (Nicolas-Alonso and Gomez-Gil 2012).

Decety et al. (2004) employed behavioral measures and fMRI to investigate cooperation and competition. The custom computer game played had three conditions: playing alone, with another player, or against another player. The age range of 12 participants (Male $= 6$) was 21–28. Both subjects of study were resulted in autonomic arousal yet the brain activated brain regions differed from cooperation to competition. Decety et al. claimed that cooperation acts as a rewarding process correspondingly to the evolutionary psychology along with developmental psychology and as it is identified in neural activity.

Klasen et al. (2008) employed fMRI during a think aloud session while 17 male participants were playing Counter Strike: Source (CSS; Valve Corporation 2004) in order to explore whether an introspective method could be supported with neurophysiological measure. They interpreted the results as there were neuronal correlates of displeasure and focus. Their subjective data of think aloud sessions were validated by the FMRI data.

10.2.3 Facial Expressions

The studies of facial expressions as emotion index go back in the literature to 1920s (Ekman and Oster 1979). Facial expressions are presumed that they can express basic emotions such as joy and anger. As expected, the techniques to measure facial expressions were developed in various science fields. Facial electromyography (facial EMG) is one of those techniques to measure facial expressions. The main objective of a measurement with an EMG is to monitor the muscle activity which is directly related to PNS activity. Facial EMG is applied by placing electrodes on three different facial muscles. Actions like closing eyelids and movements of the mouth corners may indicate happiness. Electrodes are located on orbicularis oculi where they provide data on lowering or raising eyebrows, and on zygomaticus major where they provide the data of pulling mouth corners upward or downward (Van Boxtel 2010).

Fridlund (1988) studied with zygomaticus major and corrugator supercilii, and figured out that facial muscles' strength changes due to asymmetry. Concluding that the left and right side of a face might reveal different muscle activity. Dimberg and Petterson (2000) also examined the difference in muscle strength and proposed adding a non-affective control condition to the experimental design in order to ensure that the results does not reflect any asymmetric difference. Dimberg and Thunberg (1998) studied facial response physiology and correlated happy faces to higher zygomatic major muscle activity, and angry faces to higher corrugator supercilii muscle activity.

Games are widely known for their emotional content such as narrative and music. Nacke et al. (2010) explored user experience (UX) with 2×2 experimental design, hypothesizing sound and music on and off effects measuring EMG and EDA. In addition to the psychophysiological data, a game experience questionnaire applied to all 36 participants ($M = 24$, Male $= 29$). The game used for the experiment was Half-Life 2 (Valve Corporation 2004) in first-person shooter genre. Unfortunately, the obtained EMG and EDA data could not contribute to the self-report results. They assume that their analyzing methodology for both tonic psychophysiological measures was ineffective for the experiment. They concluded that studying phasic psychophysiological data might be more promising for GUR.

Hazlett (2006) studied emotional valence with a group of 13 males aging between 9 and 15 years old ($M = 11.3$). All participants were familiar to Xbox games. They played a racing car game, Juiced (THQ 2005) via Xbox. Hazlett examined the negative and positive emotional valence during the video game play with facial EMG. The results showed that the zygomaticus muscle can provide information on a player's positive emotional valence during gameplay.

Ravaja (2009) employed facial EMG, EDA, and cardiovascular measures as well as the subjective self-report measures collected via a cross-media presence questionnaire. Sixty-nine participants ($M = 24.3$, Male $= 42$) played Super Monkey Ball Jr. (THQ and SEGA 2002) and Duke Nukem Advance (Take-Two Interactive 2002) against the computer, a friend, and a stranger. Neither friends nor strangers were co-located to the participant. Results demonstrate that gameplay against human opponent results in more positive emotional responses, supported by higher arousal, spatial presence, and engagement compared to playing against a stranger. Results revealed that playing against a friend causes more positive emotional response indicated through facial EMG data, and more arousal and engagement according to self-reports.

Point of view is another area of interest in GUR. Kallinen et al. (2007) concluded that, compared to the third-person view, players have a greater feeling that their eyes were avatar's eyes in first-person view and they are in the game scene with the help of psychophysiological methods. The study was conducted on fifty participants (Male $= 31$) between the age range of 16 and 39 years, played Elder Scrolls III: Morrowind (Bethesda Softworks 2002) while facial EMG and eye movements were recorded continuously. After that, the participants filled a spatial presence questionnaire, which showed in result that the first-person view elicits higher presence than the third-person view. However, eye-tracking data did not implicit any significant difference between the point of views investigated. On the other hand, higher level of zygomaticus major and less corrugator supercilii activity indicated that participants were more pleasant in third-person view.

Kivikangas and Ravaja (2013) investigated emotional responses to victories employing GSR and facial EMG. Participants ($M = 23.5$, $N = 99$, Male $= 51$) played Duke Nukem against a friend, against a stranger, and in single player mode. According to the facial EMG data obtained on orbicularis oculi and zygomaticus major, victory when playing against a stranger evokes higher positive responses, yet the results might be caused by strong ceiling effect that was already high in initial state against a friend. Electrodermal activity data while playing against a human rather than a computer, the increased SCL expresses that the emotions were stronger, as also indicated by facial EMG results.

Ravaja et al. (2006) investigated the characteristics of the opponent by examining ninety-nine participants ($M = 23.8$, Male $= 51$) who played Super Monkey Ball Jr. (THQ and SEGA 2002) and Duke Nukem. Participants were administered to a cross-media presence questionnaire after each game. ECG data, cardiac interbeat intervals (IBIs), and facial EMG data were also collected during gameplay. The cardiac IBI was found to be higher when the opponent is a human while the facial EMG results correlated with self-reported engagement. While the facial EMG results correlated with self-reported engagement.

Ravaja et al. (2008) studied violent game events using facial EMG and EDA. Thirty-six (Male $= 25$) young adults played James Bond 007: NightFire (EA Games 2002), a FPS game on Nintendo GameCube. The FPS genre includes two desired stimuli: first, the player kills or wounds an opponent, and the second, player gets wounded or killed. The researchers expected to obtain negatively valenced high arousal as the moral code pressures that killing somebody is wrong, the results met the researchers' expectations; killing or wounding the opponent verified to elicit negatively valenced high arousal with the body responses; increased EDA and decreased zygomaticus major and orbicularis oculi EMG activity.

Mirza-Babaei et al. (2013) developed and offered Biometric Storyboards (BioSt) method as a user test method that visualizes the facial EMG and EDA data parallel to the game content. Participants ($N = 24$, $M = 23$, all male) played three custom games. The biometric storyboarding method indicated to be provider of a higher gameplay quality according to the test results. This can be a sign for the scope of facial EMG and EDA application for GUR.

10.2.4   Electrodermal Activity and Its Measures

In this section, we will look into the information that we can get by investigating skin-related measures for GUR. Primarily, we focus on the electrical changes on the skin in relation to ANS activity.

The term electrodermal activity (EDA), referring to the electrical phenomena in skin, was introduced by Johnson and Lubin in 1966 even though the investigations on the skin and electrical potential were traced to over a hundred years ago. Today, the prevailing definition of EDA might be the one on Encyclopedia of Behavioral Medicine: "The measure of neurally mediated effects on sweat gland permeability, observed as changes in the resistance of the skin to a little electrical flow, or as differences in the electrical potential between various parts of the skin" (Critchley and Nagai 2013). Aforementioned sweat gland activity is a sympathetic nervous system activity associated with the homeostatic balance. Lang (1995) correlated EDA to arousal. According to Boucsein (2012) EDA can reflect the emotional responses and cognitive activity. Since emotions trigger the sweat gland activity the skin becomes a better conductor temporarily with a 2–5 s latency. The ANS activity increase is a sign of arousal, so utilizing skin conductance as an arousal measure is favorable (Ravaja 2004).

When analyzed anatomically, the human skin is comprised of layers that have different characteristics. It primarily has protective and sensing functions. Concerning EDA, emotional sweating is particularly significant on the palms of hands and soles of the feet (Boucsein 2012). The measurement of EDA can be done by placing electrodes near the eccrine sweat glands which are positioned in the palms of hands and soles of the feet. Its working mechanism is in general to apply a constant voltage and computing current flow to calculate the skin conductance (SC) by using Ohm's law. Of course the applied voltage is low enough for participants to recognize so that EDA can be used as a noninvasive measure (Sharma et al. 2016). By doing so, EDA measures can be divided into two: tonic and phasic skin conductance. The tonic skin conductance can be described as the low changes in the skin conductance affiliated to the participants' individual autonomic regulation, hydration, and psychological state. On the other hand, phasic skin conductance is the peaks of SC affiliated to events such as decision-making and environmental changes like smells and sounds. Skin conductance level (SCL) is derived from tonic skin conductance whereas the skin conductance response (SCR) is derived from the phasic skin conductance. While using EDA as a measurement method of research, it is strictly suggested to measure a baseline data which is basically recording of resting period (Braithwaite et al. 2013).

Peperkorn et al. (2015) disclosed that fear and presence are dependent on each other for VR medium. The participants ($N = 59$, $M = 25.18$, all female) were faced with spiders on stereoscopic and monoscopic VR for three sessions. Noting that some of the participants ($N = 22$) already had fear for spiders. Their EDA and HR were recorded, afterwards they were administered to a presence questionnaire and fear-related questionnaires. In results, HR was significantly dropped during the sessions, while SCL had shown no significant change.

Kneer et al. (2016) conducted a research of violence and game difficulty recording both IBI and EDA along with a lexical decision task and a scale. The participants ($N = 90$, $M = 24.47$, Male $= 21$) played the FPS game Team Fortress 2 (Valve 2007). The game's difficulty levels varied from low to high, a total of four conditions. The results did not indicate any effect of neither violence nor game difficulty on arousal, emotions, and behavior.

Another research using a FPS game named Left 4 Dead 2 (Valve Corporation 2009) with three game difficulty conditions: low, medium, and high challenge by Klarkowski et al. (2016). Electrodermal activity recorded during the gameplay sessions for all 66 participants ($M = 23.28$, Male $= 50$), then they were administered to a manikin. In results, high challenge condition was confirmed to be the most arousing according to the EDA measures and self-report.

The results stand in opposition to Kneer et al.'s (2016) findings. The difference might have arisen from the difference of games or difficulty in the levels or the gameplay time which was twice in Kneer et al.'s study.

Zhang and Gao (2014) investigated video game violence and music through a set of experiments. The first study was conducted with sixty male college students ($M = 21.16$) who played a violent video game (Postal 2; Running With Scissors 2003) and a non-violent video game with two different background music that were associated with high or low excitement and both with low pleasure. Several measures were taken such as aggressive behavior measurement, taste preference questionnaire, aggressive trait questionnaire. Additionally HR and EDA were taken as physical indicators of excitement. The results suggest that there was not a significant effect of game's level of violence on HR, while EDA measures were significantly higher for violent game condition. The second experiment was about physical excitement, aggression, and pleasure of background music. Thirty male college students ($M = 21.32$) participated in the second experiment. The games played were the same as the first experiment but the background songs were associated with low or high pleasure and both low excitement. As observed in the first experiment, HR measures did not yield a significant difference while EDA levels were significantly higher for the violent video game. Regardless of the background music and the game type, EDA levels were lower during the baseline compared to the after game measurements.

Granato et al. (2017) conducted a series of research on player emotions with a participant group of 9 young male adults aging between 18 and 38. Participants were administered to four 2D side-scrolling games while recording EMG on four facial muscles, ECG, respiration rate, and GSR. Their results were promising for emotion analysis during the gameplay such as psychophysiological measurement of player emotions in front of specific game events.

Terkildsen and Makransky (2019) investigated GSR and task-irrelevant event-related potentials (ERPs) as objective presence indicators. Thirty-four participants ($M = 24.63$, Male $= 23$) were assigned to PC (low presence) and VR (high presence) conditions according to their ratings on a demographic pretest. Participants were also administered to a presence scale. The GSR results suggest that there is a relation between the subjective presence experience and GSR peaks per minute. Emotional arousal indicated by phasic SCR is higher for the high presence group and arousal intensity is stimulus-dependent.

Tan et al. (2015) investigated immersion, engagement, and flow comparing a head mounted display based VR gameplay with personal computer gameplay of the game Half-Life 2 (Valve Corporation 2004) with 10 participants ($M = 27$, Male $= 7$) The sessions included EDA and HR measurements and think aloud sessions which resulted in the corroboration of think aloud date to physiological data. The researchers also claimed that cybersickness strongly affected the gameplay experience.

10.2.5 Eye-Related Measures

Eyes are visionary organ of the human body. The eyes move constantly and involuntarily even when a person tries to keep them fixated (Pinel and Barnes 2017). The sense of vision occurs at fovea centralis and its repositions are named as a saccade, while the stabilization of retina over a point is named as a fixation (Duchowski 2007). The human sight has vertical and horizontal limits and inside that limit a detailed sense of vision occurs within a specific degree. In other words, by detecting the eye movements, we can obtain information on a person's gaze area which is an indicator of their point of interest and focus of their attention. An eye-tracker, which is a device that can be attached to a pair of glasses or a screen, or even on a virtual reality headset uses video-based combined pupil and corneal reflection method to detect the position of eye. Eye-tracking investigates series of saccades and fixations, namely scanpaths, combined with their meanings. For instance, series of saccades is an indicator of searching whereas the lack of efficiency in searching is indicated by longer scanpaths (Goldberg and Kotval 1999). Measurement of the eye movements has been used in various fields such as psychology, marketing, and game research. In addition to the eye movements, there are pupillometric methods that measure the changes in the pupil size as a psychophysiological response. Pupillometry concerns memory physiologically by measuring pupil size and reactivity. Pupil dilation can tell us about sympathetic nervous system activity (Granholm and Steinhauer 2004) yet pupil size is also a correspondent of the cognitive load and affected by the light of the stimuli.

Alkan and Cagiltay (2007) investigated game-based learning with eye-tracking. Participants ($N = 15$) played Return of the Incredible Machine: Contraptions (Sierra

On Line, Inc., 2000), the game was chosen considering the decision-making and problem-solving features. All participants were interviewed and claimed that the game was easy to learn but the gameplay requires problem-solving skills and made game-relevant commentaries. The eye-tracking results were coherent to the participants' descriptive reports, for example, the fixations lasted longer during the search of a solution.

Jordan and Slater (2009) investigated presence by using both EDA and eye-tracking in a stressful VE. Twenty-eight participants (M = not stated, male = 14) experienced three conditions partially, and a 5-item presence questionnaire was administered (Slater and Steed 2000). They equipped a HMD with a camera-based eye-tracker. Results showed that the number of SCRs and scanpath entropy are negatively correlated in the stressful VE. On the other hand, the self-report did not reveal a significant difference between the conditions. The researchers concluded that eye-head movements can be an indicator of presence.

A spatial navigation study examining sex differences (Mueller et al. 2008) employed eye-tracking and pupillometry. Twenty-four participants (M = 24, Male = 12) played The Arena Maze. Pupillometry results corroborated with learning effects; however, the results did not indicate a difference between male and female. In terms of eye-tracking results, the fixation results suggested that male participants learnt spatial features faster compared to the female participants.

Mojzisch et al. (2006) investigated self-involvement during social interaction via PC by applying a virtual scene. The study included attention, arousal, and facial expression investigation through facial EMG as well as the eye movements and pupil size on male participants ($N = 23$, $M = 23.4$). Eye-related measures indicated that attention allocation is closely related to self-involvement in any social meaning. Pupil size was used to investigate arousal. Findings show that pupil size was larger when the virtual character was a female human model by comparison with a male human model. On the other hand, the participants' ($N = 23$, $M = 23.4$) activity on zygomaticus major had increased when the facial expressions' of virtual characters are socially relevant.

10.3   Conclusion and Discussion

Based on the studies reviewed above, we think that the use of psychophysiological measures in GUR is still in its infancy.

1. Some studies did not provide evidence for the effect of games as a stimuli on psychophysiological measures as in Reuderink et al. (2013).
2. Psychophysiological measures do not consistently relate with the self-report measures employed in the studies, as in Nacke et al. (2010).
3. Psychophysiological measures are taken as indicators of different mental and emotional states, as in Ravaja (2009), Lim and Reeves (2010), and Zhang and Gao (2014).

On the other hand, psychophysiological measures have an advantage over self-report measures of game user experience. Being completely involuntary and out of the control of the conscious mind, they do not depend on post-experience reflection of the user which can be biased by user's beliefs, sense of self, and memory deficits. For this reason, researchers have a great interest in employing psychophysiological measures in game user research.

However, studies that interrogate the psychophysiological measures for their relationship with the user's performance are quite a few. Except the eye-tracking studies which focus on cognitive performance of participants, cardiovascular, electrodermal, brain-related and facial muscular measures have usually been taken as indicators of emotional responses such as boredom, presence, arousal, or aggression. In our opinion, these measures can also be affected by the users' activity during the gameplay, as users struggle with the controls, obstacles, and opponents. While some of the changes on psychophysiological measures can be explained by the emotional valence, some effect might be due to the cognitive and physical task load as well as being related to negative side effects such as cybersickness (Kim et al. 2005; Tan et al. 2015; Plouzeau et al. 2018).

Also, there is a need for standardization of acquiring and reporting psychophysiological data, as these measures are sensitive to environmental factors such as room temperature or individual differences such as personality traits, participants' physical condition, or even to the participants' diet on the day of the experiment. GUR studies explored above rarely report these factors. In many of the studies, participants are not equally distributed in both genders and effect of gender differences is not reported. By standardizing and reporting these issues, it could be possible to understand controversial results obtained in different experiments and benchmark the results of GUR studies. Involvement of medical experts might also be helpful to create a convenient experimental design.

References

Alkan S, Cagiltay K (2007) Studying computer game learning experience through eye tracking. British Journal of Educational Technology, 38(3), pp 538–542

Allison BZ, Polich J (2008) Workload assessment of computer gaming using a single-stimulus event-related potential paradigm. Biological psychology, 77(3), pp 277–283

Anwar SM, Saeed SMU, Majid M (2016, December) Classification of Expert-Novice Level of Mobile Game Players Using Electroencephalography. In 2016 International Conference on Frontiers of Information Technology (FIT). IEEE, pp 315–318

Balconi M, Lucchiari C (2006) EEG correlates (event-related desynchronization) of emotional face elaboration: a temporal analysis. Neuroscience letters, 392(1-2), pp 118–123

Balconi M, Mazza G (2009) Brain oscillations and BIS/BAS (behavioral inhibition/activation system) effects on processing masked emotional cues.: ERS/ERD and coherence measures of alpha band. International Journal of Psychophysiology, 74(2), pp 158–165

Ballard ME, Wiest JR (1996) Mortal Kombat (tm): The Effects of Violent Videogame Play on Males' Hostility and Cardiovascular Responding 1. Journal of Applied Social Psychology, 26(8), pp 717–730

Boucsein W (2012) Electrodermal activity. Springer Science & Business Media.

Braithwaite JJ, Watson DG, Jones R, Rowe M (2013) A guide for analysing electrodermal activity (EDA) & skin conductance responses (SCRs) for psychological experiments. Psychophysiology, 49(1), pp 1017–1034

Cabanac M (2002) What is emotion?. Behavioural processes, 60(2), pp 69–83

Critchley H, Nagai Y (2013) Electrodermal Activity (EDA). In: Gellman M.D., Turner J.R. (eds) Encyclopedia of Behavioral Medicine. Springer, New York, NY

Decety J, Jackson PL, Sommerville JA, Chaminade T, Meltzoff, AN (2004) The neural bases of cooperation and competition: an fMRI investigation. Neuroimage, 23(2), pp 744–751

Dimberg U, Petterson M (2000) Facial reactions to happy and angry facial expressions: Evidence for right hemisphere dominance. Psychophysiology, 37(5), pp 693–696

Dimberg U, Thunberg M (1998) Rapid facial reactions to emotional facial expressions. Scandinavian journal of psychology, 39(1), pp 39–45

Drachen A, Nacke LE, Yannakakis G, Pedersen AL (2010, July) Correlation between heart rate, electrodermal activity and player experience in first-person shooter games. In Proceedings of the 5th ACM SIGGRAPH Symposium on Video Games. ACM, pp 49–54

Duchowski AT (2007) Eye tracking methodology. Theory and practice, 328(614), pp 2–3

Egan D, Brennan S, Barrett J, Qiao Y, Timmerer C, Murray N (2016, June) An evaluation of Heart Rate and ElectroDermal Activity as an objective QoE evaluation method for immersive virtual reality environments. In 2016 Eighth International Conference on Quality of Multimedia Experience (QoMEX). IEEE, pp 1–6

Ekman P, Oster H (1979) Facial expressions of emotion. Annual review of psychology, 30(1), pp 527–554

Ekman P, Levenson RW, Friesen WV (1983) Autonomic nervous system activity distinguishes among emotions. Science, 221(4616), pp 1208–1210

Fridlund AJ (1988) What can asymmetry and laterality in EMG tell us about the face and brain?. International Journal of Neuroscience, 39(1-2), pp 53–69

Gentile DA, Bender PK, Anderson CA (2017) Violent video game effects on salivary cortisol, arousal, and aggressive thoughts in children. Computers in Human Behavior, 70, pp 39–43

Goldberg JH, Kotval XP (1999) Computer interface evaluation using eye movements: methods and constructs. International Journal of Industrial Ergonomics, 24(6), pp 631–645

Granato M, Gadia D, Maggiorini D, Ripamonti LA (2017, December) Emotions detection through the analysis of physiological information during video games fruition. In International Conference on Games and Learning Alliance. Springer, Cham, pp 197–207

Granholm EE, Steinhauer SR (2004) Pupillometric measures of cognitive and emotional processes. International Journal of Psychophysiology.

Hazlett RL (2006, April) Measuring emotional valence during interactive experiences: boys at video game play. In Proceedings of the SIGCHI conference on Human Factors in computing systems. ACM, pp 1023–1026

Hazlett RL (2008) Using biometric measurement to create emotionally compelling games. Game usability: Advice from the experts for advancing the player experience, pp 187–206

Järvinen, A. (2008). Understanding video games as emotional experiences. In The Video Game Theory Reader 2 (pp. 85-108). Routledge.

Jordan J, Slater M (2009) An analysis of eye scanpath entropy in a progressively forming virtual environment. Presence: Teleoperators and Virtual Environments, 18(3), pp 185–199

Kallinen K, Salminen M, Ravaja N, Kedzior R, Sääksjärvi M (2007) Presence and emotion in computer game players during 1st person vs. 3rd person playing view: Evidence from self-report, eye-tracking, and facial muscle activity data. Proceedings of the PRESENCE, 187, 190.

Kim, Y., Kim, H. J., Kim, E. N., Ko, H. D., & Kim, H. T. 2005. Characteristic changes in the physiological components of cybersickness. Psychophysiology, 42(5), pp 616–625

Kivikangas JM, Ravaja N (2013) Emotional responses to victory and defeat as a function of opponent. IEEE Transactions on Affective Computing, 4(2), pp 173–182

Kivikangas, J. M., Chanel, G., Cowley, B., Ekman, I., Salminen, M., Järvelä, S., & Ravaja, N. (2011). A review of the use of psychophysiological methods in game research. journal of gaming & virtual worlds, 3(3), 181–199

Klarkowski M, Johnson D, Wyeth P, Phillips C, Smith S (2016, May) Psychophysiology of challenge in play: EDA and self-reported arousal. In Proceedings of the 2016 CHI Conference Extended Abstracts on Human Factors in Computing Systems, ACM, pp 1930–1936

Klasen M, Zvyagintsev M, Weber R, Mathiak KA, Mathiak K (2008, October) Think aloud during fMRI: neuronal correlates of subjective experience in video games. In International Conference on Fun and Games. Springer, Berlin, Heidelberg, pp 132–138

Kleinginna PR, Kleinginna AM (1981) A categorized list of emotion definitions, with suggestions for a consensual definition. Motivation and emotion, 5(4), pp 345–379

Kneer J, Elson M, Knapp F (2016) Fight fire with rainbows: The effects of displayed violence, difficulty, and performance in digital games on affect, aggression, and physiological arousal. Computers in Human Behavior, 54, pp 142–148

Lang PJ (1995) The emotion probe: studies of motivation and attention. American psychologist, 50(5), p 372

Lécuyer A, Lotte F, Reilly RB, Leeb R, Hirose M, Slater M (2008) Brain-computer interfaces, virtual reality, and videogames. Computer, 41(10), pp 66–72

Lim S, Reeves B (2010) Computer agents versus avatars: Responses to interactive game characters controlled by a computer or other player. International Journal of Human-Computer Studies, 68(1-2), pp 57–68

Liu Y, Sourina O, Hou X (2014, October) Neurofeedback games to improve cognitive abilities. In 2014 International Conference on Cyberworlds. IEEE, pp 161–168

Marieb EN (2010) Essentials of human anatomy and physiology pp. Pearson San Francisco, pp 356–393

McMahan T, Parberry I, Parsons TD (2015) Evaluating player task engagement and arousal using electroencephalography. Procedia Manufacturing, 3, pp 2303–2310

Meehan M, Insko B, Whitton M, Brooks FP Jr (2002) Physiological measures of presence in stressful virtual environments. In T. Appolloni (Ed.), Proceedings of SIGGRAPH 2002, San Antonio. Also in ACM Transactions on Graphics. New York: ACM Press.

Meehan M, Razzaque S, Insko B, Whitton M, Brooks FP Jr (2005) A review of four studies on the use of physiological reaction as a measure of presence in stressful virtual environments. Applied Psychophysiology and Biofeedback, 30, pp 239–258

Mendenhall Z, Saad G, Nepomuceno MV (2010) Homo virtualensis: Evolutionary psychology as a tool for studying video games. In Evolutionary Psychology and Information Systems Research. Springer, Boston, MA, pp 305–328

Mirza-Babaei P, Nacke LE, Gregory J, Collins N, Fitzpatrick G (2013, April) How does it play better?: exploring user testing and biometric storyboards in games user research. In Proceedings of the SIGCHI conference on human factors in computing systems. ACM, pp 1499–1508

Mojzisch A, Schilbach L, Helmert JR, Pannasch S, Velichkovsky BM, Vogeley K (2006) The effects of self-involvement on attention, arousal, and facial expression during social interaction with virtual others: A psychophysiological study. Social neuroscience, 1(3-4), pp 184–195

Mueller SC, Jackson CP, Skelton RW (2008) Sex differences in a virtual water maze: An eye tracking and pupillometry study. Behavioural brain research, 193(2), pp 209–215

Nacke LE, Grimshaw MN, Lindley CA (2010) More than a feeling: Measurement of sonic user experience and psychophysiology in a first-person shooter game. Interacting with computers, 22(5), pp 336–343

Neave N (2008) Hormones and behaviour: a psychological approach. Cambridge University Press, p 24

Nicolas-Alonso LF, Gomez-Gil J (2012) Brain computer interfaces, a review. sensors, 12(2), pp 1211–1279

Nijholt A, Bos DPO, Reuderink B (2009) Turning shortcomings into challenges: Brain–computer interfaces for games. Entertainment computing, 1(2), pp 85–94

Nunez PL, Srinivasan R (2006) Electric fields of the brain: the neurophysics of EEG. Oxford University Press, USA.

Parsinejad P, Sipahi R (2017) Analysis of subjects' vulnerability in a touch screen game using behavioral metrics. Applied psychophysiology and biofeedback, 42(4), pp 269–282

Peperkorn HM, Diemer J, Mühlberger A (2015). Temporal dynamics in the relation between presence and fear in virtual reality. Computers in Human Behavior, 48, pp 542–547

Pinel JP, Steven Barnes (2017) Biopsychology. Pearson education.

Plouzeau J, Chardonnet JR, Merienne F (2018) Using Cybersickness Indicators to Adapt Navigation in Virtual Reality: A Pre-study. In 2018 IEEE Conference on Virtual Reality and 3D User Interfaces (VR). IEEE, pp 661–662

Ravaja N (2004) Contributions of psychophysiology to media research: Review and recommendations. Media Psychology, 6(2), pp 193–235

Ravaja N (2009) The psychophysiology of digital gaming: The effect of a non co-located opponent. Media Psychology, 12(3), pp 268–294

Ravaja N, Salminen M, Holopainen J, Saari T, Laarni J, Järvinen A (2004, October) Emotional response patterns and sense of presence during video games: Potential criterion variables for game design. In Proceedings of the third Nordic conference on Human-computer interaction. ACM, pp 339–347

Ravaja, N., Saari, T., Turpeinen, M., Laarni, J., Salminen, M., & Kivikangas, M. (2006). Spatial presence and emotions during video game playing: Does it matter with whom you play?. Presence: Teleoperators and Virtual Environments, 15(4), 381-392.

Ravaja N, Turpeinen M, Saari T, Puttonen S, Keltikangas-Järvinen L (2008) The psychophysiology of James Bond: Phasic emotional responses to violent video game events. Emotion, 8(1), p 114

Reuderink B, Mühl C, Poel M (2013) Valence, arousal and dominance in the EEG during game play. International journal of autonomous and adaptive communications systems, 6(1), pp 45–62

Sharma M, Kacker S, Sharma, M (2016) A brief introduction and review on galvanic skin response. Int J Med Res Prof, 2, pp 13–17

Shin M, Heard R, Suo C, Chow CM (2012) Positive emotions associated with "Counter-Strike" game playing. GAMES FOR HEALTH: Research, Development, and Clinical Applications, 1(5), pp 342–347

Slater, M., & Steed, A. (2000). A virtual presence counter. Presence: Teleoperators & Virtual Environments, 9(5), 413-434.

Sztajzel J (2004) Heart rate variability: a noninvasive electrocardiographic method to measure the autonomic nervous system. Swiss medical weekly, 134(35-36), pp 514–522

Tafalla RJ (2007) Gender Differences in Cardiovascular Reactivity and Game Performance Related to Sensory Modality in Violent Video Game Play 1. Journal of Applied Social Psychology, 37(9), pp 2008–2023

Tan CT, Leong TW, Shen S, Dubravs C, Si C (2015, October) Exploring gameplay experiences on the Oculus Rift. In Proceedings of the 2015 Annual Symposium on Computer-Human Interaction in Play. ACM, pp 253–263

Terkildsen T, Makransky G (2019) Measuring presence in video games: An investigation of the potential use of physiological measures as indicators of presence. International Journal of Human-Computer Studies, 126, pp 64–80

Van Boxtel A (2010, August) Facial EMG as a tool for inferring affective states. In Proceedings of measuring behavior. Wageningen: Noldus Information Technology, pp 104–108

Wang Q, Sourina O, Nguyen MK (2010, October) EEG-based "serious" games design for medical applications. In 2010 International Conference on Cyberworlds. IEEE, pp 270–276

Weber R, Behr KM, Tamborini R, Ritterfeld U, Mathiak K (2009) What do we really know about first-person-shooter games? An event-related, high-resolution content analysis. Journal of Computer-Mediated Communication, 14(4), pp 1016–1037

Wiederhold BK, Jang DP, Kaneda M, Cabral I, Lurie, Y, May T, Kim IY, Wiederhold MD, Kim SI (2003) An investigation into physiological responses in virtual environments: An objective measurement of presence. In G. Riva & C. Galimberti (Eds.), Towards CyberPsychology: Mind, cognitions and society in the internet age. Amsterdam: IOS Press.

Zhang J, Gao X (2014) Background music matters: Why video games lead to increased aggressive behavior?. Entertainment Computing, 5(2), pp 91–100

Ludography

Bioshock, 2K, *First Released:* 2007
Counter Strike: Source, CSS; Valve Corporation, *First Released:* 2004
Counter-Strike, Valve Software, *First Released:*1999
Doom 3, id Software, *First Released:* 2004
Doom, id Software, *First Released:* 1993
Duke Nukem Advance, Take-Two Interactive, *First Released:* 2002
Elder Scrolls III: Morrowind, Bethesda Softworks, *First Released:* 2002
Half-Life 2, Valve Corporation, *First Released:* 2004
James Bond 007: NightFire, EA Games, *First Released:* 2002
Juiced, THQ, *First Released:* 2005
Left 4 Dead 2, Valve Corporation, *First Released:* 2009
Mortal Kombat, Midway, *First Released:* 1992
Postal 2; Running With Scissors, *First Released:* 2003
Prey, 2K Games, *First Released:* 2006
Return of the Incredible Machine: Contraptions, Sierra On Line Inc, *First Released:* 2000
Super Meat Boy, Team Meat, *First Released:* 2010
Super Monkey Ball Jr, THQ & SEGA, *First Released:* 2002
Tactical Ops: Assault on Terror, Infogrames Europe; U.S. edition, *First Released:* 2002
Team Fortress 2, Valve, *First Released:* 2007
Temple Run, IMANGI Studios, *First Released:* 2011
Tom Clancy's Rainbow Six: Rogue Spear Black Thorn, Ubisoft, *First Released:* 2001
World of Warcraft, Blizzard Entertainment, *First Released:* 2004

Part III
Game Design and Player Experience

Chapter 11
The Ethics of Game Experience

Sami Hyrynsalmi, Kai K. Kimppa, and Jouni Smed

Contents

Abstract Modern gaming—especially in mobile platforms—has turned into a quagmire of questionable practices. This chapter takes a look into the ethical problems brought about by the increasing importance of monetisation in game design. We recognise five factors that are threatening the player's game experience and argue how they constitute unethical behaviour on the part of game designers.

S. Hyrynsalmi
Computing Sciences, Tampere University, Pori, Finland

Software Engineering, LUT University, Lahti, Finland
e-mail: sami.hyrynsalmi@lut.fi

K. K. Kimppa
Information Systems Science, University of Turku, Turku, Finland
e-mail: kai.kimppa@utu.fi

J. Smed (✉)
Department of Future Technologies, University of Turku, Turku, Finland
e-mail: jouni.smed@utu.fi

© Springer Nature Switzerland AG 2020
B. Bostan (ed.), *Game User Experience And Player-Centered Design*,
International Series on Computer Entertainment and Media Technology,
https://doi.org/10.1007/978-3-030-37643-7_11

Keywords Game ethics · Monetisation · Business models · Game design · Online metrics · Gaming disorder

11.1 Introduction

Our motivation for this chapter is to consider the ethical aspects of the game experience. Usually articles on game experience approach the topic by building theoretical models or by addressing practical issues related to the game design and development. Our special focus is on the mobile game experience and whether it is ethically sustainable when the mobile game developers semi-openly admit that their purpose is to get the player addicted and to pay more than they realise in the first place (Kimppa et al. 2015).

Sometimes the methods catch the attention of lawmakers such as the case of loot boxes, which were deemed to be a form of gambling and should, therefore, follow the relevant regulation. At the moment, the Battle Pass monetisation model, made famous by the game *Fortnite* (Epic Games 2017), is the most popular one. Although it is likely not to be problematic in most jurisdictions from the legal perspective (like loot boxes clearly are), one could pose the question whether it and other methods of its kind are ethical and, in this chapter, we indeed do.

Ethics refers to the philosophical study of right and wrong actions. Ethical issues of digital games have been considered for decades. The previous game ethics studies have ranged from considerations from cheating in an online game (Kimppa and Bissett 2005) to discussions of how the well-being of digital chickens in games may affect the players, or misrepresent the importance of fowls in our development as a species (Fothergill and Flick 2016) as well as the ethical dark side of gamification usage (Hyrynsalmi et al. 2017).

This chapter reviews the ethical considerations of the game experience design. The *ethics of game experience* is defined to include all ethical aspects of the game experience, including the game and its mechanisms as well as its interactions with the surrounding environment such as other games and communities. This view follows and extends Lynn's (2012) view on the game experience. Included concerns are, for example, questions regarding the placements of geographical points of interests in games such as *Pokémon Go* (Niantic 2016), as they have been argued to favour wealthy areas at the cost of minorities (Colley et al. 2017) as well as endangering players (Laato et al. 2019).

The specific point at hand, in this chapter, is the impacts of the revenue and business model to the game design and, to consequently, the game experience. As the competition in the game markets has been growing and new innovative revenue and business models have been implemented into the games, the ethical consequences should also be acknowledged. This chapter will provide an overview of the state of the art for the academics as well as practical considerations for the game designers.

This chapter is structured as follows: First, we will discuss on ethical issues in games as well as define our philosophical standpoint. This discussion is followed by a review of revenue and business models of modern mobile games. After that, we present our ethical concerns of the game experience design. Concluding remarks appear in the final section.

11.2 Background

The public ethical discussion on games and playing usually revolves around issues like games and violence (or other mature content), cheating in online games, cyberbullying, game communities hostile attitude towards women and minorities (e.g., Gamergate controversy), and sexual predators utilising gaming platforms. All of these are important issues in their own right but fall out of the scope of our present paper, which focuses on the decisions made in the game design. In this regard, Adams (2014, pp. 159–162) lines out the ethical dimension of designing a game world, where the designer defines "what right and wrong means within the context of that world". Sicart (2009, p. 41) shares this view and asserts that "[t]he game designer is responsible for most of the values that are embedded in the system and that play a significant role during the game experience".

The two most problematic features of current game design—especially in mobile games—are psychological traps (Hamari 2011; Søraker 2016) and reduction of the game experience due to advertising (Palokankare 2011; Kimppa et al. 2015). One can ask does this have consequences to the game designer's character—will they treat others unfairly in other parts of their life as well (Aristotle 350 BCE/2004)? This situation constitutes cognitive dissonance, as at work they basically try to lure as much money out of their customers as possible. Heimo et al. (2018) specifically point out that these kinds of design methods are vices, not virtues. They make the game designer a worse person, rather than a better person. If their colleagues were true to them, they would stop this kind of development, as they, due to the fact that their work is drifting further away from what a good person ought to be. This, of course, sets a high bar for the colleagues at work, but professional pride ought to help towards this, as is pointed out, for example, in the ACM Code of Ethics (Gotterbarn et al. 2018).

What are the consequences of utilitarianism (Mill 1863/2001) to the customers? The so-called whales are players who use considerable amounts of their monthly income on these games. They need to also eat and pay their bills—and, possibly, they need to feed others such as minors they are responsible for. How can this kind of game design be considered right when the whole idea is to sucker the weak (Kimppa et al. 2015)? Already the intent is clearly wrong, let alone the consequences (Kant 1785/1997). On Kimppa's model (unpublished) of intentional consequentialist evaluation using a dutiful consequences model of ethical information systems (see Fig. 11.1), this is in the clearest corner of evil (bottom right in Fig 11.1.).

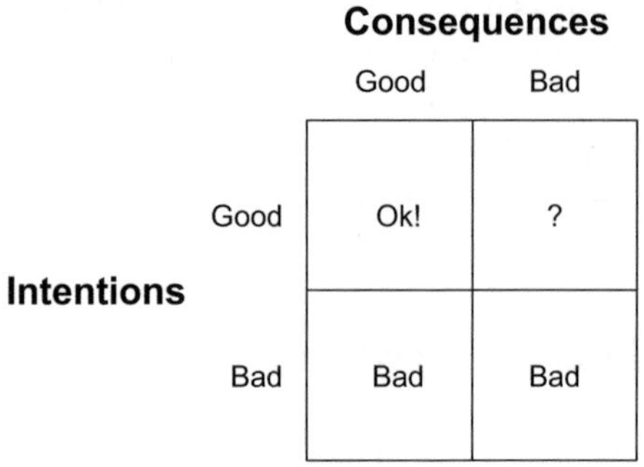

Fig. 11.1 Intentional
consequentialist evaluation of
ethical information systems

Consequences

Good   Bad

	Good	Ok!	?
Intentions			
	Bad	Bad	Bad

Capitalism is based on two different possible approaches: (1) win–win where I have something you need and both win in the trade and (2) sucker the weak and take their money. In this particular case, the latter thinking is clearly abundant. As John Maynard Keynes puts it: "Capitalism is the extraordinary belief that the nastiest of men, for the nastiest of reasons, will somehow work for the benefit of us all". Many mobile games and their functioning logic as well as their user interfaces are prime examples of this kind of thinking. Thus, it is clear that oversight on the practices used to make money is not just needed but mandatory, lest the weakest in the society (in this case those prone to addiction in games) are taken advantage of (Rawls 1999).

Karhulahti and Kimppa (2018) state that introducing elements to the game, which the players pay for, are not problematic per se, but when those elements give the players an unfair advantage, it does pose a problem. A typical example, as pointed out before, are loot boxes. If it is possible to buy ones leading the way to the victory, those who have the wherewithal will take advantage of this, but, consequently, fall for the traps built into the system. This makes the game experience poorer for both those who can do it, but especially for those who cannot.

Although interesting and critical in their own right, in the remainder of this chapter we focus on the ethical problems brought on by monetisation. It is a growing concern that there is an increasing pressure to develop games—especially mobile games—as a tool for optimised monetising. Traditionally this kind of game design has focused on gambling and (online) casinos, which have specialised in creating an environment where the player (i.e., the customer) can be persuaded to spend more money than they might have initially intended.

The reason why this has become a norm in mobile gaming is two-fold: Digital distribution and digital payments have changed the monetisation method of games and changed them from products to service. At the same time, online metrics have evolved into a highly specific "science" allowing an ever-increasing and specific observation of the players and their habits, customs and weaknesses, which has boosted the monetisation methods.

Let us next look at these two facets—monetisation and online metrics.

11.3 Revenue and Business Models

In a common use, the term "business model" refers to how a company operates, organises itself, and how it makes money (Osterwalder et al. 2005; Luoma 2013). To define the concept simply, it is a blueprint of how a business organisation is built and how it operates (Hyrynsalmi et al. 2019). In more formal terms, a business model describes how a company creates value and delivers it to the customers and captures value to itself (Zott et al. 2011).

A revenue model, or revenue logic, is a part of a business model; it reveals how a firm makes money (Popp and Meyer 2010). A revenue model consists of one or more revenue streams that indicate source, amount, and frequency of compensation. For example, a simple revenue model for a mobile game could consist of advertisement and an upfront payment, for ad-free version, revenue streams. Yet, the revenue models in mobile application stores are often complex and multifaceted (Hyrynsalmi et al. 2012).

The change from the traditional game-as-a-product to the modern game-as-a-service model has changed how these games are monetised (Smed and Hakonen 2017, pp. 307–309). Traditionally, the main monetisation model for games has been retail sale (i.e., premium games). Before the advent of digital distribution, this would have meant paying upfront for a hard copy of the game. This premium model has been transported also to digital distribution, but online games employ mainly other monetisation models. Pay-to-play (P2P) games require the player to pay periodically (typically once a month) for an access to the game. Free-to-play (F2P) or freemium games are provided free for the player. However, there are many different business models for the sources of revenue. The most obvious ones are advertising and in-application purchases, which can ease the player's progression in the game. Revenue can be generated also by selling cosmetic enhancement to the players (usually without affecting the gameplay) or giving specialised account services. Pay-to-win (P2W) is an extreme variant of F2P, where the game content is available to the player in the beginning, but, at some point, the player will hit a "pay wall". A pay wall is a challenge in the game that cannot be solved (or it is extremely hard) by playing alone and instead requires the player to pay a certain amount to bypass. In some sense, P2W can turn into P2P game if these pay walls are encountered evenly during gameplay.

The two factors that have facilitated this transition are online metrics and digital distribution. Earlier feedback from the game player had a long delay (in weeks or months), because the channels were non-digital (e.g., reviews in game magazines) or simple (e.g., a feedback form on a website). Moreover, the turn-over rate and coverage were smaller (i.e., player would typically give feedback once—if at all). This reflected the rate of change in the game design as the feedback could be accounted for possibly in the next version or in the sequel of a game. Nowadays, feedback from the players is continuous, automatic (i.e., the player does not have to initiate it), and more detailed. When this is combined with digital distribution, the design can be updated in a very short term. Moreover, it is possible to provide different instances of the game to different players to conduct (e.g., A/B testing).

Next, let us turn the discussion to the apparent—and maybe also non-apparent—ethical issues that this change from product to service has created (or amplified).

11.4 Ethical Problems

The ethical problems present in the game experience stem from how the game is taking away the player's control of their resources. We can differentiate the following resources (although they are partly overlapping):

- money,
- time and attention,
- social capital,
- mental and physical energy, and
- security.

Playing a game means that the player is willing to invest the aforementioned resources. Simply put, the player invests money to buy the game, reserves time for playing, uses social capital to invite others to join in the game, exerts mental and physical energy in the process of playing, and assumes to be secure in the real world whilst engaged in virtual risks in the game world.

In the following subsections, we will look at each of these resources from the perspective of how ethical the game design and experience is in letting the player to retain control.

11.4.1 Money

There are various ethical problems related to the inclusion of real-world money in the game design. The biggest one is the unspecific nature of the expected monetary relationship. As the player is not given upfront an expected cost but rather a (possibly partly hidden) table of prices, they are in no position to make an educated guess of the actual costs. This *design by obfuscation* hides the expectations from the player, which is understandable from the point-of-view that games are about surprise and reacting to matters as they occur. It would be unfeasible to list them out if they have not even occurred yet.

A counter-argument would be that many services work on a similar basis: When you enter a restaurant, you do not know what the bill will be at the end, because you order the courses, drinks, and dessert on the way. Similarly, when you have your car serviced, you cannot anticipate what kind of costs might occur due to replacement parts and extra work required.

The question here is not that monetising the gameplay experience is unethical per se—which it clearly is not—but what is the *intention* behind how things are priced. Design by obfuscation alters the design to hide the cost. It would be like ordering a meal where prices are not listed on the menu, but related to hidden or hard to understand factors such as the size of leftovers on your plate, the total time spent in chewing, and the number of swallowed fish bones. Moreover, these prices would vary based on the retail value of the car that the restaurant visitor parked outside. If this example seems far-fetched, consider a case where a mobile game requires the player to buy in-game resources (e.g., diamonds), which will be needed to access content otherwise unavailable, speed-up the processes that would take hours, and to avoid situations which would otherwise cause the game to end—and the real-word price of the diamonds would depend on the country and operating system of the player (i.e., the price would be higher for a player from Western Europe using iOS than for a player from a developing country using Android).

11.4.2 Time and Attention

The second concern is the use of addiction inducing mechanics. Bluntly put, the core loop of a game is trimmed to maximise the dopamine release, giving a constant flow of mini-rewards and keeping the player's mind occupied. These even have defined term like "appointment dynamics" (e.g., "come back in 1 h and claim your reward"; when the players cannot have it now, they keep thinking about it) or "fading opportunities" (e.g., "you can get this for half the price only today" or "limited edition"). In a broader sense, these issues riddle the social media as well.

Again, the key question here is the intention behind the design. Naturally, a good game is immersive and keeps the player in a flow state, but we must make a difference whether this is because of providing the player entertainment or whether it is to keep the player from leaving or putting the game aside and preventing them to play any other game. It is established that for mobile games, retention (i.e., keeping the player coming back) is the key metric (Smed and Hakonen 2017, pp. 310–311). This can be achieved by updates giving more content or by game mechanics trimmed to draw the player regularly back. For example, the mobile game *Kim Kardashian: Hollywood* (Glu Mobile 2014) requires the player to come back to the game every day to buy a present for an in-game boyfriend; failing this would cause the player to lose all the progress. Similar "streak" mechanics have adopted by also some social media sites such as Snapchat. Simply put, the problem is that the game is taking away from the player the control of their time and attention.

11.4.3   Social Capital

The social network of the player is a key for the game to spread. This was done—quite crudely—by early Facebook games such as *Farmville* (Zynga 2009), where some tasks required input from the player's friends hence allowing the game to spread among the social network. It also allowed the game to control the player's friends by shaming them into participation (e.g., "how can you leave your friend alone and not help him in this small farming task"). Further examples include, e.g., *Pokémon Go* (Niantic 2016) which allows player to send and receive gifts from friends.

A reversal aspect of misusing social capital is that mobile gaming can throw the player into a company that they would actually like to avoid. This way they could be susceptible to abuse or bullying.

11.4.4   Mental and Physical Energy

Gameplay takes energy, usually and sometimes even physical. As the control is taken away, the player can be exhausted more than is appropriate. For example, several games allow the player to perform actions after a certain time. *Travian* (Müller 2004), a browser-based massive multiplayer game, allows the player to construct a building every predefined hour. Players who ordered a monthly based premium service are allowed to queue buildings whereas those without it are known to wake up even in the middle of night to be allowed to continue playing. This and similar mechanisms can affect sleeping patterns, which is a critical question especially when we are dealing with children and youngsters. Even for adults this can be a challenge.

Related to this is game addiction, where the player has lost the control of game playing completely. World Health Organization (2018, Sect. 6C51) defines that "gaming disorder" is characterised "by a pattern of persistent or recurrent gaming behaviour ("digital gaming" or "video-gaming"), which may be online (i.e., over the internet) or offline". More specifically, its manifestations are

- impaired control over gaming,
- increasing priority given to gaming taking priority over other life interests and daily activities, and
- continuation or escalation regardless of the occurrence of negative consequences (e.g., impairment in personal, family, social, or occupational areas of functioning).

One can argue that adding *knowingly* features promoting this kind of addictive behaviour—considered a disorder by the WHO—is unethical. It resembles the stance taken by Big Tobacco in denying and discrediting the research showing that their products cause cancer.

11.4.5 Security

Typically after downloading and installing a mobile game, the player is faced with a list of permissions that the game wants to have such as the use of microphone or access to photographs and contacts. Many give these permissions without even stopping to think what they are doing. A critical review of the asked permission raises questions, why and for what purpose the game needs all this data and access. But as the game will not work without granting them, the player does not have much selective choice other than either take it or leave it.

The given access can be utilised in an alarming fashion (Sulleyman 2018). For example, the access to microphone has been used to scan the player's surroundings to create a profile of the social status and wealth of the player—which is used, in turn, in setting higher prices for the more affluent players.

Apart from collecting data from the player's in-game decisions, the game can also record the player's decisions on advertisements (e.g., whether they decide to click it or skip it). Although this data is not related to the actual gameplay, it is a valuable asset for the developer in terms of recognizing the most potential advertisers. Moreover, when this data is combined with the gameplay data, the developer can try to modify the game to be more advertisement friendly—even to the extent of blurring the demarcation between advertorial and actual content.

11.5 Concluding Remarks

Would it be possible to create ethically sound (mobile) games and game experiences? In some sense, we could try to define factors that contribute labelling a game "ethically sustainable"—in a similar fashion that we have define what constitutes food to be "ecologically sustainable". However, the best we can do is to give suggestions how an ethically sound game should be constructed—but there is no guarantee whether this practice would catch on.

The list of question to be answered by the game designers and the publisher is:

- How much does playing the game actually cost?
- How much time and attention is needed in playing the game?
- Does the game require access to the player's social network, and, if so, why?
- How mentally and physically taxing is the game?
- What kind of access to the hardware the game requires and for what purpose?

This would be a beginning towards an ethical gameplay experience—a clear statement of intent from the game designers. Who will be the first to do this?

References

Adams E (2014) Fundamentals of Game Design, 3rd edn. New Riders, San Francisco, CA, USA

Aristotle (350 BCE/2004) The Nicomachean Ethics. Penguin Classics, London, UK

Colley A, Thebault-Spieker J, Lin AY, Degraen D, Fischman B, Häkkilä J, Kuehl K, Nisi V, Nunes NJ, Wenig N, Wenig D, Hecht B, Schöning J (2017) The geography of PokéMon Go: Beneficial and problematic effects on places and movement. In: Proceedings of the 2017 CHI Conference on Human Factors in Computing Systems, ACM, New York, NY, USA, CHI '17, pp 1179–1192, https://doi.org/10.1145/3025453.3025495

Epic Games (2017) Fortnite. Epic Games

Fothergill BT, Flick C (2016) The ethics of human-chicken relationships in video games: The origins of the digital chicken. SIGCAS Computers and Society 45(3):100–108, https://doi.org/10.1145/2874239.2874254

Glu Mobile (2014) Kim Kardashian: Hollywood. Glu Mobile

Gotterbarn D, Brinkman B, Flick C, Kirkpatrick MS, Miller K, Varansky K, Wolf MJ (2018) ACM Code of Ethics and Professional Conduct. ACM, https://www.acm.org/code-of-ethics, members: Eve Anderson, Ron Anderson, Amy Bruckman, Karla Carter, Michael Davis, Penny Duquenoy, Jeremy Epstein, Kai Kimppa, Lorraine Kisselburgh, Shrawan Kumar, Andrew McGettrick, Natasa Milic-Frayling, Denise Oram, Simon Rogerson, David Shama, Janice Sipior, Eugene Spafford, and Les Waguespack

Hamari J (2011) Perspectives from behavioral economics to analyzing game design patterns: Loss aversion in social games. In: Proceedings of CHI'2011 (Social games workshop)

Heimo OI, Harviainen JT, Kimppa KK, Mäkilä T (2018) Virtual to virtuous money: A virtue ethics perspective on video game business logic. Journal of Business Ethics 153(1):95–103, https://doi.org/10.1007/s10551-016-3408-z

Hyrynsalmi S, Suominen A, Mäkilä T, Knuutila T (2012) The emerging mobile ecosystems: An introductory analysis of Android Market. In: Proceedings of the 21st International Conference on Management of Technology, International Association for Management of Technology, Hsinchu, Taiwan, IAMOT'2012, pp 1–16

Hyrynsalmi S, Kimppa KK, Smed J (2017) Gamification ethics. In: Lee N (ed) Encyclopedia of Computer Graphics and Games, Springer International Publishing, Cham, pp 1–6, https://doi.org/10.1007/978-3-319-08234-9_138-1

Hyrynsalmi S, Rauti S, Kaila E (2019) Bridging the gap between software architecture and business model development: A literature study. In: 2019 42nd International Convention on Information and Communication Technology, Electronics and Microelectronics (MIPRO), IEEE, pp 1519–1524, https://doi.org/10.23919/MIPRO.2019.8756974

Kant I (1785/1997) Groundwork of the Metaphysics of Morals. Cambridge University Press, Cambridge, UK

Karhulahti V, Kimppa K (2018) "Two queens and a Pwn, please." An ethics for purchase, loot, and advantage design in esports. In: Koivisto J, Hamari J (eds) Proceedings of the 2nd International GamiFIN Conference, Pori, Finland, May 21–23, 2018., CEUR-WS.org, CEUR Workshop Proceedings, vol 2186, pp 115–122, http://ceur-ws.org/Vol-2186

Kimppa K, Bissett A (2005) The ethical significance of cheating in online computer games. International Review of Information Ethics 4:31–37

Kimppa KK, Heimo OI, Harviainen JT (2015) First dose is always freemium. SIGCAS Computers & Society 45(3):132–137

Laato S, Pietarinen T, Rauti S, Laine TH (2019) Analysis of the quality of points of interest in the most popular location-based games. In: CompSysTech'19

Luoma E (2013) Examining business models of software-as-a-service companies. Ph.D. dissertation, University of Jyväskylä. Jyväskylä studies in computing 188, Jyväskylä, Finland, http://urn.fi/URN:ISBN:978-951-39-5562-5

Lynn D (2012) What is 'the game experience'? Gamasutra https://www.gamasutra.com/blogs/DouglasLynn/20120830/176837/What_Is_The_Game_Experience.php

Mill JS (1863/2001) Utilitarianism. Virginia Tech, Blacksburg, VA

Müller G (2004) Travian. Travian Games

Niantic (2016) Pokémon Go. Niantic

Osterwalder A, Pigneur Y, Tucci CL (2005) Clarifying business models: Origins, present, and future of the concept. Communication of the AIS 16:1–25

Palokankare T (2011) Responsible advertising in video games. Master's thesis, University of Turku

Popp KM, Meyer R (2010) Profit from Software Ecosystems: Business Models, Ecosystems and Partnerships in the Software Industry. Books on Demand GmbH

Rawls J (1999) A Theory of Justice. Oxford University Press. Oxford, UK

Sicart M (2009) The Ethics of Computer Games. MIT Press, Cambridge, MA, USA

Smed J, Hakonen H (2017) Algorithms and Networking for Computer Games, 2nd edn. John Wiley & Sons, Chichester, UK

Søraker JH (2016) Gaming the gamer?—the ethics of exploiting psychological research in video games. JICES 14(2):106–123

Sulleyman A (2018) Hundreds of smartphone apps are monitoring users through their microphones. The Independent https://www.independent.co.uk/life-style/gadgets-and-tech/news/smartphone-apps-listening-privacy-alphonso-shazam-advertising-pool-3d-honey-quest-a8139451.html

World Health Organization (2018) International Classification of Diseases 11th Revision. https://icd.who.int/en/

Zott C, Amit R, Massa L (2011) The business model: Recent developments and future research. Journal of Management 37(37):1019–1042, https://doi.org/10.1177/0149206311406265

Zynga (2009) Farmville. Zynga

Chapter 12
Death and Rebirth in Platformer Games

Edward F. Melcer and Marjorie Ann M. Cuerdo

Contents

E. F. Melcer (✉)
University of California, Santa Cruz, CA, USA
e-mail: eddie.melcer@ucsc.edu

M. A. M. Cuerdo
DePaul University, Chicago, IL, USA
e-mail: mcuerdo@mail.depaul.edu

© Springer Nature Switzerland AG 2020
B. Bostan (ed.), *Game User Experience And Player-Centered Design*,
International Series on Computer Entertainment and Media Technology,
https://doi.org/10.1007/978-3-030-37643-7_12

Abstract Failure is a central aspect of almost every game experience, driving
player perceptions of difficulty and impacting core game user experience concepts
such as flow. At the heart of failure in many game genres is player death. While
techniques such as dynamic difficulty adjustment have addressed tweaking game
parameters to control the frequency of player death occurrence, there is a surprisingly limited amount of research examining how games handle what happens when a
player actually dies. We posit that this is a rich, underexplored space with significant
implications for player experience and related techniques. This chapter presents
our exploration into the space of player death and rebirth through the creation of a
generalized taxonomy of death in platformer games—one of the genres that features
player death and respawning most heavily. In order to create this taxonomy, we
collected and catalogued examples of death and respawning mechanics from 62
recent platformer games released on the digital distribution platform Steam after
January 2018. Games selected varied equally across positive, mixed, and negative
overall reviews in order to provide a broader range of mechanics, both good and bad.
We observed gameplays of each individual game and noted the processes of death
and rebirth, respectively. A grounded theory approach was then employed to develop
the taxonomy of game death and respawning, resulting in five notable dimensions:
(1) *obstacles*, (2) *death conditions*, (3) *aesthetics*, (4) *changes to player progress*,
and (5) *respawn locations*. Finally, we discuss how the different dimensions and
mechanics highlighted in our taxonomy have implications for key aspects of player
experience, as well as how they could be used to improve the effectiveness of related
techniques such as dynamic difficulty adjustment.

Keywords Taxonomy · Platformers · Games · In-game death · Respawning ·
Player experience

12.1   Introduction

Failure in video games, often represented through death, is a central element of the
player experience (Klimmt et al. 2009). For instance, failure is well documented
to have substantial positive and negative impacts on game enjoyment (Juul 2013).

It is also intrinsically linked to challenge, and consequently a major factor in the experience of game flow (Juul 2009). While there have been various approaches to examining and manipulating this critical aspect of the gaming experience— e.g., dynamic difficulty adjustment (Denisova and Cairns 2015; Hunicke 2005), difficulty design (Wehbe et al. 2017), and challenge design (Brandse 2017) and modeling (Sorenson et al. 2011)—research understanding failure explicitly as it relates to handling in-game death is surprisingly limited. We propose that how video games actually deal with in-game death is a rich, underexplored space with significant implications for player experience and related techniques such as dynamic difficulty adjustment. With that in mind, we created a taxonomy of player death and rebirth in platformer games to better understand the current design space.

Platformers are a video game genre where players typically control a game character to jump and climb between platforms while avoiding obstacles. We chose this as our genre of focus since platformer games are generally designed around constant player death and respawning in pursuit of a goal. They are also notorious for being difficult, with many such games leading to the creation of the term "Nintendo hard"—referring colloquially to the extreme difficulty of games (particularly platformers) from the Nintendo Entertainment System era (Enger 2012). Notably, the fairness of difficulty in Nintendo hard games has been called into question in recent years (Lessel 2013), highlighting that such designs can sometimes serve more to infuriate players through frequent unfair death rather than provide an appropriate challenge. A taxonomy of player death in this space provides a tool to systematically classify death and respawning mechanics across games—helping to elucidate which mechanics may evoke positive and negative player experiences, enhance or inhibit game flow, and provide sufficient challenge or create a feeling of unfairness.

In this chapter specifically, we want to understand the essential features and types of mechanics around death in video games. This is done by employing grounded theory to analyse existing platformer games of varying user rating. We chose games as our main source of data for analysis because there is a relatively limited amount of existing literature that addresses the actual mechanics around in-game death, making expert analysis of games as artefacts a more useful source of information (Alharthi et al. 2018). We start this chapter by providing background and related work on game taxonomies, game death, dynamic difficulty adjustment, and grounded theory. This is followed by an overview of our search and analysis procedure for the corpus of platformer games. We then present our **taxonomy of death and rebirth in platformer games** that is derived from the collected dataset. Finally, we conclude with a discussion of the implications and potential application areas of our framework, as well as provide insights obtained from its use on the current dataset of platformer games. It is also important to note that we provide a ludography for the 62 games included in our dataset. Therefore, when we cite a game, the reference will be prefixed with a "G" (e.g., [G7]).

12.2   Background

In this section, we discuss existing game taxonomies and the grounded theory methodology employed to create our taxonomy, as well as highlight relevant research examining death in video games and dynamic difficulty adjustment.

12.2.1   Game Taxonomies and Frameworks

Although they are used rather interchangeably in the literature, there are some notable differences between taxonomies and frameworks. Taxonomies provide a means to organize and classify concepts while frameworks are composed of a number of concepts and the interrelations between them (Antle and Wise 2013). There can even be overlap between the two in the form of taxonomical design frameworks (e.g., Ens et al. 2014; Melcer and Isbister 2016), which treat a set of taxonomical terms as orthogonal dimensions in a design space—resulting in a matrix that provides structure for classification and comparison of designs (Robinett 1992).

In terms of games, there have been a substantial number of taxonomies and frameworks ranging from general classifications of games themselves (Aarseth et al. 2003; Elverdam and Aarseth 2007; Vossen 2004) to various aspects of games—such as core mechanics (Sedig et al. 2017), bugs (Lewis et al. 2010), player modeling (Smith et al. 2011), and external factors (Mäkelä et al. 2017)—to (most commonly) specific genres of games. E.g., serious games (De Lope and Medina-Medina 2017; Rego et al. 2010), games for dementia (Dormann 2016; McCallum and Boletsis 2013), exertion games (Mueller et al. 2008), affective games (Lara-Cabrera and Camacho 2019), idle games (Alharthi et al. 2018), and games and simulations (Klabbers 2003) to name a few. Of particular relevance to this work is the framework created by Smith et al. (2008) for analysing 2D platformer levels. Their framework consists of *components* in the form of platforms, obstacles, movement aids, collectible items, and triggers; as well as *structural representation* for how the components fit together. We utilize many of these concepts in our coding scheme and taxonomy; however, their framework ultimately focuses on rhythm and pacing to evoke challenge, rather than player death.

12.2.2   In-Game Death

Players are ultimately humans, and therefore, the player experience is tied to the human experience (Melnic and Melnic 2018). With respect to death, a notable fascination exists regarding the relationship between players' perception of in-game death and actual death. Some have argued that in-game death trivializes the seriousness of actual death (Frasca 2007). However, others believe that the inherent interactive nature of games is powerful in expressing meaningful facets of the human experience of life and death (Chittaro and Sioni 2018; Harrer 2013; Rusch 2009).

Players in particular can be impacted by death in games when they are attached to characters (their avatars or NPCs) at some emotional level or self-identify with the goals or events in the game (Bopp et al. 2016; Melnic and Melnic 2018; Rusch 2009; Schneider et al. 2004). For instance, when players are immersed in gameplay, the risk of death produces anxiety and encourages more careful decision-making, but can also evoke strong emotions from players that result in enjoyment and positive player experience despite the frustration that comes with the territory (Bopp et al. 2016).

Death is also an intrinsic part of gameplay (Mukherjee 2009) and the player experience (Klastrup 2006), with notoriously difficult level design in platformers resulting in frequent occurrences of player death (Enger 2012). These instances of in-game death generally impede player progress, e.g., through the loss of inventory items, achievements, or game functionality (Bopp et al. 2016). Notably, repetitive deaths have been found to increasingly reduce player enjoyment, as each death occurrence compounds as an evaluation of the insufficiency of a player's skills (Van Den Hoogen 2012). At even greater extremes, in-game death can completely reset player progress such as through the popular high-risk death mechanic, permadeath—i.e., the permanent in-game death of a playable character (c.f., Copcic et al. 2013)—which forces the player to restart the entire game upon dying. While the ability to have save states in some platformers has alleviated the difficulty of death and altered player strategy, the majority of platformer games still operate using linear, sequential checkpoints. As such, it is critical to examine the aesthetics and mechanics that comprise in-game death for a broader understanding of its overall effects on player experience.

12.2.3 Dynamic Difficulty Adjustment

Dynamic difficulty adjustment (DDA) describes a challenge design strategy that continuously and automatically adapts a game's difficulty level to a player's current skill level (Jennings-Teats et al. 2010; Smeddinck et al. 2016; Zohaib 2018), and as such attempts to keep the player in a constant state of flow (Denisova and Cairns 2015). There is evidence that dynamically adjusting components in games affects their perceived difficulty (Denisova and Cairns 2015; Jennings-Teats et al. 2010; Wehbe et al. 2017) and boosts player confidence (Constant and Levieux 2019). Other advantages of DDA include a decrease in the risk of players quitting a game due to frustration from constant deaths as well as an increase in a players' perceived self-efficacy (Constant and Levieux 2019; Gilleade and Dix 2004). Furthermore, it has been argued that player engagement and enjoyment can be maximized with DDA in games (Denisova and Cairns 2015; Sarkar and Cooper 2019; Xue et al. 2017). However, one notable criticism of most current DDA techniques is that they are based on designer intuition, which may not reflect actual play patterns or mechanics (Jennings-Teats et al. 2010). Therefore, a taxonomy highlighting specific mechanics and design choices around in-game death and respawning could serve to better inform and aid the design of these techniques.

12.2.4 Grounded Theory

Grounded theory methodology (GTM) is commonly used to explore new domains (Alharthi et al. 2018; Glaser and Strauss 2017). It is a data-driven and inductive research methodology where the analysis is conducted as data is collected (Hook 2015). The GTM process starts with data collection, gradually building up categories and forming a theory, before linking that theory to previous literature at the end (Hook 2015). It effectively enables a researcher to simultaneously analyse a body of artefacts (in this case platformer video games) and develop a theory about what elements of these artefacts are salient (Kreminski et al. 2019). This is usually done through the creation of a codebook which evolves over the course of the analysis and is used to note down the features of specific artefacts as they are analysed.

It is, however, important to note that GTM does not actually represent a single set of methods, as there are different philosophical schools of practice which fragment the ways it can be interpreted and deployed—often causing confusion (Glaser 1992). Notably, there are three major variants of GTM which can have major effects on the research outcome (Salisbury and Cole 2016), i.e., Strauss, Glaser, and Charmaz/Constructivist. For the creation of our taxonomy on in-game death and rebirth, we adopted the constructivist flavour of GTM (Charmaz 2006). This GTM variant frames the researcher as co-creating meaning within the domain they are studying (Charmaz 2000), focusing on providing lenses for analysis rather than a single objectively correct model of the domain (Salisbury and Cole 2016).

12.3 Methodology

We conducted a qualitative analysis of platformer games in order to identify the essential features and differing types of mechanics around death and respawning in platformer video games, as well as to highlight design choices that may be beneficial or detrimental to the player experience. We utilized a constructivist grounded theory approach (Charmaz 2006) (see related work) that started with an iterative process of finding and selecting platformer games. Games were analysed and coded by watching videos of gameplay as well as playing them when there was a lack of existing footage. Specifically, we employed open coding and conceptual memoing to identify the initial concepts around death and respawning. Axial coding—i.e., identifying relationships among the open codes and initial concepts (Alharthi et al. 2018)—was then employed to determine our initial set of categories. Finally, selective coding—i.e., integrating initial categories to form a core category that comprehensively describes the data (Alharthi et al. 2018)—was used to determine the final categories of our taxonomy.

Positively Reviewed:	Mixed Reviewed:	Negatively Reviewed:
G6, G11, G14, G18, G19, G22, G27, G28, G30, G31, G35, G36, G39, G40, G43, G47, G52, G56, G57, G60, G62	G2, G4, G7, G8, G9, G10, G12, G13, G17, G21, G24, G26, G29, G33, G34, G45, G46, G49, G51 , G53, G55, G58	G1, G3, G5, G15, G16, G20, G23, G25, G32, G37, G38, G41, G42, G44, G48, G50, G54, G59, G61

Fig. 12.1 The 62 platformer games in our corpus, categorized by corresponding critical reception: *Positively*, *Mixed*, and *Negatively Reviewed*. A ludography is included for our dataset

12.3.1   Search Strategy

In order to obtain an accurate corpus of recent popular platformer games, we utilized the extremely popular digital games distribution platform, *Steam*, for our search. We searched for all video games that were explicitly tagged as a "Platformer". In an effort to observe trends in characteristics of recent platformers, we specifically restricted the search to video games that were released within the recent period of January 2018 to May 2019. Because we wanted to observe the most popular games in terms of rating count and *Steam* did not offer the ability to sort by number of reviews, we manually selected the top twenty or so games with the highest number of player reviews for the positively, mixed, and negatively reviewed categories below.

A total of 62 games were selected based on three categories of player ratings (see Fig. 12.1): (1) *positively reviewed*, 21 collected; (2) *mixed-reviewed*, 22 collected; and (3) *negatively reviewed*, 19 collected. We chose a fairly even spread of positively to negatively reviewed games to ensure that we were collecting the broadest range of death and respawning mechanics, both good and bad, to inform the creation of our taxonomy. Games were identified as positively reviewed if they had at least 85% or higher of their player audience positively recommend the game, mixed-reviewed if they were between 60% to 84%, and negatively reviewed if they had less than 60%. We adjusted for a high approval percentage of at least 85% for positively reviewed games, because we observed that even games with the poorest reputations had about half of their players recommend them while critically acclaimed games generally had overwhelmingly positive reviews of 90% or more.

12.3.2   Analysis Procedure

12.3.2.1   Phase 1: Observations of Death and Rebirth Mechanics

We examined each game individually by watching a playthrough online or, if not available, obtaining the game and playing them ourselves. We recorded each game's approach to handling player death with information on what conditions result in death, where players were respawned, what was lost and gained, obstacle types, and visual and auditory representations of death. Other information we noted were its Steam game tags (in addition to "platformer"), game description, approval percentage, number of reviews, and basic game mechanics.

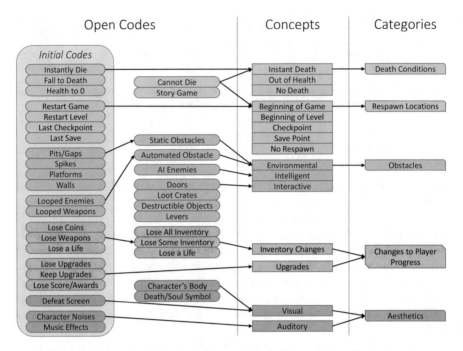

Fig. 12.2 The coding process. Starting with open coding of observations. The open codes were then related into concepts using axial coding, and were later grouped and developed using selective coding to create our five main *Death and Rebirth Taxonomy Categories*

12.3.2.2 Phase 2: Open, Axial, and Selective Coding

We started this phase by performing open coding on our observations of the 62 platformer games from phase 1. Axial coding was then employed to identify a set of emerging concepts and initial categories around death and respawning. This was followed by multiple iterative discussion sessions to explore the relationships between the open codes, emergent concepts, and initial categories—resulting in selective coding of the 5 key categories for our taxonomy of death and rebirth in platformer games. Throughout the coding process and construction of the categories, we re-observed a number of the games and reviewed related literature to refine the concepts. This coding process is further illustrated in Fig. 12.2.

12.4 A Taxonomy of Death and Rebirth in Platformer Games

Based on the concepts, common features, and mechanics that emerged from our analysis, we formed the **taxonomy of death and rebirth in platformer games** (see Fig. 12.3). Our taxonomy describes 5 major aspects of the cyclical process of death and rebirth in games: (1) *obstacles*, which are the cause of (2) *death conditions*

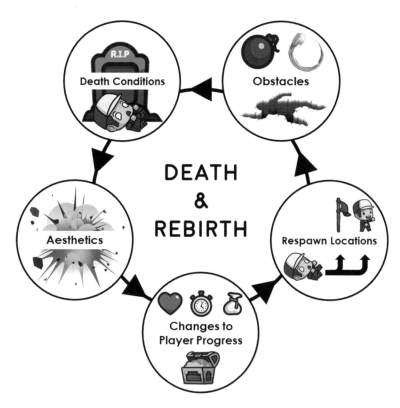

Fig. 12.3 The death and rebirth taxonomy for platformers depicted in its cyclical nature. *obstacles* are the cause of *death conditions* being met, resulting in player death. Death is depicted through *aesthetics* and causes *changes to player progress*. Players are then reborn into *respawn locations* where they must attempt to overcome obstacles again as the cycle repeats

being met and resulting in player death depicted through (3) *aesthetics* as well as causing (4) *changes to player progress* before being reborn at (5) *respawn locations* to repeat the entire process. While not every game follows this process exactly (e.g., in some games the characters cannot die but have other forms of failure instead [G23, G26–27, G43–44]), this taxonomy provides the high-level structure necessary to understand, break down, and categorize the process of death and rebirth among a variety of platformer games. We also ran the 62 games/reviews from our corpus back through some of the taxonomy categories in order to highlight certain design decisions that may be positively or negatively impacting the player experience.

12.4.1   Obstacles

Obstacles in platformers present challenges and difficulties for players to overcome (Smith et al. 2008; Sorenson et al. 2011; Wehbe et al. 2017). They are also critical elements of existing literature on analysing (Smith et al. 2008), dynamically adjusting (Hunicke 2005), and generating (Dahlskog and Togelius 2012) platformer levels. The resulting effects that obstacles have on player progress can either disrupt or encourage flow in gameplay (Isaksen et al. 2015; Lomas et al. 2013). And, ultimately, they are key factors that lead to player death (Wehbe et al. 2017). To analyse the role of obstacles in platformers, we determined what type of obstacle was the most prominent in each observed game. We identified three notably different types of obstacles that could lead to player death: (1) *intelligent*, (2) *environmental*, and (3) *interactive*.

12.4.1.1   Intelligent

Intelligent obstacles are objects in the game that actively attempt to kill the player, and their movements/actions respond in real time to player actions. Examples of these obstacles include enemy characters that follow a player and deadly moving objects, such as homing weapons and other projectiles that aim towards the player's location. Of the 62 observed platformers, 19 predominately featured intelligent obstacles with relatively positive reviews from players (11 positive, 6 mixed, and 2 negative).

12.4.1.2   Environmental

Environmental obstacles are components that are directly part of the game environment and can lead to player death. They can be either *static* obstacles that do not move or *automated* obstacles that move in rigid, fixed patterns. Of the 62 observed platformers, 34 of them predominately featured environmental obstacles with relatively negative player reviews (16 negative, 12 mixed, and 6 positive).

Static

Static environmental obstacles are immovable components of the level, such as spikes, pits, platforms, and walls. While platforms and walls do not necessarily directly result in death, their presence requires the player to make efforts to manoeuvre around them. The player can then be led to another deadly obstacle such as a pit or lose valuable resources like time as a result. Smith et al. (2008) similarly treated details such as the gaps between platforms as obstacles in their framework. Interestingly, spikes also appear to be fundamental to platformers, as they existed in some form across all of the games, regardless of their respective platformer subgenres.

Automated

Automated environmental obstacles are notably different from intelligent obstacles in that they only move in fixed patterns and do not respond or adapt to the player—

therefore remaining a relatively fixed part of the environment that the player must navigate around. Examples of automated obstacles include moving platforms or enemy characters that follow a fixed path, looping their movement and actions. In this sense, enemies act more like objects that blend in with the environment and not as actively smart characters, reminiscent of most enemies from traditional platformers.

12.4.1.3 Interactive

Interactive obstacles are objects in the game that can be activated or interacted with by the player. Examples of these include doors, levers, destructible objects, and treasure chests. While it was more common for goals in platformers to either focus on defeating enemy characters or utilizing the player's abilities to manoeuvre around a mostly static environment, platformers that were heavy on object interaction instead tended to focus on survival [G4, G40], strategy [G30], stealth [G31, G35], or simply had easily destructible objects almost everywhere in the game environment [G10, G13, G38, G53]. Only 9 of the 62 observed platformers primarily featured interactive obstacles with fairly mixed player reviews (4 positive, 3 mixed, and 2 negative).

12.4.2   Death Conditions

Platformer games heavily feature player death, to the extent that many such games have been colloquially referred to as "Nintendo hard" (Enger 2012). Player death has also been shown to evoke both positive (Bopp et al. 2016) and negative (Van Den Hoogen 2012) player experiences. As such, the primary death conditions and mechanics prevalent in these games are critical elements of the taxonomy. Specifically, we identified three distinct types of death conditions: (1) *instant death*, (2) *out of health*, and (3) *no death*. We also ran all 62 games and their review scores from the corpus back through this category of the taxonomy in order to explore if there were specific death conditions that might evoke a more positive or negative player experience (see Fig. 12.4). In Fig. 12.4, *no death* appears to be a rather neutral design choice, but using *instant death* as the primary vehicle for player death seems to create a fairly negative experience. Conversely, *out of health* appears to instill far more positive player experiences. We hypothesize that this is because *instant death* is likely to increase the frequency of player death—which has been found to subsequently decrease player enjoyment (Van Den Hoogen 2012)—over the more forgiving *out of health* death condition. However, this should be explored further in future work.

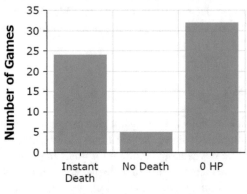

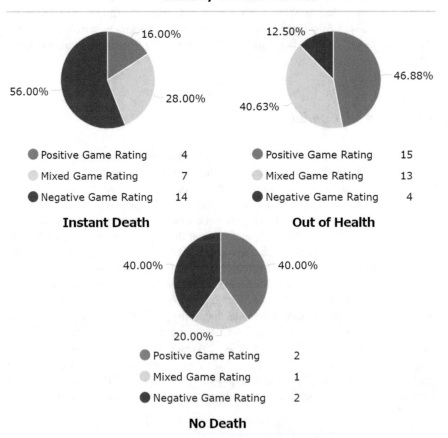

Fig. 12.4 The frequency of games in each death condition from our 62 game corpus (top), and the distribution of player ratings for each death condition (bottom)

12.4.2.1 Instant Death

Instant death describes games where the player's character dies immediately from a single injury, such as from hitting an enemy. Most of the games that applied this concept were traditional 2D side-scrolling games with puzzles and environments that relied on timing and pixel perfect platforming. One such game in our corpus was *Celeste* [G11], which had gained a reputation for being difficult to beat and applied this *instant death* concept to much critical acclaim. However, as Fig. 12.4 illustrates, this positive reception is more of an exception than the rule, where the majority of games in our corpus that employed this approach received negative player feedback overall. While this death mechanic is slowly being phased out in more recent games (e.g., only featured in 15 of the 62 observed games), there is a nostalgia factor still driving interest, mirroring classic pixel perfect platformers such as Ninja Gaiden.

12.4.2.2 Out of Health

Out of health describes games where the life of a player's character is dependent on maintaining a health bar—usually located in a top corner of the screen or represented by the character in some way. When the player runs out of in-game health, the character dies. While health is always finite in this paradigm, players are given far more chances to escape death if they make a mistake. Furthermore, games that employed the out of health approach also provided the most visual feedback of progression towards death. Therefore, this death condition may be perceived by players as one that affords more control over in-game death. Notably, this death condition also contained significantly more positively reviewed games than the other two (15 games), and was utilized in the largest number of platformers from our corpus (32 games). This suggests it might be a highly beneficial approach to incorporate into the design of platformer games.

12.4.2.3 No Death

No death describes games where death is not possible through the gameplay. It is also a fairly uncommon approach with only 7 of the 62 observed games falling in this category. However, no death also leads to fairly unique designs and mechanics in platformer games. For instance, two of the games [G23, G27] were heavily focused on narrative and sensory experiences instead of death. While two others [G26, G43] instead place focus on utilizing level design (rather than death) to enforce a high-risk potential loss of progress at all times—e.g., climbing up a mountain only to make a mistake and fall all the way down to where the game started [G26]. Interestingly, the game *Poultry Panic* [G43] features no death from the player's perspective, but instead makes the goal of the game to control multiple chickens simultaneously and turn them into food to earn points. Despite the heavy amount of death present in the game, the player's character (factory manager) never actually dies.

12.4.3 Aesthetics

Although there are a number of definitions and interpretations of game aesthetics, such as the emotional responses evoked in players (Hunicke et al. 2004), aesthetics in relation to this taxonomy refers purely to the sensory phenomena that players encounter in the game (Niedenthal 2009). Specifically, we focus on the different variations of *Visual* and *Auditory* aesthetics that occur during in-game death. However, as noted below, these aesthetic decisions can greatly impact player emotion and the overall gaming experience (Kao and Harrell 2016; Keehl and Melcer 2019; Nacke and Grimshaw 2011; Sanders and Cairns 2010), and therefore aesthetics is an important category to consider for the design of in-game death.

12.4.3.1 Visual

Visuals are a critical aspect of the aesthetic experience, where even fundamental elements—such as shape and colour—can have a substantial impact on player emotions and overall experience (Kao and Harrell 2016; Melcer and Isbister 2016; Plass et al. 2014; Um et al. 2012). With respect to visual aesthetics around in-game death, we observed that the visual changes were primarily focused on the appearance of the character and/or the use of death screens. For instance, upon death, the body of the character could undergo a dissolve, explode into pieces, fall down, or disappear. Iconography such blood, skulls, and souls was also often used to indicate character death in-game, and could remain in the environment through multiple iterations of death and rebirth to indicate where the player had previously died. A number of the platformers observed would also utilize transition effects, e.g., cutting to black or tinting corners of the screen red. Death screens were also quite commonly utilized (20 of the 62 platformers) to halt gameplay and inform players of their failed attempt, as well as potentially show changes to their in-game progress—e.g., inventory items gained or lost, running death count total, number of lives left, or achievements.

12.4.3.2 Auditory

Audio, in the form of music and sound effects, is another critical aspect of the aesthetic experience. For instance, both music and sound effects have been shown to impact player immersion and emotional response (Kallinen 2004; Keehl and Melcer 2019; Nacke and Grimshaw 2011; Sanders and Cairns 2010). In our observed games, a number of different sound effects were employed during and immediately after death such as cries or grunts, squishing or wind noises, and short electronic sounds. Music would also often be modified such as by playing a unique melody or even abruptly stopping the background music upon death. Surprisingly, a fair number of platformers did not make any auditory changes at death (21 out of 62).

Consequently, this appears to be an often overlooked category of the taxonomy that could be better utilized to improve the emotional impact of platformer games.

12.4.4   Changes to Player Progress

After a player's character dies, aspects of their progress are either retained or lost. Changes to the player's progress is an important aspect to include in our taxonomy as these types of changes have been shown to impact various aspects of the player experience (Lange-Nielsen 2011) and lead to strong emotional responses (Bopp et al. 2016). This is also a fairly prevalent category with 40 of the 62 games observed featuring some form of change to the player's progress (see Fig. 12.5). While these changes do take on a variety of forms, in an abstract sense they can be categorized as *upgrades* and *inventory changes*.

Similarly to the *death conditions* category, we ran our 62 game corpus through this category of the taxonomy in order to explore if there were specific changes to player progress that might evoke negative or positive experiences. As exemplified in Fig. 12.5, no changes to player progress appears to have a fairly even spread of game ratings while (1) changes to inventory only and (2) simultaneous upgrade and inventory changes appear to evoke increasingly positive player experiences, respectively. Surprisingly, only changing upgrades resulted in the majority of player experiences being negative and had the most negatively received games of any of the subcategories (8 games).

12.4.4.1   Upgrades

Many platformers enable retention of earned upgrades for a character after death. Examples of preserved upgrades observed in our corpus include power-ups, weapons, custom character items, skill levels, and achievements. Prior work has shown that the use of such upgrades can have significant impact on enjoyment (Ketcheson et al. 2015; Melcer et al. 2017; Melcer and Isbister 2018) and challenge (Lange-Nielsen 2011), allowing players to customize their overall experience (Denisova and Cook 2019). Notably, Smith et al. (2008) combined the use of upgrades, specifically power-ups, and inventory into one category they referred to as *Collectible Items* in their framework. We chose to separate the two as they felt distinct and might have different impacts on the player experience, as illustrated in Fig. 12.5.

12.4.4.2   Inventory Changes

Inventory systems in platformer games are another important feature to observe as they contain various explicit indicators of player progress, such as currency, lives,

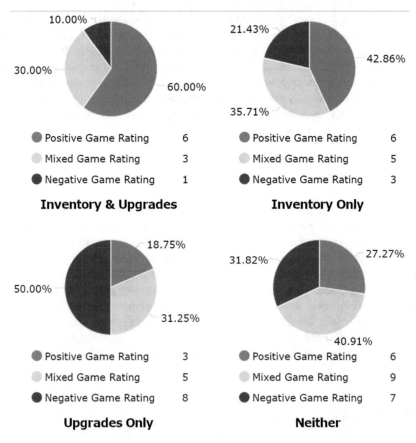

Fig. 12.5 The frequency of games for each type of change to player progress from our 62 game corpus (left), and the distribution of player ratings for each type of change to player progress (right)

and items. We observed that the changes to inventory ranged from players' keeping all of their inventory after in-game death to losing some or all of it. Conversely, a number of games from the corpus also did not have an inventory (38 games), and did not utilize this subcategory as a result.

How much inventory is maintained or lost after in-game death alters the consequence of death for the player, and ultimately impacts the overall gameplay (Keogh 2013) and game experience (Carter et al. 2013). We observed this in our corpus as well, where games in which players lose all of their inventory after death featured far more frenetic gameplay than games where players only lost some or kept all of their inventory—which tended to be slower paced and more strategic.

12.4.5   Respawn Locations

When there is death, there is also respawning in platformer games, i.e., when the player's character is brought back to life to continue gameplay. However, where the player can actually reappear varies wildly. Poor use of respawn locations (e.g., too far away or too directly into action) can lead to negative player experience (Clarke and Duimering 2006), and therefore the respawn location is another important focus of our taxonomy. For platformer games, we observed five distinct types of respawn locations: (1) *beginning of game*, (2) *beginning of level*, (3) *checkpoint*, (4) *save point*, and (5) *no respawning*.

In order to explore which respawn locations might evoke negative or positive player experiences, we ran our 62 game corpus through this category of the taxonomy (see Fig. 12.6). As illustrated in Fig. 12.6, both the use of check points and not allowing respawning at all led to fairly mixed player experiences, while respawning from the last player defined save point had quite positive player response. Surprisingly, while respawning at the beginning of a level was fairly negatively received, respawning even further back at the beginning of a game (e.g., starting over after death) had primarily positive player reviews. While there could be a number of factors contributing to this difference, we hypothesize that this may in part be due to the differences in how player progress is changed between the two subcategories (see Fig. 12.7). I.e., respawning at the beginning of the level primarily maintains upgrades only or nothing at all, while respawning at the beginning of the game primarily preserves both inventory and upgrades—giving players a stronger sense of progression.

12.4.5.1   Respawn at Beginning of Game

When players are respawned at the beginning of the game, the player's current run ends and they are usually booted to the game's initial menu screen and given options to restart the game. Players must oftentimes replay all or some sections of the game as a result. Consequently, this respawn location usually means that it requires more

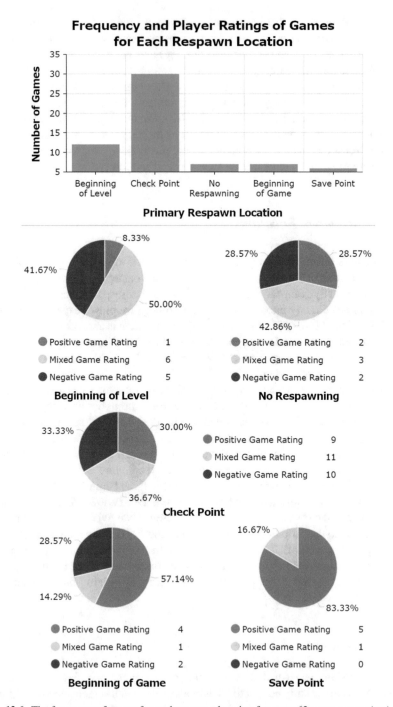

Fig. 12.6 The frequency of games for each respawn location from our 62 game corpus (top), and the distribution of player ratings for each respawn location (bottom)

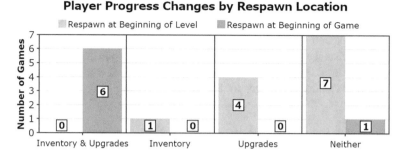

Fig. 12.7 The differences between respawning at the beginning of a level and respawning at the beginning of the game in terms of *Changes to Player Progress*. Notably, respawning at the beginning of a game primarily maintains inventory and upgrades, while respawning at the beginning of a level primarily maintains upgrades only or nothing at all

of a player's time to attempt completing the game. However, depending on whether character and inventory progress are retained after death, restarting the game may not be a back-to-square-one situation. One well known and popular subgenre of games that focus entirely around this mechanic is permadeath (Copcic et al. 2013).

12.4.5.2   Respawn at Beginning of Level

Respawning at the beginning of a level occurs in games that are explicitly split into distinct levels or stages. When players die, they are respawned at the beginning of the level that they failed to successfully complete. Usually, this respawn location also means that any character progress, such as points and inventory, achieved in that failed level are lost upon death (see Fig. 12.7). The length of levels was generally dependent on subgenre, but the pixel perfect platforming style with relatively short levels in particular was common among these games. Notably, platformers from our corpus that featured this respawning location only had 1 positively reviewed game out of 12 and was fairly negatively received by players. Many of these games, such as *Freezeer* [G24] and *Cube the Jumper* [G15], also featured *instant death—* resulting in a high frequency of player deaths per level and offering another potential explanation for the highly negative player response (Van Den Hoogen 2012).

12.4.5.3   Respawn at Checkpoint

Platformers in our corpus would most commonly respawn players at a checkpoint location not explicitly defined by the player (30 out of 62 games). Usually, this occurs when the character reaches a specific location in the game that automatically saves the progress, indicated by a brief saving animation or object that signifies the checkpoint location. Most platformers with checkpoints gradually increased their difficulty by expanding the distance between checkpoints as the game progressed; however, the distance was never so large that it forced the player to replay a lengthy portion of the level. I.e., checkpoints were used to break down levels into separate segments with smaller challenges for the player to overcome.

12.4.5.4   Respawn at Save Point

Players are given a greater level of autonomy and control in games that have save points. Save points differ from checkpoints in that they are consciously activated by the player. When players die, they are respawned at those exact locations where the save point was activated. In the observed platformers, players activated save points by having their character interact with an object in the game environment that triggers a save in that location, or by manually saving the current progress of the game with a save function—usually through a pause menu or button press during gameplay. Notably, games that employed save points in the corpus received mainly positive reviews (5 out of 6 games). We hypothesize that this may be due to the greater autonomy that this approach affords players—which has been shown to increase enjoyment (Kim et al. 2015) and motivation (Deterding 2011)—with respect to in-game death.

12.4.5.5   No Respawning

Games that had no respawning mechanics were essentially the same games that featured no death in their gameplay (see Section 4.2.3). The absence of death means that there is also no need for respawning in the game.

12.5   Discussion

We observed various components of platformer games to develop death and rebirth concepts for our taxonomy of death and rebirth in platformer games. We also ran our game corpus back through some of the taxonomy categories in order to highlight design decisions that may positively or negatively impact the player experience. Our taxonomy shows that there are a substantial number of mechanics, aesthetics, and design decisions that go into the death and respawning elements of games, despite the surprisingly limited amount of literature examining these categories directly.

12.5.1 Differentiating Roguelikes/Roguelites from Other Platformers

We observed that there were outliers of positive reception for platformers which featured high-risk gameplay. While the majority of games that employed a loss of inventory—i.e., no progress changes or maintaining only upgrades upon death—were negatively received in our corpus (see Fig. 12.5), there were two specific subsets of high-risk platformer games that still received positive reviews in this subcategory. Specifically, either pure survival games or games that applied roguelike or roguelite concepts. Although death mechanics featured in roguelikes have evolved over the years, the extremely popular mainstay features that have persisted are permadeath (Copcic et al. 2013) and procedurally generated levels (Shaker et al. 2016). Examples of these positively reviewed high-risk platformers include *Dead Cells* [G18], *Dungreed* [G22], and *Vagante* [G60].

What may seem counterintuitive makes sense when one remembers that it has been found that negative emotions triggered by in-game death can still lead to engaging positive player experiences (Bopp et al. 2016) and potential meaningful reflections of the human experience (Chittaro and Sioni 2018). The great amount of challenge is also particularly enticing to certain player types who value achievements, i.e., Advancement types (Yee 2006). Therefore, platformers with roguelike elements are high-risk, high-reward situations that certain (but not all) types of players can appreciate and actively seek out.

12.5.2 Examining Common Combinations of Design Choices

One fundamental feature of any taxonomy is its capability to categorize and describe existing designs (Melcer and Isbister 2016). In addition to running the 62 game corpus through the taxonomy to examine player experience for individual categories, we also examined common combinations of design choices for platformers (see Fig. 12.8)—further highlighting its descriptive power. Specifically, Fig. 12.8 shows the six most frequent combinations (5+ games for each) of *death conditions*, *changes to player progress*, and *respawn locations*. The most common combination (10 games) was the use of *checkpoints* with players dying once they run *out of health* and encountering changes to *upgrades* before respawning. Surprisingly, although this was the most frequent combination of design choices, the majority of games utilizing this combination were negatively reviewed (3 positive, 1 neutral, 6 negative). This illustrates how even popular platformer designs may not necessarily evoke the best player experience, and our taxonomy may be a useful tool to aid in identifying and improving these potentially problematic designs.

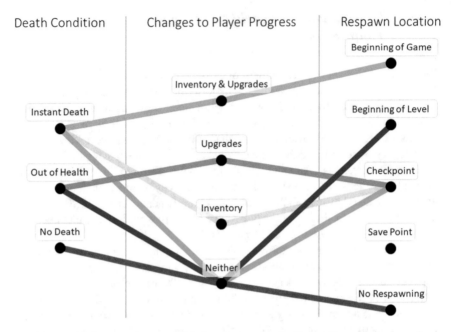

| Death Condition | Changes to Player Progress | Respawn Location |

Fig. 12.8 The top 6 combinations of design choices for *death conditions, changes to player progress,* and *respawn locations*

12.5.3 Guiding Dynamic Difficulty Adjustment and Related Techniques

Game designers must focus on the balance between inspiring confidence in players and providing sufficient challenge (Juul 2013). As mentioned earlier, techniques such as DDA attempt to effectively strike this balance for players of varying skill levels (Jennings-Teats et al. 2010; Smeddinck et al. 2016; Zohaib 2018), keeping the player in a constant state of flow (Denisova and Cairns 2015). However, current DDA techniques have been criticized for being based primarily on designer intuition rather than actual play patterns. While existing approaches addressing this issue have utilized machine learning (Jennings-Teats et al. 2010), our taxonomy presents a different opportunity since in-game death—and the categories of our taxonomy as a result—is inherently linked to challenge. Specifically, our taxonomy presents a structured tool grounded in the design of commercial platformers to categorize the different design possibilities around death and rebirth in games. As a result, it highlights novel and broadly applicable elements of a game's design that can be dynamically adjusted to improve the player experience. For instance, adjusting how far backwards a player respawns, how much of their progress is maintained, and the overall conditions for death are all approaches that have not been explored deeply in current DDA literature, but are highlighted in our taxonomy. Furthermore, future research could be done to examine how specific death and rebirth mechanics relate to various aspects of player experience to further inform DDA technique design. E.g., death and rebirth mechanics that enable a higher level of control could satisfy a player's need for autonomy (Ryan et al. 2006), or mechanics that better enable continuous successful progression in a game could satisfy a player's need for competence (Ijsselsteijn et al. 2008; Johnson et al. 2018; Ryan et al. 2006).

12.6   Limitations

It is important to acknowledge that the platformer game genre has now evolved to include multiple subgenres with distinct characteristics. This evolution of platformers may affect the way certain observed games with more "classic" designs were received by players and their resulting critical reception. Additionally, there are various player styles and preferences that are not accounted for in anonymous Steam user reviews. Positive and negative reviews may also not be related to aspects of death and rebirth, and could partially be from other aspects of the games (e.g., overall aesthetics, critical bugs, and so forth). As such, using overall Steam scores for a game to judge the efficacy of specific taxonomy categories is fairly limited. However, it does serve to illustrate how the taxonomic breakdown could be utilized to examine the impact of specific design decisions around the handling of death and rebirth on player experience. Finally, it is also important to note that the game experience is composed of many layers beyond what the five dimensions of our taxonomy covers, and has been represented by a number of factors in various game experience questionnaires. While the taxonomy is a helpful tool to guide some aspects of design for researchers and designers, further research is needed to clarify and nuance the relationship between death and rebirth design decisions and the many layers of player experience.

12.7   Conclusion

We utilized grounded theory to develop a taxonomy of death and rebirth concepts in platformer games. The goal of our taxonomy was to provide a means for game designers and researchers to better analyse and design how platformers handle in-game death. We identified 5 key categories as the basis of our **taxonomy of death and rebirth in platformer games**: (1) *obstacles*, (2) *death conditions*, (3) *aesthetics*, (4) *changes to player progress*, and (5) *respawn locations*. We also ran our 62 game corpus back through some of the taxonomy categories in order to highlight certain design decisions that may be positively or negatively impacting player experience. Further studies should be conducted to more deeply understand how categories and concepts in our taxonomy impact crucial player experience aspects such as game flow, engagement, challenge, autonomy, and self-efficacy.

Ludography

G1. Adventures of Hendri. (Mar 7, 2018). *Developed by LionAnt.*
G2. Another Sight: Hodge's Journey. (Nov 14, 2018). *Developed by Lunar Great Wall Studios.*
G3. Ascendance. (Mar 27, 2018). *Developed by ONEVISION GAMES.*
G4. Away from Earth: Mars. (Aug 23, 2018). *Developed by Only Voxel Games.*
G5. Block Shock. (Feb 6, 2018). *Developed by VoxStudios.*
G6. Bloodstained: Curse of the Moon. (May 24, 2018). *Developed by INTI CREATES CO., LTD.*
G7. Bloody Trapland 2: Curiosity. (Feb 1, 2019). *Developed by 2Play Studios and Prasius.*
G8. Bombix. (Mar 2, 2018). *Developed by Pragmatix Ltd.*
G9. Bouncers. (Jun 1, 2018). *Developed by Firehawk Studios.*
G10. Castlevania Anniversary Collection. (May 16, 2019). *Developed by Konami Digital Entertainment.*
G11. Celeste. (Jan 25, 2018). *Developed by Matt Makes Games Inc.*
G12. Chamber of Darkness. (Oct 10, 2018). *Developed by The Crow Studios.*
G13. Chasm. (Jul 31, 2018). *Developed by Bit Kid, Inc.*
G14. Crash Bandicoot N. Sane Trilogy. (Jun 29, 2018). *Developed by Vicarious Visions and Iron Galaxy.*
G15. Cube - The Jumper. (May 15, 2018). *Developed by DZEJK.*
G16. Cube XL. (Mar 12, 2018). *Developed by Timberwolf Studios.*
G17. Cybarian: The Time Travelling Warrior. (Nov 9, 2018). *Developed by Ritual Games.*
G18. Dead Cells. (Aug 6, 2018). *Developed by Motion Twin.*
G19. Death's Gambit. (Aug 13, 2018). *Developed by White Rabbit.*
G20. DeepWeb. (Sep 20, 2018). *Developed by ImageCode.*
G21. Dream Alone. (Jun 28, 2018). *Developed by WarSaw Games.*
G22. Dungreed. (Feb 14, 2018). *Developed by TEAM HORAY.*
G23. Everything Will Flow. (Jul 28, 2018). *Developed by Hont.*
G24. Freezeer. (Jun 21, 2018). *Developed by NedoStudio.*
G25. Frog Demon. (Dec 11, 2018). *Developed by White Dog Games.*
G26. Golfing Over It with Alva Majo. (Mar 28, 201). *Developed by Majorariatto.*
G27. Gris. (Dec 13, 2018). *Developed by Nomada Studio.*
G28. Guacamelee! 2. (Aug 21, 2018). *Developed by DrinkBox Studios.*
G29. I was rebuilt. (Jun 28, 2018). *Developed by Gurila Ware Games.*
G30. Iconoclasts. (Jan 23, 2018). *Developed by Joakim Sandberg.*
G31. Katana ZERO. (Apr 18, 2019). *Developed by Askiisoft.*
G32. Lightform. (Feb 19, 2018). *Developed by Shadow Motion.*
G33. Little Marisa's Disaster Journey. (Apr 28, 2018). *Developed by Dark Sky Empire.*
G34. MagiCats Builder (Crazy Dreamz). (Jul 10, 2018). *Developed by Dreamz Studio.*

G35.   Mark of the Ninja: Remastered. (Oct 9, 2018). *Developed by Klei Entertainment.*

G36.   Mega Man 11. (Oct 2, 2018). *Developed by CAPCOM CO., LTD.*

G37.   Mind Twins - The Twisted Co-op Platformer. (Jan 19, 2018). *Developed by DRUNKEN APES.*

G38.   Mines of Mars. (Sep 10, 2018). *Developed by Wickey Ware.*

G39.   Neon Beats. (May 3, 2019). *Developed by OKYO GAMES.*

G40.   Niffelheim. (Sep 26, 2018). *Developed by Ellada Games.*

G41.   Night Fly. (Jan 24, 2018). *Developed by ARGames.*

G42.   Order No. 227: Not one step back!. (Jul 3, 2018). *Developed by High Wide.*

G43.   Pogostuck: Rage with Your Friends. (Feb 28, 2019). *Developed by Hendrik Felix Pohl.*

G44.   Poultry Panic. (Jan 17, 2018). *Developed by Virtual Top.*

G45.   Razed. (Sep 14, 2018). *Developed by Warpfish Games.*

G46.   ReCore: Definitive Edition. (Sep 14, 2018). *Developed by Armature Studio and Concept.*

G47.   Return. (Aug 3, 2018). *Developed by Breadmeat.*

G48.   Richy's Nightmares. (Jul 10, 2018). *Developed by Unreal Gaming.*

G49.   Rift Keeper. (Jan 14, 2019). *Developed by Frymore.*

G50.   Riverhill Trials. (Apr 12, 2018). *Developed by Watercolor Games.*

G51.   Running Man 3D. (Aug 21, 2018). *Developed by GGaming.*

G52.   Slap City. (Mar 5, 2018). *Developed by Ludosity.*

G53.   Steel Rats. (Nov 7, 2018). *Developed by Tate Multimedia.*

G54.   Sure Footing. (Mar 30, 2018). *Developed by Table Flip Games.*

G55.   The Cursed Tower. (Feb 6, 2018). *Developed by Mohsin Rizvi.*

G56.   The Messenger. (Aug 30, 2018). *Developed by Sabotage.*

G57.   Touhou Luna Nights. (Feb 25, 2019). *Developed by Vaka Game Magazine and Team Ladybug.*

G58.   Trials of the Gauntlet. (Mar 16, 2018). *Developed by Broken Dinosaur Studios.*

G59.   Trials Rising. (Feb 26, 2019). *Developed by RedLynx.*

G60.   Vagante. (Feb 21, 2018). *Developed by Nuke Nine.*

G61.   Viral Cry. (Mar 7, 2018). *Developed by Strategy Empire.*

G62.   Wandersong. (Sep 27, 2018). *Developed by Greg Lobanov.*

References

Alharthi, S.A., Alsaedi, O., Toups, Z.O., Tanenbaum, J., Hammer, J. (2018). Playing to wait: A taxonomy of idle games. In Proceedings of the 2018 CHI Conference on Human Factors in Computing Systems (p. 621). ACM.

Antle, A.N. & Wise, A.F. (2013). Getting down to details: Using theories of cognition and learning to inform tangible user interface design. Interacting with Computers, 25(1), pp.1–20.

Aarseth, E., Smedstad, S.M., SunnanÃě, L. (2003). A multidimensional typology of games. In Proceedings of the Digital Games Research Association (DiGRA) Conference.

Bopp, J. A., Mekler, E., Opwis, K. (2016). Negative Emotion, Positive Experience? Emotionally Moving Moments in Digital Games. In Proceedings of the 2016 CHI Conference on Human Factors in Computing Systems (pp. 2996–3006). ACM.

Brandse, M. (2017). The Shape of Challenge. In International Conference of Design, User Experience, and Usability (pp. 362–376). Springer, Cham, Switzerland.

Carter, M., Gibbs, M., Wadley, G. (2013). Death and dying in DayZ. In Proceedings of The 9th Australasian Conference on Interactive Entertainment: Matters of Life and Death (p. 22). ACM.

Charmaz, K. (2000). Grounded Theory Methodology: Objectivist and Constructivist Qualitative Methods in N. K. Denzin and Y. Lincoln (eds.), Handbook of Qualitative Research (pp. 509–535).

Charmaz, K. (2006). Constructing grounded theory: A practical guide through qualitative analysis. Sage.

Chittaro, L. and Sioni, R. (2018). Existential video games: Proposal and evaluation of an interactive reflection about death. Entertainment Computing, 26, (pp. 59–77).

Clarke, D. & Duimering, P.R. (2006). How computer gamers experience the game situation: a behavioral study. Computers in Entertainment (CIE), 4(3), p.6.

Constant, T. and Levieux, G. (2019). Dynamic Difficulty Adjustment Impact on Players' Confidence. In Proceedings of the 2019 CHI Conference on Human Factors in Computing Systems. ACM.

Copcic, A., McKenzie, S., Hobbs, M. (2013). Permadeath: A review of literature. In 2013 IEEE International Games Innovation Conference (IGIC) (pp. 40–47). IEEE.

Dahlskog, S. & Togelius, J. (2012). Patterns and procedural content generation: revisiting Mario in world 1 level 1. In Proceedings of the First Workshop on Design Patterns in Games (p. 1). ACM.

De Lope, R.P. & Medina-Medina, N. (2017). A comprehensive taxonomy for serious games. Journal of Educational Computing Research, 55(5), pp.629–672.

Deterding, S. (2011). Situated motivational affordances of game elements: A conceptual model. In Gamification: Using game design elements in non-gaming contexts, a workshop at CHI.

Denisova, A. & Cairns, P. (2015). Adaptation in digital games: the effect of challenge adjustment on player performance and experience. In Proceedings of the 2015 Annual Symposium on Computer-Human Interaction in Play (pp. 97–101). ACM.

Denisova, A. & Cook, E. (2019). Power-Ups in Digital Games: The Rewarding Effect of Phantom Game Elements on Player Experience. In Proceedings of the 2019 Annual Symposium on Computer-Human Interaction in Play. ACM.

Dormann, C. (2016). Toward Ludic Gerontechnology: a Review of Games for Dementia Care. Proceedings of the 1st International Joint Conference of DiGRA and FDG.

Elverdam, C. & Aarseth, E. (2007). Game classification and game design: Construction through critical analysis. Games and Culture, 2(1), pp.3–22.

Enger, M. (2012). What is "Nintendo hard"?. http://bnbgaming.com/2011/02/08/what-is-nintendo-hard/. Accessed 8 Aug 2019.

Ens, B., Hincapié-Ramos, J.D., Irani, P. (2014). Ethereal planes: a design framework for 2D information space in 3D mixed reality environments. In Proceedings of the 2nd ACM symposium on Spatial user interaction (pp. 2–12). ACM.

Frasca, G. (2007). Ephemeral games: Is it barbaric to design videogames after Auschwitz?. Cybertext yearbook, 2, pp.172–180.

Gilleade, K. and Dix, A. (2004). Using frustration in the design of adaptive videogames. In Proceedings of the 2004 ACM SIGCHI International Conference on Advances in computer entertainment technology (pp. 228–232). ACM.

Glaser, B.G. (1992). Basics of grounded theory analysis: Emergence vs forcing. Sociology press.

Glaser, B.G. & Strauss, A.L. (2017). Discovery of grounded theory: Strategies for qualitative research. Routledge.

Harrer, S. (2013). From Losing to Loss: Exploring the Expressive Capacities of Videogames Beyond Death as Failure. Culture Unbound. Journal of Current Cultural Research (pp. 607–620).

Hook, N. (2015). Grounded theory. In Game Research Methods (pp. 309–320). ETC Press.

Hunicke, R., LeBlanc, M., Zubek, R. (2004). MDA: A formal approach to game design and game research. In Proceedings of the AAAI Workshop on Challenges in Game AI (Vol. 4, No. 1, p. 1722).

Hunicke, R. (2005). The case for dynamic difficulty adjustment in games. In Proceedings of the 2005 ACM SIGCHI International Conference on Advances in computer entertainment technology (pp. 429–433). ACM.

Ijsselsteijn, W., van den Hoogen, W., Klimmt, C., de Kort, Y., Lindley, C., Mathiak, K., Poels, K., Ravaja, N., Turpeinen, M, Vorderer, P. (2008). Measuring the Experience of Digital Game Enjoyment. In Proceedings of Measuring Behavior.

Isaksen, A., Gopstein, D., Nealen, A. (2015). Exploring Game Space Using Survival Analysis. In Proceedings of the 10th International Conference on the Foundations of Digital Games.

Jennings-Teats, M., Smith, G., Wardrip-Fruin, N. (2010). Polymorph: Dynamic Difficulty Adjustment Through Level Generation. In Proceedings of the 2010 Workshop on Procedural Content Generation in Games.

Johnson, D., Gardner, M.J., Perry, R. (2018). Validation of two game experience scales: The Player Experience of Need Satisfaction (PENS) and Game Experience Questionnaire (GEQ). International Journal of Human-Computer Studies (pp. 38–46). 118.

Juul, J. (2009). Fear of failing? the many meanings of difficulty in video games. The video game theory reader, 2(237–252).

Juul, J. (2013). The art of failure: An essay on the pain of playing video games. MIT press.

Kallinen, K. (2004). The effects of background music on using a pocket computer in a cafeteria: Immersion, emotional responses, and social richness of medium. In CHI'04 Extended Abstracts on Human Factors in Computing Systems (pp. 1227–1230). ACM.

Kao, D. & Harrell, D.F. (2016). Exploring the impact of avatar color on game experience in educational games. In Proceedings of the 2016 CHI Conference Extended Abstracts on Human Factors in Computing Systems (pp. 1896–1905). ACM.

Keehl, O. & Melcer, E. (2019). Radical tunes: exploring the impact of music on memorization of stroke order in logographic writing systems. In Proceedings of the 14th International Conference on the Foundations of Digital Games. ACM.

Keogh, B. (2013). When game over means game over: using permanent death to craft living stories in minecraft. In Proceedings of The 9th Australasian Conference on Interactive Entertainment: Matters of Life and Death (p. 20). ACM.

Ketcheson, M., Ye, Z., Graham, T.C. (2015). Designing for exertion: how heart-rate power-ups increase physical activity in exergames. In Proceedings of the 2015 Annual Symposium on Computer-Human Interaction in Play (pp. 79–89). ACM.

Kim, K., Schmierbach, M.G., Chung, M.Y., Fraustino, J.D., Dardis, F., Ahern, L. (2015). Is it a sense of autonomy, control, or attachment? Exploring the effects of in-game customization on game enjoyment. Computers in Human Behavior, 48, pp.695–705.

Klastrup, L. (2006). Why death matters: understanding gameworld experiences. In Proceedings of the 2006 ACM SIGCHI international conference on Advances in computer entertainment technology (p. 29). ACM.

Klabbers, J.H. (2003). The gaming landscape: a taxonomy for classifying games and simulations. In Proceedings of the Digital Games Research Association (DiGRA) Conference.

Klimmt, C., Blake, C., Hefner, D., Vorderer, P., Roth, C. (2009). Player performance, satisfaction, and video game enjoyment. In International Conference on Entertainment Computing (pp. 1–12). Springer, Berlin, Heidelberg.

Kreminski, M., Samuel, B., Melcer, E., Wardrip-Fruin, N. (2019). Evaluating AI-Based Games Through Retellings. In Proceedings of the Fifteenth AAAI Conference on Artificial Intelligence and Interactive Digital Entertainment (AIIDE-19). AAAI.

Lange-Nielsen, F. (2011). The Power-up Experience: A study of Power-ups in Games and their Effect on Player Experience. In Proceedings of the Digital Games Research Association (DiGRA) Conference.

Lara-Cabrera, R. & Camacho, D., (2019). A taxonomy and state of the art revision on affective games. Future Generation Computer Systems, 92, pp.516–525.

Lessel, A. (2013). Nintendo Hard, or Hardly Working?. https://venturebeat.com/community/2013/09/27/nintendo-hard-or-hardly-working/. Accessed 10 Sep 2019.

Lewis, C., Whitehead, J., Wardrip-Fruin, N. (2010). What went wrong: a taxonomy of video game bugs. In Proceedings of the fifth international conference on the foundations of digital games (pp. 108–115). ACM.

Lomas, D., Patel, K., Forlizzi, J., Koedinger, K. (2013). Optimizing Challenge in an Educational Game Using Large-Scale Design Experiments. In Proceedings of the 2013 SIGCHI Conference on Human Factors in Computing Systems (pp. 89–98).

Mäkelä, V., Sharma, S., Hakulinen, J., Heimonen, T., Turunen, M. (2017). Challenges in public display deployments: A taxonomy of external factors. In Proceedings of the 2017 CHI Conference on Human Factors in Computing Systems (pp. 3426–3475). ACM.

McCallum, S. & Boletsis, C. (2013). A taxonomy of serious games for dementia. In Games for Health (pp. 219–232). Springer Vieweg, Wiesbaden.

Melcer, E.F. & Isbister, K. (2016). Bridging the physical divide: a design framework for embodied learning games and simulations. In Proceedings of the 2016 CHI Conference Extended Abstracts on Human Factors in Computing Systems (pp. 2225–2233). ACM.

Melcer, E. & Isbister, K. (2016). Motion, Emotion, and Form: Exploring Affective Dimensions of Shape. In Proceedings of the 2016 CHI Conference Extended Abstracts on Human Factors in Computing Systems (pp. 1430–1437). ACM.

Melcer, E.F., Hollis, V., Isbister, K. (2017). Tangibles vs. Mouse in Educational Programming Games: Influences on Enjoyment and Self-Beliefs. In Proceedings of the 2017 CHI Conference Extended Abstracts on Human Factors in Computing Systems (pp. 1901–1908). ACM.

Melcer, E.F. & Isbister, K. (2018). Bots & (Main) Frames: exploring the impact of tangible blocks and collaborative play in an educational programming game. In Proceedings of the 2018 CHI Conference on Human Factors in Computing Systems (p. 266). ACM.

Melnic, D. & Melnic, V. (2018). Saved games and respawn timers: The dilemma of representing death in video games. In University of Bucharest Review: Literary and Cultural Studies Series (pp. 29–37). VII.

Mueller, F.F., Gibbs, M.R., Vetere, F. (2008). Taxonomy of exertion games. In Proceedings of the 20th Australasian Conference on Computer-Human Interaction: Designing for Habitus and Habitat (pp. 263–266). ACM.

Mukherjee, S. (2009). 'Remembering How You Died': Memory, Death and Temporality in Videogames. In Proceedings of the Digital Games Research Association (DiGRA) Conference.

Nacke, L.E. & Grimshaw, M. (2011). Player-game interaction through affective sound. In Game sound technology and player interaction: Concepts and developments (pp. 264–285). IGI global.

Niedenthal, S. (2009). What we talk about when we talk about game aesthetics. In Proceedings of the Digital Games Research Association (DiGRA) Conference.

Plass, J.L., Heidig, S., Hayward, E.O., Homer, B.D., Um, E. (2014). Emotional design in multimedia learning: Effects of shape and color on affect and learning. Learning and Instruction, 29, pp.128–140.

Rego, P., Moreira, P.M., Reis, L.P. (2010). Serious games for rehabilitation: A survey and a classification towards a taxonomy. In 5th Iberian conference on information systems and technologies (pp. 1–6). IEEE.

Robinett, W. (1992). Synthetic experience: A proposed taxonomy. Presence: Teleoperators & Virtual Environments, 1(2), pp.229–247.

Rusch, D. (2009). Mechanisms of the Soul-Tackling the Human Condition in Videogames. In Proceedings of the Digital Games Research Association (DiGRA) Conference.

Ryan, R., Rigby, C.S., Przybylski, A. (2006). The Motivational Pull of Video Games: A Self-Determination Theory Approach. Motivation and Emotion, pp. 344–360, 30(4).

Salisbury, J.H. and Cole, T., 2016. Grounded Theory in Games Research: Making the Case and Exploring the Options. In Proceedings of the 1st International Joint Conference of DiGRA and FDG.

Sanders, T. & Cairns, P. (2010). Time perception, immersion and music in videogames. In Proceedings of the 24th BCS interaction specialist group conference (pp. 160–167). British Computer Society.

Sarkar, A. and Cooper, S. (2019). Transforming Game Difficulty Curves using Function Composition. In Proceedings of the 2019 CHI Conference on Human Factors in Computing Systems. ACM.

Schneider, E., Lang, A., Shin, M., Bradley, S., 2004. Death with a Story: How Story Impacts Emotional, Motivational, and Physiological Responses to First-Person Shooter Video Games. In Human Communication Research (pp. 361–375), 30(3).

Sedig, K., Parsons, P., Haworth, R. (2017). Player–game interaction and cognitive gameplay: A taxonomic framework for the core mechanic of videogames. In Informatics (Vol. 4, No. 1, p. 4). Multidisciplinary Digital Publishing Institute.

Smeddinck, J.D., Mandryk, R.L., Birk, M.V., Gerling, K.M., Barsilowski, D., Malaka, R. (2016). How to present game difficulty choices?: Exploring the impact on player experience. In Proceedings of the 2016 CHI Conference on Human Factors in Computing Systems (pp. 5595–5607). ACM.

Smith, G., Cha, M. and Whitehead, J. (2008). A framework for analysis of 2D platformer levels. In Proceedings of the 2008 ACM SIGGRAPH symposium on Video games (pp. 75–80). ACM.

Smith, A.M., Lewis, C., Hullett, K., Smith, G., Sullivan, A. (2011). An inclusive taxonomy of player modeling. University of California, Santa Cruz, Tech. Rep. UCSC-SOE-11-13.

Sorenson, N., Pasquier, P., DiPaola, S. (2011). A generic approach to challenge modeling for the procedural creation of video game levels. IEEE Transactions on Computational Intelligence and AI in Games, 3(3), pp.229–244.

Shaker, N., Togelius, J., Nelson, M.J. (2016). Procedural content generation in games. Switzerland: Springer International Publishing.

Um, E., Plass, J.L., Hayward, E.O., Homer, B.D. (2012). Emotional design in multimedia learning. Journal of educational psychology, 104(2), p.485.

Van Den Hoogen, W., Poels, K., Ijsselstein, W., De Kort, Y. (2012). Between Challenge and Defeat: Repeated Player-Death and Game Enjoyment. Media Psychology, 15(4).

Vossen, D.P. (2004) The nature and classification of games. Avante, 10(1).

Wehbe, R.R., Mekler, E.D., Schaekermann, M., Lank, E., Nacke, L.E. (2017). Testing Incremental Difficulty Design in Platformer Games. In Proceedings of the 2017 CHI Conference on Human Factors in Computing Systems (pp. 5109–5113). ACM.

Xue, S., Wu, M., Kolen, J., Aghdaie, N., Zaman, K. (2017). Dynamic Difficulty Adjustment for Maximized Engagement in Digital Games. In Proceedings of the 26th International Conference on World Wide Web Companion (pp. 465–471). ACM.

Yee, N. (2006). Motivations for play in online games. CyberPsychology & behavior, 9(6), pp.772–775.

Zohaib, M. (2018). Dynamic Difficulty Adjustment (DDA) in Computer Games: A Review. Advances in Human-Computer Interaction.

Chapter 13
Player-Centred Design in Role-Playing Game Branching Dialogue Systems

Leanne Taylor-Giles

Contents

L. Taylor-Giles (✉)
Queensland University of Technology, Brisbane, QLD, Australia
e-mail: writer@leannectaylor.com

© Springer Nature Switzerland AG 2020   295
B. Bostan (ed.), *Game User Experience And Player-Centered Design*,
International Series on Computer Entertainment and Media Technology,
https://doi.org/10.1007/978-3-030-37643-7_13

Abstract A key focus of player-centred design from the game narrative designer's perspective is the creation of what Janet Murray has termed "dramatic agency" or the experience of Agency within a digital environment which—by virtue of its material qualities and pragmatic development constraints—remains a finite construct made in software. The tensions that arise between narrative design and player experience are particularly evident in the larger open-world type role-playing games (RPGs) where much effort is made to create richly simulated digital worlds, populated with carefully crafted characters, but where the demands of telling a story that can be accessed by player-defined characters, in sometimes no specific order, are challenging to reconcile.

Conversation architecture, as a sub-category of role-playing game design, underlies every dialogue choice that a player can make during the course of a branching narrative. Yet while the player-facing aspects of choice-based dialogues are easy to understand, decisions made during the conception of the framework behind those aspects may influence the player's Agency in unintended ways. Based on *Toward a Deeper Understanding of Branching Dialogue Systems* (Taylor-Giles, Toward a deeper understanding of branching dialogue systems, 2014), this chapter explores the manner in which architectural components of dialogue systems invisibly affect the player's possible experiences, and how player-centred design, rather than systems-centred or developer-centred design, can more fully support the player's realization of their own emergent narrative.

Keywords Agency · Branching dialogue · Conversation architecture · Creative writing · Critical path · Dramatic Agency · Emergent narrative · Emotional interface · Immersion · Interaction design · Interactive narrative · Meaningful choice · Narrative design · Player character · Role-playing video games · Writing for video games

13.1 Introduction

The position of Narrative Designer in the game development industry is a relatively recent phenomenon that has yet to be conclusively defined—some Narrative Designers write dialogue or prose, while others are more focussed on the design of the systems that support the game's narrative as a whole. All types of Narrative Designers, however, share the desire of their players for both vivid simulation of worlds in which to play and engagement in a satisfying, player-centred narrative experience. Janet Murray discusses the potential for both in her work on the future of narrative in the digital medium, suggesting that emergent storytelling systems "have reached such a degree of intricacy that they are their own description; there is no other way to predict everything they are likely to do than to run them in every possible configuration" (Murray 1997, p. 240). A complete absence of authorial control, on the other hand, provides no framework for the player to comprehend their narrative experience as a whole, and ultimately results in unsatisfying storytelling (Taylor-Giles 2014).

It was with these constraints in mind that in 2014 I outlined the Four Essential Properties of Branching Dialogues, based on the analysis of commercially success-ful role-playing games available at the time (Taylor-Giles). The titles analysed are as follows:

- *Mass Effect* (BioWare 2007);
- *Dragon Age: Origins* (BioWare 2009);
- *Deus Ex: Human Revolution* (Eidos Montreal 2011);
- *The Elder Scrolls V: Skyrim* (Bethesda Game Studios 2011).

The Four Essential Properties of Branching Dialogues were inspired by Murray's Four Essential Properties of Digital Environments (Murray 1997, p. 71) and are as follows:

- *Agency*: the ability of the player to feel they are having an impact upon the game world, applied according to Murray's definition (p. 110, 1997).
- *Ambiguity*: using ambiguous language to limit the amount of content that needs to be written while maintaining the illusion of choice.
- *Context*: information the player needs to know in order to understand how they should behave in any given scenario.
- *Lack of Judgement*: allowing the player to make the choices that you have presented without punishing them for selecting something that goes against your personal moral code. This could be considered to be a more specific, sub-definition of Authorship (Murray 1997).

Constructing a branching dialogue with these elements in mind tended to create a higher sense of satisfaction in the player; crafting a branching dialogue without any of these elements resulted in confusing and unsatisfying player experiences (Taylor-Giles 2014). The Four Essential Properties of Branching Dialogues can be considered to be player-centred, in that they foreground the player as the most important agent within any given dialogue. Since these Essential Properties were derived from analysis of the four titles mentioned previously, however, there is further insight to be gained in examining where and why these games deviate from these established best practices. Doing so will highlight common pitfalls that lead to non-player-centred design, which in turn reduces player satisfaction, and provide simple solutions to many of the problems encountered in game development when it comes to the architecture of branching conversations.

13.2 The Design of Branching Dialogue Systems

The ability to provide the player with multiple dialogue choices requires a robust backend. The game needs to call the correct non-player character (NPC) responses so that the dialogue flows as intended, set or access any variables related to available options, now or in the future, and queue up any scripted events that need to occur once the conversation ends.

The design of the branching dialogue system also delimits the player's possible interactions. Whether they can be cruel or kind, helpful or hurtful, and to what extent, is part of the overall structure of a branching conversation (Taylor-Giles 2014). Knowing the limits of the game world and the ways in which it is necessary to constrain the player is an essential part of designing conversation architecture and deciding upon best practices.

Below are three common approaches to branching dialogue system design.

13.2.1 Systems-Centred Design

Systems-centred design chooses gameplay or other mechanical aspects over developer or player comfort (Klein et al. 1997).

For example, in *The Elder Scrolls V: Skyrim* (Bethesda Game Studios 2011), players can exit any non-critical dialogue at any time. NPCs do not react, picking up their routines where they left off, and the player can restart the same conversation with them as many times as they like. Unfortunately, the player will also automatically be forced out of a conversation if they take too long to make a choice within the dialogue, leading to interrupted and fragmented interactions that bear little resemblance to what we, as human beings, would term a "conversation".

As ostensibly player-centred design, the ability to exit any conversation at any time allows the player get back to the "real" game (i.e., killing monsters and exploring) more quickly, but it also assumes that most players have little to no interest in non-violent interactions with the game's NPCs. This design decision inherently disadvantages players for whom consistent and compelling social interactions are the main goal of interactivity.

13.2.2 Developer-Centred Design

Developer-centred design, or designer-centred design, chooses the developer's comfort over the player's (Goldfarb and Kondratova 2004). These design principles can be applied to the underlying systems, or they can be applied to the structure of the conversation itself.

An example, again from *Skyrim*, is a conversation where the player's only dialogue option is "...". Since in this world every character other than the player speaks their lines aloud, an NPC would have no way of knowing when the player had replied with the "right" kind of silence for them to continue speaking. "Spoken" dialogue with no content foregrounds the constructed nature of the world, breaking player immersion and turning the interaction into a mechanism for ensuring the player's attention, rather than an actual conversation involving meaningful choices and player Agency.

Essentially, if the conversation is more fun for the developer to create, or the dialogue more fun for the developer to write, than it will be for the player to experience the end product, it is likely a case of developer-centred design.

13.2.3 Player-Centred Design

Player-centred design, then, or user-centred design, has the player's comfort and enjoyment as its primary concern (Norman and Draper 1986). Effective design, like effective conversation architecture or effective writing, is invisible: it empowers the player without seeming to have any impact at all.

It is this invisibility that makes it necessary to re-evaluate the games mentioned in *Toward a Deeper Understanding of Branching Dialogue Systems*, not only by the Four Essential Properties of Branching Dialogues that their contents informed, but also by these three different design approaches (Taylor-Giles 2014). By making the tacit decisions behind these design approaches explicit it will become possible to examine their intended and unintended consequences, with the end goal of providing a simple set of steps for the decision-making process that are likely to maximize player enjoyment while minimizing overall developer and system stress.

13.3 Necessary Distinctions Within Role-Playing Games

13.3.1 Types of Worlds

There are, broadly speaking, two types of RPGs in the current market. One type of RPG aims for simulation, i.e., a fully modelled world that the player can interact with. The other aims for replayability, i.e., an experience that changes depending on the player's choices, within a pre-determined storyline (Adams 2001).

Simulation, sometimes called randomization, is difficult. It requires interlocking systems, robust design, and can generate unexpected outcomes (Harris 2010). The player's interactions with the world are different each playthrough, because two systems will rarely come together in the same way each time without some sort of scripting to make them do so. *The Elder Scrolls V: Skyrim* (Bethesda Game Studios 2011) is a popular example of a simulated (sandbox) world.

Replayable Storylines are more confined. There may be underlying systems, but it is more likely that the game is a series of scripted events, a "situation" in which the player enters into a role, similar to the original conception of the Holodeck (Murray 1997). The interest for the player is in discovering how those big set pieces move and interact, not in puzzling out the dynamics of the (largely unsimulated) world around them. The *Mass Effect* (BioWare 2007) and *Dragon Age* (BioWare 2009) series are popular examples of replayable storylines.

13.3.2 Types of Player Characters (PCs)

There are also, broadly speaking, two types of player characters within the current RPG market. Determining which type of character the player will use to interface with the world is the first step in delimiting the available options they will have within that world.

An *Avatar* is an empty shell, waiting to be defined by the player's actions (Taylor-Giles 2014). This type of character works well in simulations because they are rarely voiced, meaning they never impose their opinions on or add unexpected nuance to the player's experience of the game. The player who controls an Avatar is usually afforded more choice regarding their in-game actions, because branching without voiceover is far cheaper and much more reactive than recording every line in advance. There are also usually fewer assumptions made about the player character, since no aspects of their personality need to be defined before the player starts the game, and in many cases the player may be allowed to choose defining elements of that character, such as gender or ethnicity. This flexibility requires the game to be written in a more generalized way, which in turn opens up the possibility of situations in which a pre-defined character would never find themselves.

The opposite of an Avatar is an *Actor*, which is a pre-existing character that the player inhabits. They have their own voice, their own morals, and their own motivations, which the player can focus but not change (Taylor-Giles 2014). This type of character works well in replayable storylines because the situations they will need to respond to are mapped in advance, and the character's voice can be recorded to match. The trade-off is that providing the character with an Actor to play as also means that the story of the game requires more authorial control, since it is impossible to pre-record dialogue for scenes which the developer has not already imagined taking place.

13.3.3 Types of Players

It is not enough to simply define the type of game world and the way in which the player will interact with that world. It is also necessary to consider the types of players who will inhabit those characters, and what kinds of activities will appeal to each of these sub-categories, which will inform the content best-suited to the game.

The co-creator of one of the earliest multiplayer RPGs (Trubshaw and Bartle 1978; Bartle 1990), Dr. Richard Bartle, spent considerable time working to understand the different types of players that interacted with the systems he designed. He categorized his results according to playing card suits:

> Achievers are Diamonds (they're always seeking treasure); explorers are Spades (they dig around for information); socialisers are Hearts (they empathise with other players); killers are Clubs (they hit people with them). (Bartle 1996)

While these player types were originally based on interactions between humans, the terms have been applied to single-player games as well (ibid.).

Each game will have something about it that appeals to each player type, and each player usually contains a mixture of those four traits—it is rare to find a person who is 100% Killer, for example. Knowing what kind of gameplay the game world or inbuilt systems encourage is key when deciding what kind of dialogue system would be most beneficial for a given game's target demographic (Taylor-Giles 2014). Also key is the manner in which the dialogue system is represented to the player—the more literal way in which the player makes their desires in the game world known.

13.3.4   Types of User Interfaces (UIs)

There is no one type of user interface that is correct for all games, just as there is no one gameplay type that suits every kind of player. The design of the conversation interface is as vital and invisible as the dialogue system itself, and can have unintended effects on how the player perceives and experiences the game (Taylor-Giles 2014). Examples from the previously identified RPGs will serve to illustrate this point.

Mass Effect (BioWare 2007) and *Dragon Age: Origins* (BioWare 2009) were both successful attempts to establish new intellectual properties (IPs) with their own dialogue conventions and visual language. They also show how the same studio can approach user interface (UI) design in very different ways based on the way they want their players to receive and process information.

The conversation system of *The Elder Scrolls V: Skyrim* (Bethesda Game Studios 2011) diverged significantly from previous *Elder Scrolls* titles, while retaining a list-based structure which has been common to computer-based RPGs since the earliest days of the genre (Taylor-Giles 2014).

Deus Ex: Human Revolution (Eidos Montreal 2011), as a successor to another long-standing franchise, also redefined how they would display their dialogue options, while at the same time acting as the re-launch of the IP. The transition from list-based choices to a honeycomb structure for the display of dialogue options is a crucial aspect of its success as a "morally ambiguous" game, i.e., one in which the authorship of the game allows for multiple correct interpretations of both in-game events and the player's actions (Taylor-Giles 2014).

Each of these games presents UIs that are distinct, memorable, and which have paved the way for RPGs since.

13.3.4.1   Mass Effect (2007) (Fig. 13.1)

Mass Effect was one of the first games to include an "Investigate" option (Hudson et al. 2011), which allows the player to ask questions without fear of progressing the conversation or incurring accidental consequences. As an information-gathering tool, it is invaluable; as a narrative device, it can break the player's immersion. For example, the first conversation of the game, pictured below, is eight times longer if the player selects every investigate option. Given the Context that the player is on their way to an important briefing with their superior officer, the ability to quiz a subordinate—and keep the Captain waiting—indirectly reduces immersion by reminding the player that the game world revolves around their actions, and that the story cannot continue without their input.

Regardless, the investigate option is cleverly designed—left to "go back", right to "go forward"—acting as a pause button for the player to get additional Context, should they desire it, before continuing the conversation.

The dialogue wheel itself suffers from unfortunate visual bias, in that the options on the lower portion of the interface are afforded more rotational real estate than those at the top. Given the convention to have positive options appear first and to have negative options appear last (Hudson et al. 2011), this results in a visual display which privileges, or gives more weight to, negative options when they appear. This convention brings with it the possible side effect of making those options appear more attractive or, in the case of controller-based interactions where the player uses a joystick rather than a mouse pointer to select their options, rendering the positive options more difficult to select.

Perhaps to counter this effect, the default dialogue option—where the player's cursor automatically falls when the conversation loads—is directly to the right,

Fig. 13.1 Mass Effect's (BioWare 2007) conversation interface

Fig. 13.2 Dragon Age: Origins' (BioWare 2009) conversation interface

meaning that if the player simply or accidentally clicks through the conversation without making a selection their character will respond in a neutral or non-committal manner.

13.3.4.2 Dragon Age: Origins (2009) (Fig. 13.2)

Dragon Age's interface borrows from earlier titles, such as *Baldur's Gate* (BioWare 1998) or *Neverwinter Nights* (BioWare 2002). As a tried-and-tested method of displaying dialogue choices, numbered lists are common. They are not, however, without visual bias (Taylor-Giles 2014).

The difference between *Dragon Age* and other games of the same fantasy RPG genre is the aggression inherent to the critical path (Option 1). Where most games use a standard good-neutral-evil layout for their dialogue options (Borland and King 2003), *Dragon Age*'s first option will exit the player from the conversation—usually into combat.

Dragon Age also straddles an interesting divide—its conversations are designed for simulation and the player character is an Avatar, yet as a whole *Dragon Age* falls into the category of replayable storylines, since the world itself is not simulated and events unfold in a set order, on an established timeframe.

13.3.4.3 The Elder Scrolls V: Skyrim (2011) (Fig. 13.3)

Skyrim's interface is an abstraction of the type found in *Dragon Age*, or even its own predecessors, *The Elder Scrolls III: Morrowind* (Bethesda Game Studios 2002) and *The Elder Scrolls IV: Oblivion* (Bethesda Game Studios 2006). Like *Mass Effect*, the

Fig. 13.3 The Elder Scrolls V: Skyrim's (Bethesda Game Studios 2011) conversation interface. The Elder Scrolls: Skyrim ® © 2011 ZeniMax Media Inc. All Rights Reserved

Fig. 13.4 Deus Ex: Human Revolution's (Eidos Montreal 2011) conversation interface. © Square Enix

option the player is most likely to want to ask appears directly under the cursor when the conversation starts. Other options take a "curiosity-downward" approach—the more obscure and lore-related questions are further from the default option, while those related to the critical path or core gameplay are closer to the top.

13.3.4.4 Deus Ex: Human Revolution (2011) (Fig. 13.4)

Human Revolution's interface is streamlined to three responses—the bottom cell is reserved for the ability to go back to a higher tier of the conversation. Once the player makes their initial selection, it is common for the player character, Adam Jensen, to continue the conversation with the same attitude, until the subject of the conversation changes. This subtly reinforces both Jensen's identity as a character, distinct and separate from the player, and the game's underlying theme that choices, when they arise, are meaningful.

The following page includes a table comparing how these different UI designs impact player engagement and how UI can purposefully (or accidentally) lead player decision-making (Table 13.1).

13.4 Player-Centred Design and the Four Essential Properties of Branching Dialogues

The above elements—world, player character, player type, and UI—were all analysed in *Toward a Deeper Understanding of Branching Dialogue Systems* to arrive at the Four Essential Properties of Branching Dialogues (Taylor-Giles 2014). The following section re-applies the Four Essential Properties, with the additional lens of designer intent—whether given examples from each game can be considered to be systems-centred, developer-centred, or player-centred.

The conversations listed come as close to the beginning of the game as possible, because it is in these first moments that the player's expectations will be set, colouring their interactions with the game world from that moment forward.

13.4.1 Agency

13.4.1.1 Letting the Player Know What is Possible

Ineffective Use of Agency. *Mass Effect*'s first skill check (Fig. 13.5).

In this example, the top and bottom options on the left are greyed out and unselectable. What the player may not yet know, and what is not made clear, is that the upper option is available if the player has a Paragon/Charm point, while the lower option requires a Renegade/Intimidation point.

These values could have been assigned during character creation or, if the player punched Dr. Manuel in the previous conversation (see Sect. 13.4.2), they would have received a free point in Intimidation.

Why is it ineffective?

This is a case of systems-centred design, where including an unmarked tutorial about the game's conversation system was judged to be more important than the frustration the player would experience on being denied the ability to choose two "available" options—being denied Agency. The options appear, but the player is unable to select them and no information is given as to why.

Table 13.1 Game comparisons

	Mass effect	Dragon age	Skyrim	Human revolution
PC type:	Actor	Avatar	Avatar	Actor
How does the UI lead the player?	The default cursor position is to the right (neutral/badass); more rotational real estate is given to the negative/evil answers at the bottom of the UI than to the positive/good options at the top	The first answer is more aggressive than the typically "good" first answers of previous RPGs	By placing lore or non-critical-path questions further away from the cursor; the player can exit at any time, the prompt for which is always visible in the bottom right	As little as possible. There is no default option nor visible hierarchy between dialogue options
What type of experience is the dialogue interface designed for?	Replayability—the difference between "I'll look into it", "Goodbye", and "Just do your job" is the draw here	Simulation—the conversations flow forward, as they would in real life, with few regressions or options to ask for more information (which is usually forthcoming anyway)	Replayability—people who know what they need from specific conversations can get it with minimal NPC interaction	Simulation—when the player can ask questions, they are limited, so the conversation moves constantly forward as it would in real life
Who benefits most from the critical path?	Killers, since the option directly to the right normally ends the conversation with minimal commitment given or information received	Killers, since the first dialogue option frequently lands them in combat	Achievers—constructing dialogues around a utility-first approach means it is very easy for the player to get what they want and get out	This is a trick question! All options are valid, so the player's path is the critical path
What player types is this interface good for?	Explorers (lore) socializers (NPC interactions), and killers (can exit directly/be a badass)	Explorers (on-screen options give Context and lore without needing to be selected), socializers (NPC interactions), and killers (can exit directly/be a badass)	Achievers (get in, get the loot, get out), killers (avoid all conversations forever)	Socializers—you need to listen to what is being said in order to respond effectively, especially during the debates (conversation battles)
What player types might find this interface difficult?	Achievers (getting the information or achievement they want requires a lot of digging)	Achievers (there is no quick way to skip through the conversation AND get all the loot on your first run)	Explorers (NPCs can interrupt conversations and wander away if the player takes too long to choose a dialogue option), socializers (no one cares about you, even your own companions)	Achievers (there is no optimal path), explorers (there are few conversational regressions), killers (conversations cannot be skipped)

Fig. 13.5 A screenshot from Mass Effect (BioWare 2007) showing greyed out conversation options on the left side of the dialogue wheel

Fig. 13.6 A screenshot from The Elder Scrolls V: Skyrim (Bethesda Game Studios 2011) showing multiple skill-based options for the player to select from *The Elder Scrolls: Skyrim* [®] © *2011 ZeniMax Media Inc. All Rights Reserved*

It is likely these prompts exist as a kind of tutorial, but the player's only options for rendering the text selectable are both metagame solutions—they must either load an earlier save and choose to punch Dr. Manuel (see Sect. 13.4.2.1, or start the game over if they want to select those dialogue options. Neither is desirable as a means of increasing player immersion and engagement.

Effective Use of Agency. *Skyrim*'s first skill check (Fig. 13.6).

When the player arrives at a specific city, Whiterun, for the first time, they are drawn into an unskippable conversation with a guard. The player is presented with several ways to get inside the city, two of which are skill checks and one of which is a bribe.

The persuasion check will succeed, while the Intimidation check will fail, but in either case the player will receive a point in the speech skill, thus introducing the game's core mechanic of "practice makes perfect".

Why is it effective?

These dialogue options introduce the skill system by maintaining the player's Agency and allowing them to make a legitimate choice. The player needs to go to Whiterun to progress the main story, so they are never truly going to be kept out, and success and failure are both contextual—the results would make sense even without the skill tags. If they try one of the skill-based options, the player is rewarded with a skill increase even on failure, encouraging them to try those options again in future. In short, the designer of the conversation considered the overall goal of the interaction and made efforts to teach the player while still allowing them full control over their decisions.

13.4.1.2 Reflecting the Player's Choices

Ineffective Use of Agency. Meeting Duncan for the first time in *Dragon Age: Origins.*

Playing as the City Elf, the first time the player meets Duncan of the Grey Wardens they have options to threaten him, question his presence, or be outright rude. When the Elder, Valendrian arrives, however, the player's only options are all respectful. If they choose "Any friend of the elder is welcome here", Duncan will respond with the line, "Oh? Changing your tune so quickly? (chuckles)" regardless of how the player treated him up to that point.

Why is it ineffective?

This is a case of developer-centred design. There are many reasons this might have happened, from lines being cut to variables being incorrectly set, but the end result is that the player's attitude is incorrectly reflected. This makes it obvious that the game, from the beginning, is not necessarily listening to the player, and reduces their sense of Agency, i.e., of having a lasting and meaningful impact upon the game world.

Effective Use of Agency. The first conversation with the player character's father in *Dragon Age: Origins.*

When the player character's cousin, Shianni, wakes them and tells them their groom or bride has arrived early, one of the player's options is "Really? That's great! The sooner the better!" while all of their other options express doubt or reluctance of some kind.

The player who selects the positive option will be able to say to "No time to talk, Father! I'm getting married!" in the next conversation. Everyone else will see "Can we talk about this arrangement?" instead.

Why is it effective?

Changing a single line may seem simple, but it makes a big difference—it brings the world into alignment with the player's attitude and heightens their sense of Agency. Even if the only players who see this difference are those who replay the game or discuss it with friends, the value remains in the fact that the game listened to the player's choice and presented the opportunity to continue with the same optimism with which they had begun.

Replacing dialogue options, rather than having mutually exclusive attitudes side-by-side, also helps the player feel as though their Avatar is consistent from one moment to the next. It is not uncommon to see multiple viewpoints represented side-by-side, from bloodthirsty to pacific (see the examples in Sect. 13.3.4), but modifying dialogue choices to provide the player with approaches that reflect their prior attitude—and without constraining them to a particular course of action—is an effective method for improving player Agency.

13.4.1.3 Resolving Trivial Choices

Ineffective Use of Agency. *Skyrim*'s "…" dialogue option.

As discussed in the introduction, dialogue lines that contain no content are sub-optimal in a game where the player character is not voiced, because other characters in the game would have no way to know when the player was done "speaking". Separate from that issue, and more important for Agency, is that having a dialogue "option" where there is only one choice is not a choice at all.

Why is it ineffective?

This is a case of either systems-centred or developer-centred design that is not unique to *Skyrim*. This conversation could have fallen prey to the game's "remove all non-critical path options until the player says the right thing" system, or the person writing the dialogue might have simply forgotten to replace a placeholder line. Regardless, forcing the player to click on the only available option makes it clear their Agency is subject to the designer's whims and can be removed at any time. In turn, this breaks the player's immersion by reminding them that the world was constructed before their arrival, and can only respond to them in pre-programmed ways.

The solution is simple: considering the conversation from the player's point of view would have revealed the issue before recording and would have made this interchange less bizarre. Alternately, since the player character's lines are never voiced, writing a line for the PC that links the two halves of the conversation organically would have been a more effective solution that helped retain player Agency.

Effective Use of Agency. Talking to Josie in *Deus Ex: Human Revolution*.

After saving Josie, an NPC who was being held hostage, the player can talk to her. The conversation begins with the player character Jensen, asking if she is all right. If the player rescued the other hostages, Jensen will also tell her they are safe before the player is offered any dialogue options.

Why is it effective?

Few people would blink if they were immediately presented with a dialogue option asking Josie if she is okay, but in this case the interaction is mandatory. This approach is more effective in games with an Actor rather than an Avatar (*Persona 5* (Atlus USA, 2016) being an exception), but what the game is telling the player is that Jensen is the kind of person who would both check on someone's well-being and relate relevant information—without the player being able to lie or omit important details.

There are no repercussions to Jensen's words, except those provided by the player's own actions (i.e., letting the hostages die, either by choice or through inability to act). In turn, the player learns more about the person they are embodying, and two unnecessary "clicks"—selecting dialogue options to relay information the player already knows—are avoided.

Several decisions like this are taken away from the player during the course of *Deus Ex: Human Revolution*. The net positive is that the player learns that their

Fig. 13.7 A screenshot from Mass Effect (BioWare 2007) showing the conversation option that leads to the circumstance of punching Dr. Manuel

choices are meaningful because the game is handling everything else—it takes away Agency at unnecessary moments to increase the impact of the moments where the player's choice *will* matter.

13.4.2 Ambiguity

13.4.2.1 Unexpected Consequences (Defining the Player's Character Without Their Consent)

Ineffective Use of Ambiguity. *Mass Effect*'s option to punch a scientist (Fig. 13.7).

This setup occurs during another dialogue tutorial in *Mass Effect*—physical interactions between characters within dialogue were, in 2007, a rare occurrence and so it is understandable that the development team would want to showcase what their new engine and conversation layout could do. In this particular case, the player is able to punch a scientist who is raving hysterically. If they do, they will receive a free Renegade point, which unlocks the Intimidate skill in later conversations and affects how NPCs view the player character for the rest of the game.

Why is it ineffective?

This is a case of developer-centred design. The player's option is clearly placed in the "bad/evil" quadrant of the dialogue wheel (Hudson et al. 2011), but since this is one of the first conversations in the game the player might not be aware of or used to the game's visual language yet. There is no indication in the line itself that it denotes an action—the line could have just as clearly been "[Punch Dr. Manuel]", but that would have ruined the surprise.

That "Surprise!" factor is a key component of what makes for developer-centred design. When the developer wants to shock the player, ideally in a way that will make the player feel an emotion—outrage, disgust, victory, etc.—it is necessary to use surprise as an element of that interaction (see Sect. 13.4.3.3). However, in this case the surprise comes not from a non-player character, but from the player character—who the player is meant to be controlling.

The way the interaction is designed requires that the player's sense of Agency be sacrificed for spectacle. Different players will, of course, have different reactions, but the fact remains that removing or obfuscating player control (via unnecessary Ambiguity) over a polarizing event (physical violence toward a civilian) does not imply that the player's reactions—certainly those which are negative—were taken into account during the design process.

The fact that this action will also automatically assign the player character a "free" Renegade point and unlock the Intimidate dialogue option mentioned in 1.4.1.1 is also developer-centred. It is encouraging the player to make use of the reputation system—which will affect how NPCs respond to the player throughout the course of the game—before explaining what that system is; essentially, it leads the player toward the developer's preferred playstyle without making it clear that other options will later become available.

Effective Use of Ambiguity. Letting Zeke Sanders escape in *Deus Ex: Human Revolution.*

For the first debate of the game, the player faces off against a desperate criminal, Zeke, who has taken a woman hostage. There are several outcomes: the player shoots Zeke, either fatally or non-fatally; the hostage is either rescued or killed; Zeke escapes with or without her. The player knows that a SWAT team is on their way, but not whether they are in position yet. It is this uncertainty that makes the situation compelling.

The interesting moment comes when the player chooses to let Zeke escape. If he has agreed to leave the hostage behind, Zeke leaves safely and contacts the player later on. If, however, he takes the hostage with him, the SWAT team is already in place and she is killed in the crossfire, while Zeke escapes.

Why is it effective?

Since the debate always lasts three rounds, all versions of the game exist on the same timeline. This means that if the SWAT team was in place when Zeke leaves with the hostage, they should also have been in place when Zeke leaves alone. However, as described above, that is not what happens.

What does happen is that the game uses ambiguous timing to preserve the player's sense of Agency. They decided to let Zeke go, so he gets away safely. The presence of the hostage does not change the player's decision, only adds consequences to that decision which were clearly stated at the beginning of the debate.

If Zeke had been killed on exiting alone, the player might have wondered what they did wrong. If they then discovered that he was doomed to die no matter their choices during the debate, it would impact how seriously they took conversations in the game from then on. They would assume none of their choices matter. Using a flexible timeline in this way to preserve player Agency allows for multiple, mutually exclusive states that all feel like the inevitable outcome of the player's choices, reinforcing the belief that their actions have consequences and therefore value.

13.4.2.2 Conversational Bottlenecks

Ineffective Use of Ambiguity. *Skyrim*'s funnelled choices.

Skyrim's critical path dialogues are funnelled, meaning that options which do not move the storyline forward will disappear after the player selects them, leaving only the lines the game "wants" the player to say. These are also conversations from which the player may not escape in the usual manner—they cannot be interrupted or restarted, meaning the player is "locked in" until they have selected the options the game needs them to select.

For example, after killing the dragon that was terrorizing Whiterun, the player has to report to Jarl Balgruuf. The dialogue options are as follows:

- "The watchtower was destroyed, but we killed the dragon".
- "Turns out I may be something called 'Dragonborn'".
- "I killed the dragon. I think I deserve a reward".

Choosing Option 3 leads to the previous Option 2 becoming Option 1:

- "Turns out I may be something called 'Dragonborn'".
- "When the dragon died, I absorbed some kind of power from it".

Choosing Option 1 leads Option 2 to again become the new Option 1:

- "When the dragon died, I absorbed some kind of power from it".
- "That's just what the men called me".

The dialogue continues in this manner until all of the relevant plot points have been addressed, at which point the player is released from the conversation, regardless of whether there may have been other questions in the list that they wished to ask.

Why is it ineffective?

This is a case of developer-centred design. The player has to hit certain story beats for the overall narrative to make sense, so the design makes sure they cannot progress without saying what needs to be said, even if the player is already aware of that information. The player will quickly realize that, unless they are saying what the game wants to hear, nothing they choose matters. It is necessary to have points where all branches of a given conversation come together to advance the plot, but Ambiguity—writing the same lines several different ways—would have made the funnelling effect less obvious.

Effective Use of Ambiguity Valendrian's intro in *Dragon Age: Origins*.

While the player is speaking with Duncan, the Grey Warden mentioned in Sect. 13.4.1.2, Duncan will comment on the player's composure, whether aggressive or calm, and ask Valendrian's opinion. Valendrian's response is always the same: "I would say the world has far more use of those who know how to stay their blades".

Why is it effective?

Valendrian is either chastising an aggressive player or commending a diplomatic player. In both cases, the Ambiguity of his response is valid. Matched with neutral voice acting, this line creates an emotion within the player that they will remember, in turn perhaps remembering Valendrian as warmer or colder than he was.

A key component of Ambiguity is engaging the player's imagination in a way that allows them to add their own nuance to the story being told, thus making them part-owner and increasing engagement and immersion (Murray 1997). Planning ahead to include effective Ambiguity in branching dialogues reduces developer workload while resulting in positive player appraisal.

13.4.2.3   Let the Player Feel the Appropriate Emotions (Sometimes Ambiguity Is Unnecessary)

Ineffective Use of Ambiguity.   The use of "hurt" in *Dragon Age: Origins.*

In the City Elf intro, if playing as a female character, the player will be kidnapped by a local human noble named Vaughan. The player must battle their way through his castle to rescue the player character's cousin, Shianni, and save the other women who were kidnapped alongside her. One of the other Elf women has already been murdered in front of the player; when the player arrives in Vaughan's bedroom it is apparent that Shianni, who is usually outspoken and defiant yet in this case is barely articulate and sobbing uncontrollably, has already been raped. The player is then offered the choice of leaving Shianni and the other women behind in exchange for their own safety and a large amount of gold.

The issue comes with the phrasing of the player's companion, Soris, if the player takes the bribe without asking after their friends: "But you won't hurt the women, right?" And, if the player refuses Vaughan's bribe and needs to convince Soris to do the same, they can say "Soris, they were going to hurt me!" In neither case is the word "rape" used.

Why is it ineffective?

This is a case of developer-centred design, masquerading as player-centred design. It makes use of unnecessary Ambiguity to soften the content the player is confronted with: the word "rape" was replaced with "hurt". Soris, as a non-player character, may be trying to distance himself from a morally reprehensible act by using neutered language, but the player who is trying to convince him has no such excuse when, in fact, the stronger word is likely to be more convincing.

The choice to use Ambiguity at this moment is in sharp contrast to an earlier dialogue choice offered to the player when speaking to the other captured women: "Chances are we'll be raped, beaten, and killed". The player character is aware of the full seriousness of the situation and can make it known to other women as well, yet when confronted by the discomfort of her male cousin can only use the more neutral term. This undermines player Agency, because the player is not able to choose the correct term that they may want to use, while presenting the player character as having inconsistent characterization.

Where this becomes particularly difficult as a concept is where one could argue that the change was made for player comfort, to reduce the impact on the perceived audience. Rape is an uncomfortable subject. Yet in choosing to frame the entire character introduction around being abducted for the purpose of being raped, there is nothing to be gained in using softer language to discuss the idea. Considering player comfort, if it was truly a concern, would have led to a different storyline entirely and avoided the unnecessary use of Ambiguity.

Effective Use of Ambiguity.   Alternate newspapers in *Deus Ex: Human Revolution* that reflect the player's actions (without placing blame).

During the lead-up to the first debate, the player has the choice to make a detour to save a group of employees who are being held hostage next to a bomb or to continue with their mission as planned. The player knows the bomb is on a timer— if they take too long, or reach the debate with Zeke before disarming it, it explodes and kills everyone in the room, including the husband of the woman being held hostage. After the mission is over, the player can read an in-game newspaper with one of two headlines:

"Hostages Rescued at Sarif Manufacturing Plant" or

"Biohazard Bomb Triggered at Sarif Manufacturing Plant"

Why is it effective?

Both newspaper articles are written in such a way as to let the player know the world is watching without blaming them for a negative outcome. If the bomb went off, the article goes out of its way to have another character both say "It was completely unexpected" and to take the brunt of the public's disapproval, while in the positive outcome the attending police officers express relief without taking ownership for the hostages having been saved. The player is free to feel however they want about their own actions, and to change their behaviour accordingly for future missions.

The Ambiguity of how the newspaper articles are written is also an effective way to avoid having multiple, very specific versions covering each of the ways the player could have approached the mission, the details of which the public realistically would not have access to anyway.

13.4.3   Context

13.4.3.1   Giving the Player Clues to Understand Their Background

Ineffective Use of Context.   *Mass Effect*'s "shakedown run".

In the opening conversation of the game, Navigator Pressly begins by saying "It's pretty obvious this shakedown run is just a cover". Even in the Investigate tree, there is no explanation of what this phrase means. Discussion of the "shakedown run" is also an important element in the next conversation with Captain Anderson, yet it likewise remains unexplained during that conversation despite being referenced later in the game as well. It appears there is no official in-game or out-of-game explanation as to what this phrase means, apart from player speculation and references to Formula 1 racing.

Why is it ineffective?

This is a case of developer-centred design. It is common to worldbuild at the beginning of the game, and it is common to overdo it and use terms and phrases the player cannot possibly understand. Working on a game for a long period of time, it is easy to forget what level of knowledge the player will come in with. Playtesting early and often with as many different people as possible—especially from outside the development team—helps reveal confusing or misleading elements that allow for a more comprehensive establishment of the Context of the game world. Reducing the number of terms and phrases that may seem common, but which are alien to people who are not working on the game or part of the same culture in which the game is being developed, will avoid the player feeling confused, frustrated, or unintelligent based purely on word choice alone.

Effective Use of Context. Telling the player who their mother was in *Dragon Age: Origins.*

Talking to the player character's father, Cyrion, in the City Elf intro can lead to this line of dialogue:

"We don't want to seem like troublemakers, after all. Adaia made that mistake".
The player can then choose from the following:

1. "Let's just get on with this, shall we?"
2. "The humans who killed her made a bigger one".
3. "Mother was a clever rogue".

If the player chose to be a warrior, the other of the two classes offered to City Elves, the last choice becomes instead: "Mother was a great warrior".

Why is it effective?

Even if the player chooses the first dialogue option, they have unwittingly absorbed lore. They know their mother was the same class as them, and that she was killed by humans.

A similar moment occurs in *Skyrim* after the player first creates their character. The soldier taking prisoner's names, Hadvar, comments on both the reasons someone of the player character's race might have come to Skyrim and, sympathetically, where he will send their remains to be buried after their execution.

As discussed in Sect. 13.4.1.2, the choice to reflect the player's decisions about how they want the game world to perceive them, within a dialogue close to the beginning of the game, is a subtle way of aligning the world with the player's desires. It tells the player that they are heard and, in an important way, *seen* as how they wish to be seen, regardless of who they may be outside of the game world.

The ability to inhabit other bodies and live different lives—experiential learning—is a vital strength of video games which no other medium has access to (Murray 1997). It is therefore in the best interests of developers to make use of the medium's strength when designing branching dialogues.

13.4.3.2 Player Character Competence

Ineffective Use of Context. *Mass Effect*: "Info's on a need-to-know basis, Pressly".

When the player speaks with Navigator Pressly during the first conversation of the game, the Investigate option allows them to ask several questions. Unfortunately, the negative player line when exiting the conversation is quoted above, and breaks the player's immersion by needlessly reprimanding a member of the crew in direct contradiction with the actions the player character themselves just took.

Even more unfortunate is that, if the player exits the conversation without asking any questions, the neutral lead-out is simply "I'd better head down and see the Captain". If the player does choose to ask questions, the neutral lead-out changes to "Carry on, Pressly", indicating that changing the line based on the player's actions during the conversation was likewise an option for the negative player lead-out line, yet this was not taken into account or implemented.

Why is it ineffective?

This is a case of developer-centred design. It is easy to lose track of what happens when and which possible lead-in and lead-out states the player character might have—in essence, the Context with which a given player is approaching the conversation—but knowing all of those states is the developer's responsibility. The downside of not tracking the possible way a player might exit your conversation is to have the player character come across as inconsistent, or as acting against the player's wishes, limiting the player's sense of Agency and breaking their immersion.

Playtesting before release would have made the disconnect between the player's actions and their words evident. Even if this oversight was not caught before recording, the hypocritical line could have simply been replaced by the neutral "Carry on, Pressly" without it deviating too far from the sentiment of the negative paraphrase, which is "Just do your job".

Effective Use of Context. *Deus Ex: Human Revolution*: "You know I can't let you go with her".

The debate between the player character and a media-proclaimed "terrorist" begins with Jensen telling Zeke that he cannot let him leave with the hostage. This is reinforced by Jensen's last line before the debate begins and before the player is able to make any dialogue choices, which is "But I can't do a thing [to help you] until you let her go".

Why is it effective?

The player knows that Jensen used to be part of SWAT, so they will immediately believe two things based on this Context: (1) Jensen knows what he is doing and (2) if the debate ends badly, it is the player's fault, not the player character's. A limited number of dialogue options—3 only—also helps here, because it constrains the player to a narrow approach, further reinforcing the belief that Jensen has been trained for something that the player would (hopefully) never attempt in real life.

All of this lead-in means that the player is given the chance to fail, but they are also given the best possible setup—a trained negotiator talking to a man who never wanted to take a hostage in the first place. The Context of the situation tells the player that the game *wants* them to succeed, and that, in fact, as Jensen they are *likely* to succeed, without ever barring the player from absolute failure or otherwise leading them toward a desired outcome.

13.4.3.3 Omitting Important Information for Emotional Impact

Ineffective Use of Context. Accepting Vaughan's bribe in *Dragon Age: Origins.*

As discussed in Sect. 13.4.2.3, the player is offered the choice to leave their friends with a known rapist and accept a large sum of money—which is considerably more than they have seen in the game up to this point—because he threatens to burn the player's village to the ground if they say no. If the player accepts the bribe, they are forced to exit the castle, Soris feels bad, and both the player character and Soris are immediately arrested by guards sent by Vaughan. A plot device saves the player character, but the guards take away the player's newfound riches and throw Soris in jail regardless.

Why is it ineffective?

This is a case of developer-centred design. Up to this point, although the players know that Vaughan is despicable, they have no reason to believe that he is a liar. The player knows that humans are prejudiced against elves, but not the extent to which this is true. It's a betrayal of both the player and the player character.

The intention of being betrayed by Vaughan is clear—it is intended to make the player dislike him even more. The issue is that both the game and Vaughan offered something they never intended to let the player keep, with no Context to understand the decision they were making. The player can neither spend the money nor give it to their elder for the community, because doing so would wreak havoc on the game's economy. In essence, the player was tricked into giving up something for nothing, and is then held accountable for their actions at the end of the game.

Obviously, leaving the player character's friends to be raped and murdered is a reprehensible choice, but if it is going to be offered it needs to be a real choice.

Effective Use of Context. Josie getting killed in *Deus Ex: Human Revolution.*

As discussed in Sect. 13.4.2.1, if the player lets Zeke escape the building with his hostage, Josie, she will be gunned down by the SWAT members that were waiting to kill Zeke. He walks out the door, the sound of gunfire plays, and then if the player exits all they find is Josie's corpse.

Why is it effective?

This surprise packs a similar emotional punch to the example with Vaughan outlined above, but avoids the pitfall of betraying the player without telegraphing the consequences of their actions. Jensen starts the debate by saying "You know I can't let you leave with her" so the stakes are already set. Zeke even refers to Josie as his "human shield" in some lines of dialogue.

Yet what the player probably did not expect, but which seems inevitable in retrospect, was that the SWAT team would open fire regardless of whether Zeke had a hostage or not. Despite the horror of the situation it is in character for both the world and the Context of a hostage situation. The player was told several times that if Josie left with Zeke she would die, so the only real surprise is who kills her.

The difference in the emotional states created by these two examples cannot be overstated. In the example from *Dragon Age*, there was nothing the player could have done to successfully leave the castle with their ill-gotten gains. Presumably intended as a comment on systemic injustice, it nonetheless instills in the player a sense of powerlessness that may be ameliorated, but never entirely erased, by their character's improvement throughout the rest of the game. In comparison, the example from *Human Revolution* tells the player explicitly what outcome they can expect if they fail to convince Zeke to let his hostage go, then allows the player to either deal with the emotional—but not material—consequences of their failure, or load their game to try for a better outcome. In either case, the player is empowered to reach the outcome they desire by the rules of engagement and the stakes being made clear before the player entered into their attempt to sway the outcome one way or another.

13.4.4 Lack of Judgement

13.4.4.1 Provide a Consistent Universe

Ineffective Use of Lack of Judgement. Cyrion withholding a gift in *Dragon Age: Origins.*

As discussed in Sect. 13.4.3.1, the player has three dialogue options in response to their father reminiscing about their mother—two which engage with the story, and one which moves the conversation forward.

If the player chooses to engage with the story, either by expressing a hatred of humans or fondly remembering their mother, Cyrion gives them their mother's boots, which will be helpful in the upcoming combat. If, however, the player says, "Let's just get on with this, shall we?" Cyrion wishes the player well and that is the end of the conversation.

Why is it ineffective?

This is a case of systems-centred or developer-centred design. It is systems-centred because it assumes a player who is uninterested in the story will not need additional help during combat, incorrectly assuming that a player who scores points in the killer sub-category will not also enjoy playing as a socializer. The decision to withhold a material reward is also developer-centred, because it judges the player for not wanting to get involved in the game world, even if that was not their motivation for choosing the first dialogue option.

The dialogue option in question is, "Let's just get on with this, shall we?" However, unintended Ambiguity allows the player to read the line in more than one way. While it may have been intended to tell the player character's father that they do not care what he is talking about—which is likely, given the aggression inherent to the critical path, as discussed in Sect. 13.3.4.2—the line could also be read as though the player finds the subject too painful to discuss, and is choosing not to engage not out of a lack of feeling, but rather an overabundance of it. As the player character in *Dragon Age* is not voiced, it is necessary that value judgements such as these be attached to lines that clearly indicate the player's disdain for the people around them, if that's the direction the developers want to take.

Further to the point, however, Cyrion has no reason to keep his dead wife's shoes if he had intended to give them to his only child. At the very least, him doing so implies that he only cares about the player character when they act the way he wants them to, which is very different from the doting father he is otherwise portrayed as. It is possible for him to disown the player later in the game, for leaving Shianni to be raped and possibly murdered, but that's certainly more deserving of parental disapproval than wanting to hurry along an unpleasant conversation.

Effective Use of Lack of Judgement. Choosing your first weapon in *Deus Ex: Human Revolution.*

Heading into the first mission after the prologue, Jensen's boss, David Sarif, provides the option of a lethal or non-lethal weapon. He explicitly says, "As far as rules of engagement go, I'll defer to you" further reinforcing the idea that Jensen is competent, capable, and trusted.

Why is it effective?

Sarif does not care what the player does as long as they protect his proprietary technology. That lead-in provides a lot of latitude for the player to approach the mission in whatever manner they would like, without the fear that the game will be judging them for their actions, or that it will punish them for playing "the wrong way". It also acts as a tutorial to the game's mechanics, letting the player know that there are different ways of engaging enemies than the usual "run and gun" of other first-person shooters without dropping the player into combat and letting them figure it out on their own.

There is also the fact that, regardless of what the player chooses, Sarif will respond positively. As Jensen's boss, after the player character is returning from a long medical leave that no one expected him to make it out alive from, the player has a vested interest in impressing him, conscious as they may be of it or not. His approval at this stage of the game reassures both Jensen and the player that they can handle the situation ahead while also providing important information that the player can use to help them throughout the mission. This is one of the few game tutorials to both mention and assuage the player's anxiety about entering an unknown situation (a new game world, with new rules and new mechanics) via a simple conversation at the game's outset. Not only does it utilize Lack of Judgement to do so, it also confers a sense of ownership over and power to the player's decisions at the same time—the judgement of placing trust in the player's abilities.

13.4.4.2 Let the Player Express Their Motivations

Ineffective Use of Lack of Judgement. Assumptions about the player in *Dragon Age: Origins.*

If the player left Shianni with Vaughan to be raped and possibly murdered, as discussed in Sect. 13.4.2.3, at the end of the game they face consequences related to their actions. If the player character is male, he will discover that Vaughan killed his fiancée. Regardless of the player's actions, Soris, Shianni, and the player character's father, Cyrion, are all bitter toward the player when they return. The player is never given the chance to explain their actions, only to apologize or move on.

Why is it ineffective?

This is a case of developer-centred design—a refusal to let go of authorial control. The ending depended on the player having done what they did for selfish reasons, so the game acts as if that is the only possible reason they could have had for making that decision. Allowing the player to counter Shianni's accusations with proof that they had left her behind for a good cause (saving the alienage and wanting to share Vaughan's money with the elder to help their people, for example) would have required a complicated series of back-and-forth exchanges, or at the very least a large attitude adjustment from Shianni, so that option was not included.

During game development, endings—and especially reactive endings to branching storylines—are usually the first to be pared back when the realities of production hit. Whether related to time, budget, or technical limitations, the task of responding to all of the possible variations on why a player might have done something is difficult at best and potentially catastrophic at worst, depending on the number of additional lines that would need to be recorded, each of which would come with its own bugs when implemented. This is to say that one way of writing around these situations is to use the distinctly human trait of having NPCs make up their own minds as to why the player did something, then let the player disabuse them of that notion when they have the chance.

The issue here is that the player is not given the chance to defend themselves in a meaningful way, or to even truly discuss their prior decision. The conversation takes place at the centre of multiple conflicts, during which the player is expected to have little time to devote to a character from the beginning of the game. Unfortunately, this oversight removes the chance for catharsis—the feeling of emotional closure that usually accompanies reaching the end of a story, whether in film, books, or video games. Considering this story element from the player's point of view—and why their initial actions might not have been entirely selfish—would ideally have given more space to these characters and this interaction, to allow catharsis to take place.

Effective Use of Lack of Judgement. Talking with Sarif after letting Zeke go.

The debrief with Sarif, Jensen's boss, does not go especially well if the player let Zeke escape, either with or without the hostage. Nevertheless, Jensen's three responses all move the conversation forward:

Sarif   "Yeah, about Sanders. What the hell were you thinking, letting him slip away like that?! I sent you in there to take care of things!"

Player Choices:

- Take charge: "You asked me to deal with the situation, and that's what I did".
- Gamble: "I'm hoping it'll pay off later. Sanders won't rest until he learns who set him up".
- Redirect: "Sanders isn't the mastermind behind this, boss".

Why is it effective?
What's obvious is that the player has no option to apologize. However, these three options also foreground the expertise that Sarif hired the player character for, and provide a Context for why the option to apologize is absent. While the player might not have known, consciously, why they let Zeke escape, these dialogue options allow them to retroactively frame their decision in a certain light, helping them build the player character's personality at the same time as they build their own understanding of how they want to engage with the game.

In the case that the player does not have any strong motivation for having let Zeke go, the first option, "Take charge" allows them to take an authoritative stance without having to expose or even identify their own motivations. There are no "wrong" answers, only rebuttals to Sarif's verbal attack. The player does not feel judged because not only are they absolved from taking a "weak", i.e., pacifist approach in the interests of getting their boss on-side, they are allowed to defend themselves using strong arguments. Consequently, Sarif backs down immediately afterward, increasing player satisfaction and their sense of Agency within the world. Few people would dare argue with their boss so directly in real life, so validating the player's arguments in this way results in the player feeling both powerful and respected.

13.4.4.3   Choose the Player's Boundaries

Ineffective Use of Lack of Judgement.   No apologies in *Mass Effect.*
In contrast with the previous example from *Human Revolution*, below are the dialogue options presented to the player if they (accidentally or purposefully) punched Dr. Manuel (Fig. 13.8).

There are no apologies here, either, but neither is there justification for the player's actions. This is due, in part, to the paraphrasing system, where the written text is meant to be only representative of the voice line that the player character will speak next, but critically absent is any sense of remorse. This could be attributed to the personality of Commander Shephard, the Actor the player is controlling, but this leaves little space for the player to interpret or influence who the player character is or might become. The most likely reason for the lack of choice in this moment is because it would be incongruous for Commander Shephard to punch someone and then immediately regret it, so that option is not available.

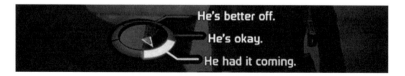

Fig. 13.8   Mass Effect (BioWare 2007)

Why is it ineffective?

This is a case of developer-centred design. Presumably the intention was to give the player a chance to feel "cool" or to showcase new features of the engine (as discussed in Sect. 13.4.1.2), but since the conversation surrounding the option to punch Dr. Manuel is not large or complex, and stopping to discuss the player's actions would have slowed down an otherwise time-critical mission, it became necessary to sweep the player's actions under the rug.

Additionally ineffective is that fact that the other NPC in the conversation has already forgiven the player for punching Dr. Manuel, i.e., the game has already judged that the player's actions were correct. It would have been more effective to segue immediately into the player character defending themselves, and have the NPC's response, than to offer a selection of options in which the ability to apologize—or justify—the player's actions is absent. Lack of Judgement does not only apply to punishing the player for actions that run counter to the developer's personal moral code—it also applies to allowing the player to behave in different ways, when the situation allows for it, without imposing the developer's morality onto the player. Unfortunately, this interaction is asserting the moral value of "might makes right", which is something not all players could be considered to agree with.

Effective Use of Lack of Judgement. The player's dialogue options once Valendrian arrives in *Dragon Age: Origins*.

While speaking with Duncan, one of the player character's elders arrives to join the conversation. Contrary to the different approaches the player could have taken with Duncan (as discussed in Sect. 13.4.1.2), they are presented only with the following dialogue options:

1. "You know this human, Elder?"
2. "I'm sorry, I had no idea".
3. "Any friend of the elder is welcome here".

Why is it effective?

One of the most difficult tasks in writing branching dialogues is to introduce the rules of the world without constraining players in a way that will make them see behind the curtain. In this instance, the player character has no reason (or need) to be rude to their village elder, so they simply cannot be. The game takes away its own opportunity to judge the player unfairly for not understanding the world.

Unlike not being able to apologize, being pleasant to someone who deserves your respect, yet who you have never met before, carries no serious emotional weight. There are also shades of nuance—a player who is still angry at Duncan can choose the first option and read it in their head in as belligerent a voice as they wish, while other players might read it as more neutral. Even though the player is constrained, they still have a large degree of latitude, within a choice that does not matter very much, with which to express themselves.

13.5   Player-Centred Design in *Deus Ex: Human Revolution's* Debate System

It may be evident by now that the conversation system in *Deus Ex: Human Revolution* is especially robust when considering the Four Essential Properties of Branching Dialogues and the concept of player-centred design. There is, however, more depth to the debate system than was able to be covered using those lenses alone, and it is a system that has yet to be implemented in other games of its kind.

The crux of system is that it is designed like a debate—verbal combat. The NPC proposes their version of reality, and the player attacks it. After a short lead-in responding to what the player has said and signalling how the player's choice was received (positive, neutral, negative), the NPC counter-attacks. The conversation progresses through three rounds until the player either wins or loses and the consequences play out from there.

Designed by Francois Lapikas and Taras Stasiuk, this conversation system's efficacy is linked to its inherent realism. The NPC's responses are randomized, so walkthroughs are (mostly) useless. The player needs to rely on what may or may not be an innate skill in order to choose the correct response: that is, the player needs to rely on their empathy.

In the first debate, Zeke gives the player specific cues about how he is feeling before the first dialogue options become available. He is a decorated veteran; someone manipulated him; he feels weak. In short, he is in despair. The player's options are different approaches to that despair: to humble him, and tell him he *is* weak; to reason with him, and tell him there is another way out; or to empathize and tell him he is stronger than he feels.

From there, it is a rock-paper-scissors mechanic of choosing the emotional tone that counteracts whatever Zeke is feeling. His responses are not flagged the same way the player's options are, so the only way to know which approach he is taking is to listen—and listen critically—to what he is saying. Is he boasting? Humble him. Is he attacking the player character personally? Reason with him. Is he in despair? Show him you understand.

Simply by the progression of the conversation, the player can learn about human interactions—specifically that the emotional tone of *how* something is said is often more important than the words being spoken. In short, this is a conversation system that was designed to teach, and reward, empathy. With the benefit of experiential learning as its base, teaching players how to better interact with their fellow human beings outside of the game world is a positive and effective model for how to design branching conversation systems in future titles.

13.6 Conclusions

13.6.1 Questions to Ask When Designing Branching Dialogue Systems

In conclusion, applying the Four Essential Properties of Branching Dialogues, as well as player-centred design, is indicated in increased player retention, satisfaction, and overall enjoyment. The following questions are aimed to smooth the way for those wishing to design their own branching conversation systems, though they can also be used by those wishing to assess the efficacy of an existing conversation system.

- Is the conversation system aimed at simulation or replayability?
- Is there inherent bias in the way the dialogue options are displayed?
- What kind of experience will the player have if they follow the critical path?
- How much latitude does the player have to define their character?
- What "world rules" is the player allowed to break, e.g., being a woman who wields a sword? How will these "world rules" be communicated to the player?
- Does each dialogue option represent a non-trivial choice with a definite consequence (dialogue or gameplay)?
- Does this moment need to be a conversation (could it have been a cinematic or other linear conversation)?
- What would each of the four Bartle player types want to say or do here?
- Are the consequences to the player's decisions adequately telegraphed ahead of time (i.e., is the player making an informed decision)?
- Is the branching efficient and leading to points where all possible versions of the conversation come together to advance the plot?
- Do the dialogue option and its consequences build trust with the player?
- Do any of the dialogue options lie to the player?
- Are the player's actions being judged based on personally held beliefs or "how the game world works" that they would otherwise have no way of knowing?

Following these guidelines, or applying them to existing systems, will provide a comprehensive understanding of the goals of the underlying branching dialogue architecture, allowing both developers and players to make informed decisions about the types of content they both create and enjoy.

References

Adams, E. (2001, May 21). Replayability, Part One: Narrative. Retrieved from: https://www.gamasutra.com/view/feature/131483/replayability_part_one_narrative.php

Atlus USA (2016, September 15). Persona 5 [Computer software]. Irvine, California, USA: Atlus Co., Ltd.

Bartle, R. (1990). Interactive multi-user computer games. MUSE Ltd for British Telecom plc, Colchester, UK, Report.

Bartle, R. (1996, August 28). Hearts, Clubs, Diamonds, Spades: Players who suit MUDs. Retrieved August 23rd, 2019 from: http://www.mud.co.uk/richard/hcds.htm

Bethesda Game Studios. (2002, May 1). The Elder Scrolls III: Morrowind [Computer software]. Rockville, Maryland, USA: Bethesda Softworks, LLC.

Bethesda Game Studios. (2006, March 20). The Elder Scrolls IV: Oblivion [Computer software]. Rockville, Maryland, USA: Bethesda Softworks, LLC.

Bethesda Game Studios. (2011, November 11). The Elder Scrolls V: Skyrim [Computer software]. Rockville, Maryland, USA: Bethesda Softworks, LLC.

BioWare. (1998, November 30). Baldur's Gate [Computer software]. Beverly Hills, California, USA: Interplay Entertainment.

BioWare. (2009, November 5). Dragon Age: Origins [Computer software]. Redwood City, California, USA: Electronic Arts.

BioWare. (2007, November 16). Mass Effect [Computer software]. Redwood City, California, USA: Electronic Arts.

BioWare. (2002, July 3). Neverwinter Nights [Computer software]. Beverly Hills, California, USA: Interplay Entertainment.

Borland, J. & King, B. (2003). *Dungeons and Dreamers: The Rise of Computer Game Culture from Geek to Chic.* New York: McGraw-Hill Osborne Media.

Eidos Montreal. (2011, August 25). Deus Ex: Human Revolution [Computer software]. El Segundo, California, USA: Square Enix.

Goldfarb, I., & Kondratova, I. (2004). Visual interface design tool for educational courseware.

Harris, J. (2010, May 18). Analysis: Purposes for Randomization in Game Design. Retrieved from: http://www.gamasutra.com/view/news/28495/Analysis_Purposes_for_Randomization_in_Game_Design.php

Hudson, C., Bishop, J., Greig, S., Karpyshyn, D., Martens, K., Muzyka, R., Ohlen, J., Roy, Y., Watamaniuk, P., Laidlaw, M. (2011). United States Patent 8,082,499. Retrieved from: http://patft.uspto.gov/netacgi/nph-Parser?Sect1=PTO2&Sect2=HITOFF&p=1&u=%2Fnetahtml%2FPTO%2Fsearch-bool.html&r=1&f=G&l=50&co1=AND&d=PTXT&s1=20070226648&OS=20070226648&RS= 20070226648

Klein, G., Klinger, D., & Miller, T. (1997, October). Using decision requirements to guide the design process. In 1997 IEEE International Conference on Systems, Man, and Cybernetics. Computational Cybernetics and Simulation (Vol. 1, pp. 238–244). IEEE.

Murray, J. H. (1997). Hamlet on the Holodeck: The Future of Narratives in Cyberspace. Cambridge: MIT Press.

Norman, D. A., & Draper, S. W. (1986). User centered system design: New perspectives on human-computer interaction. CRC Press.

Taylor-Giles, L. C. (2014). Toward a deeper understanding of branching dialogue systems (Doctoral dissertation, Queensland University of Technology).

Trubshaw, R., & Bartle, R. (1978). MUD1. Essex, United Kingdom.

Chapter 14
Designing a CAD-Enriched Empathy Game to Raise Awareness About Universal Design Principles: A Case Study

Çetin Tüker and Güven Çatak

Contents

Abstract Practicing Universal Design Principles in Design Education Through a CAD-Based Game (PUDCAD) is an Erasmus+ project organized by Istanbul Technical University with partner organizations from Turkey, Germany, Italy, and Finland. The goal of the project is to raise empathy of design students with people who have cerebral palsy, a permanent motor impairment occurred due to brain damage. The main intellectual output of the project is designing a one-day educational experience that includes a video game and an architectural design

Ç. Tüker (✉)
Mimar Sinan Fine Arts University, Department of Graphic Design, İstanbul, Turkey
e-mail: cetin.tuker@msgsu.edu.tr

G. Çatak
Department of Game Design, Bahcesehir University Game Lab (BUG), Bahcesehir University, Istanbul, Turkey

© Springer Nature Switzerland AG 2020   327
B. Bostan (ed.), *Game User Experience And Player-Centered Design*,
International Series on Computer Entertainment and Media Technology,
https://doi.org/10.1007/978-3-030-37643-7_14

workshop. The governing idea of this project is based on the user experience of the players which is also the main driving factor of teaching methodology of the game. The player experiences intentionally designed situations and experiences in the game world, and learns from these situations and experiences. Role-playing, experiential learning, educational scaffolding, and repetitive spaced-out learning methodologies are used in several stages of either the video game and the one-day learning experience. This study covers the decision process of the design team and how they approached the idea of using the design process and CAD as a part of the game mechanic. As the target audience of the project are design students, and as they are familiar with the CAD as a language while expressing and presenting their design ideas and solutions, to create a familiar universe in the empathy game, the game mechanics are enriched (supported) with a limited CAD-like environment. This makes it possible to use design itself as a part of the game mechanic.

Keywords Games for change · Universal design · Inclusive design · CAD game · Cerebral palsy

14.1 Introduction

Most of the time during the design process, due to the scope of the design brief from the client some parts of the population can be excluded nonintentionally. They were excluded because neither the client nor the designer considers their existence. Some parts of the population, the elderly, the physically disabled people, the children, or even sometimes people who cannot speak the language of the particular country can be excluded from the design goals. Ethically, the designed product or environment should be accessible for any user (unless exclusion is intentionally added to the design brief for some special reason). The idea of increasing accessibility in design is not new. It is known as design-for-all in Europe and universal design in the USA. To increase the accessibility of a product for all members of the population requires several factors. Two of these factors can be: (a) to be aware of the special needs of the previously excluded population; (b) to think and feel like the previously excluded population, in other words, empathy.

Practicing Universal Design Principles in Design Education Through a CAD-Based Game (PUDCAD) is an Erasmus+ project which was started in 2017 and will be completed in 2020. The main goal of the project is to raise the empathy of design students with people who have cerebral palsy, a permanent motor impairment occurred due to brain damage. Istanbul Technical University in Turkey is the applicant organization. Partner universities are Bahçeşehir University from Turkey, Hochschule Ostwestfalen-Lippe from Germany, Lahden Ammattikorkeakoulu Oy from Finland, Universita Degli Studi di Firenze and Politecnico di Milano from Italy. There are two non-profit organizations from Turkey; SERÇEV (Serebral Palsili Çocuklar Derneği/Association of Children with Cerebral Palsy) and Ergoterapi Derneği (Ergotherapy Association). Buratti et al. (2018) cover the previous stages of the PUDCAD project.

Beyond many workshops that were planned and applied during the three-year project, the main intellectual output of the project is a one-day design experience which is designed to: (a) raise the empathy of the design students with physically disabled people; (b) improve design skills to solve problems related with accessibility, inclusive design methodology, and universal design principles. As a decision by the project partners, the game is planned to distribute freely through the internet to be used by any design school which decides to make the game a part of their design studio.

During preliminary design meetings, the PUDCAD project partners and game design team of BAU concluded that the design objectives of the game will be: (a) to help design students empathize with physically impaired people, especially, people with cerebral palsy; (b) to train students to recognize and identify universal design problems in different contexts (environment design, interface design, product design, etc.; (c) to increase awareness of the design students about accessibility, inclusive design methodology, and universal design principles. There were also various educational objectives set by the partners and the design team. It was planned that a student who successfully completes the game and the following design activities will gain the skills: (a) to empathize with the physically impaired people by experiencing their difficulties personally within the built environment; (b) to design by using inclusive design methodology; (c) to be aware of, see and recognize non-universal design solutions; (d) to improve existing non-universal design solutions by analyzing the existing situation and by designing new solutions.

In this chapter, there will be a short description of cerebral palsy. The differences between the terms accessibility, design-for-all, inclusive design, and universal design principles will be discussed after cerebral palsy. These two contexts will give a broad insight into the borders of the context the proposed video game deals with. To support the related knowledgebase, the literature about the theoretical framework of how empathy can be raised with video games and applied examples of related video games will be presented in the literature review section. A review of CAD-based video games will also be presented in the same section. In the next section, the method of how the design team of the PUDCAD game approached the design problem will be explained based on the related educational theories. The preliminary design process and the contribution of this process to the final product will be explained in the method section. Finally, a detailed technical description of the final product, interaction decisions, application decisions of the educational methodologies will be discussed.

14.2 What Is Cerebral Palsy

Cerebral palsy is an umbrella term that covers a wide variety of disorders resulting in motor impairment (related to movement and posture) that occurred from a "defect or non-progressive lesion of the immature brain" (Bax 1964, p. 295). As Bax reports (1964), cerebral palsy is excluded from other disorders which can also affect movement and posture with these three differences: (a) not experienced for a short duration; (b) not caused by a progressive disease; (c) not caused by mental

Table 14.1 Summary of the physical impairments for ages between 6 and 12-year-old children (Palisano et al. 2007, p. 80)

Level	Abilities and limitations
I	Walks without restrictions; limitations in more advanced gross motor skills
II	Walks without assistive devices; limitations walking outdoors and in the community
III	Walks with assistive mobility devices; limitations walking outdoors and in the community
IV	Self-mobility with limitations; children are transported or use power mobility outdoors and in the community
V	Self-mobility is severely limited even with the use of assistive Technology

deficiency (p. 295). Krigger reports (2006) brain injuries that will lead to cerebral palsy can occur during the prenatal, perinatal, or postnatal periods of life. Most cases occur during the prenatal period either for unknown reasons or from birth complications such as asphyxia and these are some of the causes of cerebral palsy during the perinatal period (p. 91). Postnatal occurrence is mostly due to "brain damage from bacterial meningitis, viral encephalitis, hyperbilirubinemia, motor vehicle collisions, falls, or child abuse" (Krigger 2006, p. 91).

Studies to classify the severity of the motor disability in children affected by cerebral palsy can be dated back to the 1950s (reported by Palisano et al. 1997). Palisano et al. (1997) propose an alternative system based on "the concepts of disabilities and functional limitations" (p. 214). Gross Motor Function Classification System (GMFCS) which is based on the system of Palisano et al. is the current system that is used to classify the severity of the physical impairment of children with cerebral palsy. Physical disabilities and functional limitations can change according to the age group of the children, so GMFCS levels can have different definitions according to the age of the children. Krigger (2006) gives a very detailed overview and explanation of the GMFCS system in her article about the subject. Palisano et al. (2007) give a summary (Table 14.1) of the physical impairments for ages between 6 and 12-year-old children (p. 80). In PUDCAD game, the design team of the video game mainly relied on this summary while creating the concepts, game mechanics, and the narrative of the video game.

14.3   What Is Accessibility, Inclusive Design, Design-for-All, and Universal Design

Designers mostly prefer (or guided by the design brief) to design products, environments, and activities for a general audience like young adults to middle-aged adults, with average body height and weight, and physically able-bodied users because the largest amount of target users belong to that general population. This means at least some part of the population out of the target user group such as children, elderly, and people with several conditions of disabilities is excluded unintentionally, and they cannot use the final design product easily and effectively or at least they will experience some level of usability problems and need to work around to find a way to use the product. In this case, a design product can be an environment, a building, a digital application, or graphic design. Even in the information graphics area of the visual communication design field, it is possible to misunderstand the information conveyed by an icon, an arrow, or an information panel by an ordinary user who is a part of the general target audience.

Most of the time, the exclusion is not intentional. The process of design starts with deciding the main design criteria that lead designers to set main decisions which can be the user profile, functional requirements, and formal decisions that will shape the final product. Designers, mostly, are not educated to work with physical disabilities, as at design school, design problems are chosen from general problems rather than minor problems for educational purposes. Therefore, when they start working as design professionals, they are not accustomed to set inclusion as a design criteria.

The terms "inclusive design" and "universal design" sometimes used interchangeably. Clarkson and Coleman (2015) state that for the term "inclusive design," which generally means designing for the largest possible audience regardless of their abilities or age (including or engaging them to the activity or product), Europeans use the term "design for all" and in the USA the term "universal design" is used. As Clarkson and Coleman (2015) report, the aging of society and the motivation to integrate impaired people to society are the two main drivers of this design methodology.

There seem several designers establish different understandings of these terms. Holmes (2018a) from Microsoft explains these terms with an understanding that was developed in Microsoft, which is different from the understanding of Clarkson and Coleman. According to Holmes (2018a) accessibility is an attribute and it is defined as "the qualities that make an experience open to all" (para. 11), while inclusive design is originated from digital technologies such as creating audiobooks for deaf people and it is a (design) method (para. 12). Furthermore, universal design comes from architectural design (or several built environment design practices) and holds the meaning of "describing the qualities of the final design" (Holmes 2018a, para. 20) whereas inclusive design describes the way how the designer reaches to the final product (whether the design criteria and process focus on including the excluded population). Holmes (2018b) also discusses these terms in detail in the book named "Mismatch: How Inclusion Shapes Design." As a final word related to this terminology for a better understanding it can be said: to design a product, environment, or activity with universal qualities, the designer should adopt several interaction modalities to improve the accessibility of the final product to increase engagement with the excluded users by using inclusive design methods.

14.4 Literature Review

In this section, the literature related to several aspects of the subject will be presented in two parts. In the first part, the literature and knowledge base of psychological models about empathy and how it is possible for these models to be used as an educational method will be presented. In the same part several outstanding examples (best practices of applied video games) will also be presented. In the next part, the games which include some kind of in-game CAD-like design or modeling features will be presented. Some of these games also use these features as a part of the game mechanic but others use them just to create a technical looking atmosphere.

14.4.1 Raising Empathy with Video Games (Games for Change)

Empathy is to understand what other people think or how they feel or to understand the situation, condition, and circumstances from the first person's (the participant) point of view, rather than the third person's (the observer) view. The observer could conclude with misunderstandings or misjudgments if s/he judges the actions, feelings, or thoughts according to his/her own thoughts and experiences rather than the participant's thoughts and experiences. On the one hand, different people can conclude with different solutions under the same conditions according to their previous experience, education, feelings, biases, and prejudgments. On the other hand, it is essential but laborious or mostly impossible to create exactly the same situation and dynamics in real life because the setting and coincidences will not be the same.

A solution for this issue can be creating the exact same situation artificially and let previous observers change roles with participants to experience the same situation. As an educational strategy, this is called "role play." The roleplay model of learning is in relation to reflective learning and experiential learning. Reflective learning, as Boud et al. (1985) state, has three components such as experience, reflection process, and learning outcome. Experiences are personal feelings, thoughts, and behaviors of the participant. After any experience participant reflects on the previous experience by thinking about it, evaluating the experience, and breaking it down to understand the pieces of the experience. Experience and reflective periods are recurrent until some kind of outcome is generated. Changes in behavior and a new mindstate about the experience are the outcomes of the three-step process (Boud et al. 1985).

Experiential learning is the process of learning based on the participant's own experiences. Kolb (1984) defines experiential learning in four steps which are in a cyclic order. These are: (1) participant's own experience of any situation; (2) participant thinks about the experience and analyze it; (3) participant draws conclusion in which s/he can use next time a similar situation happens; (4) participant experiences similar situations with different behaviors for experimentation. In experiential learning, knowledge is created by the participant by transforming personal experiences (Kolb 1984).

Andersen et al. (1995) cite from Boud et al. (1993) that experiential learning is based on a set of assumptions such as learners construct their own knowledge and learning based on a particular social and cultural setting according to their own experiences which are the main stimulus for learning that is influenced by the particular context in which the situation occurred.

Although designing games particularly for change is not a very popular genre in game industry, there are some outstanding examples still being developed mostly by indie game developers. A large collection of genre can be found in http://www.gamesforchange.org/. Thinking in the frame of cerebral palsy and universal design principles, some games worth to be mentioned.

This War of Mine (2014) is a survival game that was inspired by the Sarajevo Siege during the Bosnian War between the years 1992 and 1996. The video game focuses on the daily experiences of the civilians who are trying to survive under the pressure of the military forces. The game gives a chance for players to empathize with the civilians who experienced the siege in Sarajevo by gamifying the situation.

Dys4ia (2012) is an abstract autobiographical game. The designer of the game tries to express the experiences of own gender dysphoria through the video game. The game focuses on the process of hormone replacement therapy and the designer narrates the emotional and physical changes or frustrations by reflecting gender politics, identity, personal responsibility, and personal development by a series of abstract mini-games.

Depression Quest (2014), an interactive story, was designed to spread awareness about depression, by narrating the experiences of a person suffering from depression. Also, Please Knock on My Door (2017) is a story-driven game to raise awareness and empathy about depression and social anxiety. The player controls the character who suffers from depression and social anxiety and tries to help the character to get rid of the problem. While doing this, the player experiences how people with depression and their friends and family feel like.

3D World Farmer (2006) is a farming simulation that aims to create an experience of the challenges of running a farm in a poor country. At the end of each round, the player realizes that it is becoming more and more desperate over time and it is impossible to survive. At the beginning of the game, resource management and simulation are the game's main mechanics, but as gameplay advances, the game begins to focus more on purpose and message than on a real simulation. It is a powerful idea to slowly raise the player's awareness of the challenges of farming in a poor country.

Auti-Sim (2013) is about an autistic child (game character) with auditory hypersensitivity. The player controls the character from the first-person perspective. While navigating around a playground, the character gets closer to noisy children or objects and this creates a sensory overload which was represented by audio and visual distortion. So that the player can experience and empathize with how the autistic child is affected negatively by the sound sources.

Sea Hero Quest (2016) is a game designed to collect data to let scientists understand the mental processes of three-dimensional navigation. This data then is analyzed to guess the level of a possible dementia level of the player. Although not every issue in three-dimensional navigation means the player has dementia, this is still a useful tool to understand the situation. The player rides a boat in a maze-like channel over a sea route to catch creatures, then s/he turns back and tries to point out the starting point which is way behind the player. This game was designed so that it will be faster and cheaper to collect data from anyone who played the game rather than people who have the chance and time to visit the laboratory.

14.4.2   Design Based Games and CAD-Based Games

Games are mostly designed for entertainment or educational purposes. CAD software, however, are dedicated to functionality. Although it is possible to define a very broad generalization, some researchers focus on the interactivity and engagement element of the two software groups. Kosmadoudi et al. (2012a, b) claim both systems can be similar in terms of engagement and they can interchange some elements as next generation CAD systems can borrow game-like interaction to break the limited satisfaction of complicated CAD interfaces. Although it is possible that some CAD system can borrow game-like interaction for a more entertaining CAD environment, otherwise is more common: borrowing CAD-like environment and tools into games.

In this part, maybe the most popular game is SimCity. SimCity is an open-ended city design, building, and simulation game series which was first released in 1989. This game puts the player into the shoes of a city planner and lets players make decisions about how a city can be planned and managed on a special map that represents a randomly generated geographical area. While playing SimCity, players start with the planning of the city by locating housing, business, and trade regions which were supported by the powerplant, airport, and harbors and connected by pedestrian paths, streets, and highways, all planned and constructed by the player. Players must manage the city as the mayor during gameplay (which represents years in game-time scale), and make decisions to make the citizens live happily while controlling the city economy, budget, disasters, and crime rates. Although the relations between these factors and simulations in gameplay are not precise, to foresee the problems in a real city, the game overall gives an insight into the factors to be controlled while planning and managing a city.

The game mechanics of SpaceChem (2011) are built up on the principles of chemical reactions (chemical bonds, ions, atoms, energy levels of electron orbits) and automation of the production processes as in a chemical factory. All these relations and knowledge create the parameters of a puzzle game in which players must control and solve puzzles for a successfully automated chemical production process. The idea is almost the same in Hello Quantum (2018) which is to gain an insight into how quantum computers and algorithms work while playing a puzzle game enriched with fun elements.

Fallout 4 (2015) an action role-playing game narrated in a post-nuclear apocalyptic universe and The Sims 4 (2014) a life simulation game have similar design and build modes for players to build their own architecturally designed structures. In Fallout 4 players collect items and materials from scrapyards and ruined structures to use to generate new material to be used while building new constructions. Whereas in The Sims 4, players purchase virtual items with virtual money to be used in their virtual structures which are designed and built by them. Both construction system works like simplified three-dimensional modeling software like the ones used in professional CADD software used in civil engineering and architectural modeling. The modeling tools are very simple and all construction workflow is based on predefined grid-based slots in which users can put construction materials and objects on the grid units. In this kind of a modeling environment, users can think of the spatial arrangement of the built environment in light of his/her personal decisions without concerned about the functional requirements of the architectural requirements list which is one of the important elements of the architectural design profession. Removing the functional requirements, a three-dimensional modeling software can be perceived as a playground that a player can use for personal expressive needs, which has no defined rules or missions.

The same kind of grid-based construction system exists in Minecraft (2009). Minecraft is an open world sandbox game which means the player can roam anywhere in the world without any restrictions and the world has the ability to be reshaped with the intervention of the player. In this game, all environments are based on cubes (voxels) and the player can create and remove voxels anywhere and anytime needed. This allows the player to construct structures made of cubes. In other words, Minecraft is a very simple three-dimensional modeling environment enriched with action-adventure features. A user can easily practice the basic flow of architectural design profession and modeling the architectural product in the Minecraft environment, unfortunately, the finished product will not be compatible with the details and construction techniques of the real environment, and it will not be possible to be built.

A very similar idea is Lego Worlds (2017) which is a sandbox video game. This time the player creates game worlds out of Lego bricks. The "brick-build editor tool" creates a similar CAD-like environment in which players can use to build environments or buildings out of Lego bricks. Modification possibilities are not limited to this. It is possible to modify terrain and environment by using landscape design tools.

Designing working machines or systems can be the subjects to be gamified. The three examples of these kinds of games are The Incredible Machine (1992), Kerbal Space Program (2017), and Besiege (2017). "The Incredible Machine is a puzzle game where the player has to assemble a Rube Goldberg-type contraption to solve a simple puzzle" (The Incredible Machine 2016, para. 1). The other two are more than puzzles. The player needs to design working machines to complete a functional mission. In Kerbal Space Program, players need to manage a space program in which they are assigned to design and built spaceships that will travel in the space that is restricted with real physics. Finally, Besiege is a physics-based engine-building game that lets players construct medieval siege engines.

These games are some of the examples that occupy the features of engine, game world, and system design and building that are enriched with a three-dimensional modeling feature borrowed from professional CAD modeling software. Although games mainly focused on world-building (or featuring the world-building as the main game mechanic) are not very popular in the current gaming industry, world-building is still a popular side-theme which gives opportunities for players to express themselves with their own creations and creating their own environment to fulfill their interest in designing environments.

14.5 Method

In the preliminary design period, the design team decided to prepare a workshop to discuss and think about the possible game ideas and scenarios. The 5-day workshop hosted by the University of Florence, Faculty of Architecture with the participation of the other stakeholders. Thirty-five design students coming from Turkey, Germany, Italy, and Finland attended the workshop. The students attending from Turkey were from the game design graduate program of Bahçeşehir University and were experienced in several aspects of game design. The other students have very little to almost no experience in either designing or playing games.

There were four goals of the workshop. The first one was to create an experiment to make familiar the workshop attendees to inclusive design methodology and universal design principles by designing a game. While trying to design the game, students had to analyze and adopt the inclusive design methodology and learn universal design principles, so that they can integrate all these into a game system with a scenario that reflects how the principles can be applied to an environmental context. The second is to create the opportunity for design students to experience to design games. As design experience in any kind of design field is very helpful for a design student to construct their own design knowledge, this workshop could be a chance to take look at how game designers work on a game design under time pressure and bounded by a brief. The next goal is to study and analyze how inclusive design methodology and game design principles can be gamified. This was one of the main goals of the design team. For a successful game design, it is essential to create and test various ideas. Testing is about the test of the playability of the game (can be identified as playtesting) and to see and decide if the particular idea adds value to the final product either as a fun element and an educational element. At the preliminary design level, to increase the creative and analytic power, thinking with seven student teams added value to the quality and variety of the created ideas. The fourth and last goal was to analyze what kind of scenarios can be created and to see if they can fit in the video game to be planned just after the workshop. This is very similar to the previous goal. In this case to make the game more playable, a good scenario and character profiles needed to be created. Although this will not affect the inner setup of microlearning units, an interesting scenario can help players to engage strongly with the game and higher levels of engagement can affect the attention and concentration of the player. This will result in a better transmission of the learning goals of the game to the player.

The workshop brief was to create a tabletop game in which the players can get familiar with the inclusive design methodology and universal design principles within a gamified universe. Thirty-five students divided into seven groups of five students each. In every group, one student was a game design student who is also from the Turkish student group. Professors from the stakeholders were responsible for mentoring the groups. The workshop was supported by several short lectures and presentations about various aspects of game design and universal design principles. After 4 days of the design period, seven groups presented their works as the output of the workshop as a part of the "Universal Design Practice Conference III_Design and Ergonomics—Designing for Inclusive Learning Experience" conference which was organized by UniFi. The ideas discussed during the workshop also helped the design team of the video game to gain insight into how the design process itself can be used as a part of the game mechanic to gain awareness about excluded groups and how the video game can be used as a training tool of inclusive design methodology without being didactic or boring.

14.5.1 Educational Methodology and Scenario of the Whole Day (8 h) Learning Experience

Woodbury et al. (2001) focus on using play as a tool for preliminary design teaching. This creates a playful design studio that supports the engagement of design students. Preliminary design studios can have similarities with the action of play, as most of the times students play with forms, shapes, colors, and ideas to present creative relations between concepts and their expressions. In PUDCAD project, the game is the main drive of design teaching.

Discussion and John Dewey's learning-by-doing (in other words experiential learning) methodology will be applied for the whole day experience as it fits the teaching environments of design (particularly architectural) education. The educational experience scenario is planned to start with a short presentation about universal design principles and cerebral palsy (approximately 40 min) to create a knowledge base and familiarity with the nature of the problem. After the presentation, students will play the PUDCAD video game for about 60 min. During gameplay, students will experience the physical disabilities of a cerebral palsy patient, and they will empathize with the situation in which cerebral palsy patients experience during their interaction with the objects and built environment around them. As the game mechanics of the video game is based on recognizing and correcting or improving the design errors in the (virtual) built environment, students will have the chance to improve or correct critical design errors in the game environment with a special editor that is featured in the video game. After gameplay session students and instructors will start discussions about the accessibility, inclusive design methodology, and universal design principles and problems experienced by the impaired people in the built environment (40 min).

Finally, instructors will assign a 4-h hands-on sketch problem to students to let them think and practice universal design principles and inclusive design methodology on a design problem from scratch.

14.5.2 Educational Methodology Among the Themes of the Game

Instructional scaffolding methodology is the connective approach within the different profiles and themes. Ninio and Bruner (1978) describe the framework of scaffolding, which is very broadly the expert assisting and transferring the knowledge to a novice in time. The amount of assisting decreases as the learner gains more knowledge, skills, and self-confidence. In PUDCAD game, while the player plays the first two profiles, the system (in this case the expert) will help or assist the player (learner) to recognize and learn about the inclusion problems. After successful completion of profile 1 and 2, profile 3 unlocks. While playing profile 3, the system will not assist the player. The player must recognize, identify, and solve the particular inclusion problem without getting any help from the game system. The player must play whole profiles and themes of the game for a complete learning experience.

14.5.3 The Educational Methodology Used Within the Particular Theme

Repetitive, spaced-out learning of small (micro) learning units in several contexts will be applied to help students gain the skills to recognize and identify the inclusion problems demonstrated in the virtual game environment. The spacing effect helps learners to memorize and learn the required skills and knowledge better. In this kind of teaching methodology, the tasks or the teaching sessions are short and distributed over time to let the learner make many repetitions. Greene (1989) and Crowder (1976) explain this phenomenon in detail. In the PUDCAD video game, in every theme, there are various design problems located intentionally. Every design problem is a microlearning session. It is planned that the players will experience, identify, and solve these design problems, and this will help them learn in a repetitive manner. For better learning gains, players must play all nine themes of the game for sufficient repetition.

14.6 Games Designed During the Workshop

During the workshop, a total of seven tabletop games were designed. Escape From the Campus is a Quake themed, two-player, grid-based board game. The game is about two characters who are trying to escape from the school campus just after an earthquake. One player plays each character. Every character has different skills and none of the personal skills is enough to escape from the building without the help of the other character, therefore, players have to cooperate with each other. Game mechanics are based on trading cards each turn and making a strategy due to their differences in skills and speed as quick as possible. The game has very high replayability, in addition, cooperation mechanics and the idea of creating design solutions to prevent a disaster have a high potential of contributing to the digital game (Fig. 14.1).

Fig. 14.1 The Games designed during the workshop. (Top left: A Short Daydream—Top right: Campus Challenge. Middle left: Crazy Granny—Middle right: Tsialidybi. Bottom left: The Match.—Bottom right: Campus Challenge)

The Match is a card game that has the theme of "what if." This game is designed for four players and tries to address color-blind people. Players choose a card set that has illustrations on surfaces which are drawn in black-and-white color with various themes such as animals or plants. Then each player chooses a color. Finally, the cards are laid on the board and the first one who collects six of the cards that are connected with the same color wins. Contrast recognition, alternative pictogram ideas, and symbol recognitions for color-blind people can be listed as a contribution to the game.

Fire Alarm is a four-player competitive game that is about scientists trying to escape from a science lab where an explosion occurred that caused temporary blindness and fire around them. As health resources, players have oxygen and carbon monoxide. The idea is players have to maintain a balance between the resources in order not to get poisoned and eliminated.

A Short Daydream is a four-player grid-based roll-and-move type of board game in which players are trying to reach a destination to get rid of a curse. As the story goes players understand they used to be bullying a certain person at school, who turns out to be a witch, and they were cursed by her.

Tsialidybi is about an alien invasion. Four players try to escape from an alien space ship where they are abducted. Players need to cooperate in order to win the game. Game mechanics are based on room unlocking and point-to-point movement with dicing.

Campus Challenge is about students that are on their first day on campus who are trying to reach their destination faster than other players. Characters of the game have various types of disabilities such as hearing loss, blindness, and walking disability. In every turn, players draw an event card to choose from a group of available obstacles to locate a certain obstacle on the board which can block another player's way to the destination due to the targeted characters' physical disability.

Crazy Granny is about a granny trying to find his husband in cruise ship. The game focuses on design problems that affect the elderly. Players travel in the game board with start-to-finish and roll-and-move mechanics. Players are also encouraged to think like the elderly while making their turn-based decisions not only to create empathy with the elderly but also to create a meaningful gameplay strategy.

14.7   The PUDCAD Game

The game has three profiles (different characters) and every profile has three themes (architectural environments) to be selected by the player. Therefore there are a total of nine different experiences. There is no story-driven connection between themes and profiles. All nine playable themes are unique challenges. These profiles are: (a) a teenager cerebral palsy patient using a wheelchair (Gross Motor Function Classification System-GMFCS-Level III); (b) a teenager with no physical disability, but with color blindness and experiences an environment in a foreign country in which s/he cannot speak the language and the information design of the environment

Table 14.2 Technical specifications of the game

Number of players	Single-player
Genre	Adventure (based on exploration and puzzle-solving)
General game mechanics	Exploration and puzzle-solving to earn achievement badges in a limited time (60 min)
Spatial dimensions	Three dimensional (3D)
Camera viewpoint	First person view
Camera degrees of freedom	Varied degrees of freedom based on selected player profile
Projection mode	Perspective
Reality mode	Three dimensional with perspective projection designed to run on a flat 2D personal computer screen
Character roaming freedom	In level roaming (character is free to roam anywhere in the environment limited by the level boundaries)
Environment limits	Level limited (environment is limited by the level boundaries)
Controller	Keyboard and mouse pointer
Main movement control keys	WASD (limited by design to imitate the impairment of the selected character profile)

is not designed properly (icons, language, color selection, etc.); (c) an adult inspector using crutches to walk, who is specialized in inspecting built environment with respect to their consistency with the universal design principles (Table 14.2).

Every profile has a special educational objective. Profile A and B consists of "experience-learn-solve" scenarios, Profile C consists of "experience-identify-solve" scenarios. The player will play with every profile in Profile A, Profile B, and Profile C order. To play with the Profile C (to unlock Profile C), at least one theme from each from Profile A and Profile B have to be successfully completed (one theme from Profile A and one theme from Profile B). After unlocking Profile C, the player can play any theme and profile combinations out of nine combinations.

Every theme has ten mandatory microlearning units (which are called missions or universal design problems to be unlocked) and several optional universal design problems (optional missions) which can be identified by the player during gameplay. The player will be rewarded with a "badge" every time the player successfully completes a mission (microlearning unit). The whole game has a total of 90 mandatory missions and several optional missions. To successfully complete a theme, the player must complete all ten mandatory missions in less than 60 min. To successfully complete the game, the player must complete all mandatory and optional missions in all themes.

An experience-learn-solve scenario (Table 14.3) has three steps. In the first step, the player explores the environment and encounters a design solution that excludes a target group (in this case people with cerebral palsy). This encounter can happen by chance or the player can notice the problem or at least the player can suspect that something is going wrong with the existing solution. The game system notifies the player automatically that an encounter with some kind of a design problem has occurred. Notification can be in the form of a visual signal such as a pop-up window in the center of the screen, a blinking icon, or a text message on the user interface.

Table 14.3 Experience-learn-solve and experience-identify-solve scenarios

Experience-learn-solve	Experience-identify-solve
Profile A & profile B (learning first):	Profile 3 (unlocks if the player can successfully complete at least one theme for each of the profile 2 and 3)
Experience the design problem	Experience the design problem
The system will prompt the user about the experienced design problem (problem unlocked)	Recognize and identify the difficulty correctly without getting any help
Open the designer's logbook to reach related information.	Logbook is optional
Read and learn about the possible solution	–
Solve in limited design mode	Solve in limited design mode
Earn badge	Earn badge
Continue to next mission	Continue to next mission

The second step is the activation of the microlearning unit. As the player has been notified by the game system that an encounter has occurred with a design problem, the player activates the microlearning unit to see the definition and the possible solutions to the problem. In this case, microlearning units are in the form of text and illustrations like the logbook of an architect. It is very common for designers and architects to carry small notebooks to take notes and draw sketches about the design problems, experiences, or historic places while they work or travel (mostly called a logbook). The definitions and suggestions in microlearning units are not the particular solutions of the encountered problem. Instead, it is expected from the player (in this case the designer) to create a solution for the particular problem within the knowledge base framed by the microlearning unit.

The third and last step is applying the proposed solution to the game system. The game system has a very simplified three-dimensional modeling and editing tool which can modify the existing physical layout of the game environment. This unit is called limited design mode and it imitates popular three-dimensional modeling software. As this game targets design students, to create a familiar design editing environment, a CADD-like software interface has been implemented by the game design team. The limited design mode is carefully balanced that the player cannot modify every object which can interfere negatively with the game flow. Instead, the objects to be edited and the limits of the editable environment were carefully considered by the game designers.

Experience-identify-solve scenarios (Table 14.3) are for experienced players. As game designers of the game are using the scaffolding methodology, for beginner level users (Profile A and Profile B) system helps them while finding and identifying the design problem. For Profile C, the player has to identify and mark the design problem on the game interface by herself/himself. The game system will only check if the identified design problem is already stored as a potential problem by the game designers. If the player identified it correctly the system will let the player activate the limited design mode and correct the problem.

Every profile can experience three environments (themes). All environments have been adapted from real architectural designs delivered by the stakeholders. While adapting, game designers modified the delivered architectural plans to fit in the learning goals of the particular theme. Missions (microlearning units) were created by modifying delivered architectural designs in such a way that to create problems violating universal design principles. In other words, game designers have received good designs and created bad designs from them to ensure that players create good designs again.

14.8 Interaction Decisions

In real life, people interact with their environment by movements, gestures, actions such as touching or holding objects, or moving in the environment. For able-bodied people—at this point, they can be called ordinary people—these actions, gestures, and movements can be classified as normal and ordinary. On the contrary, people who have disabilities—at this point, they can be called special people—need to create a special type of interaction with the environment and objects so that they can use them efficiently which was created for the interaction type of ordinary people. They clearly experience problems while creating their own interaction style in accordance with their special disability. They need to make an extra effort to learn or create their own interaction style with a world that was designed to have interacted with ordinary people.

Reflecting this idea to the designed game, designers decided to create a unique interaction style that is different from the industry-standard interaction schemes. For a first-person view game, the industry-standard for controlling the main character is using the keys WASD for character movement. In this case, W is used for forward, A for left and D for right move, and S is used for backward movement. This means a player who played a first-person view game at least once can get used to the controls used by the industry. For the game which is the case in this study, designers decided to create an unusual combination and interaction by using the keys to imitate the interaction of the disabled person with the wheelchair in Profile A. In other words, designers get rid of the ordinary key combination which imitate the movement of an ordinary game character, and they created a special type of key combination and interaction for the special situation of the physically disabled character. Key combinations imitate the wheelchair like A+E for left-forward-turn, Q+D for right-forward-turn, A to back-left-turn, and D for back-right-turn. To move direct-forward, the player needs to use Q+E and A+D for direct backward. In addition to these key combinations players have to "pump" the keys repeatedly to move continuously as the disabled person has to push the wheels of the chair for moving continuously. The same idea is used to imitate the crutch which is used in Profile C. To move forward with the crutch, the player needs to use A and D keys consecutively which imitates the crutch and the free leg of the disabled character in the game.

14.9 Conclusion

In this case study, the PUDCAD design team studied to raise awareness and empathy about the (intentionally or nonintentionally) excluded population by using a video game. The aim of the produced video game was to increase the accessibility of designed products, built environments, and even visual communication elements by using inclusive design methodology. The design team aimed to combine several instructional methodologies, in other words, the scientific knowledge base as the starting point of the design product, in this case, the PUDCAD game. This concept is called scientific design, which "refers to modern, industrialized design—as distinct from pre-industrial, craft-oriented design—based on scientific knowledge but utilizing a mix of both intuitive and nonintuitive design methods" (Cross 2001, p. 52).

Still, there is more room to measure the effectiveness of the designed product by means of the effectiveness as a teaching tool, as a tool to raise empathy and awareness, and as the usability and the relevance of the game itself. One of the most significant impacts of the PUDCAD game is: the game itself is about "to use design as a method to solve problems" which is probably the starting point of the design action itself. Implementing design methodology as a game mechanic is not a usual case in the game industry, probably because for the game industry, it is a very niche field and it is not very easy to implement the designing action into the game mechanics. Furthermore, design, by its nature, concludes with a "better/worse" situation rather than a "win/lose" situation which makes it very complicated to identify who wins and who loses. In this perspective, PUDCAD is a challenging experiment for the design and management team and probably one of the most unique examples of its genre.

Although the design team proposes the PUDCAD game as a solution to the research question "to raise awareness," scientifically, it is still questionable whether any game is effective in raising empathy or awareness if the player prefers to accept the experience as a game-only-experience rather than an educational experience.

Acknowledgments PUDCAD design team is Çetin Tüker, Güven Çatak, Bertuğ Benim, Poyraz Özer, Zeynep Burcu Kaya, and Yusuf Işık.

References

3D World Farmer [Computer Software]. (2006). 3D World Farmer Team. Retrieved from https://3rdworldfarmer.org/
Andersen, L., Boud, D., Cohen, R. 1995. Experience-based learning. In: Foley, G., ed. Understanding adult education and training, 2nd ed., pp. 225–39. Sydney, Australia: Allen & Unwin.
Auti-Sim [Computer Software]. (2013). Taylan Kadayifcioglu, Matt Marshall, Krista Howarth Retrieved from http://www.gamesforchange.org/game/auti-sim/
Bax, M. C. (1964). Terminology and classification of cerebral palsy. Developmental Medicine & Child Neurology, 6(3), 295–297.

Besiege [Computer Software]. (2017). Spiderling Games. Retrieved from. http://www.besiege.spiderlinggames.co.uk/

Boud, D., Keogh, R. and Walker, D., Eds. (1985). Reflection: Turning Experience into Learning. London, Kogan Page.

Boud, D., Cohen, R., & Walker, D. (1993). Using experience for learning. McGraw-Hill Education (UK).

Buratti, G., Amoruso, G., Costa, F., Pillan, M., Rossi, M., Cordan, O., & Dincay, D. A. (2018). PUDCAD Project. Towards a CAD-Based Game for the Implementation of Universal Design Principles in Design Education. In International and Interdisciplinary Conference on Digital Environments for Education, Arts and Heritage (pp. 154-162). Springer, Cham.

Clarkson, P. J., & Coleman, R. (2015). History of Inclusive Design in the UK. Applied Ergonomics, 46, 235–247.

Cross, N. (2001). Designerly ways of knowing: Design discipline versus design science. Design issues, 17(3), 49–55.

Crowder, R.G. (1976). Principles of learning and memory. Oxford, England: Lawrence Erlbaum.

Depression Quest [Computer Software]. (2014). The Quinnspiracy. Retrieved from https://store.steampowered.com/app/270170/Depression_Quest/

Dys4ia [Computer Software]. (2012). Anna Anthropy. Retrieved from http://www.gamesforchange.org/game/dys4ia/

Fallout 4 [Computer Software]. (2015). Bethesda Inc. Retrieved from https://fallout.bethesda.net/tr/games/fallout-4

Greene, R.L. (1989). "Spacing effects in memory: Evidence for a two-process account". Journal of Experimental Psychology: Learning, Memory, and Cognition. 15 (3): 371–377. doi:https://doi.org/10.1037/0278-7393.15.3.371.

Hello Quantum. [Computer Software]. (2018). IBM. Retrieved from https://apps.apple.com/us/app/hello-quantum/id1378385003

Holmes, K. (2018a). The No. 1 thing you're getting wrong about inclusive design. https://www.fastcompany.com/90243282/the-no-1-thing-youre-getting-wrong-about-inclusive-design (retrieved 19 September 2019)

Holmes, K. (2018b). Mismatch: How Inclusion Shapes Design. MIT Press.

Kerbal Space Program [Computer Software]. (2017). Take-Two Interactive. Retrieved from https://www.kerbalspaceprogram.com/

Kolb, D. 1984. Experiential learning. Prentice-Hall, Englewood Cliffs, NJ.

Kosmadoudi, Z., Lim, T., Ritchie, J. M., Louchart, S., Liu, Y., & Sung, R. (2012a). Engineering design using game-enhanced CAD: The potential to augment the user experience with game elements. Computer-Aided Design, 45(3), 777–795. https://doi.org/10.1016/j.cad.2012.08.001

Kosmadoudi, Z., Lim, T., Ritchie, J. M., Sung, R. C., Liu, Y., Stănescu, I. A., & Ştefan, A. (2012b). Game interactivity in CAD as productive systems. Procedia Computer Science, 15, 285–288.

Krigger, K. W. (2006). Cerebral palsy: an overview. American family physician, 73(1).

Lego Worlds [Computer Software]. (2017). Traveller's Tales. Retrieved from https://www.ttgames.com

Minecraft [Computer Software]. (2009). Mojang. Retrieved from https://www.minecraft.net/tr-tr/

Ninio, A. and Bruner, J. (1978). The achievement and antecedents of labelling. Journal of Child Language, 5, 1–15.

Palisano, R., Rosenbaum, P., Walter, S., Russell, D., Wood, E., & Galuppi, B. (1997). Development and reliability of a system to classify gross motor function in children with cerebral palsy. Developmental Medicine & Child Neurology, 39(4), 214–223.

Palisano, R. J., Copeland, W. P., & Galuppi, B. E. (2007). Performance of physical activities by adolescents with cerebral palsy. Physical therapy, 87(1), 77–87.

Sea Hero Quest [Computer Software]. (2016). T-Mobile. Retrieved from http://www.seaheroquest.com/site/en/

SimCity [Computer Software]. (1989). Electronic Arts. Retrieved from https://www.ea.com/games/simcity?isLocalized=true

SpaceChem [Computer Software]. (2011). Zachtronics Industries. Retrieved from http://www.zachtronics.com/spacechem/

The Incredible Machine [Computer Software]. (1992). Sierra Entertainment. Retrieved from https://archive.org/details/the_incredible_machine_1992

The Incredible Machine (2016). Retrieved from https://archive.org/details/the_incredible_machine_1992

The Sims 4 [Computer Software]. (2014). Electronic Arts. Retrieved from https://www.ea.com/games/the-sims/the-sims-4?isLocalized=true

This War of Mine [Computer Software]. (2014). 11Bit Studios. Retrieved from http://www.tlo.thiswarofmine.com/

Woodbury, R. F., Shannon, S. J., & Sterk, T. D. (2001). What works in a design game. *Supported by student reactions to being made to play, CAADRIA.*

Part IV
Case Studies of Computer Games

Chapter 15
The Relationship Between Cohesive Game Design and Player Immersion: A Case Study of Original Versus Reboot *Thief*

Ysabelle Coutu, Yangyuqi Chang, Wendi Zhang, and Sercan Şengün

Contents

Abstract Game design is a complex process, and it seems logical that the quality of the end product may be subject to the design approaches utilized. The aim of this investigation is to look deeper into fundamental design principles and identify if a cohesive, considered, and unified design philosophy can lead to a product that provides greater engagement and immersion to players. We look at the related existing research and analyze the Metacritic and Steam reviews of the 2014 *Thief* reboot (especially those reviews comparing the 2014 game to the original *Thief* trilogy) to illustrate the effects of a unified design vision on players' understanding of the game. Our findings indicate that players are primarily aware of the cohesive design decisions in each game and recognize the earlier game as having superior and more unified design.

Keywords Cohesive game design · Immersion · Thief game · Game design

Y. Coutu (✉) · Y. Chang · W. Zhang
Game Science and Design, Northeastern University, Boston, MA, USA
e-mail: coutu.y@husky.neu.edu; chang.ya@husky.neu.edu; zhang.wendi@husky.neu.edu

S. Şengün
Wonsook Kim College of Fine Arts, Creative Technologies, Illinois State University, Normal, IL, USA
e-mail: ssengun@ilstu.edu

© Springer Nature Switzerland AG 2020   349
B. Bostan (ed.), *Game User Experience And Player-Centered Design*,
International Series on Computer Entertainment and Media Technology,
https://doi.org/10.1007/978-3-030-37643-7_15

15.1 Introduction

As video games have been evolving as a medium, so too have these games' underlying design philosophies and processes changed over time. According to Kreimeier's (2003) summary of game designer Doug Church's design approach, several things must be observed when examining the concept of game design: first, it must be "applicable to the actual interaction structure and mechanics of a game, not to concerns related to marketing, production, or management." Second, game design should "have utility," addressing "specific and concrete issues occurring during the design stage of game development" (ibid.). Third, it should be abstract in that said method should be applicable to a large number of, if not all, game situations. Finally, it should have a formal structure. The design methodology of a given game is usually inherently linked to the quality of the final product, and over the years there have been a number of high-profile instances where games failed to perform as expected in the market, garnering poor sales, reviews, or both. While many factors serve to influence this, it seems in at least some of these cases design approach (specifically, failure to take the right type of design methodology for a given game) was one of the major contributing elements to game success or failure.

In this study, we analyze the design methodologies of the *Thief* 2014 reboot and their potential effects on player experience. All games in the *Thief* series are stealth games that are heavily dependent on simulating an environment and providing an immersive experience, which in turn is heavily dependent on underlying design choices made during the development process. While the original trilogy is often vaunted for its positive and long-lasting impact on the industry, the most recent entry in the franchise was met with a highly mixed reception. When attempting to diagnose why this might be the case, we noted that the original trilogy (especially the initial game, *Thief: The Dark Project* 1998) had a much different design philosophy to the reboot, and we hypothesized that this could be a major contributing factor to why the game did not succeed as well as it could have. By examining the reviews of *Thief* 2014, specifically in regards to player engagement and immersion, we explored the relationship between design methodology and product quality. We specifically hypothesized that a cohesive, considered, and unified game has the capacity to heighten player immersion and engagement, whereas a haphazard and incoherent game can lessen immersion and engagement.

15.2 Background

15.2.1 Cohesive Design

Such a concept that defines a cohesive, considered, and unified theme on drama writing has been available for a while. Lawson (1936) defines a concept called *root-action* that constitutes the reference point of the drama writing process. This was later picked up by Egri (1942) and turned into the more popular concept of *premise*. Egri argues that: "No idea, and no situation, is strong enough to carry you [the drama writer] through to its logical conclusion without a clear-cut premise. If you [the drama writer] has no such premise, you may modify, elaborate, vary the original idea or situation, or even lead himself into another situation, but you will not know where you are going" (p. 6).

In his book, The Art of Game Design, Schell (2015) discusses the notion of elements supporting a theme which he defines as "[...] what your game is about. It is the idea that ties your entire game together - the idea that all the elements must support." A central theme can be the outline of how a game will invoke sustainable interaction. Once a central theme is coined, all other design elements may be tested whether they serve to reinforce it. If any part of the game design element is obstructing or weakening the central theme, then it might require to be changed. Mitgutsch and Alvarado (2012) define this concept as "purposeful design" and suggest it as a backbone to assess serious games. Their case studies offer a successful game design as "challenging, reasonable, cohesive and coherent formal conceptual design that relates to the designers' intentions and to the purpose of the game" (p. 6).

However, a central theme should not be mistaken for a fail-safe formula to cater to all of the players. If a specific player personally does not enjoy the central theme, this may repel the player or have no effect on creating an attachment for the game. A study by Ryan et al. (2006) concludes that "there is a considerable variance between individuals in their overall experience of and motivation for computer games, and just as importantly, considerable variation within individuals as to specific game preferences."

15.2.2 Immersion in Games

Immersion has been an elusive term for video games as it has been scrutinized under very different aspects such as 3D spatial presence (McMahan 2013), perspective and point-of-view (Taylor 2002), agency (Frasca 2001), controller methods (McGloin et al. 2013), and narrative (Baranowski et al. 2008) among others. Certain concepts and terms can be mobilized by different researchers and fields interchangeably to identify nuanced experiences. Here, the immersion aspects we are looking at converge under three categories (see Table 15.1): immersion in the game rules and flow, immersion in the game's audiovisual world, and immersion in the game's story and characters.

15.3 Methodology

Our study mobilized forum posts and reviews as secondary data. We collected 70 Metacritic and Steam reviews that focused on discussing the immersion and

Table 15.1 Different uses of the term immersion

Immersion type	Related terms	References
Ludologic immersion in game mechanics and rules	Flow, Absorption	Sherry (2004), Zimmermann and Salen (2003)
Audiovisual immersion in game's graphical and aural atmosphere	Presence, Telepresence	Jennett et al. (2008), Cairns et al. (2006), Minsky (1980)
Immersion in the story and control on the story as well as the ability to change the game world	Agency, player, or narrative involvement	Murray (1997), Douglas and Hargadon (2000)

engagement of the game in comparison to its original version. The chosen material was selected if it expressed a player's opinion on the immersion and engagement of the game, whether positive, negative, or neutral. The participants articulated whatever they felt about the game after having played it.

The qualitative analysis follows the footsteps of thematic analysis as has been described by Spradley (1979) and Taylor and Bogdan (1984). According to this methodology, we treat each review as an ethnographic mini-interview and uncover patterns in the text that would later converge into sub-themes and themes. One researcher familiarized themselves with the collected data and created a codebook (MacQueen et al. 1998) for coding and theme identification (Patton 1980) of the reviews by three other researchers. Additionally, other pertinent data (such as the number of hours the player spent in-game and whether the player recommended the game or not) were also collected for reviews found on Steam, while a user score of the game (out of 10) was collected for Metacritic.[1] From both sites, researchers also noted how many people found each review helpful. These additional data helped inform the relevance of the review in question. We have also attempted to take bias in these reviews into account (e.g., nostalgia, etc.), as said bias could potentially skew results (this will be covered more in-detail in the Discussion section). Our research results should be supported by statistical formulae, such as calculating the statistical significance for scaling the accuracy of the data.

To augment our qualitative coding, we have also analyzed our code segments with AFINN-en-165 valence score library (Nielsen 2011). Additionally, we pulled insights from academic sources, such as Schell's (2015) book The Art of Game Design, to glean game designers' perspectives on this topic and find if preexisting theory and research either proves or disproves this study's hypothesis.

---

[1] The Metacritic scoring system utilized in this paper may be found here: https://www.metacritic.com/about-metascores.

15.4   Results

It is possible to posit the essential experience, or central theme, of the *Thief* franchise as: "*you are a master thief of stealth, subterfuge, and mystery*" as taken from the game's original promotional material.[2] The *Thief* games, at their core, are attempting to deliver this fantasy to players in a cohesive and immersive way. This unifying theme should thus be the driving force behind all design decisions for the game, from mechanics, to graphics and to narrative.

This study collected 70 reviews of 2014's *Thief* (35 from Steam, 35 from Metacritic, all selected by how useful other users found them). For Steam reviews, we attempted to ascertain if there is a relationship between the total hours a reviewer has played the game, and the number of players who feel the review is useful. By generating a line chart, a slight relationship was established (as shown in Fig. 15.1) that shows that the players who felt the review whether helpful or not do care about how long the reviewers played the game. The black line on the graph is the "coefficient of determination," represented by R^2, which is the statistical measurement of how two types of data are related to each other. The R^2 is between 0 and 1, and the closer R^2 is to 1, the closer the relationship between the two variables. In other words, the coefficient of determination can be represented by a line, and R^2 is the slope of this line; thus, the steeper the line is, the closer the relationship. In

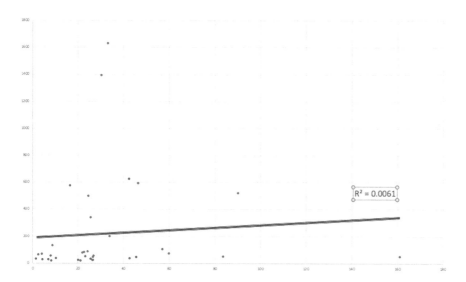

Fig. 15.1 A graph demonstrating the relationship between hours played and how useful a review was perceived as being, on Steam. X-axis: Number of hours a user spent playing the game. Y-axis: How many people found the review useful

[2]https://www.ttlg.com/Forums/showthread.php?t=149350.

this graph, $R^2 = 0.0061$, or 0.61%. This is not large, but still shows a possibility that peoples' opinions will be affected by the hours a reviewer spent playing. This result may not be significant for the overall population of reviewers, as this study contains only 35 pairs of data. As the research population increases, the results might be different, but for the scope of this data, we can determine that there is a slight relationship between the hours a reviewer plays the game and how many people find the review to be useful.

By far the biggest complaint from users was the lack of an interesting, coherent story in 2014's *Thief*. Thirty-one of 70 reviews (44.29%) cite poor plot and/or writing. Responses ranged from lukewarm to outwardly hostile, with many references to poor writing and dialogue, predictable twists, and uninteresting plot progression. For example, player #6 (P6) reports that the "story [was] a big yawn" and points out that the player character did not have any decent lines at all. P16 mentions that the existence of supernatural elements in the new game was a bad choice as compared to the realism in the original game. P19 criticizes the non-playable characters as being annoying. P21 simply concludes that "Thief [2014]'s story, setting, characters, and dialogue isn't even in the same league as the prior Thief games."

An equally common complaint found within the collected posts and reviews was the issues taken with level design, particularly in relation to linearity. Twenty-five of the 70 Steam and Metacritic reviews analyzed (35.71%) cite linearity alone as a complaint, while 31 of these reviews (44.29%) stated general issues with level design. P17 finds the character control to be "on-rails." P24 asserts that "remember all the things you love about the original Thief games: complex maps with multiple routes to success [...] it's all gone!"

Interestingly, the vast majority of reviews, both good and bad, indicate one of the Thief's major positives as high visual fidelity. Eighteen of the 70 total collected reviews mention graphics, with 16 or these 18 being positive. For example, P40 criticizes the bad level design, linear game play, artificial feel of game flow, and the lack of a sense of accomplishment while praising the graphics as stunning and "full of dark, moody environments and detailed characters."

When handling potential bias in reviews (see Discussion for more on this), this paper looked at whether the review suggested the user did or did not have major prior experience with the original trilogy, and their overall response to the reboot (either recommendation or score, depending on the platform the review was from). Figures 15.2 and 15.3 chart this relationship.

Finally, the results of the AFINN valence analysis can be seen in Table 15.2. Although the most extreme positive and negative comments were in the Steam reviews, as a total, they were found to be more sentimentally positive than Metacritic reviews.

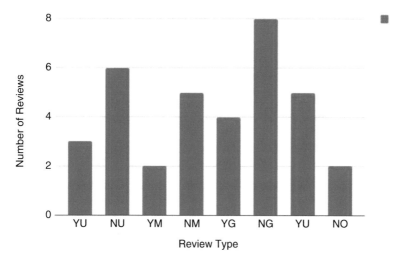

Fig. 15.2 Chart showing the number of Metacritic reviews based on prior experience with the original trilogy, and rating level. The categories are "Yes, Universal Acclaim" (YU), "No, Universal Acclaim" (NU), "Yes, Mixed or Average" (YM), "No, Mixed or Average" (NM), "Yes, Generally Unfavorable" (YG), "No, Generally Unfavorable" (NG), "Yes, Overwhelming Dislike" (YO), and "No, Overwhelming Dislike" (NO)

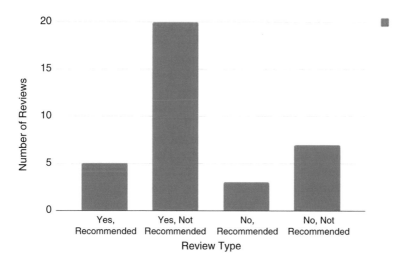

Fig. 15.3 Chart showing the number of Steam reviews either recommending or not recommending the game, in combination with prior experience with the original trilogy

Table 15.2 Measures of central tendency for the valence scores of the reviews in each platform and total

Source	μ	$\tilde{x}$	Mo	R	σ
Steam	0.3143	3	3	97 (−60/37)	20.765
Metacritic	−1	0	−3, 6	57 (−36/21)	10.894
Total	−0.3428	2	3	97 (−60/37)	16.594

15.5 Discussion

In order to examine the relationship between cohesive design and player immersion, the original *Thief* trilogy is compared with *Thief* 2014 as these games incorporate many cohesive design philosophies to create an immersive game experience. In the paper "Neo-immersion: Awareness and engagement in gameplay," Whitson et al. (2008) describe the term immersion as "a separation from the real world and the replacement of that world with a highly realistic simulation," which suggests that designs that simulate the real-world experience aim to deliver an immersion for players. The authors then present the idea of "loss of self-awareness" and "loss of game-awareness" as the two essential goals when creating an immersive game. In order for a player to lose self-awareness and game-awareness, a game provides him/her with an alternative self while avoiding the real world. A video essay, "Thief vs. AAA Gaming" by Dom Giuca (2014), describes *Thief* 2014 as an "overly simplified version of the original game," where the instructions were totally handed out to the players. For example, there are indications of hidden wires or locks inside the walls, whereas the original trilogy required players to find those game details themselves. Many players said that these changes made the experience less realistic, and that the added hints increased the game-awareness. In the real world, a thief will not have such hints but has to find ways to break-in to locations on their own. The design decisions in the original game, which are to limit the hints, are more cohesive with the thief theme and help to create a more immersive simulation for players.

The *Thief* series are stealth games that deliver a simulated experience of a thief to players, and aim to make that experience as realistic as possible through different designs. However, *Thief* 2014 failed to deliver the same experience as the original games, as the ratings are disappointing after it was released. Many players have mentioned in reviews and forum posts that they do not feel as immersed while playing the new game. In the paper "Doing While Thinking: Physical and Cognitive Engagement and Immersion in Mixed Reality Games," Hu et al. (2016) describe game immersion as "the sense of being absorbed in a game to the exclusion of all else outside of the game." As Giuca points out in his video essay, the original *Thief* game seamlessly delivers the story "through a natural dialogue between player and game," meaning that players feel immersed and less aware of anything outside of the story. This is achieved through many cohesive design decisions that reduced game-awareness for players. For example, the original game is known for letting the players find out how and where to use their gadgets. *Thief* 2014, on the other hand, simply highlights the surfaces that a certain gadget can be used on as a guide for players, which is less organic compared to the original. As a result of the less cohesive designs, players generally complain that the game felt more "gamey" and less realistic.

One issue to underline for this study is the potential presence of bias in users' reviews. A large subset of original *Thief* fans are predisposed to strong negative feelings towards the newer game, simply on the grounds that it is unlike the older games. Separating totally biased reviews from legitimate, objective reviews involving direct comparisons turned out to be a more difficult issue than initially thought, as the reviewer's intent and the extent of their bias are not always immediately clear or even able to be determined. However, even straight bashing of *Thief* 2014 could provide useful insights into genuine problems with the design methodology. Therefore, instances of bias ultimately had to be handled on a case-by-case basis. However, it is interesting to note that, while Metacritic seemed fairly balanced on the whole, Steam showed trends towards greater bias, as the vast majority of negative reviews came from individuals who had experience with the original trilogy. We had two possible methods to handle bias: one was to look for a word bank category that would help us filter out the biased comments, and the other was to categorize the reviews by players who have played the original game versus players who have not played the original game. We opted to utilize the latter approach, factoring in a player's previous experience with the original games in how they might perceive the newer game.

Problematic level design, particularly linearity in level design, was one of the most common complaints on Steam and Metacritic. Level design, in particular, is critical to the central experience of Thief, as this dictates how players interact with the world, receive content (such as narrative), and is vital to exploration (a central mechanic of many stealth games). Players seemed to feel that the linearity restricted player choice and was uninteresting, resulting in a decrease of player engagement. Furthermore, many reviews found levels and certain design decisions within them (such as the way rope arrows now work only in specific locations) to feel overly steering and "gamey." Players underline the original trilogy's more organic approach to level design and rewarding player exploration as being ultimately more compelling, since those games emphasized player motivation, thus reinforcing the essential experience (something the newer game seems to have failed at).

Plot seems to be a major contributing factor in players' perceptions of the games, and 2014's *Thief* received many complaints on this front. The presence of a lackluster plot actively clashes against the central experience of *Thief*; in order to fully convey the quintessential "thief" experience, a good central plot is necessary to provide players with a better connection to the game world. However, it is not enough for these games to have a good plot, as delivery also impacts a player's perception and consequent opinions. In his video essay, Giuca (2014) analyzes how plot on the original games was delivered through "excellent level design, art design, and sound design" without need of cinematics. 2014's *Thief* seems to lack this organic storytelling, even receiving a few complaints about the cutscenes it instead opts to employ. While not necessary for every type of game, plot seems to play an important part in user's perceptions of the overall game experience, and it seems that *Thief* 's design philosophy for storytelling failed to support the game's central theme.

One point frequently mentioned in reviews, both positive and negative, was the graphics, which for the vast majority were cited as being high-quality. Even in negative reviews, this was seen as a positive (if one of the only positives, especially in more negative reviews). Despite frequent mentions of this as a good feature of the game, most reviews mentioning good graphics still gave the game mixed to poor ratings (4 of 5 reviews on Metacritic retained a 5 or below score, and 7 of 11 reviews on Steam did not recommend the game). Two further reviews on both platforms cite the game as having poor graphics (and have an overall negative score for the game). This indicates that graphics may not be the defining factor that influences players in this type of game.

Many reviews of 2014's *Thief* also cite technical issues (i.e., bugs with gameplay and sound). While this is tied to the overall game experience, and can very much impact how a user feels about and decides to rate the game, it does not necessarily tie into design philosophy. Therefore, this study kept glitches in mind when considering overall results, but did not factor this into specific coding and analysis.

To conclude, while many elements must be harmonious to support a game's central theme, this study actually found that some elements may not be as important to player immersion, depending on game type and circumstances. We therefore believe it is important for developers to identify those elements that are central to supporting player engagement and immersion, and consequently focus on designing those elements with a cohesive and unified methodology in mind.

For a better understanding of the shift in design methodologies and subsequent player responses, a continuation of this research would likely involve a full comparison between Steam and Metacritic scores of the original three games versus the 2014 reboot. Finally, future studies may wish to expand their scrutiny to other games that similarly failed to meet expectations, in an effort to ascertain the extent of design methodology on overall product quality and critical reception.

References

Baranowski, T, Buday, R, Thompson, DI, & Baranowski, J 2008, 'Playing for real: Video games and stories for health-related behavior change', *American Journal of Preventive Medicine*, vol. 34, no. 1, pp. 74-82.

Cairns, P, Cox, A, Berthouze, N, Dhoparee, S, & Jennett, C 2006, 'Quantifying the experience of immersion in games,' In *Proceedings of Cognitive Science of Games and Gameplay Workshop at Cognitive Science*, Vancouver, Canada, July 26-29.

Douglas, Y, Hargadon, A 2000, 'The pleasure principle: Immersion, engagement, flow', *HYPERTEXT 2000 Proceedings of the Eleventh ACM on Hypertext and Hypermedia*. New York, NY: ACM, pp. 153-160.

Egri, L 1942, *How to write a play*. New York, NY: Simon & Schuster.

Frasca, G 2001, 'Rethinking agency and immersion: Video games as a means of consciousness-raising', *Digital Creativity,* vol. 12, no. 3, pp. 167-174.

Giuca, D 2014, March 16, Thief vs. AAA Gaming. *YouTube.* Available from <https://www.youtube.com/watch?v=jPqwDGXxLhU> [14 September 2019]

Hu, G, Bin Hannan, N, Tearo, K, Bastos, A, Reily, D 2016, 'Doing while thinking: Physical and cognitive engagement and immersion in mixed reality games.' In *Proceedings of Conference on Designing Interactive Systems.* ACM Press, New York, USA, pp. 947–958.

Kreimeier, B 2003, March 3, Game design methods: A 2003 survey. *Gamasutra.* Available from <https://www.gamasutra.com/view/feature/131301/game_design_methods_a_2003_survey.php> [14 September 2019]

Jennett, C, Cox, AL, Cairns, P, Dhoparee, S, Epps, A, Tijs, T, & Walton, A 2008, 'Measuring and defining the experience of immersion in games', *International Journal of Human-computer Studies,* vol. 66, no. 9, pp. 641-661.

Lawson, JH 1936 (2017), *Theory and technique of playwriting.* CreateSpace Independent Publishing Platform.

MacQueen, KM, McLellan, E, Kay, K, & Milstein, B 1998, 'Codebook development for team-based qualitative analysis', *CAM Journal,* vol. 10, no. 2, pp. 31-36.

McGloin, R, Farrar, K, & Krcmar, M 2013, 'Video games, immersion, and cognitive aggression: Does the controller matter?', *Media Psychology,* vol. 16, no. 1, pp. 65-87.

McMahan, A 2013, 'Immersion, engagement, and presence: A method for analyzing 3-D video games.' In *The Video Game Theory Reader.* Routledge, pp. 89-108.

Minsky, M 1980, 'Telepresence', *Omni,* June, pp. 45-51.

Mitgutsch, K, Alvarado, N 2012, May, 'Purposeful by design?: A serious game design assessment framework', In *Proceedings of the International Conference on the foundations of digital games.* ACM, pp. 121-128.

Murray, JH 1997, *Hamlet on the Holodeck,* New York, NY: Free Press.

Nielsen, FÅ 2011, 'A new ANEW: Evaluation of a word list for sentiment analysis in microblogs.' *arXiv preprint arXiv:*1103.2903

Patton, MQ 1980, *Qualitative evaluation methods.* Newbury Park, CA: Sage.

Ryan, RM, Rigby, CS, Przybylski, AK 2006, 'Motivational pull of video games: A self-determination theory approach', *Motivation and Emotion,* vol. 30, pp. 347-365.

Schell, J 2015, *The art of game design, 2nd edition.* AK Peters / CRC Press. Available from <http://proquestcombo.safaribooksonline.com/9781466598645> [14 September 2019]

Sherry, JL 2004, 'Flow and media enjoyment', *Communication Theory,* vol. 14, no. 4, pp. 328-347.

Spradley, J 1979, *The ethnographic interview.* New York, NY: Holt, Rinehart, and Winston.

Taylor, LN 2002, *Video games: Perspective, point-of-view, and immersion.* Graduate Thesis, University of Florida.

Taylor, SJ, Bogdan, R 1984, *Introduction to qualitative research methods: The search for meanings.* New York, NY: John Wiley & Sons..

Whitson, J, Eaket, C, Greenspan, B, Tran, MQ, King, N 2008, 'Neo-immersion: Awareness and engagement in gameplay', in *Proceedings of Future Play 2008*, ACM Press, pp. 220–223.

Zimmermann, E, Salen K 2003, *Rules of play: Game design fundamentals.* Cambridge, MA: MIT Press.

Ludography

Thief: The Dark Project, 1998, Looking Glass Studios.

Thief, 2014, Eidos Montreal / Square Enix.

Chapter 16
Empathy and Choice in Story Driven Games: A Case Study of Telltale Games

Barbaros Bostan, Önder Yönet, and Vugar Sevdimaliyev

Contents

Abstract In an attempt to find a meaningful relationship between choices in story driven games and the empathy of players, Empathy Quotient (EQ) questionnaire were used to obtain empathy scores of the 51 participants who played two chapters from one of the two Telltale games chosen for the study. The choices in these games were classified as hot and cold choices based on the hot/cold cognition dual system but the statistical tests yielded no significant relationship between the empathy scores of the participants and the number of hot/cold choices they made in the game. Data collected through semi-structured interviews that explored participants'

B. Bostan (✉)
Bahcesehir University, Department of Game Design, Istanbul, Turkey
e-mail: barbaros.bostan@comm.bau.edu.tr

Ö. Yönet
Bahçeşehir University, Department of Advertising, Istanbul, Turkey
e-mail: onder.yonet@comm.bau.edu.tr

V. Sevdimaliyev
Bahçeşehir University, Game Design Graduate Program, Istanbul, Turkey

© Springer Nature Switzerland AG 2020
B. Bostan (ed.), *Game User Experience And Player-Centered Design*,
International Series on Computer Entertainment and Media Technology,
https://doi.org/10.1007/978-3-030-37643-7_16

experiences through discussions about ethics, choices, and empathy in the games they played revealed four recurring concepts that contradict the assumption that players form an emotional bond with the story of the game they play and the characters in it. The repeating ideas identified during the qualitative coding process are: (1) the curiosity of the player, (2) the "not real" phenomenon, (3) the protagonist effect, and (4) role-playing value.

Keywords Empathy · Game choices · Story driven games · Player psychology

16.1 Introduction

Games are often framed as products bought purely for their entertainment value but emotions in games have attracted the interest of researchers in recent years. With the development of computer graphics and advances in game artificial intelligence (AI), the linear game experiences have evolved into games with stories or games with choices. As the player is provided a chance to select between a few alternatives that may affect the story or the virtual world, emotions and empathy in video games have become more important. It is critical to note here that games create a different kind of empathy when compared with the traditional media and the distinguishing feature of this medium is the ability of the player to change or affect the things that are happening in the game. So new questions arise for both the designers and the researchers: What happens when the player feels empathy towards the game characters? How can the player know what an AI controlled character is thinking and feeling? What leads the player to respond with sensitivity and care to the suffering of another character? When the player starts thinking and feeling from the protagonist's perspective (also called role-playing), does this affect the choices they make? Is it possible for an empathetic person in real life to transform into an egoist person as a player? In this regard, this paper attempts to investigate the relationship between the empathy of players and the moral choices they made in story driven games.

When we look at the etymology of "empathy," we can see that it is acquired from the Ancient Greek word "ἐμπάθεια" (empatheia). The meaning of "empatheia" is physical affection or passion. However, Edward Bradford Titchener first uses the word "empathy" in English in 1909 (Stueber 2008). He translated empathy from the German word "Einfühlung," which means "in-feeling" or "feeling into." The Austrian-American psychoanalyst Heinz Kohut approached empathy from the perspective of clinical theory and defined empathy as "vicarious introspection" or "the capacity to think and feel oneself into the inner life of another person" (Kohut 1959). Since the late 1970s empathy referred to the special type of proper vicarious emotion, which was more other-oriented than self-oriented (Batson and Coke 1981). A broader definition of empathy is provided by Batson (2009) who suggested eight different conceptualizations of empathy: (a) knowing another person's internal state, including his or her thoughts and feelings, (b) adopting the posture or matching the neural responses of an observed other, (c) coming to feel as another person feels, (d) intuiting or projecting oneself into another's situation, (e) imagining how another is thinking and feeling, (f) imagining how one would think and feel in the other's place, (g) feeling distress at witnessing another person's suffering, and (h) feeling for another person who is suffering. The conceptualizations of Batson are more suitable for interactive stories or story driven games, which aim to convey an experience rather than the interactive systems, which focus on exploring the game's mechanical depth (Fischer 2017).

Empathy is a multidimensional phenomenon and there are many different definitions from different disciplines as philosophy, psychology, and sociology. Nowak (2011) presented 57 diverse scientific definitions of empathy and Cuff et al. (2016) provided 43 different interpretations. This study accepts the basic definition well accepted by many researchers: Empathy is understanding and sharing the emotions of others (Davis 2018; Decety and Jackson 2006; Baron-Cohen and Wheelwright 2004). From a gaming perspective, others can be both the non-player characters (NPCs) and other players that the player can interact with. Another relevant debate is whether empathy is an affective or a cognitive concept. Generally, affective empathy is an emotional or reactive response to the emotions of other individuals and it is an instinctual reaction. Affective empathy is also described as emotional empathy (Davis 2018; Dziobek et al. 2008). As stated in Hoffman's (1987) definition, empathy is an affective response and more appropriate to another's situation than one's own. On the other hand, according to the cognitive approach, empathy is an understanding of the emotions of other individuals (Baron-Cohen and Wheelwright 2004) and it is a conscious attempt to put oneself in another's shoes. Ickes used the term "empathic accuracy" and defined as a one's capability to accurately infer the specific content of another individual's feelings and thoughts (Ickes 1993). In terms of the chosen games of this study, players are expected to react to the emotions of others or to understand them, whether the emotional response originated from an affective or a cognitive nature. The core of the non-critical interactions in the story driven games is caring about others and understanding how they will be affected by player decisions, which are important in fostering this sense of empathy (Ryan et al. 2016).

16.2 Theoretical Framework

In order to analyze player decisions in a story driven game, it is expected that players with high empathy will show prosocial behavior and players with low empathy will show antisocial behavior. In this regard, first the relationship between empathy and prosocial behavior will be summarized. Aiming to categorize player decisions within a story driven game, several different frameworks were analyzed and the hot cognition/cold cognition dual system is chosen for the purposes of this study. This dual system, which is supposed to facilitate the analysis of player choices in pre-scripted story driven games, is also explained in this section.

16.2.1 Prosocial Behavior and Empathy

We humans are motivated to helping others. Not only to humans, we also work hard to help and rescue animals. Why helping others is so important for us? What makes us help earthquake, hurricane, or war victims from other parts of the world? Helping is the completely voluntary act and it is a part of the prosocial behavior which consists of acts such as helping, sharing, cooperating, comforting, donating, caring, volunteering, and other positive attitudes which intended to benefit another. Many human behaviors can be explained by the empathy phenomena, and the lack of empathy is usually translated to antisocial behavior. Similarly, high empathic ability is assumed to lead to prosocial behavior. One of the first researches that focus on the connection between empathy and altruistic behavior was Krebs (1975) but it was difficult to diagnose whether egoistic or altruistic motivation caused to help others. Similar experiments on the empathy-altruism hypothesis (Batson et al. 1981, 1988, 1991) claimed that the prosocial motivation caused by empathy is aimed towards the final goal of increasing welfare of a person in need. But in a virtual world defined by the rules of a video game, are the players more interested in increasing their own welfare or the other's? It is important to note here that the morality systems of video games are inherently restricted and limited by ludic and business considerations where moral choices are usually flattened down into mere narrative flavoring rather than a reflection of an individual's ethical makeup (Heron and Belford 2014).

As stated by Batson et al. (1981), if you try to help another individual from a desire for personal gain or to avoid personal distress, then you are "egoistically motivated" and "directed toward the end-state goal of increasing your own welfare." On the contrary, if you help from a desire to decrease the distress or increase the benefit of another individual's, then you are "altruistically motivated" and "directed toward the end-state goal of increasing the other's welfare." You may be feeling empathy for another person and you may try to reduce his or her distress but if the end-state goal of your action is to reduce your own distress, this is not an altruistic behavior but an egoistic response. Altruism is utterly an unselfish act. Batson et al. (1981, p. 291) have three observations for differentiating egoism and altruism: (a) helping, as a behavior, can be either egoistically or altruistically motivated; it is the end-state goal, not the behavior, which distinguishes an act as altruistic, (b) motivation for helping may be a mixture of altruism and egoism; it need not be solely or even primarily altruistic to have an altruistic component, and (c) increasing the other's welfare is both necessary and sufficient to attain an altruistic end-state goal. Regarding these observations, games are also known for rewarding the act of helping others where increasing the welfare of others also increases the welfare of the player, which makes it more difficult to understand whether players are egoistically or altruistically motivated.

16.2.2 Hot Cognition and Cold Cognition

Hot versus cold cognition is one of the dual-system models used broadly in psychological science. Generally, this temperature metaphor is very well known in psychology and used to categorize emotion-driven and motivational processes against information-driven and cognitive processes. "Hot" cognition refers to affect-laden, emotion involved cognitive processes contrary to the "cold" cognition, which mainly related to logic-based, emotionless, rational, information-driven cognitive processes (Abelson 1963). "Hot" cognition is directed by feelings and desires, which linked with our motivations, and in conclusion, it affects our decision-making (Kunda 1999). Metcalf and Mischel classified "hot" emotional "go" system as "the basis of emotionality, fears as well as passions-impulsive and reflexive-initially controlled by innate releasing stimuli" and on the contrary, "cool" cognitive "know" system as "emotionally neutral, contemplative, flexible, integrated, coherent, spatiotemporal, slow, episodic, and strategic" (Metcalfe and Mischel 1999). However, according to the appraisal theory emotions are the result of evaluations, which makes "hot" cognition itself a little ambiguous (Scherer 1999; Roseman and Smith 2001). Players of a computer game also evaluate the situation they are in and try to guess the implications of their choices such as rewards or punishments in the form of experience points or gold, which may lead to a cold cognition oriented decision-making process.

There are also similar classifications in literature with different names. For example, another similar practice "system 1" refers to automatic, quick, and cognitively effortless operations in contrast to "system 2" which refers to more concentrated, controlled, cognitively effortful operations (Kahneman and Egan 2011). We used "hot" versus "cold" cognition system for classification of the major game choices in the selected games. The developers identified these major choices and they were also tracked for each player for demonstrating a summary of worldwide statistics on each one. After an analysis of the major choices provided in each game, they are classified into two categories: choices related with emotions like empathy, fear, anger, disgust, admiration, sadness, panic (hot cognition) and other choices related to cognitive processes as logical thinking, coherence, rationality, decision-making (cold cognition). For example, two different but similar events analyzed in this context which the player can choose is: "killing" or "not killing" an NPC. In this instance, the action of "killing" can be defined as "hot" or "cold" cognition depending on the particular game event and the emotional arousal state. It means that the action—"killing"—can be logical or emotional, based on game context. The games analyzed in this study were pre-scripted and story based, which simplified the categorization process. Besides that, the choices were analyzed from the players' point of view during classification.

16.2.3   Analyzing Games in the Context of Empathy

Research on empathy and games have usually been narrowed down to violent video games and aggression (Bartholow and Anderson 2002; Coeckelbergh 2007; Anderson et al. 2010; Happ et al. 2013) but other recent studies found that exposure to prosocial video games increases empathy and accessibility of prosocial thoughts, as well as decreasing reported pleasure at another's misfortune (Greitemeyer et al. 2010; Greitemeyer and Osswald 2011). But how do game designers create game choices that may be affected by the empathy level of the players and do the empathy level of the players really affect their choices? Games commonly use tragic events in order to create an empathic situation, such as an unfortunate accident or the loss of a character. This design perspective is quite in line with the famous proverb: "Before you criticize a man, walk a mile in his shoes." According to Bogost (2011) video games frequently ask the players to fill the "big shoes" by assuming powerful roles to achieve and experience great things in a game but Bogost (2011, p.19) also suggested that players should also try "smaller shoes":

> If a game about the Sudanese genocide is meant to foster empathy for terrible real-world situations in which the players fortunate enough to play video games might intervene, then those games would do well to invite us to step into the smaller, more uncomfortable shoes of the downtrodden rather than the larger, more well-heeled shoes of the powerful.

The games that allow players to empathize with the story or the game characters are still few since it requires intricate narrative design and believable non-player characters (NPCs). Recently, games started to use more emotion-driven narrative stories. Choice-based games give the player the chance to be more interactive and emotionally responsive during the gameplay. Meaningful choices help players to contact the game characters personally and empathize with them. Given below are some significant examples from the games industry.

This War of Mine (11 bit studios 2014) is a point and click survival-management war game created by 11 bit studios. The game is based on the siege of Sarajevo, Bosnia and inspired by the stories of real war victims. This War of Mine is one of the unique games, which gives the player a chance to look at war from a totally different perspective. Focusing on the civilian experience of war rather than common soldier's point of view in order to show the horrors of war. The player controls a group of civilians trying to stay alive in a city surrounded by the enemy.

That Dragon, Cancer (Numinous Games 2016) is a documental point and click exploration game that demonstrates the experience of parents supporting their five-year-old son Joel, who fights against cancer. The designer of the game Ryan Green is the father of Joel. The game consists of several short vignettes that show the Greens' tragedy. This game gives player a chance to look at all these events from the perspectives of parents and even doctors.

16.2.4 Selected Games: The Walking Dead and the Wolf Among Us

The two games selected for this study are The Walking Dead (Telltale Games 2012) and The Wolf Among Us (Telltale Games 2013), both developed by Telltale Games. Although they do not emphasize puzzle solving but focus on story and character development, both games are classified as episodic adventure video games. The Walking Dead is based on The Walking Dead comic book series and tells the events occurring shortly after the onset of a zombie apocalypse in Georgia. Lee Everett is the protagonist of the story, convicted for murder and being transferred to prison. The vehicle transporting Lee hits a zombie and crashes, he manages to escape and later finds a little girl named Clementine, and promises to help her find her parents. The Wolf Among Us is based on Fables comic book series, which features various characters from fairy tales and folklore that are living in a close community within New York City known as Fabletown. The protagonist of the story is the Sheriff Bigby Wolf, known as Big Bad Wolf in fairy tales, investigating the murder of a woman. Assuming that the setting of a game may affect the nature of player choices in a game, both games are used in the study where one features a post-apocalyptic Georgia and the other takes place in a hidden, magical community in New York.

These games have a special cartoon-like art style, which separates it from a realistic appearance. Both are story driven games and they are also classified as interactive movies with special emphasis on ethical decisions and interpersonal relationships. They can also be defined as story driven emotional experiences that use the Choose Your Own Adventure (CYOA) concept very successfully. Telltale tagline at the beginning of each game is: "This game series adapts to the choices you make. The story is tailored by how you play." Steam also announces one of the key features of Telltale games as: "Now, it's not only WHAT you choose to do that will affect your story, but WHEN you choose to do it." Conversation with characters is established via dialogue choices where player decisions play an important role. When the players focus on the action on-screen, it is questionable if they are going to show reactive responses to the emotions of other individuals (Newman 2002). So, the major choices in the storyline of Telltale games are usually given in off-line moments to make the player feel both emotional and cognitive empathy towards the characters (Smethurst and Craps 2015).

The selected games offer meaningful choices for the player but in terms of story structures they are more like an illusion of a choice. Player's relationship with the characters is affected by the choices but the game remains the same without a direct impact to the game's narrative. In order to motivate the player to make moral decisions for moral reasons, both games try to give the player a strong moral identity to role-play, which is defined as an effective way of achieving that end (Ryan et al. 2016). The role-playing value does not create branches in the storyline but aims to create persistent responses in the NPC dialogue options. For example, at the beginning of the Wolf Among Us game, the protagonist Sheriff Bigby responds to a public disturbance. After a small conversation with a character in front of the

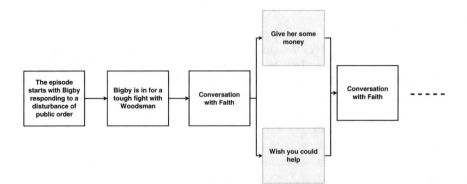

Fig. 16.1 Choice tree of the wolf among us episode one opening

building, the player heads upstairs and faces another character, Woodsman, who hits a woman. It does not matter how the player handles the conversation here, the game forces the player to fight with Woodsman. After the situation is under control, the player will learn that the woman, Faith, is a prostitute who wants his money back from Woodsman. At this point, the player must choose between "Give her some money" or just saying "Wish I could help." If the player chooses to give his money to Faith, he/she will not have a chance to use money in another point of the game. And after this major choice, the story unfolds the same way it was designed to be (see Fig. 16.1 above). The story do not branch but the game aims to create a bond between the player and the women in distress, who will be murdered later and the player will be responsible for the investigation of her death.

16.3 Participants and Methodology

Participants were volunteers from a Turkish university and they were interviewed on which Telltale games they have played before, if they played any. The selection criterion of students is that they should not have played at least one of the selected games (The Wolf Among Us or The Walking Dead) before. Those that played both games did not participate in the study and if they played one of the games before, the game that they have not experienced is selected for them. Those that have not played both games were randomly assigned to one of the two video games. At the end, 51 students (11 women, 40 men) participated in the study (mean age 21 years). Before they know the specifics of the experiment, informed consents were obtained from the participants and they were instructed to complete The Empathy Quotient (EQ) questionnaire. The measurement of empathy is a serious challenge for researchers from different disciplines and the selected EQ scale defines empathy as "the drive to identify another person's emotions and thoughts, and to respond to these with an appropriate emotion" (Baron-Cohen and Wheelwright 2004, p. 361). A team of research assistants recorded the scale results and then the participants were informed that they would take part in a study where they have to play two episodes from a selected game. During the gaming sessions all participants were tested individually and the gameplays (4–5 h for each participant) were recorded for future analysis.

There were 11 major choices for The Wolf Among Us and 10 for The Walking Dead, which were identified and tracked by the developers. The players can review their choices at the end of each chapter and see what percentage of other players made the same choice. These major choices were analyzed by three researchers separately and coded as either a cold cognition choice or a hot cognition choice. The codes were compared for inter-coder reliability and choices that were coded differently were removed from the study. At the end, 7 choices from The Wolf Among Us and 8 choices from The Walking Dead were retained in the study. The recorded gameplay videos were analyzed by both researchers: (1) to detect the dialogue options they chose, (2) to identify the major choices they made, and (3) to determine their response time to important choices provided by the game. During the gameplay analysis, interview questions were identified and notes were taken for each participant. Then the participants were called again for semi-structured interviews where the researchers discussed the choices they made, the emotions they felt while playing the game and the empathy they felt towards the game characters.

16.4 Findings and Discussion

16.4.1 Statistical Tests

Our hypothesis was that the number of hot or cold choices made by the participants would have a relationship with their empathy score. In other words, we wanted to analyze if the total number of hot or cold choices differed due to the empathy score of the participant. More specifically, we wanted to see if there is a significant difference between participants of high/low empathy in regard to the total number of hot or cold choices they made. Empathy score of the participants is a continuous (scale) variable, which ranges between 1 and 80 in the questionnaire. "Hot-Total" is conceptualized as "the total number of hot choices a player makes in the game." These are the choices coded as choices of hot cognition in the qualitative coding process. "Cold-Total" is conceptualized as "the total number of cold choices a player makes in the game." These are the choices coded as choices of cold cognition in the qualitative coding process. After such conceptualization and operationalization, we firstly started to check if any meaningful relationships existed between Empathy and "Hot-Total" or Empathy and "Cold-Total" as we have predicted in our research hypothesis.

Accordingly, we have searched for any meaningful bivariate correlations among Empathy, Hot-Total, and Cold-Total. As shown in Table 16.1, there were no

Table 16.1 Bivariate correlations among Empathy, Hot-Total, and Cold-Total

		Empathy	Hot-Total	Cold-Total
Empathy	Pearson correlation (r)			
	Sig. (2-tailed)			
	N			
Hot-Total	Pearson correlation (r)	−0.033		
	Sig. (2-tailed)	0.821		
	N	51		
Cold-Total	Pearson correlation (r)	−0.069	−0.915*	
	Sig. (2-tailed)	0.628	0.000	
	N	51	51	

*Correlation is significant at the 0.01 level (2-tailed)

Table 16.2 Relationship between two-levels of Empathy and two-levels of Hot-Total

		Hot-Total		Total
		Low number of hot choices	High number of hot choices	
Empathy	Low	11	12	23
	High	12	16	28
Total		23	28	51

Chi-square $= 0.126$, df $= 1, p > 0.05$

meaningful bivariate correlations either between Empathy and "Hot-Total" or Empathy and "Cold-Total" in spite of being predicted to exist ($p > 0.05$). Besides, a meaningful, strong (Pallant 2013) bivariate negative correlation between "Hot-Total" and "Cold-Total" ($p < 0.001$) has been observed as predicted as the normal consequence of the conceptualizations of the two concepts.

Secondly, we have categorized Empathy, Hot-Total, and Cold-Total in two sub-categories to check whether we could identify any meaningful relationships among these variables. Accordingly, Empathy has been divided as Low vs. High, based on the average empathy of participants. Hot-Total has been divided as Low Number of Hot Choices vs. High Number of Hot Choices, based on the average number of hot choices made by the participants; and Cold-Total has been divided as Low Number of Cold Choices vs. High Number of Cold Choices, based on the average number of cold choices made by the participants. Then crosstabs and Pearson Chi-Square tests have been applied with these new categorical variables. However, again no meaningful relationship has been found between Empathy and Hot-Total ($X^2 = 0.126$; df=1, $p > 0.05$] and Empathy and Cold-Total ($X^2 = 0.345$; df=1, $p > 0.05$] as shown in Tables 16.2 and 16.3.

Thirdly, we have categorized Empathy in four sub-categories (namely: Low, Average, Above Average, and High) just like it was done in the original question-naire. Then, again, we checked if we could identify any meaningful relationships between those sub-categories of Empathy and total number of hot choices in the game (Hot-Total) or total number of cold choices in the game (Cold-Total). In other words, we wanted to see if the total number of hot or cold choices in the

Table 16.3 Relationship between two-levels of Empathy and two-levels of Cold-Total

		Cold-Total		
		Low number of hot choices	High number of hot choices	Total
Empathy	Low	8	15	23
	High	12	16	28
Total		20	31	51

Chi-square $= 0.345$, df $= 1$, $p > 0.05$

Table 16.4 Relationship between four-levels of Empathy and Hot-Total or Cold-Total

		Hot-Total	Cold-Total
		Mean	Mean
Empathy (four categories)	Low[a]	4.64	2.93
	Average[a]	4.55	2.87
	Above Average[a]	4.50	2.50
	High	–	–
	Total	4.57	2.84

[a]MANOVA $p > 0.05$; The Empathy categories which have been indicated with the same superscripts do not differ significantly ($p > 0.05$) within the Hot-Total or Cold-Total

Table 16.5 Relationship between four-levels of Empathy and the player choice for choice #13

		C13		
		Revive Larry	Kill Larry	Total
Empathy (four categories)	Low	8	0	8
	Average	5	8	13
Total		13	8	21

Chi-square $= 7.953$, Phi $= 0.615$, df $= 1$, $p < 0.05$, two-tailed Fisher's exact test

game differed due to different levels of Empathy. As shown in Table 16.4, the one-way unrepeated MANOVA test between these Empathy categories and the hot/cold choice totals also yielded no significant relationship [F (4, 94) $= 1.85$, $p > 0.05$; Wilks' $\Lambda = 0.859$, partial $\eta^2 = 0.07$].

According to the findings all above, we concluded that the hot/cold dual system and the analysis based on the total number of hot/cold choices players made might not be working. So, at this final stage, instead of looking at the total number of hot/cold choices, we decided to take a look at each individual choice for a relationship between the choice and the empathy scores of the individuals with four categories (low/average/above average/high). Among the 21 choices in the selected games, only two of them show a significant relationship between the player choice and empathy, these choices are chronologically the 13th and 14th choices in the study and we named them as C13 and C14, respectively. Both choices are from The Walking Dead game and the findings are shown in Tables 16.5 and 16.6.

In Table 16.5, the relationship between four-category-empathy and the player choice (being revive or kill Larry) in choice #13 is analyzed. The relationship

Table 16.6 Relationship between four-levels of Empathy and the player choice for choice #14

		C14		
		Killed both brothers (YES)	Killed both brothers (NO)	Total
Empathy (four categories)	Low	1	7	8
	Average	9	4	13
Total		10	11	21

Chi-square = 6.390, Phi = -0.552, df = 1, $p < 0.05$, two-tailed Fisher's exact test

between these variables has been found to be significant ($X^2 = 7.953$; df = 1, $p < 0.05$, two-tailed Fisher's exact test), strong ($|Phi| > 0.50$), and in the diagonal cells. Accordingly, having low level of empathy making it more likely that the player's #13 choice is to revive and having average level of empathy making it more likely that the player's #13 choice is to kill.

This is a choice in the Walking Dead game where the NPC character Larry suffers a massive heart attack, dropping to the floor unconscious and appears to have stopped breathing. The Walking Dead Wiki[1] defines Larry as: "Though he mainly cares about the safety of his daughter and generally has good intentions, his loud, cantankerous, obstreperous, and judgmental attitude causes him to be a thorn in the side of most of the group." The player now has two choices: to help and revive Larry or assuming that it is too late to help him, killing him before he reanimates as a zombie. In this fictional setting, one becomes a zombie upon death irrespective of the manner in which one dies. So, killing Larry is coded as a cold choice since it is the rational and logical way to deal with the situation at hand and reviving Larry is coded as a hot choice, an action related with either the panic of losing a major character or the sympathy felt towards him. Although it can be concluded that players with low empathy choose to revive Larry and players with average empathy choose to kill the character, this correlation fails to explain a meaningful relationship between the empathy of players and the choice provided by the game. It can also be argued that players with low empathy should choose to make the rational choice and kill him but the relationship shows the opposite.

In Table 16.6, the relationship between four-category-empathy and the player choice (whether the player killed both brothers or not) in choice #14 is analyzed. The relationship between these variables has been found to be significant ($X^2=6.390$; df = 1, $p < 0.05$, two-tailed Fisher's exact test), strong ($|Phi| > 0.50$), and in the off-diagonal cells. Accordingly, having average level of empathy making it more likely that the player's #14 choice is killing both brothers and having low level of empathy making it more likely that the player's #14 choice is not killing both brothers.

This choice in the Walking Dead game is related with two major characters, Danny St. John and Andrew St. John. In the game, the St. John family lures unwary survivors into their farm to murder them, dismembering and trading their meat

---

[1] https://walkingdead.fandom.com/wiki/Larry_(Video_Game), Accessed on 01.08.2019.

to bandits in return for protection and supplies. The Walking Dead wiki[2] defines Andrews as: "... a cannibal who hides his true nature behind a kind and caring personality," whereas defines Danny as: "Unlike his mother and brother, who appear to commit their horrendous actions out of necessity and to survive, Danny is more sadistic and appears to relish in violence and killing and takes sick pleasure in toying with his victims before dismembering them into human meat." Killing both brothers is coded as a cold choice since the player assesses the situation and makes the rational choice since both brothers pose a danger to everyone. Not killing both brothers is coded as a hot choice since the player empathizes with their situation and desperation, deciding to spare one or both of them. Although it can be concluded that players with low empathy choose not to kill both brothers and players with average empathy choose to kill both brothers, this correlation again fails to explain a meaningful relationship between the empathy of players and the choice provided by the game. It can also be argued that players with low empathy should choose to make the rational choice and kill both brothers but the relationship shows the opposite.

16.4.2   Qualitative Analysis

The semi-structured interviews conducted for this study explored participants' experiences through discussions about ethics, choices, and empathy in the game they played. All interviews were recorded and transcribed for further analysis. Although the players were expected to form an emotional bond with the story of the game they play, four recurring concepts that contradict this assumption were identified during the qualitative coding process:

- The curiosity of the player
- The "not real" phenomenon
- The protagonist effect
- Role-playing value

The first repeating idea is the curiosity of the player. Some players wish to see what will happen if they make a good or bad choice and they were just experimenting with the game.

> If I made a very bad choice in the game, I made it because I wanted to see what would happen next. Sometimes, I just play the bad guy to play the bad guy. (P3, male)

> I tried to see the consequences of my choices, both for good and bad choices. I wondered how the game would progress. (P4, male)

> I do not do the right things in the game. I made different choices to experience different things. (P7, male)

---

[2]https://walkingdead.fandom.com/wiki/Larry_(Video_Game), Accessed on 01.08.2019.

Sometimes I do the things I can't do in real life. Normally, I am not an aggressive person but I tried to experience being aggressive in this game. (P8, female)

I intentionally made the wrong choices to see what will happen. (P36, male)

The second repeating idea is named as the "not real" phenomenon. Some players classified their experience as "just a game," so they do not feel themselves responsible for their actions and do not feel empathy towards the game characters.

I was not trying to the right thing in the game because I know that it does not effect my real life in any way. (P3, male)

I know that it was just a game and I am usually not carried away by the events of the game. (P4, male)

This is not real life. I can lie, I can do whatever I want at that moment. (P11, male)

I was not trying to the right thing because it is just a game. (P13, male)

I killed some characters because I wanted to kill them, it is just a game. (P23, male)

I am not responsible for my actions because this is a game and I tried to make the choices that I can't make in real life. (P30, female)

I never regret my choices in a game because I know that it is just fiction, just like a movie. (P37, male)

The third repeating idea is named as the protagonist effect because some players only focus on the character they play, the protagonist of the story, and their choices depend on the empathy they feel for him/her. Special emphasis was given on the control of a character. Kway and Mitchell (2018) also reported that players feel the need to ensure that their actions led to a consistent characterization of their playable character.

I was trying to feel what the protagonist should feel at the moment but I do not care for the other characters since I am not controlling them. (P5, male)

I feel more empathy towards the protagonist of the story since I play him. (P15, female)

I feel more empathy towards the protagonist because I was making choices for him and I was playing him. (P17, male)

There was only one playable character so I just feel empathy towards him. (P18, male)

You see the NPCs occasionally and you either forget them or ignore them. I feel more empathy towards the protagonist. (P40, male)

You see the world through the protagonist's eyes so you feel more empathy towards him, as for the other characters I do not feel much. (P45, male)

The fourth repeating idea was the role-play value. They imagine a role for themselves (good or bad) and try to role-play it throughout the game. In the case of The Wolf Among Us, the game gives the player a tough guy with a dark past, the Big Bad Wolf and The Walking Dead give the player a criminal convicted for murdering a state senator who slept with his wife, Lee Everett.

I do not remember most of my choices but I know that I focused on role-playing myself. (P8, female)

I tried to make the decisions my character should make. Even if my decision looks like a bad one, I chose it if it suits my character. (P12, male)

I focused on what I aim and try to make the choices the game expects of my character. (P13, male)

I was trying to role-play a bad guy, a villain. So, I do not feel empathy in any of my choices. (P19, male)

I made the choices that are 'right' for my character. I feel connected to him. (P20, female)

I tried to put my empathy aside because there is a goal to achieve and a character to role-play (P32, male)

16.5   Conclusion

Games are complex goal oriented systems where players engage in an artificial conflict that results in a quantifiable outcome. Player's motivation to reach a goal is influenced by both personal and situational factors. The needs, motives, and goals of the player are effected by the opportunities and incentives provided by the virtual world (Bostan 2009). People play games to win and to have fun in the process and this does not mean that they have to do the "right" or "moral" things that they would do in their real lives. Although story driven games are designed to strengthen the emotional bond between the player and the game, players are still constrained by the rules and the mechanics of the game. Formal constraints of a game determine the invisible borders of what "makes sense" to do within the limits of the narrative and the overall genre of the digital text (Mateas 2004). Players have their own agendas; their own goals and they expect to be rewarded at the end regardless of the nature of their choices. The classical psychological constructs such as the hot/cold cognition dual system might not work in the context of games because player decision-making process is different than how they make their decisions in real life. They usually evaluate what they will lose or what they will win at the end of a choice and they know that it is just a game, it is "not real," which is one of the recurring concepts identified by the semi-structured interviews of this study. This may also be the result of extremely shallow choice systems of games, offering few genuine opportunities for real moral reflection (Heron and Belford 2014).

When the player knows that the events that unfold in front of his/her eyes are "not real," they are also inclined to experiment with the game, such as making choices that they would never make in the real life or intentionally making a bad decision just to see what will happen next. This curiosity factor determined in the qualitative analysis of this study is also related with the fun value of a game. Some people like to experiment with the game, testing the limits of the narrative and the game mechanics. Belman and Flanagan said that people are likely to empathize only when they make an intentional effort to do so at the beginning of the game but most people play unempathetically (Belman and Flanagan 2010). With this inclination to play a game without empathy, to truly challenge a player's ethical reasoning a game should give the player opportunities to reflect, learn and improve, just as they would learn to improve other physical or intellectual skills (Ryan et al. 2016). In this regard, the protagonist of the story also effects how people make their decisions in a game. Some people like to step into the shoes of the protagonist so that they make choices not as themselves but as the character they play in a fictional world. This protagonist effect is closely related with the role-playing value identified during the interviews of this study. Some players imagine a fictional role for themselves and like to make their decisions within the boundaries of this role, which they found enjoyable. The findings of this study are also in accordance with the fact that getting the player to break the habits cultivated by playing dozens of morally inert, amoral games is not an easy task because most of the players already learned to ignore the moral dimension of their in-game behavior in favor of maximizing ludic outcomes (Ryan et al. 2016).

It should also be noted that the empathy scores of players in this study reflect the level of empathy they have in real life but players do not have to replicate their personalities in a fictional world. People of high empathy may simply experiment with the game or may desire to role-play a very different type of person since they know that this is just a game. Similarly, people of low empathy may feel connected to the protagonist of the story and make empathetic decisions that will benefit the character they play. Turkle explained this phenomenon with the differences between the "real self" and the "second self," pointing out to the unparalleled opportunities to play with one's identity and try out new ones in virtual worlds (Turkle 1994). Lastly, it should always be kept in mind that story and the characters in it usually provide a context for gameplay, a justification for the activities the player is expected to engage in the game. The distinctive feature of the medium of games is the ability to interact with it, which creates a more active experience than the passive experience of watching a movie and leads to new opportunities like experimenting with the game or role-playing a character.

References

11 bit studios. 2014. This war of mine [Computer Game].

Abelson, R. P. 1963. Computer simulation of "hot cognitions." In S. Tomkins, & S. Messick, *Computer simulation of personality*. New York: Wiley.

Anderson, C. A., Shibuya, A., Ihori, N., Swing, E.L., Bushman, B.J., Sakamoto, A. et al. 2010. Violent video game effects on aggression, empathy, and prosocial behavior in eastern and western countries: a meta-analytic review, Psychological Bulletin, 136:2, 151–73.

Bartholow, B. D and Anderson, C.A. 2002. Effects of Violent Video Games on Aggressive Behavior: Potential Sex Differences, *Journal of Experimental Social Psychology*, 38(3),283-90.

Baron-Cohen, S. and Wheelwright, S. 2004. The empathy quotient: An investigation of adults with Asperger syndrome or high functioning autism, and normal sex differences. *Journal of Autism and Developmental Disorders*, 34, 162-176.

Batson, C. D. 2009. These things called empathy: Eight related but distinct phenomena. In J. Decety & W. Ickes (eds.), *Social neuroscience. The social neuroscience of empathy*, Cambridge, MA: MIT Press, 3-15.

Batson, C.D. and Coke, J.S. 1981. Empathy: A Source of Altruistic Motivation for Helping. In: Rushton, J.P. and Sorrentino, R.M. (eds), *Altruism and Helping Behavior: Social, Personality, and Developmental Perspectives*, Lawrence Erlbaum Associates, Hillsdale, 167-187.

Batson, C. D., Duncan, B. D., Ackerman, P., Buckley, T., & Birch, K. 1981. Is empathic emotion a source of altruistic motivation? *Journal of personality and Social Psychology*, 40(2), 290-302.

Batson, C., Dyck, J., Brandt, J., Batson, J., Powell, A., Mcmaster, M., and Griffitt, C. 1988. Five studies testing two new egoistic alternatives to the Empathy-Altruism Hypothesis. *Journal of Personality and Social Psychology*, 55, 52-77.

Batson, C., Batson, J., Slingsby, J., Harrell, K., Peekna, H., & Todd, R. 1991. Empathic joy and the empathy-altruism hypothesis. *Journal of Personality and Social Psychology*, 61, 413-426.

Belman, J. and Flanagan, M. 2010, Designing games to foster empathy, *Cognitive Technology*, 14: 2, pp. 5–15.

Bogost, I. 2011. *How to do things with video games*. Minneapolis: Minnesota Press.

Bostan, B. 2009. Player motivations: A psychological perspective. *Computers in Entertainment (CIE)*, 7 (2). Article 22.

Coeckelbergh, M. 2007. Violent Computer Games, Empathy, and Cosmopolitanism, *Ethics and Information Technology*, 9(3): 219–231.

Cuff, B.M., Brown, S.J., Taylor, L. and Howat, D.J. 2016. Empathy: a review of the concept. *Emotion Review, 8*(2), 144-153.

Davis, M.H., 2018. *Empathy: A social psychological approach*. Routledge

Decety, J. and Jackson, P. 2006. A social-neuroscience perspective on empathy. *Current Directions in Psychological Science*, 15, 53-60.

Dziobek, I., Rogers, K., Fleck, S., Bahnemann, M., Heekeren, H., Wolf, O., and Convit, A. 2008. Dissociation of cognitive and emotional empathy in adults with Asperger syndrome using the Multifaceted Empathy Test (MET). *Journal of Autism and Developmental Disorders*, 38, 463-473.

Fischer, F. 2017. Solve et coagula: Ludonarrative Synthesis. Gamasutra[online]. Retrieved May 23, 2019, from https://www.gamasutra.com/blogs/FabianFischer/20171213/311360/Solve_et_coagula_Ludonarrative_Synthesis.php

Greitemeyer, T., Osswald, S. and Brauer, M. 2010. Playing prosocial video games increases empathy and decreases schadenfreude. *Emotion*, 10: 796–802.

Greitemeyer, T., and Osswald, S. 2011. Playing prosocial video games increases the accessibility of prosocial thoughts, *Journal of Social Psychology*, 151, 121–128.

Happ, C., Melzer, A. and Steffgen, G. 2013. Superman vs. BAD Man? The Effects of Empathy and Game Character in Violent Video Games. *Cyberpsychology, behavior and social networking*, 16 (10), 774-8

Hoffman, M. L. 1987. The contribution of empathy to justice and moral judgment. In N. Eisenberg & J. Strayer (Eds.), *Empathy and its development*, Cambridge: Cambridge University Press, 40-80.

Heron, M. J. and Belford, P. H. 2014. Do you feel like a hero yet? Externalized morality in videogames, *Journal of Games Criticism*, 1:2, http://gamescriticism.org/articles/heronbelford-1–2/

Ickes, W. 1993. Empathic accuracy. *Journal of Personality*, 61, 587-611.

Kahneman, D., & Egan, P. 2011. *Thinking, fast and slow*. New York: Straus and Giroux.

Kohut, H. 1959. Introspection, empathy, and psychoanalysis: An examination of the relationship between mode of observation and theory. In P. H. Ornstein (ed.), *The search for the self Vol. 1.*, New York: International University Press. 205-232.

Krebs, D. L. 1975. Empathy and altruism. *Journal of Personality and Social Psychology*, 32.

Kunda, Z. 1999. *Social Cognition: Making Sense of People*. MIT Press.

Kway, L. & Mitchell, A. 2018. "Perceived Agency as Meaningful Expression of Playable Character Personality Traits in Storygames." In International Conference on Interactive Digital Storytelling, pp. 230-239. Springer.

Mateas, M. 2004. A Preliminary Poetics for Interactive Drama and Games. In *First Person: New Media as Story, Performance, and Game*, 20–33. MIT Press.

Metcalfe J., Mischel W. (1999). A Hot/Cool-System Analysis of Delay of Gratification: Dynamics of Willpower. *Psychological Review*, vol.106, No. 1, 3-19.

Newman, J. 2002. The myth of the ergodic videogame. *Game Studies*, 2. Retrieved June 15, 2018, from http://www.gamestudies.org/0102/newman/

Nowak, A. T. 2011. Introducing a pedagogy of empathic action as informed by social entrepreneurs (PhD. Thesis, McGill University).

Numinous Games. 2016. That Dragon, Cancer. [Computer Game].

Pallant, J. 2013. *A Step by Step Guide to Data Analysis Using IBM SPSS: SPSS Survival Manual*, 5. Edition. England: McGraw-Hill.

Roseman, I. J., & Smith, C. A. 2001. Appraisal theory. In *Appraisal processes in emotion: Theory, methods, research* (pp. 3-19).

Ryan, M., Staines, D., & Formosa, P. 2016. *Four lenses for designing morally engaging games*, In Proceedings of the 1st Joint Conference of DiGRA and FDG. Dundee, Scotland. Retrieved from http://www.digra.org/wp-content/uploads/digital-library/paper_184.pdf

Scherer, K. R. 1999. Appraisal theory. In *Handbook of cognition and emotion* (pp. 637-663).

Smethurst, T. & Craps, S. 2015. Playing with Trauma: Interreactivity, Empathy, and Complicity in The Walking Dead Video Game. *Games and Culture,* 10:3, 269-290.

Stueber, K. 2008. Empathy. In A.L.C Runehov, L. Oviedo (eds), *Encyclopedia of Sciences and Religions*, Dordrecht: Springer.

Telltale Games. 2012. The Walking Dead. [Computer Game].

Telltale Games. 2013. The Wolf Among Us. [Computer Game].

Turkle, S. 1994. Constructions and Reconstructions of Self in Virtual Reality: Playing in the MUDs. *Mind, Culture, and Activity: An International Journal* 1, no. 3 (1994): 158-167.

Chapter 17
Gender Representation and Diversity in Contemporary Video Games

Ertuğrul Süngü

Contents

Abstract This study examines the effects of queer theory on the world of games, how heteronormative world-view created a certain space, and how this space evolved throughout the history of video games. queer theory, which is the subject of the study, is examined through major indie game titles, especially by people who identify themselves as queer and/or those utilizing queer perspective. Another aim of this study is to examine differences between LGBT character representation in AAA game titles and games produced by queer game developers. As a means to achieve this, "Comparative research" methodology will be utilized on AAA titles and indie games, and differences between them will be analyzed. Comparison will take place between AAA titles such as Dragon Age, Mass Effect, and The Sims and indie titles that came to the fore especially after 2010 such as Mainichi and Little Witch Story.

Keywords Gender · Indie game · Queer theory · Video game

E. Süngü (✉)
Faculty of Communication, Bilgi University, Istanbul, Turkey

© Springer Nature Switzerland AG 2020   379
B. Bostan (ed.), *Game User Experience And Player-Centered Design*,
International Series on Computer Entertainment and Media Technology,
https://doi.org/10.1007/978-3-030-37643-7_17

17.1 Introduction

Video games have been in our lives since the early 1950s. Starting with the first and very primitive video game Pong, they have changed a lot in the last 40 years (Shaw 2010). At their early stages, video games were not compact, so only a limited number of people could have access to the luxury of enjoying them. Starting with the Atari 2600 console machines and the production of games like Pong, these games have become smaller and smaller, making it possible for the general public to interact with them. In late 1970s and early 1980s people had already started playing video games at their homes (Appelcline 2014). With an increase of the interest in video games, the industry started to develop worldwide. After this, video games started to be played by millions. The diversity of consumers resulted in the creation of various genres along with different types of players and video game producers. Although few people took video games seriously until their introduction to academia in mid-2000s, feminist critics and queer video gamers started to express complaints at a much earlier time (Aaron 2004; Barton 2004; Consalvo 2003; Gross 2001; Leone 2002).

Nearly all video games were produced by (and for) young, male, and white men. Two of the most popular genres FPS (First Person Shooter video games) and TPS (Third Person Shooter video games) focused exclusively on male gameplay and story lines. There were very few female characters involved in those games and very few of them were the main characters. Even when they became main characters, like in Tomb Rider game series, the characters did not come to the spotlight because of their qualities but because of their sex appeal consisting of large breasts, small shorts, and vulnerability. Thus, feminist and queer academics started to question the nature of video games. "Are video games only male oriented? Can a woman become the main character? What about sexism and discrimination in video games? What about alienation of an entire race?"

The aim of this paper is to examine how LGBT identities are portrayed and represented differently in AAA game titles and indie games produced by queer game developers, through queer theory and by utilizing Comparative Research Methodology. This paper will include descriptive explanations about titles and headings, and comparisons about these titles will follow. In this context, AAA titles such as Dragon Age, Mass Effect, Fable, and The Sims, and games produced by queer game developers such as Lim, Mainichi, Little Witch Story, and In Bloom. Another aim of the paper is to explain and analyze a developer's effect on representation and identity.

17.2 Research Method

Comparative research in communication and media studies is conventionally understood as the contrast among different macro-level units, such as world regions, countries, sub-national regions, social milieus, language areas, and cultural thickenings, at one point or more points in time. A recent synthesis by Esser and Hanitzsch (2012) concluded that comparative communication research involves comparisons between a minimum of two macro-level cases (systems, cultures, markets, or their sub-elements) in which at least one object of investigation is relevant to the field of communication. Comparative research differs from non-comparative work in that it attempts to reach conclusions beyond single cases and explains differences and similarities between objects of analysis and relations between objects against the backdrop of their contextual conditions (Vliegenthart and Esser 2017).

This paper will include comparisons between titles that are played by people who identify themselves as queer and games produced by queer game developers though Comparative Research Methodology. Before these comparisons queer representation in modern times will be generally examined, following this AAA titles that include queer representations such as Dragon Age, Mass Effect, and The Sims will be closely examined and arguments about how diversity is used in them will be made. On the other hand, information about indie titles, In Bloom, Mainichi, Little Witch Story, and BrokenFolx, and their developers will be shared. It should be noted the aforementioned titles are still popular today but they reached a wide audience first with queercon 2013. Arguments about how queer understanding reflects in game titles, utilizing Comparative Research Methodology, in AAA games and the queer representations in them, and in games produced by queer game developers will follow.

17.3   What Is Queer Theory?

Before jumping to queer theory in video games, I believe that it would be logical to explain the concept itself. Queer theory, generally speaking, is an umbrella term which brings feminisms, LGBT, race, discrimination, and alienation under a single roof. Queer theorists try to explain that we live in a heteronormative world and attempt to answer questions about these heteronormative norms. Sex and gender have always been strange. Many people oversimplify the situation and think that this is a simple question. But a close examination of different possibilities and perspectives reveals the complexity between sex and gender. Even though the lives of straights, gays, and lesbians are not in total darkness for many people, queer theorists argue that the belief concerning gender cannot be destabilized. Nothing is what it looks like.

Queer theory arises as a response to feminism in 1970. Whereas feminists ask the question "why must we always and exclusively focus on men? What about women?" queer theorists take this question and make it more extensive. "Why do men and women have to rely on certain specific traits?" Until Michel Foucault's argument, the feminist approach of 1970s was still considered valid (Foucault 1990). However, Foucault stated that powerful people were the ones holding responsibilities in their hands. White and wealthy men were used as examples to reflect the "normal" versus the "abnormal" when it came to sex and gender. That argument was considered accurate until queer theorists put forward a new idea proposing that it was wrong to consider and divide the human body as male and female. In the 1990s Judith Butler and Eve Sedgwick stepped forward and did the groundwork for queer theory (Butler 1990). Their main argument was gender performance which can still make queer theory visible today.

Queer as a word was first used to describe homosexuality or worse, as the underestimation of homosexuality. Recently the significance of the word has started to change. It has been reformulated to define sexual identities, to gather the marginal choices under a single roof, and it is sometimes used to define a theory studying traditional gay and lesbian studies. It is clear that despite these definitions, "queer" as a word is still in the process of development. Even today, the concept is not completely formulated. The definition of the concept is full of uncertainty and elasticity, which are, in turn, essential connotations of this concept. According to the nature of this notion, an introductory evolution of the phenomena of queer can be taking a position towards intuitional and even odd. As queer theory's conceptual significance and political influence depend, to a certain extent, on its resistance against clear-cut definitions and on its refusal to get integrated into existing paradigms, queer theory becomes less and less "queer" as it inclines to become a traditional academic discipline (Jagose 2015).

17.4   Approaching Video Games and Etymology

Video game evolution has been amazing and it still finds ways to surprise us. Producers are using technology in unbelievable ways. From the days of two moving sticks and a ball, we have come to concepts like augmented virtual reality. These machines literally put players into the game and completely alter the experience of PCs and gaming consoles. But, how did this all begin? What exactly is gaming? To understand gaming and human reaction to games, we have to look at "gaming" from a different point of view. Also, we have to discuss the nature of "games" and its development.

As for games and the culture of gaming, it can be presumed that the whole process started with human beings. As a matter of fact, playing games is a common act among animals. When we look at puppies playing with each other, they are bound to obey a single rule which is to avoid biting one another's ears. Their excitement, which can be interpreted as aggression, actually is based on taking pleasure and having fun. This action represents the primitive instinct of animals. Even in the world of animals, gaming is a physical action rather than a psychological reaction. The concept of gaming, inherited from the animal world, is a complicated one which contains a duality in itself. Huizinga (2015, p. 17) wrote about this; "If we call this process mind based action, it would be an exaggeration. Yet, if we call it instinctive it does not ring any bell." Based on animal and human attitudes, the process of gaming (and video gaming) can be interpreted as an action with the aim of getting rid of extra energy, having fun, decreasing the level of stress, communicating with other players, becoming part of a virtual community, increasing self-esteem, and also living in his/her own personal space.

Terms such as "ludus," "ludere," or "lusus" are used in Latin to define games and the idea of gaming. In addition these terms "iocus" and "iocari" are also used to define having fun and pranking others. "Iocus" and "iocari" are not used to define the action of playing but rather the movement of fish in the water, flying of birds, and the movement of water. In contrast to that "ludere" refers to "not serious but pretended actions." Ludus and Ludere are specifically used for children's plays, relaxation, competition, rituals, and stage acts. "Lares Ludentes," for example, refers to the specific intention to play a role. The influence of Latin in Indo-European languages has transferred the words "iocus" and "iocari" into jeu, jouer (French), giuoco, giocare (Italian), juego, jugar (Spanish), jogo, jogar (Portuguese), joc, juca (Romanian) (Huizinga 2015).

Based on the definitions, different theories, and etymological analysis of the word "game," it would not be wrong to claim that "game" is not a material but an action. In this case, gaming is a set of personal actions which can be performed by every individual. After stating this point, I can argue that contemporary video games have not only been developed for males but also for all types of genders. At this point, queer theory, queer video game developers, and queer video game critics have the right to argue about heteronormative gaming world. It will not be logical to define contemporary video games from a single perspective. The attitude of queer interpretation is worth mentioning. Queer theorists are bringing to attention the lack of all elements which are included in the definition of LGBT such as gays, lesbians, bisexuals, and transgender in today's heteronormative norms.

17.5 Changing Heteronormative Game Playing

Video games used to share a common ground: heteronormative norms. Those norms used to stand on common ground for a long time. As Clark argues

> "'Queerness in gamers' has appeared in the media and public discourse mostly as a question of representation and inclusion: Who has been making most of our games, as opposed to who could be making them? What kind of people and experiences appear in the fictional universes that games can summon into existence, and whose life experiences are brought to bear on the stories told by or emerging from games? The status quo, to nobody's surprise, is that games have seldom been made by or for queers, or even with queers, or even with queers in mind; they're mostly created by young and middle-aged white Asian men, to be sold to similar if slightly younger and slightly browner audience of consumers." (Clark 2017)

The audience, however, diversified over the past decades across many game genres, while LGBTQ representation saw a dramatic increase. (Fig. 17.1 and Fig. 17.2) With the arrival of games like Dragon Age, Fable, and Sims this understanding has started to come under contention first, I would like to mention one of the most well-known video games of all time, The Sims. When it was published in 2000,

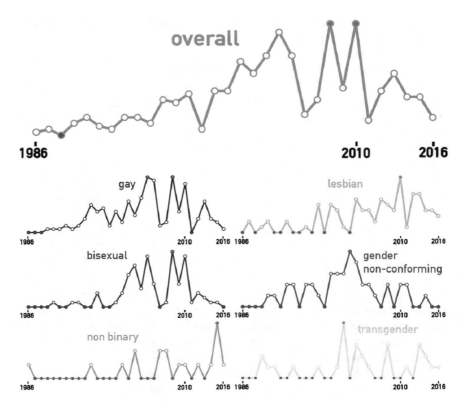

Fig. 17.1 Time series displaying the quantitative evolution of LGBTQ representation (Utsch et al. 2017)

players compared its gameplay directly with SimCity where they created cities and afterwards controlled the cities. The Sims presented the same game mechanic like SimCity but this time the players were not building cities but creating new identities. Characters in The Sims game were able to move towards any direction according to players' will. They had different needs like food, toilet, sleep, and of course sex. At first, creating identity sounded wonderful but the first Sims game was very heteronormative. Players were limited to marry the opposite sex and to act like in a routine, daily life. In The Sims 2, producers offered a "joining party" mechanic for the same-sex relationship and in the third game gay marriage became available. The latest installment, Sims 4, allowed players to have same-sex marriage.

The Sims 4 also achieved great repercussion when the game itself prevented players to share their Sims' conventions or descriptions which were related with the themes of lesbian, gay, bisexual, and transgender. This situation has been also tested by a well-known video game website Kotaku: as long as the characters had any LGBT based descriptions like gay, queertheory, homosexual, and lesbian, players were unable to upload their characters to online platforms. However, unlike the

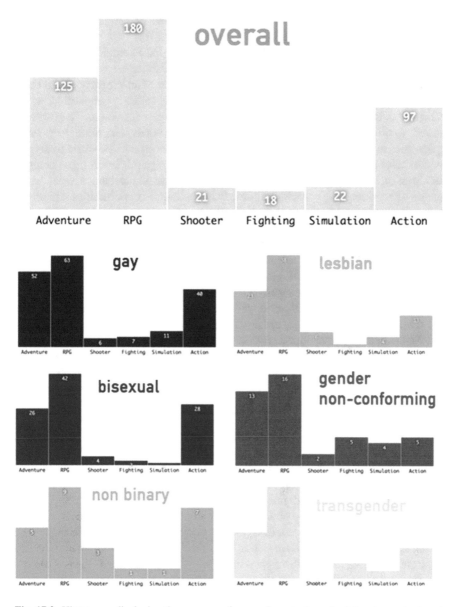

Fig. 17.2 Histograms displaying the presence of queer character in each of the six most relevant game genres (Utsch et al. 2017)

situation in 1970s and 1980s, the producer took immediate action and released an update to fix the problem. (The Sims 4 Gay Filter Fix 2014)

The video game series called Fable is another good example of queer video games and representation. Since 2004, nine different Fable titles with three of them establishing the "core" games have been released. The main property of the Fable game series is that it belongs to the category of games called "open world," which means that the players are not forced to follow a linear game structure. They are able to run in villages and other environments according to their will. Such open world mechanics in video games represent that players can run around the world freely and without any restriction. Generally world designs are gigantic and it takes hours to run from one city to other in games that utilize open world mechanics. Open world games also present players with unlimited choice-making opportunities and one of these choices is no doubt sexual. In the second game, players could choose to start their games as young boys or girls. Besides, NPC characters could be impregnated by the main hero. NPCs were not divided into two sexes but also when players inspected them, they had different personality traits based on whether the character was straight, gay, or bisexual. Homophobia was not a concern in Fable II but sex always had its own consequences. For example, if a married player had sex with a character different than his or her partner, the marriage ended with a divorce. In the third installment of Fable, same-sex marriage had become legal (Greer 2013, pp. 9–10). In third game, approach to sexuality has changed and producer Lionhead Studios has worked on options of sexualities of the protagonist. Fable II represented the NPC character's sexuality only as information but Fable III NPCs represent their sexuality before meeting with them. Their actions and reactions have been very well established in queer identity.

The Sims and Fable series belong to different video game genres and of course the representation in these games is different than a pure RPG game, like Dragon Age: Origins. The Sims is known as a simulation video game and Fable is a Third Person RPG game. In these game genres, the level of interaction is well below that of a pure RPG game like Dragon Age: Origins. Since Origins is a representation of table top RPG games in digital world, the gameplay is much more intimate and bound to player's decisions. Unlike other examples, the player not only controls a single character but also controls a group composed of five characters. Each character, even though they are controlled by computer, has his/her own unique characteristics. In the past, there were many different games like Origins. Baldur's Gate and Icewind Dale series could be good examples.

However, Origins was the first video CRPG game which offered romantic possibilities both in heterosexual and homosexual ways. Alistair, a handsome and at the same time a bashful soldier, and Morrigan, the beautiful "witch of the wilds" were able to interest game's main character in a heterosexual way. During this game, the player could talk with these NPC and get to know them better. Long and positive conservations, some quests about these characters, and some in-game gifts ended up in both emotional and sexual relationships. No matter what, they were only interested in the opposite sex. However, characters like Leliana and Zevran had intercourse with both sexes. Nevertheless, starting a romantic relationship with these two characters was not as easy as that with Alistar and Morrigan. Zevran, for example, used his sexual wiles for his own pleasure. He flirted with main character in many cases. His characteristic is very well explained by one critic on GayGamer website:

> When you encounter Zevran, he has been hired to kill you. It doesn't take long before he hits on your character, male or female. As a woman, this comes quite readily. As a male, he comes to it in a slightly more roundabout way. He compliments you, and blatantly pays you a compliment on your appearance. There are three ways to respond: turning him down, telling him that you are likewise interested, or stating that you are a man. (Greer 2013, pp. 13)

It is the last one that intrigues me, as it leads him to mention that he will stop if it bothers you. There is only one response that does not result in negative approval and that's to admit you were just surprised. He will also expand on his sexuality, admitting he prefers women.

Even if the player chooses to sleep with Zevran at the beginning of the game, there is still an option to build a long-term relationship with the character. However, more importantly, Zevran's unique behavior on sexual interest breaks any prejudiced thoughts of heteronormativity. Zevran's self-determined understanding of sexual interest, which can be described as an impulse, is provoked not only with the character of the player but also with cutting across "polysemous representation," for example, a gay forcing to have a conflict with a queer. As opposed to Reaver's bisexuality as side information of the character in Fable, the sexuality of Zevran is controlled by the player by encouraging his or her game sexuality to be more than a conjectural point.

17.6   Indie Queer Video Games

While games like Call of Duty, World of Warcraft, FIFA, Overwatch, and Battlefield are very famous in popular culture, the independent game industry has also been producing important video games. "Indie" games did not even exist in the mid-2000s because big companies like EA Games, Activision, Blizzard, and others dominated the video game industry. Especially EA Games, during their expansion period, bought different video game makers which produced well-known video games at the time; such as the creator of the Command and Conquer series, Westwood Studios. Against that capitalistic movement in video game industry, some developers came together, produced and distributed their own video games. Starting with 2008, indie game movement has increased and today we have thousands of indie video games in the industry. Indie game developers have not only created their own games but also different identities and people can raise their voices through self-published games. Some of them, inevitably, are queer video game makers. They were one of the silenced groups in the industry. However, some queer video game developers have changed this situation—although certain mainstream video games have already challenged heteronormativity, queer video game designers also had a lot to offer in terms of what a queer game should be.

> Queergaming is a provocation, a call to games, horizon of possibilities. Queergaming is a refusal of the idea that digital games and gaming communities are the sole provenance of adolescent, straight, white, cisgender, masculine, able, male and "hardcore" bodies and desires and the articulation of and investment in alternative modes of play and ways of being. Queergaming is a challenge to this stereotypical, status quo intersection of game players, developers, cultures, and technologies, what I elsewhere called the "technonormative matrix" the digitized, gamified version of Judith Butler's heteronormative matrix... Ultimately, queergaming is heterogeneity of play, imagining different, even radical game narratives, platforms, playerships, and communities. It is gaming's changing present and necessary future. (Chang 2017)

Some examples could be useful in this regard. The first example is a game developer called Caelyn Sandel. Before starting to develop video games, Sandel advocated the inclusion of social and personal themes in art. Afterwards, her gamer side surpassed her feelings and she started to develop indie video games. In her games, she generally focuses on personal journeys. She has been using the Patreon crowd funding website and has already published a few games using this method. Her first and one of the well represented queer video games was Bloom. It was published in 05.25.15 and it is still continues. Like many other queer and indie games, also Bloom does not use main stream graphic engines and 3D animations, but rather a text based game dynamics, like back at the end of 1970s and the beginning of 1980s.

In Bloom, the players witness the story of a woman named Cordelia. Apparently, she is a young trans woman who tries to explain the meaning of the world around. Not long after, we learn that she is in a different mood and trying to understand herself. Even though this mood is very hard to understand, Bloom can connect with player. Even though we do not have a 3D designed world around us, the text tells the player what she has been through. During game play, some words are highlighted. Every word is a gateway for the player to interact with the game. In this game, Cordelia's womanhood is questioned by the society, and her reaction as a trans woman under some conventional parameters gives the player a hard time. Bloom shows how the heteronormative world can be devastating for a trans woman. Her discomfort with her body also makes Bloom different than other mainstream games and underlines how hard it is to become a trans woman in a heteronormative society.

Another example is Mainichi. This game has been developed by Mattie Brice, a transgender person and an activist. Like Caelyn Sandel, she is also interested in developing video games. Mattie's video game Mainichi is one of the substantial, well designed representations of being a queer in daily life. In this game, Mattie has created a scenario based on real events from her own life—what she essentially attempted to do was to make players experience the life of a trans woman. The game begins with Mattie's character waking up. After a short indoors scene, the character gets out of her house. Then she heads for a coffee shop to meet with a friend. However, on the road, one person notices that the character is transgendered. All of a sudden, he starts to scream and swear. The character just ignores him and continues to the coffee shop. Until this guy, other people, who do not "detect" the character as a transgender, only pop up on their heads a "heart" to show that they have no problem with the character.

In the coffee shop, the barista is interested in the character while she waits for coffee. He even asks the character to go out together but the main character just wonders whether she has to give an answer. The worst part is not this dilemma but when she tells the situation to her friend and her friend gives a response. When the character asks her friend "What should we do?" her response is "I mean . . . Does he know? You know? I just don't want you to get hurt." These are the last words of this game. Then it restarts from the beginning. She wakes up in the bed and prepares herself for a meeting. The crucial thing is that whatever the player chooses at the beginning of this game, the results are always the same. At one point, the character looks at the mirror after she decides to wear makeup and says "There. I look like me again." Mattie Brice points out her alienation from society by her appearance and her gender preferences. Besides, in this game, heteronormative space is very well explained.

Snow McNally, is another queer game developer. Snow teaches narrative design, gives lectures and private classes. Snow also defends queer rights and representations and he is a queer game developer. He has already made three different games, but one of them, Little Witch Story, suits the queer aspect of game play more than the others. In Little Witch Story, magic is used as a metaphor for queerness. The story is long and text based. Explanations are really detailed and the player's responses change the game's storyline. After playing for a while, it is understood that the main character is a witch and the magic is a metaphor for queerness. When people around the character understand that she is a witch, first she is kicked out of her school and afterwards her friends start to do nasty things like forcing the character to wear different uniforms. During this transmission process, Little Witch Story shows the player what alienation means and how the way humans act can change once they learn what a person actually is. Until meeting with other witches, the mocking and the discrimination continue. However, at its core, just as developer McNally also suggests, Little Witch Story is a story about people. "It's also, I hope, a mostly optimistic story about community and support and love."

Arielle Grimes has approached queer video games a bit differently than other video game developers. In her game BrokenFolx, the gameplay is not up to the player. Every time a new game starts, there is a hybrid character and it talks to someone else. The player cannot see to whom the main character is talking to but it is not important anyway. The importance is about the subject of this conversation. The chat between the character and the invisible person is a very classic, routine conversation where a dominant person oppresses the main character. In each conversation, this game tries to represent queer experience and to reflect how the gender specific world cannot understand what they have been doing wrong and what the ground problems of the heteronormative world are.

17.7   Differences Between Indie Queer Games and AAA
Game Titles

In the digital gaming world, the interaction between the sexes started to get portrayed in different ways with titles such as Dragon Age, Mass Effect, The Sims, and Fable. The period of digital game productions that included titles such as Larry 7 has depicted a world of heteronormative standards in a fairly widespread manner. In this context, especially from the 1980s to the 2000s, digital games were thought to be consumed by middle-income white men and the games were produced according to this presumption (Fron et al. 2007; Sims 2014). At this point, it should not be forgotten that consumers were generally individuals that exist in a patriarchal system and moreover game producers were generally middle-income white men like these consumers. In other words, an economic supply and demand line can be observed in this situation. Looking back at the digital gaming world, we see that Carol Shaw is the first female game developer in the industry with a recognizable name.[1] She developed a game called River Raid (1982) for the Atari 2600 console. Although the number of prominent female developers in the modern digital gaming world has increased compared to the 80s, the only person in the media who has managed to speak for a long time as a woman in the gaming industry is Jade Raymond, founder of Ubisoft Toronto and Motive Studios. In particular, she had Executive Producer roles in The Sims Online (2002) and Assassin's Creed (2007), followed by Assassin's Creed II (2009), Assassin's Creed: Bloodlines (2009), Tom Clancy's Splinter Cell: Blacklist (2013), and Watch Dogs (2014) and she is one of the prominent women in the sector. As a matter of fact, the amount of women in a position of producer and/or manager is especially low (Chess et al. 2015). When we look at the issue not only by the consumer side but also by the producer side, we observe that there is a male-centered, dominant structure on both sides.

A similar situation exists between queer games and representations of queer identities. At this point, my argument is the difference between the games that has LGBT characters such as Dragon Age and Mass Effect, and the LGBT character representations in games produced by those who define themselves as queer and the differences between these productions. In all of the AAA game titles used in the article, LGBT genders were presented in different ways. What is done in these games is that different characters have different sexual orientation potentials. As a matter of fact, my first argument here is that only certain characters have this orientation and this orientation only finds its place in the game through sexuality. In addition, there are specific warning signs showing this orientation in the dialogue menus. In this context, in the games like Dragon Age and Mass Effect, the emergence of a relationship different from the "normal" ways is not possible to be more coincidental, but in fact it presents more "predestinated" structure. In this way, players who experience the game through a different structure knowingly select

---

[1] https://www.lifewire.com/women-in-history-of-video-games-729746.

their characters orientation. Another problem is that different orientations only go show themselves as sexual interactions and cannot be experienced in a romantic or more casual way. To give an example, living a gay relationship in these games becomes a task in itself. It is only experienced because it is "different." In addition, the representation of LGBT individuals is limited to their answers to speech options and this narrows the existence of the characters.

When we look at the games produced by queer game developers, we observe that both the representations in games and the games themselves are different. Among these differences, we see content ranging from the producer's perception of the world as a queer person to the problems they face in their daily lives. When we take the example of Mainichi, which is one of the queer games that we mentioned before in the article, as the producer says, we encounter a game that was developed without a great amount of coding knowledge. In fact, this is a small game that tells the story of designer Mattie Brice's daily life. It may be small and simple in certain perspectives, but what the developer is trying to explain is pretty big. In this little game, both the everyday troubles of the transgender persons in society and the psychological troubles in general are wonderfully represented. Another important title is the game called "Lim" produced by Merrit Kopas which is much simpler compared to AAA game titles, just like Mainichi. As a matter of fact, the game in which we move a small square in a "maze" that is formed by similar squares has an enormous queer narrative in itself. This game has different types of narrative mechanics such as other squares attacking you if you are out of norm, after these attacks getting outside of the maze and experiencing a distinctive freedom following this. In My Little Witch Story, which is developed by Snow McNally, magic is a metaphor for queerness. With a long form narrative and text based structure, it tries to explain the identity and being queer like other queer games.

17.8   Conclusion

However, until the 2000s video games were almost exclusively produced by white men and under very normative terms. This normativity generally consists of blood, gore, highly sexualized bodies of women, and masculine acts of men. On the other hand, dominant male language restricts the lifestyles of people who have other choices. This estimation was set forth by Michel Foucault in the twentieth century and remained valid until the beginning of 2010. During 2000s, many different video game developers and publishers have considered both feminist and queer elements in their games. Games like The Sims, Dragon Age: Origins and Fable series did great jobs creating a new ground for queer representation. The change began with the representation of women in games and continued with same-sex relationships and even with sexual interactions. Shaking well-known heteronormativity in video game world which has been created by mainstream companies definitely opens a new way for queer videogame developers.

In 2010s, with the rise of self-sufficient indie game developers and also the increasing technological advancements, queer video game developers have been able to raise their voices. Besides, an event called QGCON has made this industry and queer game developers more visible. Starting from 2013, every year QGCON has been home to different game developers, critics, and academics. In these events, people have made a lot of progress about queer video games and their underestimation by the heteronormative world. Developers like Caelyn Sandel, Mattie Brice, Snow McNally, and many others represent different queer aspects through their video games. What they have created does not only stand as video games but also as artistic performances. By playing these games, a player can understand what it means to be queer in the heteronormative framework. Reflection and narration in queer video games are totally different compared to the mainstream video games.

In this context, when we compare AAA game titles and games by queer developers, we see that there are different representations and narratives. AAA games undoubtedly included LGBT characters in their games, giving an important direction to the progress of the currently patriarchal gaming world and showing the gaming world that different gender identities exist. On the other hand, the games produced by queer game producers are not only contented with the representations of LGBT individuals, they also put remarkable narratives into their games and they also provide a queer narration. Although they are small and not very detailed games relatively, the metaphors used in them and the messages to convey an understanding emerge from a queer approach. Thus, there are different arguments between the representations in the AAA game titles and the games produced by the queer developers; moreover different points are addressed in these games. As a result of the comparison, there is a big difference between LGBT representation in AAA game titles and games where the game designer identifies as queer. In particular, queer designers understand the world differently, meaning that the games they produce are not at a groundbreaking level in terms of graphics, but are far more advanced in terms of meaning than most AAA game titles.

References

Aaron, Michele. *New Queer Cinema: A Critical Reader.* Rutgers University Press, 2004.

Appelcline, Shannon 2014. *Designers & Dungeons: A History of the Roleplaying Game Industry '70 and '79.* An Evil Hat Productions Publication. USA.

Barton, Matthew D 2004. "Gay Characters in Video Games." Armchair Arcade, April 1, 2004. Retrieved from http://www.armchairarcade.com/aamain/content.php?article.27

Butler, Judith 1990. *Gender Trouble: Feminism and the Subversion of Identity.* Routledge.

Chang, Edmond Y. "Queergaming" inside "Queer Game Studies" eds. R, Bonnies and Shaw, A. University of Minnesota Press, 2017.

Chess, Shira and Shaw, Adrienne 2015. "A Conspiracy of Fishes, or, How We Learned to Stop Worrying About #GamerGate and Embrace Hegemonic Masculinity.", *Journal of Broadcasting & Electronic Media,* 59:1, 208-220.

Clark, Naomi. "What is Queerness in Games, Anyway?" inside "Queer Game Studies" eds. R, Bonnies and Shaw, A. University of Minnesota Press, 2017.

Consalvo, M 2003. Hot Dates and Fairy Tale Romances: Studying Sexuality in Video Games. In: M. Wolf and B. Perron, ed., The Video Game Theory Reader. New York: Routledge, pp. 171-194.

Esser, F. & Hanitzsch, T. (2012). On the why and how of comparative inquiry in communication studies. In F. Esser & T. Hanitzsch (Eds.), Handbook of comparative communication research (pp. 3 - 22). London: Routledge.

Foucault, Michel 1990. The History of Sexuality Volume I: An Introduction. New York: Vintage Books.

Fron, Jannie, Fullerton, Tracy, Morie, Jacquelyn Ford, Pearce, Celia 2007. *The Hegemony of Play*. DIGRA: Situated Play, Tokyo, September 24-27.

Greer, S 2013. "Playing queer: Affordances for sexuality in Fable and Dragon Age", *Journal of Gaming & Virtual Worlds*. Vol. 5, No. 1.

Gross, L 2001. *Up from Invisibility: Lesbians, gay men and the media in America*. 1st ed. New York: Columbia University Press.

Huizinga, Johan 2015. Homo Ludens Oyunun Toplumsal İşlevi Üzerine Bir Deneme. Istanbul: Ayrıntı Yayınları

Jagose, A 2015. *Queer Theory: Bir Giriş*. Ed. Demir, A. A. Notabene Yayınları, Ankara.

Leone, R 2002. Contemplating Ratings: An Examination of What the MPAA Considers "Too Far for R" and Why. *Journal of Communication*. 52. Pp. 938 - 954.

Shaw, Adrienne 2010. "What is Video Game Culture? Cultural Studies and Game Studies" in *Games and Culture*. September, 2010. Pp. 403 - 424.

Sims, C. 2014 'Video Game Culture, Contentious Masculinities, and Reproducing Racialized Social Class Divisions in Middle School' in *Signs,* Vol. 39, No. 4. Pp. 848-857.

The Sims 4 Gay Filter Fix Is On The Way, IGN, 2014. Retrieved from https://www.ign.com/articles/2014/09/09/the-sims-4-gay-filter-fix-is-on-the-way

Utsch, Sofia; Bragança, Luiza C.; Ramos, Pedro; Caldeira, Pedro; Tenorio, Joao. Queer Identities in Video Games: Data Visualization for a Quantitative Analysis of Representation. Proceedings of SBGames 2017. P. 850 - 851.

Vliegenthart, Rens and Esser, Frank. Comparative Research Methods. John Wiley & Sons, Inc. Published. 2017.

Chapter 18
A Deadly Game User Experience: The Case of #BlueWhaleChallenge

Selcen Ozturkcan and Mesut Ozdinc

Contents

Abstract Lately, the Blue Whale Challenge, which is also known as the Blue Whale Game, received public attention via the countless news about teenagers all around the world harming themselves as they engage with the so-called game (Balhara et al., Asia Pac Psychiatry, 10(3), 2018; Sousa et al., Int J Soc Psychiatry, 63(8), 796–797, 2017). Though referred to as a game, it involves a series of self-harming tasks (Narayan et al., Indian J Psychiatry, 61(1), 2019), which spread via social media for completion in 50 days. The final task reported as to commit suicide (Khattar et al., White or Blue, the Whale gets its Vengeance: A Social Media Analysis of the Blue Whale Challenge, 2018). The victims of the Blue Whale Challenge, being mostly teenagers and young adults, the significant concern rising from the families calls for the topic to treated as that of a severe public health issue (Kumar et al., Psychobiological determinants of 'Blue Whale Suicide Challenge'

S. Ozturkcan (✉)
School of Business and Economics, Linnaeus University, Kalmar, Sweden
e-mail: selcen.ozturkcan@lnu.se

M. Ozdinc
School of Economics and Business, Åbo Akademi University, Turku, Finland

Department of Statistics, Mimar Sinan FA University, Istanbul, Turkey
e-mail: mesut.ozdinc@abo.fi

© Springer Nature Switzerland AG 2020   395
B. Bostan (ed.), *Game User Experience And Player-Centered Design*,
International Series on Computer Entertainment and Media Technology,
https://doi.org/10.1007/978-3-030-37643-7_18

victimization: A proposition for the agency mediated mental health risk in new media age, 2017). To this date, the blue whale challenge is perhaps the only game that demands its user to end his/her life for completing the game (Mukhra et al., Sci Eng Ethics, 25(1), 285–291, 2019). This chapter aims to explore the collection of news that involved the often-deadly game user experiences. Contributions are in several folds starting from the game user experience field to the gamer psychology as well as public health policy development and text analysis of broadcasted news surrounding a critical public concern.

Keywords BlueWhaleChallenge · MoMo · Game user experience · Deadly game · Teenage gamers · Suicide · Virtual slavery

18.1 Introduction

The incident of suicide seems to exert a great repercussion since World War II's high figures. Lately, a virtual game referred to as the "Blue Whale" is the center of public discussion, as it is said to include some 50 challenges ranging from self-mutilation to eventually suicide (Balhara et al. 2018). Allegedly this deadly game began in Russia in 2015 (Adeane 2019). It became known by the public upon teenagers starting to committing suicide by unfortunate acts such as jumping off from the top of a high building or jumping in front of a speeding train. To date, news reports indicate that many teenager suicides were results of the game, where victims come from different countries around the world. In a nutshell, Blue Whale Challenge works through instructions extended by a mentor (also referred to as a curator, master, or even a teacher) who virtually induces its "player" to perform 50 tasks, where the final mission is to take one's own life. As such, self-mutilation to inscribe acronyms such as "F57" or to engrave a whale in the skin with a sharp object followed by delivery of photographic evidence of task completion is reported as a frequent task to begin. Other dangerous tasks are then directed to the victim that range from climbing on the roof to cutting the lip as well as mind-altering tasks of watching horror movies or listening to psychedelic songs (Fon 2017; Mukhra et al. 2019; Sousa et al. 2017). While "Blue Whale" game includes much suffering, "gaming or gamified systems are often associated with the frameworks of fun, joy, or amusement against any state of boredom, which are conceptually very similar to pleasure against pain" (Ozturkcan and Şengün 2016, p. 42).

All in all, the "Blue Whale" game involves a severe factor of risk and vulnerability against children and young people. Therefore, it is of utmost necessity to research the topic for developing a better understanding of the incident. One source that offers an understanding of the ongoing discourse, where the public is both reflected upon and informed, is the traditional media. In this research, a content analysis of news on the topic is presented.

18.2   Fun in Game User Experience

Gaming is usually connected with amusement, delight, or entertainment, while involved tasks and challenges directed to gamers tend to touch upon elements that provide fun via internal sensations (Lazzaro 2009). The act of engaging in a game itself is considered an activity of prosumption (Ozturkcan 2018), where entertainment is one of the end products. The notion of fun is often depicted in close alignment with the sensation of pleasure, which is referred as the gratification that stems upon the success in becoming a winner (Wälder 1933). As the gamers match their skills with the challenges directed to them in the game, they tend to engage in a flow state (Csikszentmihalyi 1997) that involves goal clarity, instantaneous feedback, profound concentration, sense of control together with a transformed consciousness of time with results in some intrinsic rewards. Categorized in two dimensions of Players-World and Acting-Interacting (Fig. 18.1), game players can be classified as Killers, Achievers, Socializers, and Explorers in terms of the different engagements originating from the games (Bartle 1999, 2004), with aims to be the strongest among players, binding with other players, discovering the virtual game world content, and finishing the quests and goals within the game content, respectively. Such engagement can also help in the creation of relationships with other players upon identification with game content and experience of the game world and achievement of power upon tackling the involved game challenges (Yee 2006). All in all, various emotional appeals attract different players with different leads (Ryan et al. 2006).

Children demand special attention as users of technology, where joy and fun are regarded as significant motivations for them to interact with any game (Barendregt et al. 2003, p. 77). Games, in their provision of entertainment through escape, are superior to most other means of escape due to their participatory design (Federoff 2002). Immersion in the game environment is required for the game to offer the

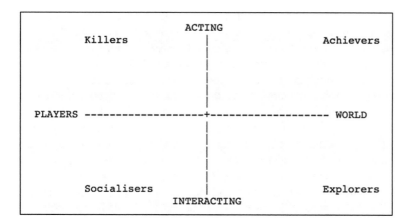

Fig. 18.1 Game player categories (Bartle 1999)

escape, that is, the player should be provided with an "illusion of non-mediation" where (s)he "fails to perceive or acknowledge the existence of a medium in his or her communication environment and responds as he or she would if the medium were not there" (Lombard et al. 2000, p. 77). Once the user forgets that (s)he is participating at a game through a medium, then the immersion in the game is created, which in turn results in the fun. However, the flow involved with fun is also argued to have a threshold in some gamers experiences, especially in cases where the players start to feel that they have to keep up with playing in order to preserve their invested efforts in gaming and results achieved so far (Ozturkcan and Şengün 2015). As a result, the fun may erode giving way to a shift of engagement from gain to avoiding losses and further punishments.

18.3 Virtual Slavery of Children and Teenagers

The ways that are reported for forcing, obliging, or tricking individuals into doing things for others are exhaustive and beyond imagination. Threats and receiving orders from figures of perceived authority are among the powerful reported ways of modern slavery of children (Dottridge 2005). Although the total number of modern slaves globally is unknown, the news indicates that more than 10,000 individuals were victims alone in the UK as of year 2014, where half of those were children (Dearden 2018). Reports by the Child Exploitation and Online Protection Centre (CEOP) outline that threats often include that information, photographs, or videos would be spread among family and friends if the victimized child chooses not to obey the directed orders, which may involve performing some rather extreme acts (BBC 2013). Accordingly, children as young as 8 years of age were revealed to have been forced to perform "slave-like acts" that also included self-harm. As indicated in different international sources, Blue Whale Challenge involves forcing the participating players to self-harm with such "slave-like acts," where the virtual slavery of engaged children and teenagers takes place. For example, Dwivedi (2017) from India reports that "a group of administrators give (the player) specific tasks like listening to a certain genre of music, waking up at odd hours, traveling without tickets and eventually it takes (the player) to self-mutilation and in the end; suicide." Along the same lines, Ngugi (2017) from Kenya indicates that the directed "tasks include watching horrific movies, self-torture, and ultimately committing suicide in order to be regarded as the winner." From Saudi Arabia, Zahaque (2018) reports that Blue Whale's "administrators threaten children and will make them feel that it is highly impossible to quit" where "finally they end up committing suicides."

Similarly, a Russian teenage girl is reported to "issued threats to her victims to murder them or their family members if they failed to complete tasks she set them involving cutting themselves with razor blades and other acts of self-harm" (Stewart 2017). In their recent article Narayan et al. (2019) point the emerging "cyber-suicide" phenomenon that they define as "the use of the Internet for matters relating to suicide and its ideation" where the highest involved risk is portrayed against the youth. Their findings indicate that the Blue Whale Challenge is on a recent cyber-suicide phenomenon. This article further extends that perspective and proposes that Blue Whale Challenge is both a cyber-suicide phenomenon, particularly for those that complete all involved challenges, and it is also a virtual slavery phenomenon for those that are in the process of being forced to gradually increasing self-harm.

18.4 The Blue Whale Challenge

In terms of the communicative models, Blue Whale is argued to tap into two models which are namely the "We-Model" and "I-Model" (Irina et al. 2017). Here, the "We-Model" articulates self-organizing network systems that are created on the grounds of common interests, eventually leading to communities. Such communities are often self-contained without any further agenda to spread externally. The "I-Model," on the other hand, utilizes the digital media portals, where extensive influence similar to that of traditional mass media is possible. Digital multimedia, in any form, is treated as a means to strengthen one's impact. Along these lines, as a form of "I-Model" communicative model, alternate reality games (ARGs) tend to embody an influential figure as an organizer (moderator), which sets the objectives for players and spectators. Blue Whale is reported as been evolved and continues to evolve as a form of ARG (Irina et al. 2017). An ARG is defined as an "analytic tool" that "focus on the pieces (or problems), platform independence or multimodal communication" where "collective action and problem-solving" result with "participatory and interactive nature of the story" (Kim et al. 2009). In their analysis of five ARGs, namely *The Beast, I Love Bees, Last Call Poker, Year Zero,* and *Free Fall,* between years 2001 and 2009, Kim et al. (2009) point to some common elements involved such as the puppet-master also known as the curator, technology-enabled distributed players, undetermined game story, and last but not the least the entry to the ARG similar to that of a rabbit hole. Szulborski (2005), in his pioneer book, argues that a state-of-the-art ARG involves interactions and in-game events that mimic real life without revealing that they are actually game elements; therefore, players start forgetting that they are playing just a game, but rather perceive the game as real life.

Along these lines, it is worth taking a closer look at the 50 challenges (Volkova et al. 2017; Yılmaz and Candan 2018) that are involved with the Blue Whale. An example list of Blue Whale Challenges directed to the players by the curators is reported by Khattar et al. (2018, p. 2) and Mukhra et al. (2019, pp. 286–287) as the following:

1. Carve with a razor "f57" on your hand, send a photo to the curator.

2. Wake up at 4.20 a.m. and watch psychedelic and scary videos that the curator sends you.

3. Cut your arm with a razor along your veins, but not too deep, only three cuts, send a photo to the curator.

4. Draw a whale on a sheet of paper, send a photo to the curator.

5. If you are ready to "become a whale," carve "YES" on your leg. If not, cut yourself many times (punish yourself).

6. The task with a cipher.

7. Carve "f40" on your hand, send a photo to the curator.

8. Type "#i_am_whale" in your VKontakte status.

9. You have to overcome your fear.

10. Wake up at 4:20 a.m. and go to a roof (the higher, the better).

11. Carve a whale on your hand with a razor, send a photo to the curator.

12. Watch psychedelic and horror videos all day.

13. Listen to music that "they" (curators) send you.

14. Cut your lip.

15. Poke your hand with a needle many times.

16. Do something painful to yourself; make yourself sick.

17. Go to the highest roof you can find, stand on the edge for some time.

18. Go to a bridge, stand on the edge.

19. Climb up a crane or at least try to do it.

20. The curator checks if you are trustworthy.

21. Talk "with a whale" (with another player like you or with a curator) on Skype.

22. Go to a roof and sit on the edge with your legs dangling.

23. Another task with a cipher.

24. Secret task.

25. Have a meeting with a "whale."

26. The curator tells you the date of your death, and you have to accept it.

27. Wake up at 4:20 a.m. and go to rails (visit any railroad that you can find).

28. Do not talk to anyone all day.

29. Make a vow that "you are a whale."

30–49. Every day you wake up at 4:20 am, watch horror videos, listen to music that "they" send you, make one cut on your body per day, talk "to a whale."

50. Jump off a high building. Take your life.

Kumar et al. (2017) investigated the above-listed tasks for understanding how players shifted from "just a game" to "real-life" perceptions. Accordingly, the players are exploited by factors of fear psychology in three different phases of Induction (tasks 1–9), Habituation (tasks 10–25), and Preparation (tasks 26–50). Task 1 being the rabbit hole, the Induction phase involves relatively safer self-harming orders, while a gradual escalation of danger leads to Habituation phase, which rips of the player from the survival instinct. In this gradual elevation of danger, the player gets immersed in the pleasure of completing a seemingly impossible task at every step. This, in turn, establishes self-confidence in the player for upcoming tasks, while obedience towards the curator is established slowly. The involved repetitive exposures to variously threatening stimuli alter the anxiety and fear, where overcoming fear is perceived as psychologically rewarding, similar to that of adventure games (Kumar et al. 2017).

18.5   Methodology

The research design adopts the approach outlined by Gillespie and Richards (2018) in conducting an analysis of news articles for sensitive topics involving victims and lost lives. Since research on the Blue Whale Challenge is still emerging, a sample was collected via keyword searches for news articles covering the Blue Whale to explore the topic further. Turkish news was scanned to further contribute to the emerging literature from a non-English speaking part of the world. This choice is also in-line with the findings of Khattar et al. (2018, p. 11), where Turkish language is listed as one of the eight languages with which Blue Whale related posts are made on social media.

Consequently, "Mavi Balina" was chosen as the keyword phrase, which translates as Blue Whale in the English language. Before the news search and article sampling, Google trend analysis was conducted with the keyword to understand if the chosen keyword had received interest (Fig. 18.2). It was revealed that the phrase was entirely related with the game topic, while related queries involved "play blue whale challenge" as the most common, followed closely by "play blue whale," "blue whale game," "what is blue whale," and "what is blue whale game" as the top ones. In terms of sub-regions within Turkey, four cities Mersin, Gaziantep, Adana, and Konya had extensive interest in searching for the phrase in Google over the last 2 years.

Once the keyword phrase is verified, the search for newspaper articles representing the phrase started. All national newspapers that have daily issues were scanned with a query of the keyword phrase. Articles identified were then extracted by the

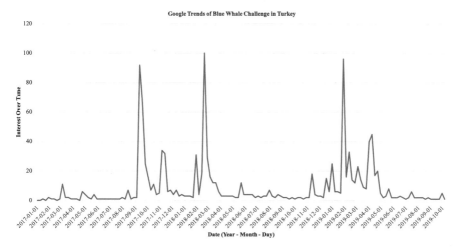

Fig. 18.2 Google Trends of Blue Whale Challenge in Turkey. *Numbers represent search interest relative to the highest point on the chart for the region of Turkey between 01/01/2017 and 11/10/2019. A value of 100 is the peak popularity for the term. A value of 50 means that the term is half as popular. A score of 0 means there was not enough data for this term

aid of NCapture extension on Chrome. Once the activity of news collection was complete, identified news was indexed to ensure there were no duplicates. At the end of this process, a sample of 205 newspaper articles was collected. In further steps, NVivo12 was utilized.

18.6 Analysis and Discussion

An exploratory content analysis of the collected news articles was conducted to understand how the news coverage was conducted, whether experts were involved as cited resources, and if the families and children were informed about preventive measures.

Theme frequency was conducted to understand which themes the news articles were related to. As illustrated in Fig. 18.3, the most relevant theme was "game," followed by Blue Whale Challenge, child, Internet, suicide, family, social media, young, age, police, Russia, threat, technology, mobile phone, app, violence, personal, and attention in descending order of meaningful frequency. There were 18 themes identified with frequency of 69–1332. In this analysis, the most frequent

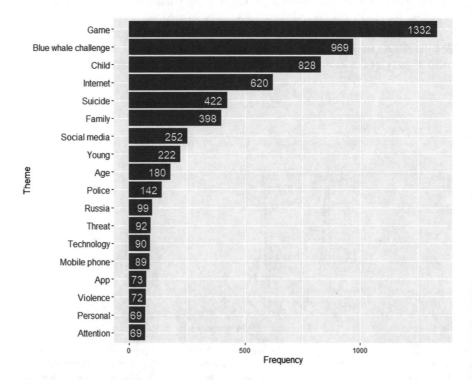

Fig. 18.3 Theme frequency of collected news articles

1000 words were first identified, then stop words were manually eliminated; finally, prefixes and suffixes were merged for stemming, and lastly, common words were themed.

Theme frequency is followed by a more in-depth analysis of each one of the top frequency themes that were above the level of 250.

Game

The game theme occurred 1332 times in the sample news articles. In almost all news articles collected, Blue Whale was portrayed as another mundane computer game. On the other hand, a substantial number of the news were about recent suicides, while there were others purely informative of the concept in general without accompanying recent suicide news. As games are often perceived in connection to definite elements of entertainment, the use of the game word in articles that were delivering news of a recent child's or teenager's suicide was contradictory, often leaving the readers confused. A possibility to misunderstand the news among the unsuspecting public raises, especially for them to conclude that a simple computer game can harm their most precious children; therefore, use of computers should not be allowed. Very few news articles involved expert opinion from a specialist on protective measures for families that would like to be informed about potentially harmful computer-based games.

Blue Whale Challenge

The chosen keyword phrase at the beginning of the sampling had a frequency of 969 in the sampled news, placing it the second most frequent theme. On the contrary, imposed selection criteria would have been expected to have the highest frequency. However, the portrayal of news mostly relied on the game element rather than the Blue Whale Challenge itself. In some articles, Blue Whale was portrayed as an app that can be downloaded to a smart device or software that can be installed on a computer. A detailed explanation of the involved virtual slavery process of the Blue Whale Challenge was quite limited.

Moreover, the use of blue dolphin imagery further strengthened that this was just another game available for kids. The public was instead left clueless about how "just a game" was transferred to some "real-life" act that may even end up with the cyber-suicide phenomenon. Hence, Blue Whale was portrayed with much confusion instead of clear identification. Traditional media chose to portray the topic as attractive one but did not adequately inform the public on available preventive measures. Indeed, there were calls to the government to ban this particular game. The resulted misunderstanding might have increased the risks involved since families might consider that government's ban will ensure their children's safety, while Blue Whale Challenge is not software or app that can be restricted easily.

Child

The child theme occurred 828 times in the sample news articles. Interestingly, young adults or teenagers were not identified among the highest frequencies. On the other hand, the age of the suicide victim and often the youngness of such age was mentioned with frequencies of 180 and 220, respectively. Children, who are often treasured as the most valuable of any society, were portrayed as being under risk. Such portrayal would have led to expectations that extensive research on child security would be in progress. However, as revealed in our literature analysis, the relevant research on the topic is only recently emerging. Children's experiences as players of Blue Whale are not yet unpacked.

Looking at the top three frequencies, news articles in the sample almost unanimously portrayed Blue Whale Challenge as a game for children. However, according to the summarized literature, players are known to exist also among teenagers and young adults. Moreover, the game user experience of children in self-harming themselves as a form of engagement is not investigated as part of the news.

Internet

The Internet theme included digital, cyber, virtual, and Internet words that had a total frequency of 620 in the sample news articles. Most news portrayed Internet as the source of evil. Deep Internet was mentioned in some news, mainly where expert opinion was included. The Internet was mentioned as the channel of threats against children in the majority of the news articles. There were even some suggesting that children should not be allowed to access to the Internet despite the invested interest they may have for better learning. Lastly, neither cyber-suicide nor virtual slavery was mentioned along with what the Internet has facilitated as a threat.

Suicide

The suicide theme included both suicide and death, with a total frequency of 422 in the sample news articles. Most articles delivered suicide news as thriller stories. The cyber-suicide phenomenon was not mentioned in any of the articles. Very few articles mentioned the pre-suicide experiences of children where they self-harmed themselves. Virtual slavery was not mentioned in full scope to inform the public about why the victims had chosen to commit suicide.

Moreover, the suicidal nature of some of the victims is expressed, almost in an attempt to normalize the reported suicide in the news as an expected outcome without many linkages to the Blue Whale. Most of the families that were interviewed were suffering from loss of a child due to committing suicide. Detailed warning information raised by them to prevent any future victims from committing suicide was mentioned in a few, but not in the majority of the news.

Family

The family theme occurred 398 times in the sample news articles. Families of deceased Blue Whale Challenge players were included in the news. Mostly parents that were in severe pain due to their recent loss were quoted. Mourning was the common element in these quotes. The context where families are given a voice in the news points that the suicide victim was an introvert, the lack of the communication and attention of the family may have resulted in the terrible incident. There were also members of the larger families quoted and interviewed, such as aunts and uncles, where such interviews were further informative in understanding how participation in the Blue Whale Challenge may have led to self-harm with virtual slavery. To conclude, family theme is accompanied by strong emotions of sadness, mourning, and loss, but the preventive measures that those families might find useful for protecting their children are available only in a few news articles.

Social Media

The social media theme included social media itself as well as specific media such as Facebook, Twitter, and Instagram, with a total frequency of 252 in the sample news articles. Social media is portrayed as the disguised evil, from where those with a hidden agenda have found their way into communicating with the vulnerable children. Some news takes it even to the extent of suggesting banning the social media participation of kids. In some news, Blue Whale Challenge is described as a game that could be played on a social media platform.

The overall picture depicted in the news with the highest frequency of seven themes is as follows: Blue Whale Challenge is a game for children that they get to know through their engagement at social media over the Internet, and parents are left with nothing but profound sadness and mourning once the player child completes the game by committing suicide.

18.7   Conclusion

In this chapter, the deadly game user experiences of Blue Whale Challenge players are explored. Conclusions indicate that the global public concern demands improved understanding of the gamer psychology and game user experience to develop protective measures.

We propose that virtual slavery be used as a description of the involved game dynamic, in addition to the cyber-suicide phenomenon suggested by Narayan et al. (2019). Further research is needed to identify efficient and effective ways of understanding the players of the Blue Whale Challenge itself and its players. Most news involved the suicide victim; however, the involved curator is also a part of the game though generally disguised. International research, statistics, and co-operation are needed to better understand the involved dynamics and communication channels of the players. Social media should not be the scapegoat as the migration between different communication channels might be possible. However, the "Rabbit Hole" should be identified to prevent any future virtual slavery or cyber-suicide. Along the same lines, it is crucial for news articles to assume a rather informative perspective with useful practical tips to raise awareness.

References

Adeane, A. (2019). Blue Whale: What is the truth behind an online 'suicide challenge'? Retrieved from https://www.bbc.com/news/blogs-trending-46505722
Balhara, Y. P. S., Bhargava, R., Pakhre, A., & Bhati, N. (2018). The "Blue Whale Challenge"?: The first report on a consultation from a health care setting for carrying out "tasks" accessed through a mobile phone application. *Asia Pacific Psychiatry, 10*(3). doi:https://doi.org/10.1111/appy.12317

Barendregt, W., Bekker, M. M., & Speerstra, M. (2003). Empirical evaluation of usability and fun in computer games for children. In M. Rauterberg, M. Menozzi, & J. Wesson (Eds.), *Human-Computer Interaction – INTERACT'03* (pp. 705–708). Amsterdam: IOS Press.

Bartle, R. A. (1999). Hearts, clubs, diamonds, spades: Players who suit MUDs. Retrieved from http://mud.co.uk/richard/hcds.htm

Bartle, R. A. (2004). *Designing virtual worlds*. San Francisco: New Riders Publishing.

BBC. (2013). Cyber-blackmailers 'abusing hundreds of UK children'. Retrieved from https://www.bbc.com/news/uk-24163284

Csikszentmihalyi, M. (1997). *Finding flow*. New York: Basic Books.

Dearden, L. (2018, 26 March 2018). British children being forced into modern slavery in UK as 5,000 potential victims found. *Independent*. Retrieved from https://www.independent.co.uk/news/uk/crime/modern-slavery-uk-british-children-sexual-labour-exploitation-5000-record-nca-a8271331.html

Dottridge, M. (2005). Types of Forced Labour and Slavery-like Abuse Occurring in Africa Today. *Cahiers d'études africaines* (179–180), 689–712.

Dwivedi, V. (2017). What is Blue whale challenge? Retrieved from https://www.indiasopinion.in/blue-whale-challenge/

Federoff, M. A. (2002). *Heuristics and Usability Guidelines for the Creation and Evaluation of Fun in Video Games*. (Master of Science). Indiana University, Bloomington.

Fon, R. (2017). Here's how the 'blue whale' suicide game is killing teens on social media. Retrieved from http://iheartintelligence.com/2017/02/22/blue-whale-suicide-game-social-media

Gillespie, L. K., & Richards, T. N. (2018). *Using Content Analysis to Examine News Media Portrayal of Femicide: Sampling and Coding Considerations*. doi:https://doi.org/10.4135/9781526449214

Irina, V., Kadyrova, S., Rastorgueva, N., & Algavi, L. (2017). From The Silent House meme to The Blue Whale-Game: the storyworld's transformation. In *4th International Multidisciplinary Scientific Conference on Social Sciences and Arts SGEM 2017* (Vol. 1, pp. 253–260).

Khattar, A., Dabas, K., Gupta, K., Chopra, S., & Kumaraguru, P. (2018). White or Blue, the Whale gets its Vengeance: A Social Media Analysis of the Blue Whale Challenge. Retrieved from https://arxiv.org/abs/1801.05588

Kim, J., Lee, E., Thomas, T., & Dombrowski, C. (2009). Storytelling in new media: The case of alternate reality games, 2001–2009. *First Monday, 16*(6). doi:https://doi.org/10.5210/fm.v14i6.2484

Kumar A, Pandey, S. N., Pareek, V., Faiq, M. A., Khan, N. I., & Sharma, V. (2017). Psychobiological determinants of 'Blue Whale Suicide Challenge' victimization: A proposition for the agency mediated mental health risk in new media age. *PsyArXiv*. Retrieved from https://doi.org/10.31234/osf.io/8xh92

Lazzaro, N. (2009). Understand emotions' in Beyond game design: Nine steps towards creating better videogames. In C. Bateman & R. Bartle (Eds.), (pp. 3–47). Hampshire: Cengage Learning.

Lombard, M., Reich, R. D., Grabe, M. E., Bracken, C. C., & Ditton, T. B. (2000). Presence and Television. *Human Communication Research, 26*(1), 75–98.

Mukhra, R., Baryah, N., Krishan, K., & Kanchan, T. (2019). Blue Whale Challenge': A Game or Crime? *Science and engineering ethics, 25*(1), 285–291. doi:https://doi.org/10.1007/s11948-017-0004-2

Narayan, R., Das, B., Das, S., & Bhandari, S. S. (2019). The depressed boy who accepted "Blue Whale Challenge". *Indian Journal of Psychiatry, 61*(1). doi:https://doi.org/10.4103/psychiatry.IndianJPsychiatry_234_18

Ngugi, F. (2017). Kenya Bans Online Game 'Blue Whale Challenge' After Teen Commits Suicide. Retrieved from https://face2faceafrica.com/article/blue-whale-app-kenya

Ozturkcan, S. (2018). Game Prosumption. In N. Lee (Ed.), *Encyclopedia of Computer Graphics and Games* (pp. 1–2). Cham: Springer International Publishing.

Ozturkcan, S., & Şengün, S. (2015). Gaining rewards vs avoiding loss: When does gamification stop being fun? In D. Davis & H. Gangadharbatla (Eds.), *Handbook of Research on Trends in Gamification* (pp. 48–71). Hershey: IGI Global.

Ozturkcan, S., & Şengün, S. (2016). Pleasure in Pain: How Accumulation in Gaming Systems Produce Grief. In Barbaros Bostan (Ed.), *Gamer Psychology and Behaviour* (pp. 41–55). Cham, Switzerland: Springer International Publishing.

Ryan, R. M., Rigby, C. S., & Przybylski, A. K. (2006). Motivational pull of video games: A self-determination theory approach. *Motivation and Emotion, 30*, 347–365.

Sousa, D. F. d., Filho, J. o. d. D. Q., Cavalcanti, R. d. C. P. B., Santos, A. B. d., & Neto, M. L. R. (2017). The impact of the 'Blue Whale' game in the rates of suicide: Short psychological analysis of the phenomenon. *International Journal of Social Psychiatry, 63*(8), 796–797.

Stewart, W. (2017). At home with Blue Whale's 'administrator of death': Russian police release footage of teenage girl accused of convincing dozens of vulnerable children to kill themselves. Retrieved from https://www.dailymail.co.uk/news/article-4835980/Teen-convinced-dozens-children-commit-suicide.html

Szulborski, D. (2005). *This is Not a Game: A Guide to Alternate Reality Gaming*: Lulu.com.

Volkova, I., Kadyrova, S., Rastorgueva, N., & Algavi, L. (2017). *From the Silent House Meme to the Blue Whale-Game: The Storyworld's Transformation*. Paper presented at the 4th International Multidisciplinary Scientific Conference on Social Sciences and Arts SGEM 2017.

Wälder, R. (1933). The psychoanalytic theory of play. *The Psychoanalytic Quarterly, 2*, 208–224.

Yee, N. (2006). The psychology of MMORPGs: Emotional investment, motivations, relationship formation, and problematic usage' In R. Schroeder & A. Axelsson (Eds.), *Avatars at Work and Play: Collaboration and Interaction in Shared Virtual Environments* (pp. 187–207). London: Springer-Verlan.

Yılmaz, M., & Candan, F. (2018). Oyun Sanal İntihar Gerçek: "The Blue Whale Challange/Mavi Balina" Oyunu Üzerinden Kurulan İletişimin Neden Olduğu İntiharlar Üzerine Kuramsal Bir Değerlendirme. *Akdeniz Üniversitesi İletişim FakÜltesi Dergisi, 30*, 270–283.

Zahaque, T. (2018). The Deadly Arrival of the Blue Whale Challenge. Retrieved from http://www.albiladdailyeng.com/deadly-arrival-blue-whale-challenge/

Chapter 19
Exploring Experiential Spaces in Video Games: Case Studies of Papers, Please, Beholder, and Mirror's Edge

Simay Gizem Çavuşoğlu and Güven Çatak

Contents

Abstract Video games offer unique experiences for players with their participatory nature. Their spaces can be considered as experiential spaces because of this characteristic. Video game spaces take place in the center of player experience. This study attempts to define experiential spaces of video games with a suggested framework. This framework includes not only relations between video games and different fields such as cinema and architecture, but also unique characteristics of video games. The purpose of this framework is to look closely at experiential spaces and provide a base for player experience researches. Reliability and consistency of the framework are tested in three different video games: Papers, Please; Beholder; and Mirror's Edge.

S. G. Çavuşoğlu (✉)
Department of Game Design, Bahcesehir University, Istanbul, Turkey

G. Çatak
Department of Game Design, Bahcesehir University Game Lab (BUG), Bahcesehir University, Istanbul, Turkey
e-mail: guven.catak@comm.bahcesehir.edu.tr

© Springer Nature Switzerland AG 2020
B. Bostan (ed.), *Game User Experience And Player-Centered Design*,
International Series on Computer Entertainment and Media Technology,
https://doi.org/10.1007/978-3-030-37643-7_19

Keywords Video games · Experiential spaces · Analysis framework · Interaction

19.1 Introduction

The first explanation for worlds created by games is the magic circle (Huizinga 1949). It is the separated space that occurs when a player starts to play a game (Juul 2008). Although Huizinga used the term as an example of different playground types, not in the meaning of today, the term became increasingly popular. It can refer to tangible spaces such as a chessboard, or intangible spaces created by players when they interact with each other. Juul (2008) suggests an alternative metaphor instead of the magic circle: a puzzle piece with "different interfaces on its sides." This definition fits because games can be examined from many perspectives.

Video game spaces are interfaces between players and the real world. Video game worlds are virtual spaces where games take place and they are shaped by the player experience. An opinion on video game spaces can be reached through similarities between theme parks and especially three-dimensional video games. Theme parks offer experience in physical environments which emotionally stimulate their guests (Carson 2000). A video game creates a similar virtual environment with the player's own agency (Pearce 2007). In a similar way, Jenkins (2004) determined video game spaces as spatial stories.

There are three main dimensions of video game spaces: representation, navigation, and interaction. Representation relates to how the video game is represented. Aarseth et al. (2003) explain video game spaces into three subcategories: perspective, topography, and environment. Representation includes not only visual characteristics but also cinematic techniques. Also, narrative elements can be added in this category. Not only the world created by the game but also all the components of that world and how they are presented are the subjects of representation. Another opinion related to space depends on similarities of video games and architecture (Nitsche 2008; Wolf 2011; Götz 2007). Although there are various common characteristics between video games and architecture such as vision or sound (Adams 2003), the pivot of this relation is navigation which mainly points out the movement in the space. Wolf's (2011) navigational logic depends on spaces in the game world and connections between them. Although navigation is one of the ways to interact with a video game, the interaction term usually refers to direct manipulation of game components.

Zagal et al. (2005) clarify spatiality in video games within three levels: representation, game world, and gameplay. While representation is related to the characteristics of space and game world refers to movement, gameplay explains the actions of the player in the space. Game spaces can be best explained through interaction (Günzel 2008), in other words player experience in the represented space (Leino 2013; McGregor 2007).

Player experience in video games is closely related to four terms: engagement, flow, immersion, and presence (Bostan and Berkman 2017). Engagement is defined as the lowest level of involvement by Brown and Cairns (2004). Flow is the state that occurs when someone is deeply engaged with an activity and based on total involvement (Csikszentmihalyi 2014). Presence is the sense of surrounding caused by a virtual world and immersion is related to losing the sense of being in the real world (Calvillo-Gámez et al. 2015). These terms have similarities and they sometimes are used interchangeably. They are used to define and evaluate the player experience. A video game is discerned with two elements: gameplay and environment (Calvillo-Gámez et al. 2015). This study argues that game space is the base where the player experience is shaped.

Game space is the main characteristic that leads to immersion. As Schmidt (2007) suggests "any immersive action can be divided into two parts: the contribution of the human being and the tool of immersion." In this case, the player and the game space form two parts because spatiality is the defining element of computer games (Aarseth 2001). Gameplay experience needs active participation (Ermi and Mäyrä 2005) and game space is where the player participation occurs. Also, immersion is about being in the moment (Schmidt 2007) and players can do that in the game with their avatars (Leino 2013; Vella 2013) or in other words, with their representations. Experience is placed between the avatar and the environment. Engagement with a game is shaped by activity in the space (Nitsche 2008) because "a game without an arena is only a potential (Aarseth 2001)." Video games create environments for players to explore (Newman 2004; Jørgensen 2013). This exploration comes with opportunities in gameplay and depends on three main activities like in the definition of game space: scrutinize, navigation, and interaction (Jørgensen 2013). To evaluate the player experience, first, it is necessary to understand the space in which the experience is shaped and the interactions that shape the experience.

The purpose of this study is to define experiential spaces of video games with a holistic approach according to how they are represented and experienced. Different frameworks and explanations were brought together to create a new framework which comprehensively clears up the elements mentioned above. After that, the reliability and applicability of the framework will be tested on three selected video games: Papers, Please, Beholder, and Mirror's Edge. All video games offer diversity for the analysis with their spatial characteristics.

19.2 Methodology

To understand the player experience, we need to understand how the player experience is shaped. For example, when a player opens Super Mario Bros (Nintendo 1985), they see the player character Mario in a plumber outfit standing on a brown platform. There are blue skies and green bushes in the cartoonish world of Mushroom Kingdom. In the beginning, the player discovers there is a two-way movement in the game. Mario can go forward and back horizontally, and jump.

Fig. 19.1 Relations between the different layers of the framework

The transition between screens (movement) is continuous. Also, there are several ways to interact with the game: the player can break bricks, collect coins, or jump on Goombas, etc. If the player experience in Super Mario Bros is studied, some questionnaires or scales would be used to evaluate the player experience. However, the player experience is shaped by the experience in the Mushroom Kingdom and it depends on how the game is represented and interacted with. The aim of this study is to understand how experiential spaces affect the player experience.

The player experience in video games consists of two aspects: observation and interaction. Observation provides a passive experience similar to cinema. It is about environment, settlement, and style. Built or natural environment, characters, objects, and economy create the game world. Interaction with every component in the game world offers an active experience. Also, movement can be reviewed in this category because it needs active participation, too. The methodology has four layers according to how players experience the mediated space: what they see (representation and style), how they navigate (navigation), and what they can do (interaction) (see Fig. 19.1). Representation and style are connected to each other directly unlike others because they complete each other. The navigation part is based on the movement, and the interaction is related to the participatory nature of video games.

19.2.1   Representation

Every game "must take place inside a clearly defined game world" (Aarseth 2003) and this section clarifies how the game world is represented. Although the book is about how to design virtual worlds, Bartle (2004) explains all aspects of game worlds in general. He divides constituents of virtual worlds into several categories such as geography, population, etc. Furthermore, this section uses a similar method with the Diverse Worlds Project (Brand et al. 2003). This study, differently from the Diverse Worlds, not only identifies the components of the game world but also offers a comprehensive vocabulary by grouping them according to their functions within the game. The representation part of the analysis is shaped as follows:

- Setting

  - General characteristics
  - Terrain: Elevation, vegetation, hydrography
  - Built environment

- Settlement

  - Population: Population density, characters
  - Economy: Resources, currencies

The setting is used in the most general sense: information of place and time (time in the game world and time in the gameplay). Physical world is related to the natural and built environment. First, some questions should be answered to understand general characteristics such as: How big is the space of the game? What is the dominant surface? Are there any specific topological rules? Terrain and built environment are significant parts of the experience, for example, playing in a forest or a metropolis will not be the same. Because of this diversity, games can offer unique experiences. Settlement refers to the life of the community created by the game. In character analysis, their representations are explained by their form, gender, visibility, and roles.

19.2.2 Style

This section handles style analysis in the experiential spaces from two different perspectives: the style of the game designer (visual modes) and style of the game world (visual style). The style of the game designer refers to the player's perspective within the game. Visual modes explain framing, while visual style relates to esthetic concerns in the framed screen:

- Visual modes

  - Projection angle
  - Framing mechanisms: Anchor, mobility

- Visual style

  - Style
  - Color
  - Light: Quantity of light, contrast level

The article by Arsenault et al. (2015) is used for the items in visual modes section. Items belonging to the projection angle section are bird's-eye view, top-down view, isometric, horizontal view, first person view, and third person view. The anchor is about framing positions. If the camera frames one character or subject, it is subjective; moreover, more than one subject means intersubjective framing. The framing is objective if the camera is "centered on a given location or environment"

(Arsenault et al. 2015). Lastly, if the camera moves freely or randomly, it is called anchorless. The other analysis item, mobility, is related to movement in framing. The player can control the framing (unrestrained), mobility can be connected to the anchor (connected), the mobility can be given by the game itself (authoritarian), or the framing can be immobile (fixed).

The visual style of the game is explained in three subcategories: style, color, and light; and there are proper vocabularies for categorizing video games according to their styles (Lee et al. 2014; Keating and Windleharth 2017). The style has 10 elements: abstract, realistic, stylized (anime, cartoon, handicraft, Lego), map-based, silhouette, watercolor, cel-shaded, low-poly, pixel art, and pre-rendered. Color consists of three items: achromatic, monochromatic, and colorful. Also, the light will be clarified according to the quantity of light (bright or dark) and contrast level (high or low).

19.2.3   Navigation

Navigation includes both movements in space and navigation between spaces. Fernández-Vara et al. (2005) evaluate spatial configurations in video games considering technological development and its effects on space design. They use a historical approach because video game spaces have increasingly diversified and became complicated from past to present. It is possible to track all aspects of their analysis in today's games because cardinality in game space is a preference-based decision. On the other hand, navigation is related to interaction with space itself (Wolf 2011). Wolf (2011) explains spatial cells as 2D or 3D spaces which "allows non-contingent two-way movement between all possible positions within that space" with boundaries. The second part of this section includes these boundaries and connections between different spaces:

- Movement in space: Gameplay, the transition between screens
- Movement between spaces

  - Boundaries
  - Connections

Whether a game is single-screen or not, movement in the game space could be categorized into three categories: one-dimensional movement (in the direction of one axis), two-dimensional movement (in the direction of two axes), and three-dimensional movement (in the direction of three axes). Also, the transition between scenes can be derived into two: discrete and continuous. If the player reaches the edge of the screen and the movement continuous, it is continuous. However, if the screen refreshes, it is discrete. Boundaries between spaces could be tangible barriers or they can be provided by the game itself such as screen edges. The analysis of a connector located between spaces could be done according to the following questions: Can the player pass from one space to another? Is the connector visible? Does the player need some additional item to open that? (Wolf 2011).

19.2.4 Interaction

Interaction defines the player experience in the video game because it is the fundamental characteristic which makes the medium unique. Understanding interaction in games also means understanding how much freedom the player has and uses for shaping the direction of each game (Consalvo and Dutton 2006). Interaction can be analyzed in four parts:

- Physical world
- Objects
- Characters
- Time

All subcategories in this section also explained in the representation part except objects. The reason for not including objects in the representation part is their complexity. A game can provide thousands of different objects; however, without interaction they only provide a passive experience. Some questions are used for each item belonging to this section to analyze the interactive nature of the game world. What are the interaction options? Are these interaction options temporary? Do these options change during the gameplay? (Consalvo and Dutton 2006).

19.3 Game Analysis and Findings

19.3.1 Papers, Please

Papers, Please (3909 LLC 2013) is an indie "dystopian document thriller" game. The player plays as an immigration inspector at a border checkpoint of 1980s fictional Arstotzka. The player needs to examine the documents of entrants and foreigners and decide to approve, deny, or detain according to the deceptions, forgeries, or accuracy of the information on the documents. Papers, Please is a point-and-click simulation game. It has simple yet powerful mechanics. As Moralde (2014) mentioned "*Papers, Please* provides a gameplay experience that helps the player cultivate and internalize that mindset yet also gives the space to step back and examine that attitude, the reasons for it, and the consequences it carries."

Representation Papers, Please is set in the fictional communist country called Arstotzka. The game starts on 23rd November 1982 and ends at the latest on 24th December 1982. Every workday starts at 6 a.m. and ends at 6 p.m. unless it finishes early because of an attack to the border. In real life, the duration of one game day

Fig. 19.2 Environment categorization in Papers, Please (with permission of 3909 LLC)

is between 3 and 8 min. The game does not give detailed information about world size. The player can see only names and places of other countries in the regional map section of the rule book and passports. The game's environment is the checkpoint area. There are no specific topological rules. Also, there is no vegetation in the game.

Papers, Please has one built environment: the checkpoint. The game space is divided into three parts: the queue, the booth, and the desk (see Fig. 19.2). The queue part is located at the top and it is where the travelers wait. On the left bottom side of the screen, there is the booth. Travelers come, present their documents, and answer the questions. The right bottom side is the close-up desk where the player examines the documents and decides between further examination, deny, detain, or approve.

There is no information on population density. The protagonist of the game is the unnamed inspector who works for the Ministry of Admission. The inspector is seen as a silhouette at the beginning of each day while walking to his booth and appears in a family photo. Also, there are some fixed characters. Fixed characters can be entrant or non-entrant. Some fixed characters are randomly generated, and they look different in each gameplay. All non-entrant characters and entrants who are seen more than once during the gameplay are analyzed in Table 19.1 and their representations can be viewed in Fig. 19.3. When the character representations are viewed in general, the majority of them are males.

The currency of the game is credits. The player earns five credits for each person they make the right decision on. There is no penalty for the first two wrong decisions each day. The player can make money from other sources such as bribery, efficiency wages for each detention, etc. It is important because, at the beginning of the game, the player has four dependents: wife, son, mother-in-law, and uncle. At the end of

Table 19.1 Character analysis of Papers, Please

	Character	Form	Gender	Visibility	Role/organization
1	Jorji Costava	Human	Male	✓	Entrant/unknown country
2	Calensk	Human	Male	✓	Arstotzkan guard
3	Dimitri	Human	Male	✓	Supervisor
4	EZIC messenger	Human	Unknown	✓	EZIC member
5	M. Vonel	Human	Male	✓	Arstotzkan investigator
6	Messof Anegovych	Human	Male	✓	Arstotzkan entrant
7	Filipe Hasse	Human	Male	✓	Arstotzkan entrant
8	Sergiu Volda	Human	Male	✓	Arstotzkan guard
9	Danic Lorun	Human	Male	✓	Republican citizen
10	Vengeful father	Human	Male	✓	United Federation citizen

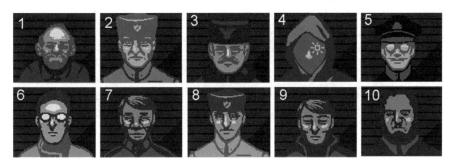

Fig. 19.3 Representation of characters in Papers, Please (with permission of 3909 LLC)

each day, the player must pay for rent, food, and needs (such as medicine). If the player cannot meet the needs, dependents die. Excess money is transferred to the next day.

Style While the queue and the desk have a top-down perspective, the booth's projection angle is first-person. Framing mechanisms of all three screens are objective and fixed. There are three immobile screens with limited object movement options. The visual style of the game is pixel art. Although it is colorful, dark colors are mostly used. Especially the game environment has two main colors: black and gray. This gives the game a pessimistic atmosphere. There are six color patterns in the representation of the travelers. All travelers appear randomly in accordance with these color patterns: pink clothing/brown face, green clothing/blue face, red clothing/green face, gray clothing/dark brown face, dark green clothing/gray face, and purple clothing/brown faces (see Fig. 19.4).

Navigation There is no player-based character movement. The player can see all three screens simultaneously and move the objects between the booth and the desk. The transition between spaces is discrete. The edges of the screens create boundaries. While the objects cross the boundary between the booth and the desk, they scale up and vice versa.

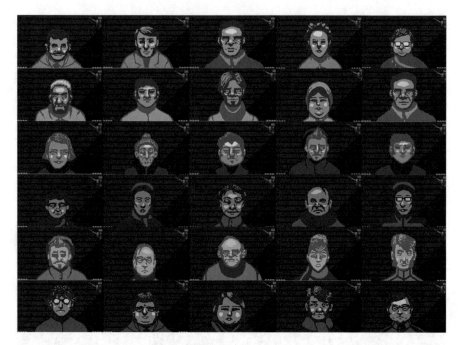

Fig. 19.4 Groups of color palettes in character representations (with permission of 3909 LLC)

Table 19.2 Interaction with the environment

Elements	Interaction options	Duration	Changeability
Stamps	Open, stamp	Permanent	×
Drawer	Open, close	Permanent	×
Call button	Press	Temporary	×
Highlight discrepancy	Press	Permanent	×

Fig. 19.5 Environmental elements of Papers, Please (with permission of 3909 LLC)

Interaction There are two main mechanics in the game: point-and-click and drag-and-drop. All interaction options are based on these two mechanics. Although it takes part especially in the desk area, it is possible to interact with the environment for all three spaces (see Table 19.2 and Fig. 19.5).

Table 19.3 Interaction with objects

Object	Interaction options	Duration	Change
Objects involved information for the inspector			
Audio transcript	Move, select discrepancy	Permanent	×
Official bulletin	Move, open	Permanent	×
Rulebook	Move, open	Permanent	×
Documents			
Passport	Move, select discrepancy, stamp	Temporary	×
ID card	Move, select discrepancy	Temporary	×
Entry permit	Move, select discrepancy	Temporary	×
Work pass	Move, select discrepancy	Temporary	×
Authorization	Move, select discrepancy	Temporary	×
Identity supplement	Move, select discrepancy	Temporary	×
Grant of asylum	Move, select discrepancy	Temporary	×
Certificate of vaccination	Move, select discrepancy	Temporary	×
Access permit	Move, select discrepancy	Temporary	×
Temporary visa slip	Move, stamp	Temporary	×
Investigator ID	Move	Temporary	×
M.O.A. citation paper	Move	Temporary	×
Objects given by NPCs			
Notes	Move, give	Temporary	×
EZIC code	Move, solve	Temporary	×
Press ID	Move, give	Temporary	×
Locket	Open, move, give	Temporary	×
Token	Move	Temporary	×
Credits	Move	Temporary	×
Flyers	Move, keep, turn backwards, give	Temporary	×
Business card	Move, keep, turn backwards, give	Temporary	×
Plagues	Move, hang	Permanent	×
Pennant	Move, hang	Permanent	×
Drawing	Move, hang	Permanent	×
Family photo	Move, hang	Permanent	×
Keys	Move, use	Temporary	×
Photo	Move, keep, give	Temporary	×
Watch	Move, keep, give, sold	Temporary	×
Weapons			
Guns	Take, move, shoot	Temporary	×
Bomb	Move, deactivate	Temporary	×
Poison	Open, move, use	Temporary	×

Objects are the most important entities of the game. Interaction with objects is analyzed in four categories (see Table 19.3). Objects which involve information for the inspector are readable and include rules of the current date for the investigator. Documents mostly include information of travelers and the player must decide

Table 19.4 Interaction with characters

Elements	Interaction options	Duration	Changeability
Interrogate mode	Open	Temporary	×
Entrants	Press buttons to interrogate, give documents	Temporary	×
Attackers	Shoot	Temporary	×

Fig. 19.6 Interaction with characters in Papers, Please (with permission of 3909 LLC)

whether the traveler may or may not enter according to the accuracy of given information or excuses. If there is a discrepancy or forgery, the player can open investigation mode. Objects given by NPCs have no effect on gameplay except hangable objects, EZIC notes, and business card. Weapons are seen at certain times. For example, the gun drawer opens, and the player can take and use guns when there is an attack against the checkpoint.

As is seen in Table 19.4 and Fig. 19.6, interaction options with characters are limited. Interrogate mode is not connected with characters directly; however, when it is activated, search or fingerprint buttons become usable. Most days come with new rules. There is no interaction option related to time in the game. When a workday starts, it will continue until it ends.

19.3.2 Beholder

Beholder (Alawar Premium 2016) is a 2D point-and-click adventure video game. Carl Stein, the player character, is assigned as the landlord of a building with six apartments run by Ministry of Allocation and his tasks are peeping, spying, profiling, and reporting tenants according to often updated state laws. While doing his job, he also should meet the expectations of his family and tenants. Every choice comes with a consequence. The gameplay depends on the given tasks and balancing is an important part. The player can choose what to do and there are several endings depending on these choices.

Representation The game occurs in a totalitarian state and starts on September 1st. Every day in the game lasts approximately seven and a half minutes. It takes place in a building which is masonry construction with seven apartments in three storys and a basement. The dominant surface consists of walls and there are no specific topological rules. It is a residential building and it is possible to discover both inside and outside of it. Carl Stein lives with his family at the basement level. All apartments are furnished with similar objects. There are three modes of apartments: needs repair, ready to move in, and occupied (see Fig. 19.7). The game world consists of apartments of tenants, Carl's apartment, entrance halls, and the street.

Population density is unclear. One of the interesting things about the game is its character representations. All characters are almost silhouettes, only their eyeholes, facial hair, accessories, and neckbands are in white. All information related to their emotions is given by their shape of eyeholes (see Fig. 19.8). There are five types of characters: Carl Stein (the protagonist), his family, tenants, ministry workers, and NPCs. There are 25 potential tenants during the gameplay, some of them come according to specific tasks. All characters appearing on the first day are available in Table 19.5.

There are two currencies: money and reputation points. The player can earn money by completing tasks, blackmailing, profiling and reporting tenants, or

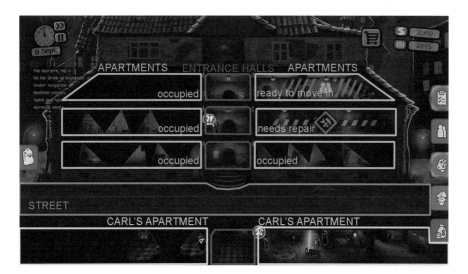

Fig. 19.7 Three modes of apartments (with permission of Alawar Premium)

Fig. 19.8 Representations of characters in Beholder (with permission of Alawar Premium)

Table 19.5 List of characters appearing on the first day

	Character	Form	Gender	Visibility	Role/organization
1	Carl Stein	Human	Male	✓	Landlord
2	Martha Stein	Human	Female	✓	Family member
3	Patrick Stein	Human	Male	✓	Family member
4	Anna Stein	Human	Unknown	✓	Family member
5	Policeman	Human	Male	✓	Family member
6	Bruno Hempf	Human	Male	✓	Ministry worker
7	Rosa Ranek	Human	Female	✓	Ministry worker
8	Mark Ranek	Human	Male	✓	Tenant
9	Maria Schimmer	Human	Female	✓	Tenant
10	Klaus Schimmer	Human	Male	✓	Tenant
11	Jacob Manishek	Human	Male	✓	Tenant
12	Nathan Kehler	Human	Male	✓	NPC

stealing items from tenants and selling them. The player can use the money to do some tasks and buy items. Reputation points can be earned with tasks as well as talking to the tenants. It can be spent on buying surveillance cameras, convincing tenants, and bribing the police. Some tasks have a time limitation. If the player cannot complete these tasks in time, there is a penalty.

Style Projection angle of Beholder is horizontal. The anchor of the framing mechanisms is anchorless, it does not depend on the movement of Carl Stein. The mobility of the screen is fixed. There is one fixed screen and the player can move and zoom in/out the camera within that screen.

There are two different yet compatible art styles in the game. While the style of character representation is in silhouette, the game world looks sketchy and cartoonish. Furthermore, characters are achromatic, black and white are used heavily. The game world is colorful and has cold colors. The game has a very dark look with a low contrast level; however, contrast levels of character appearances are high due to their art style.

Navigation Movement in the game is two-dimensional: horizontal and vertical. The transition between spaces is continuous. Different spaces are considered in three different parts: apartments, entrance halls, and the street. The movement between

Table 19.6 Analysis of connectors in Beholder

Connector	Passability	Visibility	Reversibility	Open/closed	Movement	Connection
Door (first, second, third floors)	✓	✓	✓	Closed	↔	Outside ↕ Inside ↕ Inside
Door (basement floor)	✓	✓	✓	Open	↔	Inside ↕ Inside
Stair	✓	✓	✓	Open	↕	Inside ↕ Inside

Table 19.7 Interaction with the environment

Elements	Interaction options	Duration	Changeability
Apartments of tenants	Repair, find a tenant	Temporary	×
Doors	Peep, knock, unlock	Permanent	×
Mailbox	Read	Temporary	×

spaces part is derived from analysis of Wolf (2011) because smaller spaces are accepted as spatial cells in suggested framework. Boundaries are walls (between apartments and halls) and the edge of the building (between the building and the street). All doors have the same characteristics and they are either open or closed. Doors belonging to tenants are closed but they can be opened by a master key; however, the two doors located in the basement are always open because they lead to Carl's apartment (see Table 19.6).

Interaction The player can interact with the game environment through apartments, doors, and the mailbox. (see Table 19.7 and Fig. 19.9). Doors have important roles in the gameplay because of almost every action in the game related to interaction with doors. The player should knock or peep the door if he/she wants to know if somebody is in the apartment. If there is nobody, surveillance cameras can be placed or the apartment can be searched after unlocking the door with the master key.

Objects in the game can be used for Carl's duties (surveillance cameras, furnishes, small objects), communicating with the government (desk and telephone), fixing things (repair kit), or making money (small objects) (for all interaction options with objects see Table 19.8). There is also a bus coming and leaving every day and it carries tenants; however, there is not an interaction option with it. Character interactions (see Fig. 19.10) are shaped by tasks and based on dialogues. This creates a need for UI analysis. The protagonist's walking pace is adjustable. If the player clicks somewhere, Carl Stein starts walking at a normal pace. He walks faster to the point of arrival if the player double clicks. Lastly, the player can stop time. However, there is no time manipulation option.

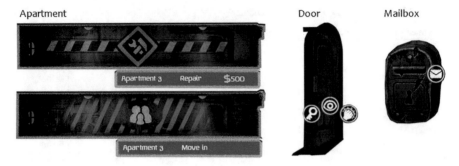

Fig. 19.9 Interaction with the environment (with permission of Alawar Premium)

Table 19.8 Interaction with objects

Elements	Interaction options	Duration	Changeability
Surveillance camera	Purchase, place in, displace, sell	Permanent	×
Furnishes	Search, repair	Permanent/temporary	×
Desk	Search, repair, write a document	Permanent/temporary	×
Telephone	Dial the number, pick up, reference	Permanent/temporary	×
Repair kit	Purchase, use, sell	Permanent	×
Small objects	Take, steal, sell, give, use as evidence	Permanent/temporary	×

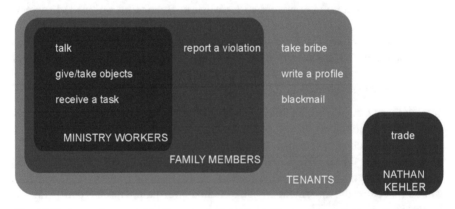

Fig. 19.10 Interaction sets with characters in Beholder (with permission of Alawar Premium)

19.3.3 Mirror's Edge

Mirror's Edge (Electronic Arts 2009) is an action-adventure video game and has unique characteristics compared to video games belonging to the platformer genre. The City is controlled by the authoritarian city regime. They control the media and govern the City with strict rules. Runners are an independent, illegal courier group and they carry documents across the city from senders to receivers. The players run, jump, swing, or cling all over the city to escape government forces and solve the

Fig. 19.11 Districts of the City (with permission of Electronic Arts, Inc.)

mystery behind the death of Robert Pope through the game. The game represents a familiar world in a different practice. As Bogost (2008) mentioned, "And because Mirror's Edge is a video game instead of a photograph, it is able to extend a way of looking into a way of moving as well."

Representation Mirror's Edge is set in a near-future metropolis called "The City." The game takes place in a built environment which has a modernist style. The game environment is limited to the city and there are some districts which are mentioned in the game: Financial District, West Arlington, Lower East Side, Ryding Park, Downtown, the Docks, Harbor, Looking Glass Garden, and the Shard (see Fig. 19.11).

The dominance of the white color in the game can be seen best throughout its representations of districts. The dominant surface is built environment which is a mix of buildings and construction materials made of concrete, steel, and panels. There are no specific topological rules in the game except Faith's incredible skills as a runner. The vegetation of the game includes trees and decoration plants. They are sparsely placed to the environment both inside and outside. Also, there is a river which crosses the City. There are lots of structural elements in the environment because the City is still under construction. All elements belong to the built environment are listed in Table 19.9 and their representations can be seen in Fig. 19.12.

Table 19.9 Built environment of the City

	Element	Type	Part
Buildings			
1	Robert Pope & associates building	Commercial	Inside
2	City eye building	Commercial	Inside
3	Centurion plaza	Commercial	Inside
4	Z. Burnfield international shipping building	Commercial	Inside
5	New Eden mall	Commercial	Inside
6	PK building	Commercial	Inside
7	Shard	Government	Inside/outside
8	Unfinished plaza	Other	Inside
9	Abandoned building	Other	Inside
10	Unknown buildings	Unknown	Inside/outside
Circulation			
11	Elevator	–	Inside
12	Stairs	–	Inside/outside
13	Terraces	–	Outside
14	Elevator shaft	–	Inside
Others			
15	Rooftops	–	Outside
16	Ground level (squares, streets)	–	Outside
17	The harbor	Transportation	Inside/outside
18	Subway	Transportation	Inside/outside
19	Drain	Infrastructure	Outside
20	Tunnels	Infrastructure	Inside
21	Canal passage	Infrastructure	Outside
22	Maintenance rooms	Transportation	Inside/outside
23	Boat	–	Inside/outside
24	Ventilation	–	Inside

The City is sparsely populated. There are several factions such as City Protection Force (CPF) and Pirandello Kruger (PK) which are connected to the city regime and they control the lives of the citizens. There are different characters who have important roles in the story. Players play the game as Faith Connors who is the protagonist. She is partially visible in the game unless some shiny surfaces reflect her image. Kate Connors is the twin sister of Faith and she is a member of CPF. She has a similar physical appearance with Faith except she is seen wearing the CPF uniform. Mercury is a former runner and a guide for Faith. He can be seen in the cut scenes, there is only his voice during gameplay. All characters in Mirror's Edge are represented in normal sizes and appearances (see Fig. 19.13 and Table 19.10).

Style The player plays the game from the first-person angle during the gameplay. The anchor of the game is anchorless and its mobility is connected to the dot in the center of the screen. The style of Mirror's Edge is close to realistic style even if

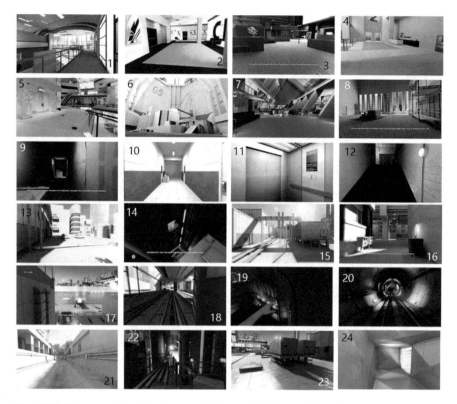

Fig. 19.12   Representation of environmental elements (with permission of Electronic Arts, Inc.)

it has some unrealistic touches because of the runner vision. The dominant color of the surfaces is white even though some objects that are not normally white are also white, such as plants (see Fig. 19.14). This gives the game a bright look. High contrast is created with various colors: black, blue, yellow, green, orange, and red. Although environmental elements usually have two dominant colors, interior environments are represented as more colorful than exterior ones. Allison (2015) mentions that colors have different meanings for Faith. According to the article white color represents the background of the game, things that are irrelevant for Faith. Some red objects "act as landmarks." While blue objects mean slow down, black ones represent the danger.

Navigation The game allows three-dimensional movement during the gameplay. Transitions between cut scenes and gameplay or between different episodes are discrete; however, movement during gameplay is continuous. One of the most important things about movement in the game is runner vision. It visualizes the correct path for the player by coloring certain objects red. In addition to runner vision, the player can get a hint about where the correct path is by pressing the left alt key. There are two main boundaries between spatial cells: walls and spaces

Fig. 19.13 Representations of characters (with permission of Electronic Arts, Inc.)

Table 19.10 List of characters in Mirror's Edge

Character	Form	Gender	Visibility	Role/organization
Faith Connors	Human	Female	Partially	Runner
Kate Connors	Human	Female	✓	CPF
Mercury	Human	Male	✓	Runner
Celeste Wilson	Human	Female	✓	Runner
Miller	Human	Male	✓	CPF
Travis Burfield	Human	Male	✓	Founder of project Icarus
Jacknife	Human	Male	✓	Independent
Robert Pope	Human	Male	✓	–
Clarence E. Kreeg	Human	Male	✓	Runner
Cops	Human	Male/unknown	✓	PK

between buildings. The connectors are ventilation halls, doors, ladders, stairs, bars, springboards, zip lines, pipes steel shapes, and panels. Connectors are mostly passable, visible, and reversible (for analysis see Table 19.11; for representations see Fig. 19.15).

Interaction Because the game experience is shaped by movement in Mirror's Edge, interaction with the physical world depends on navigational elements (see Table 19.12). Most objects in the game are also related to navigation (see

Fig. 19.14 Representation of plants (with permission of Electronic Arts, Inc.)

Table 19.13). Objects which lead the player are seen in red and they have some options such as step upon, jump, rotate, etc. Although runner's bags are collectable and have importance in the story, if the player chooses to not collect them, it does not have an impact on the gameplay. Players rotate valves, press buttons, and break glasses to open a path for themselves. In addition, weapons can be used for combat but there is no option for carrying them during gameplay. If the player does not drop the weapon, it spontaneously falls from their hands.

The player can interact with PK Forces; other characters are seen mostly in the cut scenes. Although there are some combat options, players can finish the game without interacting with any NPCs. It is possible to avoid and run away from enemies. Interaction options with PK Forces are punching, kicking, shooting, and disarming. Player can manipulate time by slowing down the flow of time during the combats.

19.4   Conclusion

This study has attempted to provide a holistic approach for defining experiential spaces in video games. The aim of this study is to provide a base for player experience research. As mentioned earlier, it is crucial to understand the structure of the game space and the experience in that space to understand the player experience. This framework could help understand experiential spaces of video games because it enables the detection of various factors. In addition, it is possible to use different layers individually according to the perspective of the research. Applicability and reliability of the framework were tested on three different video games. Each game highlights different layers of the framework.

Table 19.11 Analysis of connectors in Mirror's Edge

	Connector	Passability	Visibility	Reversibility	Open/closed	Movement	Connection
1	Door	✓	✓	✓	Open	↔	Outside ↕ Inside ↕ Inside
2	Elevator door	✓	✓	×	Closed	↔	Inside ↕ Inside
3	Emergency gate	✓	✓	×	Closed	↔	Inside ↕ Inside
4	Ventilation hole	✓	✓	✓	Open	↔	Inside ↕ Inside
5	Springboard	✓	✓	×	Open	↔ ↕	Outside ↕ Outside
6	Zip line	✓	✓	×	Open	↔ ↕	Outside ↕ Outside
7	Pipe	✓	✓	✓	Open	↔↕	Outside ↕ Outside Inside ↕ Inside
8	Ladder	✓	✓	✓	Open	↕	Outside ↕ Outside
9	Stair	✓	✓	✓	Open	↕	Outside ↕ Outside Inside ↕ Inside
10	Bar	✓	✓	✓	Open	↔	Outside ↕ Outside Inside ↕ Inside
11	Steel shape	✓	✓	✓	Open	↔	Outside ↕ Outside Inside ↕ Inside
12	Panel	✓	✓	×	Open	↔	Outside ↕ Outside

Fig. 19.15 Representations of connectors in Mirror's Edge (with permission of Electronic Arts, Inc.)

Table 19.12 Interaction with the environment

Elements	Interaction options	Duration	Changeability
Door	Open	Temporary	×
Ramp	Jump	Temporary	×
Zipline	Descent	Temporary	×
Pipe	Balance walk, climb, descend	Temporary	×
Ladder	Climb, descend	Temporary	×
Bar	Grab, swing	Temporary	×
Steel shape	Balance walk	Temporary	×
Panel	Wall run	Temporary	×

Papers, Please is about balancing different factors and it has simple gameplay with a variety of objects. In the analysis, representation and interaction layers worked in harmony. A variety of objects were supported by simple mechanics and they created a decent gameplay experience for players. Beholder has a particular representation style: the game has two different visual styles in the representation of characters and the game environment. Also, it reveals a weakness of the framework: UI analysis. Because almost all character interaction options are done by dialogues, it could be useful to add UI analysis for future studies for similar cases. Mirror's Edge is explored by navigating the environment. Dominant color palettes and extreme brightness in the representation layer contribute to the sense of being in the game world. The game highlights the navigation and interaction parts of the framework.

Table 19.13 Interaction with objects in Mirror's Edge

Image	Object	Interaction options	Duration	Changeability
	Runner's bag	Collect	Permanent	×
	Weapon	Shoot Pick up Drop	Temporary	×
	Helicopter	Jump	Temporary	×
	Valve	Rotate	Temporary	×
	Handrail	Jump	Temporary	×
	Box	Step upon	Temporary	×
	Buttons	Press	Temporary	×
	Crane	Climb Jump	Temporary	×
	Truck	Get in	Temporary	×
	Chair	Step upon	Temporary	×
	Glass	Break	Temporary	×
	Brick	Step upon	Temporary	×

After examining three different games, the applicability of the framework was tested successfully. The framework helps to understand various games with different genres, styles, and gameplay experiences. Also, it works better on Mirror's Edge than the other two games because the game provides more data for each layer. Explaining experiential spaces can be useful for player experience studies because it is important to understand how players' experiences are shaped and changed by the game world as well as the experiences themselves.

References

Aarseth, E (2001) Allegories of Space. The question of spatiality in computer games, In: Eskelinen M & Koskimaa R (eds) Cybertext yearbook 2000, Saarijärvi: Publications of the Research Centre for Contemporary Culture, pp 152–171

Aarseth E (2003) Playing research: Methodological approaches to game analysis. In: 5th International Digital Arts & Culture Conference, RMIT University, Melbourne, May 2003

Aarseth E, Smedstad S M, Sunnanå L (2003) A Multi-dimensional typology of games. Level Up Digital Games Research Conference, Utrecht, 4 – 6 November, pp 48–53

Adams E (2003) The Construction of Ludic Space. Proceedings of the DiGRA Conference. http://www.digra.org/wp-content/uploads/digital-library/05150.52280.pdf Accessed 10 June 2019

Allison F (2015) Whose mind is the signal? Focalization in video game narratives. DIGRA International Conference, Lüneburg, 14–17 May 2015

Arsenault D, Cote P, Larochelle A (2015) The Game FAVR: A framework for the analysis of visual representation in video games. The Journal of the Canadian Game Studies Association. 9 (14): 88–123

Bostan B, Berkman M I (2017) Explorations in Game Experience: A case study of 'Horizon Zero Down'. In Proceedings of the Eurasia Graphics 2017, Istanbul, 4 – 6 November

Bartle R A (2004) Designing virtual worlds. Berkeley, New Riders

Bogost I (2008) Persuasive Games: Windows and Mirror's Edge. Gamasutra, http://www.gamasutra.com/view/feature/132283/persuasive_games_windows_and_.php Accessed 23 December 2018

Brand J E, Knight S, Majewski J (2003) The diverse worlds of computer games: A content analysis of spaces, populations, styles and narratives. Proceedings of the DiGRA Conference. http://www.digra.org/wp-content/uploads/digital-library/05150.06387.pdf Accessed 15 April 2019

Brown E, Cairns P (2004). A grounded investigation of game immersion. In CHI'04 extended abstracts on Human factors in computing systems, ACM, pp 1297–1300

Calvillo-Gámez E H, Cairns P, Cox A L (2015) Assessing the core elements of the gaming experience. In Game user experience evaluation, Springer, Cham, pp. 37–62

Carson D (2000) Environmental storytelling: Creating Immersive 3D Worlds Using Lessons Learned from the Theme Park Industry. Gamasutra, https://www.gamasutra.com/ view/feature/131594/environmental_storytelling_.php Accessed 18 December 2018

Consalvo M, Dutton N (2006) Game analysis: Developing a methodological toolkit for the qualitative study of games. Game Studies: *The International Journal of Computer Game Research*. 6 (1):1–17

Csikszentmihalyi M (2014) Play and intrinsic rewards. In Flow and the foundations of positive psychology, Springer, Dordrecht, pp 135–153

Ermi L, Mäyrä F (2005) Fundamental components of the gameplay experience: Analysing immersion. Worlds in play: International perspectives on digital games research. 37(2): 37–53

Fernández-Vara C, Zagal J P, Mateas M (2005) Evolution of spatial configurations in videogames. Digital Games Research Association Conference, Vancouver, 16–20 June http://www.digra.org/digital-library/publications/evolution-of-spatialconfigurations-in-videogames/ Accessed 22 December 2018

Götz U (2007) Load and support: Architectural realism in video games. In Borries F V, Walz S P, Böttger M (eds) Space, time, play: Computer games, architecture and urbanism, pp 134–137

Günzel S (2008) The Space-Image. Interactivity and Spatiality of Computer Games. In Günzel S, Liebe M, Mersch D (eds) Conference Proceedings of the Philosophy of Computer Games Conference, Potsdam, pp 170–88

Huizinga J (1949) *Homo Ludens: a study of the play-element in culture*. London, Boston & Henley: Routledge & Kegan Paul

Jenkins H (2004) Game design as narrative architecture, In Harrigan P, Wardrip-Fruin N (eds) First person: New media as story, performance, and game, Cambridge: MIT Press, pp 118–130.

Jørgensen K (2013) GWI: The Gameworld Interface. Proceedings of the Philosophy of Computer Games, Bergen: University of Bergen, 2–4 October 2013

Juul J (2008) The magic circle and the puzzle piece. Conference Proceedings of the Philosophy of Computer Games. Potsdam: Potsdam University Press, pp 56–67

Keating S L W, Windleharth T (2017) The style of Tetris is … Possibly Tetris? : Creative professionals' description of video game visual styles. Proceedings of the 50th Hawaii International Conference on System Sciences. Hawaii, 4–7 January 2017, pp 2046–2055

Lee J H, Perti A, Cho H et al. (2014) UW/SIMM video game metadata schema: controlled vocabulary for visual style Version 1.5. http://gamer.ischool.uw.edu/official_release/ Accessed 7 February 2019

Leino T O (2013) From game spaces to playable worlds. The Philosophy of Computer Games Conference, Bergen, University of Bergen, 2–4 November

McGregor G (2007) Situations of play: patterns of spatial use in video games. Situated play: Proceedings of DiGRA 2007 Conference, Tokyo, Digital Games Research Association, 24–27 September 2007, pp 538–545

Moralde O (2014) Cause No Trouble: The Experience of "Serious Fun" in Papers, Please. Proceedings of the DiGRA 2014 Conference, Utah, Digital Games Research Association, 3–6 August 2014

Newman J (2004) Videogames, London & New York: Routledge, p 108

Nitsche M (2008) Video game spaces: Image, play, and structure in 3D worlds, London & Cambridge: The MIT Press

Pearce C (2007) Narrative environments: From Disneyland to World of Warcraft. In Borries F V, Walz S P, Böttger M (eds) Space, time, play: Computer games, architecture and urbanism, Basel, Boston & Berlin: Birkhäuser, pp 200–205

Schmidt F (2007) Use Your Illusion: Immersion in Parallel Worlds. In Borries F V, Walz S P, Böttger M (eds) Space, time, play: Computer games, architecture and urbanism, Basel, Boston & Berlin: Birkhäuser, pp 146–149

Vella D (2013) The Wanderer in the Wilderness: Being in the virtual landscape in Minecraft and Proteus. In Proceedings The Philosophy of Computer Games Conference Bergen

Wolf M J P (2011) Theorizing navigable space in video games. In Günzel S, Liebe M, Mersch D (eds), DIGAREC Series 06, Keynotes 2009 (10), Potsdam: Potsdam University Press, pp 18–49

Zagal, J P, Mateas M, Fernández-Vara C, Hochhalter B, Lichti N (2005) Towards an ontological language for game analysis. 2005 Conference: Changing Views – Worlds in Play, Vancouver, Digital Games Research Association, 16–20 June

Ludography

Alawar Premium (2016) Beholder. [video game] Novosibirsk, Barnaul: Alawar Premium Limited

Electronic Arts (2009) Mirror's Edge. [video game] California: Electronic Arts Inc.

Nintendo (1985) Super Mario Bros. Nintendo Entertainment System

3909 LLC (2013) Papers, Please. [video game]

Part V
New Technologies and Player Experience

Chapter 20
Immersiveness and Usability in VR: A Comparative Study of *Monstrum* and *Fruit Ninja*

Ysabelle Coutu, Yangyuqi Chang, Wendi Zhang, Sercan Şengün, and Ray LC

Contents

Abstract VR is a new medium, and standards and techniques for understanding the power of VR are just beginning to be adopted. The aim of this study is to look at the immersive potential of VR games physiologically and perceptually, using the horror game *Monstrum* and the arcade game *Fruit Ninja*. Players were run through *Monstrum* while talking aloud about the gameplay and then surveyed about their experience. To make a comparative study of VR and non-VR experiences, another study saw participants play *Fruit Ninja Mobile* and *Fruit Ninja VR* while recording galvanic skin response (GSR) during gameplay. It was found that, while *Monstrum* is immersive, issues like unintuitive UI and unappealing game AI dampened the experience, with motion sickness being a chief complaint. Meanwhile, *Fruit*

Y. Coutu (✉) · Y. Chang · W. Zhang
Game Science and Design, Northeastern University, Boston, MA, USA
e-mail: coutu.y@husky.neu.edu; chang.ya@husky.neu.edu; zhang.wendi@husky.neu.edu

S. Şengün
Wonsook Kim College of Fine Arts, Creative Technologies, Illinois State University, Normal, IL, USA
e-mail: ssengun@ilstu.edu

Ray LC
College of Art, Media, and Design, Northeastern University, Boston, MA, USA

Parsons School of Design, New York, NY, USA
e-mail: rayLC@newschool.edu

© Springer Nature Switzerland AG 2020
B. Bostan (ed.), *Game User Experience And Player-Centered Design*,
International Series on Computer Entertainment and Media Technology,
https://doi.org/10.1007/978-3-030-37643-7_20

437

Ninja VR was conducive for player engagement and immersion, with comparable instances of action gameplay sequences showing elevated numbers of GSR peaks per minute over the 2D Mobile version. This shows that emotional arousal for the same game is elevated in VR. Qualitative user responses corroborate the idea of a more immersive VR experience due to increased role taking over the 2D version, giving rise to possible design strategies for VR.

Keywords Video games · Immersion · VR · Virtual reality · Monstrum · Fruit Ninja

20.1 Introduction

VR technology faces various challenges, ranging from "enabling technologies [to] systems engineering and human factors." Consequently, there are questions surrounding best practices for designing for VR (Ali and Nasser 2017). Some studies focus on the best control schemes for VR (Martel and Muldner 2017), while others focus on storytelling, with relation to empathy and immersion that depends on participant personalities (Shin 2017). VR technology bears academic scrutiny to better establish standards, baselines, and usability for crafting the most effective and immersive experiences possible.

This study attempts to establish elements in VR experiences that are more or less conducive to immersion. A game in VR should be more immersive to players compared to a Mobile version, as it would give them a more intense feeling of being "in the experience," especially during action gameplay, where 2D games are emotionally isolating . Our initial study with *Monstrum* (2015) raised some important issues with control schemes as being highly impactful of end user experience, though this did not necessarily denote immersion. Rather, motion sickness was a factor that needed to be eliminated to get more cohesive results. Further, the inclusion of paired VR and non-VR gameplay allows a more controlled study of the physiological effect of the medium.

Fruit Ninja was chosen due to accessibility, familiarity to gamers, and lack of virtual movement, i.e., movement with a joystick, which contributes heavily to motion sickness. It was also thought that a comparison between the VR (2016) and Mobile (2010) versions of the game might lead to more coherent insights than a comparison between VR and PC, as Mobile is a more haptic experience than traditional mouse-and-keyboard inputs and creates less degrees of separation between player and game. If any major differences could be discovered, this would lend itself well to understanding the reason for VR's immersiveness.

20.2 Background

VR as a medium has been used in diverse settings such as architectural visualization, storytelling, and content creation where its ability to create immersive environments is unique. However, in relation to VR's role in gameplay, it is still relatively difficult to see what VR adds to the game experience other than a 360° display. To highlight the key differences, we must examine both VR and Mobile versions of the same game to gain insights about how VR changes aspects of gameplay interaction and elicits different physiological responses from players.

What marks out VR as a medium may be its ability to transport players to a setting where they otherwise would have no access to, be it in the real world or the virtual world. This allows us to gain empathy with a viewpoint that we previously did not have access to due to emotional response to the view from the headset (Torisu 2016). VR content creates greater engagement and empathy compared to 2-dimensional films (Schutte and Stilinovic 2017), leading to the question of whether this occurs in VR games vs. 2D games as well. It was found that VR facilitates perspective-taking in an experience involving color blindness (Ahn et al. 2013), raising the possibility that interactive experiences also produce psychologically different experiences in VR over 2D. Indeed, a study has shown that EEG beta-waves were elevated in frontal areas when viewing VR content compared to 2D video content (Kweon et al. 2017), suggesting physiologically different states when participants viewed content in VR.

The use of VR in the game context compared with 2D involves the question of how well players can effect changes in the environment. A study showed that in a horror VR game, the ability to cope with fright (self-efficacy) is a determining factor in how fearful (and enjoyable) the game is (Lin et al. 2018). Because VR is closer to the real world than 2D games, it can bring about emotional reactions, which is determined by how well players can cope with their own feelings in the immersive environment. Avatars have been used to express the emotions of players using biometric sensors integrated with gameplay (Bernal and Maes 2017). A comparison of the GSR sensor activity during gameplay in VR (as opposed to non-interactive content) would allow us to surmise whether these arousing emotional states are associated with immersive gameplay in VR.

20.3 Methodology

Six graduate students with varying gameplay background from Northeastern University participated in the *Monstrum* experiment. Informed consent was obtained, giving info on procedure, risks, data acquisition, contact info, and participant rights. A 10-question survey was also given. For this experiment, the researchers used two computers in the Northeastern Usability Lab: one for letting participants play *Monstrum*, and the other for recording the gameplay and the player. An Oculus Rift headset was used to play Monstrum in VR, and a standard Xbox controller was used to interface with the game (the Oculus Rift controllers were incompatible). Recording is done in Morae software.

After giving informed consent, participants went through a relatively short segment of the game. They were asked to say whatever came into their minds during their experience, especially regarding the user interface and game progress. As one researcher closely recorded the verbal observations from think-aloud, the other took notes regarding qualitative nonverbal data. Each session lasted 10–15 min, varying with regard to how long players could either survive in the game or stomach gameplay before having to rest. A post-game survey and interview followed. This worked well for an initial assessment of VR immersivity and set a baseline for further investigation.

However, in light of the *Monstrum* study's shortcomings, it was decided a second study should be run where users play through both VR and non-VR versions of a game, allowing for a direct comparison of the media. This would allow researchers to more accurately correlate immersiveness with the medium (VR or 2D monitor). Additionally, a different game was chosen utilizing a different movement system to minimize player discomfort, as motion sickness was the foremost complaint for breaking immersion in *Monstrum*. *Fruit Ninja* was the game selected for this, as not only did it support the use of the Rift touch controllers, but it also involved gameplay not requiring players to move virtually. Any movements they made would be one-to-one, which tends not to induce sickness in users.

Fourteen participants of varying levels of experience were run through *Fruit Ninja* and *Fruit Ninja VR*. After being briefed, participants were fitted with Shimmer3 wireless GSR (galvanic skin response) sensors, which provide real-time biometric feedback on a user's skin conductivity, measured by two electrodes attached to the fingers. Physiological arousal (stress, excitement, sadness, etc.) results in greater GSR activation, serving as a potential indication of a user's interest or emotional state at a given moment. Using Peak Analysis data (calculating where significant "spikes" occur in GSR conductance) researchers can further refine potential instances of arousal and begin to determine what stimuli might be resulting in increased user engagement.

After being fitted, participants were then asked to play both Mobile and VR versions of *Fruit Ninja* for however long they felt comfortable (though not exceeding 5 min per game). Half the participants started with VR, while the other half started with Mobile; this was randomly assigned. The Mobile version of the game was played on an iPad and recorded with a Tobii eye-tracking headset (for video only, as eye-tracking was not possible with VR and thus no comparisons could be made), while the VR version of the game was played using an Oculus Rift headset and an Oculus touch controller. Data (including screen footage and GSR metrics) was collected and partially analyzed in iMotions 7.0. Video, as well as Raw and Peak Analysis GSR data are then exported and analyzed in depth in R 3.6 using the pracma and signal libraries.

20.4 Results

With the *Monstrum* study, participants were able to provide their thoughts on many aspects of the game. All of them reported motion sickness caused by the game after 5–10 min of playing, and four out of the six participants mentioned that it may have been caused by the controls. *Monstrum* lets players use the Xbox controller stick to run and turn around in-game. Participants said the controls made the game feel "disorienting" and "not intuitive." Those who tried to physically turn around instead of using the controller stick described the experience as "inconvenient."

Despite the fact that the participants were all satisfied with the graphics and sound, all six of them reported the game to be less immersive due to the lack of instructions. Participants mentioned they felt confused because the short tutorial section did not provide full instructions on how to use the controls before the game starts. They then had to spend extra time figuring out how to move around, open the inventory, use items, etc., making the gameplay experience poor.

Three of the six participants also commented on the floating text instructions in the game. Researchers initially thought minimizing floating text might increase immersiveness, though due to the lack of a dedicated tutorial level, testers indicated they actually wished there was more floating text to help guide them with where to go, what to grab, how to explore, and so on, despite the text's non-diegetic nature.

With *Fruit Ninja*, both qualitative (user feedback and survey response) and quantitative (GSR biometrics) data were collected, to gauge participant engagement and immersion. Averaged GSR peak data over the entire trials of gameplay did not show significant differences between VR and Mobile ($p = 0.3209$). However, when focusing on 60-s segments of similar gameplay during fruit-whacking episodes, it was found that VR elicited a greater GSR response (peaks per minute) from participants (paired t-test, $p = 0.0197$, Fig. 20.1). This shows that subjects were aroused to a greater extent during VR gameplay over Mobile, making the experience more emotionally relevant for the participant during applicable gameplay sequences.

To see in depth how the GSR responses evolve over a trial, GSR conductances relative to the start of the trial are plotted for both VR and Mobile. After capturing the peaks of GSR responses, we then plot the GSR conductances integrated over the parts of the trial where GSR peaks occurred. As seen in Fig. 20.2, VR experiences generated greater GSR peaks integrated over the duration of the peaks, showing that VR produced sustainably more arousing responses over the course of a trial as well.

For qualitative data, participants both filled out a brief Google survey (20 questions) after having completed both the VR and Mobile portions of the study. Survey results indicated VR as being more immersive than Mobile (t-test, $p = 0.0001138$) when participants were asked to rank immersivity on a scale of 1–10 (one being least immersive, 10 being most immersive). Additionally, 64.3% of respondents indicated they preferred VR to Mobile.

The greatest vector for confusion in VR seemed to stem from the limited field of view and requirement for the player to utilize head movement in ascertaining the position of game elements (e.g., fruits and bombs). Two participants also commented on additional game mechanics in both Mobile and VR impacting their experience. One mentioned how a player can "accidentally bump things away with the flat of the blade you are given, which can knock fruits out of reach if you aren't careful," while the other also indicated "an omnidirectional blade like in Beat Saber" would perhaps have improved their game experience.

After completing the survey participants were also briefly interviewed, allowing them to provide more open-ended feedback and to express their final thoughts on

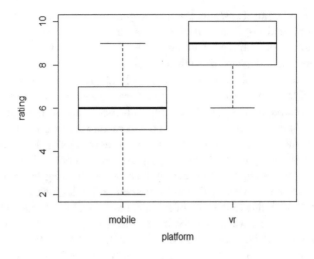

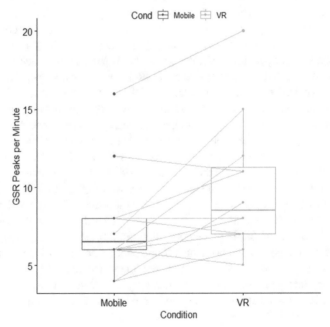

Fig. 20.1 The first figure depicts qualitative survey data scoring immersivity ("rating") for both Mobile and VR platforms. The second figure depicts GSR peaks per minute for 60-s fruit-whacking sample intervals for Mobile and VR gameplay of each participant in the Fruit Ninja study

the games and their experiences. From here, feedback was compiled and coded, as illustrated in Tables 20.1 and 20.2.

Of the 13 collected interview responses, seven cited VR as being objectively more immersive than Mobile. Six also cited VR as being more realistic than Mobile,

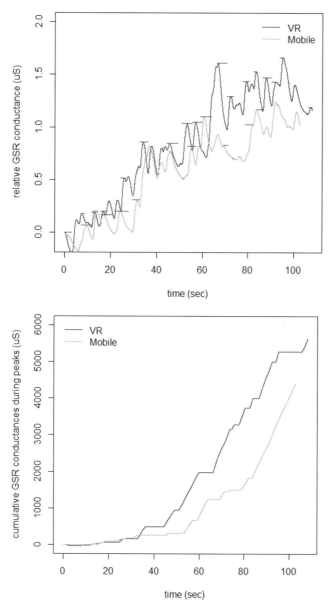

Fig. 20.2 Example GSR traces for participant 14, showing entire trial of VR and Mobile gameplay in real time (up). Red bars are GSR peak periods used to compute the plot on the down. GSR conductances (in micro Siemens) are integrated over periods of the peak calculate on the left. VR gameplay showed greater integrated conductances, indicating a greater overall GSR response over the course of the trial (down)

Table 20.1 An example of how interview data was coded

Feedback	Mobile	VR	General
Creates two different experiences Mobile is 2D, more control VR: Never know what is coming Forget you are slicing with a sword in Mobile More realistic in VR VR is more immersive In the environment Feel like actual ninja Arm movements	More control, less thematic	More realistic, limited view, more immersive	Two different experiences

Table 20.2 Coded interview data

Mobile	VR	General
All info on one screen, more clarity	Limited view, weird camera	
	Sound and visuals, intuitive, interactive	
	Harder than Mobile, more realistic, added physics mechanic	
More control, less thematic	More realistic, limited view, more immersive	Two different experiences
	Limited view, different dimension, more complex, more engaging, more immersive	Two different experiences
	More realistic, limited view, different dimension, interactive, fun, more immersive	
	Less control, no outside distractions, physical hardware limitations, more immersive	
Boring	More immersive, more realistic	
All info on one screen	Harder than Mobile, needed clearer instructions, more immersive	
	Intuitive, physical hardware limitations, needed clearer instructions, different dimension, added physics mechanic	
	Limited view, added physics mechanic, more immersive, worse gameplay	
More control, better feedback	More realistic, graphics	Two different experiences
Engaging	More realistic, harder than Mobile, minimal UI	

with four of these specifically attributing this to being able to see and swing around a sword in-game (one respondent mentioned that Mobile lacked this aspect, thus somewhat separating the experience from the theme of "being a ninja").

Five respondents also noted that, given the 3D nature of the VR game, this resulted in a limited field of view at a given point in time (versus Mobile where all information is presented on one screen). Interestingly, opinions were split as to whether or not this was a good thing: one participant cited this as an explicitly negative thing, while two thought this added to the experience and two were somewhat on the fence (more neutral).

20.5   Discussion

When looking at the first study, *Monstrum* (and VR games in general) are relatively immersive simply by virtue of the medium, as the vast majority of this study's participants stated VR directly impacted their experience. However, perhaps one of the biggest factors contributing to confusion among players was a lack of clear direction on mechanics and controls. Gameplay needed to be discovered through experimentation, and some players were not even able to perform simple tasks like opening their inventory without prompting from the researchers. A more minimalist UI would negatively impact the game experience, therefore indicating that properly indicated directions and HUD elements are important to minimizing confusion and increasing immersion. It should be noted that *Monstrum*'s UI is a mixture of diegetic elements (e.g., pulling up readables in the player's journal) and spatial elements (e.g., floating text in the game world explaining how certain game mechanics work, such as crawling under furniture to hide). Diegetic elements exist within the diegesis of the game world, and spatial elements exist outside of the game's diegesis but are still present within the game world's geometry (Stonehouse 2014).

Sound and graphics were most well-received when players were questioned about what they found most appealing in the game. These likely had a positive impact in increasing player immersion. Conversely, the game's AI was the most negatively received, though this was likely due to minimal contact with said AI, and in all but one case that contact being a sudden and non-telegraphed player death. This lack of clear feedback on what had gone wrong, how the AI operates, and how players can adapt in the future likely was detrimental to the experience.

One of the most impactful aspects of *Monstrum* in regard to player experience was motion sickness. Every participant experienced some degree of discomfort during play, largely owing to the smooth artificial locomotion system (using thumbsticks to navigate through the game's world). This movement system likely induced a temporary vestibular mismatch (perceiving movement while remaining stationary), resulting in headache, dizziness, nausea, and other adverse effects on testers (Carbotte 2018). *Monstrum* also did not support Oculus Rift Touch controllers, which would have provided a more natural way of engaging with the game world.

Results from the *Fruit Ninja* study were far more promising, as both the Touch controller and motion sickness issues were rectified through choice of game, while running a paired study allowed for direct comparison between a VR and non-VR experience. The majority consensus among participants, both through survey and interview, is VR felt more immersive. Being able to see and physically interact with in-game elements (the sword being the most commonly cited and praised) led users to feel they were engaging in a more realistic experience, therefore strengthening the game's core premise (in this case, "being a ninja"). These results seem to indicate VR heavily feeding into players' sense of ilinx, this being "the pursuit of vertigo" and "an attempt to momentarily destroy the stability of perception" (in other words, play in an attempt to stimulate the senses through such means as excitement, adrenaline, fear, etc.) (Caillois 2006).

GSR responses in *Fruit Ninja VR* during VR action gameplay sequences are significantly higher than responses in Mobile, but when averaged over the entire course of experiments, they do not differ. This shows that VR is only effective when players are asked to adopt particular roles (such as a ninja whacking fruit). This suggests that self-efficacy of actions in VR make the VR experience more arousing. The trial-by-trial analysis also shows that VR appears to activate greater GSR responses when integrated over the entire trial, showing that the effect of VR may not lie at the beginning of gameplay, but rather further into the experience, when subconscious role taking takes effect, and the actions become more arousing than they would be in Mobile. However, this can also be due to the Mobile version feeling more like a toy compared to the VR version, where players actually adopt the idea that they are ninjas.

This carries through into qualitative data, which shows the majority of participants emphasized they felt a high level of immersivity in VR, both when surveyed and interviewed. Many of these respondents specifically cited being able to see and swing around a sword as contributing to this higher level of engagement. As one participant stated, "There is less of a disconnect between you and the gameplay (you really feel like you're swinging a sword around, rather than just swiping a screen with your finger)." The addition of a fully realized and tracked 3D environment also seems to have impacted users' experiences (some positively, some negatively). These two factors contributed to creating more realistic game experience in VR compared to Mobile.

Some of the negative pushback to the added dimension, and the requirement for head movement to navigate that dimension, may have to do with hardware limitations; VR is still not on the same level as real-world vision and interaction, and limited field of view or headset calibration might have contributed to a somewhat suboptimal experience. An adjusted FOV may have remedied some of these concerns, though the possibility of players missing information because it appeared outside their range of vision is still a major issue which might call for more robust haptic (e.g., controller vibration) or audio cues.

There may have been some bias in participants, as almost all had previously had experience with the Mobile version of the game (some participants indicated they may have had extensive experience with the game prior). While this lent itself well to running the study with little need to coach participants, this may have also impacted their engagement with the Mobile portion of the study.

In future research, a similar study could be run involving the collection of other biometric data (such as EEG (Electroencephalography), eye-tracking, facial expression analysis, etc.). This would allow researchers to gauge the charge of participant responses to stimuli (either positive or negative) as well as gauging the type of brain activity present during gameplay. Additionally, running another horror game (or a game meant to stimulate a more pronounced emotional response) might benefit further GSR collection, as this would likely lead to more dramatic peaks. One study does just this, utilizing both GSR and EEG to gauge VR immersion using a virtual roller coaster, with their findings indicating overall higher engagement in VR (Farnsworth 2017). By applying these biometrics tools to more interactive experiences, the hope is both researchers and developers can more accurately pinpoint what makes VR so immersive, and how VR game design can better deliver a given desired experience to users.

20.6   Conclusions

This study studied how VR game experiences affect us physiologically and perceptually. We showed that gameplay usability such as UI and motion sickness affect the immersiveness of VR experiences. In a comparative study of the same game in VR vs. Mobile, we found greater arousal in players during action sequences, as well as greater GSR responses integrated within a trial. What's more, players appear to adopt their roles in the VR game better, taking actions with greater deliberation, and using the limited point of view as indicative of increased immersion in their character.

Acknowledgements We thank Fan Ling, Riddhi Padte, and Jason Duhaime for their assistance in running this study at the NEU Usability Lab. We also thank Dr. Casper Harteveld (Northeastern University) for his insights and support.

References

Ahn, S. J., Le, A. M. T., and Bailenson, J. (2013). The effect of embodied experience on self-other merging, attitude, and helping behavior. *Media Psychology.* 16 (1): 7-38.

Ali, N. S., & Nasser, M. (2017). Review of virtual reality trends (previous, current, and future directions), and their applications, technologies, and technical issues. *Journal of Engineering and Applied Sciences, 12*(3), 783-789. Available from <https://www.researchgate.net/publication/313349469_Review_of_virtual_reality_trends_previous_current_and_future_directions_and_their_applications_technologies_and_technical_issues>

Bernal, G., and Maes, P. (2017). Emotional Beasts: Visually Expressing Emotions through Avatars in VR. *Proceedings of the CHI Conference Extended Abstracts on Human Factors in Computing Systems*, 2395-2402. Available from <https://doi.org/10.1145/3027063.3053207>

Caillois, R. (2006). The definition of play and the classification of games. In K. Salen, & E. Zimmerman (Eds.), *The game design reader : A rules of play anthology* (). Cambridge, Massachusetts: MIT Press.

Carbotte, K. (2018). Do the locomotion: The 19 ways you walk and run in VR games. Available from <https://www.tomshardware.com/picturestory/807-virtual-reality-games-locomotion-methods.html#s2>

Farnsworth, B. (2017, Jan 17,). Measuring the power of virtual reality immersion [A case study]. Available from <https://imotions.com/blog/measuring-virtual-reality-immersion-case-study/>

Kweon, S. H., Kweon, H. J., Kim, S. J., Li, X., Liu, X., Kweon, H. L. (2017). A Brain Wave Research on VR (Virtual Reality) Usage: Comparison Between VR and 2D Video in EEG Measurement. *Advances in Human Factors and Systems Interaction*, 592: 194-203.

Lin, J. H. T., Wu, D. Y., Tao, C. C. (2018). So scary, yet so fun: The role of self-efficacy in enjoyment of a virtual reality horror game. *New Media and Society*, 20(9). <https://doi.org/10.1177/1461444817744850>

Martel, E., & Muldner, K. (2017). Controlling VR games: Control schemes and the player experience. *Entertainment Computing, 21*, 19-31. doi:https://doi.org/10.1016/j.entcom.2017.04.004

Schutte, N. S., and Stilinovic, E. J. (2017). Facilitating empathy through virtual reality. *Motivation and Emotion*. 41: 708. DOI: https://doi.org/10.1007/s11031-017-9641-7.

Shin, D. (2017). Empathy and embodied experience in virtual environment: To what extent can virtual reality stimulate empathy and embodied experience? *Computers in Human Behavior, 78*, 64-73. doi:https://doi.org/10.1016/j.chb.2017.09.012

Stonehouse, A. (2014, Feb 27,). User interface design in video games. Available from <http://www.gamasutra.com/blogs/AnthonyStonehouse/20140227/211823/User_interface_design_in_video_games.php>

Torisu, T. (2016). To what extent can virtual reality and machines stimulate empathy? UCL Interactive Architecture Lab. Available from <http://www.interactivearchitecture.org/to-what-extent-can-virtual-reality-and-machines-stimulate-empathy.html>

Ludography

Monstrum, 2015, Team Junkfish.
Fruit Ninja, 2010, Halfbrick Studios Pty Ltd.
Fruit Ninja VR, 2016, Halfbrick Studios Pty Ltd.

Chapter 21
Interactive Storytelling in Extended Reality: Concepts for the Design

Natasha Skult and Jouni Smed

Contents

Abstract Extended reality (XR) covers many techniques, such as virtual reality (VR) and augmented reality (AR), for creating mixtures of physical and synthetic realities. In this chapter, we present the work done in realizing interactive storytelling in XR. In addition to a literature review, we discuss how user experience (UX) and game design can be transformed to these new application areas.

N. Skult
Department of Art History, University of Turku, Turku, Finland

MiTale Ltd., Turku, Finland
e-mail: nabutr@utu.fi

J. Smed (✉)
Department of Future Technologies, University of Turku, Turku, Finland
e-mail: jouni.smed@utu.fi

© Springer Nature Switzerland AG 2020   449
B. Bostan (ed.), *Game User Experience And Player-Centered Design*,
International Series on Computer Entertainment and Media Technology,
https://doi.org/10.1007/978-3-030-37643-7_21

Keywords Interactive storytelling · Extended reality · Virtual reality ·
Augmented reality · Gamification · Interactive narratives · Digital storytelling

21.1   Introduction

In interactive storytelling, the generated story depends on the pre-prepared content
and the interactor's (e.g., player's or user's) choices in the storyworld. This differs
from conventional storytelling, where the audience is not given choice but the
content of the story stays the same in each instance. Interactive storytelling has been
researched since the 1990s focusing on presenting the stories in two-dimensional
screens (Smed et al. 2019). Figure 21.1 illustrates the difference between conventional storytelling, where the author constructs the story presented as such
the spectator, and interactive storytelling where a designer creates a storyworld
populated with characters and events that together with interactor's choices generate
the story. With the advent of more consumer-oriented and technically feasible
devices, the research interest in interactive storytelling is shifting also to *extended
reality* (XR).

XR combines different approaches to extend the physical reality with synthetic
components, which can be partial as in augmented reality (AR) or complete as in
virtual reality (VR). In comparison to other media for digital storytelling, XR poses
a fundamental challenge of catching the interactor's attention and directing it to
the right place at the right time. Storytelling in such a medium possesses unique
challenges that we previously did not have to consider. Conventional storytelling
practices, from books to movies and including as well most of the digital games, is
presented on a 2D screen, where interactor receives the information as a separate
entity from the story setting and takes part in it as an avatar. In XR, the interactor
becomes an active part of the storyworld, fully immersed in the social network of
its fictional characters and interactive elements in a virtual environment.

Fig. 21.1 A comparison of
(**a**) conventional storytelling
and (**b**) interactive
storytelling

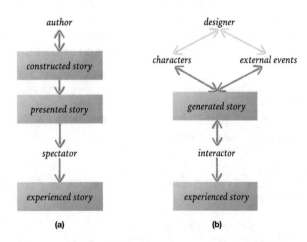

This brings multiple challenges for developers in both technical and creative side. Technically, the fidelity of presence and the feeling of inclusiveness are essential—from the quality of graphics and 3D sound design, to motion-tracking (especially head and eye movements). This must be applicable for all specific requirements from handheld devices to fully VR setups. For example, storytelling in AR usually depends on the location, and the interactor's route in the real world can be interpreted as choices also in the superimposed storyworld.

From the creative side, the first challenge is the constant availability of 360° view that can easily distract the interactor from the main parts of the story. The content creators must also consider the transitions between the scenes or actions having in mind the time the interactor needs to adjust to new surroundings and the new content that they should engage with. Providing acknowledged presence for the interactor is one of the laborious tasks facing the content creators, because the XR experience should feel "real." Another challenge is finding the right way and time when the interactor should be actively involved in the story (and when not). This includes keeping the interactor focused on the plot despite being able to direct their attention anywhere, along with the possible desire for the "six degrees of freedom"—the ability to move forward and backward, left and right, and, depending on a story, even up and down. An equally important challenge is creating content with which the interactor will bond—creating such emotions that the interactor will care about the characters, the storyworld, and the outcome of the narrative experience.

In this chapter, we analyze the challenges of interactive storytelling in XR and propose approaches how they can be addressed in the design and content creation practices based on both theoretical work and practical implementations. In Sect. 21.2, we present a review of the previous work, which has mainly conducted within the last few years. In Sect. 21.3, we take a closer look at designing user interface (UX) in XR. This is followed by three case studies in Sect. 21.4. Concluding remarks appear in Sect. 21.5.

21.2 Background

Figure 21.2 illustrates a hierarchy of needs in XR by Cronin (2015) modelled after Maslow's hierarchy of needs. The feeling of comfort and interpretability of the environment are the basic needs of XR. The XR hardware developers usually offer information for the application developers on the best practices to avoid common problems in the user experience; for example, see Oculus (2019).

Being a new area for narrative design, XR still lacks defined and refined working methods. The most important element in the design process is prototyping and user testing according to Rouse and Barba (2017) who interviewed 15 designers working with mixed reality (MR) experiences. Moreover, their approaches to the design varied along an opportunistic–deterministic spectrum, where the opportunistic approach is less structured and highly flexible, whereas deterministic design favors scientific or research-oriented approach.

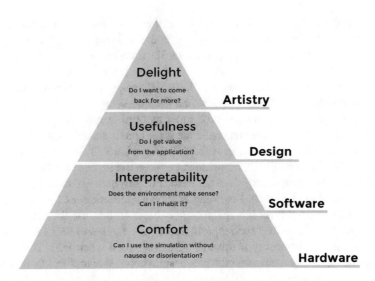

Fig. 21.2 The hierarchy of needs in VR development (Cronin 2015)

In this section, we present the previous work on XR and storytelling. Although some of this work has focused on *cinematic virtual reality* (CVR), where one or more users are watching 360° movies with VR devices, the ideas are also applicable to the cases where the view is created synthetically and in real time.

21.2.1 Field of View

The key challenge for XR is that the field of view is limited and the interactor cannot pay attention to the entire virtual scenery at once. For this reason, the traditional filmmaking techniques (i.e., methods that directors commonly use to direct the viewer's attention) that largely define current movie-making industry are not suitable (Fearghail et al. 2018). Filmmakers have traditionally relied on four core tools to tell stories:

- cinematography,
- sound,
- mise-en-scène (i.e., the arrangement of the scenery, props, etc. in the scenery), and
- editing.

If the interactor is free to explore the scene by looking wherever they want, all of these core approaches need to be reconsidered (see Fig. 21.3).

In XR, rather than having a window to a world, the viewer is present in it. Conveying narratives in XR is difficult because of the freedom given to viewer of being able to choose their own vantage point in the scene (Fearghail et al. 2018; Ko

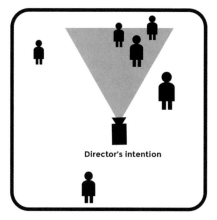 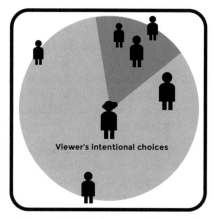

Fig. 21.3 Traditional film environment in comparison to an XR environment (Ko et al. 2018)

et al. 2018). For example, the story could be carried onwards in traditional cinema by moving from a cut to cut, which allows the director to control the viewers' attention, whereas in XR the viewer might not be looking at all where the director wants. For this reason, conventional approaches need to be re-evaluated for XR and new ones to be considered so that there is an understanding on how to use the appropriate techniques to maximize the quality of the user experience.

The orientation of the viewer is more important in directing the viewer to conceptualize the environment rather than presenting a series of images itself (Fearghail et al. 2018). The orientation plays a crucial role especially in cuts, since every cut requires the viewer to re-orientate themself in the new environment. Excessive or quick cuts may result in disorientation both in terms of the environment and the narrative and further negatively affect the quality of immersion. For this reason, utilizing the spatial nature of XR is essential for the directional approach, rather than basing it on time-based sequence of images. The pacing and playing should be more like in traditional theater, with a focus on cinematography (Dowling et al. 2018).

When the characters are performing the same task for a long time or are silent, the viewer tends to explore the environment, which is a good moment to direct their attention to the narrative (Bala et al. 2016).

21.2.2 Spatial Storytelling

Slater and Wilbur (1997) divides the process of achieving spatial presence into three phases:

- place illusion ("I am here"),
- plausibility ("this is happening"), and
- body ownership ("it is my body").

"Spatial storytelling" means engaging the viewer inside a spatial environment in which are contained non-linear narratives that can be discovered by exploring the provided space (Hameed and Perkis 2018). The narrative can be formed by using the space and movement over a temporal period, which makes spatial storytelling a promising way to develop more cohesive models for immersion. Spatial storytelling can stimulate presence in immersive environments, because it creates preconditions for narrative experiences in different immersions. According to Hameed and Perkis (2018) spatial stories can

1. evoke pre-existing narrative associations,
2. provide a backdrop where the narrative events unfold,
3. embed narrative information within their mise-en-scène, and
4. provide resources for emergent narratives.

21.2.3   Eye-Contact and Gaze

The viewer's attention is naturally drawn to the acting persons and the attention in XR can be directed by the character's eyeline or by the character directly addressing the interactor (Ko et al. 2018; Fearghail et al. 2018); see Fig. 21.4. Long takes, which tend to be preferred in XR, are not employed so much in traditional filmmaking. It is possible to draw comparisons to immersive theater where actor's eye-contact with the audience can be a means of strong non-verbal communication, and actor's (i.e., the principal character in the scene) eye-contact and gaze could be used to direct the viewer's attention for narrative storytelling (Ko et al. 2018). This would

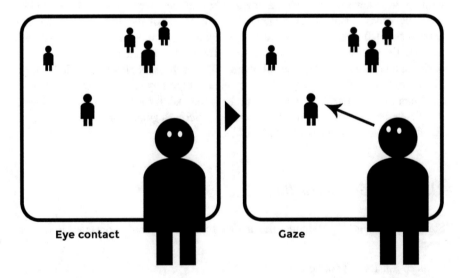

Fig. 21.4 Perception on directing the user's attention using eye-contact and gaze (Ko et al. 2018)

also facilitate more immersive and co-present feeling with the actors making the narrative more realistic.

21.2.4 Sound Cues

Sound is a crucial part of guiding narratives in XR, because sound cues not only contribute to the level of presence the viewer experiences, but also provide peripheral awareness of their surroundings by directing the user through the narrative (Fearghail et al. 2018). Pre-rendered audio, however, does not allow for immersive interaction, but audio elements should have interactive roles in the narrative since they can guide the user attention (Nakevska et al. 2014; Bala et al. 2018). Sound should take into account the plot and the interactive context of the user experience by allowing interactivity during the viewing.

Bala et al. (2018) list two modalities of listening: musical listening and everyday listening. In everyday listening, people pay more attention to what the sound source is communicating rather than the inherent sound itself. Thus, sound can be thought of as an object of hearing that informs the listener about events in the surrounding environment.

21.2.5 Social Aspects

For many people, watching films is a social experience: they enjoy discussing the events of the presented material as they occur. In XR (and especially in VR), using the devices requires that one person is using a personal head-mounted display (HMD) to immerse themself within the scene. This means that the viewers get isolated of their surrounding environment during the experience. Even if viewers are watching the same content simultaneously, they are not getting the same experience, due to the user's freedom to choose to move their field of view to look where they want to. Rothe et al. (2018) state that this is a drawback of XR systems because it separates the viewer from other people socially. Human interaction, such as pointing out interesting details or seeing what other people are focusing on, do not work as one cannot see the other people through the screens. Therefore, supporting social communication is crucial when developing VR applications.

For this purpose, Rothe et al. (2018) identify seven key challenges and design aspects that must be taken into account when considering social awareness and interaction in shared XR experiences:

1. *Viewport sharing*: The difference in users' field of view and missing awareness of the other's view is a main problem for shared XR experiences. There are two approaches for this problem: to frame the other's viewport (e.g., as a highlighted

rectangle) or to overlay the co-watcher's field of view as a small screen (which takes away valuable visual space).

2. *Communication*: While voice chat can be a good tool for increasing social awareness, it can also cause distraction and decrease the viewing experience. Replacing the (possibly disruptive) voice chat with a simple sign language could be a possibility as well.

3. *Social Awareness*: The feeling of being together is usually experienced by observing the postures and gestures, as well as perceiving the other's presence in the periphery of one's view. People watching the same screen can have silent interaction through body language, which cannot be seen when the watchers are wearing HMDs.

4. *Synchronization/navigation*: Social viewing could be possible even when communicating between multiple devices. By implementing this, users can see the same thing as anyone else viewing the content in real time, so it is as if they would be watching together. It must be preserved in the case of using navigation controls like pausing or playing the scene.

5. *Input device*: Navigation and communication require input methods. Graphical elements on the display or speech control disturb the viewing experience in this context. Instead, non-disturbing input methods should be implemented, and, for example, the use of gestures could be a natural form of interaction.

6. *Role concept*: Relation between the viewers can be defined as non-guided, guided, or slave. In a non-guided approach, the viewers have the same roles and permissions (i.e., everyone has control over their actions), which can cause that conflicts emerge in highly active communication. In the guided approach, one user is a guide that acts as a reference for communication and synchronization and is also responsible for the navigation (i.e., guides and followers form a hierarchy in the experience). In the slave mode, the camera is locked to be the same for all of the followers, which is not ideal as it allegedly causes simulator sickness but works well for third-party collaborators not using HMDs.

7. *Asymmetric Environments*: Shared CVR experiences should be possible across different devices, which can be achieved by assigning different roles to the viewers. For example, one could be in an observer role viewing through a TV while the other would be in an inspector role with the HMD and have their view be streamed to the TV.

21.3 Designing UX in XR

User experience (UX) in games consists of multiple layers of complexity in design choices that rely on the developers' aim to provide a desired overall game experience. In practice, the majority of UX is influenced by the individuals' previous experiences, personal tastes and preferences, interests and abilities as well as expectations from the game. Before addressing the UX design in XR, let us first discuss the fundamental elements of conventional UX design practices.

21.3.1 UX in Game Design

For a designer, a game is a way to interact and to have a dialogue with the players—from getting the players to understand the game to having them play the game in a way the designer has intended them to do. Communication between the designer and the player is one of the core elements of gameplay, and it consists of conveying the information in several ways. Unlike in other media of creative industries, gameplay uses multiple elements to convey the information to the player through visual and audio effects, emotion and anticipation of the performers, composition and dynamic point-of-views. The player is an active interactor with that environment making an impact through actions and the received feedback from these actions. Therefore, composing a game as a medium of entertainment carries more depth in its dialogue with the players.

Giving and receiving *information* is the key element of this dialogue. Games are filled with information given in the form of visual, audio, and interactive clues with the aim to confirm to the player the following aspects (Adams 2014, pp. 259–260):

- Where I am and what is my immediate goal?
- What shall I do next in order to fulfill the task ahead?
- Am I doing things right or shall I improve something?
- Am I in danger in losing or not progressing?

The more complex the gaming experience, the more carefully these questions need to be answered by the designer providing the players with adequate clues throughout the gameplay. The most common clues are given through

- in-game dialogues with other characters,
- quests and calls for action,
- sounds and music,
- secondary display and pop-ups,
- props and inventory, and
- visual narrative within the gameplay environment.

Whatever the clues are, they are meant to affect the players' experience, and they aim at sparking curiosity and empower exploration—simply, giving a sense of satisfaction in achieving the set goals. Some of the clues are focused on giving more sense to the story, a sense of emotion and mood, and an element of surprise and unknown. All this tries to keep the game fresh and unpredictable and maintaining players motivated to continue with their gaming experiences.

Often the clues are directive and used to control the players' movement and actions throughout the game environment. These clues are meant to lead the player to the "correct" path to meet the set goals. Regardless of the genre, games are in essence exploratory: the player is meant to find new ways and new solutions to the given task (not necessarily foreseen by the designer). That is why games are a continuous dialogue between the designer and the player, where both lead each other to new experiences.

21.3.2 Challenges in XR

The process of designing games based on a screen and given control inputs (e.g., a gamepad, mouse, or keyboard) has been evolving for decades. This evolution has created best practices, which are often genre and platform specific. Enabling the players to physically interact inside a virtual game environment provides new challenges for implementing these conventional practices to produce completely new gaming experiences. UX design in XR is a collective experimental process, where the developers are currently working on to find best practices in solving a completely new set of challenges. Each new medium of immersive experience have faced a new set of challenges for which the conventional practices used before are not fitting. We can look back to the evolution of cinematic conventions and language for more than a century ago. Starting with the practices of stage theater, the directors and moviemakers found the solutions through decades of experimenting and figuring out what feels best for the audience. This is exactly what is happening with the XR game developers who are taking part in a collaborative effort through inclusiveness and discovery each day, sharing best practices in ongoing technical improvements.

In XR, the interaction with the environment itself brings multiple challenges. The first challenge is that each individual player does not start with a default setup but is unique in their height and posture. The input streams have a natural mapping view, where free head movements and the observation of 360° space around the player are possible. If the player uses a gamepad or mouse and a keyboard in XR, the movement is not in the right connection between the actions and what the brain perceives, which can cause physical discomfort to the player.

This brings us to the second challenge: fidelity to the movement and interaction with the virtual world. Any sudden errors that may occur by rotating views, unbalanced change of frames, and scaling of items in the given environment can break the immersion and affect the player's experience. Interacting inside a virtual world is memorable and intuitive due to the richness in movement. The game world is now being observed through our own view—just like in real life—using our own eyes and head movements, twists and turns of whole body towards the direction of choice. Moreover, the input of the headset itself is intuitive allowing to explore clues the same way as we do in day-to-day life. This has a great impact on the UX design, since physical body perception is easy to get used to—we know how to move and interact with objects around us. It gives the feeling of an unbraced and unconstrained field of motion that the player can explore with their own individual preferences—it brings *presence*. Presence of the player as an embodiment in the virtual world gives a new layer to the game design practices that need to focus on the emotional and sensory aspects—a concept of a *body*—in the game design process. To feel fully immersed in a virtual experience, the player needs to feel like themself, needs to be in control of their own body as would be the case in the real world. If the game world does not give an adequate feedback to the player actions according to the expectations based on interacting with the real world, the player experiences a *disconnection.* Therefore, one important aspect is to avoid risks for the player of disconnecting with the game world while being present inside the game.

21.3.3 Finding a Balance in the Design

In order to create the best possible user experience in XR it is important to create a balance of shared information between audio-visual components and interactions (Yi et al. 2007). Moreover, movements and gestures must be meaningful to the player as much as to the immediate feedback they provide in the game environment. Therefore, the representation and the visual narrative of the game world are crucial. If the game has a high fidelity to the real world, it sets up expectations for the player on how to interact and behave so that the environment will be more like in the real world. This could be a cause for a bigger discomfort if some interaction does not fulfil the player's expectations. On the other hand, if the environment has a more abstract setting, adopting senses to the new rules inside of the abstract world is more appealing and has a lower risk of disconnection.

One of the best known examples is giving virtual hands to the player. Hands and fingers, especially fingertips, are a big part of how we communicate with the world (Wolf et al. 2011). Once the player has no connection to their own hands in the virtual world with full fidelity, they may experience disembodiment in which brain does not receive the information about interactions with the given object and environment. Therefore, creating virtual hands—that can be more abstract, like in the *Job Simulator* game for HTC Vive—provides a better connection to the world and interaction with its elements. Currently, the best virtual hands with realistic movement is provided by Oculus Quest, where the controllers allow interaction with precision not just a grip. While grip calls for action, more tangible and precise finger movements bring forth the cognitive side of interaction as it makes the player to think not just act. These are also another improvements and implementations of the intuitive clues that designers can have when creating a game.

Besides giving control to the player with a 360° view to the environment and control over its objects, there is still a need for haptic feedback which enriches the sense of presence in the space and objects around. By having haptic feedback on touchpads or controllers we can provide senses of friction, texture, and elasticity. With the newest technical achievements in XR development, it is possible to trick the player's brain in believing that touching the object is real. This also refers to the feeling of presence in the game environment, the distances of the objects around as well as play areas. While the physical play area has a maximum size within a room scale, the virtual area of the gameplay is unconditional. This means player can move throughout the virtual world beyond the physical space which is limited by VR headset setup, therefore interactivity with virtual environment need to aligned with the setup in a physical/real world.

There are multiple approaches to realize movement through the virtual environment. The most common one is to simply walk towards close-range objects or "teleport" to the further distance spot by pointing to the specific location in the environment. Unlike in more conventional game design practices, in XR the player is a part of the experience and not just following the clues made by designer. Every player can interact differently to their own desired preferences and pacing; other players are likely to notice different objects and give them different priorities even if some were intentionally highlighted by the designer to follow. This brings forth the most significant challenge in UX design: being able to design an experience that can be recognized by different players equally important by following the clues left by the designer. Furthermore, this design approach opens opportunities for creating tailored gaming experiences for specific needs and interests of each player individually.

In creating a meaningful, immersive, and intuitive UX in XR, one of the main goals is focusing on the player's ability to make meaningful choices. Once again enabling free body movement and gestures have utmost importance in creating these choices. For example, if the player were in a chemical laboratory conducting an experiment with several chemicals, giving the ability to mix ingredients in a specific manner would give a more meaningful result of successful experiment than clicking one button on a controller to produce the final result. In XR, the player immerses in a realm between fantasy and reality at the same time, knowing that the game is taking place and no actual harm can be caused even if a mistake happens, while, at the same time, carefully attempting the best possible practices to achieve the goal requiring both physical and mental concentration. Games so far also have been challenging the players to use both their physical and mental focus, but this is mainly based on reflex skills and the training of the fine motorics using specific controls input. Now, the whole body takes place inside the virtual world—or at least that is what the player's senses are communicating to the cortex.

To empower the game designer truly with tools to tackle presented design challenges we need tools that enable to generate various sensory stimuli. Sounds and 360° audio design serves the player to orient themself in the environment and it also gives various clues to what may be the task with the highest priority. Visual elements and highlights, use of light, and the building up of an atmosphere can serve in collecting the right items, avoiding danger, and providing additional narrative-driven content that needs not to be presented textually.

The presentation of textual content is particularly challenging in a virtual environment since it should not extend beyond the textual information we are surrounded in the real world. The use of established systems of communication with conventional signs and symbols is highly recommended. Because of this most of the user interface and signs are still available as 2D objects in a 3D environment. Having a narrator explaining the content in more detail through audio is more convenient than making the player to read long text instructions and descriptions.

When creating a training environment in a VR or AR setup, there is often a need to use multiple user interfaces. For example, in a VR safety training environment (see Sect. 21.4.2) the player may have an interface only visible to themself, such as hints, instructions, or inventory and secondly having various written information on the boards and screens in actual virtual environment. Studies and reports from gamification practices emphasize that personal UI elements visible only to the player should be curved and closer to the player's reach and not in the direct line of sight. Recommended approach is to have it available for player in a slightly in periphery areas which head movement would trigger and become static interface while player is keeping the focus on. Other signs and guidance in the environment are locked to the specific location points and the player must approach them either by walking towards or teleporting next to them. Naturally, the complexity of the UI design depends on the complexity of the virtual training world. Nevertheless, it is possible to have multiple layers of clues of audio-visual stimuli but only extensive testing can reveal which are needed in order to have the most beneficial results in the training sessions.

21.4 Case Examples

The development of XR environments plays a big role in the evolution of game technology, but its implementation is even more present outside of the game industry and the fields of entertainment. Much of the development is taking place to support to other industries from simple visualizations of work spaces and possible improvements in construction work to interactive simulations for learning and training practices. There are various reasons for this shift of consumer demands, but the main reason is the lowered cost of the equipment needed for VR or AR presentations. The required hardware and a computer powerful enough to run the applications, which are not yet affordable for common consumer market, are affordable enough for companies and institutions. Moreover, a VR setup needs a physical space for the player to move around freely, which can be an issue for the use in a home environment but usually not for commercial companies.

In the following three case studies, we will discuss several different approaches in UX design and the use of XR technology for specific requirements of the clients (which we cannot disclose due to restrictions in sharing the project details and parties involved). The application areas vary from logotherapy to safety training and the use of XR from AR to VR.

21.4.1 Location-Based AR Experience

In the project "Sanalanka Adventures—Speech and Language Therapy Tool," we have been developing an interactive environment for 3–6 year old children that have difficulties in language learning and speech development (see Fig. 21.5). It serves the children to overcome communication challenges through engaging them in a gaming experience, where we utilize AR content, speech recognition, and neural networks. A child can practice various tasks assigned by the therapists, who have

Fig. 21.5 A screenshot from *Sanalanka Adventures*

own dashboard where they can set up and adjust tasks for each individual client and follow the therapy progress.

With respect to the AR technology, we have utilized interactive storytelling from the game content with a real-life setting. Certain tasks can be completed in different environments such as the child's home or outdoor playground. AR serves as an additional form of interactive learning and utilizes the most important parts of it: curiosity, finding a solution for the given challenge, discovery, the feeling of accomplishment and showing/teaching one's own experiences to others. In general, AR is a good tool for educational and therapy practices, because it can be used by different target groups and it is self-explanatory by having virtual content available in a real-life environment. Used in combination with other technologies such as speech recognition it opens up new areas of accessibility for those children who have issues with their fine motoric skills. Being able to control and interact using speech—especially in speech and language therapy—evokes bigger motivation to improve the speech elements such as pronunciation by assigning own self-governed goals such as completing fun tasks within the game environment. No character or asset in the game gives negative feedback if the user fails. Instead it encourages the child to try again and gives positive feedback. This way the child often forgets that they are even playing an educational or therapy game and wish to continue with their adventures towards new discoveries.

In *Sanalanka Adventures*, we have created several different approaches using AR, of which we present here two. The first example includes a building game that takes place inside an area that the child decides to use, which can be indoors (e.g., their own room) or outdoors (see Fig. 21.6). One can think of this as playing *Minecraft* (Mojang 2011) but with the twist of having game mechanics from *Thomas Was Alone* (Bithell 2012). The child gets virtual building blocks which each have different qualities and specifications (e.g., size and colors) and also "skills." These skills determine whether some blocks are better with different aspects and features

Fig. 21.6 A screenshot from the building game of *Sanalanka Adventures*

the player wants their building to have (e.g., some blocks are good to hold heavy weight but cannot float on water, or those that are good to float are not good with strong winds). A combination of having different blocks when building one's own fantasy world requires lots of tinkering and strategizing, while trying to solve different challenges that virtual environment may give.

In the second example, we use AR technologies together with the existing material used in speech therapy. Traditionally, this material is provided to the families in the form of stickers and images, which parents should place in the right places at their home, with the purpose of explaining different everyday activities around the household. They serve as communication tools in explaining various activities from guiding how to wash hands and which tab gives hot and cold water to being cautious around kitchen appliances. In our platform, we have used one of the main characters in the game as a child's friend and personal assistant, who explains each activity. Having scanned an image with a mobile device, the friend provides additional information about the item that is scanned and warns about a possible danger. This way the child remains interested to explore and learn on their own what each image or item is meant for and how to properly interact with it.

Although the evaluations of results are still in the process, we have seen encouraging results in testing various AR solutions with young children, which seems to indicate potential in providing immersive content for other sectors and subjects in education and healthcare practices.

21.4.2   VR Safety Training

Simulations and training programs in VR are already in common use. The main reason why companies see a benefit in using VR in their training programs is its cost efficiency, because it makes it possible to train multiple employees at the same time while giving individual input to each employee. As an example we will discuss here the UX design of a fire safety training simulation.

Fire safety training simulation is usually carried out in a controlled environment with sources of smoke and fire occurring according to the training protocols. In some training protocols, only one person at a time can take part in the training and resetting the training room is rather costly and time consuming when each employee needs to go through the training individually. In a virtual safety training, we can have simultaneous training sessions with no risk of malfunctioning fire systems and easy-to-reset training programs (i.e., simulations). The UX design is based on the high accuracy of replicating virtually the real building used the real-world training. It also follows fully the safety protocols, air conditioning systems and other specifications that can provide realistic simulations of smoke and fire behavior inside the building. The emergency exists among with all other features of the building are identical to the real-world building. The training does not even have to wait for the building to be finished in the real world, but VR training can use a virtual environment based on the existing plans and construction specifications. It is also possible to create different scenarios and conditions with ease and run the training sessions on demand.

In order to provide realistic training sessions, proper UX design is crucial. Besides the hyper-realistic approach of representation of the environment and the simulations of the smoke and fire behavior, it is equally important to provide an experience that would guide the player and give the right responses to their actions in the virtual world. Therefore, one must make sure that there is no snap-turning nor motion blur in the movement. Moreover, breaching through the walls or moving through the items in the environment cannot be allowed. Each object should be interactable with its own specifications and the game audio is properly implemented in 360° soundscape. As we mentioned earlier in Sect. 21.3.3, the control and representation of hands is of great importance which affects the feeling of realistic interaction across the virtual environment.

21.4.3   Collaborative Multiplayer XR Storygame

Creating a multiplayer environment in XR is based on the notion that games commonly played in groups (e.g., sports or board games) can now be set in a real-world environment with virtual content that would be of accurate size, location, and behavior (i.e., its actions with respect to each player). In practice this means that each device used in a game needs to track the exact location and have a real-time synchronization with all inputs that the players in a group make. This is rather complicated and challenging from the perspective of software development and usually results with numerous obstacles preventing the game to perform as intended. However, in a smaller scale (e.g., table-top or small room scale environments) we have successfully utilized collaborative XR gaming experiences (see Fig. 21.7).

Fig. 21.7 The collaborative
multiplayer XR storygame in
classroom use

We are presenting here a project that focuses on the educational content from a school curriculum. The aim of the game is to show the pupils how different actions from each player such as making "good" and "bad" decisions can affect the other player's actions and their progress as much as the whole game environment. Since this project is aimed for elementary school children, we have created a solution that they can use in their own smartphones by installing the game on their own device and giving permission to use the device's camera for AR purposes. In this project, the game can be played by two to four players. Each player's actions produce a reaction in the virtual environment and the results are visible to the other players allowing them to interact if wanted. This responsive interactive environment serves in both collaborative and competitive setup. The game objectives are set in the beginning by the teacher (e.g., selecting the tasks, win conditions, and choosing a collaborative or competitive mode). In the collaborative mode, the pupils are required to collaborate and the tasks are designed to utilize each player's input in solving the tasks. In the competitive mode, there are commonly competing sides (individuals or groups of two) that try to solve the tasks as fast as possible.

Collaborative XR learning environment gives opportunities for training smaller and bigger groups. It also allows also to engage in exercises and other learning activities. The location-based tracking makes it possible to set the game area to cover bigger outdoor quests, depending on the desired tasks and learning objectives.

This approach has shown improvements in teamwork and empowering fellow players to show support and encouraging them to teach one another during the exercises. Here, the biggest challenge in the UX design is the remaining accuracy in interactivity and the correspondence among the players and virtual assets they have control over in the real world. With technical improvements we see a high value of creating interactive XR content, since it is engaging and immersive for users of different ages, interests, and skill sets.

21.5 Conclusion

There are three important factors that must be considered in the design of interactive storytelling in XR. Firstly, the design has to utilize the locations in the (virtual) world, because the story will take place in space and the interactor will be actively engaged in *moving through the story*. Secondly, the characters in the storyworld has to be able to show realistic, human-like responses—even in surprising situations and actions from the human interactor. Shortly put, the characters have to be *round*, not flat. Thirdly, the design of the environment is crucial, which is already well-mastered in the level design of videogames. However, there is an extra challenge if the environment is based on the real world such as a realistic VR model in simulation training or a real-world environment in AR.

This chapter collected research work done in realizing interactive storytelling in XR and our observations in creating various XR applications. Obviously, this work is still in its early phase and best practices are currently taking their form. Still, it is possible to say already that this process will require—and create—a new language to allow the designers of interactive XR storytelling to express themselves.

References

Adams EW (2014) Fundamentals of Game Design, 3rd edn. New Riders, San Francisco, CA, USA
Bala P, Dionisio M, Nisi V, Nunes N (2016) IVRUX: A tool for analyzing immersive narratives in virtual reality. In: Nack F, Gordon AS (eds) Interactive Storytelling: 9th International Conference on Interactive Digital Storytelling, ICIDS 2016, Los Angeles, CA, USA, November 15–18, 2016, Springer-Verlag, Lecture Notes in Computer Science, vol 10045, pp 3–11, https://doi.org/10.1007/978-3-319-48279-8_1
Bala P, Masu R, Nisi V, Nunes N (2018) Cue Control: Interactive sound spatialization for 360° videos. In: Rouse R, Koenitz H, Haahr M (eds) Interactive Storytelling: 11th International Conference on Interactive Digital Storytelling, ICIDS 2018, Dublin, Ireland, December 5–8, 2018, Springer-Verlag, Lecture Notes in Computer Science, vol 11318, pp 333–337, https://doi.org/10.1007/978-3-030-04028-4_36
Bithell M (2012) Thomas Was Alone. Mike Bithell
Cronin B (2015) The hierarchy of needs in virtual reality development. Web page, https://medium.com/@beaucronin/the-hierarchy-of-needs-in-virtual-reality-development-4333a4833acc
Dowling D, Fearghail CO, Smolic A, Knorr S (2018) Faoladh: A case study in cinematic VR storytelling and production. In: Rouse R, Koenitz H, Haahr M (eds) Interactive Storytelling: 11th International Conference on Interactive Digital Storytelling, ICIDS 2018, Dublin, Ireland, December 5–8, 2018, Springer-Verlag, Lecture Notes in Computer Science, vol 11318, pp 359–362, https://doi.org/10.1007/978-3-030-04028-4_42

Fearghail CO, Ozcinar C, Knorr S, Smolic A (2018) Director's cut—analysis of aspects of interactive storytelling for VR films. In: Rouse R, Koenitz H, Haahr M (eds) Interactive Storytelling: 11th International Conference on Interactive Digital Storytelling, ICIDS 2018, Dublin, Ireland, December 5–8, 2018, Springer-Verlag, Lecture Notes in Computer Science, vol 11318, pp 308–322, https://doi.org/10.1007/978-3-030-04028-4_34

Hameed A, Perkis A (2018) Spatial storytelling: Finding interdisciplinary immersion. In: Rouse R, Koenitz H, Haahr M (eds) Interactive Storytelling: 11th International Conference on Interactive Digital Storytelling, ICIDS 2018, Dublin, Ireland, December 5–8, 2018, Springer-Verlag, Lecture Notes in Computer Science, vol 11318, pp 323–332, https://doi.org/10.1007/978-3-030-04028-4_35

Ko D, Ryu H, Kim J (2018) Making new narrative structures with actor's eye-contact in cinematic virtual reality (CVR). In: Rouse R, Koenitz H, Haahr M (eds) Interactive Storytelling: 11th International Conference on Interactive Digital Storytelling, ICIDS 2018, Dublin, Ireland, December 5–8, 2018, Springer-Verlag, Lecture Notes in Computer Science, vol 11318, pp 343–347, https://doi.org/10.1007/978-3-030-04028-4_38

Mojang (2011) Minecraft. Mojang

Nakevska M, Funk M, Hu J, Eggen B, Rauterberg M (2014) Interactive storytelling in a mixed reality environment: How does sound design and users' preknowledge of the background story influence the user experience? In: Mitchell A, Fernández-Vara C, Thue D (eds) Interactive Storytelling: 7th International Conference on Interactive Digital Storytelling, ICIDS 2014, Singapore, Singapore, November 3–6, 2014, Springer-Verlag, Lecture Notes in Computer Science, vol 8832, pp 188–195, https://doi.org/10.1007/978-3-319-12337-0_19

Oculus (2019) Design. Web page, https://developer.oculus.com/design/

Rothe S, Montagud M, Mai C, Buschek D, Hußmann H (2018) Social viewing in cinematic virtual reality: Challenges and opportunities. In: Rouse R, Koenitz H, Haahr M (eds) Interactive Storytelling: 11th International Conference on Interactive Digital Storytelling, ICIDS 2018, Dublin, Ireland, December 5–8, 2018, Springer-Verlag, Lecture Notes in Computer Science, vol 11318, pp 338–342, https://doi.org/10.1007/978-3-030-04028-4_37

Rouse R, Barba E (2017) Design for emerging media: How MR designers think about storytelling, process, and defining the field. In: Nunes N, Oakley I, Nisi V (eds) Interactive Storytelling: 10th International Conference on Interactive Digital Storytelling, ICIDS 2017, Funchal, Madeira, Portugal, November 14–17, 2017, Springer-Verlag, Lecture Notes in Computer Science, vol 10690, pp 245–258, https://doi.org/10.1007/978-3-319-71027-3_20

Slater M, Wilbur S (1997) A framework for immersive virtual environments (FIVE): Speculations on the role of presence in virtual environments. Presence 6(6):603–616, https://doi.org/10.1162/pres.1997.6.6.603

Smed J, Suovuo T, Trygg N, Skult P (2019) Lecture notes on interactive storytelling. TUCS Lecture Notes 29, Turku Centre for Computer Science (TUCS), http://bit.ly/LectNotesIS

Wolf K, Naumann A, Rohs M, Müller J (2011) A taxonomy of microinteractions: Defining microgestures based on ergonomic and scenario-dependent requirements. In: Campos P, Graham N, Jorge J, Nunes N, Palanque P, Winckler M (eds) Human-Computer Interaction—INTERACT 2011, Springer-Verlag, Lecture Notes in Computer Science, vol 6946, pp 559–575, https://doi.org/10.1007/978-3-642-23774-4_45

Yi JS, Kang Y, Stasko J, Jacko JA (2007) Toward a deeper understanding of the role of interaction in information visualization. IEEE Transactions on Visualization and Computer Graphics 13(6):1224–1231, https://doi.org/10.1109/TVCG.2007.70515

Chapter 22
Using AR Mechanics and Emergent Narratives to Tell Better Stories

Matthue Roth

Contents

Abstract In games like *BioShock* and *Half-Life 2*, most storytelling does not happen with words. Graphic design, sound design, environmental architecture, and experiential cues put the player in the space, tell the story, and teach users to play the game. Together, these components tell the player what to afraid of, when to run or when to approach with caution, when to draw your gun, and when to jump on a monster's head.

With illustrations by Kurt Loeffler, Eugene Meng, and Germain Ruffle.

M. Roth (✉)
Google LLC, Mountain View, CA, USA

© Springer Nature Switzerland AG 2020   469
B. Bostan (ed.), *Game User Experience And Player-Centered Design*,
International Series on Computer Entertainment and Media Technology,
https://doi.org/10.1007/978-3-030-37643-7_22

Augmented reality, or AR, does not merely introduce users to a new world. It introduces users to a new world every time they start a new play session. These design techniques present a basic layout for a new physical vocabulary of game design and user interaction.

How do traditional game experiences, and this existing well-defined vocabulary, transfer to augmented reality experiences? In AR, the user's main game mechanic is simply existing in the space. Moving your phone or device around is an act of exploration and discovery. Each physical movement leads to a new variation on the experience, revealing a new slice or a new aspect of the AR world.

Keywords Augmented reality · Storytelling · Realism · Environmental design · Experience design · Game mechanics · Player choice

22.1 The Emergence of Emergent Mechanics

Today I am thinking about the game *VVVVVV*. It is a slight variation on Pac-Man and Super Mario Bros., designed and developed almost entirely by one person, Terry Cavanagh, and released back in 2010. The player controls a tiny, cute space traveler, Captain Viridian, who is stranded in a sort of two-dimensional maze (Fig. 22.1).

You can run left or right, though there is one more action, a face-palmingly simple mechanic that forms the heart of the game: instead of jumping, you can stand on ceilings. (In the game, it is stylized as reversing the flow of gravity. But essentially, you get to stand on ceilings, okay?)

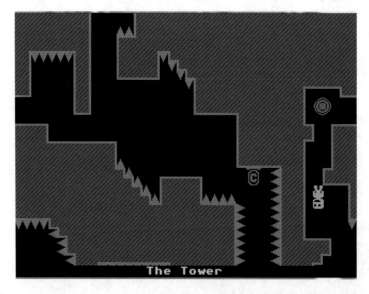

Fig. 22.1 A simple reversal of gravity in *VVVVVV* (used with permission of Terry Cavanagh)

The remarkable thing about *VVVVVV* is not the simplicity of the game, nor its retro graphics or devastatingly hard gameplay. All these things are important, to be sure—its narrative is simple and elegant, a straightforward mission with a few clever twists, turns, level design, and quirks (in one room, for no apparent reason, you meet a crying elephant).

But the reason that *VVVVVV* occupies my mind is not its novel mechanic. It is the confluence of story and motion, the parallel between the player's ultimate *goal of the game* and *what you actually do* from one moment to the next. The game's object is to explore the map, un-strand yourself, and collect your stranded crew; the moment-to-moment action is a kind of targeted falling, pushing yourself in one direction or another, then trying to simultaneously explore each new screen and avoid the million spikes and flying objects that are trying to kill you.

The most unexpected thing about the game is that it took 29 years to be made—that is, since the first platforming game was released (generally thought to be *Donkey Kong* (Nintendo 1981), followed by *Jumpman* in 1983 (Jensen 2018)).

Jensen (2018)). Video games are evolving and iterating faster than we can keep track of. In the late 1980s, Nintendo rattled the world by announcing that you could save a game-in-progress with writable files embedded in *The Legend of* (Nintendo 1986), eliminating the potential danger of not completing a game of Super Mario Bros. before we were called to dinner. The latest iteration of the *Zelda* series contains literally hundreds of hours of content. The game has more polished graphics, quicker reaction times, a control scheme exponentially more complicated than the original's two-button layout. But the mechanic is the same: you roam around grass- and monster-filled lands. You collect stuff. You search for a princess.

More recently, a genre of games sometimes disparagingly called "walking simulators" has given rise to an even more basic function (Clark 2017). Put simply, you walk. Imagine Pac-Man without the ghost monsters, Call of Duty without enemy armies, Dead Island without zombies. All you have, in the last case at least, is an island. But there might be tons of things on that island to explore: caves and caverns, animals and plants, people living out their own lives that you can follow, watch, and, unintruding, discover their stories.

It is no accident that in a lot of walking simulators, as well as a lot of early VR games, you play the role of an explorer or a ghost. But even ghosts and explorers, while stumbling through an alien world, are changed by it.

That is where story comes from.

22.2 A Game Is a Story That the Player Tells Themselves

Immersive computing[1] offers us a whole new world of gameplay possibilities. Walking simulators were a deconstruction of what it meant to play a video game, where exploring the world could function as its own reward—the challenge for game designers was building a world that was exciting, surprising, and rewarding enough to pay off to players without having to resort to combat, weapons, and skill trees (or, at least, a conventional set of skill trees).

Sometimes, walking simulators succeed in creating a good game with minimal interaction, and sometimes not so much. (Some of my favorites, for the record, are *Gone Home*, *Amnesia: The Dark Descent*, and *The Norwood Suite*.)

And then there are immersive games, which sometimes do not even require you to walk—you play the game, or experience the experience, simply by looking around and existing in the space.

So what makes a game a *game,* and not a book or a movie or an art exhibit? It is not the existence of a story—games have stories, even games as minimalist as *Pac-Man* and *VVVVVV*. It is that, when you play a game, you experience the story by telling it to yourself. Sometimes, the variation in stories can be huge: in open-world games such as *Just Cause* or *Borderlands,* your character's journey can take as many branches and twists as there are roads and pathways in the game. Games such as *Gone Home* are more traditional: although players can find or skip different rooms or artifacts, there is a single linear story lying behind the facade.

22.3 Things That Go Bump in Your Phone

Augmented reality offers a whole collection of game mechanics—constructing, crafting, discovery, and more. At its simplest, AR is a way to see virtual content in the physical world. Here is the easiest way to explain it:

Virtual reality: real YOU in an imaginary world

Augmented reality: imaginary objects in YOUR world

---

[1]The nascent field of experiential reality includes a lot of acronyms and variations on a theme: AR (augmented reality), VR (virtual reality), MR (mixed reality), and more. At Daydream, we try to sidestep all these terms and their various baggage and instead focus on the type of experience we're making. For that reason, throughout this chapter I will refer to XR experiences (see?) as "immersive experiences" or "immersive computing."

ARCore is a platform for building AR apps.[2] It keeps track of three variables to construct its AR worlds:

- Motion tracking
- Environmental understanding
- Light estimation

When you are designing game mechanics, AR gives you access to basically any gesture or action that the user can perform in the real world,[3] but it's helpful to think of possible user actions in terms of those three variables.

22.4   Onboarding in Games

Tutorials might be the worst thing to happen to games. Tutorials are like the fat, cheaply printed instruction manual that comes with your kid's bike—you would rather get the setup completely wrong than sit through and read this perfect-bound book before you actually *do* something.

In UX, we call this process "onboarding," but it is the same idea. Stop telling me what I can do! Just step aside and let me do it.

The moment an AR experience begins *is not* the moment in the app that the user gets launched into AR. It is not even the opening screen of the game.

It is the first moment the user sees screenshots from the game, or sees your Play Store page, or hears their friend talking about it.

As game designers, we might not have control over every screenshot and Let us Play video that a player sees or does not see before they enter your game. But, in whatever visuals we *do* create, we can show players what to expect.

Manage their expectations. Show players the size of the experience. Once they have started playing, the first moments of the game set the rules for the rest of the game.

We generally think of AR experiences in three sizes: tabletop, room-size, and world-size (Fig. 22.2).

Try to think of an in-game way to show users the limits of the world. Open-world games will often give fetch quests that get progressively more expansive, encouraging players to take bigger and bigger bites of the world. The first-person shooter *BioShock* is the opposite: the player enters a lighthouse, then a bathysphere,

---

[2] A quick word about AR development: ARCore is Google's engine for running AR, which appears on newer Android phones, and which most of the following design techniques are focused on. Apple has a similar engine called ARKit that is packaged with iOS, and there are a few others, too. Each engine has different features and annoyances, but basically what they do is they look at what your camera's seeing—at any given moment, in the moments just before, the moments after—and they look at all that information to put together a picture of the world around you in 3D.

[3] For instance, picking up objects, playing catch, or picking up a phone and calling someone. No jumping from one roof to another, though, *please.*

Fig. 22.2 AR experiences can exist in table-scale, room-scale, or world-scale settings. (From the app *ARCore Elements* by Google LLC)

Fig. 22.3 Convince the user to detect their real-world surroundings. (From the app *ARCore Elements* by Google LLC)

then ventures deeper and deeper into the heart of a closed system. This mirrors the player's experience of exploring the undersea city of Rapture, getting closer and closer to its heart, and finally (spoiler, but not really) encountering its creators (Fig. 22.3).

Once your playspace is established, you need to convince the user to detect their real-world surroundings. This is a problem we do not have in conventional games: the user's already plugged in the power cord. When you have opened a Google Doc, you see the blinking cursor. They know what to do.

So give your player a mission. An excuse to discover the world.

That is right: give them a fetch quest.

Why do we hate fetch quests in games? Because they so often fill up the dead space between fighting. It is like saying to the player, "The thing you usually do is run around and kill people. Now, let's just get rid of the killing-people part and focus on the running around."

In AR, however, the user journey—the running around, that is—serves exactly the same purpose as the technical functionality of scanning for surfaces. Your device and your brain are both discovering the world in harmony.

22.5 Onboarding in Stores

These AR techniques—finding surfaces, setting up experience boundaries—do not necessarily feel like storytelling techniques. But they are!

There is a three-act structure that can be overlaid atop virtually every story. It was elucidated by Aristotle in his *Poetics,* which, despite the name, is the basis for pretty much every motion picture. You can take the skeletal outline of the three-act structure, pretend it is a piece of clear mimeograph paper, lay it on top of any movie, book, or even lots of pop songs, and the outline will fit (Aristotle 1961). (If you are wondering about pop songs, the second-act bridge is the all-is-lost moment.)

At the beginning of Act I, there is an inciting incident—an explosion, a birth, a death, your house getting lifted up by a tornado and landing on a witch. Something happens. Something that the main character does not have control of.

Then the character reacts to it. Our hero swallows the red pill, enters the magic mirror, and rebels against the Matrix. Or she straps on the witch's slippers and follows the Yellow Brick Road! That is the Act I climax.

And then Act II, which is most of the experience—this is the million quests in a video game, or the middle hour and a half of a 2-h movie—is a series of events where the character faces challenges. Each one gets harder than the last. And each one reveals a new part of a character, a part that the audience has never seen before.

That is also why, the more fights there are, the more repetitious and grindy a game gets, since it is no longer revealing something new and unseen.

Each episode or interaction gets more challenging, until the end of Act II, when the character faces complete despair. It is the lowest moment, when all is lost, the dark night of the soul. "You must fall completely before you get up again," says Blake Snyder, who wrote *Save the Cat,* one book about writing theory.

The climax of Act II comes with a complete reversal, from the darkest night into the final blaze of glory. The hero wins! They achieve what they have been after all along.

Except that, somehow, the hero discovers that what they have wanted all along is not what they *truly* want. Dorothy finds the Wizard and he is not a wizard at all. Freeing the world inside the Matrix does not actually free the world outside it. Instead, the hero needs to use what they have learned along the way, the person they have grown into, in order to conquer (or be defeated by) the new ending, the twist ending.

So that is the story of every story, whether it is a novel or movie or video game. Here is another idea: it is also the story of *each moment* of a video game.

The greater story of *Borderlands* is finding a mystical key and opening a giant vault. The greater story of *BioShock* is overthrowing a society of people who thought they were better than everyone else and turned themselves into mutants. But the moment-to-moment story, of finding weapons and power-ups, of fighting skags or splicers or other monsters, is the story that the player comes away with, the parts that stick with the player afterward.

These single moments, pieced together, are what tell the story of your game. And the onboarding, the way you teach the player how to handle those moments and react to them—effectively, the way you teach them to play the game—is how you teach them to tell the story to themselves.

22.6 Building a World

But how do you create a game that sticks with your player and tells a good story? By designing a world that is both amazing to look at and reacts to your presence.

Give your world a feeling of being lived-in, livable, and malleable. The essence of any AR experience is crafting a combination of virtual and real-world objects. So let your virtual creations interact with the real world.

Let a virtual frog hop from the real-world coffee table to the floor. Let virtual waterfalls flow from the headboard of your bed and your kitchen sink. Let CGI goblins hide beneath your bed...although be careful how you deploy that, because you can turn your phone off but you might not be able to shut off your imagination.

The more that real and virtual objects play together—the more they interact and fit together and bounce off each other—the more your world will feel like an actual, living, inhabited place.

And it *is* inhabited! To some extent, all AR-designed environments are procedurally generated, even those that simply materialize as a portal hanging in midair or a Pokémon loosely sitting on (or a few inches above) the front lawn. Seeing a virtual object or character can transform the real-world environment, either physically—a brick wall in the middle of a sidewalk, for instance—or thematically, like a dragon hovering in a bathroom that you *thought* was unoccupied.

Inserting virtual content into the real world is only the beginning of an AR experience. In order to make it feel real, we need to add the third dimension—the user. Let people touch, manipulate, and change as many virtual objects as they can (and as many as it makes sense to be changed and manipulated).

If you are making a beach scene, let users pick up seashells and crabs and hurl them into the water. If you are in the Wild West, let users nearly bump into a horse, and then let the horse snort and gallop away. Make the user feel like the world is *there*, just like the non-virtual world. Make it even more so. Invite them to interact with it.

When we see an empty soda can or a stuffed animal lying out in the real world, we do not feel the need to pick it up or interact with it, since we do not question the validity of its existence. On the other hand, when you put a virtual soda can on the table, the first thing that any player will want to do is pick it up, throw it against the wall, or crush it. That is okay! As a matter of fact, it is awesome. Sprinkling your scene with these objects is a great way to encourage users to explore, experiment, and spend more time in your experience.

It also encourages users to mess around with the scene. One of the joys of inhabiting an augmented reality is the joy of messing it all up and never having to clean it up. You can have a barroom brawl in your kitchen and not have to sweep up any glass.

22.7 Get Players Out of Their Heads (By Getting Them Out of Their Seats)

Here is the single biggest obstacle to playing games or creating an effective experience in AR.

How do we hold our phones? With one hand extended, stretched out in front of us, our bodies craned over in a posture that is the stuff of a first-grade teacher's worst nightmare.

How *can* we hold our phones? Any way we want. Any way our arms can stretch, any way our heads can turn, and any way our bodies can move. Phone-based AR experiences can occur in four different physical positions:

1. Sitting down, with hands resting
2. Sitting down and moving your head/device/torso
3. Standing still, in one place
4. Standing and walking around

The more openness you place into an experience, the tighter your visual storytelling has to be. In the 2D *Super Mario Bros.,* there is only one possible direction to run in—forward. The screen does not even move backward! Once that fire flower is out of sight, you have lost it forever. On the other hand, in a first-person game, and even more so in an AR experience, players can go in any direction they want. It is up to you, the designer, to provide breadcrumbs, hints, and visual storytelling elements to show them where you *want* them to look.

So you should constantly remind users that they are in a 3D space. Design your mechanics to convince players to move around—to get out of their seats, move *in* their seats, or even just move their heads and phones around. By changing your players' physical position, you will also change their mental experience.

In other words, blow their minds by blowing their bodies out of their seats. One of the greatest advantages you have in AR is the size of your space. It is theoretically infinite. The problem is most users do not remember that.

So give them something to chase.

22.8   Player Mechanics and Story Mechanics

Once you have taught your player how to play the game, you can start getting crafty. Game mechanics are what players can actually *do* in AR. Remember, the story of the player's experience is the player's experience and actions that are happening at any given moment. And, like every story, you can break down each moment into a first, second, and third act—a call to action, a hero's quest, and a culmination.

The story mechanic is the running in *Mirror's Edge*. It is the searching for Pokémon in *Pokémon Go*. It is the dying over and over again in *Dead Souls*. When you think about the AR mechanic that you are developing for your game, break it down into that 3-act method. Even the simple act, as discussed before, of encountering an empty can of soda:

Act I
INCITING INCIDENT (*The first big thing that happens, setting the plot in motion*): The player sees a virtual bottle of soda sitting on the kitchen table.
   ACT I CLIMAX (*The hero's call to action*): The player picks it up.

Act II
RISING ACTION (*A series of challenges that challenge the hero and deepen the quest*): The player bangs it on the table and hears a tinny thud. They shake it. They bang it into the wall.
   ALL IS LOST MOMENT (*The darkest our*): The player decides to abandon the soda can and sets it back down.
   REVERSAL (*The moment where everything changes*): Setting it down, the player sees a bottle opener half-hidden between the table and the wall, glinting in the light.

Act III
BLAZE OF GLORY (*The twist ending*): The player lifts up the bottle opener and opens the bottle. Surprise! The soda explodes out and fizzes all over the player.

Think of the three-act structure of the hero's quest for each of these mechanics. And think of each of these as jumping-off points to design mechanics of your own. Because you are creating a world with as many possible inputs as the real world, you can turn almost anything into a mechanic. Even standing still can count as a mechanic when it is deployed well.[4]

22.8.1   Play Hide and Seek

Take advantage of the real-world environment. Send players looking for a virtual object, or create a *Where's Waldo*-style hunt in the existing scene for an object that

---

[4]Not to say that *we* deployed it well, but if you ever happen to be visiting the Daydream space at Google NYC, say hi to our AR robot and try standing in front of the screen without moving for, oh, about 45 s. I am not saying you *will* unlock a really cool Easter egg! But I am not saying you will not.

is there, but not *there*. Create a scavenger hunt and send users scrambling to find real-world objects, then let their phone detect images to pass or complete tasks.

Use anchors to remember a real-world location and have users return to it. The AR game *ARrrrrgh* is a multiplayer game on a single device: one player takes the phone, taps a location, and buries a treasure chest; then they hand the phone to another player, who goes around the room tapping on spots and digging for treasure.

Or do a simple hide-and-seek game or a fetch quest. You can place virtual objects just out of reach, or just out of sight. Use vertical plane detection to hide something just behind a corner or a door (Fig. 22.4).

You can even hide virtual objects behind other virtual objects! Video games have a longstanding tradition of placing power-ups and bonuses behind walls that can be punched or blown up or decimated. Why should the real world be any different?

AR is an inherently visual medium, and hide and seek missions work perfectly within AR because, essentially, every time you move your phone to look for a new object, that is exactly what you are doing.

22.8.2   Make Virtual Creatures Reactive

Remember that first moment of joy when you hit a joystick, and right away, a character on a screen did exactly what you told them to? It was a seamless blend of the real and virtual worlds. You were controlling imaginary characters.

It was also a moment of ultimate player agency. It put you in the driver's seat of this pixelated character's life. You have the power to affect the character. No matter what you tell it to do, it complies right away. And that character, in turn, has the

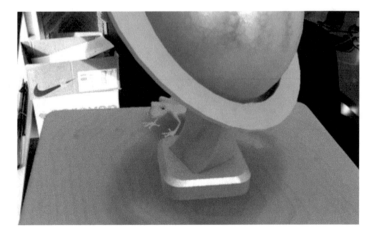

Fig. 22.4 Virtual objects can be hidden behind other virtual objects. (From the app *ARCore Elements* by Google LLC)

power to affect the world. Each time Mario smashes a brick, it changes the shape of the world and the dynamics of your platforming.

It also means that every game is, in some sense, a first-person game. You are a part of it. The player is not a virtual object, but in some way, they are being equated with virtual objects. They are existing in an environment together with them. And, just like players should be able to interact with virtual objects, the objects should also be able to interact with the player.

This is not just a way to make the AR scene superficially or cosmetically fun. The more non-necessary stuff that users can pick up and interact with, the more they will want to hunt for the objects that they *do* need to pick up and interact with.

22.8.3 Break Reality Carefully

It is great to create a world-scale environment where users can go anywhere. But for your game narrative—whether it is a tightly controlled mystery or an open-ended exploration—you should always let players know where they should be looking next.

You can always plant direct hints: a character running in a certain direction, just out of camera.

You can also alter lighting, coloring, or perspective. As a worldbuilder, you are empowered to decide when you want your world to look realistic, and when you want to withhold that realism. If you need to draw the user's attention to an object or an area or an evil robot, the entire world is at your command (Fig. 22.5).

Fig. 22.5 Break reality selectively in order to draw your users' attention to certain areas or objects. (From the app *ARCore Elements* by Google LLC)

At your disposal are lighting, shading, texture, and physics—not to mention the layout of the area itself.

Highlight objects. Play objects down and move them into the shadows. Give a treasure chest intricate detail. Make backgrounds plain and dim. Be natural. Be unnatural. You can tell a whole story with just a setting.

When we learn to design, we are given skills and techniques to make objects and environments blend together and look uniform. By selectively withholding these skills, or *un*-using them, we can draw the player's eye, either subconsciously or consciously, in a certain direction or to a certain object.

22.8.4 Selective Surprises

When the first horror movies were made, one of the first cinematic techniques that directors seized upon, to varying degrees of effectiveness, was jump scares. Jump scares are great! Technically, it is a sudden variation of perspective, forcing the player (or viewer) to suddenly and completely alter their spatial conception in relation to the screen. Storytelling-wise, it causes an instant emotional reaction.

That emotional reaction can take several forms:

- *Discomfort*. This is the classic, visceral horror-movie response. Suddenly, nothing seems sure to the player. The characters are larger than life, and way closer than the player ever thought possible.
- *Inspired*. Think of the camera pulling back on a beautiful island paradise as a helicopter lands atop a mountain, or the first time the human protagonists of *Jurassic Park* leap out of their jeep to see an 80-foot-tall Apatosaurus taking a morning stroll.
- *Funny*. The first time you ever opened a Jack-in-the-box, this was ideally your response. (In reality, for most kids it is closer to discomfort.)

The best jumpscares, all the best moments of connection, happen when you forget there is a screen separating you from the experience. Having the action right in front of you makes that separation even easier to forget.

Just one warning: in AR experiences, do not make the user move backward without looking behind them! It is all too easy to trip over a rock, a piece of furniture, or a kid or roommate lying on the floor behind you.

22.8.5 Any Spatial Variable Can Be a Strategy

In early video games like *Wolfenstein 3D* or *Zelda*, it was easy to figure out the movement patterns behind enemy AI. Put bluntly, their artificial intelligence was not very intelligent.

As games (and game programming) became more sophisticated, sneaking skills got more sophisticated. Enemies could detect you, or not detect you, and entire games, from first-person sneakers such as *Dishonored* and *Thief* to weirder games such as *Volume* and *Tattletail,* were founded on hiding and sneaking.

The game itself could track the player's visibility percentage. Lines of sight were established by designers and evaded by players. Sneaking around became an actual, measurable mechanic.

That is just one way to turn movement itself into a mechanic. Think about how many variables figure into simple movement: the player's height, in relation to the height of any detected surfaces. The light estimation. How stable or wobbly we are at any given moment. Our line of sight, and our awareness of any obstacles, real or virtual, that we might be about to step on or bump into.

Do not worry! You do not have to account for all these things in your game mechanic. In fact, the more you focus on one single variable, the more easily both you and your players will have paying attention to it, and keeping track of it. Any of these things can be a major factor in your game. It is up to you to pick which ones.

22.8.6   The World Is a Shared Space

When your players create or play in a single virtual world, it opens up the potential to interact with other players. After all, we all inhabit the shared multiplayer space of the real world.

You can bring that experience to your AR game with cloud anchors. By matching virtual content with real-world locations, then serving the same content to different users, cloud anchors create a shared virtual space to complement the shared real-world space.

The transformation of an AR space from single-player, single-phone to multiplayer will force you—and challenge you!—to reevaluate every step of your experience. Will the experience be competitive, player vs. player? Will it be competitive where players form teams? Where they all work together?

One other possibility: it could be incidentally multiplayer. You can create the same experience for every player, a game that exists on its own, but that happens to exist in every player's space at the same time. One player could just happen upon another player in a shared maze, and trade tips . . . or try to steal each other's gold. In many cases, the computing power and shared internet bandwidth might not be worth it. On the other hand, it *might* be a crazy amount of fun.

22.8.7   Make Your World Accessible to Everyone

In some ways, AR is a great way to create an all-access world. When a player scans for surfaces, they are effectively setting their own boundaries.

It is a uniquely accessible value proposition: players first set their own limits, then play within them.

It is also a great way for players with special physical limits to see things in their own scale. AR, and especially phone-based AR, gives the user control of establishing scene and boundaries. If the area they scan during the initial surface-finding is an area that is accessible to them, they are literally setting their own limits. If the player is in a wheelchair, or if they are playing while sitting or lying on the ground, that is the zenith of the camera angle. The initial angle that the player establishes will, by and large, establish the angle at which they will be perceiving the rest of the experience.

However, that comes with a whole set of new challenges. If you tell users to reach up and grab something, or to take two steps forward, what happens when your user cannot reach their device out or take steps? In mixed reality, every environment is fundamentally a procedurally generated environment, a collaboration between the app and the user.

When you design your experience, and when you craft specific challenges within the experience, try to allow for different paths to success. When your players have to reach a far-off or high-up object, do not just anticipate that they will be tall enough, or be able to jump high enough. Add a reticle for reaching that object, to stretch and extend the user's virtual grip based on the angle of their phone. Or add a tap-and-drag mechanism where the user can "hold" an object from far away and bring it closer to them.

Establishing multiple paths to success is not solely a concept for disabled users. It also just makes gameplay cooler. Think of different ways people can play your game: moving or still, sitting or standing or lying on their back, staring at the ceiling. Shooting or sneaking, or using a gun or crowbar. My brain, again, goes back to *BioShock*, where instead of using a pistol, the user can summon tornadoes or launch a swarm of bees with their hands—they are not just weapons; they can ideally affect the environment, and change the interaction, in fundamentally different ways.

22.9 Conclusion

What is the perfect ending to an AR game?

If classic stories spring from the relationship between character and plot (Henkin, undated), then games spring from the relationship between the player and their quest. So each quest, every mechanic that we employ and every moment that the player plays the game, can be a new moment of discovery of the world, a moment of revelation of the character, a new story, and a new mini-game inside itself.

The object of this chapter is not to convince you to neglect the major story of your game, nor to convince you that you need to think about a complete story arc for every time that your player knocks over a virtual vase of flowers or sneaks through a dark room.

Instead, it is to consider the relationship between who you *are* in a game and what you *do*. And how one leads to the other, and how the other can teach you more about the first.

Lastly, if you are interested in experiencing actual AR techniques that complement this chapter, search the Google Play Store for ARCore Elements, a free app made by the Daydream AR Platform team that includes all the mechanics mentioned here, and several more.

Acknowledgements Many thanks are due to the Google Daydream AR Platform UX team: Alex Faaborg, Yvonne Gando, Patrick Gunderson, Khushboo Hasija, Kurt Loeffler, Eugene Meng, Germain Ruffle, and Alesha Unpingco.

References

Aristotle. *Aristotle's Poetics*. New York: Hill and Wang, 1961.

Clark, Nicole. A Brief History of the "Walking Simulator," Gaming's Most Detested Genre. Salon.com. November 11, 2017. https://www.salon.com/2017/11/11/a-brief-history-of-the-walking-simulator-gamings-most-detested-genre/

Henkin, Josh. From the Roots of Character Grow the Branches of Plot. *Glimmer Train*. Undated. https://www.glimmertrain.com/bulletins/essays/b127henkin.php

Jensen, K. Thor. Run, Jump, and Climb: The Complete History of Platform Games. Geek.com. October 25, 2018. https://www.geek.com/games/run-jump-and-climb-the-complete-history-of-platform-games-1748896/

Index

© Springer Nature Switzerland AG 2020
B. Bostan (ed.), *Game User Experience And Player-Centered Design*,
International Series on Computer Entertainment and Media Technology,
https://doi.org/10.1007/978-3-030-37643-7

Printed in the United States
by Baker & Taylor Publisher Services